Critical Survey of Graphic Novels
Independents & Underground Classics

Critical Survey of Graphic Novels
Independents & Underground Classics

Second Edition

Volume 3
Shortcomings – Zot!
Appendixes and Index

Editors
Bart H. Beaty
University of Calgary

Stephen Weiner
Maynard, Massachusetts

SALEM PRESS
A Division of EBSCO Information Services, Inc.
Ipswich, Massachusetts

GREY HOUSE PUBLISHING

Cover photo: iStock/Grandfailure. Blue man walking through a futuristic city.

Copyright © 2019 by EBSCO Information Services, Inc., and Grey House Publishing, Inc.

Critical Survey of Graphic Novels: Independents & Underground Classics, Second Edition, published by Grey House Publishing, Inc., Amenia, NY, under exclusive license from EBSCO Information Services, Inc.

All rights reserved. No part of this work may be used or reproduced in any manner whatsoever or transmitted in any form or by any means, electronic or mechanical, including photocopy, recording, or any information storage and retrieval system, without written permission from the copyright owner. For information, contact Grey House Publishing/Salem Press, 4919 Route 22, PO Box 56, Amenia, NY 12501.

∞ The paper used in these volumes conforms to the American National Standard for Permanence of Paper for Printed Library Materials, Z39.48 1992 (R2009).

Publisher's Cataloging-In-Publication Data
(Prepared by The Donohue Group, Inc.)

Names: Beaty, Bart, editor. | Weiner, Stephen, 1955- editor.
Title: Critical survey of graphic novels : independents and underground classics / editors, Bart H. Beaty, University of Calgary, Stephen Weiner, Maynard Public Library.
Other Titles: Independents and underground classics | Critical survey of graphic novels.
Description: Second edition. | Ipswich, Massachusetts : Salem Press, a division of EBSCO Information Services, Inc. ; Amenia, NY : Grey House Publishing, [2019] | Includes bibliographical references and index.
Identifiers: ISBN 9781682179130 (set) | ISBN 9781682179147 (v. 1) | ISBN 9781682179154 (v. 2) | ISBN 9781682179161 (v. 3) | ISBN 9781682179581 (ebook)
Subjects: LCSH: Graphic novels--History and criticism. | Underground comic books, strips, etc.--History and criticism.
Classification: LCC PN6710 .C754 2019 (print) | LCC PN6710 (ebook) | DDC 741.5/9--dc23

FIRST PRINTING
PRINTED IN THE UNITED STATES OF AMERICA

Contents

Master List of Contents vii

Shortcomings 675
Shutterbug Follies 679
Signal to Noise 683
Sin City 687
Skim 692
Skitzy: The Story of Floyd W. Skitzafroid 696
Sloth 700
Small Killing, A 704
Smile 708
Exit Stage Left: The Snagglepuss Chronicles 712
Snowman, The 715
Stitches: A Memoir 718
Strangers in Paradise 722
Stray Bullets 727
Stray Toasters 732
Streak of Chalk 736
Stuck Rubber Baby 740
Suckle: The Status of Basil 745
Summer Blonde 749
Summer of Love, The 753
System, The 756
Tale of One Bad Rat, The 760
*Tales of the Beanworld: A Most Peculiar
    Comic Book Experience* 764
Tamara Drewe 768
Tank Girl 772
Tantrum 776
30 Days of Night 780
Three Fingers 784
300 788
Three Shadows 792
*Tragical Comedy or Comical Tragedy
    of Mr. Punch, The* 796
Transit 800
Treasury of Victorian Murder, A 803
Tricked 807
Twentieth Century Eightball 811
Usagi Yojimbo 815
Violent Cases 820
Walking Dead, The 823
Wall, The: Growing Up Behind the Iron Curtain 828
Waltz with Bashir: A Lebanon War Story 832
We Are on Our Own 836
What It Is 839
When the Wind Blows 842
Whiteout 846
Why I Hate Saturn 850
Wilson 853
Xenozoic Tales 857
Yossel 860
You Are Here 864
*You'll Never Know
    Book One: A Good and Decent Man* 867
Zombies Vs. Robots 871
*Zot! The Complete Black and White Collection,
    1987-1991* 875

Appendixes
Bibliography 881
Guide to Online Resources 905
Timeline 907
Major Awards 911
Works by Artist 1002
Works by Author 1014
Works by Publisher 1021
Index 1027

MASTER LIST OF CONTENTS

Volume 1

Master List of Contents	vii
Publisher's Note	xi
Introduction	xv
Contributors	xvii

A.D.: New Orleans After the Deluge	1
Adventures of Luther Arkwright, The	5
Adventures of Tintin, The	9
Age of Bronze: The Story of the Trojan War	15
Age of Reptiles	20
Airtight Garage of Jerry Cornelius	24
Alan's War: The Memories of G.I. Alan Cope	28
Alec: The Years Have Pants	32
Alice in Sunderland: An Entertainment	37
Aliens	41
American Born Chinese	46
American Splendor: From off the Streets of Cleveland	50
Anya's Ghost	55
Arrival, The	59
Asterios Polyp	63
Asterix	67
Aya of Yopougon	72
Bacchus	77
Ballad of Doctor Richardson, The	82
Berlin: City of Stones	86
Binky Brown Sampler	89
Black Hole	93
Blackmark	97
Blankets: An Illustrated Novel	101
Blueberry	105
Bone	112
Book of Genesis, The	117
Boulevard of Broken Dreams, The	121
Box Office Poison	125
Boxers and Saints	128
Burma Chronicles	133
Cages	137
Cancer Vixen: A True Story	141
Cartoon History of the Universe, The	145
Castle Waiting	149
Chicken with Plums	154
City of Glass	158
Clumsy	162
Color Trilogy, The	166
Complete Essex County, The	170
Complete Fritz the Cat, The	174
Contract with God, And Other Tenement Stories, A	179
Curious Case of Benjamin Button, The	183
David Boring	187
Dead Memory	190
Dear Julia	194
Deogratias: A Tale of Rwanda	198
Diary of a Mosquito Abatement Man	202
Dropsie Avenue: The Neighborhood	205
Dykes to Watch Out For	209
Ed the Happy Clown: The Definitive Ed Book	214
Elk's Run	218
Embroideries	222
Epileptic	226
Ethel and Ernest: A True Story	231
Exit Wounds	234
Far Arden	238
Fax from Sarajevo: A Story of Survival	242
The Fixer: A Story from Sarajevo	246
Flaming Carrot Comics	250
Flood! A Novel in Pictures	255
Footnotes in Gaza: A Graphic Novel	259
Frank Book, The	263
Friends with Boys	267
From Hell: Being a Melodrama in Sixteen Parts	271
Fun Home: A Family Tragicomic	276
Gemma Bovery	281
Get a Life	286
Ghost World	290
Give It Up! And Other Short Stories	296
Glacial Period	300
Golem's Mighty Swing, The	304
Goliath	308
Good-Bye, Chunky Rice	311
Hard Boiled	315
Harum Scarum	319
Harvey Kurtzman's Jungle Book: Or, Up from the Apes! (and Right Back Down)	323
Hate	327

Haunted	332
He Done Her Wrong: The Great American Novel—And Not a Word in It	336
Hey, Wait	340
Hicksville	343
History of Violence, A	347
Home after Dark	351
Houdini: The Handcuff King	355

Volume 2

Master List of Contents vii

Ice Haven	359
Incognegro: A Graphic Mystery	363
I Never Liked You: A Comic-Strip Narrative	367
In the Shadow of No Towers	370
It Rhymes with Lust	374
It's a Bird . .	377
It's a Good Life, If You Don't Weaken: A Picture Novella	380
It Was the War of the Trenches	384
Jar of Fools: A Picture Story	388
Jew in Communist Prague, A: 1. Loss of Innocence	391
Jew of New York, The: A Historical Romance	395
Jimmy Corrigan: The Smartest Kid on Earth	398
Journey: The Adventures of Wolverine MacAlistaire	402
Journey into Mohawk Country	407
Julius Knipl, Real Estate Photographer: Stories	411
Kabuki	414
Kafka	419
Kampung Boy	424
Kane	428
King: A Comics Biography	431
Kings in Disguise	434
Laika	437
La Perdida	441
Last Day in Vietnam: A Memory	445
Leave It to Chance	448
Life and Times of Scrooge McDuck, The	454
Life Sucks	459
Like a Velvet Glove Cast in Iron	463
Long Time Relationship	467
Lost Cause: John Wesley Hardin, the Taylor-Sutton Feud, and Reconstruction Texas	470
Lost Girl	474
Lost Girls	477
Louis	482
Louis Riel: A Comic-Strip Biography	487
Love and Rockets	491
Lucky	498
Mail Order Bride	502
Market Day	506
Maus: A Survivor's Tale	509
Metropol: The Complete Series + Metropol A.D.	514
Minor Miracles: Long Ago and Once Upon a Time Back When Uncles Were Heroic, Cousins Were Clever, and Miracles Happened on Every Block	518
Monologues for the Coming Plague	522
Mouse Guard	526
My Mommy Is in America and She Met Buffalo Bill	531
Nat Turner	535
Night Fisher	540
9/11 Report, The: A Graphic Adaptation	543
Notes for a War Story	547
Omaha the Cat Dancer	551
One! Hundred! Demons!	556
Our Cancer Year	560
Owly	564
Palestine	569
Palomar: The Heartbreak Soup Stories	573
Passionate Journey	577
Paul	581
Paying For It: a comic-strip memoir about being a john	585
Pedro and Me: Friendship, Loss, and What I Learned	588
Percy Gloom	591
Perfect Example	595
Persepolis	598
Photographer, The: Into War-Torn Afghanistan with Doctors Without Borders	602
Plain Janes, The	605
Playboy, The	608
Poor Bastard, The	611
Predator	615
Pride of Baghdad: Inspired by a True Story	619
Pyongyang: A Journey in North Korea	622
Queen and Country	626

Rabbi's Cat, The 632	Roughneck 656
Rex Mundi 637	Safe Area Goražde
Richard Stark's Parker 642	The War in Eastern Bosnia 1992-95 659
Road to Perdition 646	Scary Godmother: The Boo Flu 663
Robot Dreams 649	Scott Pilgrim 666
Rose 652	Shenzhen: A Travelogue from China 671

Volume 3

Master List of Contents vii	Transit 800
	Treasury of Victorian Murder, A 803
Shortcomings 675	Tricked 807
Shutterbug Follies 679	Twentieth Century Eightball 811
Signal to Noise 683	Usagi Yojimbo 815
Sin City 687	Violent Cases 820
Skim 692	Walking Dead, The 823
Skitzy: The Story of Floyd W. Skitzafroid 696	Wall, The: Growing Up Behind the Iron Curtain 828
Sloth 700	Waltz with Bashir: A Lebanon War Story 832
Small Killing, A 704	We Are on Our Own 836
Smile 708	What It Is 839
Exit Stage Left: The Snagglepuss Chronicles 712	When the Wind Blows 842
Snowman, The 715	Whiteout 846
Stitches: A Memoir 718	Why I Hate Saturn 850
Strangers in Paradise 722	Wilson 853
Stray Bullets 727	Xenozoic Tales 857
Stray Toasters 732	Yossel 860
Streak of Chalk 736	You Are Here 864
Stuck Rubber Baby 740	You'll Never Know
Suckle: The Status of Basil 745	Book One: A Good and Decent Man 867
Summer Blonde 749	Zombies Vs. Robots 871
Summer of Love, The 753	Zot! The Complete Black and White Collection,
System, The 756	1987-1991 875
Tale of One Bad Rat, The 760	
Tales of the Beanworld: A Most Peculiar	**Appendixes**
Comic Book Experience 764	Bibliography 881
Tamara Drewe 768	Guide to Online Resources 905
Tank Girl 772	Timeline 907
Tantrum 776	Major Awards 911
30 Days of Night 780	Works by Artist 1002
Three Fingers 784	Works by Author 1014
300 788	Works by Publisher 1021
Three Shadows 792	Index 1027
Tragical Comedy or Comical Tragedy	
of Mr. Punch, The 796	

Critical Survey of Graphic Novels
Independents & Underground Classics

SHORTCOMINGS

Author: Tomine, Adrian
Artist: Adrian Tomine (illustrator)
Publisher: Drawn and Quarterly
First serial publication: 2004 (in *Optic Nerve*)
First book publication: 2007

Publication History
Shortcomings was originally serialized as issues 9-11 of Adrian Tomine's comic book series *Optic Nerve*, before being released as a whole in 2007. An excerpt from the story appeared in *McSweeney's Quarterly Concern*, issue 13. Though his work has appeared in major publications such as *Pulse, The New Yorker*, and *Rolling Stone*, Adrian Tomine has earned most of his recognition from his self-published work and his series *Optic Nerve* that he started in 1991 and that was picked up by Drawn and Quarterly in 1995. The first issues of *Optic Nerve* contained short stories with little to no connection between characters; not until issue 9 did Tomine decide to create a longer story arc.

Shortcomings represents the first time that Tomine focused directly on non-Caucasian characters. Though Tomine is Asian American and drew himself in comics before *Shortcomings*, he often drew his glasses opaque to hide his eyes and his racial identity. The fact that *Shortcomings* does focus so much on race was a major departure for Tomine, and many critics have drawn connections between the story's protagonist, Ben Tanaka, and Tomine, suggesting that the character can be seen as partly autobiographical.

Plot
Shortcomings centers on Ben Tanaka, a thirty-year-old movie theater manager in Berkeley, California, and his relationships with girlfriend Miko Hayashi and best friend Alice Kim. Ben lives with Miko, who has recently become politically active. The story opens at the final screening of a film at an Asian American film festival that Miko has helped organize. After the screening, Ben and Miko's differing views on the film and the festival evolve into a fight that causes Miko to wonder if Ben is ashamed of being Asian.

Adrian Tomine at the 2011 Brooklyn Book Festival. (By David Shankbone, via Wikimedia Commons)

The next day, Ben has lunch with Alice, a Korean American lesbian and graduate student. Alice listens to Ben as he discusses his growing resentment toward Miko's newfound activism. Alice is happy to listen to Ben complain, but is more interested in flirting with the waitress. Back at home, the rift that is growing between Miko and Ben becomes more apparent. After dinner, instead of accepting Miko's offer to go to bed, Ben buries himself in a number of new DVDs he has received in the mail.

Soon, a new employee at the theater, Autumn Phelps, becomes a distraction for Ben. When Miko sees how Ben acts around Autumn and finds a number of pornographic DVDs, she confronts him again about his potential self-hatred and accuses him of being obsessed with Western ideals of beauty that include blond hair and white skin. The two resolve to try to stop pushing each other's buttons and to avoid arguments, but Miko begins to resent what she sees as a rejection of her Asian heritage and herself. Soon afterward, Miko tells Ben that she has been offered, and has accepted, a four-month-long internship in New York City. Ben refuses to move to New York for only four months; Miko informs him that she had not asked him to. Chapter 1 ends with Ben driving Miko to the airport; he is unable to keep the agreement they made not to argue. Miko leaves for New York frustrated, and Ben returns home angry and lonely. However, with his newfound freedom, Ben decides to pursue Autumn.

Autumn is an aspiring artist, and chapter 2 begins with Ben attending one of her performance-art shows. At coffee with Alice, Ben talks about Autumn, and Alice asks how seeing her fits into his relationship with Miko. Ben deflects the question by pointing out that Miko said they should take some time off. Ben and Autumn's relationship does not last long, though. Ben mistakes her friendship for romantic interest; he tries to kiss her, but she retreats from the attempt.

Hoping to take Ben's mind off Autumn and Miko, Alice takes him to a party. The party is attended exclusively by lesbians, and Ben finds himself alone, sitting outside, where he meets and starts to flirt with Sasha. Alice tries to dissuade Ben from pursuing Sasha, whom she calls a "fence sitter," Alice's term for bisexuals. Ben thinks that makes Sasha the perfect candidate to be the first white woman with whom he sleeps.

Ben's relationship with Sasha progresses, and they eventually sleep with each other. Ben calls Alice to brag about his conquest, but Alice is distracted by the fact that she has been kicked out of school for fighting with another woman. Alice also informs Ben that she is going to move to New York City. With his best friend preparing to move across the country, Ben feels his life start to unravel. The theater he manages is closed down for seismic reinforcing, and Sasha breaks up with him when her former girlfriend returns to California. All of this sends Ben into a state of depression. Now in New York, Alice calls Ben and urges him to visit her because there is something that he has to see.

That which Ben has to see is a series of erotic photographs of Miko, taken at their home in California and displayed in the window of a clothing store in New York. Determined to find and confront Miko, Ben goes to the offices where she is supposedly interning; however, the company has no records of her having interned there. Ben and Alice decide to stake out Miko's apartment, and they catch her leaving with the man who took the photographs, Leon Christopher, a clothing designer. Ben confronts Miko and Leon. To avoid a public confrontation, Miko brings Ben up to the apartment she shares with Leon to explain what is happening. Miko admits that she and Leon met in California when he took the pictures, but they did not want to start anything until her relationship with Ben had been resolved. The two argue, and Miko asks Ben to leave. He begs her not to do this to him. Ben spends one last evening in New York with Alice, and she asks him to move there. He still cannot bring himself to leave California and instead catches a plane back to what little he has left.

Characters

- *Ben Tanaka*, the protagonist, is a thirty-year-old Japanese American who manages a theater in Berkeley, California. He has been dating Miko Hayashi for two years, but the relationship has started to sour. Ben is also best friends with Alice Kim, who is one of the few people willing to put up with his negative attitude and constant complaining.
- *Miko Hayashi* is Ben's Japanese American girlfriend. She has recently become politically active in the Asian American community. She works with a group to put on an Asian American film festival and leaves for New York City for an internship related to the festival.
- *Alice Kim* is Ben's best friend. She is Korean American and a lesbian. She is a perpetual student, working on a graduate degree until she is kicked out of school for hitting the roommate of a former lover. Her expulsion from school prompts her to move to New York, where she meets and commits to a relationship with an old acquaintance. She is usually the force that tries, however unsuccessfully, to get Ben to change or try something different from his usual routine.

- *Autumn Phelps* is an employee at the theater Ben manages. She is an aspiring artist and invites Ben to one of her performance-art pieces. After a couple of dates, Ben tries to kiss her but is deflected.
- *Sasha Lenz* is a bisexual woman. Ben meets her at a party and decides to pursue her, even though Alice thinks doing so is a bad idea. She is the first white woman with whom Ben sleeps, and their relationship eventually ends when her former girlfriend returns to Berkeley.

Artistic Style

Tomine works almost exclusively in black and white, and his artwork focuses heavily on detail. Though much of his early work could be called rough, his style has become much cleaner and succinct with time. Tomine uses the clear-line style of drawing, using strong lines of uniform importance and no hatching.

Tomine's panel structure maintains a clean and uniform style, frequently using an eight-panel-per-page structure with two rows of three panels and one row of two panels. Slight variations of this panel structure dominate the pages of *Shortcomings* and highlight and reinforce the real-world problems and experiences of Ben and of the people he encounters.

Tomine's attention to detail also draws attention to the world in which his characters live. Not only does Tomine draw his character with distinct features that can change with their situation (for example, Ben becomes grittier and is slightly unshaven as he becomes more depressed), but also he draws them in clothing that fits with their personalities. Hoodies, T-shirts, jewelry, and even glasses are given the same attention as a character's expressions. The necklace that one character wears in a panel is meticulously drawn in every panel in which the character wears it.

The same attention to detail is given to interiors and exteriors of buildings. Cupboards and fridges are drawn to look as though they actually open, and apartments are filled with accurate decorations and appliances. Because Tomine writes stories about real people, his art also reflects a real and recognizable world, with actual Berkeley and New York buildings depicted. Tomine's art has also been compared to the work of his friend Daniel Clowes, to the point that he has even been accused of stealing Clowes's style.

Adrian Tomine

One of the most important cartoonists of the 1990's, Adrian Tomine began publishing mini-comics as a teenager and garnered an enormous following (this work was later collected as *32 Stories*) before launching a comic book series with Drawn and Quarterly. *Optic Nerve* began as a series of short stories (collected as *Sleepwalk and Other Stories*) and then as a sequence of longer stories (*Summer Blonde*) before featuring the serialization of *Shortcomings*. *Shortcomings*, released as Tomine's first graphic novel, was his first substantial work to address his Asian American heritage. More recently, Tomine has published a short collection of gag material about his wedding and a stand-alone issue of *Optic Nerve*, one of the last remaining comic books to have survived the shift to graphic novels in the 2000's. Tomine's art is strongly influenced by that of his friends Dan Clowes and Jaime Hernandez, and it features clean lines and naturalistic representations. He has also produced several covers for *The New Yorker*.

Themes

Shortcomings is most notable for how it deals with race and sexuality. For both Ben and Miko, their Asian heritage is something that defines them, but in different ways. Miko considers her heritage something to be embraced and celebrated, but for Ben, it is something from which he is constantly running. He is accused of being self-loathing and of fetishizing Caucasian women. While Miko is almost hypersensitive about her heritage, Ben is consciously ignorant. When he accompanies Alice to a family function, he does not fully understand why her Korean parents would have issues with him as a Japanese person. Even as he tries to forget his own race, he is uniquely concerned with the race of those around him. Even when he is with Miko, his eye is constantly wandering, especially toward Caucasian women. Ben is obsessed with the idea of dating and having sex with a Caucasian woman, a fact that also plays into the emphasis on sexuality in *Shortcomings*.

Ben's best friend is a lesbian, and one of the girls he dates, Sasha, identifies as bisexual. However, Ben has turned his obsession with Caucasian women into a race-based sexuality. While most characters are comfortable with their particular sexuality, Ben initially denies that he is attracted to Caucasians, but the goal of sleeping with one soon becomes a driving force for him. Sexuality is one of the few lenses through which Ben is able to see race. However, this is usually a way for Ben to highlight the negative stereotypes of his own heritage. One of Ben's major concerns with dating a Caucasian woman comes from stereotypes about Asian men being less endowed than their Caucasian counterparts physically. This also highlights Ben's belief that it is impossible for individuals to escape the bounds of socially inscribed identities based on race.

Impact

Shortcomings was well received, gaining high praise from many reviewers of both graphic novels and books in general. It won a position on multiple "best of" lists in 2007, including those organized by *Publisher's Weekly* and *The New York Times*. Before *Shortcomings*, Tomine had been criticized for his resistance to confronting racial identity. In fact, the largest impact of *Shortcomings* has been the debate surrounding portrayals and ideas of race—especially for Asian Americans—presented by both the characters and Tomine himself. Largely because of an absence of both Asian American writers and characters in graphic novels, many people either defended or panned the work. An essay published by the Society for the Study of the Multi-Ethnic Literature of the United States asserts that Tomine, like his character Ben, has a pessimistic view of the possibilities and limitations that have been ascribed to Asian Americans. At the same time, David Shook of Oxford University praised Tomine and his effort to "ask questions important enough to be asked." Tomine has been receptive to both praise and criticism of his work, going so far as to print both positive and negative letters he receives in the letters section of *Optic Nerve*.

Joseph Willis

Further Reading

Clowes, Daniel. *Ghost World* (1997).
Tomine, Adrian. *Sleepwalk and Other Stories* (1998).
_____. *Summer Blonde* (2002).

Bibliography

Oh, Sandra. "Sight Unseen: Adrian Tomine's *Optic Nerve* and the Politics of Recognition." *MELUS* 32, no. 3 (2007): 129-151.
Shook, David. "*Shortcomings*." *World Literature Today* 82, no. 3 (2008): 65-66.
Tomine, Adrian. "Adrian Tomine." Interview by Nicole Rudick. *The Believer*, October, 2007, 42-51. http://www.believermag.com/issues/200710/?read=interview_tomine.

See also: *Ghost World*; *Scott Pilgrim*; *American Born Chinese*; *The Arrival*

SHUTTERBUG FOLLIES

Author: Little, Jason
Artist: Jason Little (illustrator)
Publisher: Doubleday Graphic Novels
First serial publication: 2000-2001
First book publication: 2002

Publication History

In 2000, on the heels of his award-winning *Jack's Luck Runs Out* (1998), Jason Little introduced readers to Bee, a quirky young woman working as a photo processor. *Shutterbug Follies* began as a free serialized Web comic that ran in weekly episodes on Little's Web site, beecomix.com. It was also inked in a number of layouts and color formats for weekly newspapers. Little ended each *Bee* Web comic page (12-14 panels) with a cliff-hanger, enticing readers with "continued next week" and putting up a new episode on Sunday mornings. When collected into *Shutterbug Follies*, the installments tell a darkly funny and mysterious story.

In 2002, the strips were gathered into a hardcover Doubleday Graphic Novel (a defunct imprint of Random House that only published two other graphic novels). Little moved to Dark Horse Comics for his next installment of Bee's adventures. He features Bee in *Motel Art Improvement Service* (2010), presenting readers with another mystery, this time with a more mature heroine.

Plot

Bee has just graduated high school and is working as a photo processor in a Lower Manhattan one-hour photo shop. She is an aspiring photographer and gets a voyeuristic slice of life every time she develops a roll of film. She begins keeping copies of the more titillating and strange photos: breasts at bachelor parties, puking frat boys, and before-and-after photos taken by a local mortician. The mortician's handiwork is followed by even more corpses, this time crime-scene photos taken by a Russian newspaper cameraman. There is something not quite right about these latter photos, which sets Bee on the trail of Oleg Khatchatourian.

Jason Little

Jason Little first came to fame with his 1998 Xeric Award-winning comic book *Jack's Luck Runs Out*, which featured characters whose images were derived from playing cards (the jack, queen, and king). In 2002 he published the work for which he is best known, *Shutterbug Follies*, after serializing it online and in several alternative newspapers. *Shutterbug Follies* tells the story of a photo lab technician, Bee, who becomes embroiled in a mystery after she develops pictures of a dead body. A sequel, *Motel Art Improvement Service*, was published in 2010, which finds Bee working as a cleaning lady and involved in a drug deal gone awry. Little's style has been characterized as bubblegum noir for its combination of dark themes and slickly inviting art. His visual style is strongly influenced by the clear-line style of Hergé but with a slightly more cartoony edge, and he uses vibrant colors to establish a sense of space.

After trailing Khatchatourian to his apartment, Bee sets up surveillance across the street and snaps her own photos when the Russian cameraman receives a visit from a redheaded woman and a wheelchair-bound boy. As Bee spies through her viewfinder, a pill-wielding Khatchatourian confronts the woman.

Bee's tedium resumes at the photo shop until she eventually develops another set of the undertaker's before-and-after photos. This time, the corpse is the redheaded woman. With the help of Rodney, a taxi driver, Bee follows Khatchatourian to his photo exhibit entitled "Recent Atrocities," a show consisting entirely of ostensible crime-scene photos.

Bee does some investigating and discovers the dead redheaded woman was Daisy Papavasilou, Khatchatourian's wife, a famous artist, and mother of their ailing son. When the Russian shows up with another roll of film starring his dead wife, Bee is back on the case and tails Khatchatourian to Brighton Beach, where he becomes involved in an apparent kidnapping. Bee listens in as one of the men is murdered.

The next day, Khatchatourian shows up with another roll of film, and, after developing the film, Bee comes across a photo of the bullet-ridden corpse of one of the men from the previous night.

Out of the blue, Khatchatourian calls and offers Bee a night job babysitting his sick son, Yuri. Once Khatchatourian leaves, Bee's curiosity gets the better of her, and she snoops around until she discovers a stash of pills. They are diuretics. It seems Papavasilou had been switching them for the boy's anticonvulsive medication, thereby causing her son's illness. Bee also finds the negatives that prove Khatchatourian murdered his wife.

Khatchatourian is not going to let Bee stand in the way of his "art," and he tries to murder her. She gets away using a homemade WD-40 "torch" and locks herself inside a file cabinet, temporarily escaping Khatchatourian and his Russian mob buddies. She pages Rodney, and he calls 911. However, the Russian discovers and overpowers Bee, bringing a heroin-filled syringe closer to her, until Yuri appears in the doorway and distracts Khatchatourian, allowing Bee to escape. The apartment door is forced open and cops pour in. Bee is saved, the bad guys are taken to jail, and the last panel of *Shutterbug Follies* shows Bee in Rodney's cab, looking back as Yuri is taken away by social services.

Characters
- *Bee,* the heroine, is a normally proportioned young woman, with a preference for striped T-shirts and jeans. Wide-rimmed green glasses complement her short-cropped red hair. She works at a photo-processing lab and is nosy to the point of voyeurism, making copies for her own collection of the more titillating photographs she processes. Her curiosity lands her in the middle of a murder mystery.
- *Oleg Khatchatourian,* the antagonist, is a bearded Russian who speaks in heavily accented English. He is an artist and assassin who operates under the occupational ruse of a newspaper cameraman, setting up his victims in poses fit for his exhibit "Recent Atrocities." He is the father of Yuri and the husband and murderer of Daisy Papavasilou.
- *The Mortician* is a horse-toothed, white-haired, dapper old man. He takes before-and-after pictures of his "latest preparations," some of which Bee saves to share with her best friend. He is Daisy Papavasilou's undertaker.
- *Daisy Papavasilou,* the redheaded wife of Khatchatourian and mother of Yuri, is also an artist. She is mentally ill, having Munchausen syndrome by proxy, and substitutes her son's anticonvulsive medication for diuretic pills that keep him wheelchair bound. Daisy is trampled to death by a horse, but it may have been murder.
- *Lyla* is Bee's dark-haired best friend. She is sexually precocious and sports tattoos and urban chic outfits. She looks forward to the day that Bee saves up enough money to become her roommate. Bee seeks advice on several topics from her.
- *Rodney Plaster,* is a scruffy, cigarette-smoking cab driver that Bee enlists to track down Khatchatourian. He is a member of the music group the Polymers. He often gives Bee cautionary advice and ultimately saves her life by calling the cops when she is trapped in Khatchatourian's apartment.
- *Huey,* Bee's love interest, is a brown-haired young man who changes his looks to match his current situation. He fancies himself a photographer but seems to be nothing more than a Peeping Tom. He is Khatchatourian's assistant and tells Bee that there is nothing fake about Khatchatourian's bloody photographs.

Artistic Style

Shutterbug Follies's full-color, horizontal hardcover format is reminiscent of a photo album, such as those found on the shelves of the fictional "Mulberry Photo" where Bee works. The front cover's depiction of a filmstrip, with its negative images of atrocities, highlights Bee's penchant for snooping, but when the film wraps around to the back cover, readers recognize the main characters.

Between the covers, a substantial rounded black line surrounds the narrative panels. Bee's photo-inspired panels are less encumbered, using only a thin outline. Thirty-five millimeter film and photographs are just a few of the photo formats in *Shutterbug*; some panels are Polaroids, and others are black-and-white Brownie Hawkeye stills. The only deviation from the square, left-to-right, top-to-bottom photo-album style occurs in nightmare and action scenes, when Rodney has to "follow that car," when Bee is risking her neck to get to the bottom of kidnapping and murder, or when she is being menaced by Khatchatourian.

The book also contains panels of red negatives with sprocket holes, emphasizing the photographic nature of Bee's work and her voyeuristic tendencies. Many panels are seen through a camera's viewfinder, as Bee utilizes her telephoto lens to spy on the bad guys. There are even panels that resemble television screens as Khatchatourian watches Bee on closed-circuit surveillance cameras.

The straight-on perspective rarely deviates and pulls the reader into the pictures, while many panels tell the story without words. Speech bubbles add to, instead of repeat, the story. Text boxes communicate the passage of time ("eighteen minutes later") and space ("fifteen blocks later"). Shouting is rendered in bold text, sound effects are colored, and sweat (or stress) beads fly throughout. The photographic panel style is essential to the narrative of Bee.

Themes
Little calls *Shutterbug Follies* "bubblegum noir," a Nancy-Drew-meets-Sam-Spade kind of story. Even though Bee may rival Miss Marple in sleuthing ability, this is no cozy mystery; her guts and spunk are reminiscent of a Raymond Chandler character as, for example, she wields a phone to knock her attacker senseless. Her cartoonlike visual identity may remind some readers of Velma Dinkley, but her exploits take her beyond *Scooby Doo* since characters from R-rated movies, not Saturday-morning cartoons, populate her world. Bee is an amateur detective who uses reasoning and logic like any good investigator.

Shutterbug Follies is a story in which good triumphs

Cartoonist Jason Little, photographed at the 2003 Alternative Press Expo (APE) in San Francisco. (By GeoffreyMason, via Wikimedia Commons)

over evil, but that does not mean it qualifies for the Comics Code seal of approval. Like any first-rate noir detective, Bee has a secure sense of right and wrong when battling criminals in the gritty world of the city. She is ambivalent about morality, and even though she may be a "good girl," it is not by choice.

Photography is both a narrative and stylistic theme in *Shutterbug Follies*. Developing film is the perfect career for the voyeuristic Bee, and Little exploits photography and film in the book's layout and narrative. On a larger scale, Little seems to be asking, "What constitutes art?"

Bee is a feminist hero. She is the guts and brains behind a loose band of compatriots. The taxi-driving Rodney not only vomits at the sight of blood but also never wants to get involved in hunting down the criminals. He waits in the car while Bee risks her neck to see what the Russian mob is up to. Huey, Bee's love interest, wilts at the slightest provocation, including criticism of his "art." Lyla is always cautioning Bee against taking chances, unless they are sexual in nature. In the end, it is Bee who infiltrates the lair of the assassin and brawls her way to his ultimate capture.

Impact

Little appreciates *The Adventures of Tintin* (1929-1976), and it shows. His characters and settings have the saturated hues and clear line that made Hergé famous, with lots of full-bodied oranges, reds, purples, and greens. There is no cross-hatching, skies are blue, sidewalks are gray, and shadows are dark tones on top of the original color. Little's art may fool some readers (those who expect *Tintin*-esque story lines), but *Shutterbug Follies* is an adult-rated adventure taking place on the streets of New York. *Shutterbug Follies* earned the dubious honor of being banned in Texas schools for profanity, inappropriate language, and sexual content, as well as in Arizona for material that Little supposes is "prurient in nature [because] all the panels with violence and blood have been left in."

When *Shutterbug Follies* first appeared on the Web as a serial comic it featured a vertical layout and always ended with a cliff-hanger. These once-a-week comics, delivered each Sunday, kept readers coming back for more and, with few exceptions, constitute the hardcover edition of *Shutterbug Follies*.

Bee is a new kind of hero, a woman with a normal shape who wears flat shoes. Little's phrase "bubblegum noir" is spot-on, with Bee in noir trouble, but shown in bubblegum colors and art reminiscent of the Sunday newspaper comics. Little's narratives are best when they are shown, not told, allowing the reader to sit next to Bee as she rides on the subway and look over her shoulder as she peruses her catalog of the grotesque.

Doré Ripley

Further Reading

Bendis, Michael Brian. *Alias* (2001-2004).

Little, Jason. *Motel Art Improvement Service* (2010).

Mills, Christopher. *Femme Noir: The Dark City Diaries* (2009).

Bibliography

"Book Review: *Shutterbug Follies*." Review of *Shutterbug Follies*, by Jason Little. *Librarianaut*, March 24, 2009. http://librarianaut.com/2009/03/24/book-review-shutterbug-follies.

Little, Jason. "An Interview with Jason Little." Interview by Mark Bryant. *Popimage*, Fall, 1999. http://www.beecomix.com/comics/infoframes.htm.

Seven, John. "Motel Art Improvement Service Goes from Web to Print." *Publisher's Weekly*, December 14, 2010. http://www.publishersweekly.com/pw/by-topic/book-news/comics/article/45504-motel-art-improvement-service-goes-from-web-to-print.html.

See also: *Ice Haven*; *Jimmy Corrigan*; *The Adventures of Tintin*

SIGNAL TO NOISE

Author: Gaiman, Neil
Artist: Dave McKean (illustrator)
Publisher: VG Graphics; Dark Horse Comics
First serial publication: 1989-1992
First book publication: 1992

Publication History

Signal to Noise has sustained a variable life, extending through different formats. Conceptually inspired by a short work, entitled "Wipe Out," composed by Dave McKean for the fashion magazine *The Face*, it developed into a series written by Neil Gaiman for sequential publication in *The Face* in 1989. VG Graphics brought out a collected edition in 1992, in tandem with Dark Horse Comic's American edition, and the work has continued to be reprinted by Dark Horse Comics through 2007.

Following the first collected version of the work in the United Kingdom, a BBC Radio 3 drama based on the work was broadcast in 1996, with input from both Gaiman and McKean. McKean later released a recording of the radio drama as an audio CD through his own record label, *Feral*, and it has since been distributed by Alan Spiegel Fine Arts. Various other permutations of the work include a stage play produced by the NOWtheatre Group in Chicago.

The Dark Horse Comics 2007 edition contains "Wipe Out," prose poems by Gaiman and McKean, a final "millennial" chapter, and a "remastering," which was necessary when the original "film" for the book was lost and the work needed to be recomposed. Both Gaiman and McKean have seen the graphic work as a project with a life of its own, transmuting and becoming "interactive" in the years following its original publication, a concept in keeping with the themes of the work itself.

Plot

Signal to Noise depicts the final days of a film director in London who learns that he is dying of cancerous tumors. Refusing treatment, the director finishes his final script at the cost of personal relationships, but he dies

> **Neil Gaiman**
> Neil Gaiman has written in a dizzying number of genres and formats, meeting critical and popular success in all of them. His characters are memorable and complex, and find themselves in surreal, often supernatural, settings. Gaiman evokes a creepy, sometimes horrifying, atmosphere, but balances this with whimsical interludes and comic relief. The novels are complex, with frequent use of literary and cultural references. Despite its complexity, Gaiman's prose is straightforward and reader-friendly, and the stories move quickly with multiple storylines resolving just in the nick of time.

with his personal vision and creative legacy intact. The eleven-part sequence utilizes first-person narrative and flashback memory sequences to illustrate the director's impressions of his own illness as well as the conceptual processes behind his final film project.

The director narrates the opening sequences of his "mental film," a subject dealing with the year 999 A.D., set in a village in the middle of Europe, where townspeople await the end of the world. Waking in his Islington apartment after a nightmare, the director ignores a call from his doctor and friend, Julia, who insists he accept treatment for his condition. He asks himself about the "sense" of life, introducing the title questions "What's signal? What's noise?" He recalls learning of his condition, refusing treatment, and going home. Meeting with friend and producer Inanna at his home, he cancels the film project and relates the grim news of his sickness.

Thinking of millennial celebrations to occur ten years in the future, the director realizes he will be dead; he becomes frustrated with his body and his work, wishing for more time to get his final project "right." Three months following his diagnosis, the director begins to write, delineating the characters of the village.

The director's upstairs neighbor, Reed, visits him, and they discuss the possibility of a "pattern" in life's chaos, a premise that the director rejects. Inanna continues to contact the director, but he denies that he is writing the film script. He completes more than half of his film script and settles on *Apocatastasis* as the title for his film, a term meaning renewal or return to an original position. He agrees to allow Julia to do a blood test but refuses treatment again when the results appear bleak.

The director completes his film script with great satisfaction, feeling that it can now live independently of him. He finds himself among the villagers awaiting the apocalypse in silence. As the moment passes, the villagers begin to realize that their world has not ended, but the director has died. Reed gives Inanna the envelope left behind for her by the director. At home, Inanna opens the envelope, finds the script for *Apocatastasis*, and begins to read.

Almost ten years later, Inanna narrates her experiences, having seen the director's film through production and moved on with her life. Approaching the millennium, he has been impossible to forget, as a stage play based on his diaries and a flurry of interviews has accompanied a documentary and retrospective about him. The events give her a sense of art's function, allowing the living to commune with the dead. The millennium comes and goes, much as the director predicted, with human beings moving on along the same path, as in *Apocatastasis*.

Characters

- *The Director*, the work's protagonist and narrator, is a veteran and award-winning filmmaker approaching a major project when he learns he is terminally ill. Living in London in an Islington apartment, he continues work on the film script, regardless of whether or not it will see publication, and he considers the concept of apocalypse and of "apocatastasis," or renewal. He wears large glasses, has a graying moustache and disheveled salt-and-pepper hair, and dresses in simple clothing of blue, black, white, or gray-brown.
- *Julia* is the director's doctor and friend whom he loves but keeps at arm's length. She diagnoses the director's tumors and attempts to treat him, but she is denied. The director envisions her as an attractive snow leopard, but she is never portrayed visually in the text.
- *Inanna Shah-Leshy* is the director's producer who intends to facilitate his current project. She has a great attachment to the director, may have at some time been his lover, and admits that she loves him after his death. She is portrayed with long, dark, wavy hair and in light-colored, feminine clothing. She also acts as narrator for the final, posthumous chapter of the work.
- *Reed* is the director's upstairs neighbor and friend. His idealistic belief in possible "patterns" in the universe contrasts with the agnostic views of the director and the rationalist views of Inanna, who is described as his "opposite." He confesses his love for the director following his death, and appears with long hair in a ponytail, a short beard, and light-colored clothing.

Artistic Style

The style of *Signal to Noise* is partly patterned after the short work "Wipe Out" that McKean designed for *The Face* magazine. Features of the original work include the random cutting and pasting of language and the cinematic effect of shifting angles around a central figure. These features became a stylistic template for the new work, leaving room for reader interpretation of the significance of seemingly random language to the story line; extra material added to later versions of *Signal to Noise* shows the evolution of complementary stylistic elements in McKean's work.

Like Gaiman's and McKean's *Violent Cases* (1987), *Signal to Noise* includes the use of multilayered pencil sketches, mixed-media collage and photography, and a grid effect of sequential narrative with some large, full-page spreads. *Signal to Noise* is divided into strict white-framed grid patterns for about two-thirds of its contents, interrupted by striking half-page or full-page open images, usually depicting the director. A lavish, painted, double-page spread shows the villagers waiting at a distance at the time of the director's death.

Color scheme is also similar between *Violent Cases* and *Signal to Noise*, focusing on blues, grays, and browns. *Signal to Noise* displays a washed effect of ink

Author Neil Gaiman. (By Kyle Cassidy, via Wikimedia Commons)

and blue watercolor, giving the film sequences a richer texture than the external narrative. McKean's broader style within the work consistently evokes luminous surfaces against a dark background, while the final "millennial" chapter appears more celebratory, with a bold use of gold, purple, and green backgrounds.

Lettering includes white narrative text overlaying dark panels, whereas reported speech appears in white speech bubbles. The final "millennial" chapter, however, presents text narrative as black on a streaming red banner. Photographic elements appear both as purely photographic collage and as part of mixed-media imagery, particularly implemented in "storytelling" sequences dealing with religious content or the remote past.

Themes

The title *Signal to Noise* introduces what may be the most general theme of the work, the relationship between meaning, signals, and the "background noise" of daily life. The title is part of a phrase describing the ratio between transmitted signal and background static. Locating the division between signal and noise, however, proves problematic for the director, for whom this is a recurrent line of questioning. Images reinforce the signal/noise concept, including the snowstorm that opens the director's screenplay, obscuring the reader's view of the villagers awaiting apocalypse in a television static effect. Gaiman and McKean reinforce this dominant concept by flooding the text with the "noise" of garbled sentences opening each chapter title page in word combinations without a clear established meaning that, nevertheless, add to the work. All daily life becomes "noise" to the director as he attempts to focus on the "signal" of his final work until the "silence" of death, which concludes both signal and noise.

Another significant grouping of concepts in the work involves the relationship between apocalypse and "apocatastasis," which is defined in the text as a restoration, or return, to a previous position or condition. Apocalypse is what the director's villagers most fear, and it is the subject of the director's film, but he chooses to reframe the apocalyptic situation as not "one big" apocalypse in human history but a series of "little ones" that conclude each human life. Human history operates in a cycle of feared apocalypse resulting in "apocatastasis," a circular return to original positions to begin the cycle again.

Several situations in *Signal to Noise* give rise to a discussion of the role and function of artistic creation and the survival of artifacts following the death of their creator. The director notes in dream sequences that he has no offspring and that his films have been his children and loved ones. This suggests that for the director, his "obsession," film, is a form of "signal" whereby he communicates meaningful aspects of himself. Inanna, in her epilogue, concludes that art exists as a form of necessary communication with the dead, prophetic in its observation of cyclical human history.

Impact

In the late 1980's, Gaiman and McKean set out to highlight the vast potential of the comics medium and the ways in which comics have matured in subject matter and format. Conceived of as serialized works (rather than graphic novels), works such as *Violent Cases* and *Signal to Noise* exemplify new directions in comics. In terms of subject matter, they introduce the psychological first-person narrative and handle universal human themes, including the dark aspects of life and a questioning of the modern human condition. *Signal to Noise*, in particular, takes on a historical perspective at the approach of the millennium, emphasizing the continuity of human experience over time, and it assumes that comics have the potential gravitas to depict the relationship between the visual arts, including film, drama, and sequential narrative, in a meaningful way.

In terms of format and content, *Signal to Noise* addresses the boundaries between language and image intrinsic in comics by providing disjunctive, nonlinear text as a form of commentary on image and plot and by necessitating reader participation in establishing interpretation. The multimedia life of the work emphasizes this boundary-crossing possibility in comics, living on in several emended editions, a radio play, and a stage play.

McKean's innovative and experimental artwork brings a much wider range of media to comics illustration than that of the traditional Golden Age and Silver Age of comics, introducing photography, collage, and computer technology such as text sampling to the medium. McKean's work has helped raise comics illustration to a level of "high art," suggesting that comics illustration, as a whole, is intrinsically worthy of classification alongside more established art formats.

While the subject matter of *Signal to Noise* reinforces nonsuperhero content and presents significant universal human themes as a relevant commentary on modern life, its format establishes visual experimentation and a variety of media as acceptable aspects of comics illustration. McKean's serialized works *Cages* (1990-1996) and *Pictures That Tick* (2009) further explore the relationship between comics illustration and multimedia context.

Hannah E. Means-Shannon

Further Reading

Gaiman, Neil, and Dave McKean. *The Tragical Comedy or Comical Tragedy of Mr. Punch* (1994).

_____. *Violent Cases* (1987).

McKean, Dave. *Cages* (1998).

Bibliography

McCabe, Joe. *Hanging Out with the Dream King*. Seattle: Fantagraphics Books, 2005.

Olsen, Stephen P. *The Library of Graphic Novelists: Neil Gaiman*. New York: Rosen, 2005.

Schweitzer, Darrell, ed. *The Neil Gaiman Reader*. Rockville, Md.: Wildside Press, 2007.

See also: *The Tragical Comedy or Comical Tragedy of Mr. Punch*; *Cages*; *Violent Cases*

SIN CITY

Author: Miller, Frank
Artist: Frank Miller (illustrator); Lynn Varley (colorist, cover artist); Chip Kidd (cover artist)
Publisher: Dark Horse Comics
First serial publication: 1991-2000
First book publication: 1993-2000

Publication History

Sin City's first appearance was in *Dark Horse Presents, Fifth Anniversary Special* in 1991 and consisted of the first chapter of what would become *Sin City: A Hard Goodbye*. Comics creator Frank Miller was a rising star at this point in his career, after the success of *Batman: The Dark Knight Returns* (1986) and *Batman: Year One* (1988). Miller had built his career as an artist working for DC Comics and then for Marvel Comics, notably on the *Daredevil* (1986) series. Dark Horse Comics was created in 1986 and has become the largest independent publisher of American comics.

After the initial appearance of *Sin City*, Miller produced the entirety of the first *Sin City* arc in *Dark Horse Presents*, issues 51-62. The *Sin City* tale was well received, and Miller continued to produce the stories, often referred to as "yarns." Dark Horse published the next yarn, *A Dame to Kill For*, as a limited series in 1993. Miller wrote yarns of varying lengths with one-shots appearing in anthologies, such as *Dark Horse Presents* and *Tales to Offend*, but longer arcs were printed in miniseries format. The series' popularity resulted in the limited-series issues being reprinted as graphic novels and the one-shots being published in an anthology in graphic novel form called *Sin City: Booze, Broads, and Bullets*.

Plot

Sin City is a collection of stories concerning the inhabitants of the crime-blighted metropolis Basin City (commonly referred to as Sin City) and its outlying regions. The different tales were published out of chronological order, but a time line can be pieced together based on the interaction of the characters.

Frank Miller. (By pinguino k from North Hollywood, USA, via Wikimedia Commons)

The first yarn, *The Hard Goodbye*, opens with the street tough Marv expressing his gratitude for finding Goldie, a prostitute. Marv wakes up the next morning feeling as if he has been drugged and notices that Goldie has been murdered sometime during the night. The police quickly close in on Marv's apartment; realizing he has been set up, Marv swears vengeance for Goldie and begins his violent assault on the swarming police force. He hunts for those responsible for Goldie's death and begins interrogating increasingly well-connected individuals. After meeting Goldie's twin sister, Marv is provided with the tools and information needed to kill a cannibalistic serial killer named Kevin and his benefactor, the powerful Patrick Henry Roark. Marv is arrested, and the story ends with Marv's death in the electric chair.

In *A Dame to Kill For*, Dwight McCarthy's former lover, Ava, persuades him that her new husband, Damien Lord, is an abusive sadist who plans to torture her to death. Dwight enlists the aid of Marv to infiltrate the heavily secured home of Ava's wealthy husband. Dwight kills Damien and is immediately shot by Ava, as she explains that she has set him up in order to gain Damien's wealth. Dwight receives multiple gunshot wounds but is able to escape with Marv's aid. He makes it to Old Town, and his life is saved through the medical help of the prostitutes there. He reveals that two of Old Town's most influential citizens, Gail and Miho, are indebted to him, so he is able to enlist their help to get revenge and start a new life. Ava seduces a police officer in order to get him to kill Dwight. Dwight eventually returns and, through an intricate plan, infiltrates the Lord compound again and manages to kill Ava.

The Big Fat Kill features Dwight after the events of *A Dame to Kill For*, in which he begins a new life with the face given to him by the women of Old Town. Dwight's new girlfriend, Shellie, has been getting harassed and beaten by a man named Jack. Dwight follows Jack and his friends as they make trouble in Old Town and are quickly trapped and killed by Miho the assassin. Dwight discovers that Jack is "Iron Jack" Rafferty, a hero cop; thus, he must hide the bodies of Jack and his friends or else a truce between the prostitutes of Old Town and the police will be destroyed. Dwight has a hallucination-filled trip to some tar pits and is attacked by mercenaries. Gail is kidnapped and tortured to force the surrender of Old Town in the face of the impending conflict. Dwight is rescued by Miho and retrieves the remaining evidence, Jack's severed head, from the mercenaries. Using classic battle tactics, Dwight and his allies are able both to destroy all the evidence and to eliminate all the witnesses.

That Yellow Bastard opens years before the other stories of Sin City, with the last workday of Detective John Hartigan. Hartigan has tracked down a serial pedophile and murderer and has decided to bring him to justice while saving the latest intended victim, Nancy Callahan. Unfortunately for Hartigan, the killer is the only son of Senator Roark, the most powerful man in Sin City, and is thus untouchable. Hartigan rescues Nancy and disfigures the younger Roark by shooting off his ear, hand, and genitals. Senator Roark frames Hartigan for the kidnapping of the young girls taken by his son. Hartigan struggles in prison but keeps sane through the weekly letters Nancy sends him. When the letters stop abruptly and Hartigan is visited by a yellow, putrid-smelling man, he signs a confession to the crime and is immediately released. Hartigan tracks down Nancy, realizing too late that his release is a trap, and he is eventually incapacitated by the Yellow Bastard. The Yellow Bastard is revealed to be the younger Roark; he has mutated in an effort to remake his mutilated body. Hartigan escapes his death trap, tracks down the Yellow Bastard, and kills him. Hartigan kills himself in one last attempt to save Nancy by protecting her from the inevitable wrath of Senator Roark.

In *Family Values*, Dwight and Miho track down those responsible for the death of Carmen, one of the prostitutes of Old Town. They learn of the assassination of a hit man-turned-politician, which resulted in Carmen's needless death. Miho acts as the enforcer as Dwight follows the trail of informants and thugs to the head of the Sin City mafia. After relating the tale of Carmen to the mob heads, Dwight leaves the execution of the men to Carmen's mourning lover, Daisy.

Booze, Broads, and Bullets is a collection of short one-shots that provide additional tales about Marv and Dwight's exploits in Sin City. The assassin Delia is introduced and appears in a few short stories. The collection also includes the short piece "Silent Night," which, though containing only a single line of text, relates the story of Marv rescuing a child from slavery.

Hell and Back is the love story between Wallace and Esther. Wallace, a poor war hero, saves Esther from committing suicide, and they soon fall in love. Two men wearing medical services uniforms are pursuing Esther and eventually incapacitate Wallace and kidnap her. Arriving at Esther's address, Wallace finds Delia; both are quickly set upon by the monstrous Manute, whom Wallace is able to defeat. Wallace leaves with Delia and recruits the help of his former captain in the Army. Wallace suspects Delia of working against him but is ultimately unable to prevent himself from being drugged, placed in a car, and thrown off a cliff. Although he survives the crash, he suffers from severe hallucinations as he is attacked by corrupt police officers. Wallace defeats the corrupt cops, Delia, and her allies with the help of the captain. He locates Esther in a base that seems to produce and distribute human slaves and human organs. Wallace informs the police of the Wallenquist group's operation and disrupts the base through the destruction of certain buildings and the eventual police action. Wallace is finally reunited with Esther, and they drive off into the desert.

Volumes
- *Sin City: The Hard Goodbye* (1993). Also known as *Sin City*. Collects issues 51-62 of *Dark Horse Presents*. Relates the story of Marv's quest to avenge Goldie's death.
- *A Dame to Kill For: A Tale from Sin City* (1994). Collects issues 1-6 of *Sin City: A Dame to Kill For*. Covers Dwight's fall back into the filth of Sin City and attempt to kill those responsible.
- *The Big Fat Kill: A Tale from Sin City* (1996). Collects issues 1-5 of *Sin City: The Big Fat Kill*. Dwight and the Old Town prostitutes cover up their murder of a hero cop.
- *That Yellow Bastard: A Sin City Yarn* (1997). Collects issues 1-6 of *Sin City: That Yellow Bastard*. Relates Detective Hartigan's attempt to save Nancy Callahan's life by standing against the powerful Roark family.
- *Family Values: A Sin City Yarn* (1997). Dwight and Miho team up to track down a hit man and exact revenge for the senseless killing of an Old Town prostitute.
- *Sin City: Booze, Broads, and Bullets* (1998). Collects one-shots that provide further adventures of Marv and Dwight as well as glimpses of the supporting characters of Sin City.
- *Hell and Back: A Sin City Love Story* (2000). Collects issues 1-9 of *Sin City: Hell and Back*. Features a new character named Wallace, a war hero and Medal of Honor recipient, who falls in love with Esther and must destroy a criminal enterprise to get her back.

Characters
- *Marv* is a central character in some of *Sin City*'s yarns. He is a hulking man with a broad chest and a deeply scarred face. He was raised in the most dangerous part of Sin City and grew up with a twisted sense of fun and an unstoppable drive to fight. He suffers from some kind of mental disorder, which seems to cause memory loss, hallucinations, and confusion. He is extremely loyal to his friends and defends women and children.
- *Dwight McCarthy* is a central figure in Sin City. He is athletically built, with well-defined muscles, and is initially shown bald with a pointed chin; however, after plastic surgery, his chin is squared and his hair grows out. He often fights to protect women, whether or not they ask for help, and he has formed a close relationship with Gail and Miho of Old Town.
- *John Hartigan* is a retired detective with angina. He is tall with wide shoulders and a large, X-shaped scar over his right eye. He is an honest cop in a corrupt department and decides to sacrifices his entire life to save Nancy Callahan.
- *Wallace*, the central character in *Hell and Back*, is a long-haired, bearded man of above-average height. He is a Medal of Honor recipient and thus has impressive combat skills and stamina. He is portrayed as an unemployed artist and chef.
- *Goldie* is the woman of Marv's dreams and the twin sister of Wendy. A prostitute of Old Town, she has blond, curly hair and a curvy body. Marv seeks to avenge her murder.
- *Kevin* is a cannibalistic serial killer. He has a blank expression and cropped hair and wears glasses.
- *Wendy* is Goldie's twin sister and one of the leaders of Old Town.
- *Patrick Henry Roark* is a Catholic cardinal and influential member of the Roark family. A short, fat, balding man, he uses his influence to control the people in power across Sin City.
- *Ava Lord* is Dwight's former lover and the wife of the wealthy aristocrat Damien Lord. She is a manipulative woman who uses her sexual charms to control others and describes herself as evil.
- *Jack*, a.k.a. *Iron Jack Rafferty* and *Jackie Boy*, is a hero cop who assaults Dwight's girlfriend, Shellie, and is killed by Miho.
- *Manute* is a hired enforcer for Ava Lord and later the Wallenquist group. He is likely the largest

character in Sin City, with impressive strength and great loyalty to his employers.
- *Gail* is a leader in Old Town. She is a tall woman with a slim, athletic body and short, spiked hair. She is passionate but loyal to the women she leads.
- *Miho* is the deadliest assassin in Sin City and works for the women of Old Town as an enforcer of their laws. She is Japanese and shorter than five feet and has long, flowing hair.
- *Nancy Callahan* is the girl saved by Detective John Hartigan. She grows up to be the beautiful exotic dancer at the local bar, Kadie's, visited by all of the characters of Sin City.
- *The Yellow Bastard*, the son of Senator Roark, is the serial pedophile and murderer who turns yellow and fetid after experiments are performed on him to restore his missing body parts.
- *Senator Roark* is the short, fat brother of Patrick Henry Roark and father of the Yellow Bastard. His connections with all the powerful organizations in the city give him authority and make him the most powerful man in Sin City.
- *Esther* is Wallace's love interest in *Hell and Back*. She is a beautiful African American woman. She is an actor and a target for the human slave operation of the Wallenquist group.
- *Delia*, a.k.a. *Blue Eyes*, is an assassin working for the Wallenquist group. She is a slim, beautiful woman with bright blue eyes.

Artistic Style

Sin City was produced in black and white, with a few elements touched with a single color to draw the eye of the reader. The sharp delineation between the black-and-white regions of each illustration is created through the use of crisp straight lines and a lack of shading. Each image is created by voids within a black space, with figures seemingly rising from the background. The figures are drawn in a generally realistic manner but with exaggerations of masculine features.

Scenes containing snow are particularly interesting, as Miller creates unique patterns of voids within the illustration through a technique using the application and removal of white rubber cement. Rain is represented by long streaks of white, creating voids that obscure the characters and background alike.

Essentially, characters are formed by scraping away the darkness of a background to reveal details; the precipitation is created through sharp voids and so takes on its own organic quality. The addition of points of color in a predominantly colorless work allows Miller to create intensity in certain physical features, such as blue or red eyes. The final volume, *Hell and Back*, uses a large amount of pastel color to represent Wallace's hallucinations, and the effect is immediate, as it drags the reader from the bleak portrayal of *Sin City* into a world of bright colors and pop-culture references.

Themes

Sin City addresses concepts of gender identity and gender roles as well as the part of a society that rejects traditional concepts of law and order. Some critics have referred to Sin City as hypermasculine, overly violent, and misogynistic. While masculinity and masculine roles are important to the characters in Sin City, the protagonists are most often driven by vengeance, loyalty, or altruism. Dwight is driven by a need to protect the women around him, and the complexity of his relationship with the women comments on classic masculine gender roles within a world of egalitarian female agency. The use of the word "retard" in the text indicates a complete lack of political correctness, which is likely Miller's act of rebellion against both the loss of traditional masculine identity and the overemphasis on emotional sensitivity.

Sin City explores the concept of a "good madman" in the character of Marv, who is governed by a moral code of protecting women and children yet driven by intense homicidal urges. Marv's actions in *The Hard Goodbye* are not fueled by any selfish desire but a fixation on the complete removal of a perceived evil force, so Marv essentially ceases to be a man and becomes a force of pure violence. The characters in *Sin City* are so hyperbolic that they simply become manifestations of the ideals that they hold at their core.

Impact

Sin City solidified a growing trend in superhero comic books that focused on the grit and street crime of cities. The popular reception of each successive yarn caused Miller to increase the pulp-fiction nature of the comics. The final yarn, *Hell and Back*, reveals a certain change in Miller's perception of his own work, as he begins to hyperbolize his own style. The character Wallace seems to be an amalgamation of each of the preceding male protagonists, possessing Marv's toughness, Hartigan's devotion, and Dwight's control. This final volume satirizes the hypermasculine concept, or at least comments on its overuse. Miller's inclination to mock his own characters continues in *Batman: The Dark Knight Strikes Again* (2002).

Films

Sin City. Directed by Robert Rodriguez and Frank Miller. Dimension Films/Troublemaker Studios, 2005. The film was loyal to the source material, and the comics served as a storyboard during the production process. The film mirrors the novels' black-and-white format with splashes of color appearing on key elements. The cast included Bruce Willis as Hartigan, Clive Owen as Dwight, and Benicio Del Toro as Jackie Boy, and Mickey Rourke won a number of awards for his portrayal of Marv.

Joseph Romito

Further Reading

Miller, Frank, and Klaus Janson. *Batman: The Dark Knight Returns* (1986).

Miller, Frank, and David Mazzucchelli. *Batman: Year One* (1988).

Miller, Frank, and Lynn Varley. *Batman: The Dark Knight Strikes Again* (2002).

Bibliography

Dargis, Manohla. "A Savage and Sexy City of Pulp Fiction Regulars." *The New York Times*, April 1, 2005. http://movies.nytimes.com/2005/04/01/movies/01sin.html?_r=1&ex=1153281600&en=7e266ef33d532f3a&ei=5070&oref=slogin.

Eisner, Will, Frank Miller, and Charles Brownstein. *Eisner/Miller: A One-on-One Interview*. Milwaukie, Ore.: Dark Horse Books, 2005.

Wandtke, Terrence R. *The Amazing Transforming Superhero! Essays on the Revision of Characters in Comic Books, Film, and Television*. Jefferson, N.C.: McFarland, 2007.

See also: *300*; *Hard Boiled*

Skim

Author: Tamaki, Mariko
Artist: Jillian Tamaki (illustrator)
Publisher: Groundwood Books
First book publication: 2008

Publication History

In 2005, Emily Pohl-Weary, editor of *Kiss Machine*, a popular Toronto "zine," wanted to publish a series of graphic novellas featuring Canadian writers and artists who had no previous experience working on comics. Mariko Tamaki, a columnist for *Kiss Machine* and a friend of Pohl-Weary, had the idea for a Gothic Lolita story told through the eyes of a Japanese Canadian teenager. She approached her cousin, Jillian Tamaki, a New York-based graphic artist with whom she had never worked, to illustrate the book. The pair produced a twenty-four-page protoversion of *Skim* that was distributed on newsstands in Canada. This early version of *Skim*, about one-third of the final story, came to the attention of Patsy Aldana, publisher of Groundwood Books, who signed the book based on the strength of the published comic book and a synopsis of the rest of the story. The book was redrawn for consistency and published in 2008.

Plot

Kimberly Keiko Cameron, also known as Skim, is a sixteen-year-old daughter of separated parents who attends an all-girls Roman Catholic high school. Skim shares a cynical view of school and her fellow students, as well as an interest in Wicca with her only friend, Lisa Soor.

Shortly after the breakup between Katie Matthews, one of the popular girls at school, and John Reddear, a star athlete from a neighboring all-boys school, John kills himself, sending the girls' school staff into a panic. Students involved with Gothic culture, including Skim, are deemed fragile by the school's guidance counselor, Mrs. Hornet. Seeking some relief from the stress of her school, Skim skips class to smoke in a nearby ravine and is joined by Ms. Archer, the only teacher with whom Skim feels a kinship.

The friendship between Lisa and Skim begins to fray as Skim becomes increasingly more distant and secretive about her frequent out-of-school meetings with Ms. Archer, with whom she later shares a kiss. Skim begins obsessively visiting Ms. Archer at her home, when she stopped showing up for work.

The tense environment at school continues when Katie falls off a roof and breaks both her arms. Many, including Katie's best friend Julie Peters, assume her accident was a suicide attempt. In response to Katie's accident, Julie organizes a new club called Girls Celebrate Life, but Skim and Lisa see through the group's superficiality.

The school staff continues to search for a way to prevent another tragedy by bringing in grief counselors. Attending one of these sessions, Skim realizes both the growing gap between her and Lisa and her strong romantic feelings for Ms. Archer. Ms. Archer eventually returns to school but barely acknowledges Skim. This prompts Skim to visit Ms. Archer's home again, leaving her valued tarot cards behind as a sign of affection. The next day at school, Skim is devastated when Ms. Archer tells her not to come to her home anymore and when Lisa reveals that Ms. Archer has taken a new job and will be leaving.

During a memorial ceremony, Skim and Lisa discuss the rumors that John may have been gay. Feeling alienated from Lisa and upset about Ms. Archer leaving, Skim eats alone and then returns to school to discover she missed seeing Ms. Archer for the last time.

Lisa and Anna Canard, another popular girl, have become close, and Skim finds a new friend in Katie. Skim attends the big dance with Lisa but discovers Katie outside the gym, destroying the Girls Celebrate Life bulletin board. Skim and Katie leave the dance together after they are confronted by Julie, who accuses Katie of not appreciating her friends. Katie reveals to Skim that she feels harassed by her friends and wants to be left alone.

> **Mariko and Jillian Tamaki**
>
> In 2008, cousins Mariko and Jillian Tamaki produced the award-winning graphic novel *Skim*, a remarkable debut work. Writer Mariko Tamaki was already established as a Toronto-based writer of creative nonfiction, while Jillian, who trained at the Alberta College of Art and Design, had previously published a collection of illustrations and short comics titled *Gilded Lillies*. *Skim* is drawn in a moody black-and-white style and is celebrated for the quality of its compositions, which range from naturalist to expressionistic styles. Since finishing *Skim*, Jillian Tamaki has worked as an instructor at the School of Visual Arts in New York and has published illustrations in the *New York Times* and *The New Yorker*. A collection of these illustrations, *Indoor Voice*, was published by Drawn and Quarterly in 2010. Mariko Tamaki published *Emiko Superstar* (art by Steve Rolston) in DC Comics' Minx line of graphic novels.

The next day, Ms. Archer leaves Skim's tarot cards on her locker with a note that says "I hope you understand." Now accepted by the popular girls, Lisa shares her love of boys with Anna, while Skim and Katie discover a genuine friendship with each other. Skim abandons witchcraft and accepts that her friendship with Lisa has changed.

Characters
- *Kimberly Keiko Cameron*, a.k.a. *Skim*, is a sixteen-year-old Japanese Canadian girl and the protagonist of the book. In addition to dealing with separated parents, she is struggling with both her role in high school and her sexual orientation. She is an introspective loner.
- *Lisa Soor* is Skim's best friend. She is abrasive and volatile and struggles with her social identity. On the surface, she is cynical toward the popular cliques, but deep down she wants to be a part of them, a fact that results in an unstable friendship with Skim.
- *Ms. Archer* is an eccentric, bohemian English and drama teacher who develops a bond with Skim that later evolves into a romantic relationship. She comes to regret giving into her impulses, causing her to leave her teaching job.
- *Katie Matthews* is the most popular girl in school but is also extremely depressed and alienated by the fact that her former boyfriend commits suicide. She finds an unlikely friend in Skim after realizing the superficiality of her friends.
- *John Reddear* is a star volleyball player who commits suicide, which creates the overreactive, anxious environment at Skim's school. He is Katie Matthews's former boyfriend, though rumors that he is gay persist.
- *Julie Peters* is Katie's best friend and the founder of the Girls Celebrate Life club. She is bossy and self-righteous.
- *Anna Canard* is a popular girl and a member of the Girls Celebrate Life club. She is obsessed with boys and school gossip and later befriends Lisa.
- *Mrs. Hornet* is an overprotective yet oblivious guidance counselor who supports the school programs set up to help students deal with recent tragic events.

Artistic Style
Jillian Tamaki's background in design and illustration is reflected in *Skim*'s fluid, expressionistic style. Tamaki also cites as influences the work of Will Eisner, Seth, Dan Clowes, and Chester Brown. Her delicate pen-and-ink strokes convey a strong sense of movement and are highly suited to the book's use of the diary format. The informal, handcrafted feel to her comics helps readers sympathize with the book's teenagers. Tamaki uses a wide range of panel sizes and layouts, depending on the content of the page; pages with a defined panel structure usually indicate conversation or outward events, while depictions of Skim's inner world have a fluid or loose structure, sometimes with no panels at all. Single-page and double-page spreads are used for emphasis, as in the silent double-page spread of the first kiss shared between Ms. Archer and Skim. Tamaki's use of unusual panel composition,

skewed perspective, and extreme close-ups add to the anxious atmosphere of the book. The moody tone of the book is further enhanced by Tamaki's use of heavy darks and negative space to convey isolation, loneliness, and emptiness, such as in the stark white scene of the outdoor memorial service.

Tamaki's unique design delivers a series of adolescent characters that resemble eighteenth-century Japanese wood-block prints, with erotic undertones and grotesque distortion that places characters in the awkward physical state between childhood and adulthood. Skim is a story of intensely dramatic emotions that are often hidden, understated, or repressed, and Tamaki successfully conveys these emotions through her characters' facial expressions and body language.

Themes

As a work for young adults, *Skim* primarily examines identity. Throughout the book, Skim and Lisa explore their identities as outsiders, expressing their cynicism and choosing to dabble in Wicca, a marginal religion. However, Lisa's exploration of identity is somewhat superficial. By the end of the book, she rejects her outsider status and embraces life with the popular girls, leaving Skim behind. Skim not only explores her cultural identity through Wicca but also her physical identity (as when she bleaches her hair for the school dance) and her sexual identity (as in her romance with Ms. Archer). Sexual identity comes up again when the text indicates that John may have killed himself because he could not accept that he was gay. His suicide causes panic in the school community but also destabilizes the identity of Katie, who has built a persona as "the most popular girl." Faced with depression, she begins to question who she really is.

Skim also explores authenticity as connected to the theme of identity. Adolescence is a period when teens not only try to discover who they really are but also look for genuine meaning or purpose in their lives. John's death sets into motion a series of events that cause Skim to question the authenticity of the world around her. Powerless to challenge the surface events in her life, Skim responds with cynicism and indifference that thinly disguise her true feelings of sadness and isolation. Ms. Archer's rejection eventually forces Skim to question the authenticity of relationships and intimacy. By the end of the book, Skim does find a form of intimacy in her growing friendship with Katie.

Impact

Considered one of the first literary graphic novels for young adults, *Skim* has been highly praised in both Canada and the United States. The book was well reviewed and has been called convincing, poetic, poignant, and an honest view of adolescence. In addition to winning three prestigious graphic novel awards, *Skim* was nominated for four Eisner Awards and a Harvey Award in 2009.

Skim was included on *The New York Times* list of the top ten illustrated books and the *Publisher's Weekly* list of the best books of the year in 2008. In 2009, it was also featured on American Library Association (ALA) lists—Best Books for Young Adults and Great Graphic Novels for Teens—as well as the Texas Library Association's Maverick Graphic Novels Reading List. The book was selected for ALA's Gay, Lesbian, Bisexual, Transgender Round Table Rainbow list for its portrayal of homosexuality. *Skim* received strong praise in Canada and was selected as one of the Canadian Children's Book Centre's Best Books for Kids and Teens and was nominated for the Canadian Library Association's Young Adult Book of the Year, both in 2009.

The book was nominated for a Governor General's Literary Award in the category of Children's Literature—Text, the first nomination ever for a graphic novel. Media attention was brought to the fact that only the text was recognized, while Tamaki's illustrations were not. This oversight prompted a discussion about the interdependent relationship between text and art in graphic novels. Acclaimed Canadian cartoonists Seth and Brown wrote an open letter to the Canada Council for the Arts, objecting to the exclusion of Tamaki on the ballot and stressing the importance of the contribution of both writer and artist. While the two managed to get support from many other Canadian and American graphic novelists, including Lynda Barry, Dan Clowes, and Bryan Lee O'Malley, the Canada Council did not add Tamaki to the official list of nominees. While the book did not win the award, this passionate call to arms illustrates *Skim*'s importance as a graphic novel with strong literary and artistic value.

Scott Robins

Further Reading

Clowes, Daniel. *Ghost World* (1997).

Schrag, Ariel. *Potential* (2000).

Tamaki, Mariko, and Steve Rolston. *Emiko Superstar* (2008).

Bibliography

Chan, Suzette. "This Is the Story of Mariko Tamaki and Jillian Tamaki. So Read On." *Sequential Tart*. http://www.sequentialtart.com/archive/oct05/art_1005_3.shtml.

Tamaki, Jillian. "The Jillian Tamaki Interview." Interview by Chris Randle. *The Comics Journal*, July 5, 2011. http://www.tcj.com/the-jillian-tamaki-interview.

Tamaki, Mariko. "Graphic Scenes: In Conversation with Mariko Tamaki." Interview by Zoe Whittal. *Herizons* 22, no. 2 (2008): 37.

Taylor, Jessica. "Skim, a Beautiful Graphic Novel." *Xtra!*, March 13, 2008. http://www.xtra.ca/public/Toronto/Skim_a_beautiful_graphic_novel-4468.aspx.

See also: *Ghost World*; *The Plain Janes*; *Dykes to Watch Out For*; *Scott Pilgrim*

Skitzy: The Story of Floyd W. Skitzafroid

Author: Freeman, Don
Artist: Don Freeman (illustrator)
Publisher: Self-published (1955); Drawn and Quarterly (2008)
First book publication: 1955; 2008

Publication History

Don Freeman was born in San Diego in 1908. He moved to New York in 1928 and studied at the Arts Student League with noted social realist artists John Sloan and Harry Wickey. Freeman concentrated his drawings on Depression-era working men and women, predominantly from the theater district. He was an illustrator for the *New York Herald Tribune* and *The New York Times* and became known as the "Daumier of New York City" for his entertaining caricatures and images that resembled nineteenth-century French printmaker and caricaturist Honoré Daumier. He was also a book illustrator, noted for his drawings in William Saroyan's *My Name is Aram* (1940) and *The Human Comedy* (1943). Freeman also illustrated numerous children's books, including the popular *Corduroy* series.

Skitzy was self-published in 1955 and printed at John D. Hooper Lithographers in San Francisco. It was originally a spiral-bound book with dimensions of 5.25 × 4 inches. The 2008 edition by Drawn and Quarterly extended the dimensions to 9 × 7 inches and included an illustrated hard cover and an afterword by illustrator Dave Kiersh.

Plot

Skitzy, a nearly wordless book, begins with the text, "As we look in on Mr. and Mrs. Skitzafroid they appear to be blissfully sleeping," and portrays a middle-aged couple in bed. Mr. Skitzafroid has a smile on his face, but when he turns over to his left side, he displays a frown and scratches his head in unsettled slumber, which awakens his wife. She sits up in bed and shows an expression of worry as she notices his mouth displaying a slight frown on the right side and a smile on the left. When they both awaken, she helps him dress, makes his breakfast, and pauses for a kiss, which she

American illustrator Don Freeman, 1908–1978. (By Roy Freeman, via Wikimedia Commons)

never receives as he rushes off to work. Mr. Skitzafroid races to catch a train, and while reading a newspaper, he splits into two men (one with a disgruntled expression and the other with a smile). When both men step off the train, the smiling Mr. Skitzafroid races downtown, and the disgruntled Mr. Skitzafroid walks uptown.

The smiling Mr. Skitzafroid takes the West Side subway to Greenwich Village. He stops and picks up grapes from a fruit vendor before entering a tenement building under the scrutiny of his neighbors. He unlocks the door to an apartment and enters a studio with an easel and a painting of a naked woman on the wall. A young, attractive woman, who was also on the subway with Skitzafroid, walks up the stairs to his room. She enters the room, where the smiling Mr. Skitzafroid has changed into a beret and painter's frock. He shakes the young woman's hand and begins to mix paints on his palette while she undresses. He hands her the cluster

> **Don Freeman**
>
> One of the most acclaimed children's book illustrators of all time, Don Freeman's contribution to comics stems from a proto-graphic novel produced for adults. Through a series of mostly wordless pages, *Skitzy* presents a day in the life of Floyd W. Skitzafroid, a man who is both an office worker and artist. Originally published by John D. Hopper Lithographers in 1955, the work was relatively unknown until it was republished by Drawn and Quarterly in 2008. Freeman's illustrations in the book are full-page pen drawings produced in a sketchy and unpolished style. His children's books, of which *Corduroy* and *A Pocket for Corduroy* are undoubtedly the most celebrated, differ in their look from *Skitzy* and feature detailed images complete with watercolor washes.

of grapes, which she holds over her head in a naked pose. After she finishes posing, Skitzafroid works on his canvas as the model relaxes while sipping from a cup and reading a book entitled *Piece of Mind*.

When Skitzafroid completes his work, he shows the woman the painting, which she admires. He pays her for posing, and as she leaves, he calls her back and offers her the grapes in a kind gesture. He changes back into his street clothes and rushes off with his painting. He receives mixed reactions from people on the subway, who gaze over his shoulders at the painting. He arrives at an art gallery and sells his painting to the owner, who is captivated with the piece. The owner immediately places the piece in the display window.

When Mr. Skitzafroid passes a jeweler, he sees a necklace, which he buys with the profit he earned from his painting. When he steps outside, he notices a policeman looking at his painting, labeled, "Grape Susette by Skitza," in the gallery window and admits to being the artist. Although he is initially disappointed that the policeman does not believe him, he walks away in a happy mood and whistles as he reaches the train station early to have his choice of seats.

The second part of the book opens with the text, "During all this time in another part of the city" and displays the disgruntled Skitzafroid working at a desk with a stack of accounting paperwork. Skitzafroid's frustration is depicted with imaginary numbers spinning around the top of his head. These numbers then take the shape of naked female figures and sinister monsters, finally dissolving and being replaced by his boss, who stands behind him in judgment and scolds him in front of the other workers who then leave for the day.

Mr. Skitzafroid joins a crowd of people, who push one another in a mob to the train station. He squeezes through the crowd and barely manages to jump on the crowded train. The only seat available is next to his artistic self. When he sits down, his two selves come together, and the smiling self takes over the expression of both men.

When he reaches home, the smiling Mr. Skitzafroid takes his wife in a warm embrace and kisses her passionately, much to her surprise. She is dressed for an occasion, perhaps an anniversary, with candles burning on their dining table. He offers her the necklace he bought, and she proudly wears it during dinner. After they have eaten and he relaxes in his chair, she opens a curtain, and presents him a gift—the painting that he sold to the gallery. When she leaves the room, he looks down at his painting and discovers that she paid eight hundred dollars for the work for which he was paid one hundred dollars.

After he goes to bed, he ponders the rise in cost. His wife sheds a tear, thinking that she has done something to upset him. He tosses and turns all night until he awakes in the morning and comes up with the idea to open his own gallery, Froid Art Gallery, with his artistic side doing the artwork and his accountant side managing the business. With a contented smile on his face, he looks over to his wife who beams with admiration and love.

Characters

- *Mr. Skitzafroid* is a middle-aged man with two personalities. One is a frazzled accountant who cannot concentrate at work and is neglectful to

his wife. The other is a smiling artist, dedicated and proud of his artwork, who is friendly to everyone he meets and attentive to his wife.
- *Mrs. Skitzafroid* is a stay-at-home, caring wife who is concerned over her husband's lack of interest and the toll that his job is having on his health and on their relationship.
- *Susette* is a 1950's stereotype of a model. She has large breasts, wavy hair that is long and blond, and she wears a fluffy slip, a dress, and high heels.

Artistic Style

Freeman used pen and ink on white cardboard for the *Skitzy* drawings, which are not framed inside a panel but float freely on each page, which gives the narrative a relaxed flow. His simple line work, without the use of shading, and the open layout of the pages allow him to create different facial expressions in his characters that change the mood of the story. Freeman expertly displays feeling and emotion in facial expressions, as seen in the critical stares of people on the subway as they judge Mr. Skitzafroid's nude painting. Freeman begins the book with a few lines and a dominant use of white space. This minimalist approach immediately directs readers' attention to the couple in bed. The pages fill with more objects as Mr. Skitzafroid enters the city, and Freeman displays realistic street scenes that depict activities such as children playing behind garbage cans and street vendors selling fruit and vegetables. One of the more skillful examples of his line work is in the sequence in which the accountant mind of Mr. Skitzafroid is shown in rebellion with his artistic side. Freeman accomplishes this in a display of numbers that twist and turn above Mr. Skitzafroid's head and transform into naked female models with the number 8 on its side depicting their breasts and the number 6 portraying a woman's right arm that is raised over her face.

Freeman indicates action and emotion with a variety of lines, such as speed lines when Mr. Skitzafroid the artist races down the street, motion lines when the policeman twirls his baton or shakes his thumb, and beaming lines from Mr. Skitzafroid to indicate an idea or surprise. Freeman's use of stereotypes is easily recognizable in his caricatures, as, for example, with the policeman's authoritative disposition.

Finally, Freeman includes signs and store displays that provide narrative support and character insight. One example is when Mrs. Skitzafroid, concerned about her husband's lack of interest, reads a magazine article that is titled, "Is Your Husband Culturally Starved?"

Mr. Skitzafroid's split personality is made clear not only in the title of the book but also in the way he is rendered. There are two chapter openings with text—one in the beginning and the other when the story switches from artist to accountant—though these could be omitted because the visual narrative is strong enough to avoid any plot confusion.

Themes

Skitzy centers on an alienated white-collar worker who is part of a mass of other workers who live in the suburbs and scramble to and from their jobs on a train. His wife remains at home, cleaning and cooking. This monotonous routine has been referred to as the "rat race" and was something sociologists focused on during the 1950's to research whether a healthy balance between work and play was attainable. Freeman presents this idea dramatically in the psychological breakdown and the creation of the two personalities in Mr. Skitzafroid. Although this drama is presented in a lighthearted manner and ends happily, it nevertheless displays the debilitating feeling most men and women feel when trapped in jobs that offer few rewards. Many never find the freedom to do something they actually want and love to do. Freeman presents the balance —the integration of work and creativity and the possibility of a happy life for the Skitzafroids once Mr. Skitzafroid envisions a way to make a living combining his business background and his artistic skills.

Impact

At the time of its original publication in 1955, *Skitzy* was an overlooked wordless graphic novel. It would have remained out of print if not for the growing number of wordless comics published in the 2000's, which has encouraged an interest in past works of this genre. Publishers such as Drawn and Quarterly, Fantagraphics Books, and Dover Publications have republished largely forgotten wordless graphic novels.

Freeman also published an illustrated book in 1945 called *It Shouldn't Happen* that parodies the life of a soldier in the guise of a dog. This illustrated book with limited text was an early example of Freeman's skillful use of pen and ink and white space that he developed further in *Skitzy*.

David A. Beronä

Further Reading

Gropper, William. *Alay-oop* (1930).

Gross, Milt. *He Done Her Wrong: The Great American Novel and Not a Word in It—No Music, Too* (1930).

Waldman, Myron. *Eve* (1943).

Bibliography

Clough, Rob. "Art and Commerce: Skitzy." Review of *Skitzy*, by Don Freeman. *High-Low* (December 25, 2008). http://highlowcomics.blogspot.com/2008/12/art-and-commerce-skitzy.html

Freeman, Don. *Come One, Come All!* New York: Rinehart, 1949.

———. "Oral History Interview with Don Freeman, 1965 June 4." Interview by Betty Hoag. *Smithsonian Archives of American Art*. http://www.aaa.si.edu/collections/interviews/oral-history-interview-don-freeman-12155.

See also: *Passionate Journey*; *He Done Her Wrong*; *Ethel and Ernest*

SLOTH

Author: Hernandez, Gilbert
Artist: Gilbert Hernandez (illustrator); Jared K. Fletcher (letterer)
Publisher: Vertigo
First book publication: 2006

Publication History

Gilbert Hernandez's *Sloth* (which followed his 2003 *Palomar* series) was published in July, 2006, as a hardcover and in December, 2008, as a paperback. The work was released by Vertigo, which is an imprint of DC Comics that caters to mature audiences because of adult themes such as graphic violence, verbal profanity, and sex. *Sloth* was simultaneously published in the United Kingdom by the London-based company Titan Books, without any changes to the original publication; the hardcover was released in October, 2006, and the paperback was published in January, 2009.

The size of *Sloth* is somewhat smaller than that of standard-formatted comics, with a page dimension of 9 × 7 inches. Consequently, the pages often have fewer panels than standard comics, which Hernandez uses to his advantage with the repeated incorporation of long horizontal panels that stretch across whole pages.

Sloth differs from Hernandez's usual serialized form of publication; it is the first stand-alone project of his career. In several interviews, he has stated that the choice to create a stand-alone comic was based on a desire to have a work with a concise narrative arc and one that is completely independent from his ongoing *Love and Rockets* (1985-) story line.

Plot

Bored with mundane suburban living, Miguel Serra decides to will himself into a coma. When he wakes up a year later, not much has changed, that is, except for his own pace: His walk, lovemaking, and songwriting have all slowed, earning him the nickname Sloth. He resumes his life with his girlfriend, Lita, and his best friend, Romeo, and the three teens decide to investigate a bizarre urban legend about a "goatman," a supernatural figure who can convince his victims to switch places with him. To add to the mystery, the goatman resides in a nearby lemon orchard that is rumored to hold the bodies of various murder victims; the body of Miguel's absent mother is suspected to be there. At the moment when readers start to grasp the dark world of these three teens, Hernandez unexpectedly presents readers with a sudden narrative twist in which his main characters experience an unexplained identity switch. While the physical appearances of the characters remain intact, their identities and roles are completely altered. It is no longer Miguel who wakes up from a coma, but Lita, a teenage girl who has been abandoned by her parents and raised by her unsupportive grandparents. As readers follow the new protagonist Lita, familiar faces resurface: Miguel is now a popular boy at Lita's school, and Romeo is now Romeo

Comic book creator Gilbert Hernandez at a signing at Midtown Comics Times Square in Manhattan, April 24, 2010. (By Luigi Novi, via Wikimedia Commons)

X, a famed rock star. While the circumstances of these three teens change, the story remains fundamentally the same: Lita struggles to find a way out of her everyday existence while juggling a complex love triangle in which she is involved with Miguel and Romeo X. Before the conclusion of the graphic novel, Hernandez inserts one last narrative twist by having both Lita and Romeo X fall into comas after a physical confrontation between Romeo X and Miguel. By doing so, Hernandez allows readers to view the life of the suburban teenager from three different vantage points. Readers realize that not much has changed because the issues at hand remain largely the same. Ultimately, the trading of circumstances highlights the continuum of teenage life, where switching identities does not alter, or ease, the underlying difficulties of daily existence.

Although the format of the graphic novel suggests a more complete or contained story, Hernandez complicates this tendency by presenting readers with an open-ended narrative that is packed with ambiguity and uncertainty, suggesting a significant tension between the format and the contents of the work.

Characters
- *Miguel Serra*, the protagonist, is a teenager with straight black hair who has a calm, pensive, and reserved personality. Abandoned by his parents at a young age, he was raised by his grandparents, Armando and Bea, in an unnamed suburban neighborhood. He is haunted by the vague memory of his mother and the mystery surrounding her disappearance and possible murder in the lemon orchard. After an identity switch with Lita, he maintains the same name and appearance, but becomes much more popular in high school. However, underneath this newfound popularity, Miguel remains the same quiet individual he was before the identity switch.
- *Lita* is a freckled teenager with blond hair who is Miguel's girlfriend and possibly Romeo's love interest. She is a drummer and displays a passionate interest in urban legends and the supernatural. Halfway through *Sloth*, she switches places with Miguel and becomes the protagonist after waking up from a self-induced yearlong coma. After the switch, she is active, outgoing, and determined to be in control of her life.
- *Romeo* is a friend of Miguel and Lita. He is tall with curly blond hair and has an outgoing personality. In the first section, he is the "third wheel" in a love triangle that involves Lita and Miguel. In the second section, he becomes Romeo X, a popular rock musician who grew up in the same suburban neighborhood as Miguel and Lita. After running into the two teens in the lemon orchard late one night, he quickly develops a romantic interest in Lita, thereby reinstating the original love triangle between the three teens. As Romeo X, he is less self-assured and cocky around Lita.

Artistic Style

Hernandez's storytelling has often been described as Magical Realism, which is clearly reflected in *Sloth* through the stunning depiction of surrealist dream sequences and dreamlike moments in waking life where, for example, characters physically take flight into the sky. In terms of mood, the work is often compared to the films of David Lynch, especially *Mulholland Drive* (2001) and *Lost Highway* (1997). This comparison stems from the similarities in style and storytelling, such as the unexplained character switch, the use of surrealism, and the weaving together of reality and dreams. The overall artistic style of the work is carried out visually through a remarkable balance of black and white spaces. The contrast between black and white is especially dominant in dream sequences and moments of deep questioning, uncertainty, or fear, which mirror the interior emotions of the characters. Although Hernandez's lines are simple and clean, they remain expressionistic and gestural and add to the obscure and gloomy mood of the work. A good example of this can be seen in the swirling skies above the lemon orchard, which visually complement the inner turmoil of the three teens.

Characters are often depicted in a cartoonish fashion with exaggerated doughy eyes and simplified mouths that are reminiscent of Dan DeCarlo's and Harry Lucey's *Archie* series. The straightforward look of the characters is enhanced by their lack of shading, giving them a two-dimensional or cutout appearance. However, the characters are not flat; rather, Hernandez reduces complex individuals to their bare essence. As with all of his work, Hernandez excels in the use of body language to convey important character traits and emotions. This can be seen in his use of silences, where readers are often left to deduce the internal state of characters through subtle visual clues, such as the direction of the characters' gaze or the positioning of their bodies.

Themes
The themes within *Sloth* focus on such things as tumultuous teen romance and risky teen love triangles, the difficult transition between childhood and adulthood, the breakdown of the family, and the mundane boredom of suburban life that produces a numbing effect brought on by safety and predictability.

Throughout the work, characters attempt to escape the pain and absurdity of their teenage years through a variety of methods such as heavy rock music, dream worlds, comas, and suicide. These attempts at escape are symptomatic of a struggle for meaning in a world that does not always make sense. *Sloth* portrays an environment in which parents are absent, jailed, or fading out of mind; bullies are friendly one day and hostile the next; and love triangles among friends render everything uncertain. These themes underscore the existential mood of the entire work, as teenagers often perceive their lives as fleeting and meaningless.

Urban legends and the difficulty of differentiating reality from fiction are also significant themes in *Sloth*. By juxtaposing the supernatural figure of the goatman with the possibility of actual murders in the lemon grove, an overlap between fact and fiction is created, heightening the sense of darkness and ambiguity in the work. Furthermore, Hernandez aptly links the murky space between reality and fiction to the question of free will. More specifically, this can be seen in the unresolved mysteries in the work, such as the question of whether these teens can choose to will themselves into comas and whether the goatman can actually convince his victims to switch places with him.

Impact
Although Hernandez's *Sloth* was not a huge commercial success when first published in 2006, it did receive very favorable critical reviews for its outstanding storytelling and art. *Sloth* is a high-quality graphic novel that attests to the long-lasting legacy of the author who is known to have mastered the skill of visual storytelling in both serialized and stand-alone formats. Furthermore, *Sloth* contributes to the overall status and reputation of the Hernandez brothers, who began producing and self-publishing comics in the early 1980's, marking them as pioneers in the world of alternative comics.

Arguably, one of the most important contributions of Hernandez to the genre of alternative comics is his innovative portrayal of the human psyche. More specifically, in his focus on complex characters that exhibit both positive and negative personality traits and in his ability to construct the visual passage of time through character aging and weight gain, Hernandez has once again proven his overall understanding of the human condition. This standard of excellence is clearly maintained in *Sloth*, since the three teens are far from being flat characters; they are complex individuals who struggle with existential dilemmas and identity crises that are universally representative of the human condition. Hernandez is often cited as a major influence in the world of alternative comics for his artistic mastery and uncanny ability to capture psychological realism.

Marie-Jade Menni

Further Reading
Hernandez, Gilbert. *Human Diastrophism* (2007).
_____. *Poison River* (1997).
Hernandez, Jaime, and Gilbert Hernandez. *Flies on the Ceiling* (2003).

Bibliography
Hernandez, Gilbert. "*Palomar* and Beyond: An Interview with Gilbert Hernandez." Interview by Derek Parker Royal. *MELUS* 32, no. 3 (Fall, 2007): 221-246.
_____. "Pleased to Meet Them: The Hernandez Bros. Interview." Interview by Gary Groth, Robert

Fiore, and Thom Powers. *Comics Journal* 126 (January, 1989): 60-113.

Hernandez, Jaime, and Gilbert Hernandez. *Ten Years of Love and Rockets*. Seattle: Fantagraphics Books, 1992.

Royal, Derek Parker. "To Be Continued. . . .: Serialization and Its Discontent in the Recent Comics of Gilbert Hernandez." *International Journal of Comic Art* 11, no. 1 (Spring, 2009): 262-280.

See also: *Palomar*; *Love and Rockets*; *The Complete Fritz the Cat*

SMALL KILLING, A

Author: Moore, Alan
Artist: Oscar Zarate (illustrator)
Publisher: VG Graphics
First book publication: 1991

Publication History

A Small Killing first appeared in 1991 as a graphic novella, published by VG Graphics in the United Kingdom. It was reprinted in 1993 by Dark Horse Comics in its first American edition and again in 2003 by Avatar Press, the latter version also containing an interview with writer Alan Moore and illustrator Oscar Zarate on the genesis of the work. Moore's first non-superhero comic work followed the termination of his publishing company Mad Love Press, through which, prior to its demise, he had released the anthology work *AARGH* (*Artists Against Rampant Government Homophobia*, 1988) and his ambitious but short-lived project *Big Numbers* (1990). *A Small Killing* coincided with publication of Moore's *From Hell* (1991-1998) and was prompted by Zarate's suggestion that he and Moore work on a story in which a child pursues an adult; Moore paired the idea with a dream he recalled in which he was confronted by his childhood self. The structure and detail of the work proceeded from mutual input in order to capture the atmosphere and culture of the final years of the 1980's.

Plot

The basic story of *A Small Killing* is of an adult being pursued by a child. It develops into a deeply psychological work, critiquing the passivity of Timothy Hole, an advertising executive in New York who has landed the account of the Flite soft drink company in Russia. The nonlinear narrative, opening with Hole's trip back to his native Britain before beginning his position in Russia, is arranged in a four-part format. The chapters cover his life in New York, London, and Sheffield, with the latter locale figuring in two parts, both in his childhood and his early adulthood. Each chapter uses a specific method of conveyance, devolving from airplane to train to car to bicycle along Hole's journey into the past.

> **Oscar Zarate**
>
> Born in Argentina, Oscar Zarate is best known as the illustrator of the Alan Moore-written graphic novel, *A Small Killing*, which won the Eisner Award in 2004. *A Small Killing* tells the story of an advertising executive searching for inspiration for a diet cola campaign and emphasizes his psychological interiority and childhood memories. Zarate's art is strongly influenced by artists like Jacques de Loustal, Lorenzo Mattotti, and other masters of the direct-color tradition that emerged in the 1980's. His figures are slightly grotesque and his compositions tend to emphasize the subjective experience of the lead character through the use of vibrant colors. Additionally, he produced an adaptation of William Shakespeare's *Othello* in 1985 and illustrated a graphic novel by British comedian Alexei Sayle, *Geoffrey the Tube Train and the Fat Comedian*. In 2003 he published *Freud for Beginners*.

In the opening chapter, set in New York and concerning the years 1985 through 1989, Timothy waits on a crowded airplane for takeoff. He recalls both a recent party at which a display case of bird eggs is shattered and a dream featuring a man and a boy in which one is struck by lightning. While in New York, Timothy notices a young boy in a school uniform who seems to be following him, and he pursues the boy unsuccessfully through the airport.

In the second chapter, Timothy arrives in London, where he lived from 1979 to 1985, and travels by train. He tours the Docklands in search of Sylvia's art studio and recalls their extramarital liaisons. While exploring London nightlife, he pursues the same young boy and remembers leaving his employer in London for the job in New York. Timothy concludes that the boy is trying to kill him. He considers his ambivalent role in an unplanned pregnancy, which resulted in a package from Sylvia containing the aborted fetus of their child.

Taking a train to Sheffield the next morning, Timothy finds that he has mistakenly purchased a child's ticket.

In the third chapter, Timothy returns to Sheffield, where he lived with Maggie from 1964 to 1979, during which time he carried on a secret affair with Sylvia. When he confronts the boy in a local pub, the boy admits that he is trying to kill Timothy. While driving his old car around town, Timothy recalls a happier era with Maggie and his worst deed in early life: burying, then releasing, a bottle of live insects. Perusing his mother's old photo album, he finds, to his horror, that the final picture is of the boy who has been pursuing him.

The fourth and final chapter addresses Timothy's childhood, from 1954 to 1964. While riding his father's bike, Timothy encounters a present-day Maggie, now married and a mother of two children. Approaching the ruins where he used to play as a child, Timothy realizes that he did not release the insects he had buried alive. He finds the buried bottle and giant insects pour forth. The boy appears and attacks Timothy with a club. After waking up in morning sunlight, Timothy returns to town, where he enters a world with a "new pulse" where "everything is pregnant."

Characters
- *Timothy Hole*, pronounced "Holly," the protagonist, is a worried, lean, bespectacled man of early middle age with short dark hair. At first, he wears black, brown, or beige clothing with loudly patterned ties; later in the story, his clothing changes to purple and red. His glasses often reflect light, creating a whiteout effect around his eyes. His lean lips and wrinkled, high forehead reinforce his emotional responses to stimuli.
- *Lynda* is a tall, elegant African American woman working for the Flite soda advertising agency in New York. She has multicolored hair and wears brightly colored clothing. She avoids becoming involved in a casual relationship with Timothy.
- *Bob Levine* is Timothy Hole's boss in New York. He is portrayed in a dark suit with dark hair and a slightly sinister expression. He is responsible for breaking Timothy's case of bird eggs at Timothy's farewell party.
- *Sylvia*, a former girlfriend of Timothy Hole, has short auburn hair and large green eyes. She has a studio in London, where she specializes in creating jewelry with organic motifs.
- *Maggie Hole*, later *Davies*, is Timothy Hole's childhood friend, whom he marries and later divorces. When she first appears, she is dressed in yellow and has dark hair with a widow's peak. Later, she wears horn-rimmed black glasses. An artist specializing in handmade toys, she establishes a successful business in Sheffield.
- *Barry Forbes* is Timothy's first boss in London, the founder of the Forbes-McCauley Agency. A genial, kindly man, he appears in a gray-black suit or green sweater with a loose red tie, with disheveled white-grey hair and a beard.
- *The boy*, a version of Timothy Hole in childhood, first appears in a navy blue school uniform with short trousers, striped school tie, brogues, and socks. He has dark hair and a wicked, menacing expression. He relentlessly lures Timothy to follow him in New York, London, and Sheffield.

Artistic Style

Zarate's chosen medium in *A Small Killing* is watercolor, with pencil used to reinforce edges and lines. Livid pastel colors set the tone for the work in the opening scene of a sunset and recur in crowd scenes, wherein Timothy Hole is presented in realistic tones but his crowded surroundings appear in luminous mixtures of yellow, orange, and red. Instances of surprise are in white, while violence is presented in oranges and reds. The narrative frequently calls for night scenes, which Zarate illustrates with intense blues and greens, often with a light green or yellow tracing to emphasize facial expression.

Zarate is partly responsible for the nonlinear and image-based structure of the work, often returning to symbolic objects for thematic resonance. Photorealism is occasionally implemented in Timothy's exploration of cityscapes but does not maintain a dominant role in the work. To guide the reader through psychological space, memory is conveyed through black-and-white pencil drawings and dream sequences are rendered in a slightly muted tone.

The writer Alan Moore. (By Fimb, via Wikimedia Commons)

The color schemes coordinate with Zarate's depiction of humanity, which is largely carnivalesque verging on the grotesque, particularly in body posture and facial expressions. Figures en masse tend to have features of a nearly animalistic nature, although characters who interact with Timothy often assume expressions of great warmth. Neither warmth nor the grotesque characterizes the depiction of Timothy Hole, whose own angularity and predominantly muted colors stand in contrast to his wider setting. Zarate's use of color and line suggests a certain ferocity and passion typical of humanity, which renders Timothy Hole's own passivity even more distinct. On the whole, the collaborative artistic freedom Zarate exercises in *A Small Killing* contributes greatly, through fine detail and sweeping use of tone, to the expression of Timothy Hole's psychological state and his own impressions of the world in which he moves.

Themes

Both Moore and Zarate acknowledge several dominant themes in *A Small Killing*, including the nebulous nature of memory, the consequences of avoiding responsibility for one's actions, and the movement of a generation from a "hippie" to a "yuppie" identity.

The inherent instability of memory is introduced repeatedly in the text. As Hole journeys through his past, he repeatedly questions his memories and finds his motivations unclear, until a final collapse of memory ends in the realization that he did not, as he had previously believed, release insects from a jar as a child. Falsified and corrected memory is associated with Timothy's first realization of responsibility for his past actions.

The concept of taking responsibility for one's actions may be the strongest theme present in the work, as it determines the trajectory and purpose of Timothy's personal journey. Timothy revisits several key events in his life as a way for Moore and Zarate to explore this theme. The first, engaging in an affair with Sylvia and lying to Maggie, his wife, is described as Sylvia's "fault." The second, betraying Barry Forbes in order to take a more upwardly mobile job in New York, is presented as a sensible thing to do. The third, failing to make a decision about whether or not to have a child with Sylvia, which leads to their subsequent breakup, is ascribed to Sylvia's fickle nature. Finally, the memory of Timothy's childhood transgression, burying a bottle of insects alive, forces him to admit his responsibility for destructive behavior and enables him to achieve a fresh start in life.

The hippie-to-yuppie transformation is highlighted in the narrative through the use of settings and contrasting memories. Sheffield, notably a "red town," contrasts with Timothy Hole's choice to commute to London and later move to New York to pursue global advertising. As a young artist, Timothy harangued the "crucifying" aspect of capitalism, whereas his job in London represents an exploratory departure, flirting with advertising and overestimating his potential as a conceptual genius. In moving to New York, Timothy physically removes himself from his "red" roots and distances himself from earlier ideology. Returning to London, and then to Sheffield, elucidates his estrangement from his former self, as well as his lack of guiding ideology as a "yuppie" in middle age.

Impact

Following the publication of *Watchmen* (1986-1987) and his work on *The Swamp Thing* (1984-1987), Moore pursued his first nonsuperhero graphic work in *A Small Killing*. The adaptation of several of Moore's prose works to the graphic medium followed, including *Hypothetical Lizard* (2007), *The Birth Caul* (1999), and *Snakes and Ladders* (2001), alongside complete works dealing with subject material alternative to superheroes, such as *From Hell*. This movement away from superhero subject matter seemed out of character for Moore at the time and puzzled his fan base, resulting in *A Small Killing*'s emergence as a lesser-known work in 1991. However, it received more critical attention following Moore's success with the *From Hell* series. The release of an American edition in 1993 gained public attention, and its re-release in 2003, with a reflective interview on its composition, has reached an even wider audience.

Though the work was an anomaly for Moore at the time of its release, other authors were already experimenting with semiautobiographical accounts of life experiences in the graphic medium, including Harvey Pekar and Robert Crumb in *American Splendor*, which first appeared in 1976. Timely forays into the psychological aspects of narrator-guided comics include writer Neil Gaiman and artist Dave McKean's *Violent Cases* (1987), *Signal to Noise* (1989-1992), and *The Tragical Comedy or Comical Tragedy of Mr. Punch* (1994). Arguably, Gaiman and Moore paved the way for psychologically narrated graphic works at the turn of the millennium by illustrating methods for communicating memory, implementing stream-of-consciousness narrative, and depicting psychological realities discrete from quantifiable daily life. *A Small Killing*, while illustrating the harsh realities of failed relationships and the collapse of individual ideology, also reflects on the context of late 1980's commercialism and Britain's troubled identity during the Margaret Thatcher era. Because of its challenging format and subject matter, *A Small Killing* establishes an influential model for both psychological narrative techniques and the informing role of cultural context in nonsuperhero comics.

Hannah E. Means-Shannon

Further Reading

Gaiman, Neil, and Dave McKean. *Violent Cases* (1987).

Moore, Alan, and Eddie Campbell. *A Disease of Language* (2006).

Moore, Alan, et al. *Alan Moore's Hypothetical Lizard* (2007).

Bibliography

Di Liddo, Annalisa. *Alan Moore: Comics as Performance, Fiction as Scalpel*. Jackson: University Press of Mississippi, 2009.

Khoury, George, ed. *The Extraordinary Works of Alan Moore*. Raleigh, N.C.: TwoMorrows, 2008.

Millidge, Gary Spencer, and Smoky Man, eds. *Alan Moore: Portrait of an Extraordinary Gentleman*. Marietta, Ga.: Top Shelf Productions, 2003.

See also: *Violent Cases*; *Lost Girls*; *From Hell*; *Signal to Noise*

SMILE

Writer: Raina Telgemeier
Artist: Raina Telgemeier
Colorist: Stephanie Yue
Publisher: Graphix (a division of Scholastic).
First book publication: 2010.

Publication history
Raina Telgemeier had published short self-published comics (called "mini comics") when she met an editor from Scholastic publishing who invited her to submit a full length graphic novel to the Graphix imprint at Scholastic.

Plot
After a Girl Scout meeting, Raina knocks out her front teeth while racing some girls to her door. Her dentist, Dr. Golden, puts a temporary cast in her mouth to hold her remaining teeth in place while her mouth heals. While removing the cast Dr. Golden discovers that the bone above her teeth has been damaged, so Raina is referred to an Endodontist, Dr, Dragoni, who performs oral surgery on Raina as he tries to save her teeth. Soon after, Raina is fitted with braces and gets her ears pierced as a reward.

Summer passes uneventfully, and Raina enters seventh grade. As a member of the school band, Raina is befriended by a sixth grader named Sammy, who also wears braces. Sammy is interested in Raina and Raina reciprocates, though she is teased by her friends.

That October, an earthquake rocks San Francisco, shaking Raina's house. Her family survives with minimal damage, but they lose power and school is canceled for several days. A few days later Sammy implies that he's going to ask Raina out on a date, but she disappoints him by telling Sammy that she has an orthodontist appointment. The days pass uneventfully, until a few weeks later when Raina's Orthodontist informs her that her teeth aren't responding well to traditional methods. He recommends pulling her front teeth and replacing them with false teeth while pulling the remaining teeth together to close the gap. Over winter break, Raina's teeth are pulled and fake ones implanted,

Raina Telgemeier. (By Niccoló Caranti, via Wikimedia Commons)

as the rest of her teeth were treated according to routine methods. One afternoon, Raina sees the movie "The Little Mermaid," with her little sister and her mother. The movie makes such a strong impression on Raina that she decides to become an animator when she grows up. At school, Raina discusses the movie with her friend Emily. Sean, a classmate, joins the conversation enthusiastically. Raina is drawn to Sean, and as the Valentine's Day Dance approaches, she hopes that he will ask her to go as his date. At the same time, Sammy wants to ask Raina to go to the dance with him but he's too shy to ask her. The two make noncommittal plans to attend the dance independently. But Raina decides not to go to the dance and stays home. The next day Sammy sees Raina at band practice and expresses his disappointment. He also gives Raina a Valentine Day present, but the incident ends their friendship. Raina hardly notices; she distracts herself by going to Sean's basketball games and obsessing about her braces, all the while fantasizing that Sean is her boyfriend. At her thirteenth birthday party, Raina's friends urge her to more aggressively pursue Sean. They give her a fashion makeover, making Raina believe that they know Sean's fashion preferences. Later that night, her friends admit that they have no idea what kind of clothing Sean prefers, and Raina grows angry.

The summer between seventh and eighth grade passes harmlessly, and Raina hopes that Sean will call her but her phone doesn't ring. Raina finds eighth grade markedly different from seventh grade. Personal appearance and hygiene are the topics her friends seem most interested in as all the girls' bodies are changing, and not always in the same ways at the same time. Still drawn to Sean, Raina tries out for the basketball team because Sean is a basketball player. But she isn't selected for the squad. In class, when she writes a note to Sean, her teacher reads n it aloud to her class, embarrassing Raina.

Although she can't attract Sean's attention, Raina is friendly with lots of boys who offer her video game tips and are interested in discussing things other than personal hygiene and appearance.

Raina's braces appear to be working correctly, but Dr. Dragoni notices that her gums are damaged. Next, Raina sees a periodontist. The procedure the doctor uses is so painful that Raina passes out. This makes her mother very angry and she scolds the periodontist loudly in front of his patients, much to his chagrin. On the way home in the car, Raina thanks her mother for her support.

That summer, Raina is a counselor at Girl Scout camp for the last time. Her false teeth are removed as her other teeth have grown closer together. As ninth grade starts, she sports a new look and a hopeful sense of confidence. One drawback of high school is that she and her friend Melissa will be attending different schools. Raina initially spends her free time with her friends from middle school, while worrying whether or not she can get her schoolwork completed. When her middle school friend play a mean prank on her, Raina realizes that they have always had a cruel side and she decides to find a new group of friends.

Weeks pass and Raina feels lonely. She is befriended by a new girl, Theresa. Theresa invites Raina into her circle of friends. The circle includes Sean from Raina's middle school. Raina's braces are removed, but her teeth have a blueish hue. Her teeth are made white again through bonding a few interminable months later.

Raina continues to make new friends in high school and works hard to develop her artistic skills. When the ninth grade dance is scheduled, she attends with a group of her friends, and is able to smile when a group photo is taken.

Characters

- *Raina*: The protagonist of *Smile*, twelve-year-old Raina lives a fairly normal pre-teen life in San Francisco with her parents and two younger siblings, until she knocks her two front teeth out in a freak accident while running. What follows over the next four years is a series of dental emergencies, as her orthodontic treatment becomes more and more complicated and includes oral surgery, specialists, temporary teeth, and headgear. While Raina undergoes this treatment she navigates middle school. Rejects her first boy, experiences her first crush, separates from her middle school friends, and enters a new social circle in high school.
- *Melissa:* Raina's friend from middle school who is supportive of her. When the girls enter ninth grade they attend different high schools.
- *Karin and Nicole:* Raina's friends during middle school, they playfully ridicule Raina. Following a prank the girls pull on her in high school, Raina minimizes her interaction with them.
- *Raina's mother:* Raina's mother is kind and supportive that she'll emerge from her complex orthodontic problems successfully.
- *Theresa:* A friend Raina makes after she starts high school and decides to minimize her friendships with Karin and Nicole.
- *Sammy:* A sixth grader flute playing bandmate of Raina, Sammy is interested in her, and expects

her to attend the Valentine's Day dance. When Raina doesn't go to the dance, Sammy ends their friendship.
- *Sean:* A boy in Raina's class who she has a crush on, Sean isn't interested in Raina, and prefers playing basketball. When the two enter high school, they develop the same circle of friends.
- *Dr. Dragoni:* The Endodontist who takes on to Raina's teeth problems after Dr. Golden refers her to him. Dr. Dragoni provides a multi-stepped solution to Raina's complex dental issues over a period of four years. When Raina finally has her braces taken off, and her teeth problems resolved, Dr. Dragoni is quite pleased with his work.

Artistic Style

Telgemeier's style bears influences of Saturday morning cartoons, newspaper comic strips (especially Bill Watterson's comic strip *Calvin and Hobbes* and Lynn Johnson's *For Better or Worse*) as well as graphic novels such as Jeff Smith's *Bone*. The figures are cartoony with expressive faces and bodies rendered in a cartoony but also realistic style. Although the characters have similar visual qualities, Telgemeier gives each one an individual signature. The coloring is soft and pleasing to the eye. The backgrounds are sparse: more often than not there is only a blank soft color for a background. The light colored backgrounds give this emotional story an ongoing sense of optimism. Conversely, pages with dark backgrounds, especially full page illustrations, indicate darker, more complex emotions. The pages are generally divided into five to seven small panels, giving each page a feeling of movement. Each chapter is introduced with a full page illustration setting the tone for the following chapter, and very rarely, a full page illustration is included as part of the story. The lettering is unobtrusive, except in instances where the letters are bigger, indicating strong emotion.

Themes

One theme of *Smile* is a developing sense of self-confidence. Raina's self-confidence is shattered by the fall that precipitates her very complicated dental work. Her confidence grows as her orthodontic issues are resolved. This is evident as she parts ways with her middle school friends and makes new friends in high school. It's also demonstrated in the way she is willing to openly smile as the graphic novel resolves and resistant to opening her mouth as the story begins. Raina's sense of self confidence is evident in her relationship with Sean as well. What begins as a heart-rending school girl crush in middle school concludes as a friendly relationship in high school. Another theme of *Smile* is that things get better over time. The moodiness of middle school is replaced by the promise of a better world in high school as childhood allegiances end and personality traits emerge fueled by growing intellectual curiosity and other interests.

Impact

The impact of *Smile* was multi-faceted: because *Smile* was on the New York Times Book Review best seller list for 220 weeks, it made Raina Telgemeier into a star in the graphic novel firmament, enabling her to follow up with more autobiographical best sellers such as *Sis-*

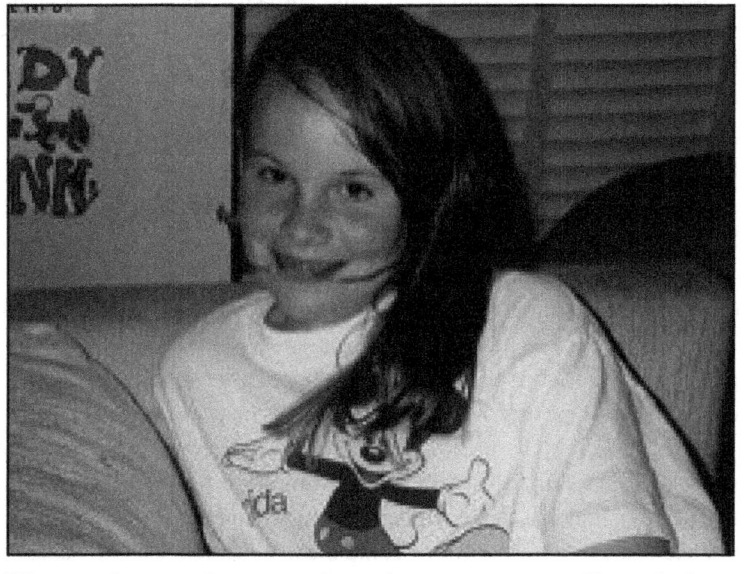

Telgemeier has posted pictures on her website, goraina.com, of her orthodontia at the time of Smile. (Raina Telgemeier)

ters and *Drama*. The success of *Smile* demonstrated that the trade book market for children's graphic novels was expanding, as the comic book readership had previously leaned heavily toward graphic novels with adult themes and concerns. *Smile* also solidified the place of Scholastic's graphic novel imprint, *Graphix*, as Smile was a natural book to follow Jeff Smith's *Bone* series and Kazu Kibuishi's *Amulet* series.

Further reading
Hicks, Faith Erin, *Friends with Boys*
Rablagliati, Michael, *Paul Joins the Scouts*
Telgemeier, Raina, *Sisters*

Bibliography
Bird, Elizabeth, "Blood, Sweat, and Teeth": New York Times Book Review, May 14, 2010. https://www.nytimes.com/2010/05/16/books/review/Bird-t.html.
Wildsmith, Snow, "Smile": School Library Journal, December 30, 2009. http://blogs.slj.com/goodcomicsforkids/2009/12/30/review-smile/.
"Smile by Raina Telgemeier": Kirkus Reviews, February 1, 2010. https://www.kirkusreviews.com/book-reviews/raina-telgemeier/smile/.

Exit Stage Left: The Snagglepuss Chronicles

Writer: Mark Russell
Artist: Mike Feehan
Inkers: Mark Morales, Sean Parsons, and Jose Marzan Jr.
Colorist: Paul Mounts
Letterer: Dave Sharpe
First serial publication: Originally published in Exit Stage Left: the Snagglepuss Chronicles, 1-6, and Suicide Squad/Banana Splits Special 1, 2017.
First book publication: DC Comics, 2018.

Publication history

Snagglepuss was one of a series of animated cartoon characters produced by Hanna-Barbara studios in the late 1950s and 1960s. Writer Mark Russell had written a modern day storyline featuring *The Flintstones*, another animated cartoon from the Hanna-Barbera studios. When Russell's editor saw some quotes Russell had posted on Facebook, he suggested framing a story around them. The quotes became part of the Snagglepuss story.

Plot

In this re-invention of the Hanna-Barbera Television cartoon character Snagglepuss is recast as Mr. Snaggle Puss, a very successful southern playwright tiger living in the United States during the 1950s. Snaggle Puss speaks English and interacts successfully with humans and other anthropomorphic animals. As the story begins, Snaggle Puss has been called before the House Committee on Un-American Activities and is questioned about his ties to the Communist party and whether or not his colleagues in the theater have ties to the Party. Then the story becomes a flashback, and the scene shifts to an opening night of a new Broadway hit written by Snaggle Puss. After the play ends, Snaggle Puss and his wife separate and Snaggle Puss goes to a gay bar he frequents in the village, the Stonewall. In the bar he meets his lover, a human named Pablo. Pablo has escaped persecution in Cuba by coming to America and fears the Communist witch hunt in the United States while Snaggle Puss doesn't. Next Snaggle Puss has a drink with Dorothy Parker, who tells him that she's washed up as a writer, and that will be his fate too, sooner than he imagines. Returning home, Snaggle Puss is surprised to find Huckleberry Hound, another re-imagined animated television cartoon character, at his door. Huckleberry is a successful novelist, and a very old friend of Snaggle Puss's. The two haven't seen each other for a very long time. Snaggle Puss, his wife Lila, and Huckleberry attend a party thrown by Peggy Guggenheim. At the party, Snaggle Puss speaks with a dispirited playwright, Lillian Hellman, who has appeared before the House Committee on Un-American Activities. Next Snaggle Puss goes to an age old home and visits an Alzheimer patient. The patient asks Snaggle Puss who he is, not realizing that Snaggle Puss is his own son, who he disinherited. On his way out Snaggle Puss discovers a musician friend playing at the home because he's unable to get other work in the theater. That night Snaggle Puss, Pablo, and Huckleberry Hound go into the city. Huckleberry approaches a man hoping for a gay encounter and is rebuked. At a delicatessen, the three of them run into Lillian Hellman. She tells them that she is leaving the United States: her appearance before the House Committee on Un-American Activities has destroyed her career. A few days later, Snaggle Puss meets with Gigi Allen, counsel to the House Committee on Un-American Activities. Allen tells Snaggle Puss that he will be subpoenaed to appear and that she hopes he cooperates with the committee. Snaggle Puss is firm that he will not cooperate. The two part and a few days later as Snaggle Puss watches a play rehearsal a telegram arrives informing him that he is to appear before the House Committee on Un-American Activities. In the next scene, Snaggle Puss's friend the playwright Arthur Miller asks him to pretend that he was with the actress Marilyn Monroe in place of Miller, as Miller is afraid that Monroe's boyfriend, the baseball star Joe Di Maggio, will seek revenge. Snaggle Puss complies. Next he takes his friend Huckleberry Hound to the Stonewall, the gay bar he frequents, and introduces him to a Police horse, Quick Draw McGraw, a third re-invented animated cartoon character. The horse and the dog become involved. As the hound has come out, Snaggle Puss and Huckleberry reminisce about the day many years earlier, when Snaggle Puss left Mississippi because he couldn't hide the fact that he was gay. While this is happening, Gigi Allen plans a raid on the Stonewall bar because she wants to get incriminating evidence that will force Snaggle Puss to cooperate with the House Committee on Un-American Activities. Coincidentally, Snaggle Puss is not at the bar when the raid occurs. Officer McGraw is among the Police implementing the raid. In an effort to hide the fact that he is gay, McGraw beats his lover, Huckleberry Hound. Next the scene switches to Counsel Gigi Allen, who meets her own gay lover in the wee hours of the morning. The ensuing humiliating publicity from the raid at Stonewall sends Huckleberry Hound into a state of despair which ends in suicide. As this happens, the flashbacks have ended, and Snaggle Puss testifies before the House Committee. He decides not to give the committee names of colleagues who have ties to the Communist Party; even as he worries that his stance will destroy his career as a playwright. Because he will not cooperate, Snaggle Puss is branded a traitor by popular news columnists, and he is blacklisted. He divorces his wife, and his father dies never realizing that the volunteer who visited him was his own distant son. The scene moves forward a few years, and Snaggle Puss eats a TV dinner alone in anonymity while wondering whether his refusal to comply with the House Committee on Un-American Activities accomplished anything at all, there is a knock on the door. When he opens it he finds a repentant Quick Draw McGraw, the former Police horse, who was removed from the Police force when it was discovered that he was gay. However, the horse has a new career, as an animated television character, and he tells Snaggle Puss that many blacklisted writers are now getting work in television cartoons. Quick Draw invites Snaggle Puss to join him in the television studio. With resignation, Snaggle Puss agrees, while bringing along his old friend Huckleberry Hound's son, Huckleberry Jr.

Characters

- *Snaggle Puss:* Originally an animated television cartoon character first appearing in 1961 who's battle cry was, "Exit Stage Left!" in this incarnation Snaggle Puss is a gay Southern playwright modeled after Tennessee Williams. When he is asked to incriminate his friends, colleagues and fellow artists for their alleged involvement in anti-American activities, Snaggle Puss refuses. As a result, he fails commercially. Eventually, he finds work as a writer of television cartoons.

- *Huckleberry Hound:* Another reinvention of a 1960s cartoon character, in this version, Huckleberry Hound is a Southern novelist based in part on the life and career of the Nobel pize winning novelist and short story writer William Faulkner. Cast as Snaggle Puss's oldest friend, Huckleberry is a repressed homosexual who finally comes out when he visits Snaggle Puss in New York City. During the Police raid the Stonewall, a bar that Snaggle Puss and Huckleberry Hound frequent, Huckleberry is beaten by his lover, the Police horse, Quick Draw McGraw. Thrown into a suicidal despair over this rejection, Huckleberry ends his own life.

- *Quick Draw McGraw:* A third character based on a Hanna-Barbera television cartoon, Quick Draw McGraw first appeared on television in 1959. In *Exit Stage Left the Snagglepuss Chronicles*, McGraw is a Police officer who also goes to the Stonewall bar, sometimes seeking companionship, other times to take a payoff. When he becomes involved with Huckleberry Hound, he believes he has found true love. After Huckleberry Hound's death, McGraw is discovered as a homosexual, and leaves the police force. Eventually, McGraw finds his way into television cartoons, and invites Snagglepuss to join him.

- *Gigi Allen:* A federal prosecutor determined to keep Communist ideology from infiltrating American culture through the arts, Allen tries Lillian Hellman and Snaggle Puss, because she be-

lieves that their plays are subversive. In one scene it is revealed that Allen herself is a lesbian.
- *Lillian Hellman:* A playwright who was blacklisted during the McCarthy hearings in the 1950s, Hellman continued to work although her plays were less popular after she appeared before the House Committee on Un-American Activities.
- *Arthur Miller:* Author of the play, T*he Crucible*, a play ostensibly about the Salem witch trials in Salem, Massachusetts in 1692, but also a commentary on the work of the House Committee on Un-American Activities. Miller appeared before the committee in 1956 and was found to be in contempt of court.

Artistic Style

The artistic style of *Exit Stage Left: the Snagglepuss Chronicles* is complicated and arresting. The animals are portrayed as if they are humans, and endowed with human expressions. The page layouts vary: some pages are multi-paneled while others have one or two panels in order to focus on character rather than movement. Backgrounds are detailed and build credibility to this story of talking animals. Color is an important element as well, and often used to give a scene a prevailing mood. Television is a critical component of this story, and it appears as realistic black and white box, generally in one corner of a panel and contrasting with the characters and backdrops that are depicted in color.

Themes

The theme of *Exit Stage Left: the Snagglepuss Chronicles* is the many forms of repression. In the world of 1950s United States of America, to be a homosexual was to live a life of fear and of secrecy. Although the gay community in New York City openly attended the Stonewall bar, they paid off the Police to prevent raids and public humiliation. However, even this practice did not ultimately deter raids, violence perpetrated on them, or public humiliation. The activities of the House Committee on Un-American Activities amplified those fears, not only felt by homosexuals, but by many types of people whose lifestyle, beliefs, or politics ran contrary conservative American culture.

Impact

Exit Stage Left: the Snaggle Puss Chronicles was the last in a series of books based the animated Hanna-Barbera characters, and it was critically acclaimed, placing on several year-end best lists, including those compiled by National Public Radio, Forbes Magazine, and the New York Times and the New York Public Library. *Exit Stage Left: the Snaggle Puss Chronicles* cemented the reputation of writer Mark Russell as a creator of strange, nostalgia-tinged stories, and it enhanced DC Comics reputation as a publisher of literary, adult-centered stories as opposed to being solely a publisher of genre materials, so the book widened the range of DC's Comics' readership as well.

Further Reading

Chaykin, Howard, *American Flagg*

Gaiman, Neil, et al, *The Sandman: Volume 2: the Doll's House*

Russell, Mark, *the Flintstones*

Bibliography

Abad-Saritos, Alex, "The SnagglePuss Chronicles is the first great comic book if 2018":*VOX*, December 22, 2017. https://www.vox.com/2017/12/22/16795830/the-snagglepuss-chronicles-comic-review.

McMillan, Graeme, "DC Reviving Hanna-Barbera's 'Snagglepuss' as a gay playwright," October 16, 2017. https://www.vox.com/2017/12/22/16795830/the-snagglepuss-chronicles-comic-review.

Spacetwinks, Colin, "Review in progress: Exit Stage Left-the Snagglepuss Chtonicles." *Medium.Com*, February 12, 2018. https://medium.com/@spacetwinks/review-in-progress-exit-stage-left-the-snagglepuss-chronicles-d5d396c513e6.

SNOWMAN, THE

Author: Briggs, Raymond
Artist: Raymond Briggs (illustrator)
Publisher: Random House
First book publication: 1978

Publication History

The Snowman, by Raymond Briggs, was originally published in hardcover in Great Britain by Hamish Hamilton in 1978. The book's first U.S. printing was through Random House Children's Books. In 1985, Hamish Hamilton sold the rights to Penguin Books, which was interested in its mass-marketing potential. However, Random House remains the sole U.S. publisher. In 1980, Snowman Enterprises Ltd. was formed to control the merchandising for products based on the book. The book has sold more than two million copies in the United Kingdom and the United States combined and has been published in more than twenty countries.

In 1977, Briggs released the graphic novel *Fungus the Bogeyman*, which incorporated lengthy passages of prose text mixed among the panels. After its publication, the book received a great deal of criticism for its gory and explicitly detailed life of a bogeyman that lives in a slimy, filthy underground dwelling. During the writing and release of *Fungus,* Briggs had also maintained a file of ideas for what would become *The Snowman*, and then one morning when he discovered it had snowed the night before, Briggs decided that it was a good time to begin work on a new project. He also felt the need to create a clean and pleasant work, especially after the negative reception that *Fungus* had received.

Plot

When a boy wakes one morning, looks out his window, and discovers that snow is falling, he decides to get dressed and run outside to play. He rolls a ball of snow and packs snow on top of it to build a large mound. After a quick retreat inside, he returns to continue work on his creation. He shows his mother what he has made and then places a hat and scarf on the snowman, finishing it off with a tangerine for the nose and coal for the eyes and the buttons.

That evening, the boy spends time with his parents, but he keeps looking out the window at his snowman. After going to bed, he wakes in the middle of the night, runs to the window, and looks at his snowman. He grabs his robe, goes outside, and is greeted by the snowman who has come alive and tips his hat. The two shake hands, and the boy invites the snowman inside. The boy shows the snowman around the living room and kitchen and teaches the snowman about household electronics and appliances.

After a snack of ice cubes, the boy leads the snowman upstairs. They sneak into the boy's parents' room, where the snowman tries on some clothing, and then they go to the boy's room where they play with his toys.

The boy leads the snowman downstairs to the garage, and they play in the family car. Then the snowman retreats to the freezer and lies down to cool off. As the snowman gets out of the freezer, the boy takes out some frozen food and prepares a candlelight meal in the kitchen.

Having had enough of being inside, the snowman leads the boy outside. They start to run, then take off into flight. High in the snowy sky, they fly over a meadow, above the city skyline, and land at the end of a pier. Seeing that the sun is rising, the snowman grabs the boy's hand, and they take flight again and land in the front garden of the boy's home. The snowman leads the boy to the front door, and they hug and wave good-bye. The snowman returns to his original stance in the yard.

The boy retreats to his bedroom, looks out the window at the snowman, and then gets into bed. When he wakes the next morning, he runs down the stairs, past his parents in the kitchen, and out the door; he finds that the snowman has melted and is now a small heap of snow. The hat and scarf are on top of the snow with pieces of coal nearby.

Characters

- *Young Boy* (a.k.a. *James* in later versions of the book and in film and stage productions) is the protagonist of the story. He appears to be six or seven years old and has reddish hair and is the only child in the family. He is excited to see newly fallen snow, and he runs out to the front yard to construct a snowman. He is consistently fascinated with the snowman throughout the novel.

- *Mother* is usually seen around the house wearing her apron. She takes care of her son's everyday needs by feeding and dressing him and tucking him into bed at night. When the novel was written in the 1970's, this was considered the traditional role for a mother, and it would have been usual for her to stay at home during the day cleaning the house, cooking, and taking care of the emotional and physical needs of her children. She enjoys watching her son play and encourages his use of imagination.
- *Father* is seen only a few times throughout the story. He plays what was then the stereotypical fatherly role of being the family provider and head of household. Each time he appears in the story, he is spending time with his wife.
- *Snowman* is the robust, friendly snowman that the boy creates. His larger-than-life body has sculpted arms and legs. He wears a green hat and a scarf and has a tangerine for a nose and black coal for eyes and buttons. He comes to life in the middle of the night as a playful, intriguing, and adventurous friend to the young boy.

Artistic Style

The Snowman is completely wordless and is comprised of neatly arranged frames that are square- and rectangle-shaped with rounded edges. Muted shades of pastels give the book a light, soft quality, while the air and the snow are presented in hazy softness. When the story climaxes with the flight over city lights, the colors darken, signifying the night sky.

Briggs felt that pencil drawings with ink would introduce harshness to the book and would take away from the freshness of the snowman, giving the drawings a rough look. Instead, Briggs used soft pencil crayons to illustrate the book. Using this medium, the color tends to grow into the pictures and lends softness to the images.

While there are no text blocks or speech bubbles in the book, each frame imparts just enough information to further the story. The frames are a variety of sizes, and the panels tend to increase in size with the intensity of the storyline, which also serves to advance the pacing of the story. When the story climaxes, a single frame covers a full page. As the story comes to a close, the panel sizes decrease. The story concludes with a single square frame, surrounded with white space.

Themes

Childhood excitement, innocence, and imagination are major themes of the book. When the boy first sees that snow has fallen, he cannot wait to go outside and play; he dresses quickly and runs out the door. He uses his imagination to build the snowman, and he works meticulously to make the shape by carving arms and legs into the snow.

After the snowman is built, the boy becomes preoccupied with it. For the rest of the day and into the night, he returns to look at the snowman. After being tucked into bed, he abruptly wakes in the middle of the night and runs to look out the window.

The relationship between the boy and the snowman is unique. The snowman is the size of an adult and to a certain extent guides the boy as an adult would, but the snowman is also playful and curious like a child. The two friends learn from each other's worlds. They have fun playing with everyday objects and use their imaginations to create new games.

The Snowman is also thematically driven around fantasy. Common fantasy themes are prevalent such as when the inanimate snowman comes to life, becomes a companion for the boy, and then flies the boy through the night sky on a wonderful adventure.

A final theme in the book is loss. On the last page of the book the single frame shows the boy with his back to readers looking down at his melted snowman. This image is left open to interpretation. Most readers would believe the boy to be disappointed or perhaps heartbroken that his friend is gone. Its realism is a life lesson, however: All relationships end at some point. There cannot be life without death.

Impact

Comics were not as readily accepted as an art form in the United Kingdom as they were in other European countries when *The Snowman* was first published in the late 1970's. The term *comics* had negative connotations because sequential art was not valued in the same manner that fine art was. However, with the commercial success of *The Snowman*, Briggs broke boundaries by expanding picture-book illustration to now include sequential art and wordless text, which then helped shape the artistic styles of such British illustrators as Shirley Hughes, Jan Ormerod, Peter Collington, Posy Simmonds, Philippe Dupasquier, John Prater, and Colin McNaughton.

In 2005, Briggs was inaugurated into Britain's Royal Society of Literature and is recognized as one of the country's most respected graphic novelists and as a pioneer in the comics art form. Comics and graphic novels have increasingly garnered respect in the United Kingdom, and publishers are releasing more titles each year.

Variations of the original title were published from 1985 to 1999, including board books, story books with text, and numerous novelty titles. Activity books and a CD-ROM based on the book were also released. The snowman character has also been transformed into many collectibles and toys as well as stationary, clothing, kitchenware, household goods, and bedding.

A stage musical production of *The Snowman* by the Birmingham Repertory Theatre premiered in London's West End in 1993 and has been performed every Christmas since. The troupe has also toured England, Japan, and the United States.

Films

The Snowman. Directed by Dianne Jackson and Jimmy T. Murakami. Snowman Enterprises/TVC London, 1982. This unrated film adaptation was originally made for television. The film begins with a short introduction by Briggs. David Bowie acts as the narrator in a re-released version, and the song "Walking in the Air," sung by Peter Auty, is featured in the original film and became a top-ten record in the United Kingdom. While the film maintains the pastel colorings of the book and follows the majority of the plot, it includes a number of omissions and some major additions. The film was nominated for an Academy Award for Best Animated Short Film in 1982.

Janet Weber

Further Reading

Briggs, Raymond. *The Bear* (1994).
_____. *Father Christmas* (1973).
Tan, Shaun. *The Arrival* (2007).

Bibliography

Briggs, Raymond. "Big Kid, 'Old Git,' and Still in the Rudest of Health." Interview by Rachel Cooke. *The Observer* (August 9, 2008) http://www.guardian.co.uk/books/2008/aug/10/booksforchildrenandteenagers.

Irvine, Louise. *The Snowman Collector's Book*. Somerset, England: Richard Dennis, 2004.

Jones, Nicolette. *Raymond Briggs: Blooming Books*. London: Jonathan Cape, 2003.

See also: *Ethel and Ernest*; *The Arrival*; *Robot Dreams*

STITCHES: A MEMOIR

Author: Small, David
Artist: David Small (illustrator)
Publisher: W. W. Norton
First book publication: 2009

Publication History
Prior to writing *Stitches*, David Small submitted a children's-book proposal for a novel about a child who wanders alone in a hospital ward while he waits for his father and then finds a fetus in a jar. The proposal was rejected, but for Small it was the beginning stages of writing *Stiches*. Though he was not a huge fan of graphic novels, Small was impressed with Art Spiegelman's *Maus* (1986) and the artwork of Chris Ware, who wrote and illustrated *Jimmy Corrigan: The Smartest Kid on Earth,* and Small soon realized that the only way to tell his story was through a graphic memoir.

As Small began to draw and write, the memories of his family and his dysfunctional childhood became tangible, and the rage that had been repressed for decades was stirred up and brought to the surface. Despite the intense emotional pain, Small believes that reliving the memories helped his creative process. When published, *Stitches* became David Small's first graphic novel and first book for adults.

Small said he chose W. W. Norton to publish *Stitches* because of its history of producing nonfiction works. Small's manuscript was delivered to the editor at Norton in a box with the corners stitched together to resemble wound sutures.

Prior to publication, Norton insisted that Small show an advance reading copy of *Stitches* to anyone who could possibly refute the story. The only person alive was Small's brother Ted, with whom he had been estranged for fifty years. After reading the book, Ted said to his brother that *Stitches* was a snapshot of his own youth. The book had thus helped to mend a broken bond, and as a result, the brothers were able to reconcile.

Stitches was first released by W. W. Norton in 2009, and a paperback edition followed in 2010. Renowned independent bookstore Powell's Books in Portland, Oregon, released 850 copies of the book in a special slipcase edition, making it the thirteenth book in Powell's slipcase program and the first graphic novel.

Plot
Small offers an autobiographical sketch separated into chapters that represent periods of his life. The book concludes with a brief glimpse of the author as an adult. Small is first seen at the age of six in Detroit, Michigan, where he lived in a home in which communication was nonexistent and silence reigned. As a child, David had ongoing respiratory ailments, which his radiologist father treated with radiation.

On days when he waited at the hospital for his father to finish work, David would roam the halls. On one occasion, he wanders into the pathology department and

---

David Small
David Small is the acclaimed children's book author and illustrator who won the Caldecott Honor Award for *The Gardener* (written by his wife, Sarah Stewart) and the Caldecott Medal for *So You Want to Be President?* (written by Judith St. George). Though his drawings have appeared in *The New Yorker* and *The New York Times*, he is best known in the comics industry as the creator of the autobiographical graphic novel *Stitches* (2009). In that work, Small records his experiences as a sickly child who, at the age of fourteen, had one of his vocal chords removed and was told that he was expected to die from cancer. Widely praised, *Stitches* was one of the most acclaimed graphic novel debuts in history. Small's illustrations in *Stitches* make great use of the small size of his pages, often employing page-width panels. He creates pen images to which he adds gray tone and washes and he frequently composes his panels from odd angles, giving the book a somewhat alienating feeling.

discovers a fetus-like creature in a jar. This scene becomes embedded in David's mind and later haunts him in his dreams.

When David is eleven, his mother hosts a bridge club meeting. David is responsible for greeting guests and taking their coats; while doing so, one of the guests discovers a bulging growth on David's neck and urges his mother to have it seen by a doctor. David's mother's high spirits from the meeting are squelched by the discovery, and David is later taken to a doctor who believes it to be a cyst that must be removed surgically. The cyst is not removed for another three years, and because the surgeon is unable to remove all of it, a specialist is recruited to perform a second surgery. David wakes from the surgery to discover he has lost a vocal cord and his thyroid gland, and he is unable to speak.

While recuperating at home, David finds a letter his mother had written to his grandmother, telling her that David had cancer. When he questions his parents about the cancer, they tell him he did not need to know about it.

The loss of his voice makes David feel like an outcast at school, which causes him to be angry. This anger leads him to skip classes, to suffer from recurring dreams of being trapped, and to spend a night in jail for driving the family car without a license. He is sent to an all-boys school, from which he runs away multiple times

At the age of fifteen, David visits a psychologist, and it is here that he comes to terms with the fact that his mother does not love him. Through therapy he finds the courage and confidence to escape his family, live on his own, and complete his high school education. He discovers art, which helps him regain his voice.

Characters

- *David Small* is the protagonist of the story and a slender, curly headed boy. During his childhood, he is given radiation by his father that eventually causes throat cancer.
- *Betty Small*, a.k.a. *Mama*, is David's mother. She is silent and withdrawn and never speaks her mind. She is constantly slamming doors and cabinets and banging pots and pans. She is always angry and unhappy and smokes constantly despite the fact that she was born with a heart problem and has only one functioning lung. She lives as a closet lesbian and dies when David is thirty.
- *Edward "Ed" Small*, a.k.a. *Dad*, is a tall man, who is always smoking his pipe. He works as a radiologist. Every day after work he retreats to the basement in the family home to hit his punching bag. He believes David's respiratory problems can be cured through radiation.
- *Ted Small* is David's older brother and is drawn as an older version of David. He spends most of his time in the basement banging on his drums.
- *Grandparents* live in rural Indiana and are Betty's mother and stepfather. David's grandmother is physically forceful and speaks rudely to David. David is afraid of her and believes she is crazy. David's grandmother intentionally kills her husband by setting fire to the house, and she is then sent to a mental institution.
- *The Murphys* are Betty's paternal grandparents who were said to be cruel to their daughter-in-law, Betty's mother. Mr. Murphy tried to kill himself by drinking Drano, which merely destroyed his vocal chords, leaving him unable to speak. Mrs. Murphy is revealed to have been a petty thief.
- *Papa John* is David's step-grandfather and Betty's stepfather. He works as a greeter at a funeral home and knows everyone in town. He is kind and gentle to David, and is the only closely related family member who treats David with respect. He is killed by David's grandmother when she sets fire to their home.
- *Mrs. Irene Dillon* is a member of the bridge club and is married to a surgeon. She points out the growth on David's neck. In a later scene in the book, she is in the bedroom with Betty.
- *Dr. Joe Dillon* is the first doctor to diagnose the growth on David's neck, which he says is a cyst and suggests it be removed. He asks David's father to take an X-ray of it. He is married to Irene Dillon.
- *Hospital Nurse* is the flamboyant and pudgy lady who takes care of David in his hospital room. She is outgoing, friendly, energetic, and continuously happy.

- *Dr. Blyss* is the first surgeon to operate on David's neck. He is unable to remove the entire mass and recruits a specialist for a second, more invasive surgery.
- *Psychologist* is David's therapist. He tells David that his mother does not love him. He becomes David's father figure, and his office becomes a safe haven for David and is the first step in separating from his family.

Artistic Style

Through the use of brush and wash and a dominant pallet of grays, *Stitches* captures each character's strong emotions. Small also used a fine-point dip pen and created every drawing and speech bubble by hand without the use of computer-generated artwork. Most of the sketches were done on card stock, and the final art was completed on Bristol board.

The book is almost wordless, making the visual experience and characters' body language of primary importance to the advancement of plot. Small hallucinogenic images and varying panel sizes impart a dreamlike structure to the story. One-page panel images enforce realism and depth. The total effect of Small's illustrations has prompted artists and critics to compare *Stitches* to a silent movie.

Symbolism is used to convey difficult childhood memories. A telephone placed within numerous panels and the pages containing telephone lines, for example, are representative of the lack of communication in Small's family. Similarly, the smoke from his father's pipe is symbolic of his father's vacuous explanations and the missed opportunities in Small's life.

Themes

The themes within *Stitches* relate directly to Small's development from childhood through his teen years and into adulthood. Generational dysfunction within families stemming from a lack of communication, abuse, helplessness, and physical and emotional pain is explored. Conversely, *Stitches* explores the themes of hope, coming of age, and rebirth.

Small shows the reader a childhood and adolescence filled with unusual trauma and abuse at the hands of his parents, which is illustrated in his parents' stark facial expressions as well as in a complete lack of remorse by his father despite acknowledging that he has given his son cancer through the radiation treatments.

Following his second surgery and after learning that his voice has been taken from him, David is outraged and forced into a life of silence, terror, and helplessness. Unable to speak, his mind floods with cries of anger (effectively seen through full-page panels of screaming heads) that are so loud, he is afraid his family can hear the voices in his head.

The reader is also presented with hope, which is seen in David's young face and again as an adult and which indicates David's ultimate survival—especially through his therapist's help and support. Eventually, David comes of age by discovering his life passion and realizing that his art has saved him and has given him the confidence needed to persevere, which ultimately results in a rebirth and redemption.

Impact

Almost immediately upon publication, *Stitches* was praised by such well-known art directors, writers, and cartoonists as François Mouly, Robert Crumb, Harry Bliss, Jack Gantos, Jeff Rivera, Stan Lee, and Jules Feiffer. The book received multiple starred reviews in popular review journals and garnered respect from critics.

At the end of 2009, *Stitches* was on a variety of top-ten and best-of lists, especially through the American Library Association, which chose Small to be a panelist for its annual auditorium speaker's event in 2010. *Stitches* was also nominated for numerous top awards, such as the National Book Award in 2009 and two Eisner awards in 2010. The book has been published in over eight languages. While the book is aimed at adult readers, it has garnered a wide readership from young adults.

Stitches has also paved the way for other writers and illustrators such as Tracy White (*How I Made It to Eighteen: A Mostly True Story*, 2010) and Raina Telgemeier (*Smile*, 2010) to use the graphic novel medium to share their traumatic childhood and teenage experiences.

Small did not expect *Stitches* to garner such widespread fame and attention. On a more personal level, however, *Stitches* allowed David Small to come to terms with his past, rekindle a relationship with his brother, and, as he conveyed during an interview with *Graphic Novel Reporter,* go through "the most passionate artistic experience I ever had."

Janet Weber

Further Reading

B., David. *Epileptic* (2005).

Barry, Lynda. *One Hundred Demons* (2002).

Bechdel, Alison. *Fun Home: A Family Tragicomic* (2006).

Brabner, Joyce, and Harvey Pekar. *Our Cancer Year* (1994).

Marchetto, Marisa Acocella. *Cancer Vixen: A True Story* (2006).

Telgemeier, Raina. *Smile* (2010).

Walls, Jeanette. *The Glass Castle* (2005).

White, Tracy. *How I Made It to Eighteen: A Mostly True Story* (2010).

Bibliography

Small, David. "David Small Talks with The White Rabbit's Grandniece." Interview by Danica Davidson. *The Comics Journal*, October 6, 2010. http://classic.tcj.com/interviews/david-small-talks-with-the-white-rabbits-grandniec/.

_____. "The Powells.com Interview with David Small." Interview by Dave Weich. *Powell's Books*, August 13, 2009. http://www.powells.com/blog/?p=7543.

_____. "Why I Write. . . ." *Publishers Weekly* 256, no. 35 (August 31, 2009): 23-25.

See also: *Epileptic; One! Hundred! Demons!; Fun Home; Our Cancer Year*

STRANGERS IN PARADISE

Author: Moore, Terry
Artist: Terry Moore (illustrator); Josh Wiesenfeld (inker); Jessica Kindzierski (cover artist)
Publisher: Antarctic Press; Image Comics; Abstract Studio
First serial publication: 1993-2007
First book publication: 1995-2007

Publication History

Strangers in Paradise began as a single issue in 1993. Its first three issues were published individually by Antarctic Press of San Antonio, Texas. Moore then decided to self-publish Volume 2 under the imprint Abstract Studio. In 1996, Moore moved the series to Homage Comics, an imprint of Image Comics, to publish issues 1-8 of Volume 3. Moore then returned to Abstract Studio to finish the series with issues 9-90. *Strangers in Paradise* has been collected in trade paperbacks, and the entire series was published in 2004-2007 as a set of six Pocket Editions.

Strangers in Paradise Treasury Edition was published in 2004 by Perennial Currents (HarperCollins), which includes Moore's original manuscript for the first issue and reprints a special issue from 2000 (not included in trade paperbacks) called "When Worlds Collide!" Moore has also published two guides to *Strangers in Paradise*: the *Strangers in Paradise Source Book* (2003) and *Strangers in Paradise: Lyrics and Poems* (1999). In 2009, Moore released a limited run of a *Strangers in Paradise Omnibus*, which collects the entire story in two hardcover volumes.

Plot

Strangers in Paradise centers on Katchoo and Francine and their friend David and the portrayal of the relationships among the characters. Its title comes from a fictional play within the series, which in turn takes its name from the song "Stranger in Paradise." The play contains the line, often repeated in the series, "Without love, we're never more than strangers in paradise."

The first scene of the first issue takes place as a flashback when Katchoo and Francine were in high school.

Terry Moore signing a hardcover edition of Strangers in Paradise at 2010 San Diego Comic-Con. (By Dave & Margie Hill, via Wikimedia Commons)

Ten years later, Katchoo and Francine live as roommates and are best friends. The situation that dominates the entire series is introduced in the first three volumes: Katchoo has rejected men and is in love with Francine. Francine believes in marriage and "happily ever after," despite a string of unsuccessful relationships. She clearly loves Katchoo but struggles throughout the series with how, and whether, to express that love in a sexual or romantic way. In the first three issues, Francine ends a relationship with Freddie Femurs, who is a recurring character. Katchoo shows her propensity for violence by retaliating physically against Freddie and later meets David at a museum. In spite of her rebuffs, he wins her friendship, and Volume 1 ends with the three characters happy and together.

Volume 2 begins with *I Dream of You*, which departs from romantic comedy and explores crime and suspense. Katchoo's complicated and secret past is revealed through a series of flashbacks interspersed with present-day scenes. Katchoo once belonged to the Parker Girls, an organization headed by rich widow Darcy Parker. Katchoo confesses to David that she fell into life as a "high-priced call girl" when she ran away at the age of fifteen to escape her abusive stepfather. Katchoo eventually also escaped her life with Darcy, but with a good deal of Darcy's money. Darcy tracks down Katchoo, and the volume ends with a bloody standoff in which Katchoo is shot and it is revealed that David is Darcy's brother. Other central characters introduced in this volume are Tambi and Bambi who are twins and Katchoo's half sisters and work as Darcy's bodyguards

Volume 3 opens with a scene years into a future that will become known as "Version One." Francine has not seen Katchoo since her wedding ten years prior. In the present, Katchoo and Francine continue to dance around a romantic relationship, and Katchoo exposes Darcy to the media. When the story breaks, Tambi kills Darcy. There is a brief return to the "future" where Francine's mother reunites Francine and Katchoo.

The present-day story shows the series of fights that led to Katchoo and Francine's separation. David and Katchoo survive a plane crash, and Francine meets her future husband, Brad. Francine wavers between Brad and Katchoo, but she chooses Katchoo. The arc ends in the future with the phrase "The End . . . of Version One."

Moore then offers two more "versions" and a scenario in which Francine stays with Brad and becomes pregnant. Tired of waiting for Francine, Katchoo begins sleeping with another woman, which drives Francine back to Brad. Before their wedding, Francine miscarries. *Heart in Hand* ends with the death of Katchoo's stepfather and Brad and Francine's wedding.

Tattoo sees David, Katchoo, and Katchoo's former lover Casey in Las Vegas, where a near-marriage with David makes Katchoo realize that she can only be with women. When David discovers he has cancer, Tambi and Katchoo make plans to carry on his line by having his child. On the same day, Francine discovers that Brad is cheating on her, and his brother, musician Griffin Silver whose songs figure prominently in the series, has been murdered. Seeing a painting of herself by Katchoo in Griffin's house, Francine realizes where her heart lies and leaves Brad.

During the final issues of the series, David dies, and Francine follows Katchoo to Santa Fe and finally commits to a relationship with her. They buy a house and discover that they are both pregnant. The last scene of the series shows them peaceful, happy, and with their children.

Volumes

- *The Collected Strangers in Paradise,* Volume 1 (1995). Collects Volume 1, issues 1-3. Originally developed as a stand-alone miniseries.
- *Strangers in Paradise: I Dream of You* (1996). Collects Volume 2, issues 1-9. Introduces the crime plot and Katchoo's association with Darcy Parker.
- *Strangers in Paradise: It's a Good Life!* (1996). Collects Volume 2, issues 10-13. Includes the first installment of the "Molly and Poo" story in issue 13.
- *Strangers in Paradise: Love Me Tender* (1997). Collects Volume 3, issues 1-5. Includes a superhero fantasy sequence.
- *Strangers in Paradise: Immortal Enemies* (1998). Collects Volume 3, issues 6-12. Features the implosion of the Parker Girls.
- *Strangers in Paradise: High School!* (1998). Collects Volume 3, issues 13-16. Features the origin of Katchoo and Francine's friendship and their starkly different home lives in high school.
- *Strangers in Paradise: Sanctuary* (1999). Collects Volume 3, issues 17-24. Includes scenes from "Version One" of Katchoo and Francine's future.
- *Strangers in Paradise: My Other Life* (2000). Collects Volume 3, issues 25-30. Takes place mostly in Nashville, the site of David and Katchoo's plane crash, and Francine's mother's house.
- *Strangers in Paradise: Child of Rage* (2001). Collects Volume 3, issues 31-32 and 34-38. Takes place a year after *My Other Life.*
- *Strangers in Paradise: Tropic of Desire* (2001). Collects Volume 3, issues 39-43. Contains the

end of "Version One," in which Katchoo and Francine end up together.
- *Strangers in Paradise: Brave New World* (2002). Collects Volume 3, issues 44, 45, 47, and 48. Contains a glimpse of "Version Two," in which Francine marries Brad and stays with him.
- *Strangers in Paradise: Heart in Hand* (2003). Collects Volume 3, issues 50-54. Introduces Cherry Hammer and Griffin Silver as major characters.
- *Strangers in Paradise: Flower to Flame* (2003). Collects Volume 3, issues 55-60. Includes a parody of the Disney film *Snow White* (1937).
- *Strangers in Paradise: David's Story* (2004). Collects Volume 3, issues 61-63. Details David's violent family and past and his subsequent conversion to Christianity.
- *Strangers in Paradise: Tomorrow Now* (2004). Collects Volume 3, issues 64-69. Features several of Katchoo's paintings.
- *Strangers in Paradise: Molly and Poo* (2005). Collects Volume 2, issue 14; Volume 3, issues 46 and 73. Includes two-sided stories of murder.
- *Strangers in Paradise: Tattoo* (2005). Collects Volume 3, issues 70-72 and 74-76. Takes place in Las Vegas and features Katchoo opening her own studio.
- *Strangers in Paradise: Love and Lies* (2006). Collects Volume 3, issues 77-82. Includes Griffin Silver's murder.
- *Strangers in Paradise: Ever After* (2007). Collects Volume 3, issues 83-90. Includes David's death and Francine and Katchoo's final reconciliation.

Characters

- *Helen Francine Peters* is a curvy, dark-haired optimist. She spends the series oscillating between her belief in the stability of men (despite all evidence to the contrary) and her undeniable love for Katchoo. She represents the hopes, fears, and ideals of the average woman.
- *Katina Marie Choovanski*, a.k.a. *Katchoo*, is an artist and earned her nickname from her father, Chicago mobster Sonny Baker. Her petite frame and long blond hair belie her physical strength and violent past. She distrusts men (beginning with her stepfather, who abused and raped her). She spends the series trying to escape her past and to persuade Francine to be in a relationship with her. She is also a recovering alcoholic.
- *David Qin*, a.k.a. *Yousaka Takahashi*, is a gentle Japanese American art student. He was born Yousaka Takahashi and took the name of "David Qin" from a young man he killed as a teenage gang member. Unlike his half sister Darcy, he shows contrition for his youthful crimes and becomes a Christian. He falls in love with Katchoo and impregnates her before he dies.
- *Darcy Parker* is an attractive, Japanese American woman who lives for money and power. Unlike her half brother David, she embraces violence and brands the women who work for her with tattoos of lilies. She despises men and considers them weak. Katchoo was Darcy's lover and closest confidant before betraying her.
- *Gwynnethina Casey Bullocks-Femur* is a perky blond aerobics instructor with large breasts and a small nose (both the result of plastic surgery). She enters the group by marrying Freddie but remains friends with Francine, Katchoo, and David after their divorce. She is presented as cheerful and uncomplicated, but she keeps a secret that she works for Tambi.
- *Mary Beth Baker,* a.k.a. *Tambi*, is a tall, heavily muscled woman with long, bleached-blond hair. She can be distinguished from her twin sister, Sara Beth or "Bambi," by the scars on her arms (from cutting herself). She and Bambi both serve as Darcy Parker's bodyguards and are Katchoo's half sisters.
- *Frederick "Freddie" Stanley Femur* is an average-looking, curly haired lawyer. He dates Francine, marries and divorces Casey, and performs legal services for several characters. He maintains his macho, conservative views throughout the series; though he desires women

(particularly Francine), he does not understand them.

- *Veronica Bouedaue*, a.k.a. *Rachel Hampton* and *Beverly Pace*, is a beautiful Asian woman with long hair. Darcy's cousin, she rises from a lowly chauffeur position to reviving the Parker Girls after Darcy's death. She uses the aliases Rachel Hampton and Beverly Pace in her deceitful rise to power. Rejected in some way by almost every character, she is consumed by her lust and rage and eventually dies a slow death.
- *Bradley Silver* is a tall, handsome doctor who woos Francine at a vulnerable time in her life. He is a decent person, but after their marriage, he proves himself to be like all of Francine's other boyfriends and cheats on her. He is Griffin Silver's brother.
- *Griffin Silver* is taller and more handsome than his brother. He is an aging rock star, and he has a dedicated fan base and artistic integrity. His songs appear frequently throughout the series. He is murdered onstage by a stalker.
- *Emma Glass* is a slim, dark-haired woman who discovered Katchoo on the streets of Los Angeles and brought her in to work for Darcy Parker. She and Katchoo worked as partners and escaped to Hawaii with some of Darcy's money. A drug addict, she was infected with AIDS by Veronica and dies early in the series.

Artistic Style

Strangers in Paradise is drawn almost entirely in black-and-white line drawings. Throughout the series, Moore uses devices such as sound effects and varying dialogue styles for different tones of voice while parodying superhero comic books and Disney animation. From time to time, he also draws in other cartoonists' styles such as Charles Schulz and Bill Watterson.

Moore often displays parallel visual sequences or intersperses two different sequences to show contrast. In *High School!*, for example, Katchoo's stark and empty house and morning routine are presented alongside Francine's crowded, lighter, more supportive environment. Later on, Francine and Katchoo have a phone conversation in which the visual of each character contrasts with their small-talk dialogue.

Moore's overall style is realistic and cinematic. He makes a point of drawing women with varying body types such as Francine's whose stomach bulges over her jeans. Moore also uses several cinematic techniques such as close-ups, dissolves, and fade-outs. In *It's a Good Life!*, Moore draws the border of a film reel around a sequence of scenes. Text outside dialogue bubbles illustrate characters' thoughts (like voice-overs), and occasionally there is use of screenplay-style dialogue bordered by "stills" of the characters talking. Sheet music and lyrics often weave through sequences like a sound track.

Themes

The major theme of *Strangers in Paradise* is the complexity of human relationships. Many of the relationships and characters defy easy labels or definition. When labels are applied—for example, Katchoo as a lesbian or Francine as a heterosexual—they do not last and only cause grief and confusion. There is an emphasis, instead, on the authenticity of relationships, life, or art.

Both Katchoo and Griffin Silver struggle with the idea of remaining true to one's art in the face of commercialism. Music, visual art, and poetry are all important to the main characters. Many issues begin with a Griffin Silver song or a poem by Katchoo or David.

Terry Moore

Best known for his long-running adult series *Strangers in Paradise*, Terry Moore often focuses on strong central female characters with complex problems and relationships. His work includes several stories containing superhero, science-fiction, and supernatural elements, but he has mainly concentrated on fully developing the characters in his work. A writer-artist, Moore has sometimes incorporated unique design elements into his stories, such as sheet music for songs of his composition.

Quotations from real-life songs and written works open issues and serve as sound tracks for scenes.

Strangers in Paradise also deals with male/female relationships. Katchoo and Francine represent opposite sides of a spectrum of women's feelings about men—Katchoo cannot live with them, and Francine cannot live without them. While Francine responds to male characters by becoming hurt and insecure, Katchoo responds with hostility and violence. The whole Parker Girl organization is an exaggerated response and a warning to women to acquire the resources to counteract centuries of male power. Only two male characters do not eventually disappoint—Mike Walsh and David Qin. In fact, the series can be seen as a protest against modern society's injustices toward women. Multiple story lines show the effects of sexual and emotional abuse against women in the form of incest, stalking, rape, or domestic violence. Women's bodies are the object of scrutiny by individual men and by society. Objectifying women is manifested in characters' obsession with their weight and in Francine's accidental and intentional exposures of her body. Katchoo, on the other hand, makes an effort in her art to paint the body as something to be admired instead of scrutinized.

Power, money, and their effects on people is another theme. Darcy Parker thrives on both, while her brother David sees money as a way to help others. Katchoo's finances ebb and flow throughout the series and only near the end of the series is she able to have money without succumbing to drugs and indolence. In general, those who love money and power meet bad ends, while those who value relationships and love are, if not rewarded, at least respected.

Impact

Strangers in Paradise is notable for its readership, which extends beyond the typical graphic novel audience. For many readers, the series was their introduction to graphic novels, and more than half of the readership is female.

Strangers in Paradise drew early praise from such diverse sources as Kevin Smith and Neil Gaiman for its faithful depictions of women's relationships and inner thoughts. Moore has also gained praise for featuring lesbian, gay, bisexual, and transgender characters at a time when graphic novels and mainstream film and television did not include these groups in their storylines.

Elizabeth Galoozis

Further Reading

Bechdel, Alison. *Fun Home* (2006).

Thompson, Craig. *Blankets* (2003).

Vaughan, Brian K., et al. *Runaways* (2003-2009).

_____. *Y: The Last Man* (2002-2008).

Bibliography

Duffy, Damian, and John Jennings, eds. *Out of Sequence: Underrepresented Voices in American Comics*. Seattle: University of Washington Press, 2009.

Hatfield, Charles. *Alternative Comics: An Emerging Literature*. Jackson: University Press of Mississippi, 2006.

Moore, Terry. "The Terry Moore Interview." Interview by Dirk Deppey. *The Comics Journal* 276 (May, 2006): 60.

Tramountanas, George A. "Strangers No More, as Moore Brings *Strangers in Paradise* to an End." *Comic Book Resources*, March 17, 2006. http://www.comicbookresources.com/?page=article&id=6652.

See also: *Fun Home; Blankets*

STRAY BULLETS

Author: Lapham, David
Artist: David Lapham (illustrator); Maria Lapham (cover artist)
Publisher: El Capitán
First serial publication: 1995-2005
First book publication: 1996-2004

Publication History

David Lapham and his wife Maria created the El Capitán publishing company in order to self-publish *Stray Bullets*. *Stray Bullets* came out on an irregular schedule for its first ten years, averaging about four issues a year. In 2001, *Stray Bullets* went on hiatus while Lapham produced the nine-issue mystery series *Murder Me Dead*.

Each issue of *Stray Bullets*, especially those in the first arc, is a stand-alone story that ends with the text, "The End. . . ." However, the characters and events of the single issues intertwine to form story arcs of seven to ten issues. El Capitán collected the first three story arcs in hardback and trade paperback. A fourth collection was to be published in 2003. El Capitán also published eight smaller paperbacks that collect four issues each without regard to story line.

Since 2005, Lapham has reluctantly placed *Stray Bullets* on hiatus to write comics about mainstream superhero characters such as Batman, Daredevil, the Punisher, the Spectre, Wolverine, and Spider-Man. Lapham has completed some created-owned work for DC Comics imprints with the graphic novel *Silverfish* (2007), the series *Young Liars* (2008-2009), and the limited series *Sparta: USA* (2010).

Plot

Stray Bullets is primarily a coming-of-age story about Virginia Applejack, whose story has spanned from the summer of 1977 to April, 1986. Virginia first appears in the second issue as a seven-year-old coming out of the movie theater after watching *Star Wars*, and she sees Spanish Scott walking away from a double murder in a Baltimore alley. Her silence after the murder and the emotional and physical abuse she suffers from her mother leads to her violent reaction against third-grade bully Kevin Leeds.

Kevin and a gang of friends respond by brutally attacking Virginia on Halloween night. Virginia becomes a rebellious child who creates an ultraviolet fantasy world in which her alter ego, Amy Racecar, dabbles in bank robbing, presidential politics, science-fiction adventure, clown killing, and adventures modeled on Akira Kurosawa's samurai films. Amy's adventures refract Virginia's misadventures in satiric and hyperbolic ways, and Virginia takes on the name Amy when she successfully runs away from home after her beloved father's death in late 1982, chronicled in "Innocence of Nihilism."

Virginia does not provide the only focus for the story. "Innocence of Nihilism" also introduces a cast of small-time criminals in late 1970's and early 1980's Baltimore who are connected to the mysterious crime

---

David Lapham

Best known for his work on the crime comic book series, *Stray Bullets*, David Lapham began his career working for the short-lived Valiant Comics and Defiant Comics companies in the early 1990's. In 1995 he began publishing *Stray Bullets*, a collection of interconnected crime stories, through his own El Capitan Books. Forty issues of that series were published by 2005 and later collected in a number of volumes, although the work remains incomplete. In 2000 he produced a murder mystery, *Murder Me Dead*, as a nine-issue serial. Since 2005 he has taken on a large amount of freelance work in the superhero genre, working on *Detective Comics*, *Daredevil vs. Punisher*, and *Tales of the Unexpected*. Lapham's stories are tremendously dark in tone and feature characters from the margins of society in noir-inspired settings. His art tends toward the naturalistic, and he uses blacks extensively to create dark moods and settings.

boss Harry. Harry's girlfriend, Nina; her best friend, Beth; and Beth's boyfriend, Orson, steal two suitcases of cocaine from Harry and flee west to the desert town of Seaside. They hide in Seaside from the spring of 1982 to October, 1983, events that provide much of the story of "Somewhere Out West." Virginia joins the fugitives in the summer of 1983 and bonds with both Beth and Nina.

After the violent conclusion of "Somewhere Out West," Beth and Virginia continue west to Los Angeles and live together until July, 1985. Over the course of the following two story arcs ("Other People" and "Dark Days"), the two women become intertwined in networks of adulterous couples and sexual perversion, events that end with Beth in another standoff with Monster. Virginia and her young friend Bobby are abducted.

Virginia is rescued by the police and returned to her mother in Baltimore, where she resumes high school in the fifth arc, "Hijinks and Derring-Do." Over the course of the school year—from September, 1985, to late April, 1986—Virginia finds that her high school presents almost as much danger and sexual violence as the underworld of Los Angeles. In a strategy reminiscent of that used in Dashiell Hammett's *Red Harvest* (1929), she starts a war between the school's major factions: the jocks and the burnouts. This war results in her capture by Kevin and Hussey at the end of issue 40, which is also the cliff-hanger on which the series halted with one issue left in the fifth story arc. The *Stray Bullets* short story in *Noir* shows how Virginia escaped from the duo. It is not known how or when Lapham will continue the series, but he stated in a letter column that the sixth arc would have been entitled "Total War."

The comic has had two issues that occur after April, 1986. In issue 20, set in August, 1986, Monster attempts to coerce a mathematics professor into deciphering a code for Harry, and in issue 1, set in summer 1997, a grown-up Joey turns a mission to dispose of the corpse of Harry's latest girlfriend into a massacre.

Volumes

- *Stray Bullets,* Volume 1: *Innocence of Nihilism* (1996). Collects issues 1-7. Features a series of interrelated stand-alone stories that introduce a cast of small-time criminals in Baltimore.
- *The Collected Stray Bullets,* Volume 1 (1998). Collects issues 1-4. Paperback versions of issues collected previously in *Stray Bullets: Innocence of Nihilism.*
- *Stray Bullets,* Volume 2: *Somewhere Out West* (1999). Collects issues 8-14. Features Nina, Beth, and Orson hiding out in the small desert town of Seaside after stealing Harry's cocaine.
- *The Collected Stray Bullets,* Volume 2 (1999). Collects issues 5-8. Paperback versions of issues collected previously in *Stray Bullets: Innocence of Nihilism* and *Stray Bullets: Somewhere Out West.*
- *The Collected Stray Bullets,* Volume 3 (2000). Collects issues 9-12. Paperback versions of issues collected previously in *Stray Bullets: Somewhere Out West.*
- *Stray Bullets,* Volume 3: *Other People* (2001). Collects issues 15-22. Features Beth and Virginia navigating through the secret and violent sex lives of adulterous married couples in Los Angeles.
- *The Collected Stray Bullets,* Volume 4 (2001). Collects issues 13-16. Paperback versions of issues collected previously in *Stray Bullets: Somewhere Out West* and *Stray Bullets: Other People.*
- *The Collected Stray Bullets,* Volume 5 (2001). Collects 17-20. Paperback versions of issues collected previously in *Stray Bullets: Other People.*
- *Amy Racecar Ultimate Collection* (2002). Collects issues 6, 10, 18, and *Amy Racecar Color Special*, issues 1-2. Features Virginia's fantasy alter ego, Amy Racecar.
- *The Collected Stray Bullets,* Volume 6 (2002). Collects 21-24. Paperback versions of some of the issues collected in *Stray Bullets: Other People.*
- *Stray Bullets,* Volume 4: *Dark Days* (2003). Collects issues 23-30. Features Virginia being kidnapped twice, as Beth, Ian, and Roger scramble to find her.
- *The Collected Stray Bullets,* Volume 7 (2003). Collects 25-28. Paperback versions of issues collected previously in *Stray Bullets: Dark Days.*

- *The Collected Stray Bullets,* Volume 8 (2004). Collects issues 29-32. Features the conclusion of "Dark Days" and the beginning of "Hijinks and Derring-Do." Virginia returns to Maryland and starts high school.
- *Noir: A Collection of Crime Comics* (2009). This black-and-white anthology of crime comics published by Dark Horse Books contains Lapham's short story "Open the Goddamn Box," which provides some resolution for the cliff-hanger in issue 40.

Characters

- *Virginia Applejack*, a.k.a. *Amy Racecar*, is the imaginative and daring young runaway who the series has followed from age seven to sixteen. She has a soft spot for nebbish kids and reacts violently against threats of bullying and molestation. She carries a knife and wants to be a writer.
- *Joey* goes on a killing spree in the first issue. The series shows his traumatic childhood as an unwanted hanger-on in the Baltimore underworld of the 1970's and the 1980's.
- *Harry* is an unseen crime boss who employs Scott, Monster, Blue Ed, Desmond "The Finger" Dees, and others as enforcers. The actions of many of the series' small-time criminals are driven by their fear of Joey.
- *Spanish Scott* is a trusted enforcer for Harry and Joey's uncle. A knife or a cigarette lighter is his weapon of choice, and he has a fearsome reputation.
- *Celia Applejack* is the long-suffering, emotionally disturbed mother of Virginia. She resents Virginia's close relationship with her father. She enjoys life after her husband dies and Virginia runs away.
- *Leon Murray* is an African American classmate of Virginia throughout elementary and high school. His race and timidity make him an outcast, but he assists in Virginia's war against jocks. He and Virginia share a mutual attraction.
- *Kevin Leeds* is a bullying football player who manifests his attractions for girls in elaborate and violent schemes of blackmail and rape that he fails to carry through.
- *Rose* is a nymphomaniac who is in love with Orson and introduces him to parties and drugs. She is also Joey's neglectful mother, and she sometimes assists in the schemes of Harry, her brother Scott, and Monster.
- *Monster* is the fearsome, relentless, anti-Semitic misogynistic enforcer for Harry. He is jealously in love with Beth and opts not to kill her on at least two occasions.
- *Nina* is Harry's closely watched girlfriend and Beth's best friend. Scott discovers her cheating on Harry; she claims it was rape, and Scott kills the boy in front of her. Guilt drives her into cocaine addiction.
- *Beth Kozlonowski* is Orson's girlfriend who feels protective of both Nina and Virginia (whom she knows as Amy). She is vivacious, outspoken, business savvy, and often disgusted by Orson's caution.
- *Orson* is an acquiescent high school senior with an engineering scholarship to Duke before he sees Scott murder someone and Rose and Beth draw him into drinking and drug use, unleashing his wild side.
- *Nick Giardelli* is a foolish and courageous Seaside resident who is unlucky in love and business until Orson and Nina put him up as their candidate for Seaside sheriff.
- *Ian* has a siblinglike relationship with the film star Holly, and they meet Beth "Out West," where Beth tries to set him up with Nina. Later in Los Angeles, Beth enlists Ian's help to find Virginia.
- *Janet McGraw* is Benny's wife, whose affair with the nebbish Hank awakens her adulterous and sadomasochistic proclivities. She is close friends with Roger and Kathy Boggs.
- *Bobby McGraw* is Janet's son, and he draws comic books. He becomes friends with Virginia/Amy and draws Amy Racecar comics for her. Virginia inadvertently leads him into Ron's clutches.
- *Amelia* is a waitress-cum-stripper who resents men's wandering eyes and responds by

- specializing in seducing men who are already in a relationship. She dates Beth's former boyfriend, Ricky Fish, and becomes embroiled with Monster.
- *Detective Roger Boggs* is a police officer who falls in love with Ricky Fish's wife Kathy and eventually marries her. After being shot, he becomes embroiled in the search for Virginia and Bobby.
- *Ron*, a.k.a. *Ronacles*, abducts Virginia/Amy and Bobby and forces them to participate in mock incestuous, misogynistic games in which he rapes Bobby and tortures Virginia/Amy.
- *Mike Hussey* is a homosexual football player who represses his desires by raping and killing men and women. He transfers to Virginia's high school and becomes Kevin's partner against her.

Artistic Style

Lapham uses a panel layout of four rows with two panels per row. Frequently at the beginning and end of issues and at important story points, Lapham varies this structure. For example, issue 2 opens with three rows, each with a single elongated panel. This format allows Lapham to highlight the movie marquee for *Star Wars* (1977) and introduce the characters of Spanish Scott and Manny, while Lapham's drawing of a streetlight serves to bisect the bottom two panels. Twice later in the issue, Lapham combines four of a page's usual eight panels into a single large panel to showcase an important scene, such as the introduction of Virginia's parents or the aftermath of Virginia stabbing Kevin with a pencil. Lapham ends issue 2 with a rare splash page, showing Virginia's unconscious body after she is assaulted on Halloween. Despite *Stray Bullets*'s reputation for the use of gratuitous, twisted ultraviolence, Lapham's layouts often emphasize the brutal aftereffects and chaotic results of violence rather than the acts of violence themselves.

Lapham's black-and-white art has clean lines and a cinematic quality enhanced by the framed panels. He specializes in drawing distinctive and slightly cartoony human forms that mostly adhere to a conventional realism. Exceptions to this realism come from the occasional use of swirled lines and hearts to suggest falling in love, drunkenness, and other extreme emotional states. This general realism is abandoned during Amy Racecar fantasy sequences, which use a science-fiction cartooning style. Lapham's situations and artwork often reference his cinematic predecessors. A prominent example of this allusiveness occurs in issue 39 as Lapham's art recalls visuals from Kurosawa films such as *Seven Samurai* (1954), *Throne of Blood* (1957), and *Yojimbo* (1961).

Themes

Lapham's predominant theme in *Stray Bullets* is the struggle between stupid and confused men and savvy and sexually assertive females. Lapham's male characters tend to be updated versions of the male dupe in classic films noirs. Their fear and bewilderment can range from simple cowardice to outright mental illness, and most of them struggle to understand the women in their lives. Lapham's male characters are not created equal, and some of them, such as Orson and Leon, manage to overcome their fears and act heroically, if not effectively. Others (such as Joey, Kevin, Monster, Ron, and Hussey) perpetuate violence, often with misogynistic overtones.

Despite being violent and outrageous, Virginia's fantasy life as Amy Racecar appears to be a coping mechanism for the traumas of her past. The fantasies of Joey, Monster, Janet's husband Benny McGraw, and Ron are just as unreal but often result in real-world violence, such as Joey's shooting spree in issue 1 and Ron's rape of Bobby and torture of Virginia in issue 29.

Impact

Stray Bullets is the longest-running self-published crime comic. Along with its contemporary *Sin City* (1991-2000), *Stray Bullets* helped pave the way for the renaissance in creator-owned crime comics with titles such as *100 Bullets* (1999-2009), *Criminal* (2006-   ), and *Scalped* (2007-   ). Both *Sin City* and *Stray Bullets* are similar in their alternating focus on multiple characters in a shared universe; however, their differences are striking. *Sin City* has gained more notoriety because of creator Frank Miller's superstar status and the film adaptation. *Stray Bullets* has attracted a cult following but is completely out of print. *Sin City*'s protagonists are essentially superheroic knights in trench coats, while *Stray Bullets* and its successors give significant focus to doomed lower-class criminals in a less fantastic world. Women in *Sin City* may be strong characters, but they also tend to be hyperviolent fantasies of scantily clad prostitutes that are side characters. *Stray Bullets* spoofs that fantasy to some degree with the character of Amy Racecar; however, it has two main female protagonists who are tough yet vulnerable and human, Virginia and Beth.

Bob Hodges

Further Reading

Azzarello, Brian, and Eduardo Risso. *100 Bullets* (2000-2011).

Brubaker, Ed, and Sean Phillips. *Criminal* (2007-   ).

Cooke, Darwyn. *Richard Stark's Parker* (2009-   ).

Bibliography

Benton, Mike. *Crime Comics: The Illustrated History*. Dallas, Tex.: Taylor, 1993.

Horsley, Lee. *The Noir Thriller*. New York: Palgrave Macmillan, 2009.

Lindenmuth, Brian. "The Fall (and Rise) of the Crime Comic." *Mulholland Books*, December 14, 2010. http://www.mulhollandbooks.com/2010/12/14/a-history-of-and-appreciation-for-crime-comics.

Moore, Stuart. "Graphic Violence: A Talented New Generation of Writers Brings Crime to the Comics." *Mystery Scene* 77 (2002): 32-35.

See also: *Parker*; *Sin City*; *A History of Violence*

STRAY TOASTERS

Author: Sienkiewicz, Bill
Artist: Bill Sienkiewicz (illustrator); James Novak (letterer)
Publisher: Marvel Comics
First serial publication: 1988
First book publication: 1991

Publication History

Bill Sienkiewicz's *Stray Toasters* originally appeared in 1988 as a four-issue miniseries published monthly by Epic Comics, an imprint of Marvel Comics. Installments were numbered models 1 through 4, punning on the title of the series as well as the satirical advertisements for toasters manufactured by the fictional Bolle-Happel Appliances company that appeared on the back of each issue.

This title, like most in the Epic Comics catalog, treats a story line and characters independent from the Marvel Universe. Sienkiewicz's longtime affiliation with the parent publisher and his distinctive visual style offer the only recognizable continuity between the content of *Stray Toasters* and his previous work for Marvel, most notably his penciling work for the *New Mutants* (1984-1985). Though readers and collectors had for years recognized Sienkiewicz's status as an illustrator, *Stray Toasters* represented his first published venture as sole artist and author.

In 1991, Marvel published all four issues of *Stray Toasters* in one volume, entitled *Stray Toasters: Designer Edition*, which included concept sketches for the series from Sienkiewicz's notebooks. Graphitti Designs, a company that specializes in licensing pop-culture and comics-related merchandise, released a one-volume edition of *Stray Toasters* in 2003. Image Comics republished the collection in 2007, again as a single volume.

Plot

Founded in 1982, creator-owned Epic Comics provided Marvel Comics with an outlet to market and publish content targeted to mature audiences while allowing creators to retain creative control and ownership of

---

Bill Sienkiewicz

Few superhero artists in the 1980's had a more expressionistic and individualized graphic style than Bill Sienkiewicz. Hired by Marvel when he was only nineteen, Sienkiewicz debuted on *Moon Knight* before making a name for himself on the X-Men spin-off title, *The New Mutants*. His 1988 miniseries, *Stray Toasters*, for Marvel's Epic imprint signaled a move away from the mainstream of superhero imagery, while his 1986-1987 collaboration with writer Frank Miller, *Elektra: Assassin*, is one of the most stylistically unusual superhero comic series ever published by Marvel. In 1990 he produced two issues of the miniseries *Big Numbers* with Alan Moore before abandoning that labor-intensive project. More than almost any other single artist, Sienkiewicz revolutionized the aesthetics of superhero comics in the 1980's, breaking from the legacies of the 1960's and 1970's that privileged a house style, and pursuing his own form of self-expression.

---

their work. Sienkiewicz's highly stylized renderings of an ensemble of flawed characters connected by a series of bizarre murders make *Stray Toasters* ideally suited for readers who value darker themes, psychologically complex characters, and nontraditional comics art.

The story takes place in a violent and depressed version of New York City, an indeterminate future in which cars fly, dogs are extinct, cats proliferate, homelessness has escalated, and the mortality rate among newborn girls is 80 percent. Sienkiewicz projects several plots onto this dystopian backdrop, all of which are more or less resolved by the story's conclusion.

As Phil the demon arrives in New York for an extended holiday, Egon Rustemagik investigates the brutal slaying of Deborah Dissler, whose body has been mutilated with power tools and wired like an electrical appliance. Rustemagik discovers that Dissler was a patient of his former lover, the psychiatrist Abby Nolan.

Bill Sienkiewicz. (Public domain, via wikicommons)

He seeks her out for information about the victim, whose death may be connected to the recent mutilation and murder of eleven boys. Abby refuses to discuss her patient with Rustemagik, citing client confidentiality, though she does allude to Dissler's son, Todd.

While reviewing forensic evidence of the murders, Rustemagik learns that the child victims have been drained of blood and viscera. Phil, in the form of an old woman, beats up Rustemagik for accidentally killing one of the cats that Phil intended to deliver to his sons as a vacation souvenir. Dr. Montana Violet reveals that he feeds on the liquefied remains of the murdered boys; these are supplied to him by Dahlia, who is killing them in a symbolic attempt to eradicate her own apparently deceased son.

Rustemagik links Dahlia to the child murders. Fearful of being implicated, Violet abducts Rustemagik and attempts to destroy his mind with hallucinogens. Meanwhile, Harvard Chalky devises a scheme to claim Abby's affections by killing Rustemagik but shoots Phil instead. Phil identifies Chalky as the perfect souvenir lawyer to take back to Hell. Big Daddy attempts to murder Abby, who has uncovered the bizarre relationship between Todd and the construct.

Finally aware of Violet's manipulations, Dahlia resolves to murder him. Rustemagik, however, having emerged from his drug-induced incapacitation, destroys Violet's putrescent body with a pipe but spares his cybernetic head. Rustemagik attempts to apprehend Dahlia, but he is too late; Dahlia confronts Violet, and when he reveals that her son, Todd, not only is still alive but also has been technologically enhanced, she kills him. The mortal characters engage in a standoff at Abby's house, in which Rustemagik destroys Big Daddy, Abby stabs Dahlia to save Todd, and Chalky shoots Rustemagik in the head without killing him. *Stray Toasters* closes with Big Daddy disassembled, Abby adopting Todd, and Rustemagik and Chalky institutionalized. Empty-handed, Phil returns to Hell.

Characters

- *Egon Rustemagik* is the main protagonist, a physically imposing figure with a white walrus moustache and an austere haircut. He is a criminal psychologist, author, and alcoholic who has recently been discharged from Bosley Mental Institution. Dahlia is his lover.
- *Abigail Nolan*, a.k.a. *Abby*, is Rustemagik's former lover and the mother of their deceased child. Her allegations of abuse against Rustemagik formed the basis of the case that sent him to Bosley. She works as a psychiatrist.
- *Dahlia* is a wealthy, religious widow. Aside from her relations with Rustemagik, she primarily interacts with robot servants that wear formal attire and masks resembling human faces. She is a patient of Dr. Montana Violet.
- *Dr. Montana Violet* has blue skin as the result of self-induced cyanosis. He is immobilized by obesity and assisted by a flock of cybernetic crows. A freakish amalgam of flesh, appliances, and wires, he appears on television to dispense medical expertise.
- *Todd* is a boy of indeterminate age. He is tow-headed and wears overalls, and his only words are "toast and jam." Abby discovers him sitting on her doorstep after the murder of his mother.
- *Harvard Chalky*, an assistant district attorney, craves boundaries and values rules. A small, weedy man with large eyeglasses, he is a client of Abby Nolan.

- *Phil* is a demon. He shares his experiences in the mortal realm on postcards addressed to Hell. He is happily married with two sons and has healthy, functional relationships with his family and friends. He is red, horned, and enormous in stature, with hooves and a pointed tail.
- *Big Daddy* is a foul-mouthed, misogynistic construct that murders women. His head is a toaster and he wears a pin-striped suit. He shares a strong bond with Todd.

Artistic Style

Stray Toasters showcases the synthesis of fine-art techniques, multimedia, and traditional comics illustration that has since become Sienkiewicz's hallmark. His formal artistic training is evident throughout, as is his appreciation for and mastery of anatomical painting. The illustrations in *Stray Toasters* are painted, enabling Sienkiewicz to utilize techniques uncommon in comics, apart from in cover art, as well as imitate some of his artistic influences. For example, his paintings of Dahlia often incorporate colors and imagery that call to mind Egon Schiele's portraits of women, while Violet's entries in his medical journal feature illustrations that evoke Pablo Picasso's explorations of primitivism. Utilizing the distinctive palettes and imagery of other artists in reference to certain characters conveys both thematic consistency and visual variety.

Sienkiewicz's use of multimedia in *Stray Toasters* embellishes the freedom from line and composition demonstrated by artists such as Ralph Steadman. In addition to the dribbles and splatters characteristic of Steadman's work, Sienkiewicz's artwork also incorporates hardware, textiles, ink-pad stamps, mimeographed images, and organic materials, all of which serve to introduce depth and texture to traditional comics design.

Despite these many innovations, *Stray Toasters* still offers readers a sequential narrative. Even though Sienkiewicz plays with conventional comics panels by varying their size and shape, interspersing full-page illustrations among them, and utilizing collage, the work remains recognizable as a comic book, especially in terms of its depiction of dialogue and narrative.

Sienkiewicz uses the usual bubbles to indicate characters in conversation, although most of the narration in *Stray Toasters* occurs in characters' heads. He represents each character's thoughts in colored boxes that correspond to each individual consciousness; Abby's thoughts, for example, are pink, and Dahlia's are violet. While lettering is consistent among most characters, notable exceptions include Sienkiewicz's childlike printing of Todd's impressions and Big Daddy's evil ideas, which are presented in Courier typeface. These variations in internal speech underscore the deceptions and misunderstandings among characters while helping readers to navigate through these characters' minds.

Themes

The narrative of *Stray Toasters* is bookended by Phil's departure from and return to Hell, reinforcing the idea that the earthly mortal realm is even more hellish than his nightmarish supernatural home. His words "The family circle is a triangle" are the first and last in the series, and they emphasize the notion that family, and relationships in general, are central themes, if ironic ones. In contrast to Phil, none of the mortal characters exhibit the ability to have healthy or at least conventional relationships. Rustemagik, for example, tells Dahlia that "Domesticity makes me puke," while Chalky's relationships are strictly transactional.

By making each character loosely represent a social institution that traditionally supports human well-being—Violet corresponds to science and medicine, for example—Sienkiewicz suggests that these institutions are, at their worst, insidiously controlling, with individuals being complicit in their institutionalization. Todd's perverse enslavement to Big Daddy exemplifies this complicity, while Rustemagik ultimately demonstrates the self-knowledge required to escape the control of these institutional powers when he overcomes Violet's drug-induced manipulations.

Sienkiewicz complicates this theme, however, by further implying that the self can also be an institution that exerts a passive control over an individual. Again, it is Rustemagik who most obviously suggests this, with his persistent utterance of the name Mona;

although to what or whom this name refers remains a mystery in *Stray Toasters*, it is evident that the word represents whatever traumas Rustemagik continues to repress. Phil contends that Rustemagik's brain injury, which has erased his memories, has given him a second chance to be a child and live his life over again—in other words, he has come full circle to a state of innocence. The other mortal characters who exhibit unhealthy attachments to their pasts either die or are institutionalized by the end of the book. Abby and Todd are the notable exceptions to both Rustemagik's ironic restoration to innocence and the others' damnation.

Impact

Since its publication, *Stray Toasters* has been read and commented on as definitive of Sienkiewicz's strengths as an artist. It demonstrates an elaboration of the experiments with design and layout that he introduced in *Elektra: Assassin* (1986-1987), notably in his use of multimedia. His uses of and tributes to other artists' work, especially that of James McNeill Whistler, Schiele, Picasso, and LeRoy Neiman, have not been as widely addressed but remain significant, as Sienkiewicz blurred the distinctions between popular and fine art and arguably expanded the comics lexicon by incorporating both nontraditional illustration techniques and visual allusions into this work.

Stray Toasters references other cultural works as well, namely literary and cinematic works such Dante's *La divina commedia* (c. 1320; *The Divine Comedy*, 1802), the Bible, Ridley Scott's *Blade Runner* (1982), Alfred Hitchcock's *The Birds* (1963), and Orson Welles's *Citizen Kane* (1941). In addition, Sienkiewicz's satirical rendering of the "News with Punch" segment calls to mind Frank Miller's scathing treatment of cable news cycles and personalities in *Batman: The Dark Knight Returns* (1986). These references to other works accomplish at least two aims: First, they reinforce the idea that the distinction between high and low culture is arbitrary; and second, they promote a more inclusive concept of cultural literacy that deems popular films, classic films, and canonical literary works to be equally deserving of critical attention.

Admittedly, Sienkiewicz's kinetic juxtaposition of imagery and references has been distracting for some critics. Other readers have contended that the narrative in *Stray Toasters* cannot hold its own with the design, layout, and execution of Sienkiewicz's illustrations. Still, this work's imaginative allure persists, as its multiple republications suggest.

Greg Matthews

Further Reading

Díaz Canales, Juan, and Juanjo Guarnido. *Blacksad* (2010).

Gaiman, Neil, and Dave McKean. *Signal to Noise* (2008).

Mignola, Mike. *The Amazing Screw-On Head and Other Curious Objects* (2010).

Miller, Frank, and Bill Sienkiewicz. *Elektra: Assassin* (2000).

Bibliography

Berthold, Michael C. "Color Me Ishmael: Classics Illustrated Versions of *Moby-Dick*." *Word and Image* 9, no. 1 (January-March, 1993): 1-8.

Johnston, W. Robert. "Splash Panel Adventures!" *Smithsonian Studies in American Art* 3, no. 3 (Summer, 1989): 38-53.

Robinson, Tasha. "Bill Sienkiewicz: *Stray Toasters*." Review of *Stray Toasters*, by Bill Sienkiewicz. *A.V. Club*, October 14, 2003. http://www.avclub.com/articles/bill-sienkiewicz-stray-toasters,5404.

Szadkowski, Joseph. "For Illustrator, Brush Is Mightier Than Word." *Washington Times*, September 29, 2007.

_____. "Master of Sequential Art Influences Generations." *Washington Times*, September 22, 2007.

See also: *Signal to Noise*

STREAK OF CHALK

Author: Prado, Miguelanxo
Artist: Miguelanxo Prado (illustrator)
Publisher: Norma Editorial (Spanish); NBM (English)
First serial publication: *Trazo de tiza*, 1992-1993
First book publication: 1993 (English translation, 1994)

Publication History

The English translation of Miguelanxo Prado's *Trazo de tiza* (*Streak of Chalk*), translated by Jacinthe Leclerc, was published by NBM under its imprint ComicsLit in 1994. A second edition was published in 2003. NBM was one of the first companies to introduce European graphic novels in the United States. Although it publishes works of general interest, it is still considered an alternative publishing house, since the firm does not publish superhero comics.

The original Spanish edition, *Trazo de tiza*, was published by Norma Editorial in 1993. Founded in 1977 by Rafael Martinez, Norma Editorial is an independent publishing house in Barcelona, Spain. The company began as an agency representing writers and graphic artists and has become one of the most important European publishing houses of graphic novels, comics, and manga. In addition to being published in English, *Trazo de tiza* has appeared in German, French, Finnish, and Catalan translations. *Trazo de tiza* first appeared from 1992 to 1993 as a serialized story in *Cimoc*, a Spanish magazine that published adult comics and was edited by Martinez.

Plot

Written for a mature-adult audience, *Streak of Chalk* is a graphic novel of fantasy and inquiry into the human condition. Prado uses an unreliable narrator who shifts from being omniscient to being Raul, Sara, Ana, and back to being omniscient; thus, readers are unable to determine reality from fantasy and past from present. The characters are ordinary people caught in a world between reality and fantasy and are unable to control their lives.

Miguelanxo Prado. (By Alberto Ramos, via Wikimedia Commons)

The plot centers on a love affair between Raul and Ana that is thwarted by their inability to interact with each other and express their emotions. While sailing alone, Raul drifts off course during a storm and lands on a mysterious, uncharted island with a long, white pier that looks like a streak of chalk in the ocean. On the small island, there is an abandoned lighthouse and an inn and general store run by a middle-aged woman named Sara. She and her son, Dimas, a sinister young man who kills seagulls with arrows, are the only inhabitants of the island. When Raul arrives, Dimas helps him tie up his boat, then immediately disappears. Raul discovers graffiti written on the wall of the pier, much of which appears to be messages left by lovers.

Raul goes to the inn, where he encounters Sara standing behind the counter, apparently waiting for customers, but, as he soon discovers, there is only one person besides Sara and her son on the island. Ana, who was there the previous year, has returned and is waiting for someone. The inn and its proprietor appear to be there waiting in a sort of purposeless, almost useless way. The next day, Raul sees Ana from the window of his room and goes in search of her, but she has disappeared. Raul discovers a dead seagull lying in a pool of blood, an arrow piercing its neck. He is appalled by such savagery. Meanwhile Ana has come to the inn to eat. She and Sara have a conversation about Raul.

Upon returning to the inn, Raul attempts to befriend Ana, but she rejects him and leaves. Sara observes them. In a brief conversation with Raul, she gives contradictory details of how they get their supplies and of who comes to the island. A seagull enters the building; Raul befriends the bird and names him Lucas. Raul goes for a walk and runs into Ana, who is writing. They talk briefly about the strangeness of the island and about literature. She then leaves abruptly.

The next day, Raul looks for Ana at the inn. Sara advises him to forget about Ana; Raul rejects Sara's advice, goes in search of Ana, and discovers another dead seagull. Ana and Raul meet, spend time together, and discuss the strange musical pipes on the pier (which Sara calls flutes) and the strangeness of the island. Sara worries that another boat will arrive and bring misfortune, for she insists that three boats are an ill omen.

By the next morning, another boat has arrived, and Sara's prediction proves correct. Tato and Berto, the new arrivals, beat up Raul; attempt to rape Ana, who forces them away with a gun; and then succeed in raping Sara. Ana and Raul meet again the next morning, and she rejects him. Dejected, Raul goes to the inn and gets drunk. Taking advantage of Raul's disappointment and drunkenness, Sara seduces him. She also tells him about the rape and says Dimas killed Tato and Berto. Hoping to make amends to Raul for her rudeness, Ana goes to his boat and finds him with Sara. Too ashamed to face Ana, Raul leaves the island. Raul left Ana a note, which Sara fails to give her, and Ana leaves.

Raul decides to return to the island to see Ana. When he arrives, her boat is gone. Sara does not recognize him and knows nothing about Ana. Raul sees two couples walking on the island; the men resemble Tato and Berto. At this point, Raul can no longer distinguish what actually happened from what he imagined. He blames the island for his confusion. However, before he leaves, Raul writes a message to Ana on the pier wall, which appears to be the same message that was there when he arrived. The graphic novel ends with Sara gazing out the window at the sea; a wine bottle and glass are on the table.

Characters
- *Raul*, the protagonist, is a thin, dark-haired, young man who lacks self-confidence and is retiring. He is a sensitive individual appalled by violence, especially Dimas's savagery. Raul is romantically attracted to Ana and attempts to become involved with her, but he always says or does something that drives her away.
- *Sara* is the middle-aged proprietor of the island's one building, which serves as an inn, a bar, a hotel, and a general store. She has red hair, somewhat coarse features, and a stocky build. She may be in love with Raul and definitely is sexually attracted to him, succeeding in seducing him when he is rejected by Ana. She may have been raped by Tato and Berto.
- *Ana* is Raul's love interest. Young, slender, and blond, she provides a sharp physical contrast to Sara. She is also better read, more intellectual and sophisticated, and more competent at self-defense than Sara is. However, she is incapable of expressing her feelings for Raul and is afraid to interact with other people. She is writing a novel and waiting for someone. She prefers to be alone. During most of the story, she rejects Raul's attempts to interact with her.
- *Dimas*, Sara's son, is physically reminiscent of a Neanderthal. He is protective of his mother. He likes to hunt and kills seagulls at night. He is perpetually watching and waiting. He imbues the novel with a sinister atmosphere of danger and foreboding.
- *Lucas* is a seagull that becomes Raul's companion.
- *Tato* acts as one of the two antagonists. Both psychologically and physically, he provides a sharp contrast to Raul: He is muscular, self-confident,

overbearing and sexually aggressive, loud, and violent.
- *Berto* serves as Raul's other antagonist. Like Tato, he contrasts sharply with Raul both physically and psychologically.

Artistic Style

Prado masterfully combines written text and visual narration in *Streak of Chalk*. Quotations from novels and references to other literary works link *Streak of Chalk* to various traditions and novel theories. However, the visual narration contains all of the information necessary to the story. Prado's use of single panels as introductions to each chapter creates a synopsis of the narrative within the novel. The use of variously sized panels without any precise order reflects the chaos and confusion of the characters. Prado does not use bubbles linking dialogue to specific characters. Dialogue appears in the panels in such a way that it is sometimes difficult to decide which character is speaking. Prado's use of black pages, either empty or containing only words, at the beginning of each chapter gives a sense of entering into a world of illusion through either dreams or the imagination.

Color plays a major role in the visual narration of *Streak of Chalk*. Prado uses color to shift the mood of his story, to foreshadow events, and to depict the psychology of his characters. Sara and Dimas are always portrayed in dark browns and reds, while light blues and pinks are used to portray Ana. The more primitive and physically oriented Sara and Dimas are linked to the earth and to basic instincts of survival, while the intellectual, sophisticated Ana is presented in colors that reflect sentiment, illusion, and quest. The sea and sky change from light blues, white, and pinks, to deep blues, violets, and dark purples, and the interiors become dark reddish brown as danger, failure, and disappointment take over the characters' lives.

Prado uses facial characteristics and expressions to depict the personalities and emotional states of his characters. Sara, Dimas, Tato, and Berto have broad, heavy, short faces, while Ana and Raul have long, pointed faces. Dimas's face changes little, always reflecting cruelty and a lack of intellect. He is a static representation of the primitive aspects of the human being.

Sara's, Ana's, and Raul's faces contort in expressions of fear, anger, and disappointment. Prado also establishes a rapport between the reader and Raul by facing him away from the action of the panels and looking out, as though he is asking advice from the reader.

Themes

Streak of Chalk is a graphic novel that can be read as a mystery, a fantasy, an inquiry into the human condition, and a study of the creative act of writing a novel. The surface theme of the work is the unsuccessful love affair between Raul and Ana. At this level, it is the story of a man and a woman who meet on a mysterious island. Sara, Berto, and Tato function as disruptive elements in their relationship. However, Prado is more interested in examining the difficulties that human beings encounter in attempting to interact with each other and in expressing their emotions than in simply recounting a story of events. Ana and Raul inevitably

---

Miguelanxo Prado

Born in Spain, Miguelanxo Prado was an architect and a novelist before entering the comics industry in the late 1980's. He published his earliest works with the French press Les Humanoïdes Associés. He is best known for his award-winning 1992 graphic novel *Streak of Chalk*, a story of a man on an island who is unable to distinguish fantasy from reality or the past from the present. Prado was one of the most influential figures in the direct-color movement that characterized European comics at this time. Rather than producing images in pen and ink that were subsequently colored in a separate process, his pastel drawings were fully produced on the page and reproduced in book form. His serene images are notable for their classical compositions. He followed this work with an adaptation of *Peter and the Wolf* and three volumes of his series *Chroniques absurdes*, before significantly reducing his output in the comics field. In 2007 he released an animated feature film titled *De Profundis*.

say the wrong things to each other; they both appear to be searching for something. Both Ana and Raul are closed off to meaningful communication.

By bookending the story with the same message written on the pier Prado complicates the readers' ability to understand the meaning and to differentiate reality from illusion and past from present. The story is full of factual inconsistency and raises numerous questions. Does this mysterious island actually exist? Do Sara, Dimas, Ana, Lucas, Tato, and Berto exist, or has Raul imagined all of them? Has the entire story been an illusion experienced by the weary Raul after the storm? Are Sara and Dimas actually a part of reality, and the story of Ana and Raul and the others part of the daydreams and fantasies of a lonely woman on a rarely visited island?

Both the creation of a novel and reader participation in the novel are important themes of the story. Prado prefaces the book with quotations from S. S. Van Dine's *The Kidnap Murder Case* (1936) and Jorge Luis Borges's "Tlön Uqbar, Orbis Tertius," signaling the multiple layers of meaning in *Streak of Chalk* and inviting readers to interpret meaning freely. At the end of chapter 6, Prado includes the advice of Ana's editor about rewriting after having read her manuscript. He concludes his graphic novel with a note from the author about his purpose and method of writing.

Impact

For Prado, the graphic novel, with its combination of written text and visual narration, offers the most complete means of artistic expression possible. The work of Moebius, Hugo Pratt, and the team of José Muñoz and Carlos Sampayo first attracted the young architecture student to a career in comics. In the 1980's, he began writing short comics and publishing them in magazines. Prado sees the graphic novel as a creative medium that combines literature and the visual arts. His graphic novels are influenced by the work of several literary authors including Borges, Adolfo Bioy Casares, and Virginia Woolf. Prado's drawing and painting reveal the influence of a wide variety of artists, ranging from Dutch realist Johannes Vermeer to French post-Impressionist Henri de Toulouse-Lautrec. *Streak of Chalk* has played an important role in elevating the graphic novel to serious literature. The work is an exercise in artistic creation and a study of the human condition as well as a good story.

Streak of Chalk, Prado's first book-length comic work, was well received both in Spain and throughout the world and earned him global exposure and recognition; in 1994, the French translation of the novel, *Trait de craie*, won the Alph-Art Best Foreign Comic Book Award at the Angoulême International Comics Festival. Prado has subsequently become a major international graphic novel artist and worked in related media as well. He has worked on such successful animation projects as *Men in Black: The Series* and produced his own animated film *De Profundis* (2007). He has also worked with Laura Esquivel on the novel *The Law of Love* (1996) and with Neil Gaiman on *The Sandman: Endless Nights* (2003).

Shawncey Jay Webb

Further Reading

Esquivel, Laura. *The Law of Love* (1996).
Prado, Miguelanxo. *Daily Delirium* (2003).
_____. *Tangents* (1995).

Bibliography

Eisner, Will. *Graphic Storytelling and Visual Narrative*. New York: W. W. Norton, 2008.
Groensteen, Thierry. *The System of Comics*. Translated by Bart Beaty and Nick Nyugen. Jackson: University of Mississippi Press, 2007.
McCloud, Scott. *Making Comics: Storytelling Secrets of Comics, Manga, and Graphic Novels*. New York: Harper, 2006.
_____. *Understanding Comics: The Invisible Art*. New York: HarperPerennial, 2010.

See also: *City of Glass*; *Far Arden*; *Asterios Polyp*

STUCK RUBBER BABY

Author: Cruse, Howard
Artist: Howard Cruse (illustrator)
Publisher: DC Comics
First book publication: 1995

Publication History

Howard Cruse appeared on the national underground comics scene during the 1970's, most notably with his series *Barefootz*. In 1979, he began editing *Gay Comix*, an anthology of works by openly gay and lesbian comics creators. Throughout the 1980's, *The Advocate* ran his series *Wendel*, a comic that addressed a range of issues, including gay rights, HIV/AIDS, and same-sex relationships, through the perspective of the affable title character and his circle of friends. When he began working on *Stuck Rubber Baby* in 1990, Cruse intended to publish the graphic novel with editor Mark Nevelow of Piranha Press, an imprint of DC Comics active from 1989 to 1994 that featured an eclectic line of alternative comics. Cruse anticipated the book would take two years to complete, but the complexity of the project led him to work nearly twice as long.

Because Piranha Press was defunct by the time of the book's completion, in 1995, Cruse published *Stuck Rubber Baby* with Paradox Press, another short-lived DC Comics imprint created to publish graphic novels outside the superhero purview of the parent publisher or titles with science-fiction and fantasy elements handled by the Vertigo imprint. Hardback and paperback editions with an introduction by acclaimed playwright Tony Kushner were released under the Paradox imprint in the late 1990's. In 2010, a fifteenth-anniversary hardback edition of the book was published by Vertigo with a new introduction by Alison Bechdel.

Plot

In *Stuck Rubber Baby*, Toland Polk, a young white man in the fictional town of Clayfield, Alabama, struggles to come to terms with his sexual orientation against the backdrop of the African American civil rights movement. From the vantage point of the early 1990's, Toland (with some gentle needling from his unnamed partner) narrates his coming of age during the 1960's—the period he referred to sardonically as "Kennedy-time."

After his parents are killed in a car accident, Toland works as a gas-station attendant while living in his childhood home with his sister, Melanie, and her husband, Orley. He is openly humiliated when he indicates that he is a homosexual during his U.S. Army draft physical and resolves to stop being gay. In an effort to avoid conflict with the congenial but deeply prejudiced Orley, Toland accepts his friend Riley's invitation to move into "The Wheelery," the house he shares with his girlfriend, Mavis.

Mavis introduces Toland to her friend Sammy Noone, an openly gay man returning to work as a church organist in Clayfield after serving in the U.S.

> **Howard Cruse**
>
> A mainstay of the American underground comics movement, Howard Cruse played a key role in bringing gay and lesbian issues into the comics world as the founding editor of *Gay Comix*. During the 1970's, Cruse had published his *Barefootz* work, a cute-style series featuring a character with enormous bare feet in a variety of underground titles. With the launch of *Gay Comix* in 1979, he began addressing the topic of gay rights in his work, notably in *Wendel*, a strip that ran in *The Advocate* and featured the titular lead, an idealistic gay man. In the early 1990's he worked to produce his most ambitious graphic novel, *Stuck Rubber Baby*, the story of a young man growing up in the American South in the 1960's. The work combines the history of the civil rights movement and a story of one young man's growing awareness of his homosexuality. Cruse's art features characters drawn in a naturalistic yet cartoony style. His panels are almost always filled with detail and he employs a painstaking approach to stippling and cross-hatching in order to create depth.

Navy. Sammy invites the residents of the Wheelery to a party, where Toland meets a host of Clayfield's civil rights activists, members of the local gay community, and burgeoning folk singer Ginger Raines. Toland pursues a friendship with Ginger that quickly turns romantic.

Shortly after Riley returns from his stint in the Army, Sammy takes his friends on a tour of Clayfield's nightspots, including the Rhombus (a gay bar) and the Alleysax, a jazz club that welcomes an interracial audience. Soon after, Ginger and Toland attempt to consummate their relationship, but when the condom that Toland has carried in his wallet for years fails, he panics and "comes out" as gay to Ginger. Though Toland is certain that he can be in love with Ginger, she refuses to be his "lifeline" to the straight world.

Following the lead of his friends, Toland becomes more aware of and involved in the civil rights movement, even attending the historic 1963 March on Washington. When the Melody Motel, a rallying point for Clayfield's integrationist community, is bombed, killing several young members of the local Freedom Chorus, Sammy confronts the news media, unleashing an angry torrent against the violent actions and ideas that led to the deaths of innocents. In a moment of frustration and denial, Ginger and Toland have unprotected sex that results in the conception of a child.

Soon after his public tirade, Sammy becomes the target of Ku Klux Klan intimidation and loses his job at the church. Ginger reveals that she is pregnant and, although she does not want to abort the pregnancy, she also does not want to marry Toland or keep the child because she fears such decisions would end her dream of becoming a professional singer. Toland seeks advice and solace with local civil rights leader Reverend Harland Pepper and his wife, Anna Dellyne Pepper, a former jazz singer who gave up her career to be a wife and mother but who has advised Ginger to pursue her professional ambitions. Anna and Harland's son Les encourages Toland to embrace his sexuality, and despite Toland's initial resistance, the two have sex.

Mavis and Toland accompany Sammy to ask for financial assistance from his estranged father. The Noone family is not at all supportive, and following this rejection, a drunk and depressed Sammy asks Toland

Howard Cruse at Columbia University. (By Alex Lozupone, via Wikimedia Commons)

to have sex with him. When Toland turns him away, Sammy leads them to the home where Clayfield's segregationist tabloid, *The Dixie Patriot*, is published and makes a scene on the property. Toland and Sammy return to the Wheelery, where later that night Toland is knocked unconscious and Sammy is lynched.

In the final chapters, Toland tries to make sense of Sammy's murder. Melanie reveals that though she had wanted to adopt Toland and Ginger's baby, she feels incapable of raising the child alone, as she is divorcing Orley. Years later, during a chance encounter between Toland and Orley in San Francisco, Orley reveals that he feels responsible for Sammy's death because he had provided *The Dixie Patriot* with the damning information about Sammy's sexuality. Toland also recalls his one encounter with his infant daughter when he visits Ginger briefly after she gives birth to the child. Having worked through his story, Toland recalls the words of advice given him by Anna: Though his life has changed dramatically since the Kennedytime, he will never be able to escape his past.

Characters
- *Toland Polk*, the primary protagonist, is the middle-aged, openly gay narrator of the framing story. He is a somewhat aimless man in his early twenties who struggles with his sexual identity in the framed narrative. He is a white southerner living in Clayfield, Alabama, who becomes involved with the civil rights movement after forming a romantic attachment to Ginger Raines.
- *Ginger Raines* is a plucky white college student and aspiring folk singer who is passionately committed to the cause of the civil rights movement. Her complicated friendship and romance with Toland helps him come to terms with his sexuality and clarify his ideas about social justice.
- *Sammy Noone* is an openly gay man whose vocal opposition to the injustices perpetrated against racial and sexual minorities inflames the discourse surrounding civil rights in Clayfield. His romantic advances complicate Toland's understanding of his own sexuality. Eventually, his lynching serves to clarify Toland's moral values and inspires him to accept his own homosexuality.
- *Riley Wheeler* is Toland's friend and a liberal-minded Army veteran who subscribes to Hugh Hefner's "Playboy philosophy," though he is committed to his longtime girlfriend, Mavis. He invites Toland to live with him in his home, "The Wheelery," which is the site of many philosophical debates, Toland's coming out to Ginger, and Sammy's hanging.
- *Melanie Polk* is Toland's sister and is fiercely protective of her younger brother. She wants to adopt Toland's baby, as she is unable to have children of her own, but after ousting her intolerant husband, Orley, she decides it is not in the best interests of her or the child.
- *Orley* is Melanie's congenial but bigoted husband. He provides *The Dixie Patriot* with information that leads to the persecution and murder of Sammy Noone.
- *The Reverend Harland Pepper* is an African American minister and the leader of Clayfield's civil rights movement. He is the spiritual heart of local activism and also provides Toland with moral ballast.
- *Anna Dellyne Pepper* is a former jazz singer and the wife of Reverend Pepper. She advises Ginger to stay true to her professional ambition, which leads Ginger to decide to give up her child for adoption. She also provides Tolland with advice about being true to himself and embracing his past, no matter how painful it may be.
- *Les Pepper* is the gay son of Harland and Anna. He encourages Toland to accept his homosexuality and is Toland's first male sex partner.

Artistic Style

With *Stuck Rubber Baby*, Cruse departs from the more whimsical style of *Barefootz* and *Wendel*. In these earlier works, Cruse established a trademark cartoony style that is clean, dynamic, and often visually hyperbolic with its pliable forms. *Stuck Rubber Baby* is characterized by a more complex neorealistic technique. The lush, richly detailed line work is complemented by scrupulous cross-hatching and shading to render a grittier visual—a perfect accompaniment to the book's narrative. Cruse's distinctive playfulness is not entirely abandoned, as his characters maintain a roundness reminiscent of the sensual and voluptuous figures of American artist Paul Cadmus. The stippling effect that Cruse uses to round his forms also allows for subtle play between light and shadow, another departure from his earlier work and one that provides more complex dimensionality.

Stuck Rubber Baby is presented as Toland Polk's oral memoir, so captions allow the character to narrate events. In another departure from his earlier work, Cruse uses few verbal thought balloons, though Toland's musings and reveries are often represented pictorially. Cruse's meticulous hand-lettering allows for subtle differences in voice among characters, a sensuous representation of the music that underscores the narrative, and the fluid integration of sound effects into the visual iconography of the book. In general, *Stuck Rubber Baby* relies upon conventional panel layouts to advance its narrative. However, at key moments, Cruse disrupts the visual progression by using devices such as jagged, fractured images to represent traumatic experiences or superimposed "photographic artifacts" to substantiate memories. These idiosyncrasies blend seamlessly into the more traditional layout to create a visual representation of memories pocked with disruptive artifacts. Like other Paradox releases, *Stuck Rubber Baby* was published in black and white.

Themes
Stuck Rubber Baby is significant for plumbing the gray areas of discourse and actions surrounding identity politics (particularly race and sexuality) in the mid-twentieth-century American South. One of the book's central concerns is the link among all civil rights crusades and the fundamental human rights that all marginalized minorities seek. Through his complicated and problematic characters, Cruse unsettles clear-cut dichotomies of good and evil, morality and sin, and truth and lies. Cruse also works to render visible the tapestry of complex human stories that underlie large historical narratives.

In his portrayal of Toland Polk's fumbling quest for identity, Cruse demonstrates that the road to self-understanding is often meandering. In addressing the violence of the civil rights era, *Stuck Rubber Baby* acknowledges an ineffable quality of trauma that defies a definitive understanding. Toland is deeply affected by Sammy's lynching, but he is never capable of fully remembering or understanding the events of Sammy's death. Ultimately, *Stuck Rubber Baby* is a document of witnessing—one that encourages an uprooting and evaluation of trauma by narrating past experience. Cruse asks the reader to consider to what degree the past should be abandoned when it is marked by pain and regret and to what degree the past should be embraced, as those same painful events are integral to identity formation in the present.

Impact
Stuck Rubber Baby enjoyed critical acclaim when it first appeared in 1995. In addition to winning major industry awards, the work was lauded by many critics in the lesbian, gay, bisexual, and transgender press for its candid exploration of queer themes, thoughtful portrayal of civil rights issues, and careful consideration of the subtleties of sexual identity. The book has been compared favorably to Art Spiegleman's *Maus* (1986), given its ability to tell a nuanced story of personal development against the backdrop of traumatic historical events.

Additionally, *Stuck Rubber Baby* earned international acclaim for its translations in French (*Un Monde de différence*), German (*Am Rande des Himmels*), Spanish (*Stuck Rubber Baby: Mundos diferentes*), and Italian (*Folio di un Preservativo Bucato*). Despite its critical success, however, *Stuck Rubber Baby* did not enjoy widespread sales in its initial printings. One of the most significant legacies of the book is its making acceptable the frank discussion of queer themes in mainstream graphic novels. Though the work is not an autobiography, *Stuck Rubber Baby* set a precedent for the burgeoning number of graphic memoirs that have appeared since the late 1990's. Cruse's comfortably confessional style in narrating the intimate details of an individual's life certainly influenced Alison Bechdel's *Fun Home* (2007) and Judd Winick's *Pedro and Me* (2000), works that unflinchingly confront issues of sexuality, family, and the role of culture in mediating identity.

Ben Bolling

Further Reading
Bechdel, Alison. *Fun Home: A Family Tragicomic* (2007).

Cruse, Howard. *The Complete Wendel* (2011).

_____. *From Headrack to Claude: Collected Gay Comix by Howard Cruse* (2009).

Fish, Tim. *Cavalcade of Boys: Complete Collection* (2006).

Kirby, Robert, and David Kelly, eds. *The Book of Boy Trouble: Gay Boy Comics with a New Attitude* (2006).

Rucka, Greg, and J. H. Williams. *Batwoman: Elegy* (2010).

Winick, Judd. *Pedro and Me: Friendship, Loss, and What I Learned* (2000).

Bibliography

Anderson, Ho Che. "Rings True." *The Comics Journal* 182 (November, 1995): 103-105.

Brayshaw, Chris. "The Struggle to Communicate." *The Comics Journal* 182 (November, 1995): 94-98.

Mescallado, Ray. "Easy Comparisons." *The Comics Journal* 182 (November, 1995): 99-102.

Rubenstein, Anne. "Matters of Conscience: A Howard Cruse Interview." *The Comics Journal* 182 (November, 1995): 106-118.

See also: *Fun Home; Pedro and Me; Maus*

SUCKLE: THE STATUS OF BASIL

Author: Cooper, Dave
Artist: Dave Cooper (illustrator)
Publisher: Fantagraphics Books
First book publication: 1996

Publication History

After producing three issues of his comic *Pressed Tongue* for Fantagraphics Books, self-taught comics creator Dave Cooper was approached by the company's founder, Gary Groth, to write a full-length graphic novel. The first edition of *Suckle: The Status of Basil* was released by Fantagraphics in 1996, and the book was reprinted in 2001. In 2008, Delcourt published a French translation in a single volume with Cooper's subsequent graphic novel, *Crumple: The Status of Knuckle* (2000), which is sometimes viewed as a kind of sequel to *Suckle*.

Plot

Suckle follows the coming-of-age of Basil, a smiley and naïve adolescent, as he navigates a hallucinogenic world of virile aliens, ectoplasmic vaginas, demonic insects, sociopathic men, and sexually aggressive women. Basil is born from an egg laid by a fly in a labia-shaped bump in the earth. He wanders nude through a forest until he finds a futuristic city. He nourishes himself with strange vaginal fruit that gives him erotic nightmares. This vagina symbol haunts him throughout his adventures: Whenever he sees it, he melts into a giddy puddle of desire. He is also stalked by the Demon that sporadically materializes out of shapes in the cityscape and tries to enter him, causing terrifying erotic experiences.

He stumbles upon a cabin, where he is invited in to eat by the Scottish couple who live there. The woman befriends him, offering him a friendship bracelet, and the man teases him when he smells the vaginal fruit on his breath. Basil is deeply touched by the idea of having a friend. In the city, he falls in love with the Angelic Woman, who is the leader of a New Age sect connected with the vagina symbol: She wears a pendant with the symbol around her neck. He also meets an urbane, leprechaunish Brit who takes him away from the Angelic Woman and tries to initiate him into sexuality by taking him to visit prostitutes, while simultaneously embezzling his money. Basil is uninterested in the prostitutes but is pleased to meet a woman who gives him a massage, until the moment is lost, when she demands he lick a sweet liquid off her body. He manages to escape when the liquid pours out of a machine in impossible quantities.

Basil is left derelict in the red-light district, revolted by the crass sexuality on sale around him, until one of the sect's members, the friendly Jessica, finds him and takes him back to their temple. Inside, the Angelic Woman is reading to a group of women from a book with the vagina symbol. Jessica takes him away to nurse his wounds and put him to bed. That night, he dreams that the Angelic Woman desires him. He sleepwalks out and enacts his fantasy with Jessica, who is masturbating on the couch. Suddenly, the Demon climbs out of the Angelic Woman's mouth, and Basil wakes up, horrified to see Jessica in front of him. The next day the Demon will not leave him alone. Even when he masturbates, and the Demon shoots out of his urethra, it still wants more. Basil runs all around town but sees the Demon everywhere. Finally, the Angelic Woman finds him and leads him back to the temple, where the two make love in a hallucinogenic scene in which she offers him her vagina. He suckles it, and their two bodies disintegrate into shapes in motion and ecstatic smiles.

The depraved world outside no longer bothers the giddy Basil, until he meets the Brit again, who takes him to a sadomasochist (S and M) dungeon. He escapes this, but the world seems hopelessly corrupt again. In a rage, he stamps on the friendship bracelet given to him by the woman in the cabin, and the crushed bracelet reveals a secret shape. He takes the shape and uses it to unlock the most sacred door in the temple, but when he opens it, he sees the Demon sodomizing the Angelic Woman. He vomits violently and collapses, lying unconscious for several weeks. When he regains consciousness, he is delighted to be back in the woods with

Jessica, who promises to take him somewhere nice to settle. The story ends with Basil overjoyed to see Jessica, who is a real friend.

Characters
- *Basil*, the protagonist, is a spiky-haired teenager with big innocent eyes and a wide grin. He dresses in mid-1990's slacker chic, wearing a grimy T-shirt and an earring. He begins his journey as an innocent set adrift in a surreal, highly sexual universe. Though he dreams obsessively of vaginas, he is repulsed by aggressive, vulgar, and commercial sexuality. He is easy to manipulate and needs to be cared for by a friend. Through the course of his adventures, he becomes more aware of what he desires and is more able to stand up for himself. He is haunted by the Demon, who destroys his idealized sexual fantasies.
- *Jessica* is a helper. She has long, curly black hair and a round face with big cheeks, which gives her an innocent and friendly look. She is a mother figure who takes care of Basil, taking an interest in his drawings and telling him the rules of the vagina sect. Basil does not see her as sexual until he mistakes her for the Angelic Woman and undresses her while sleepwalking.
- *The Brit* first appears to be a helper but is increasingly revealed to be an antagonist. The anonymous character is rotund with a small, leprechaunish head and weaselly eyes and speaks in an East London accent. He tries to initiate Basil into machismo culture by taking him to brothels and S and M dungeons, but he extorts money out of him. Toward the end, when Basil is fed up with the vulgar, commercial world of the sex industry, he fantasizes about chopping the Brit's face in half.
- *The Angelic Woman* is the anonymous spiritual leader of the vagina sect. She is tall, with light, flowing hair, and she radiates confidence and calm. She has the vagina symbol tattooed on her forehead and wears it on a pendant and around her waist. Readers never hear her speak, but Basil obsesses over her image. His dream is smashed when he sees her being sodomized by the Demon, and in this scene, she no longer appears beautiful. She seems much older, with serpentine hair, sagging breasts, and a snout.
- *The Demon* is a black devil character, with long horns and an evil grin. He stalks Basil's imagination, forming out of shapes in the landscape or from his fantasies. The Demon pollutes Basil's angelic sexuality, leading him into morally questionable behavior that he later regrets or tries to cover up. By sodomizing the Angelic Woman, the Demon manages to infect Basil's most idealized fantasy.

Artistic Style
Suckle: The Status of Basil continues some of the surreal treatment of sexual angst and William S. Burroughs-like aliens that Cooper was exploring in his "zine" *Pressed Tongue* and his earlier *Cynthia Petal's Really Fantastic Alien Sex Frenzy* (1993). The comic makes use of a similar mid-1990's stoner-culture aesthetic. Cooper's landscapes alternate from urban scenes reminiscent of *Futurama* to fantastical "nowhere lands" that recall works by comics creator Jim Woodring. Bodies burst apart, merge, inflate, or otherwise transform in hallucinogenic scenes, and bodily fluids frequently explode all over the page. Cooper's portrayal of bewildered male sexuality and assertive female sexuality is reminiscent of Robert Crumb's comics, as are the scenes of strange erotic ritual, such as when a woman is having an orgasm on a giant spliced tongue.

Layout and color are used to great effect in *Suckle*. The book is small, and Cooper usually crams six to eight frames on each page, making the fictional world seem busy. The panels are mostly different-sized rectangles, but different shapes and proportions appear throughout. Only two fundamental scenes are rendered on a full page. Cooper plays effectively with light and dark contrasts, which correspond to moments of innocence and depravity. The lightest points occur when Basil is walking through the desert and when he makes love with the Angelic Woman. The page darkens whenever the Demon appears and in a disturbing sequence in an S and M dungeon. On the last few pages, this contrast is even starker, as Basil is passed out and

> **Dave Cooper**
>
> Dave Cooper began producing comics professionally as a teenager for Aircel Publishing and, after a stint in a band, returned to the field in his twenties with a series of richly detailed underground comics, including *Puke and Explode* and *Cynthia Petal's Really Fantastic Alien Sex Frenzy*. His breakthrough work was the science-fiction graphic novel *Suckle*, in which a naïf is confronted with a series of horrors that gradually peel away his innocence. *Crumple*, originally serialized in *Zero Zero*, depicted a world overrun by militant feminists, while *Ripple* was a sexually frank depiction of an artist who becomes obsessively possessive of one of his models. Cooper's career trajectory has meant that each of his books is darker in subject matter and tone than its predecessor and his art has become increasingly complex, detailed, and lushly cartoony. More recently, Cooper has turned his attention to a career as an easel painter but, in 2007, he published a children's book under the pseudonym Hector Mumbly.

dreaming of a dark vagina that slowly transforms to Jessica's light lips. The only use of color is to illustrate a picture Jessica draws of Basil on yellow paper. The book ends with Basil filling in her image on the same page, symbolizing their friendship.

Themes

Suckle is a surreal exploration of male anxiety about coming-of-age and the mystery of female sexuality. When the story begins, Basil wanders nude through a desert: It is only his contact with civilization that gives him the idea to clothe himself. Likewise, he is ignorant of his own sexuality, but as he is inducted into different forms of sexuality, he gradually learns about his own desires. The foil to this is played by the Demon, who shrouds his fantasies in guilt. There are nods to adolescent shame about masturbation: When Basil eats a vaginal fruit, an old farmer teases him that everyone knows what he has been doing. Basil is shocked when he experiences unexpected erections and surprised when other people reveal their sexual interest in him. Without understanding why, he becomes programmed to seek out the vagina symbol.

In the world of *Suckle*, women are mysterious and distant. Basil is in awe of the ones he desires and often repulsed by those who desire him. Only at the end of his journey do male and female desires begin to correspond. While the women Basil meets are either sexual deviants or mother figures, the angel/whore dichotomy is continually disrupted by his experiences. When apparent mother figures suddenly become sexual, as happens with Jessica, Basil is particularly perturbed. Even his ideal, the Angelic Woman, who seems to have a pure sexuality, turns out to have nasty desires, as he discovers when he sees her with the Demon.

Basil's maturation also happens in the shadow of machismo and the sex industry. Though Basil is motivated by seeking out the symbol of a vagina, he is not satisfied by finding sex in brothels or S and M dungeons, not necessarily because of the commercial nature of the transaction but because of the crassness and aggressiveness of the women. The closest the commercial world can come to impressing him is when he sees a picture of a vagina on the Brit's wall, which he declares to be beautiful.

Impact

Suckle was a major turning point in Cooper's career. After years of working on other people's projects and his own minicomics, Cooper became a serious artist in his own right. The book earned him his first Harvey Award nomination in 1997, paving the way for Harvey and Ignatz awards for his next comic series, *Weasel* (1999). Success with the 136-page format led to *Crumple: The Status of Knuckle* and *Ripple: A Predilection for Tina* (2003), both of which also address sexuality and sexual anxiety. The three similarly titled works are sometimes referred to as a trilogy, despite *Ripple* having an entirely different artistic style.

Matt Jones

Further Reading

Brown, Chester. *Ed the Happy Clown* (1989).
Burns, Charles. *Black Hole* (2005).
Matt, Joe. *The Poor Bastard* (1997).

Bibliography

Cooper, Dave. "The Dave Cooper Interview." Interview by Gary McEown. *The Comics Journal* 245 (August, 2002): 76-105.

_____. "Dave Cooper." Interview by Nicolas Verstappen. *L'autre bande dessinée* (August, 2008). http://www.du9.org/Dave-Cooper,1028.

McInnes, Gavin. "Gavin McInnes Explains Dave Cooper." *Juxtapoz* 113 (June, 2010): 132-142.

See also: *Ed the Happy Clown*; *Black Hole*; *The Poor Bastard*; *The Complete Fritz the Cat*; *The Frank Book*

SUMMER BLONDE

Writer: Adrian Tomine
Artist: Adrian Tomine
First serial publication: The stories included in *Summer Blonde* were originally published in issues five through eight of his self-published magazine *Optic Nerve*.
First book publication: Drawn and Quarterly, 2002.

Publishing history

Cartoonist Adrian Tomine had been self-publishing stories beginning in his teenage years. Many of these stories were collected into graphic collections, *32 Stories, Sleepwalk and Other Stories*, and *Killing and Dying*. *Summer Blonde* is another graphic collection by Tomine.

Plot

Summer Blonde consists of four short stories, each with a different set of characters. The book is tied together by a prevailing mood and themes. In the first story, "Alter Ego," fledgling author Martin is having a very difficult time producing a follow up novel. Martin lives with his girlfriend Erin, writing articles for pay. Martin has also ghost-written a book for an up and coming actor. When a postcard, ostensibly sent from an old crush arrives, it sends Martin into a confused state. While in his hometown looking for his old crush he becomes involved with her younger sister still in high school. When Martin's girlfriend tries to get him to clarify their romantic situation, Martin is unable to do so and she leaves him. When Martin's agent calls, presumably about Martin's novel in progress, he tells Martin to put the novel on the back burner: a publisher is anxious for Martin to ghostwrite a second book with the same young actor. The second story, "Summer Blonde" tells the story of Neil, Carlo, Whit and Vanessa. Aspiring musician Carlo moves into the same apartment complex as Neil and the two are initially friendly. Neil is a very depressed young man who sees a counselor regularly to help manage his life. Neil has a crush on Vanessa, a pretty young woman who works in a card shop and is involved with a graduate student named Whit. Neil often buys cards at Vanessa's shop pretending that one of his many relatives is having a birthday, but in reality he hopes to work up the courage to ask Vanessa out on a date. When Carlo becomes involved with Vanessa, Neil is very jealous, and one day realizes that she is pregnant with Carlo's child. Seeing Neil in a public place, Whit and Vanessa feel Neil is stalking Vanessa, and Whit warns Neil to stay away from her. Whit learns that Vanessa is pregnant from Neil and beats Carlo senseless. Vanessa visits Carlo in the hospital and he crudely breaks it off with her. The final scene takes place sometime later: Neil and Vanessa run into each other on the subway; Neil says he's not stalking her, and Vanessa tells him to just stay away from her. The next short story, "Hawaiian Getaway," features a young Asian-American protagonist named Hillary, who is fired from her job as a phone operator after two and a half years for being flippant with a famous client. Stopping at her regular coffee shop, Hillary is impressed at the ease in which some people can start up conversations, something she is unable to do. Talking to her mother long distance a few days later, Hillary learns that her roommate informed her mother that she had

Adrian Tomine signs copies of Summer Blonde *at the MoCCA Festival, 2011.* (By Alex Lozupone, via Wikimedia Commons)

been fired. Hillary is frustrated further when she receives an interpersonal instructional guide from her younger sister a week or so later. She finds unemployment a bore, and develops a habit of calling a pay phone and delivering a false story to any passerby who answers the pay phone. She offers unsolicited (and unappreciated) advice to her roommate Lloyd about his relationship with his girlfriend Stephanie. One night, Hillary has an unsatisfying sexual encounter with a middle-aged DJ. The next day Hillary's roommate, Lloyd, informs her that he is moving out of the apartment. Hillary assumes that Lloyd is moving in with Stephanie, of whom she disapproves, but she is wrong. Lloyd is moving out because he finds living with Hillary too depressing. A call from her mother, letting Hillary know that her grandmother, who lives close by, has had a heart attack, sends Hillary back to calling a pay phone again for distraction. A young man named Sam answers the phone realizes that Hillary is playing a joke, and the two meet, have dinner, and then go back to Hillary's apartment and make love. Hillary asks Sam to go to her grandmother's funeral with her, and they make plans. But on the day of the funeral Sam doesn't come to Hillary's apartment or call her. The last story in the collection, "Bomb Scare," focuses on Scotty, an isolated sixteen year old boy who lives with his mother. Scotty spends most of his time socializing with Alex; an older boy whom other students believe is gay. Scotty works part time at a sandwich shop and is friendly with Cammie, a popular girl. During a conversation, Cammie makes it clear to Scotty that their classmates think he is gay. Scotty adamantly denies this. One night Alex invites Scotty over to his house and offers pornography as entertainment. Scotty is shocked. In the days that follow Scotty and Alex see less of each other. The next day at school Cammie becomes inebriated and removes her clothes. Days later, at a party, Cammie passes out after relieving herself on the couch, making her group of friends avoid her. While at work Scotty talks with Cammie. He tells her that he's not interested in sex. Dubious, Cammie asks Scotty to help her run for class treasurer. He complies and the two become better friends. One school day the principal announces that there's been a bomb threat. Everyone leaves the building. While waiting out the bomb threat Cammie tells Scotty that her parents are divorcing and that she's moving away. When the bomb scare is over, she and Scotty go to his house instead of returning to the school. Cammie asks Scotty is he wants to see her naked. Scotty doesn't answer, and Cammie takes off her shirt and holds him as he looks dumbfounded.

Characters

Alter Ego

- *Martin*: A frustrated novelist unable to produce a satisfying second novel. When a postcard from an old crush arrives, Martin's life is turned upside down as he tries to find the sender of the post card. While he's struggling with his novel and his emotional life, a book he ghostwrote for pay has become surprisingly successful, sending him into an artistic as well as emotional maelstrom.
- *Erin*: Martin's girlfriend, she is hurt by his pursuit of a teenage crush, and his subsequent love affair with teenage Jenna. As a result, Erin moves out of their apartment and is noncommittal when Martin tries for reconciliation.
- *Ryan:* Martin's friend who is also a novelist. Ryan works a day job as he can't support himself with by writing. Ryan is both supportive and envious of Martin's commercial and critical success, but he is disapproving of Martin's affair with Jenna and advises him to "grow up".
- *Jenna:* The teenage sister of Samantha, the high school crush that Martin pursues, Jenna flatters Martin but later offers more genuine opinions of his writing. When Martin realizes that his affair with Jenna has deeply affected his relationship with Erin, he breaks off their relationship.

Summer Blonde

- *Neil:* Very depressed young men, Neil's crush on Vanessa borders on obsession, and he invents reasons to buy cards at the shop where Vanessa is employed. When Neil sees her getting a pregnancy test he offers to help her. Later, when he bumps into Vanessa and her boyfriend Whit, he is warned to stay away from her. Neil informs Whit that Vanessa is pregnant. Much later, after Neil has moved away from Vanessa's neighborhood, the two find themselves in the same subway car, Neil tries to apologize for his behavior, but Vanessa is cold to him.

- *Carlo:* an aspiring musician who moves into Neil's apartment complex, Carlo is very successful with women, and begins an affair with Vanessa, inspiring Neil's jealousy. After Vanessa becomes pregnant, Carlo is hospitalized after being attacked by Vanessa's boyfriend. When Vanessa visits Carlo in the hospital he tells her that their affair is over.
- *Vanessa:* A pretty young woman who works in a card shop, Vanessa is unaware that Neil is obsessed with her. When she and Carlo have an affair she doesn't tell her boyfriend Whit. When Whit learns that Vanessa is pregnant, he wants to keep the baby even as Vanessa doesn't.

Hawaiian Getaway

- *Hillary:* A depressed young woman fired from her job as a telephone operator, Hillary is plagued by her own depression, her more successful younger sister, and her prying mother. When her grandmother passes away, Hillary must attend the funeral alone as she has no close friends.
- *Lloyd:* Hillary's apartment mate, who had a very short love affair with Hillary after she moved in to the apartment. Hillary disapproves of Lloyd's girlfriend Stephanie and is very critical of their relationship. When Lloyd moves out of the apartment, Hillary assumes that it is so he and Stephanie can move in together, but she is wrong: Lloyd wants to move away from Hillary.
- *Sam:* A young man whom Hillary meets through her phone pranks, the two have a one night stand. When Hillary asks Sam to go to her grandmother's funeral with her, he agrees but then stands her up.

Bomb Scare

- *Scotty:* a sixteen year old boy who is confused about his sexuality, Scotty lives with his mother and isn't supportive of his mother's evolving relationship with her boyfriend Phil. Scotty is most comfortable with Alex, a gay classmate whom he eventually shuns. When Cammie, another classmate, offers to show herself to Scotty naked, he is uncomfortable as opposed to interested, making Cammie question his sexuality.
- *Alex:* Scotty's gay friend. When Alex indicates that he is interested in Scotty sexually, Scottie breaks off the relationship.
- *Carrie*: A classmate and a co-worker of Scotty's, Cammie is ridiculed after a drunken incident at a party. Hoping to get into a good college, Cammie enlists Scottie's help as she runs for class treasurer. While trying to determine whether or not Scotty is gay, she removes her shirt and holds him.

Artistic Style

The artistic style throughout *Summer Blonde* is consistent throughout the four stories, contributing to the persistent mood. The illustrations are black and white, the only color in the book is on the cover, and those colors are soft. Pages are broken down into six to nine small panels focusing on characters. This layout mirrors the conflicted and constricted emotions the characters feel. Characters from story to story are drawn similarly, again contributing to the persistent mood of the overall collection. Backgrounds are realistically rendered while remaining unobtrusive. There are no splash pages, again emphasizing the claustrophobic lives of these characters.

Themes

The recurring theme of these stories is depression In "Alter Ego," Martin is so depressed that he can't make any headway with his second novel that he jeopardizes his relationship with Erin. In "Summer Blonde," Neil's depression is evidenced by his seeing a therapist and by his inability to act on his fantasies about Vanessa. In "Hawaiian Getaway," Hillary's depression is presented as a chronic state: she is fired from her job because of her inappropriate behavior, she is unable to make small talk with people she interacts with, and her roommate moves out of their apartment because he finds living with her a depressing experience. Finally, in "Bomb Scare," both Scotty and Cammie are depressed about

Tomine's art style is distinctive. (By dalcrose, via Wikimedia Commons)

their parents' respective divorces, but Scotty's greater feeling is confusion: he doesn't know whether he's gay or not, he doesn't know who he wants for friends, and he doesn't know whether or not he can be positive about his mother's new relationship. In "Alter Ego," Martin's depression seems to be chronic, as does Neil's and Hillary's in the stories "Summer Blonde" and "Hawaiian Getaway." Scotty's depression in "Bomb Scare," seems more temporary, a kind of byproduct of his teenage years. Scotty is also the youngest of the four protagonists: while he is sixteen the others appear to be in their late twenties or early thirties.

Impact

Summer Blonde was published in 2002, the same years that YALSA (the Young Adult division of the American Library Association) held its first day long conference on graphic novels in public libraries. It was also the year the first *Spider-man* movie arrived in theaters, so *Summer Blonde* appeared on the cusp of widespread mainstream acceptance of the graphic novel form. What *Summer Blonde* accomplished specifically was to carve out a niche in the trade book market for literate graphic novels. The book also propelled the career of cartoonist Adrian Tomine and his publisher, Drawn and Quarterly, outside of the comic book marketplace, as the book received notices in mainstream media outlets.

Further reading

Burns, Charles, *Black Hole*
Forney, Ellen, *Marbles: Mania, Depression, Michelangelo and Me: a Graphic Memoir*
Tomine, Adrian, *32 Stories*

Bibliography

"Adrian Tomine's Summer Blonde": *Asian American Literature Fans*, January 20, 2011. https://asianamlitfans.livejournal.com/91490.html.

Anam, Nasia, "Tomine's *Summer Blonde* no romp on the beach": *the Chicago Maroon*, July 26, 2002. https://www.chicagomaroon.com/2002/07/26/tomines-emsummer-blondeem-no-romp-on-the-beach/.

Perring, Christian, PHD, "Review-Summer Blonde": *Metapsychology Online Reviews*, August 7, 2003. http://metapsychology.mentalhelp.net/poc/view_doc.php?type=book&id=1829.

SUMMER OF LOVE, THE

Author: Drechsler, Debbie
Artist: Debbie Drechsler (illustrator)
Publisher: Drawn and Quarterly
First serial publication: 1996-1999
First book publication: 2002

Publication History
The Summer of Love began as a five-issue series for Drawn and Quarterly called *Nowhere*. The first twenty-six-page issue came out in October, 1996, and the rest were released sporadically, with two issues in 1997, one in 1998, and one in 1999. The five issues then became five parts of a single story, which was published by Drawn and Quarterly in hardcover in 2002. A paperback edition was published the following year. Creator Debbie Drechsler wrestled with the coloration, changing it with each edition. For the *Nowhere* issues, she used green and brown. The hardcover of *The Summer of Love* was gray and turquoise, and the paperback was green and another shade of brown. From the hardcover to the paperback, the name of the town was changed from Mayfield to Woodland. The book has been translated into French, published by L'Association in 2004, and Spanish, published by La Cupula in 2007.

Plot
Summer of Love is a semiautobiographical story based on Drechsler's adolescence. The Maier family has just moved to a new town called Woodland, a sleepy suburban area built around a mysterious and alluring forest. Lili Maier, the oldest of four children, is in her early teens and has an intense sibling rivalry with Pearl, two years her junior. The family's arrival immediately solicits the interest of the neighborhood's teenage flaneurs, including the amicable Kim, who is Pearl's age, and the unfriendly sophomore Keith Dunham.

One day, Lili goes to explore the woods and ends up frolicking around, only to find that she is being surveyed by a boy in a high-up tree house. She feels suddenly awkward about her juvenile behavior and struggles to maintain composure more fitting to a growing young woman. The observer turns out to be Stevie, a handsome

> **Debbie Drechsler**
> One of the most powerfully original voices in the comics field in the mid-1990's, Debbie Drechsler was in her forties when she began publishing her first comics. *Daddy's Girl*, her first graphic novel, was released in 1996 to tremendous critical acclaim. The semi-autobiographical story of a victim of incest was shocking in its remarkable frankness and its ability to deal with tough topics without sentimentality. Her follow-up, *Summer of Love*, was a meandering work depicting teenage experiences of alienation. It was serialized by Drawn and Quarterly in the late 1990's and collected in 2002. Drechsler's comics are highly expressionistic, with extremely detailed images that eschew traditional perspective. She uses heavy black lines that are reminiscent of scratchboard. *Summer of Love* was printed with color overlays intended to evoke certain emotions, and broke from naturalism in that regard.

and serious boy who plays in a band. Lili later meets him while hanging out on Dunham's lawn, and the two bond over their mutual affection for Jefferson Airplane. They end up kissing while listening to a record that Stevie brings over, and he invites her to join his band. Lili declines because she cannot sing, but that does not stop her from fantasizing about them getting famous. Lili is conscious of her every move, wary that doing the wrong thing could push Stevie away. Stevie takes her to the tree house. They kiss again, but when he tries to touch her breast, she flinches; he apologizes for moving too fast. Lili does not know how to tell him that she liked it, and he decides to leave. He does not come to see her again.

As Lili agonizes over the reasons for Stevie's change of heart, she happens upon Pearl and Kim kissing in the woods, which horrifies her. The next time she meets Stevie he casually dismisses her, which prompts her to take up Dunham's relentless offer to give her a tour of the woods. Despite thinking that he is a jerk, she lets him kiss her and is surprised to find she enjoys it. She agrees to go back to his place where they make out on the living room sofa, and when he goes for her breast, she does not flinch.

Back at school, things start to go well for Lili when she befriends the beautiful and popular Claire Kessler. However, when she stands up Claire to make out with Dunham under the stairs, Claire tries to ostracize her from her group. Lili tries to pry her way back in by helping Claire's art club with the decorations for the school dance. While she is working, she overhears Dunham gossiping about her, claiming that she left her last school because she was pregnant. She is devastated but feels powerless to counter the rumor or to get revenge on Dunham.

At the dance, Kim abandons Pearl for a boy named Paul, and Lili has to sit through a set by Stevie's band, now fronted by his new girlfriend, Ev. Lili leaves to sulk under the stairs, where she is cornered by Dunham. She wrestles her way past him; he calls ominously after her, saying she will be sorry. The next day after school everything erupts. Dunham accuses Kim and Pearl of being lovers. They deny it, but the accusation has already tarnished them. As Lili gets on the school bus, Dunham proposes to forget about the rumor he spread, if she agrees to be nice to him. She dismisses the offer, and the book ends with Pearl and Lili walking home alone, fantasizing about moving away.

Characters

- *Lili Maier*, the protagonist and the author's alter ego, is a petite ninth grader who wants to fit in and make friends in her new community. She maintains a nervous inner monologue that runs in contrast to the sarcastic, irritable demeanor she carries on with her family. She is easily surprised by her own desires: She does not expect to be attracted to Dunham but finds herself drawn in by his confident male power.
- *Pearl Maier* is Lili's slightly younger sister. She and Lili squabble incessantly and bounce their frustrations off each other. When Lili finds out that Pearl is gay, she is initially worried about the effect this will have on people's perceptions of her. She almost outs Pearl to a friend but restrains herself. When the two find themselves ostracized, though, they return to a state of sisterly solidarity.
- *Keith Dunham* is a tall, loudmouthed teen who lives down the street from the Maier family. He keeps a close watch on the comings and goings that take place in the woods and uses this information to his advantage. He flirts aggressively with Lili, who cannot stand him but finds herself drawn to him physically. He bets with his friends that he can "score" with her, but he also makes up lies about her behind her back. When Lili stops seeing him, he becomes vicious and tries to blackmail her into seeing him again.
- *Steve Farley*, a.k.a. *Stevie*, is a good-looking, quietly cool boy on whom Lili develops a crush. He is a junior who plays in a band, which means he ranks high on the local gossip network's hierarchy. His laconic manner makes it difficult for Lili to judge what he is thinking. She worries constantly that he will lose interest in her, and when he does, the change in his behavior is barely noticeable. He is a loyal, if slightly indifferent, friend to Dunham. When Lili asks him if he finds anything strange about Dunham, he prefers to stay neutral.

Artistic Style

Much more realistic than her earlier *Daddy's Girl* (1996), with its haunting woodcut-like lines and swirls, *The Summer of Love* aims for naturalism in its depiction of suburban teen life, in a style not unlike Daniel Clowes's *Ghost World* (1997). The comic is rendered in a palette of tree green, brown, and burnt orange that initially looks like a peculiar film negative but also gives the comic the allure of a distant summer memory taking place sometime in the late 1960's. Drechsler did the illustrations in gray scale and had the colors added by the printer. In her work as an illustrator and graphic designer for newspapers and magazines, she has become increasingly interested in using digital techniques, and *The Summer of Love* is no exception: She used Photoshop to design background patterns, most notably the motifs on the female characters' dresses.

Drechsler's eye for the details of teenage gestures is what gives her work such striking verisimilitude. The teens stretch their bodies awkwardly to look older, but their shaky confidence is betrayed by big vulnerable eyes, shy smiles, and timid postures. While the scenes in town capture the patchwork squareness of the suburbs with delicate minimalism, the woods are rendered in overpowering swirls of brown and orange that highlight their power as a place of erotic seclusion.

Drechsler frequently divides her pages into a grid of four or five equal panels and then a single double-sized panel, stretched either vertically or horizontally. She attributes this style to her background in graphic design. The pacing of *The Summer of Love* is slower than *Daddy's Girl*, and Drechsler makes effective use of silent panels that highlight important visual moments and stress the sense of awkwardness of other scenes. Thought bubbles play an important role in juxtaposing characters' actions and intentions. After Stevie apologizes for touching Lili's breast, there is a long pause where she thinks about how much she liked it, but all she tells him is not to worry. The vagueness of teen language is also a strength in Drechsler's dialogue. Characters are always going nowhere and doing nothing, and those who insist on finding out are told it is "none of their beeswax."

Themes

The Summer of Love is about the difficulties of coming-of-age, but it also offers a harsh judgment of gender relations in high school. Boys are endowed with a tremendous sense of agency, which they use without remorse. Girls must be hyperconscious of their behavior, as the slightest slip could tarnish their reputations, and this leads to petty competition and deep insecurity. Lili seems powerless to defend herself from Dunham's vindictive rumormongering. Faced with his claim that Pearl is gay, the two sisters find the only solution is to stick together and fantasize about leaving town. Drechsler shows how the rumor mill enforces compulsory heterosexuality and produces sexuality of a certain kind in the girls, who must construct their sexual identities within a space bordered by accusations of frigidity and homosexuality on the one hand and "sluttiness" on the other. Lili's slight flinch when Stevie tries to touch her marks the end of his interest in her, and it seems there is little she can do to change that.

If female heterosexuality is difficult enough, homosexuality is worse. Drechsler's rendition of Lili's reaction to seeing her sister kiss another girl is revealing. Not only is she disgusted by it, but also amazed: She had no idea that girls could be homosexual. The next time Lili sees Pearl, she is inexplicably aggressive with her, as if she herself is unaware of what she feels or why she feels it. Lili is clearly concerned about the effect that having a gay sister could have on her reputation. Meanwhile, Pearl's sexuality is infantilized by her partner, who leaves her when a boy asks her out.

Impact

As a follow-up to her acclaimed and shocking *Daddy's Girl*, *The Summer of Love* established Drechsler as an important contemporary comics artist. In the blurb for *Daddy's Girl* Drechsler had written that she did not think she had any more stories she needed to tell, so another book was by no means inevitable. Reviewers compared *The Summer of Love* to the work of Lynda Barry, Phoebe Gloeckner, and Clowes. Drechsler cites those artists as influences, as well as Julie Doucet and Richard Sala, though their styles are quite different. *Nowhere*, the "zine" version of the book, was greeted with eagerness and nominated for the Ignatz Award for Outstanding Graphic Novel or Collection in 2002, while the book itself was nominated for the Best Script Award at the 2005 Angoulême International Comics Festival.

Matt Jones

Further Reading

Barry, Lynda. *One! Hundred! Demons!* (2002).
Clowes, Daniel. *Ghost World* (1997).
Drechsler, Debbie. *Daddy's Girl* (1996).

Bibliography

Arnold, Andrew D. "What It Feels Like for a Girl." *Time*, October 11, 2002. http://www.time.com/time/arts/article/0,8599,364159,00.html.
Drechsler, Debbie. "The Debbie Drechsler Interview." Interview by Gary Groth. *The Comics Journal* 249 (December, 2002): 82-107.
———. "Debbie Drechsler." Interview by Nicholas Verstappen. *L'autre bande dessinée* (July, 2008). http://www.du9.org/Debbie-Drechsler,1018.

See also: *One! Hundred! Demons!*; *Ghost World*; *Long Time Relationship*

System, The

Author: Kuper, Peter
Artist: Peter Kuper (illustrator)
Publisher: DC Comics
First serial publication: 1996
First book publication: 1997

Publication History

Lou Stathis, an editor from DC Comics, originally asked comics creator Peter Kuper in the mid-1990's to create a work for a new DC imprint called Vertigo Vérité, which would publish material designed to reach a mature audience of readers. After riding on the subway in New York, Kuper had an idea for a work about the interconnections of people's lives. The result was *The System*, originally published in 1996 in a three-issue series and as a graphic novel the following year.

Plot

The System is a lengthy wordless comic and one of the finest examples of overlapping plots in a comic. It focuses on the lives of twenty characters living in New York City in the late twentieth century against the backdrop of a scandalous presidential election between candidates Muir and Rex and a corporate battle between two major corporations, Syco and Maxxon. The ensuing political and corporate battles are described in newspaper headlines and television reports.

The first part introduces both the murder of a stripper on her way to the subway and the subsequent events in the lives of characters as they move around the city. At first, little connection exists between the characters except a physical closeness as they pass one another on the street. Kuper slowly begins to link characters together, beginning with the shakedown of a drug dealer by a corrupt policeman and the discovery of a terrorist plot by a rival corporation to detonate a bomb and destroy the Syco landmark building.

In the second part, another stripper is brutally murdered in the subway. A middle-aged detective named MacGuffin, responsible for an earlier accidental shooting of an innocent boy, is assigned to investigate these murders.

Peter Kuper

A well-known illustrator, Peter Kuper is a politically engaged cartoonist who co-founded the influential anthology *World War 3 Illustrated* in 1979. Though he has worked in a variety of genres, he is particularly famous for his wordless comics, including *Eye of the Beholder* (which was originally serialized in *The New York Times*) and *The System*. *The System* is typical of his graphic style and represents one of the pinnacles of his creative career. Working without dialogue, Kuper has constructed a detailed political parable with graffiti-inspired images. Initially influenced by woodcut artists like Frans Masereel and Lynd Ward, Kuper has increasingly worked with stencils and spray paint. His color work has a vibrant but ragged look, with shapes constructed out of layers of paint. Among his other works are a comics adaptation of Upton Sinclair's novel *The Jungle* and several collections of short stories, including *Topsy Turvy*, *Give it Up!*, and *ComicsTrips*.

A friendly gay man visits his partner in a hospital, where the latter is being treated for AIDS. A stockbroker's payment for insider trading in his online account is hacked by a skateboarding gamer who transfers the funds to his own account. The drug dealer, who is a close friend of graffiti artist Lil Bro is killed by a rival drug gang in a drive-by shooting. A gang of young skinheads kills a young African American man for walking down a sidewalk with his white girlfriend in a predominantly white neighborhood. This killing results in protest demonstrations by a group of black men.

In the third part, MacGuffin finds a bloody scrap of text from the Bible, which is a clue to solving the murders. Black demonstrators, angry over the murder of the African American man, take over a subway train that stalls on the tracks. The drunken subway operator of a fast-approaching train crashes into the stalled train

Peter Kuper at Columbia University. (By Alex Lozupone, via Wikimedia Commons)

with the protestors, resulting in a catastrophic wreck that kills the operator, the stockbroker, and the terrorist. In a series of concluding events that brings together the lives of the characters, the gay man's partner recovers after a near-death experience; the corrupt policeman is arrested in a corruption scandal; and MacGuffin discovers the evangelist's son has murdered the strippers. The evangelist's son runs out into the street after being sprayed with mace by an assaulted stripper and is accidentally struck and killed by a cab driven by an Indian man.

The story concludes with the merging of the corporations into SYMaxx and the election of Rex for president after the mysterious death of Muir. The girl from the interracial couple sobs in a taxi as she reads about the acquittal of the gang of skinheads and the jailing of the protestors, who have been charged with causing the train accident. The assaulted stripper and her son leave the city on a plane. MacGuffin retires a hero for saving the stripper. Lil Bro weeps as he sprays red paint under the phrase "Rest in Peace," in memory of his murdered friend. The gamer, with cash from the stockbroker's bank account, upgrades his vehicle from a skateboard to a motorcycle. The gay couple raises a champagne toast to themselves. The missing woman, Betty Russell, closes a window blind in her brightly lit room.

In the final pages, a homeless man lights a match and opens a suitcase that contains the terrorist's radioactive bomb, which he took from the scene of the subway accident. As he opens the suitcase, his dog accidentally activates the bomb. This eighty-four-page wordless comic concludes with three disturbing onomatopoeic words, "tic tic tic," displayed in the lower left corner of a solid black page. In the lower right corner are also the words "The End," which have a double meaning: Not only do the words refer to the end of the narrative but also to the end of many lives after the anticipated explosion.

Characters

- *A homeless old man and his dog* appear in the beginning and end, as well as at various times throughout the narrative, but they are always in the background of unfolding events.
- *The strippers* include two who are murdered and one who eventually escapes and gratefully leaves the city with her son.
- *The interracial couple* is attacked by a gang of skinheads, resulting in the death of the African American man.
- *The stockbroker* is a dishonest employee guilty of insider trading.
- *Detective MacGuffin* is haunted by guilt from the accidental shooting death of a boy. His intuition leads to the discovery of the murderer, which saves the life of the third stripper.
- *Lil Bro* is a young, black graffiti artist whose artwork covers building walls and subway trains.
- *The drug dealer* is a close friend of the graffiti artist who is killed by a rival gang.
- *The corrupt policeman* is guilty of robbing drug dealers and taking protection money from local businesses.

- *The young gay man* is casually dressed and friendly with everyone he meets. His partner is in the hospital being treated for AIDS.
- *The singer in the subway* narrates in song the destruction of the global environment.
- *The Indian cab driver* accidentally kills the murderer when he runs out in front of the cab.
- *The drunken subway operator* is responsible for crashing into another train.
- *The terrorist* is hired to set off a bomb and destroy the Syco high-rise.
- *The long-haired gamer* on a skateboard disrupts traffic and pedestrians and hacks into the stockbroker's account.
- *The evangelist and his son* stand at a subway entrance and accuse strippers, the interracial couple, and the gay man of sinful acts. The evangelist's son is responsible for murdering two strippers.
- *The missing woman* is named Betty Russell. Her name and face are displayed on posters throughout the story. At the conclusion, she is shown in a room, happily alive.

Artistic Style

The System displays Kuper's distinctive use of stencils and spray paint, which he skillfully renders in dynamic color, capturing heartfelt moments such as a mother embracing her son or, in contrast, the powerful crash of subway trains. His use of lines provides additional insight into the characters. Diagonal lines provide a sense of tension in a panel, as with the renegade skateboarder racing past upset pedestrians on the sidewalk or the eager hands reaching out for a stripper on stage. In another example, wavy lines around the panels that display the subway operator indicate his intoxication as he steps out of a bar.

Kuper cleverly introduces new characters by displaying them in the background of a panel from an event that involves a different character. The new character is subsequently placed in the foreground, and an event unfolds in his or her life until another character is introduced and the story follows that person. This overlapping of characters and events increases readers' attention to details in the story. At first, the characters appear to have little to do with one another, as in a panel where the gay man rides in a taxi driven by the Indian cab driver that passes the homeless man in an alley. Kuper subtly increases the involvement of the characters throughout the story until the subway accident and the death of the evangelist's son, which illustrate the intended connection between the characters.

With the multitude of characters in this story, Kuper relies on stereotypes that provide a means to identify and predict behavior. Examples include the gang of skinheads who harass and brutally attack the interracial couple and the overweight, cigar-smoking policeman guilty of harassment and extortion. In contrast, Kuper challenges readers' stereotypes by presenting a drug dealer with a tender heart and a stripper who returns home as a loving mother to her son in a well-kept apartment. The mixture of heartfelt and tragic events encourages readers to question their own prejudicial stereotypes.

Kuper also uses word images that include marketing slogans, brand names, graffiti, posters, newspaper headlines, news on television, electronic ticker tapes, and online banking transactions. These words are essential elements in the plot and provide important clues about characters, events, and cultural norms. One example is shown at a bodega corner market advertising "Candy" and "Beer," implying a childhood dependence on candy that may progress to alcohol dependence. Another example is a poster of a missing woman named Betty Russell, an image in the beginning panel and one that surfaces nine times throughout the narrative and is not resolved until the end, which invites multiple interpretations.

Themes

One of the major themes is the power of money and the dysfunctional compulsion that drives people to accumulate cash in the capitalistic "system." Many of these diverse characters are involved in making money, whether legally or illegally. This is conveyed in a constant exchange of dollars, from the extortion of local businesses by the corrupt policeman to the transfer of virtual currency in an online transaction. The dollar bill is one of many visual motifs used in the narrative and is behind every motivation, from buying a newspaper to the underhanded schemes of business transactions and cutthroat presidential elections.

Intolerance is another theme portrayed throughout this comic. Narrow-mindedness is displayed in a variety of events, including through the raised eyebrows of people in the subway judging the racially mixed couple, the public reprimand of the gay man by the evangelist, and the harassment of the homeless man by the corrupt policeman.

Another theme is the destruction of the natural environment by large corporations such as Syco. This theme is presented by a street singer in a song about a peaceful jungle that is torn apart by bulldozers that slaughter birds and animals and uproot plants and trees.

Impact

Along with Eric Drooker's award-winning graphic novel *Flood! A Novel in Pictures* (1992), Kuper helped revitalize the genre of contemporary wordless graphic novels with a social focus and modern themes. In subsequent years, many comic artists have adopted the wordless medium for their storytelling ideas. To celebrate the new millennium, the French publisher L'Association published a two-thousand-page wordless volume, *Comix 2000*, with more than 324 international contributors. Marvel Comics even jumped on the wordless trend by publishing all its issues in December, 2001, without words. The series was named *'Nuff Said*, based on a quote by renowned comics creator Stan Lee.

David A. Beronä

Further Reading

Drooker, Eric. *Flood! A Novel in Pictures* (1992).

Kuper, Peter. *Sticks and Stones* (2004).

L'Association. *Comix 2000* (1999).

Bibliography

Beronä, David A. "Wordless Comics: The Imaginative Appeal of *The System*." *Critical Approaches to Comics and Graphic Novels: Theories and Methods*, edited by Randy Duncan and Matthew J. Smith. New York: Routledge, 2011.

Kuper, Peter."This Is Not a Comic Book: Jarret Lovell Interviews Graphic Artist Peter Kuper." Interview by Jarret Lovell. *Crime Media Culture* 2 (April, 2006): 75-83.

_____. *Speechless*. Marietta, Ga.: Top Shelf Productions, 2001.

See also: *Flood!*; *Give It Up! and Other Stories*; *He Done Her Wrong*; *Passionate Journey*

T

TALE OF ONE BAD RAT, THE

Author: Talbot, Bryan
Artist: Bryan Talbot (illustrator); Ellie DeVille (letterer)
Publisher: Dark Horse Comics
First serial publication: 1994-1995
First book publication: 1995

Publication History

The Tale of One Bad Rat, written and illustrated by Bryan Talbot, was initially published monthly as a four-part series from October, 1994, to January, 1995, and issued in a collected edition exactly one year after the appearance of its first issue. Both the series and the graphic novel were published by Dark Horse Comics, with the latter appearing under the Dark Horse Books imprint. The graphic novel was published by Titan Books in the United Kingdom. Within a few years of its publication, the book was translated into several languages, including French, Spanish, and Swedish. In addition to receiving American and British awards, both the book and Talbot have obtained recognition on an international scale.

Bryan Talbot at the 2008 Big Apple Convention in Manhattan. (By Luigi Novi, via Wikimedia Commons)

Plot

The Tale of One Bad Rat is a nongenre graphic novel originally stemming from Talbot's desire to create a book set in England's Lake District. Instead of creating a documentary comic, Talbot chose to present a story connecting one of the many artistic personalities who settled in the region, the writer Beatrix Potter, with a parallel, modern character, the sixteen-year-old Helen Potter. Initially included as the reason Helen ran away from home, the issue of child sexual abuse eventually became the book's chief focus. Divided into sections titled "Town," "Road," and "Country," the book narrates Helen's journey from London to the Lake District, punctuating it with some of her key, most painful memories of home and school.

The book opens with an almost suicidal Helen and her pet rat begging at a train station. When a preaching Christian touches her, she violently pushes him away and runs out. The Christmas tree in Trafalgar Square reminds her of the Christmas her aunt gave her a set of Beatrix Potter books. Another flashback hints at an incestuous relationship with her father and the tension between her parents. Four boys save her from a harassing, drunk man but rob him in the process. Lacking alternatives, she eventually moves into an abandoned house in Kensington with them. A friendship develops between Helen and one of the boys, Ben, who plans on starting his own band. Nonetheless, she remains a recluse, detests human contact, and leaves the city when a cat kills her rat.

The second section opens with a flashback to when she adopted the rat at school. Nightmares and flashbacks continue to plague her as she hitchhikes northward. The first person to offer her a ride tells her about the significance of rats in Hinduism. Panicked by a pass another driver makes at her, she forces the car to crash into a tree; she runs away, only to faint from hunger and fatigue behind a house.

The third section begins with a contrasting, bright depiction of Helen working as a waitress in a country inn. Its owners, Sam and Ruth McGregor, offer her a place to stay and encourage her to explore the area. Aware that she is troubled, they provide support without forcing her to voice her problems. Through reading and musing, Helen eventually finds the strength to talk about her disturbing experiences, invites her parents for lunch at Herdwick Arms, and confronts her father. Though her relationship with her parents does not change, Helen feels liberated and is content to remain with the McGregors. Later, she visits Hill Top, Beatrix Potter's home, and imagines discovering a manuscript titled "The Tale of One Bad Rat." Unfolding in a visual and literal style identical to Beatrix Potter's, this story-within-a-story mirrors Helen's experiences and has a happy ending, as does the graphic novel, which ends as Helen paints the breathtaking scenery with her massive rat beside her.

Characters
- *Helen Potter*, the protagonist, is a blond and blue-eyed teenager whose life roughly follows that of Beatrix Potter, her source of inspiration. Unloved by her mother and molested by her father, she is distant, distrustful, and artistic. Over the course of the graphic novel, she comes to terms with both her past and herself.
- *The Rat* is a two-year-old hooded rat adopted by Helen after she frees all the rats in school from their cages. Dying toward the end of the first section, the rat becomes Helen's imaginary, larger-than-life pet. The rat is a constant companion of Helen, except during her brief emotional release in the third section, and their closeness is highlighted by Helen's identification with rats as misunderstood creatures.
- *The Potters* are Helen's parents. Unable to get along, they are too occupied by their own problems to realize the effects of their behavior on their daughter. Maintaining a middle-class, unhappy household, Mrs. Potter never hesitates to remind Helen that she is unwanted, while Mr. Potter uses his daughter for pleasures missing from his marriage. Both are heavy smokers and drinkers.
- *Ben* is one of the boys who prevent a man from harassing Helen. A lanky, bespectacled teenager wearing torn jeans, he looks out for Helen and takes a keen interest in her artwork and knowledge about rats. He tries to kiss her, but he is pushed away. Ultimately, he fulfills his dream of becoming a famous musician by starting a band called "Rat Kings," a name alluding to one of his conversations with Helen.
- *Sam and Ruth McGregor* are the childless, cheerful, middle-aged innkeepers who offer Helen a job and the same room that Beatrix Potter once occupied in Herdwick Arms. In complete contrast to the Potters, both are sensitive and accommodating. While Sam provides facts regarding the countryside, Ruth gently encourages Helen to confront the roots of her sadness.

Artistic Style

Talbot's art is characterized by his attention to detail, which persists despite the diverse stories and styles of his works. Although the harsh realism discernible in many underground comics is preserved, *The Tale of One Bad Rat* is devoid of the travestying features that also prevail over many underground works. Because of the book's topic, extra effort is put into achieving accuracy, and the characters and settings are based on real-life models and locales. The rat, for example, emerged from sketches of Talbot's own pets that were rendered in a manner akin to Beatrix Potter's affectionate delineations of domestic animals. In addition to the recurrent references to Beatrix Potter's settings and drawings in the book, her style of art and page layouts are closely impersonated in the imaginary Beatrix Potter manuscript.

While Talbot regards Alfred Bestall's *Rupert Bear* comics as having the greatest impact on *The Tale of One Bad Rat*, the book also displays the influence of comics such as the cartoonlike works of Leo Baxendale and Dudley D. Watkins. Aspects of the book, including its grand landscapes, moments of expressive emotionality, and nightmare sequences, recall superhero comics by such artists as Jack Kirby, Jim Steranko, and Jim Starlin.

Although the panel transitions are kept simple, the arrangements of the panels are varied and subtly sophisticated. The consistently quadrilateral frames appear in different sizes and frequently overlap or are superimposed and function as partial backgrounds for the pages. Visual symbols are used to indicate Helen's inner state; these include dandelions, which allude to her changing emotions, and shattering glass, which appears during her outburst in the third section. In order to make *The Tale of One Bad Rat* accessible to a broader readership, Talbot claims to have employed a clear-line style. However, in accordance with his literary inclinations, the significance of the clear line for Talbot comes not from Hergé but from William Blake.

Themes
The nature and effects of child sexual abuse and the ways of overcoming it are the book's main concerns. Related problems include coping with fighting parents, living in dysfunctional families, and believing oneself to be different and bad. Given its focus on a teenage protagonist who succeeds in demonstrating her maturity and independence by freeing herself from her childhood issues, the book is similar to a coming-of-age novel. The matter-of-fact tone imbues the book with realism, making it easier for readers to identify with the story. Helen is not a victim but a survivor. Since her strength calls for admiration instead of pity, the story is affirmative and inspirational. Moreover, by tactfully avoiding a moralistic edge, Talbot enhances the possibilities for reader empathy.

In addition, an atemporal dimension is included through the interweaving of Beatrix Potter's life and stories. This intertextuality emphasizes the darker elements of her childhood and work, including the serious difficulties that all of Beatrix Potter's animal protagonists must overcome. Furthermore, these intertextual references exemplify Talbot's attempts to incorporate specifically British features into his works.

The soothing, inspirational characteristic of the Lake District and nature in general is an auxiliary theme. The importance of art as an expressive outlet is also underscored. Like many underground comics, *The Tale of One Bad Rat* explores a taboo topic. However, unlike many underground works, the book has a serious tone generally free of underlying jibes.

Impact
Regarded as one of the leading figures of the British underground comics movement, Talbot is known for experimenting with the potential of sequential art. His literal and visual innovations in cross-genre and nongenre storytelling make him one of the earliest, most significant graphic novelists, particularly as a representative of the British underground scene, which is often overshadowed by its American and French counterparts.

Appearing in 1995, *The Tale of One Bad Rat* heralded the boom in adult-oriented, powerful graphic novels. The nonautobiographical nature of *The Tale of One Bad Rat* exemplifies the ability of fictional graphic storytelling to be equally moving and effective. The praise that it attracted in spite of its atypical subject matter was indicative of the increasing critical interest in graphic novels tackling serious issues and frequently featuring ordinary but disturbed or marginalized protagonists.

Though occasionally erroneously placed in the children's section of libraries, the book nonetheless deals with a child's story with regard to both narration and illustration. Consequently, the book is also found in the libraries of counseling centers in the United Kingdom, the United States, and other countries, where it is used to spread awareness of child sexual abuse. As noted in its afterword, *The Tale of One Bad Rat* is an unusual graphic novel, even for Talbot, but he regards it as his most meaningful book because of its successful thematization of a problem that requires attention but is rarely discussed due to social taboos.

Maaheen Ahmed

Further Reading
B., David. *Epileptic* (2005).
Burns, Charles. *Black Hole* (2005).
Talbot, Bryan. *Alice in Sunderland* (2007).

Bibliography
Huxley, David. *Nasty Tales: Sex, Drugs, Rock 'n' Roll, and Violence in the British Underground*. Manchester, England: Critical Vision, 2001.
Sabin, Roger. *Adult Comics: An Introduction*. London: Routledge, 2011.
Sorensen, Lita. *Bryan Talbot*. New York: Rosen, 2005.
Talbot, Bryan. *The Art of Bryan Talbot*. New York: NBM, 2007.
_____. "Engraving the Void and Sketching Parallel Worlds: An Interview with Bryan Talbot." Interview by Roger Whitson. *ImageTexT Interdisciplinary Comics Studies* 3, no. 2 (2007). http://www.english.ufl.edu/imagetext/archives/v3_2/talbot.

See also: *Epileptic*; *Black Hole*; *Alice in Sunderland*; *The Adventures of Luther Arkwright*

TALES OF THE BEANWORLD:
A MOST PECULIAR COMIC BOOK EXPERIENCE

Author: Marder, Larry
Artist: Larry Marder (illustrator)
Publisher: Beanworld Press; Dark Horse Comics; Eclipse Comics
First serial publication: 1985-1993
First book publication: 1990 (issues 1-16); 2009

Publication History

Tales of the Beanworld, originally a black-and-white comic book series, was initially self-published by Larry Marder under the publisher name Beanworld Press. The production schedule was irregular, as Marder worked on the comic while also maintaining a full-time career in advertising. Although Marder intended to publish the comic twice per year, the first three issues were published in 1985. After 1986, issues 5-21 of *Tales of the Beanworld* were published by Eclipse Comics. Issue 5 indicates that the comic was to be published on a quarterly basis, but 1989 was the only year in which four issues were released. In 1990, *Tales of the Beanworld* was collected into four volumes published by Eclipse Comics; these included additional artwork and stories that were not part of the comic's original run. Dark Horse Comics published the full collection of *Tales of the Beanworld* in a two-volume, hardcover set titled *Larry Marder's Beanworld* in 2009. A volume of new stories, *Larry Marder's Beanworld* Book 3: *Remember Here When You Are There!* was published later that year.

Plot

Marder first developed the beans that populate *Tales of the Beanworld* for a series of editorial cartoons published in his campus newspaper during the 1970's. The Beanworld, which Marder refers to as a "process," began to take shape over time, particularly after the introduction of Gran'Ma'Pa as the sole food source for the beans. The stories incorporate elements from popular culture, ecology, and various world mythologies, particularly western Pueblo cosmology. *Tales of the Beanworld* is accessible to readers as young as eight, but the series is intended for readers of all ages. From the first issue, Marder cautioned readers not to look for deeper political meaning in the comic, noting that "it is what it is."

Tales of the Beanworld is an ecological fantasy about beans and those upon whom they rely for survival. The spiritual guardian Gran'Ma'Pa is the center of bean life. Each day, Mr. Spook assesses Gran'Ma'Pa to determine whether a "sprout-butt" will fall. If no sprout-butt falls, he declares a "goof-off day" during which beans relax and have fun. If a sprout-butt falls, Mr. Spook attempts to catch it with his trusty fork on the first bounce. The sprout-butt will be unhappy if he does not catch it quickly, and this will lead to bad-tasting chow at the end of the process.

Once he catches the sprout-butt, Mr. Spook leads the Chow Sol'jers over the legendary edge of Beanworld, into the Thin Lake, past the Four Realities, past

---

Larry Marder

Launched in 1984, *Tales of the Beanworld* made Larry Marder one of the great cult successes of the American alternative comics scene. Marder's characters, the Beans, are minimalistic figures living in a fictional universe. Marder's art in the series is extremely lively but consists of characters who are little more than elaborately constructed stick figures. The work also contains a great deal of slang and made-up language. His stories borrow freely from a number of mythologies and tell an elaborately detailed story with strong ecological overtones. The series was published through 1993 and then relaunched, on more than one occasion, as a series of special issues. In the 1990's Marder became involved with the Direct Line Group, a comics retailers organization, then became executive director of Image Comics and, later, president of McFarlane Toys. Marder remains an important cult author and has a particularly devoted fan following.

the Bone Zone, and finally in among the Hoi-Polloi Ring Herd. The Hoi-Polloi are one-armed gambling folk whose currency happens to be chow, the foodstuff of the beans. The Chow Sol'jers attack a ring of Hoi-Polloi and steal their chow. In exchange for the pain, loss, and suffering, the Chow Sol'jers leave behind the sprout-butt. The Hoi-Polloi surround the sprout-butt with love, and it eventually makes the ultimate sacrifice: turning itself into chow.

The Chow Sol'jers return to the Proverbial Sandy Beach, where they are greeted by Professor Garbanzo and the Boom'r Band. They deposit the fruits of their chow raid into the chowdown pool, the communal feeding place. The beans all soak in the pool, absorbing vitamins and nutrients through their heads and trace elements through their feet. Professor Garbanzo spends her time creating and repairing tools for the Chow Sol'jers and other beans, using the elements of the Four Realities as building materials.

The beans encounter various threats to their orderly way of life, eventually learning that they are not the center of the universe. As the beans discover, there is more to life and the "Big-Big-Picture" than their own food chain.

Characters

- *Mr. Spook*, a protagonist, is the hero of Beanworld and leader of the Chow Sol'jers. His origin story and appearance suggest that he is a mutated bean who was later trained to be a hero and assigned to the Beanworld. As the hero, he sometimes feels justified in taking action without consulting others. He has a trusty fork that serves as his weapon, but he must cope with the transformation of his fork halfway through the series.
- *Professor Garbanzo*, a.k.a. *Proffy*, a protagonist, is the bean charged with inventing, repairing tools, treating the wounded, and thinking. She wears a unique hat that is decorated with symbols representing the elements of the Four Realities. She is obsessed with finding a purpose for twinks, star-shaped items that are connected to the mysterious float factor phenomenon. A distractible but rational individual, she often tries to temper the rash actions of Mr. Spook.
- *The Boom'r Band* is a trio of musician beans and former Chow Sol'jers that provides music for dancing and recreation. The band uses the power of music to help heal injured beans and release some of the powers within the mystery pods.
- *Beanish* is a former Chow Sol'jer and the artist in residence of Beanworld. He earns his share of chow by contributing to the artistic culture of Beanworld, staging fabulous "look-see-shows" for the other beans. He has a secret friend named Dreamishness whom he meets in the sky each day.
- *Gran'Ma'Pa* is the spiritual and culinary guardian of Beanworld and the parent of the beans. This treelike entity is the source of sprout-butts, which are eventually converted into chow. Its condition must be interpreted by Mr. Spook, as it does not speak except occasionally through the sprout-butts.
- *Big Fish* is a large fish that swims through the skies looking for "notworms." He is the source of Mr. Spook's trusty fork, which had gotten stuck in his tongue and required the bean's assistance to remove.
- *Dreamishness* is Beanish's secret friend and muse. She lives in the midday sky and gives Beanish new knowledge and special powers in exchange for his efforts to help her to become something more.
- *Goofy Service Jerks* are creatures who reside in service stations that are part of the Big-Big-Picture and service many worlds besides Beanworld. They bring reproductive propellant to entities such as Gran'Ma'Pa who want to reproduce and expand their worlds. Like the other Goofy Jerks, they are composed of notworms.
- *Mr. Teach'm* is a teacher within the Big-Big-Picture beyond the Beanworld. He has three large growths resembling leaf fronds on top of his large-mouthed, floating head. He trained Mr. Spook to be a hero.
- *Goofy Survey Jerks* are Goofy Jerks who investigate customer satisfaction after the reproductive propellant has been delivered by the Goofy Service Jerks.

- *The Goofy Sermon Jerk* is the Goofy Jerk in charge of the service stations and the other, smaller Goofy Jerks.
- *Goofy Surveillance Jerks* are investigators who are sent out when a complaint reaches the Goofy Sermon Jerk.
- *Heyoka* is a former Chow Sol'jer who begins to talk and act backward after leaving the army. She asks Gran'Ma'Pa for help and eventually floats away to a service station.

Artistic Style

Marder's artistic style is highly iconic and abstract. The high-contrast black line work and occasional gray screen tones are often put in relief by the liberal use of white space on the page and within the frame. Few of the objects or characters have direct referents in the "real" world, although some characters, including Gran'Ma'Pa, Big Fish, and the beans themselves, are recognizable as abstractions of objects most readers would recognize. This abstract style easily conveys the idea that Beanworld is a fantasy world.

The beings and objects that are native to Beanworld tend to be smoother, rounder, and less angular than creatures or objects originating within the broader expanse of the Big-Big-Picture. Mr. Spook has sharp features and is in stark contrast to his surroundings, while the beans are rounded like their guardian, Gran'Ma'Pa. Beans are at times depicted differently based on their roles in Beanworld. When Beanish leaves the Chow Sol'jers, he uses native materials to alter his appearance and transform into the artist in residence of Beanworld; the Boom'r Band likely underwent a similar transformation. Professor Garbanzo's origin story is vague but clearly demonstrates her affinity with the elements of the Four Realities, from which she makes most of the tools for the beans. When she unlocks the door to her fix-it shop, her hat begins to sport images that represent the Four Realities.

Marder utilizes many one-page panels that include a great deal of detail and often depict simultaneous events, offering the reader a "big-big-picture" of the scene. Most of the panels are angular, but their diversity of size creates a dynamic visual style. He frequently takes a cinematic approach to framing, presenting extreme close-ups and similar camera-like angles. This dynamic and complex approach to framing meshes well with the abstract character and object designs.

Over the course of eight years, Marder produced twenty-one issues with a style that remains consistent throughout, even after the broader Big-Big-Picture and the characters who live there are introduced. This consistency is at least partly due to Marder's role as the sole writer and illustrator of the series.

Themes

The major themes of *Tales of the Beanworld* are interdependence, cooperation, and evolution. As Marder notes, the comic is about the affinity of life. The Beanworld begins as an orderly cycle of life in which every bean and adversary has a role to play. The early issues depict the beans as they struggle with a few minor external threats and with overabundance, exploring the ways in which these challenges shape their world and their understanding of it. By issue 8, it becomes clear that the Beanworld is part of the Big-Big-Picture; Beanworld is not the center of the universe, and there is more to life than keeping the food chain intact, though that is certainly important. Much of the rest of the series focuses on how the beans cope with their changing understanding of their place in the world. The gift of the Pod'l'pool Cuties—baby beans that need to be cared for and socialized—changes everything in Beanworld.

The comic also explores the ways in which different styles of management and leadership sometimes come into conflict. As the hero of Beanworld, Mr. Spook is accorded respect by all of the beans. However, both Beanish and Professor Garbanzo come into conflict with him because of his attitude toward the mystery pods and the float factor. Professor Garbanzo believes these phenomena are important to study and analyze, while Mr. Spook is much more conservative in his attitude toward the unknown. Mr. Spook attempts to ban all experimentation with the float factor without even calling a council meeting, while both Beanish and Professor Garbanzo continue to experiment behind his back, reasoning that there are potentially valuable uses for the float factor despite Mr. Spook's concerns about safety and fear of the unknown.

Impact

Tales of the Beanworld was first published during the late 1980's black-and-white boom in independent comics publishing. While Dave Sim is likely the best-known and most successful creator of that era, Marder has also been an important figure in independent self-publishing. Despite the relatively few published issues, the comic has been identified as a favorite by comics creators such as Scott McCloud, who praised it for being open to such a variety of interpretations. The reprinting of the original run of stories and the publication of a new volume attest to the lasting impact of *Tales of the Beanworld*.

June M. Madeley

Further Reading

McCloud, Scott. *Zot!* (1984-1990).
Millionaire, Tony. *Maakies* (1994-   ).
Smith, Jeff. *Bone* (1991-2004).

Bibliography

Boerner, Leigh Krietsch. "Ecology: A Story of Symbiosis." *Science* 324, no. 5932 (June, 2009): 1270.

McCloud, Scott. "Introduction." In *Larry Marder's Beanworld* Book 1: *Wahoolazuma!* Milwaukie, Ore.: Dark Horse Books, 2009.

Smith, Jeff. "Introduction." In *Larry Marder's Beanworld* Book 3: *Remember Here When You Are There!*, Milwaukie, Ore.: Dark Horse Books, 2009.

See also: *Zot!*

TAMARA DREWE

Author: Simmonds, Posy
Artist: Posy Simmonds (illustrator)
Publisher: Jonathan Cape
First serial publication: 2005-2007
First book publication: 2007

Publication History
Tamara Drewe and its predecessor *Gemma Bovery* were conceived when, after years of writing cartoons for *The Guardian*, author Posy Simmonds approached the editors of *The Guardian* with the desire to write a story with a definite ending. *Tamara Drewe* was originally published as a weekly cartoon strip, unfolding in 110 installments between September 17, 2005, and October 20, 2007. As the strip's newspaper run came to an end, Simmonds collected and edited the comic, creating the story that was published as a single volume by Jonathan Cape in 2007. Like *Gemma Bovery*, which was based on Gustave Flaubert's *Madame Bovary* (1856), *Tamara Drewe* began as a reworking of a nineteenth-century novel, Thomas Hardy's *Far from the Madding Crowd* (1874). While first drafts adhered closely to Hardy's plot, Simmonds began to deviate from Hardy's novel as her story developed, making *Tamara Drewe* entirely her own work.

Plot
As it is modeled after *Far from the Madding Crowd*, *Tamara Drewe* tells the story of a strong, proud young woman in the country who is wooed by three suitors and goes through heartbreaking experiences, emerging in a state of relative domestic bliss at the end. However, Simmonds's story closely represents Hardy's in only the briefest of summaries. Simmonds's twenty-first-century version opens at Stonefield, an idyllic writer's retreat near Ewedown, as Nicholas Hardiman's wife, Beth, discovers yet another of his affairs. Just as this drama comes to an end, a burglar alarm sounds at the nearby Winnards Farm, announcing the return of Tamara Drewe, who arouses the interests of everyone in the area.

Posy Simmonds. (By Ade Oshineye, via Wikimedia Commons)

Though her initial plan is to sell Winnards Farm after her mother's death, Tamara begins to enjoy her life there and decides to write her column from the country. On a trip back to London, she encounters Ben Sergeant, the former drummer of a hip rock band; they begin a relationship, soon becoming engaged. Ben spends most of his time in the country and becomes a spectacle for Jody Long and Casey Shaw, two Ewedown teenagers who often sit in the graffitied bus shelter near Tamara's house, waiting for opportunities to take pictures of the star with their cell phones.

On Valentine's Day, Jody and Casey's interest in Ben and Tamara's relationship turns from voyeuristic to criminal when a bored Jody breaks into Winnards, accesses Tamara's e-mail account, and sends a "valentine" to Ben, Nicholas, and Andy Cobb that reads, "I want to give you the biggest shagging of your life." The e-mail causes a break between Tamara and Ben. Nicholas is interested, however, and he begins pursuing Tamara. Uninterested at first, Tamara eventually invites Nicholas into her bed.

Jody and Casey discover the affair. Disgusted by this infidelity, Jody presses her friend to capture proof of Tamara and Nicholas's relationship and send it to Beth, which she does. As the entire situation approaches its breaking point, Jody sends another counterfeit e-mail from Tamara's computer, causing Ben to return to Ewedown.

Beth confronts her husband, demanding a divorce. Though Nicholas has confessed to Tamara that he wants to leave his wife, he is infuriated by the revelation that another writer, Glen Larson, has informed Beth that Nicholas lied about how a previous affair ended. Meanwhile, Ben discovers Jody breaking into Winnards and convinces her to promise to stop meddling. During this conversation, Ben's dog, Boss, chases some nearby cows. In their anxiety, the cattle stampede over a hill and down to where Glen and Nicholas are heatedly arguing. A shoving match ends with Nicholas falling and being trampled by the cattle.

In the aftermath of this tragedy, Jody is found dead from huffing air duster, her way of celebrating for having finally met Ben. Ewedown is barraged by television crews and reporters; the news from the village portrays Tamara as a man-eater. In her desperation, she turns to Andy, who has quietly pursued her from the beginning of the novel.

Characters
- *Tamara Drewe* is a young, beautiful columnist who returns to her hometown of Ewedown. Though charmed by the country, she seeks out companionship that is advantageous to her aspirations of celebrity. Her relationships with Ben and Nicholas disrupt both rural and marital tranquility, with disastrous results.
- *Beth Hardiman* is the plump, fiftysomething proprietor of Stonefield. She is responsible for the retreat's effortless peace and tranquility, constantly nurturing and encouraging her husband, the writers, and everyone else by offering jobs, food, dictation, and kind words.
- *Nicholas Hardiman* is a successful writer of popular crime novels that fund Stonefield's existence. He hides his deep dissatisfaction with his career and his marriage to Beth behind a facade of smug superiority and habitual womanizing.
- *Andy Cobb* is a self-professed "loser" and a product of the dying town of Ewedown. His parents once owned Winnards Farm, and he once owned a design studio. Bereft of both, he works for the Hardimans as a gardener and handyman during the day; by night, he drinks at the local pub and laments the influx of moneyed Londoners. He is attracted to Tamara, but she continually rejects or ignores him.
- *Jody Long* is a spunky but bored teenager who is determined to make "something" happen in Ewedown. Obsessed with Tamara's boyfriend, Ben, she and her friend Casey break into Winnards Farm. Their meddling accelerates the adult dramas going on around them.

Artistic Style

The initial publication of *Tamara Drewe* as a weekly newspaper cartoon greatly influenced the form and content of the work. The pages are square, having been created to fit within the allotted three-column space in *The Guardian*. Every page is a ministory or sketch in and of itself, and most pages begin and end with a "hook": a humorous comment, a mysterious statement, or a significant look, all meant to keep readers waiting for the next week's installment. Limited to 110 episodes by her contract, Simmonds uses long narrative passages to develop the multiple plotlines. Traditional layouts featuring speech balloons are frequently used when a character is reminiscing or when an intimate conversation is taking place. Traditional panel layouts are often interspersed with page-long or -tall illustrations with irregular borders.

Simmonds's artistic style is in keeping with her careful study of human relationships and reactions. *Tamara Drewe*'s pages are full of close-ups that emphasize facial expressions and postures. Crowd scenes such as Nicholas's Christmas book signing are excellent portrayals of the interactions of a certain subset of literary society. However, Simmonds is also a master of settings, and many pages depict quaint, rural landscapes reminiscent of the type used by Hardy: open spaces with hills, gnarled trees, stone barns, paddocks, and cattle.

Colors in *Tamara Drewe* are muted, with many greens and browns used for outdoor scenes, warm oranges for scenes of domestic comfort, and gray-blues for memories. Only teenagers and gossip magazines are colored with bright reds, pinks, and yellows, seemingly indicating that anyone wearing these colors is an interloper upon the rural tranquility of Ewedown.

Themes

Taking a cue from Hardy's novel, *Tamara Drewe* explores the literary theme of rural life versus urban life. The representations of and relationships between country and city found in British literature are updated and played out in a contemporary setting. Ewedown is a dying town, kept alive by rich Londoners who own vacation homes there. What Ewedown affords them is what Stonefield sells as a commodity: the tranquility and nostalgia of a supposedly simpler life. As indicated by the Drewe family's ownership of Winnards Farm, once the property of the Cobb family, an agricultural economy has given way to one based upon a twenty-first-century version of landed gentry, who hire the local "peasantry" to do most of the work on their hobby farms. As do many of Hardy's works, *Tamara Drewe* shows a rural Britain at a time of change in the interaction between rural and urban life.

Another powerful theme, one that separates Simmonds's work from Hardy's, is the novel's honest portrayal of teen culture. The slow death of Ewedown particularly affects the lives of its teens, and this lack of opportunity fuels Jody's boredom and, thus, her delinquency. Simmonds captures these adolescents' lingo and realistically depicts Jody and Casey's family lives, discussions of sex, worship of popular culture and its stars, and experimentation with drugs. When Beth provides Ewedown's teens with a place to gather after Jody's death, Simmonds seems to promote providing teens with more responsibility and more socially acceptable methods of entertainment.

Tamara Drewe is concerned with relationships between men and women, but since three of the four voices narrating the novel are female, the commentary often turns to an exploration of issues that particularly affect women. For example, Tamara's nose job implicates standards of beauty, Beth's nurturing actions invite discussions of domesticity versus career, and Jody and Casey's discussions of sex often include typical judgments of female sexuality.

Impact

Though her popularity is firmly established in Britain, Simmonds is less known in the United States. With its interesting position as both a popular episodic cartoon and a revision of classic literature, *Tamara Drewe* does not fit any particular niche. In a literary sense, the novel takes part in the rash of popular revisions of canonical literature that has taken place in the twenty-first century. Simply by using Hardy as a source of inspiration, Simmonds includes him in her simultaneous mockery and appreciation of a whole array of literary traditions. More strictly in the world of graphic storytelling, *Tamara Drewe* mixes modes that carry certain stigmas or prestige (cartooning is simple or for marketing purposes; the classics are "good" literature; columnist journalism is fluffy) and by doing so lends credence to the increasing perception of graphic novels as literature.

Films

Tamara Drewe. Directed by Stephen Frears. Ruby Films, 2010. This film adaptation stars Gemma Arterton as Tamara Drewe, Dominic Cooper as Ben Sergeant, Tamsin Greig and Roger Allam as Beth and Nicholas Hardiment, Luke Evans as Andy Cobb, Bill Camp as Glen McCreavy, and Jessica Barden as Jody Long. Many of the actors bear striking resemblances to their graphic novel counterparts, and the film differs from the graphic novel only in subtle changes in plot, characterization, and names. Glen's character is also used more often for comic relief, and he and Beth begin an affair.

Anna Thompson Lohmeyer

Further Reading

Simmonds, Posy. *Gemma Bovery* (1999).
_____. *Literary Life* (2003).

Bibliography

Chute, Hillary L. *Graphic Women: Life Narrative and Contemporary Comics*. New York: Columbia University Press, 2010.

Imlah, Mick. "Tamara Drewe's Wessex." *The Times Literary Supplement*, November, 2007.

Simmonds, Posy. "Posy Simmonds." Interview by Daneet Steffens. *Mslexia* 37 (April/May/June, 2008). https://secure.svr9-speedyservers.com/~mslexia/magazine/interviews/interview_37.php.

See also: *Gemma Bovery; La Perdida; The Summer of Love*

Tank Girl

Author: Martin, Alan
Artist: Jamie Hewlett (illustrator); Chris Chalenor (colorist)
Publisher: Penguin; Dark Horse Comics
First serial publication: 1988-1995
First book publication: 1993-1996

Publication History

Jamie Hewlett and Alan Martin met in the 1980's and began working on the black-and-white comic *Tank Girl*. *Tank Girl*'s original appearance was a one-page advertisement in a fanzine *Atomtan* and was simply an image of Tank Girl, drawn by Hewlett and captioned with the phrase "She'll Break Your Balls and Your Back." The *Tank Girl* series was first published in 1988 in the first issue of *Deadline*, a British magazine started by Steve Dillon and Brett Ewins and published by Tom Astor that provided a forum for new comics. Penguin purchased the rights to *Tank Girl*, publishing the series in book format in the United Kingdom; in 1991, Dark Horse Comics acquired the rights to publish *Tank Girl* in the United States. Penguin and Dark Horse Comics changed the format to color, bringing Chris Chalenor into the project.

The *Tank Girl* issues originally published in *Deadline* were collected into three volumes—*Tank Girl: The Collection*, *Tank Girl 2*, and *Tank Girl 3*—which comprise the "classic" *Tank Girl* comics created by the team of Martin and Hewlett. The miniseries *Tank Girl: The Odyssey* (1995), written by Peter Milligan and illustrated by Hewlett, and *Tank Girl: Apocalypse* (1995-1996), featuring the work of Alan Grant, Andy Pritchett, and Philip Bond, were collected and reprinted in 2003. A *Tank Girl* comic based on the film adaptation of the series employed Tedi Sarafian's screenplay and was written by Milligan and drawn by Pritchett. While Martin and Hewlett were credited with character creation, they were not involved with the writing or artwork. *Tank Girl* was revitalized in 2007, and a slew of graphic novels and miniseries have been published, written by Martin, and, for the most part, illustrated by Rufus Dayglo. Given the seminal nature of the original series, only its collections are highlighted in the volumes section.

Jamie Hewlett in 2014, signing copies of "The Cream of Tank Girl" at a Tank Girl lecture at the British Library. (By GorillazMonkeyZ, via Wikimedia Commons)

Plot

Tank Girl had only a vague plot in its incarnation from 1988 to 1995. The basic concept, which Hewlett and Martin sometimes ignored, is that Tank Girl works for an unspecified, potentially government agency that allows her to embark on missions riding in a tank in near-future Australia. She often fails at these missions and spends most of her time drinking, cursing, fighting, and having sex with her kangaroo boyfriend, Booga.

Considered to be part of both science fiction and female superhero genres, *Tank Girl* has only two major science-fiction elements: its futuristic setting and a kangaroo that has mutated into compatibility with a human woman. (The comic series includes multiple unexplained kangaroo-type beings; incidentally, the movie places the action in a science-fiction setting that includes a tribe of kangaroo-humans who have mutated through human intervention.) The other genre with which *Tank Girl* is often identified (female superhero) is also a somewhat misleading affiliation given that Tank Girl has no superhuman powers and excels at what she does simply by being stronger, faster, and better than anyone she encounters. The character of Tank Girl is most appropriately labeled an antihero because she is in the habit of committing a number of mostly victimless crimes that advance her agenda.

Tank Girl achieved a cult following and was quickly branded, attracting a number of musicians. Adam Ant provided a blurb for the first collection, and Graham Coxon of Blur provided one for the second collection.

In the first graphic novel, Tank Girl attacks a group of barbeque-crashing kangaroos, killing them and declaring herself a bounty hunter. The next issues involve Tank Girl failing to deliver a consignment of colostomy bags to the prime minister of Australia, being tracked by bounty hunters for her failure, stealing a religious relic (God's Dressing Gown), having sex with Booga, killing ninjas, and meeting an Aborigine. In 1989, two new characters, Sub Girl and Jet Girl, were introduced, and they joined Tank Girl in causing mayhem.

In "The Australian Job," Tank, Sub, Jet, Booga, Stevie, Camp Koala, Mr. Precocious, and Squeaky the Toy Rat go to see the "ultimate criminal mastermind" in order to pull off their idea of a major heist: stealing beer from the Mafia in Sydney. After committing the robbery, they promptly drink all the beer. Tank Girl and Booga then spend some time in what they consider to be domestic bliss: drinking, having sex, and making tea.

Tank Girl 2 is more disjointed than the first collection, allowing Tank Girl to simply enjoy herself while committing mostly petty crime. The issues include several parodies; however, there are two multi-part story lines: "Summer Love Sensation," in which Tank Girl carjacks and kills a man for his convertible, and "Blue Helmet," in which Tank Girl robs a convenience store.

Volumes

- *Tank Girl: The Collection* (1993). Collects issues published in *Deadline* from 1988 to 1990, including episodes such as "Whatever Happened to Good Intentions?," "Dumpster," "Big Mouth Strikes Again!," "Bob's Your Uncle," "Here Today, Gone Tomorrow," "Built Like a Car," "The Australian Job," "Hard Boiled," "Up Jumped a Jolly Swag Man," "The Preposterous Bollox of the Situation," and "The Day Nothing Happened."
- *Tank Girl 2* (1995). Collects issues published in *Deadline* from 1990 to 1992, including episodes such as "I've Got Friends at Bell's End," "Force Ten to Ringarooma Bay," "Half a Pound of Tupenny Rice," "Jet Gurl In: Hairy P——," "Summer Love Sensation," "Sunflower," "Askey and Hunch," "Blue Helmet," "F——ed Up Afro Zombies from Nowhere," "The Fall and Rise and Fall and the Ship in a Bottle," "Hewlett and Martin's the Guide to Joy!," and "Booga's Christmas Carol."
- *Tank Girl 3* (1996). Collects the last issues published in the original *Deadline* series, published from 1992 to 1005.

Characters

- *Tank Girl*, a.k.a. *Rebecca Buck*, is the protagonist of the series. Her appearance changes throughout the series, but some of her general characteristics are a thin frame, a mostly bald head with brightly colored hair as an accent, and a willingness to be naked. Her joys in life are simple: violence, sex, and alcohol.
- *Booga* is the kangaroo-mutant boyfriend of Tank Girl. He was once a member of a roving kangaroo gang, but he failed his initiation when he stayed with Tank Girl after a marathon sex session. He is a follower and is often assigned (by Tank Girl) to unpleasant tasks.
- *Jet Girl* is one of Tank Girl's friends. She has black hair, but otherwise she looks very similar

to Tank Girl. She makes only brief appearances, although in a letter home to her mother, Tank Girl mentions her as a childhood friend. Her main purpose is to pilot a jet and help Tank Girl with her adventures.
- *Sub Girl* is one of Tank Girl's friends. Hair color aside, she also looks like Tank Girl. Like Jet Girl, she is mentioned in Tank Girl's letter home to her mother. She pilots a submarine and helps Tank Girl.
- *Stevie* is Tank Girl's former boyfriend. He is a blond-haired Aborigine who Tank Girl uses on occasion for her own benefit. He owns a convenience store and chain-smokes. He is responsible for some tension in the series because Booga is jealous of him.
- *Camp Koala* is a brown talking stuffed animal. He dies tragically in a baseball game that involves live grenades. He is replaced with another stuffed koala, but he makes a few appearances as an angel after his death.
- *Squeaky Toy Rat* is a toy rat that squeaks. He helps with the beer heist in Sydney.
- *Mr. Precocious* is an oddly drawn stuffed animal that speaks; he may be a pink elephant with only two feet. He assists in the Sydney beer heist.

Artistic Style

Tank Girl began as a black-and-white comic in a magazine. Color was added when the comics were gathered into graphic novels. Possibly because of this, the artwork includes broad strokes and a lot of contrast. There are also often brightly and single-colored backgrounds for scenes.

Hewlett's drawing style has the visual effect of graffiti and psychedelic-punk visual art. It mimics the comic's style and lack of coherence. The comic uses bubbles for lettering, which is in all capital letters, but there are also block-style colored words, such as "MASH," "STAB," and "SQUIRT," to indicate actions. Hewlett often uses these to add small humorous details. Interspersed with the strips are often full-page images or scrapbook-style collages that include fake Polaroid photos.

The early issues are drawn with a tight and sharp style. Most pages have a complex layout and appear "busy," with up to twelve panels of varying sizes, but other pages are a single image. The images and layout are used to enhance the chaotic style.

Hewlett's style changes and becomes experimental as the episodes progress. The page layouts still vary and retain their anarchistic style, but the images become rounder and the coloring is less brash and bold. The colors are watercolor in style, with muted tones and backgrounds that appear to have a "wash" over them, generating blue or green tones.

Themes

Tank Girl became a major influence on "riot grrrls," Guerrilla Girls, and other feminist groups who celebrate "girl culture" and work against the patriarchy in power. Tank Girl is rebellious and fights for what she wants. She takes on stereotypical male characteristics such as cursing, committing crimes, and ignoring rules that woman are generally expected to follow. Tank Girl is aggressive and sexual but still feminine. She has sex with men, women, and kangaroo mutants. She is an action hero who is somehow both loved and feared.

The plot follows a feminist bent by letting Tank Girl do what she wants to do; she is the aggressor in her relationships, she confides to her mother that she has no plans to marry, and she does not cook or clean.

All of the characters fall in line with Tank Girl's presentation of feminist ideology. Jet Girl and Sub Girl, while followers, are also riot grrrls. They fight and take part in the legal and illegal shenanigans that Tank Girl endorses. Booga and other male characters, such as Stevie, follow her lead and often take on traditionally female roles: Booga is responsible for cooking, cleaning, and making tea. The only "bad guys" involved are just that: guys. Tank Girl does not battle other women. Instead, there is a sense of camaraderie among the women of the series.

Impact

Tank Girl belongs to the Modern Age of comics. Its popularity reflected the rise of riot grrrl and small comics' presses. In the 1990's, self-published comics known as "zines," with a circulation generally no greater than five thousand, often presented gender-based topics and helped to usher in the development of riot grrrls and bring them to the attention of mass media. *Tank Girl* became part of the daily popular culture and was discussed in the news. Thus, *Tank Girl*, with its counterculture appeal, was often emulated during this time period.

Another comics character that has used *Tank Girl* as a blueprint, albeit with less success, is Lady Death. *Barb Wire* (1996) was a film that attempted to capitalize on *Tank Girl*'s popularity. Despite *Tank Girl*'s underground success, the comic never rose above its cult status, even after the movie of the same name. Tank Girl's willingness to stand up for herself was also noted by groups in England who opposed Prime Minister Margaret Thatcher's antihomosexual legislation. They created T-shirts with Tank Girl's likeness for a march against Section 28.

Films

Tank Girl. Directed by Rachel Talalay. Trilogy Entertainment Group, 1995. This film adaptation stars Lori Petty as Tank Girl and Malcolm McDowell as Kesslee. The film differs from the series in that the kangaroo mutants are given a backstory and Tank Girl first has a human boyfriend, living on a commune with a group fighting against the government entity Water and Power that controls the postapocalyptic world in which the story is set. The world in the movie is similar to those in *Mad Max* (1979) and *Blade Runner* (1982), but the images evoke the original *Tank Girl* as it exists in the comics world. The movie began with a blueprint from Hewlett and Martin but was instead based on a screenplay by Tedi Sarafian.

Katherine Sanger

Further Reading

Breeden, Jennie. *The Devil's Panties* (2001-   ).
Morrison, Grant, and Philip Bond. *Johnny the Homicidal Maniac* (1995-1997).
_____. *Kill Your Boyfriend* (1995).

Bibliography

Driscoll, Catherine. "Girl Culture, Revenge, and Global Capitalism: Cybergirls, Riot Grrls, Spice Girls." *Australian Feminist Studies* 14, no. 29 (1999): 173-193.

Helford, Elyce Rae. "Postfeminism and the Female Action-Adventure Hero: Positioning Tank Girl." In *Future Females, The Next Generation: New Voices and Velocities in Feminist Science Fiction Criticism*, edited by Marleen S. Barr. Lanham, Md.: Rowman & Littlefield, 2000.

McGovern, Celeste. "You've Come a Long Way, Baby." *Alberta Report/Newsmagazine* 22, no. 33 (July, 1995): 24.

Romney, Jonathan. "Tanked Up on Attitude." *New Statesman and Society* 8, no. 358 (June, 1995): 35.

See also: *Love and Rockets*; *Omaha the Cat Dancer*; *Sin City*

TANTRUM

Author: Feiffer, Jules
Artist: Jules Feiffer (illustrator)
Publisher: Alfred A. Knopf
First book publication: 1979

Publication History

Originally labeled a "comic book novel," as the term "graphic novel" had not yet been popularized, Jules Feiffer's *Tantrum* was first published as a black-and-white book-length cartoon story by Alfred A. Knopf in 1979 under the Borzoi imprint. *Tantrum* was one of the first adult graphic novels published by a trade publisher and was afforded standard trade-book treatment. *Tantrum* is also significant in that it was not serialized prior to the book's publication. The novel was reprinted by Fantagraphics Books in 1997. The Fantagraphics edition, also in black and white, includes an introduction by Neil Gaiman and is paperbound, while the Knopf book is hardbound.

Jules Feiffer, American cartoonist, seated with proof sheets from Sick Sick Sick (1958), his first book. (By Dick DeMarsico, World Telegram staff photographer, via Wikimedia Commons)

Plot

In chapter 1, "Metamorphosis," Leo, the forty-two-year-old protagonist, sits at an upper-story window, apparently contemplating a jump. He finds no comfort in his success and family life because they offer "no danger, no mystery." His wife's statement that he is a "decent, thoughtful, responsive man" frightens him. When asked what he wants, Leo responds, "Mommy!" Unable to cope with the pressures of adulthood, he transforms into a two-year-old. His wife, Carol, takes him to a doctor, who refuses to believe that Leo is not a normal toddler.

In chapter 2, "Homecoming," unable to get solace from his wife and children, Leo visits his parents; they refuse to believe that the two-year-old they see is their middle-aged son. Leo tries repeatedly to enter the house and even considers burning it down. Finally, he decides to stop pestering his parents and leaves.

In chapter 3, "Plans," Leo visits his brother, Charlie, and asks for help. Although he is a successful businessman, Charlie is bogged down with an impending divorce, extramarital affairs, and a cocaine habit. He is unable to help Leo. In chapter 4, "Rescue," Leo's sisters, Norah and Natalie, try to help him but end up fighting pointlessly between themselves. In chapter 5, "The Law," Leo returns home but finds his family in turmoil: His daughter, Ruthie, is dealing hashish, and his son has impregnated a girl. Considering a divorce, Leo and Carol consult a lawyer. When the lawyer tells Leo that alimony law applies to him even though he has the appearance of a child, he flees in terror.

The next chapter, "The Others," begins with Leo running aimlessly. He is picked up by an ambulance and taken to "the others": other middle-aged people who have reverted to two-year-olds. The others attempt to convince Leo to join them, but he refuses.

In chapter 7, "Flight," Leo fights off more middle-aged two-year-olds and stows away on a flight to Palm Springs, where he hopes to find his sister-in-law, Joyce. In chapter 8, "Dream's End," Leo finds Joyce, but she

> **Jules Feiffer**
>
> A legendary figure in the world of cartooning due to his more than forty years at *The Village Voice*, Jules Feiffer is an acclaimed novelist, playwright, screenwriter, children's book author, and graphic novelist. Feiffer broke into the world of comics in the 1940's as an assistant to Will Eisner before turning to the arena of editorial cartooning in the 1950's. His work for the *Village Voice* made him a literary celebrity in New York and collections of his strip—including *Sick, Sick, Sick* and *The Explainers*—were important cultural landmarks. *Passionella*, originally published in 1957, was one of the earliest proto-graphic novels and retold the Cinderella story in a Hollywood setting. *Tantrum*, his most important graphic novel, tells the story of a career man who reverts to the form of a child. Feiffer's drawings are incredibly loose and sketchy, as if produced very quickly, and he is widely praised for his dialogue and characterization.

is no longer the beautiful woman that he remembers and lusts after; rather, she is starving herself. Worried, Leo implores Joyce to seek medical attention. She refuses, but Leo feeds her by the spoonful, and she gains weight. Leo wakes in chapter 9, "Epiphany," to discover that Joyce has gone into the desert to starve and punish herself. Leo finds her, and Joyce finally begins to eat. She becomes the voluptuous woman Leo desires, but now Leo is aging at a quick pace. He realizes that he cannot bear the responsibility of another person's happiness and returns to New York City, landing on the doorstep of Charlie's mistress, Miss Swallow. Miss Swallow takes Leo into her home, deceived by a note stating that the two-year-old is Leo's son.

In the next chapter, "Epiphany II," Miss Swallow finally gives Leo the attention he craves, nurturing and playing with him as one would a toddler. However, when they bathe together, Leo becomes attracted to Miss Swallow and reverts back to his forty-two-year-old body while in the bathtub. Leo flees, screaming.

In Chapter 11, "Comeuppance," Leo returns home to find his apartment in shambles. Carol refuses to eat. Leo makes the children clean the apartment and then returns to sitting on the windowsill as he had before. He begs Carol for forgiveness and vows to try harder to make their life work, but Carol does not want him to try harder. Like Leo, she is tired of all the responsibility and wants to be a two-year-old. They both revert to their two-year-old selves, and the story closes as Leo and Carol leave the apartment, deciding to offer their children financial but not emotional support.

Characters

- *Leo*, the protagonist, is a middle-aged man who transforms himself into a two-year-old through the force of his will, as he no longer wants to accept the responsibilities associated with being a husband and father.
- *Carol* is Leo's wife. She is initially critical of Leo's transition into a toddler but later succeeds in also becoming a two-year-old.
- *Phil* is Leo's teenage son. He impregnates a girl.
- *Ruthie* is Leo's daughter. She is suspected of dealing hashish.
- *Charles* is Leo's brother, to whom Leo goes for help. He physically resembles Feiffer. Laden with problems of his own, including a divorce, he is unable to help Leo.
- *Joyce* is Leo's sister-in-law, whom he desires. When Leo visits her, he finds she is starving herself.
- *Miss Swallow* is Charles's secretary, with whom he is having an affair. Leo is attracted to her.
- *Norah* and *Natalie* are Leo's sisters. They try to help him but are ineffective.

Artistic Style

Feiffer was a seasoned cartoonist by the time he created *Tantrum*, and it was his practice to draw panels in pencil first and then ink over them. However, to convey the urgency Feiffer deemed necessary in *Tantrum*, he eliminated the pencil step and drew directly in ink. If a drawing seemed wrong, he redrew it on another piece of paper, cut it out with a knife, and pasted it onto the background. Almost without exception, *Tantrum* is composed of single-panel pages, another departure for the artist. Feiffer's earlier comics typically use multiple panels or multiple drawings within a single panel to create an effect, but in *Tantrum*, large single panels better convey the immediacy required. The drawings focus on characters, with only intimations of backgrounds, further creating a sense of urgency and isolation. The bold pen lines strike a sharp contrast to the white background, and the unpolished drawings magnify the sense that the story could be anyone's midlife crisis. To express a sense of futility, Feiffer often places characters at one end of a large white page, thus conveying their emotions and feelings of powerlessness.

Themes

The resolution of a midlife crisis is one theme of *Tantrum*. With the exception of Leo's children and parents, all the characters face dilemmas posed in middle age. Charles's marriage and career are in ruins, although he appears ignorant of the havoc in his life; his estranged wife, Joyce, starves herself in order to become more attractive. Leo reverts to toddlerhood to rid himself of his responsibilities. However, he finds it difficult to enjoy infancy because he responds to women in a sexual way and not the way a child would. Leo's return to middle age is determined by a sexual response while bathing with his brother's mistress. Only Carol seems comfortable in her age for most of the book, caring for her two children and attempting to help Leo mature. In the end, while Charles copes with the hardships of middle age by having an affair and Leo's sisters meet the challenge with hopelessness, Leo and Carol respond to middle age by utterly rejecting it.

Another theme of the book is responsibility to others. Although Leo tries to be a good man and provide for his family, responsibility wears on him, making him unhappy and dissatisfied. His attempts to be a responsible parent are shown to have failed; his daughter deals drugs, and his son has impregnated a girl. Ultimately, both Leo and Carol reject midlife responsibilities and return to infancy. By the end of the novel, they acknowledge their responsibility to financially support their children, but they accept that they can no longer guide their children emotionally.

Impact

At the time of *Tantrum*'s original publication, comics were mainly superhero stories, romance stories, funny animal stories, and adaptations of popular films. Comic strips, appearing both in newspapers and as collections, covered the same ground as comic books, although some offered political perspectives. *Tantrum* told a story different from those to which readers of the time were accustomed and delivered an unusual message: Life is difficult, some things cannot be resolved, and parents can do only so much for their children. The book also made an impact with its presentation, jarring the reader with its unpolished, direct drawing style and bleak visual tone. As most stories told in comic book form at that time resolved neatly and without complications, featured pleasant or funny drawings, and were packaged in pleasing colors, *Tantrum* was ahead of its time.

Marketed as a "comic book novel," *Tantrum* sold reasonably well but not well enough to be reprinted. In general, the book-buying public was not ready for comic books that explored serious issues. However, as the graphic novel form gained recognition and respectability in the mid-1990's, *Tantrum* was acknowledged as both a stepping stone to respectability for the genre and an important work in itself. Coupled with Feiffer's memoir of his early days in comics, *The Great Comic Book Heroes* (1965), *Tantrum* secured his place as a seminal figure in the history of the graphic novel.

Stephen Weiner

Further Reading

Burns, Charles. *Black Hole* (2005).
Eisner, Will. *The Contract with God Trilogy: Life on Dropsie Avenue* (2006).
Lemire, Jeff. *The Complete Essex County* (2007-2008).

Bibliography

Feiffer, Jules. *Backing into Forward: A Memoir*. New York: Doubleday, 2010.

_____. "The Jules Feiffer Interview." Interview by Gary Groth. *The Comics Journal* 124 (1988).

Weiner, Stephen. *Faster Than a Speeding Bullet: The Rise of the Graphic Novel*. New York: NBM, 2003.

See also: *A Contract with God, and Other Tenement Stories*; *The Complete Essex County*; *Black Hole*

30 Days of Night

Author: Niles, Steve
Artist: Ben Templesmith (illustrator); Robbie Robbins (letterer)
Publisher: IDW Publishing
First serial publication: 2002
First book publication: 2003

Publication History

30 Days of Night was originally published as a three-part limited series by IDW Publishing in 2002 and collected as a graphic novel in 2003. While Steve Niles and Ben Templesmith pitched their vampire story to a number of publishers, they experienced difficulty interesting a major publishing house in the project, given the extreme violence inherent in the story line. The comic was also originally envisioned as a film, but that idea was initially unsuccessful as well. Sensing that the project would be sellable, IDW Publishing ultimately agreed to publish the comic book as a limited series, which the authors could then use to pitch a feature film. The comic book was enormously successful and led to a feature-film adaptation as well as numerous comic book sequels, some produced by the original creative partners and some by Niles with other artists. These comics and graphic novels were nominated for several Eisner Awards. *30 Days of Night* was the first major project for both Niles and Templesmith and helped them become two of the most highly sought-after creators in the horror comic genre.

Plot

Like other cities in the extreme Northern Hemisphere, Barrow, Alaska, is subject to periods of absolute darkness for up to thirty days. When the story begins on November 17, 2001, the sun will not rise again over the town until December 17. The local sheriff, Eben Olemaun, and his deputy and wife, Stella Olemaun, find that all of the town's cell phones have been stolen and destroyed. Meanwhile in Louisiana, a psychic, Miss Judith, and her son are troubled by an e-mail inviting unknown people, including a man named Vincente, to a mysterious gathering in Barrow.

Steve Niles

A leading figure in the resurgence of horror comics in the 2000's, writer Steve Niles is best known for writing *30 Days of Night* (with artist Ben Templesmith), a graphic novel in which vampires travel to a town in Alaska where the sun does not rise for thirty days. The work was originally written as a screenplay and only optioned for the big screen after it was produced in comic book form. Niles is also the writer of Criminal Macabre, a horror comic featuring a paranormal investigator in the tradition of John Constantine. In the mid-2000's, Niles collaborated with singer Rob Zombie to produce comics through IDW, including The Nail and Bigfoot. In the realm of mainstream American comics, Niles has worked extensively with DC Comics, notably on the Batman miniseries *Gotham County Line* and *Simon Dark* (both with Scott Hampton), and *Batman: Gotham After Midnight* (with Kelley Jones).

The Olemauns are watching the final sunset when they get a call informing them of a disturbance at the local diner. At the diner a mysterious man is attempting to order alcohol, which is illegal in Barrow, as well as a bowl of raw hamburger meat. After refusing to leave, the man is taken into custody. At the same time, Gus Lambert, who is in charge of the telecommunications center of the town, is disturbed to find equipment vandalized. When confronted by several strange men, he tells them that the center controls all signals in and out of Barrow. He is disemboweled by one of the men, who then proceed to destroy the rest of the center.

At the sheriff's office the imprisoned stranger becomes increasingly belligerent, claiming that a group of people are coming to destroy the town. When the man bends the bars of his cell to attack those in the office, Stella shoots him several times in the head, killing him. Investigating the dead man's claims, the

Comic book illustrator Ben Templesmith at a signing for Choker, *his collaboration with writer Ben McCool, at Midtown Comics East in Manhattan.* (By Luigi Novi, via Wikimedia Commons)

Olemauns drive to the telecommunications center, where they find Lambert's head on a pole and the center destroyed. Eben notices a strange light in the distance and, looking through binoculars, sees a group of vampires approaching the town. They drive back to warn the town, but the massacre has already begun.

In Barrow, the vampires quickly kill as many humans as possible, literally tearing many of them apart and throwing their bodies to the side. Some humans try to escape, to no avail; others try to fight back, but they soon find that the vampires are largely immune to gunshots. In Fairbanks, Alaska, Taylor, Miss Judith's son, rents a helicopter to collect evidence about the vampire massacre.

A few survivors, including the Olemauns, hide in an industrial furnace for several weeks. Running low on food, Eben goes to collect more and is confronted by a large vampire, who tries to find out where the others are hiding. Eben shoots the vampire, only wounding him, and escapes back to the hideout.

The vampires postpone the rest of their hunt to welcome Vincente, an older vampire and clearly one of their leaders. Roderick Marlowe, the vampire who organized the hunt, welcomes Vincente and tells him that he thinks Barrow would make the perfect place to hunt because of the lack of sunlight. Vincente is not pleased by the idea, believing that it would expose the vampires to greater scrutiny and lead to further persecution of the vampire community. He fights and kills Marlowe and then demands that the remaining humans be killed and the town burned down.

In the hideout, one of the survivors, who has been scratched by a vampire, complains of feeling cold; he becomes a vampire and attacks the group. The others kill him, but not before Eben, who has a plan, uses a syringe to extract blood from the vampire. Outside, Vincente sees someone taking pictures from the helicopter. He jumps on it, forcing it to crash, but not before it transmits data back to Miss Judith.

Realizing that all the townsfolk will die unless something is done, Eben injects himself with vampire blood. He is quickly transformed into a vampire and goes outside to confront Vincente and the others. Although it seems that Eben is no match for the ancient vampire, his love for the town gives him the strength to kill Vincente and several other vampires. He orders the remaining vampires to leave the town and not return. They quickly retreat into the night, and Barrow is saved.

After the vampires have fled, Eben and Stella sit together and talk. Eben realizes that he is losing what is left of his humanity and does not want to live like the other vampires. The sun rises as Eben and Stella hold each other, killing Eben and leaving Stella sitting in the snow, devastated.

Characters
- *Sheriff Eben Olemaun*, the protagonist, is a tall Eskimo of medium build. He is dedicated to his wife, Stella, and his town, Barrow, and is willing to do anything in his power to defend both of them. During the vampire invasion, he leads the other survivors to safety and tries to provide for them, going outside to search for food at great risk. His courage and nobility are demonstrated

by both his self-imposed transformation into a vampire, which gives him enough strength to expel the other vampires, and his choice to die rather than to live as a vampire.
- *Deputy Stella Olemaun* is an attractive Eskimo woman with dark red hair. While she is not as fearless as Eben, she does everything in her power to save the town. Early in the comic, she demonstrates her fierce desire to keep the town safe by killing the first vampire.
- *Miss Judith* is a mysterious, middle-aged African American woman. She attempts to prove that vampires exist, even sending her son to collect evidence with a video camera and a helicopter. Her motives are not revealed in the book.
- *Taylor* is a tall, handsome African American man with a shaved head. Apparently Miss Judith's son, he attempts to gather evidence to prove that vampires really exist. He is killed when Vincente attacks his helicopter and causes it to crash, but he manages to send the images to Miss Judith before he dies.
- *Roderick Marlowe*, an antagonist, is a tall, thin, bald vampire. He organizes and plans the massacre of Barrow, considering the town easy prey because it resides in darkness for a month. He sends Vincente an invitation to the massacre, possibly in an attempt to curry favor. He is killed by Vincente for revealing the existence of vampires.
- *Vincente*, an antagonist, is a tall, bald, and evidently ancient vampire leader. He disrupts Marlowe's plans and orders that Barrow be destroyed. Although he is apparently the strongest of the vampires, Eben kills him.

Artistic Style

Templesmith's visuals are stunning in their intricacy. The overall mood is set by the limited color palette and the splashes of red that punctuate particularly bloody scenes. The art is reminiscent of the more abstract work of Bill Sienkiewicz, especially his work in the *New Mutants* and *Moon Knight* series in the 1980's, in which normal characters are transformed into abstract shapes in order to demonstrate mood or emotional turmoil.

Inspired by the bleak setting of John Carpenter's film version of *The Thing* (1982), Templesmith often leaves the backgrounds vague, as if the snow and cloud cover have made Barrow into a virtual wasteland even before the vampires arrive. His character designs are greatly influenced by Dave McKean's 1990's style as well as by the work of Ashley Wood. Overall, Templesmith emphasizes a sense of bleakness, tying the art into the story through his use of computers for both backgrounds and color adjustment in addition to traditional pencil and ink work. The lettering is also effective, with human speech set in a traditional font and the vampires' words set in a twisted, meandering font, emphasizing their inhuman nature. In addition, Templesmith's vampires are not "sexy" monsters but instead parodies of the humans they once were, with hideous sets of barbed fangs jutting out at angles and long claws instead of fingernails. Since the publication of *30 Days of Night*, Templesmith's highly evocative style has significantly influenced the field of modern adult-oriented horror comics.

Themes

The overall themes of *30 Days of Night* are the triumph of love over evil, courage and nobility in the face of danger, and sacrifice for the greater good of the community. The first is reflected in the relationships between Eben and Stella and Eben and the rest of the town of Barrow. Although Eben and Stella could easily flee the town in their car at the start of the vampire invasion, they choose to stay and fight an enemy that seems undefeatable. In choosing to stay and putting their own lives in danger, Eben and Stella make their love for the town clear. When Eben becomes a vampire, he knowingly chooses to die rather than lose his sense of humanity or his love for Stella.

When Eben fights the other vampires, his love of the town and the townspeople's support for him give him the strength he needs to kill Vincente. At the end, realizing he is a danger to the town, he chooses to die as the sun rises. Stella also demonstrates her love and courage, allowing Eben to take his own life even though it means living without him.

Impact

Incredibly influential within the comics industry, *30 Days of Night* inspired a new wave of sophisticated horror comics for adults. It also established the reputation of newcomer Templesmith as a worthy successor to artists such as Bernie Wrightson and McKean in his macabre but effective use of muted color and extravagant exhibition in pencils and inks. Templesmith's influence can be seen in many modern artists, particularly those working for smaller companies that allow creative latitude, such as IDW. The success of *30 Days of Night* also allowed Niles, who had been at the margins of the industry, to become a successful horror writer and work across the industry in a variety of genres.

The series was also instrumental in inspiring many gothic- and horror-themed titles and prompting the major comic book companies to revive their vampire and other horror characters for a mainstream audience. Lastly, the series' success also led many more creators, particularly Mark Millar, to pitch their projects as films shortly after or even before publication.

Films

30 Days of Night. Directed by David Slade. Columbia, 2007. This film adaptation was written by Niles, Stuart Beattie, and Brian Nelson and stars Josh Hartnett and Melissa George. The film largely follows the plot of the original series, but it eliminates the character of Vincente and has Marlowe survive until the final battle. The film received mixed reviews, and many comic book fans were disappointed by the lack of subtlety present in the original series. A sequel, based on the comic book sequel *Dark Days*, was released straight to video in 2010.

Web Series

30 Days of Night: Blood Trails and *30 Days of Night: Dust to Dust*. Fearnet.com, 2007-2008. These Internet-only miniseries star a variety of actors and serve as a prequel and sequel to the original film, respectively. Many fans of the original series criticized the Web series for their low production values.

Brian A. Cogan

Further Reading

Chaykin, Howard, David Tischman, and David Hahn. *Bite Club* (2005).

Kirkman, Robert, Tony Moore, and Charles Adlard. *The Walking Dead* (2004-).

Niles, Steve, and Ben Templesmith. *Criminal Macabre* (1990-).

Bibliography

Barker, Clive. Introduction to *30 Days of Night*. New York: IDW Publishing, 2003.

Barsanti, Chris. "The Graphic Report." *Kirkus Reviews* 72, no. 19 (October 1, 2004).

Gilland, Blue. "30 Days of Night/Tim Lebbon." Review of *30 Days of Night* by Steve Niles. *Dark Scribe Magazine*, October 22, 2007. Available at http://www.darkscribemagazine.com/reviews/30-days-of-night-tim-lebbon.html

See also: *Walking Dead*

Three Fingers

Author: Koslowski, Rich
Artist: Rich Koslowski (illustrator)
Publisher: Top Shelf Comics
First book published: 2002

Publication History

Rich Koslowski got his start in the early 1990's at Animagination, where he worked on commercials, instructional videos, and children's books. He soon began drawing and inking comic books, primarily *Sonic the Hedgehog* from Archie Comics. In 1997, Koslowski self-published a forty-page one-shot comic book called *How to Pick Up Girls If You're a Comic Book Geek*. The name of his publishing company was 3 Finger Prints, since he was already thinking about the story that would become *Three Fingers*. The comic was a success, leading Koslowski to feature the three characters introduced in *How to Pick Up Girls If You're a Comic Book Geek* in the ongoing, award-nominated series *The 3 Geeks* and *Geeksville*.

In 2001, he decided to create *Three Fingers*. An impetus for *Three Fingers* was Koslowski's work on children's books, during which time he went to schools to talk to students and do drawing demonstrations. Often children would ask why the characters were drawn with only three fingers. He would tell them that it was easier to animate three fingers than four. The question got him thinking, and several years later, *Three Fingers* was born. Koslowski approached Chris Staros, publisher of Top Shelf Comics, with a proposal for the book, which Staros accepted. When *Three Fingers* was released in 2002, it garnered positive reviews and award nominations, winning an Ignatz Award. It has been translated and published in several different languages, including Italian, Spanish, and Portuguese. It was out of print for a time, but a new edition of *Three Fingers* was published in 2010.

Plot

Three Fingers is a "documentary" that takes place in a world similar to that of the film *Who Framed Roger Rabbit* (1988), in which cartoon characters exist alongside human beings. Most of the characters are based on well-known cartoon characters, mainly from Disney or Warner Bros. Through both "historical footage" and interviews with both humans and the aged Toons, the story begins by discussing the rise of filmmaker "Dizzy" Walters and his star, the Toon actor Rickey Rat, who gains fame in *Railroad Rickey*, the first feature film starring a Toon. The film's success leads to more films starring Toons (called cartoons), but at first, none of them are as successful as *Railroad Rickey*.

A legend begins to grow around Rickey: That his film success is based on him having three fingers on each hand instead of four, which was the number of fingers that unsuccessful Toons have. Soon, more three-fingered Toons begin making successful pictures. However, there is speculation that these Toons were not born this way but, instead, had their fourth fingers surgically removed. Apparently, some Toon parents even have their children's fourth finger removed after birth to guarantee future success. While the Toons deny the allegations, it becomes apparent that the studios not only know about this procedure but also encourage it. Several of the Toons interviewed tell of how they had to make the decision between mutilating themselves and not getting work. The studios say that they will not work with actors who have undergone the "ritual"; however, after "Warmer Brothers" has a hit with the three-fingered Portly Pig, three-fingered Toons become the norm in films.

Public outcry over the ritual leads to Senate hearings on the subject, with studio personnel and Rickey Rat called to testify. However, the main Toon to appear is the popular "Buggy" Bunny, who denies having undergone the procedure. In the present-day interviews, Portly and another Toon, Carhorn Armwhistle, take Buggy to task; Portly mentions Buggy's role in the disfigurement of Dapper Duck. Marilyn Monroe also speaks against the ritual at the hearings and is among the humans to speak up about the mistreatment of the Toons. Others to do so include President John F. Kennedy and Martin Luther King, Jr., and the documentary speculates that their deaths may have been the result of them speaking up for the Toons.

The hearings lead to a legal ban on the procedure, with strong penalties against any doctor who performs it. However, since only three-fingered Toons are getting work, four-fingered Toons try other methods, including undergoing illegal surgeries, which in the case of some, such as King Lion, ends in disfigurement. For a short time, there are rumors of a man known as "the Specialist" who would not only perform the surgery but also fake the Toon's past records to say that they were born with three fingers. During this period, more three-fingered Toons make their debuts, and while the Specialist is never caught, some speculate that it is Walters.

After Walters dies, the new people in charge of the studio produce *The Rainforest Story*, whose Toon star, Chow-Mow Glee, has four fingers. The film is a success and proves that a four-fingered Toon can be successful. This leads to other successful films starring four-fingered Toons, and soon both three- and four-fingered Toons are doing well. In the end, "Teen Toon Star" M. C. Wak-O hints that the ritual is still practiced, but among the younger generation of Toons it is known as "The Rickey."

Characters
- *Reginald Desmond "Dizzy" Walters* is a filmmaker analogous to Walt Disney. He is the only one of the main characters who is not interviewed, because he died years before the documentary.
- *Rickey Rat* is the main character of the story and resembles Mickey Mouse. His fame is what leads to the ritual.
- *Beatrice Clarke* is a human being and a Toon historian.
- *Carhorn Armwhistle* is a roosterlike cartoon character.
- *Portly Pig* is a stuttering pig who worked for Warmer Brothers Studios.
- *Beatrice Clarke* is a film historian interviewed for the documentary.
- *Chester Chimp* is a Toon who was Rickey's childhood friend.
- *Freidrich Von Katze* is a German-born cat Toon who eventually has to work in pornographic films.
- *Rapid Rodriguez* is a Spanish-accented Toon who uses his size and speed to take pictures of the ritual. While interviewed, he appears in shadow as an "unidentified former Toon actor."
- *Ned Kerney* is a dog Toon who plays the role of Rickey's pet dog "Jupiter."
- *Sly Vester, Jr.*, is a Toon cat who was a child actor who worked with his father; he is one of the interviewees.
- *Bartholomew Baxter "Buggy" Bunny III* is a famous rabbit Toon who denies undergoing the ritual.
- *Dapper Duck* is a Toon who was Buggy's friend and who underwent the ritual.
- *King Lion* is a former Toon actor who had illegal surgery on his hand, which ended in his disfigurement.
- *Hans Wurstmacher* is a human cinematographer who is interviewed for the documentary.
- *Regis P. Redbreast, Ph.D.* is a Toon bird who is a professor of toonistics.
- *The Specialist* is a rumored individual who performed the ritual on Toons after the procedure was made illegal. Some say that he and Walters are the same.

Artistic Style

With its documentary style, *Three Fingers* is done in black and white but in two styles. The historical parts are presented as photographs and film stills with text written on the side of and, occasionally, over the images. In most cases, there are three pictures per page. The majority of the interviews are drawn in six-panel format, with three panels on top of three. Some pages have only three panels centered in the middle of the page, and a few have less. The Toons are anthropomorphic animals, and they are shown as being elderly in the interviews. Some, such as Portly Pig and Dapper Duck, are shown to be in ill health. Whenever Rickey is shown, he is in shadow and holding a cigarette. The humans are drawn realistically both in the past photographs and in the modern-day interviews.

Themes

Parody is a major theme of *Three Fingers*; most characters in the book are obviously based on characters from cartoons, mainly those from Warner Bros. and Walt Disney studios. However, while the book is a parody, the characters are not shown in a humorous way.

Another theme concerns the lengths to which people will go to become famous. In *Three Fingers*, characters mutilate themselves in order to get work and achieve success in the motion-picture industry. In real life, actors undergo various procedures—such as plastic surgery, liposuction, and breast augmentation—in order to begin, advance, or continue their careers. In *Three Fingers*, parents perform the ritual on their children to help them to achieve fame. This is an equivalent to the phenomenon of "stage parents," who put their children through psychologically damaging and dubious activities to win pageants and get into show business. The willingness of those in power to encourage such activities, or, at least, to turn a blind eye toward them, is also an issue covered in the book.

Impact

Three Fingers has had a positive effect on Koslowski's career. It garnered positive reviews and won Koslowski an Ignatz Award (along with nominations for a Harvey Award and an Ursa Major Award). The title also had a good deal of positive word-of-mouth feedback among comic book readers. Since *Three Fingers* was published, Koslowski has continued his comics works. As a writer, he has produced additional stories with the 3 Geeks, told the adventures of Omega Flight for Marvel Comics, and created the Elvis-themed original graphic novel *The King* (2005) for Top Shelf Comics. As an artist, he penciled and inked the original graphic novel *B. B. Wolf and the Three LPs* (2010) and inked the adventures of various Archie Comics characters, including Archie, Jughead, Betty, and Veronica. He is also the author of the 2007 illustrated, Christmas-themed novel *The List*.

David S. Serchay

Rich Koslowski

After working in the animation industry, Rich Koslowski got started in comics as an inker for Archie Comics. While working in a comic book store, he created the self-published, stand-alone comic book, *How to Pick Up Girls If You're a Comic Book Geek*. The success of that endeavor led him to create the *Three Geeks* series, which was a popular title at the end of the 1990's. In 2001 he released his first graphic novel, *Three Fingers*, about the prejudice against "cartoon actors" in Hollywood in the 1930's and 1940's. The work was nominated for several awards and won the Ignatz. In 2005, Koslowski released a follow-up graphic novel, *The King*, which was a satirical take on Elvis Presley. Koslowski's work is characterized by its broad humor and use of stereotypical characters and situations for satiric effect. *Three Fingers* is a departure from much of the rest of his work because of its exploration of serious themes and issues, albeit with great irony.

Further Reading

Arnold, J. D., and Rich Koslowski. *B. B. Wolf and the Three LPs* (2010).

Koslowski, Rich. *The King* (2005).

Bibliography

Koslowski, Rich. "Rich Koslowski Counts Down to *Three Fingers*: *3 Geeks* Creator Tackles an Animation Icon." Interview by Beau Yarbrough. *Comic Book Resources*, May 6, 2002. http://www.comicbookresources.com/?page=article&id=1114.

Lyga, Allyson A. W., and Barry Lyga. *Graphic Novels in Your Media Center: A Definitive Guide.* Westport, Conn.: Libraries Unlimited, 2004.

Serchay, David S. *The Librarian's Guide to Graphic Novels for Adults.* New York: Neal-Schuman, 2010.

See also: *Maus*; *It's a Bird*; *Flaming Carrot*; *Boulevard of Broken Dreams*

300

Author: Miller, Frank
Artist: Frank Miller (illustrator); Lynn Varley (colorist)
Publisher: Dark Horse Comics
First serial publication: 1998
First book publication: 1999

Publication History

Frank Miller's *300* was published by Dark Horse Comics in 1998 as a five-volume serial. At the time he released *300*, Miller was already well known in the comics world, having published with Marvel Comics, DC Comics, Epic Comics, and Dark Horse Comics. With its violent imagery, warrior philosophy, and freewheeling interpretation of a famous event in ancient Greek history, *300* reaffirmed Miller's reputation as a fearless innovator. A hardcover edition was published in 1999.

Plot

300 tells the story of the famous Spartan warrior-king, Leonidas, whose small, elite force nearly defeated the vast armies of Persian king Xerxes and helped frustrate Xerxes's quest to conquer the Greek city-states.

In chapter 1, entitled "Honor," the primary narrative of the war between the three hundred Spartan warriors and the Persians begins when an arrogant Persian ambassador and his retinue gallop into Sparta with an ultimatum: promise submission to Xerxes or be destroyed. Amused and insulted at this proposal, Leonidas and his soldiers throw the Persians into a hole to the city's sewer system.

In chapter 2, entitled "Duty," Leonidas, although a secular ruler, must obtain the permission of the priests of the "old gods" to go to war. The corrupt priests forbid Leonidas to fight Xerxes, but he goes anyway—ostensibly taking a stroll to the north with three hundred men as his bodyguards. At the edge of town, he is joined by a boisterous but amateurish force of seven thousand Arcadians led by his old friend Daxos. This chapter ends with the arrival of the combined Greek army at Thermopylae, the "Hot Gates" that will help obstruct the Persian attack and negate the huge numbers advantage held by the Persians.

Frank Miller at 1982 San Diego Comic Con. (By Alan Light, via Wikimedia Commons)

In chapter 3, entitled "Glory," Leonidas and his forces round up and slaughter the Persian scout in the hills around Thermopylae. These hills are also home to the physically grotesque but brave Ephialtes, a refugee from Sparta's cruel laws against infant deformity. Ephialtes has waited a lifetime to prove himself as a worthy Spartan warrior. He partly succeeds by showing Leonidas a hidden path behind the Spartan lines, but when Leonidas asks him to raise his shield high enough to contribute to the Spartan phalanx battle formation, Ephialtes is unable to do it. Leonidas sends him away as gently as possible, but this rejection will have serious consequences for the Spartans.

In chapter 4, entitled "Combat," the focus is on all-out warfare. This chapter vividly depicts both the physical action of intense warfare and the mental cat-and-mouse games that form the strategic and tactical aspects of combat.

In the opening battle of "The First Day" section, the Spartans are ready and waiting for the Persians in full battle formation. They shape their phalanx of interconnected shields and spears into a broad rectangle and drive the unprepared Persians over a cliff and into the sea.

Immediately after this rout, the Persians counterattack with archers and cavalry. These attacks also fail, and the first day ends with three defeats for the Persians and a burst of jubilation among the Spartans.

The first day's activities have not ended yet, however, for Xerxes makes an unexpected personal call on Leonidas, offering to make him the warlord of all of Greece and the general of Xerxes's armies in Europe. Unimpressed, Leonidas rejects the offer.

In the section called "The First Night," Xerxes's wounded pride leads him to commit his elite soldiers, the Immortals, to a premature night attack on the still fresh and confident Spartans. Leonidas is ready with a surprise, two-front ambush by Spartans and Arcadians. The resulting rout leaves Xerxes shaken; however, when rejected Ephialtes sees the Spartan victory, he angrily decides to take his knowledge of the secret path to the Persians.

The final chapter is entitled "Victory." In "The Second Day" portion, the Persians are desperately throwing man and beast at the Spartan position. Nothing works, however, until Ephialtes betrays the Spartans' weak spot to Xerxes in exchange for wealth, pleasure, and Persian acceptance.

The catastrophic results of this betrayal on the Greeks are felt on the second night. Upon learning from a dismayed Daxos that the Persians are moving to surround them, Leonidas rejects Daxos's request that all the Greek forces retreat so as not to be annihilated. Instead, he orders all Greeks except the Spartans to return home and leave the final battle to the three hundred. This is the key to Miller's paradoxical title "Victory," for the chapter graphically shows the Spartan contingent meeting its end.

To transform this defeat into victory, Leonidas sends his great friend, the warrior and storyteller Dilios, back to Sparta to tell the heroic story of the three hundred Spartans' last stand to bring unity and inspiration to all Greeks, so they will defeat the Persians and give birth to a new age of reason, justice, and law.

Characters
- *Leonidas*, the protagonist, is the king of Sparta and is its fearless and brilliant military commander. He is the complete embodiment of the Spartan philosophy of freedom, reason, courage, and warrior pride. He is also presented as a prophet of a coming age of Western rationality and civilization.
- *Xerxes*, the antagonist, is the Persian king whose imperial ambitions bring him into conflict with the freedom-loving Greek city-states. Despite his over-the-top vanity, he is a formidable opponent, physically commanding, cunning, seductive, and courageous.
- *Dilios* is a trusted Spartan warrior who is also Sparta's storyteller, memory keeper, and mythmaker. Just hours before the final battle, Leonidas sends him home to tell the story of the three hundred as an inspiration to the embattled Greek resistance.
- *Stelios* is a bumbling novice fighter at the start of the story, but through the trials of war, he becomes one of Leonidas's fiercest and most effective warriors.
- *Ephialtes* is the grotesquely deformed Spartan traitor. His parents went into exile to save him from infanticide, but he was raised to identify with Spartan warrior values. Rejected by Leonidas as a fighter, Ephialtes takes his knowledge of the hidden path behind Spartan lines to Xerxes.

Artistic Style

300 appeared first as a five-volume serial in 1998 from Dark Horse Comics. Each page of the comic book form was designed to be one-half of a page in the book version, which came out the following year. Thus, the hardcover version has a distinctive wide-screen format that gave it a cinematic feel and allowed Miller and Varley to create individual panels that have an epic scope that is difficult to achieve in more standard formats.

The imagery of *300* has a blunt force that supports the story's violent subject matter. Miller's line work is used functionally to create contrasts and mark distinctions that add nuance and texture to both the parts and the whole. For instance, Miller's heroic Spartan warriors are characteristically presented in uncluttered and strongly geometric designs. The simplicity and uniformity of the soldiers' garb and weaponry (round shields and straight spears) reinforce this sense of geometric power and symmetry.

In contrast, the Persians rarely look organized. They move in great numbers, but they appear without geometrical organization, scrambling from place to place with their weapons askew, wearing attire that is anything but uniform and that does nothing to protect them from the clean lines of Spartan spear thrusts.

Interestingly, this contrast between the geometric formations of the Spartans and the chaotic masses of the Persian soldiers disappears in death. For most of the novel, the Spartans win and live, while the Persians are drawn as anonymous masses of hacked-up bodies. At the end, when death comes to the three hundred Spartans, they too are reduced to a scattered heap of empty, disorganized human remains.

This vision of all-encompassing death comes close to nihilism, but the book's final image shows a new generation of Spartan warriors leaping forward to war, with spears thrust upward and brilliant red capes flying in the wind. Here, color and line create a form of rebirth.

Themes

Frank Miller's *300* is an imaginative re-creation of a famous episode in the history of ancient Greece. Thus, it is not surprising that many of the most important themes in the book are historical and political in nature. The master theme is a major historical one: The Greek republics of the fifth century B.C.E. were "the world's one hope for reason and justice," and the Persians were trying to destroy the people who embodied these values. Leonidas has the most powerful prophetic vision of both the unfolding of history and the unique place of his three hundred warriors in that history: "A new age is begun. An age of great deeds. An age of Justice. An age of law. And all will know that 300 Spartans gave their last breath to defend it." Whether one agrees with this assessment or not, it gives the work a powerful thematic center.

Finally, there is the quintessential writer's theme: the power of language and of story. Thus, Dilios the storyteller is the most important character at the end of the tale, for Leonidas has ordered him home before the final battle specifically to ensure that everybody in the Greek federation understands the full significance of the sacrifice of the three hundred: "You have a talent unlike any other Spartan. You will deliver my final orders to the council—with force and verve—and you will make every Greek know what happened here," meaning a great moral victory in the midst of a military defeat.

Impact

By 1998, when the comic series *300* appeared, anything that Miller wrote, drew, or said in interviews had an impact in the comics world. The immediate influence of *300* was shock and awe. Positive recognition came first when Miller, colorist Lynn Varley, and the work won a number of major comics industry awards from their peers. However, negative attention came almost immediately as well, particularly since the story touched some sensitive nerves regarding ethnic stereotyping and male homosexuality. Never one to back away from a good argument, Miller kept the controversy going with pointed and irreverent verbal counterpunches in a variety of venues.

Films

300. Directed by Zack Snyder. Warner Bros., 2006. Miller has always been one of the most "cinematic" of comics creators and consciously built an effective working relationship with the film industry in Hollywood. With Miller co-producing and consulting, director Zack Snyder and his writers developed an expanded role for Leonidas's wife (Lena Headey), drew a strong performance from little-known Scottish actor Gerard Butler (as Leonidas), and created a unique visual style with eye-catching surprises. The cunningly promoted film set a March opening-weekend record at the box office by earning nearly $71 million. Unsurprisingly, it also drew a lively mix of positive and negative commentary. In interviews, Miller all but identified the ancient Persians with the al-Qaeda terrorist organization, and the film's distribution was banned in Iran.

Roger Stilling

Further Reading
Miller, Frank. *Batman: The Dark Knight Returns* (1986).
_____. *Sin City* (1992).
_____. *Ronin* (1983).

Bibliography
Gabilliet, Jean-Paul, Bart Beaty, and Nick Nguyen, trans. *Of Comics and Men: A Cultural History of American Comic Books*. Jackson: University Press of Mississippi, 2010.
George, Milo, ed. *The Comics Journal Library,* Volume Two*: Frank Miller*. Fantagraphics Books, 2003.
Herodotus. *The Histories*. Translated by Aubrey de Sélincourt, revised by John M. Marincola. New York: Penguin Books, 1996.
Miller, Frank, and Hal Schuster. *Frank Miller*. San Bernardino, Calif.: Borgo Press, 1986.

See also: *Sin City*; *It Was the War of the Trenches*

Three Shadows

Author: Pedrosa, Cyril
Artist: Cyril Pedrosa (illustrator)
Publisher: Delcourt (French); First Second Books (English)
First book publication: *Trois Ombres*, 2007 (English translation, 2008)

Publication History
Though French artist and writer Cyril Pedrosa established his career in European comics through his collaborations with writer David Chauvel and his solo debut, *Les Coeurs solitaires* (2006), *Three Shadows* became his first graphic novel to be exported to the United States. Originally published in 2007 as *Trois Ombres*, *Three Shadows* was partially inspired by an event in Pedrosa's life. After watching friends endure the death of their child, Pedrosa sought to explore the unpredictable dynamics of mortality. In all, it took six months for Pedrosa to compose the tale and one year to complete the art. The graphic novel was translated from French to English by Edward Gauvin.

Plot
In an unspecified location in a premodern era, Louis and Lise enjoy a "simple and sweet" life of pastoral bliss with their son, Joachim. They spend their time working the rolling fields of their farm, relaxing in the shade, and swimming in the river. It is a peaceful existence. Joachim awakens one evening and tells his parents about three unmoving, ominous horse riders he saw on the distant hill overlooking the house. During a hunting excursion, the family dog, Diego, goes missing. Later that night, the shadowy figures appear again. Louis seizes an ax and pursues the three shadows, but they disappear. Louis advises Joachim never to go outside alone.

The next night, Joachim hears a mysterious scratching noise. Thinking it is Diego, he opens the door and faces the three shadows. Louis frightens them away. Lise goes to town to consult the mystical, elderly Suzette Pike, who warns Lise not to resist the shadows. Lise also learns that Pike has been protected

Autograph session with Cyril Pedrosa at Delcourt festival 2007 (Paris, France). (By Georges Seguin (Okki), via Wikimedia Commons)

from the shadows her entire life, but the old woman now accepts her own mortality. When Lise shares this information with her husband, Louis refuses to allow the shadows to take his son. Louis and Joachim flee the farm with the shadows seemingly in pursuit. The shadows locate Pike, and she gives herself to them.

Louis and Joachim go to a crowded port to catch a ferry to the west, where they may be safe from the shadows. Once Louis and Joachim enter the port, they witness the worst of humanity, such as slave traders and thieves who profit from others' pain. After obtaining a ticket through a bribe, Louis and Joachim board a ship that holds the weak and the elderly. In an attempt to help a sick old man, Louis tries to locate medical supplies. He meets the kind, helpful bosun of the ship, who prides himself on his civility. Louis also discovers a slave who is being held in the captain's cabin.

Louis next meets a boisterous yet repugnant slave trader, Manfred. After Manfred violently attacks a woman selling charms, he is murdered by the woman's colleagues. The next morning, Louis is accused of being the killer. During a storm, the slave kills the captain, and the boat sinks. Louis and Joachim are rescued by an old man who lives in a hut on the beach. Blaming the shadows for all the deaths, Louis realizes his mistake in fleeing and decides to return home to cherish his remaining moments with his son.

The old man strikes a deal with Louis: If Louis gives the man his "good heart," then the man will give Louis the strength and power to protect Joachim. When he agrees, Louis is transformed into a massive, black golem without a heart. He flees through the countryside, carrying Joachim in his fist. After months, Joachim pleads for his monstrous father to release him. Louis collapses and allows the shadows to take Joachim. The shadows are revealed to be three women, who note that they have an appointment with the "one who cheats."

After obtaining Louis's good heart, the old man has transformed into a young and powerful baron. One of the three women, Aurore, requests a seat at the baron's table and makes a bet with him. If the baron wins the bet, he will receive a kiss; if Aurore wins, she can have any object owned by the baron. Aurore changes places with her fellow "shadow" Fate, and the bet is won. The baron discovers the ruse, but the women demand his prized necklace. In the pendant on the necklace resides the essence of Louis's good heart. The baron refuses and flees. He is struck down by a carriage, and the women take the pendant and give it to Joachim.

The women and boy find Louis lying on a mountaintop. Joachim pours the elixir containing Louis's good heart from the pendant into his father's nose. His father is revived, and Joachim leaves with the shadows. Years later, Louis and Lise have two daughters and recognize the tenuous nature of life. The story concludes with an image of petals fluttering off a cherry blossom tree.

Characters

- *Louis* is the hulking, bearded patriarch of a rural family. His dedication to the survival of his son, Joachim, leads the two on a grueling physical and spiritual journey. He eventually makes an ill-advised exchange and is transformed into a golem. At the end of the journey, he learns to accept the transitory nature of life and existence.
- *Joachim* is the young son of Louis and Lise.
- *Lise* is the wife of Louis and the mother of Joachim. Haunted by the appearance of the three shadows, she visits the mysterious Suzette Pike for guidance. After speaking with Pike, she realizes that she and Louis should value the time they have remaining with Joachim before he is taken by the shadows.
- *Suzette Pike* is a shrunken old woman whom Lise visits for advice regarding the shadows. Outside her home is a plaque that reads "Midwife, Exorcist, Sympathetic Ear." She advises Lise not to fight the shadows and to value every moment that remains with Joachim. She has kept the shadows in waiting for many years, but after her session with Lise, she willingly faces her fate and goes with the shadows.
- *Manfred* is an intelligent, yet prideful and violent, slave trader that Louis encounters on the voyage to the west. After violently attacking a woman, he is murdered during the night. Louis is blamed for the murder.
- *The Bosun* is a massive man with a kind heart who prides himself on his sensitivity and his sophisticated dress. During the dehumanizing boat ride across the expansive river, he is one of the few people to help Louis and the other degraded travelers. During the storm, he releases Louis and Joachim from their cage, attempts to save people, and refuses to abandon the sinking ship.
- *The Slave* is a woman being transported by Manfred. She serves as a cook for the ship's captain. Her testimony implicates Louis in the murder of

Manfred. She eventually exacts revenge upon the captain by stabbing him during the storm.
- *The Three Shadows* are initially ominous, foreboding figures on horseback that hold vigil on the hill near the family's home. Despite Louis's efforts to evade them, they eventually seize Joachim and are revealed to be three kind women representing the three fates. After the old man deceives Louis, they locate and restore Louis's "good heart" before returning him to human form.
- *The Old Man*, a.k.a. *the Baron*, is first introduced as a withered hermit living on the beach. He rescues Louis and Joachim after the destruction of the ship. Once the old man obtains Louis's good heart, he is transformed into a wealthy baron. The three shadows eventually reclaim the good heart and return it to Louis, while the baron's spirit is dragged off to be punished for eternity.

Artistic Style

Three Shadows falls into a European tradition of emotionally sophisticated, yet accessible, literary works that utilize allegory to ruminate on an existential concern. Pedrosa's black-and-white art is characterized by fluid, swirling lines that display the frenetic, consuming nature of the father and son's journey as well their increasing anxiety as the shadows pursue them. Pedrosa uses brush, pen, and charcoal and effectively balances both joy and grief while alternating between bold, broad strokes and fine line work.

The phantasmagoric nature of the father and son's epic journey becomes evident as Pedrosa employs dynamic inking, stark shadowy scenes with high contrast, and unorthodox comics techniques such as drybrushing to create a psychological portrait of desperation. The atmosphere achieved through the line work and swooping, kinetic landscapes is highly effective. Black spaces seem to consume the characters as the graphic novel progresses. Pedrosa's caricature, or cartoon, style places emphasis on certain traits that indicate the essence of each character. The disgusting and disturbing visages of corrupted individuals stand in contrast to the kindly faces of the innocent Louis and Joachim.

Cyril Pedrosa

Having studied animation at the Gobelins School, Cyril Pedrosa began his career in France's Disney studios as an assistant animator on films including *The Hunchback of Notre Dame* and *Hercules*. After meeting writer David Chauvel, Pedrosa abandoned animation for a career in comics, collaborating with him on the four volumes of *Ring Circus* beginning in 1998 and the three volumes of *Les Aventures spatio-temporelles de Shaolin Moussaka*. In 2006 he published his first graphic novel, *Les Coeurs solitaires*, and followed it up the next year with *Three Shadows*, a breakthrough work about a young boy and his parents whose life in the country is disrupted by the arrival of three figures determined to claim the boy. Pedrosa's comics show a strong influence from his time in the Disney studios. They are skillfully rendered in a classic animation tradition and convey a great deal of vitality. Since 2008, he has been publishing the humorous autobiographical comic *Autobio* in the comics magazine *Fluide Glacial*.

Pedrosa's artwork is influenced by Japanese woodcuts, European caricature and cartooning traditions, and the animation of Disney and Studio Ghibli. In addition, *Three Shadows* displays aesthetic links to the grotesques of Francisco de Goya, the elongated bodies and use of blacks by El Greco, and the circular, kinetic movements of Vincent Van Gogh's canvases. The literary aspects of *Three Shadows* can be traced to a number of influences, including European folktales, medieval morality plays, Voltaire's *Candide* (1759), John O'Hara's novel *Appointment in Samarra* (1934), and the Magical Realism of Gabriel García Márquez.

Themes

Three Shadows concerns the corrupting forces of society, the love of parents, and the inescapability of mortality. The most prominent theme of *Three Shadows* is the transitory and fleeting nature of life. At the beginning of the tale, the family leads an idyllic life separate from larger society. During their flight from the shadows, Louis and Joachim encounter the most repugnant elements of humanity.

Three Shadows also serves as a meditation on the extreme measures loving parents will take to protect their children from death. It is only through Louis's transformation into a monstrous golem that the desperate father learns of the inescapability of death. Once Louis realizes that his son deserves freedom from the literal grip of the golem, he accepts that a life of flight and fear is less desirable than a peaceful death. These trials teach Louis both to value the remaining time he has with his son and to embrace life by accepting death as an inevitable component of existence. With that knowledge, Louis recognizes the true nature of life.

Impact

Beyond a smattering of titles (such as René Goscinny and Albert Uderzo's *Asterix* series, 1961-1979, and Hergé's *The Adventures of Tintin*, 1929-1976) and a few celebrity artists (such as Moebius or Jacques Tardi), French comics and their creators have yet to achieve popular recognition in the United States. Lauded at 2008's Angoulême International Comics Festival and revered by the European comic literati, *Three Shadows* received strong reviews in the United States. Despite this critical acclaim, the work reached only a limited audience in the country. A sophisticated pastiche of literary genres and artistic styles, *Three Shadows* serves as a unique example of European comics art and graphic storytelling in the twenty-first century.

Shannon Blake Skelton

Further Reading

Kelly, Joe, and J. M. Ken Niimura. *I Kill Giants* (2009).

Tan, Shaun. *The Arrival* (2006).

TenNapel, Doug. *Ghostopolis* (2010).

Bibliography

Croonenborghs, Bart. "The Three Shadows of Cyril Pedrosa." *Broken Frontier*, May 28, 2008. http://www.brokenfrontier.com/lowdown/p/detail/the-three-shadows-of-cyril-pedrosa.

Pedrosa, Cyril. "There's No Such Thing as a Graphic Novel." *First Second Books: Doodles and Dailies*, April 14, 2008. http://firstsecondbooks.typepad.com/mainblog/cyril_pedrosa_guest_blogger.

Wheeler, Andrew. "Review: *Three Shadows* by Cyril Pedrosa." *Comic Mix*, April 2, 2008. http://www.comicmix.com/news/2008/04/02/review-three-shadows-by-cyril-pedrosa.

See also: *The Rabbi's Cat*; *The Adventures of Tintin*; *Asterix*; *My Mommy Is in America and She Met Buffalo Bill*

Tragical Comedy or Comical Tragedy of Mr. Punch, The

Author: Gaiman, Neil
Artist: Dave McKean (illustrator)
Publisher: Gollancz; DC Comics
First book publication: 1994

Publication History

First published in 1994 by science-fiction and fantasy publisher Gollancz, *The Tragical Comedy or Comical Tragedy of Mr. Punch* has been published in hardcover and paperback by both Gollanz and the DC Comics imprint Vertigo (1995), and it was republished in paperback by Bloomsbury Publishing in 2006. This reissue is indicative of the graphic novel's more mainstream acceptance, as Bloomsbury does not frequently publish comic books or graphic novels. The book has also been translated into German and French.

Plot

The story begins as a young boy, purportedly the young Neil Gaiman himself, ventures to the English seaside with his grandfather for a fishing excursion. Bored with fishing, the young boy strays from his grandfather's side and encounters a small tent in which a Punch and Judy puppet show is taking place. While the boy watches, Mr. Punch and Judy argue, and Mr. Punch throws a baby from the window, killing it. The boy runs.

However, he is unable to escape the nightmarish comedic horror of the Punch and Judy show. As he returns again and again that summer to the seaside arcade that his grandfather owns, he encounters a strange and alluring Punch and Judy man, known as the Professor, whose dark past seems quite unfortunately entangled with that of the boy's grandfather and uncle. As the boy watches the Punch and Judy show and becomes more involved in the lives surrounding it and affected by it, he learns more than he may have wished about the secret lives of adults and their sudden betrayals.

The Professor offers the boy an opportunity to be a bottler, collecting money for the show, and it is through this proximity to the show and its production that the boy repeatedly views Mr. Punch's horrifying violence. In the Punch and Judy show, Mr. Punch kills his baby and then his wife, Judy, when she complains. When a police officer arrives to arrest Mr. Punch, the puppet dispenses with him too. Mr. Punch then proceeds to outwit a ghost, a crocodile, a doctor, and the hangman. Finally, Mr. Punch triumphs over the devil himself. Whether the Punch and Judy show comes to resemble the boy's experiences that summer or whether the boy's experiences come to resemble the Punch and Judy show, readers are left to discern for themselves. From the time he first watches the show, the boy comes to see a series of strange deceptions and defeats that mask a darkly mysterious past and an adult world of secrecy and lies.

Dave McKean

Despite the critical success of Dave McKean's graphic novel *Cages*, which he both wrote and illustrated, many readers will best recall McKean for his elaborate and innovative collaborations with writer Neil Gaiman, including the covers of the seventy-five issues of *Sandman*. A multimedia artist, McKean blends line drawings with paint, collage, photography, and sculptural elements to produce truly distinctive original images, many of which eschew traditional representational realism. With Gaiman, he has produced a number of graphic novels, including *Violent Cases*, *Signal to Noise*, *Black Orchid*, and *Mr. Punch*. His collaboration with writer Grant Morrison, *Arkham Asylum: A Serious House on a Serious Earth*, pushed the limits of comic book expressionism in order to represent the instability and danger of an asylum filled with supervillains. Also renowned for his work in illustration and film, McKean has one of the most distinctive visual styles of any current cartoonist.

Author Neil Gaiman. (By Kyle Cassidy, via Wikimedia Commons)

While looking for his grandfather one day, the boy enters a room in which he overhears a dramatic conversation that he does not understand. What he sees there—a brutal victimization of the arcade mermaid whose belly has begun to expand in a telling and inconvenient way—haunts him for the rest of his life, not only because he does not fully understand what he has seen but also because he is witness to his grandfather's profound response. When again he sees the Punch and Judy show, it is through more mature and wiser eyes, and he is even more susceptible to the horror of the extraordinary violence of the show. Though the boy returns home at the end of the summer to his mother and new baby sister, he is forever shaken by the secrets he has unearthed and forever burdened by his inability to piece together the missing shards of truth that are lost to the passage of time.

Characters

- *The boy*, a semiautobiographical representation of Neil Gaiman in his youth, is a mature and intelligent child with a wide-eyed curiosity that leads him straight into the middle of some challenging and confusing situations. Narrating from the perspective of his adulthood, but reflecting on his memories of these childhood experiences, the protagonist leads readers through the metaphorical re-creation of the Punch and Judy show, played out at the hands of his relatives.
- *Grandfather Arthur*, the boy's grandfather and owner of the seaside arcade in which the Punch and Judy show appears, serves as the catalyst for many of the boy's adventures that occur during the summer the boy spends in his care. He is depicted as both an austere-looking man, gray-haired and stoic, and a raving madman, as he appeared in the protagonist's later memories.
- *Uncle Morton*, a hunchback, is the boy's favorite relative and the one who leads him most deeply into the intriguing and seemingly dangerous world of adults. He interacts little with the boy but seems to be present anytime strange things happen.
- *Swatchell*, a.k.a. *the Professor*, runs the Punch and Judy show and apparently has a sordid and mysterious history with the boy's grandfather. He teaches the boy about the Punch and Judy show and offers him the opportunity to be his "bottler," or money collector; in doing so, he reveals tantalizing tidbits about the boy's grandfather and his past.
- *The mermaid*, one of the many human attractions at the arcade, sings to passersby for coins. The boy eventually learns that she is, in fact, human and then witnesses as she becomes the victim of a malicious and violent outburst when it is discovered that she is carrying an illegitimate child.
- *Mr. Punch*, sneaky, malicious, and prone toward extreme violence, is the protagonist of the Punch and Judy show and the antagonist of the main character's boyhood. A flat character, he serves as the physical representation of the protagonist's fears and as a metaphor for the unexplainable violent tendencies of all adults.

Artistic Style

This graphic novel showcases the work of comics creator Dave McKean, longtime collaborator with Neil Gaiman and well-known for his work in a variety of graphic media. To create the mystifying, nightmarish world of *The Comical Tragedy or Tragical Comedy of Mr. Punch*, McKean blended line art, photography, and a variety of styles. What results is a shattered portraiture of a series of confused and confusing memories brought back from the mind of a child and represented in a montage of harrowing scenes.

The inconsistent styles depict the protagonist's unreliable memories and distrust of what he has seen and heard. The characters with whom he interacts—primarily his family members—are depicted in one of two ways: as sketched, comic-style portraits or in garish, sepia-toned photographs. Though McKean rarely delivers one medium without some interruption from the other, the sketches tend to represent the protagonist's narration of the events he experienced as a child, while the photographs tend to represent specific memories he has recollected in his adulthood. The lines between the two media blur increasingly as the plot progresses and as the protagonist becomes more distrustful of the memories he calls to mind.

The lettering, which McKean and Emigre Fonts developed especially for this text, changes from character to character to represent different voices. The words often overlay but never interfere with the well-spaced images, which enhance the narration through thematic color (such as bright red during particularly violent scenes) and sharpness or blurring (as in the soft-focus photographs of scenes the boy may or may not have fully understood). The oversize pages are dense and cluttered with images, and a second or even third reading may be necessary to appreciate fully the richness of detail for which McKean is so well known.

Themes

Based as it is on the historical Punch and Judy show and drawing specifically from the script of an early nineteenth-century puppet show, this graphic novel provides fertile ground for an exploration of various elements of culture and history. Such topics of possible examination include the history of these puppet shows, the 1960's era in which the protagonist was growing up, and the prewar era of his grandfather's and uncle's youth.

As in many of his works, Gaiman explores the theme of faulty memory and of the natural tendency to wish to come to terms with the past even when the necessary clues have expired. The protagonist's recounting of childhood experiences represents not only a coming-of-age but also a return to one's roots and a search through family memories to resolve the secrets that disappear into the void between childhood and adulthood. It is in this confusing in-between space that most of the story occurs; this element is emphasized through McKean's imagery and graphic design.

Touching on themes of corruption, unwanted pregnancy, violence, and murder, the Punch and Judy show allegorizes the horrifying family secrets the protagonist discovers during his summer with his grandfather. Through this allegory, Gaiman examines the hidden family dynamics that shape a human life and forge its inescapable and often haunting past. There is no condemnation, only a tacit understanding that such secrets haunt the reader. Though the family history is never fully realized, confused as it is by the passage of time and other adults' varied perspectives on what may have happened, what the boy learned about his family that summer continues to haunt him and serves as the starting point for his adult inquiry into secrecy, betrayal, and the pursuit of truth.

Impact

Though not one of Gaiman's more widely recognized works and far less notable than Gaiman's *The Sandman* series, *The Comical Tragedy or Tragical Comedy of Mr. Punch* gained quite a bit of attention for McKean, who was hailed for incorporating some of the most advanced graphic design techniques and styles into the graphic novel format. The novel heralds a dynamic artistic approach to graphic novels—an approach more fully and more frequently realized in many recent film adaptations of earlier comics and graphic novels. McKean's merging of various artistic and graphic media to create such haunting imagery has since been emulated widely; however, he remains at the forefront of artists using this style.

This graphic novel marks a significant departure from the rough-hewn sketches in some of McKean's earlier work and demonstrates the full scope of his abilities not only as a graphic artist but also in creating a full story-world to accompany Gaiman's minimalist narrative. Gaiman and McKean challenge the boundaries of what may be considered children's literature, treating some sensitive issues—such as the vicious termination of an unwanted pregnancy—through subtle imagery and innuendo to maintain a veil of innocence for those not yet prepared to seek the full truth in the text and graphics.

Rachel E. Frier

Further Reading

Carey, Mike, and John Bolton. *God Save the Queen* (2007).

Gaiman, Neil, et al. *The Sandman* (1989-1996).

Kwitney, Alisa. *Destiny: A Chronicle of Deaths Foretold* (2000).

Bibliography

Gaiman, Neil. "It's Good to Be Gaiman: A Revealing Interview with Newbery Winner Neil Gaiman." Interview by Roger Sutton. *School Library Journal*, March 1, 2009. http://www.schoollibraryjournal.com/article/CA6640441.html.

Howard, Elise. "Neil Gaiman." *Horn Book Magazine* 85, no. 6 (November/December, 2009): 351-354.

Wagner, Hank, Christopher Golden, and Stephen R. Bissette. *Prince of Stories: The Many Worlds of Neil Gaiman*. New York: St. Martin's Griffin, 2009.

Zaleski, Jeff. "Comics! Books! Films!: The Many Faces of Neil Gaiman: The Arts and Ambitions of Neil Gaiman." *Publishers Weekly* 250, no. 30 (July, 2003): 46.

See also: *Tamara Drewe*

Transit

Author: McKeever, Ted
Artist: Ted McKeever (illustrator)
Publisher: Image Comics; Vortex Comics
First serial publication: 1987-1988
First book publication: 2008

Publication History

Ted McKeever entered the comics scene with the publication of the first issue of *Transit*, which established his distinctive artistic style, dark humor, and recurring themes. The chapters of *Transit* were originally published individually as part of what was intended to be an ongoing series. Issue 1, "Smoke Rings," was published in April, 1987, and was followed by issue 2, "Potato at Ground Zero" (June, 1987); issue 3, "Corruption for Beginners" (August, 1987); issue 4, "Incidents and Accidents" (November, 1987); and issue 5, "Sign of the Teaspoon" (March, 1988).

After publisher Vortex Comics went out of business following the publication of issue 5, McKeever abandoned the project to pursue other endeavors. However, in October of 2008, McKeever republished these works in a single volume that also included a newly drawn issue 6, "Final Throes." Under the editorship of Kristen Simon and with the graphics and design talent of publisher Jim Valentino, the compilation showcases the progression of the series' art, as the illustrations become increasingly detailed and intricate and McKeever's unique style becomes more distinctive. The new edition was issued in hardback by Shadowline/Image Comics; the text is the first volume in the Ted McKeever Library, which also includes *Eddy Current* (2008) and *Metropol* (2009).

Plot

Spud, an urban rebel and graffiti artist with a hint of a temper and a mild violent streak, suddenly finds himself witness to a politically charged murder as he flees from a police officer he has inadvertently spray painted. Though shaken by the experience, he does not realize the significance of the act he has witnessed until he is targeted as the prime suspect and becomes a hunted man. By then, his memory of the specific details has become blurry, and he cannot quite remember the name of the killer or determine why the murder occurred. This confusion lays the path he is to follow as he tries to protect himself and put the pieces together.

The pieces start to fall into place unexpectedly, but Spud does not put them together quickly enough to protect himself. Spud pursues Reverend Grisn, a man whose identity remains murky but who seems to be using his political platform to cover up his criminal activity. However, Spud makes the mistake of going after him in plain sight, evidently unaware of Grisn's mob ties and network of protection. Spud is captured and brainwashed. While Spud's friends Nigel and Sam search for him and are questioned by the police as accomplices, Grisn's megalomania and failed allegiance to mob boss Traun are revealed.

As Grisn becomes an increasing threat to Traun's control, the mob secures an early release from prison for Joe Bone, who is then sent to kill Grisn. As Bone struggles to readjust to life outside of prison and acclimate himself to the role of a killer, an accidental murder precipitates the dissolution of social order, and Traun's control proves to be far weaker than he had expected. In the final chapter, the city descends into chaos. Spud, freed from the mob's clutches but brainwashed and devoid of identity, proves to be neither the only victim nor the most tragic.

Characters

- *Spud*, the protagonist, is an average urban punk and self-proclaimed "cool subway arteest" who happens to be in the wrong place at the wrong time. The only witness to a politically motivated murder, he becomes its prime suspect.
- *Reverend Grisn*, the primary antagonist, is a mayoral candidate running on the platform of religious renewal and the promise of a return to a more moral society. However, he is responsible for a string of immoral acts and is eventually revealed to be at the core of the city's criminal underbelly.

- *Joseph "Joe" Bone* is a violent mobster who was incarcerated after loyally taking the fall for his superiors. When he finds himself inexplicably paroled six months early, he knows that more is to be requested of him, soon finding that his next assignment is to stop the very threat that the mob had created.
- *Nigel* is a blind accordion player and one of Spud's few trusted friends. He helps Spud get back on his feet, avoid the police, and begin to piece together the puzzle of Grisn's identity and plans.
- *Sam the Meatman* is a hulking former professional wrestler and now a resident of the city's slums. He agrees to let Spud stay with him and suddenly finds himself at the center of a criminal investigation and a string of unsettling murders.
- *Traun* is the mob boss, the puppet master under whose influence the city begins to descend into chaotic rioting and violence.

Artistic Style

While each chapter demonstrates a progression in the development of McKeever's artistic style, and though many of the illustrations in the book edition of *Transit* have been enhanced by Jim Valentino, a number of trademark features are consistent throughout. All of McKeever's illustrations are black and white; color is used in the cover image of each issue of the original series but is omitted from the collected volume. McKeever's use of page space remains consistent through the final chapter. In general, pages are laid out with adequate space between each of the illustrations and with few full-panel spreads. Because his formatting is generally standardized, McKeever is able to emphasize specific images or plot points by making only minor changes to the format or layout of the illustrations.

McKeever seems to hone his skill as an illustrator across the first five chapters: Background details become sharper and characters' identifying traits more distinctive. The final chapter, published twenty years after the original publication of the series, attests to McKeever's mastery of his style. The imagery becomes more haunting as society dissolves into chaos, and McKeever borrows stylistically from manga and Japanese animation in depicting the violence of this dissolution. The most significant changes in his illustrations across the series are evident in the appearance of his characters, whose depictions become increasingly realistic and less cartoonlike, and in his adaptation of page space in the final chapter to emphasize the vastness of the city's destruction and the significance of his biblical references.

Themes

The story's many themes evolve and intensify as the series progresses. Initially, McKeever introduces themes of urban chaos and social decay, depicting destructive events ranging from the mild (Spud's reasonably harmless vandalism) to the more severe (Grisn's murder of a hit man in the subway station). As the series progresses and the plot unfolds, it becomes clear that these two examples of social destruction pale in comparison to those enacted by the deeper criminal underbelly of society. By the end of the story, McKeever has revealed the vastness of destruction that can be caused by one man's love of power, by the strength of his political and religious corruption, and by the passivity of those who choose not to stand in his way. At each turn, one individual's selfish disregard for morality proves to be the catalyst for further immoral acts and the progressing decline of social order.

Underpinning these subjects is the recurring theme of religion and religious corruption, which is introduced with Reverend Grisn's character and culminates in the final chapter as the city burns and falls to ruin at the hands of one maniacal and misguided religious figurehead. As the series progresses, the religious message seems to evolve much as does McKeever's artistry, demonstrating the artist's growth and development. By the final chapter, McKeever's artistic style has become more distinctive than in the beginning, and the religious theme is more overtly depicted than in previous issues. Biblical quotations, overlaid on panels depicting the city's ruin and abandonment, reinforce themes of judgment and human responsibility that have been only gently alluded to at earlier points in the narrative, leaving readers with a message that continues to resonate long after the reading experience has ended.

Impact

In addition to launching McKeever's career, introducing the works of a graphic artist who would later win many awards and influence many subsequent artists and works, *Transit* stands at a pivotal point in the comics industry. First published in 1987, it is an early example of Modern Age comics and is simultaneously groundbreaking and typical of its period. McKeever excels at incorporating popular urban culture into the comics genre and blending graffiti art with comics art. While none of his artistic methods is groundbreaking in its own right, his blending of formats established a standard that was much imitated in the works of later comics artists.

Though McKeever's name is little known among mainstream readers, those within the comics industry and filmmakers such as the Wachowskis often cite his works, especially *Eddy Current* and *Metropol*, as the inspiration for many of their ideas and for the progression of the comics genre into the Modern Age. By depicting the nonhero, the average man who suddenly finds himself faced with extraordinary circumstances, McKeever helped launch the comics industry into the 1990's and into more mainstream accessibility, bringing the genre to a broader body of readers. While McKeever saw only sparse critical acclaim at the beginning of his career, he has come to be revered as one of the preeminent figures of the Modern Age.

Rachel E. Frier

Further Reading

Burns, Charles. *Black Hole* (2005).

McKeever, Ted. *Metropol* (2009).

Moore, Alan, and Dave Gibbons. *Watchmen* (1987).

Bibliography

Lamm, Spencer, et al. *The Matrix Comics*. Brooklyn, N.Y.: Burlyman, 2003.

Ligotti, Thomas, Stuart Moore, and Joe Harris. *The Nightmare Factory*. New York: Harper Paperbacks, 2007.

McKeever, Ted. "Finishing *Transit* and More—Talking to Ted McKeever." Interview by Vaneta Rogers. *Newsarama*, September 18, 2008. http://www.newsarama.com/comics/090818-TedMcKeever.html.

Saccio, Tatjana, and Dennis Seese. "Tag Team Review No. 9: Ted McKeever's *Transit*." Review of *Transit*, by Ted McKeever. *Library Journal*, December 17, 2008. http://www.libraryjournal.com/article/CA6623680.html.

Schuytema, Paul C. "Looking for a Hero: Modern Comic Book Characters Toil in an Imperfect World." *Omni* 16, no. 12 (1994): 27.

See also: *Black Hole*; *Metropol*; *Sin City*

Treasury of Victorian Murder, A

Author: Geary, Rick
Artist: Rick Geary (illustrator)
Publisher: NBM
First book publication: 1987-2007

Publication History

Nantier Beall Minoustchine (NBM) published the first volume of Rick Geary's *A Treasury of Victorian Murder* in 1987. This anthology was republished in a smaller format in 2002, making it consistent in size with the other volumes in the series. The second volume, *Jack the Ripper*, was also reprinted after it initially went out of print. The second edition of *The Borden Tragedy* included a selection of newspaper clippings concerning the original case. The ninth and final volume of the series was published in 2007, and Geary began to publish graphic novels based on twentieth-century murders the following year. All of the titles in *A Treasury of Victorian Murder* were released in both hardcover and paperback editions in 2008. Several volumes were also made available as e-books.

Plot

A Treasury of Victorian Murder presents famous murder cases from the Victorian era (1837-1901) in both Great Britain and the United States. With a deadpan delivery and often flowery narration reminiscent of the writing style of the era, Geary's treatment of these cases is not lurid but provides background context that is accessible to both young adult and adult readers. The separate volumes may be read in any order, as they do not follow any discernible time line. However, the first volume offers valuable background information on this era, providing a concise look at celebrated events and illustrious personages of the Victorian age and illuminating eighteen famous murderers. Of the eighteen cases, Geary highlights only two in subsequent volumes: those of Jack the Ripper and Madeleine Smith.

The introductory volume consists of three stories of unequal length. The first story introduces the unsolved 1873 murder of the Ryan siblings in New York City. The second tale involves the murderous physician Edward William Prichard, who kills his wife and mother-in-law in 1865. Despite the suspicions of Prichard's medical colleagues, nothing is done to save the lives of his victims. Prichard, an inept doctor and self-absorbed sociopath, becomes the last person to be publicly executed in Scotland. The final story is that of Mary Eleanor Pearcey, who brutally kills her lover's wife and youngest child in 1890.

Jack the Ripper is the subject of Geary's second volume. Geary presents the story through the lens of a faux journal of an unknown British gentleman and armchair detective. While many theories about Jack the Ripper are presented in Geary's rendition, he does not favor any as the ultimate solution, leaving such speculation to his reading audience.

The subject of an equally infamous murder case, Lizzie Borden, is also presented through the lens of a "recently discovered" memoir, this time of a female acquaintance of the young woman. The account begins with the murders and Borden's arrest and then explores the family background and dynamics of the case, as narrated by the young woman "playing detective." Extensive research is put forth, including a time line of two days before the tragedy and an hourly diary of the events of the day of the murders.

In the fourth volume, Geary focuses on the personal and political motivation behind the assassination of President James A. Garfield in 1881. Charles Julius Guiteau shoots the president as a "political necessity" and feels that he is not guilty of murder because the bullet takes several months to kill Garfield. The topic of the fifth volume is the unsolved 1841 murder of the young clerk Mary Rogers, whose story was superficially adapted by Edgar Allan Poe as the short story "The Mystery of Marie Rogêt." Again, Geary dispassionately presents the numerous theories proposed by the media at the time of the murder, highlighting the changes Poe made to his short story to concur with contemporary speculation.

The sixth volume follows the path of a known murderer, this time the proprietor of a rooming house built to his own peculiar specifications. H. H. Holmes reinvents himself numerous times to victimize mostly young women. He continuously flees compromising situations and danger until he is arrested for insurance fraud. The Pinkerton Detectives are brought on the case and uncover more than fifty missing people dispatched by Holmes.

The assassination of Abraham Lincoln is the focus of Geary's next volume. Geary provides the reader with contextual information and compares Lincoln's dream of his own assassination with the actual event. The story also details the aftermath of the assassination.

An unsolved murder and a classic case of class differences is explored in the story of Madeleine Smith, a young woman who becomes enthralled with an unsuitable man. She pens 198 passionate letters to Pierre Emile L'Angelier, sixty of which are read at her trial. When he refuses to destroy the letters or return them to her, she allegedly resorts to arsenic to rid herself of his persistence. Her guilt cannot be proved by the courts, and she goes free.

The final volume takes place in Kansas and concerns the bloody Bender family. Geary provides maps and historical context, illuminating several theories regarding the family members and the various murders.

Volumes

- *A Treasury of Victorian Murder*, Volume 1 (1987). Three murder cases that exemplify the Victorian era and its fascination with murder are explored.
- *Jack the Ripper: A Journal of the Whitechapel Murders* (1995). The infamous unsolved serial murders of Whitechapel are presented along with maps and contextual information concerning the area, the people involved, and the various theories regarding the possible identity of Jack the Ripper.
- *The Borden Tragedy: A Memoir of the Infamous Double Murder at Fall River, Mass., 1892* (1997). The double murder of Lizzie Borden's father and stepmother is explored, with particular focus on the subsequent trial of Borden both in court and in the media.
- *The Fatal Bullet: The Assassination of President James A. Garfield* (1999). The life paths of Garfield and his assassin, Guiteau, are compared and contrasted.
- *The Mystery of Mary Rogers* (2001). The unsolved murder of Rogers is played against the background of the inefficient New York Police Department and the various theories regarding her death.
- *The Beast of Chicago: The Murderous Career of H. H. Holmes* (2003). The lives and deaths of Holmes and his victims are explored in the context of the World's Columbian Exposition of 1893.
- *The Murder of Abraham Lincoln* (2005). The assassination of Lincoln and the events surrounding it are chronicled, beginning with the development of the conspiracy and ending after the death of the assassin, Booth.
- *The Case of Madeleine Smith* (2006). Smith's arrest for poisoning her lover, failure to be convicted, and later life are examined.
- *The Saga of the Bloody Benders* (2007). The crimes of the notorious Bender family are contrasted with the everyday details of pioneer life of Kansas in the early 1870's.

Characters

- *Nicholas Ryan* is a young man who lives with his sister, Mary, in New York City. The 1873 murders of Ryan and his pregnant sister go unsolved; there is speculation, however, that Ryan may have been the father of Mary's child.
- *Dr. Edward William Prichard* is a successful and charming physician living in Glasgow, Scotland; he poisons his mother-in-law and wife in 1865. The murder trial uncovers the depths of his misrepresentations regarding his education and personal relationships.
- *Mary Eleanor Pearcey* is an unattractive widow fixated on her neighbor, Frank Hogg. Hoping that he will return her passion, she murders his wife and their baby.
- *Narrator* is an unknown British gentleman who lives in London during the time of the Jack the

Ripper attacks and subsequent investigation. He is an amateur detective and crime buff with contacts in police departments.
- *Lizzie Borden* is a spinster living with her father, stepmother, and sister when her father and stepmother are murdered. She is the prime suspect for the murders but is acquitted.
- *James A. Garfield* is the twentieth president of the United States. He is known as an honest, courageous, humble, and steadfast person, having demonstrated these qualities throughout his political career. He is assassinated in 1881.
- *Charles Julius Guiteau* is an ambitious lawyer with a limited conscience who attempts to gain a foothold in politics through any means necessary. Seeking fame, he fatally shoots President Garfield.
- *Mary Rogers* is a clerk known as the "Beautiful Cigar Girl" who works in John Anderson's tobacco store in New York City. Her unsolved murder becomes a national sensation.
- *Herman W. Mudgett*, a.k.a. *H. H. Holmes*, is a con artist, bigamist, and serial killer. He turns his Chicago boarding house into a "murder castle."
- *Abraham Lincoln* is the sixteenth president of the United States. Although highly regarded as a passionate and wise leader, he is assassinated in 1865.
- *John Wilkes Booth* is an actor who is outraged by the South's defeat in the American Civil War and strongly opposes the abolition of slavery. He assassinates Lincoln and later dies while attempting to escape pursuit.
- *Madeleine Smith* is a woman from a wealthy family who breaks societal conventions by falling in love with the working-class L'Angelier. She is accused of poisoning him with arsenic but is acquitted.
- *Pierre Emile L'Angelier* is Smith's working-class lover. He resorts to blackmail attempts to stop Smith from breaking off their affair, using the passionate letters she had written to him over the course of their two-year relationship. He dies of arsenic poisoning.
- *Kate Bender* is an attractive and outgoing woman who orchestrates the murder of visitors to her family's Wayside Inn. She and her family are responsible for eleven known murders, but they escape before the victims are discovered and are never apprehended.
- *Colonel Ed York* is the brother of murder victim Dr. William York. He inadvertently alerts the Bender family to their upcoming discovery while tracing his brother to the Wayside Inn. His brother's body is the first to be uncovered when the property is searched.

Artistic Style

The sole creator of the *Treasury of Victorian Murder*, Geary researched, wrote, illustrated, and lettered the pages and covers of all nine volumes. Geary's clean and stark black lines on a white background produce a woodcut quality that is evocative of old newspaper engravings and reminiscent of the style of artist Edward Gorey. His finely detailed illustrations lack shading and, surprising for a comic, speech balloons. There is no direct dialogue; all of the text appears in narration boxes or in long listings of questions collected for the reader.

Geary uses a consistent format for all of the stories. The cover of each volume is printed in full color. The splash page introduces the characters and the specific setting; a wide variety of rectangular panels follows, interspersed and often overlaid with circular panels that introduce characters and provide a portal into the past. The characters and individual settings are immediately recognizable, and both contain moody and distinct nuances, expressing the often sinister aspects of the story. Geary utilizes half pages, full pages, and double-page spreads to add suspense and horror to the narrative. Rarely do two consecutive panels illuminate the same character or setting; these frequently changing images create a detached sense of urgency and suspense. The detailed and dark illustrations are graphic enough to convey the severity and violence of the crimes, but the art is neither morbid nor gruesome. Geary's use of language, often overblown and flowery, provides a counterpoint to his restrained images.

> **Rick Geary**
>
> Cartoonist Rick Geary has long employed a smooth, clean style to depict some of history's most horrible events. A veteran at adapting classic novels and short stories for the all-ages Classics Illustrated line, Geary has found his greatest acclaim in his series *A Treasury of Victorian Murder* and *A Treasury of XXth Century Murder*, biographical examinations of such infamous murderers as Lizzie Borden and Jack the Ripper. Geary often employs narrative techniques similar to the classic works he has adapted for these stories.

Themes

The title of the series sets out the thematic parameters: infamous murders that took place in the Victorian era in Great Britain and the United States. The murder victims and their killers are essentially from all walks of life, but the upper-middle-class stratum is the focus of the majority of the cases. In addition, each of the cases selected for inclusion in the series is shown to have been the subject of much public interest and speculation in the contemporary press. In his introduction to the first volume, Geary asserts that such crimes were characterized by interpersonal anxieties triggered by the rapidly industrializing, sexually repressive Victorian society and encouraged by the frenetic energy and sensational attentiveness of the popular press. Geary's comparison of Victorian newspaper coverage of murders to modern media coverage of similar crimes is an underlying theme throughout the series.

Along with public sensationalism, the series explores true crime, history, and mysteries. Geary's fascination with the darker elements of the Victorian era, the advent of sensationalized press coverage, and the macabre rationales for many of the murders is clearly reflected in his dispassionate but engaging exploration of these crimes. His meticulous research and illumination of the people, places, and events bring the seedy edge of the Victorian era to life.

Impact

Geary's work on *A Treasury of Victorian Murder* and other historical nonfiction titles has aided in the acceptance of the comic book format as a viable and vital reading material in schools and libraries. His treatment of the evidence offers an accurate and detached, but horrific, view of the murders and demonstrates a strong affinity for illuminating the images, mood, and language of Victorian society. Geary's presentation of the fascination that Victorians had with death never waivers through the nine volumes, nor does his attention to detail, as evidenced by the numerous maps, floor plans, and character studies provided for background. His inclusion of bibliographical information further indicates the serious intent of the work. This entertaining and educational series has been frequently recommended for inclusion in history classes.

Gail A. de Vos

Further Reading

Bendis, Brian Michael, and Marc Anderyko. *Torso* (2002).

Geary, Rick. *A Treasury of Twentieth Century Murder* (2008-   ).

Moore, Alan, and Eddie Campbell. *From Hell* (1999).

Bibliography

Geary, Rick. "The Power of Old-Fashioned Storytelling." In *The Education of a Comics Artist: Visual Narrative in Cartoons, Graphic Novels, and Beyond*, edited by Michael Dooley and Steven Heller. New York: Allworth Press, 2005.

Scott, Gini Graham. *Homicide by the Rich and Famous: A Century of Prominent Killers*. Westport, Conn.: Praeger, 2005.

Tabachnick, Stephen E. "The Graphic Novel and the Age of Transition: A Survey and Analysis." *English Literature in Transition, 1880-1920* 53, no. 1 (2010): 3-28.

See also: *From Hell; Houdini; The Book of Genesis*

Tricked

Author: Robinson, Alex
Artist: Alex Robinson (illustrator); Bwana Spoons (cover artist); Brett Warnock (cover artist)
Publisher: Top Shelf Comics
First book publication: 2005

Publication History
After garnering critical acclaim and industry recognition for *Box Office Poison* (2001), Alex Robinson released the structurally complex *Tricked* in 2005. The graphic novel took four years to complete. After abandoning two variations on themes presented in *Tricked*, Robinson connected loose narrative strands to knit a tapestry of interwoven stories. Robinson's publisher, Top Shelf Comics, decided to release *Tricked* in one volume instead of serializing it in order to create an "event" around its release. Robinson has commented that the characters Ray and Steve represent two sides of his own personality and that the most challenging character to create was Nick because of the character's inability to empathize with other humans.

Plot
Tricked takes place in an unspecified modern American city and begins by providing brief glimpses of the novel's many characters. After a chance meeting in which Lily refuses Ray's sexual advances, he hires her as his personal assistant. Unbeknownst to his wife, Nick has been laid off and now works at a shop called The Dugout, forging signatures on sport memorabilia and stealing money from his cruel Russian boss, Boris. Phoebe travels to the city in search of her father, Richard. Steve holds silent grudges against those around him. Lily quickly becomes Ray's muse and inspires a series of new recordings. Caprice meets Boyd, and they begin a relationship. Boris has Nick assist him in viciously assaulting a man whom he wrongly believes has stolen money from him. While meeting an old friend, Steve reveals his sociopathic proclivities. Phoebe arrives in the city and goes to The Little Piggy to locate Richard.

Steve receives an autographed photograph of Ray in the mail and believes that the autograph is a forgery. Richard's friends are surprised to learn of Phoebe's existence, and his longtime companion, Frank, temporarily leaves him. Lily accompanies Ray to the island of St. Hubbins to record new material. Caprice and Boyd's relationship grows more serious. Phoebe and Richard visit the zoo together, and Richard reveals to his daughter that he is gay.

Steve has increasingly disturbing dreams, is fired from his job, and holds imaginary conversations with Ray. Boyd tells Caprice that he loves her. Ray proposes marriage to Lily; she accepts. A fellow forger reveals to Nick that Boris once killed a man. Caprice and Phoebe go to The Dugout to buy a gift for Boyd. Nick sells Caprice a signed baseball, but he then admits that the signature is a forgery. Nick introduces himself as "Ray" and convinces Caprice to meet for a date. Richard arranges for Frank to meet Phoebe formally. Steve's actions become more erratic. Caprice helps throw a birthday party for Boyd, but she has doubts about their relationship.

Ray and Lily go on their honeymoon. Lily accidentally discovers a room full of "groupies" waiting for Ray, and she storms away in anger. Meanwhile, Ray ruminates on the emptiness of his celebrity lifestyle. He then realizes that he has been set up by his former personal assistant in an effort to sabotage his marriage.

Nick worries that Boris has learned of his deceptions. Caprice and Nick meet for their date. Phoebe becomes a waitress at the diner. Steve slips further into madness. On a second date with Caprice, Nick concocts even more lies. Caprice realizes that Boyd does indeed love her. Lily agrees to meet with Ray at The Little Piggy to try to save their new marriage.

When Boris demands that Nick run an errand, the suspicious Nick believes that Boris will kill him. Nick murders Boris with a baseball bat and flees with money from the shop. Richard invites Phoebe to move to the city and live with him and Frank, who are now reconciled. Richard notes that the diner is closing early for a private party organized by Ray Beam. Steve learns of

Ray's imminent visit to The Little Piggy. Lily reveals that she loves Ray, and the two meet at the empty diner. A bloodied Nick arrives at the diner in an attempt to convince Caprice to leave town with him, but she refuses. Nick sees Ray and approaches him. At the same time, Steve enters the restaurant and aims a gun at Ray. Steve accidentally shoots Nick, killing him.

A few years later, Steve is in prison, Phoebe lives in the city, and Caprice and Boyd are still in a relationship. Ray is happily married to Lily and now devotes time and energy to social causes. He accepts that he is indeed happy with himself.

Characters
- *Ray Beam* is a handsome, alternately self-possessed and self-loathing twenty-nine-year-old. He is the former lead singer of the popular rock band the Tricks. After the band's dissolution, Ray earned critical acclaim and popular success with two solo recordings. It has been four years since his first solo album, and he is in need of another hit. He desperately attempts to write new music, but his creativity is stymied, and he indulges in an endless succession of one-night stands and drug abuse. With the help of Lily, he begins recording again and learns to live an authentic, fulfilling life.
- *Lily Rivera* is an attractive, diminutive, and kind young woman who accidentally meets rock star Ray Beam while working as a temporary employee at a talent agency. Lily is unfamiliar with Ray and his music and is not impressed by his celebrity status. As a result, she views him not as a famous musician but as a fellow human. They later fall in love and are married.
- *Steve* is an overweight, balding, and bespectacled office tech worker and an obsessive fan of both the Tricks and Ray Beam. He harbors great animosity toward his fellow humans, especially those who do not agree with his taste in music. When he decides to suspend the use of medication that keeps his psychosis under control, he is fired from his job and becomes delusional. He eventually attempts to assassinate Ray.
- *Nick* is a slightly pudgy but rather handsome man who lost his office job some time ago. Unwilling to confess his joblessness to his wife, he continues to fabricate stories about work. In actuality, he is employed at The Dugout, a sports memorabilia shop, where he forges autographs of sports stars. He is later shot and killed by Ray's would-be assassin, Steve.
- *Caprice* is a cute, intelligent, insecure woman who works as a waitress at the diner The Little Piggy. Because of a history of failed relationships, she is hesitant to become involved in a committed relationship with Boyd. When Nick pursues her, she realizes the value of Boyd's love.
- *Richard* is the co-owner and co-manager of The Little Piggy. A gay man previously married to a woman, he fathered a child but has neither seen nor contacted his daughter, Phoebe, for more than a decade. When Phoebe comes to the restaurant and introduces herself, Richard's world is thrown into crisis, as neither his longtime companion, Frank, nor his friends know that he has a daughter.
- *Phoebe* is a thin, blond teenage girl from Carrizozo, New Mexico. She travels to the city to find her father, Richard. She is stunned to learn that her father is gay, but she seeks to establish a meaningful relationship with him. She eventually becomes a waitress at The Little Piggy, forging a connection with her long-absent father.

Artistic Style
Tricked literalizes and visualizes the way in which seemingly unconnected lives are woven together through chance, coincidence, and serendipity. Each character is introduced individually in the first of the fifty chapters. As *Tricked* progresses, the lives of the characters begin to subtly intertwine. Structurally, *Tricked* bears a resemblance to ensemble work by such filmmakers as Robert Altman and Paul Thomas Anderson.

The characters are highly developed and possess intricate personal lives, yet they are portrayed in a cartoonlike, caricature style reminiscent of Dan DeCarlo's tenure on *Archie* and the oeuvre of Will Eisner, a former

> **Alex Robinson**
>
> Trained at the School of Visual Arts, Alex Robinson began serializing his graphic novel *Box Office Poison* with Antarctic Press in the 1990's before it was collected by Top Shelf in 2001. Robinson's work is strongly literary, focusing on typical individuals from his own generation. *Box Office Poison* depicts a series of slacker characters on the fringes of the comics industry, while his subsequent graphic novel, *Tricked*, revolves around a diverse collection of six characters whose lives variously intersect over the course of several weeks. *Too Cool to Be Forgotten* tells the story of a man transported back to his high school in the 1980's when he uses hypnosis to try to quit smoking. Visually, Robinson uses a cartoonishly naturalist design in which the figures of his characters are slightly exaggerated. His pages are generally composed as discrete units and he uses word balloons to divide space.

instructor of Robinson. Robinson's use of expressive, deceptively simple black-and-white line work to evoke engaging characters genealogically links *Tricked* to the Hernandez brothers' *Love and Rockets* (1981-1996). In the climax, the characters find themselves sharing both time and space. The ensuing pages depict defining moments from each character's life. All of these images eventually swirl together. As this occurs, Ray utters, "I understand," as if he has reached a moment in which he can clearly see the connections between all of humanity. The volume concludes with a single image on an otherwise blank page: a lemniscate, the symbol of infinity.

Themes

In accordance with its title, *Tricked* concerns deception. All of the characters grapple with the dynamics of deception, be it self-deception or the deception of others. Ray has deceived himself through indulgences afforded by his rock-star lifestyle. This self-deception has led to a sense of alienation from his music, rendering him unable to access his creativity. Lily chooses not to deceive anyone, and because of that trait, her life is both authentic and fulfilling. It is only through Lily that Ray relinquishes his self-deception and achieves actualization as an artist.

Steve also deceives himself, choosing to blame others for his failures in life. He is unable to confront himself honestly, and this leads to his psychological breakdown and attempt to kill Ray. Nick's deception of others has become more than a method of coping with his life; he has turned to deception as a profession, deceiving his wife and family while also earning income through forgery. Even when he pursues Caprice, Nick is unwilling to reveal any truth about himself. He has deceived so many people that it is almost impossible to separate his "true" identity from his various alter egos.

Caprice has deceived herself into believing that a healthy, loving relationship is unattainable. When Boyd declares his love for her, she retreats into self-deception and indulges in a fling with Nick. Only when Caprice recognizes Nick's deceptive ways does she realize her love for Boyd. Richard's deception regarding his former life creates a serious rift in his relationship with Frank. Only through Frank's love for him and acceptance of Phoebe is Richard able to earn forgiveness. The arrival of Phoebe, who has deceived her mother by leaving Carrizozo to find her father, serves as a sort of reckoning for Richard. At the conclusion, the characters' various decisions regarding truth and deception determine their fates.

Impact

Tricked is a paradigmatic example of the adult-oriented, alternative graphic novel focused on character and structure. It offers modern commentary on celebrity, the music industry, violence, petty crime, psychosis, the role of the artist in society, romance, and sexual identity. Both Robinson's art and narrative approach had an immediate impact upon creators in independent and small-press comics. As an experiment in structure and a register of the societal concerns of its time, *Tricked* serves as an intriguing document of postmillennial American graphic storytelling.

Shannon Blake Skelton

Further Reading

Hernandez, Gilbert, Jaime Hernandez, and Mario Hernandez. *Love and Rockets* (1981-1996).

Robinson, Alex. *Box Office Poison* (2001).
Thompson, Craig. *Blankets* (2003).

Bibliography

Robinson, Alex. "Alex Robinson." Interview by Gavin J. Grant. *Indie Bound*. http://www.indiebound.org/author-interviews/robinsonalex.

_____. "Alex Robinson Chat Transcript." Interview by Brian Cronin, Brandon Harvey, and Adam P. Knave. *Comic Book Resources*, September 8, 2008. http://goodcomics.comicbookresources.com/2008/09/08/alex-robinson-chat-transcript.

_____. "The Alex Robinson Interview." Interview by Tom Crippen. *The Comics Journal* 293 (November, 2008): 64-99.

_____. "Alex's Robinson's *Tricked*." Interview by Hilary Goldstein. *IGN*, March 17, 2005. http://comics.ign.com/articles/596/596989p1.html.

_____. "New Tricks: An Interview with Alex Robinson." Interview by John Hogan. *Graphic Novel Reporter*. http://graphicnovelreporter.com/content/new-tricks-interview-alex-robinson-interview.

See also: *Love and Rockets; Box Office Poison; Blankets*

TWENTIETH CENTURY EIGHTBALL

Author: Clowes, Daniel
Artist: Daniel Clowes (illustrator)
Publisher: Fantagraphics Books
First serial publication: 1988-1996 (partially published in *Eightball*)
First book publication: 2001

Publication History

Eightball was Daniel Clowes's second series for Fantagraphics Books, the first being *#$@&!: The Official Lloyd Llewellyn Collection* (1989). Whereas *Lloyd Llewellyn* is based around a single character and has a consistent style, *Eightball* is an anthology comic with varied content: Most issues contain one part of an ongoing narrative strip plus several shorter, one-off strips, sometimes in the style of newspaper "funnies." Issues 1-10 feature *Like a Velvet Glove Cast in Iron* (1989-1993), while issues 11-18 serialize *Ghost World* (1993-1997), both of which were later collected in book format. The style also leaves room for some relatively long one-offs such as "Caricature" (issue 15) and "Gynecology" (issue 17), which were later collected under the title *Caricature* (1998).

After Clowes completed *Ghost World*, he stopped including shorter strips in *Eightball*, and issues 19-21 were entirely given over to the three parts of *David Boring* (1998-2000). In issues 22 and 23, Clowes fused the two approaches. Each issue is a single narrative but is told in a kaleidoscopic style via a series of short strips, using varying styles and character viewpoints (often presented as if they were one of a regular series starring those characters). The last issue (23) was published in June, 2004.

The *Twentieth Century Eightball* book, published in 2002, collects short strips from *Eightball*, issues 1-16, all of which are five pages or less (*Caricature* had featured strips of six pages or more), with the emphasis on humor. A handful of the strips were published in places other than *Eightball*. For example, "The Operator," was published in *Twist*, issue 3 (October, 1988); "Frankie and Johnnie," in *Young Lust*, issue 7 (1990); and "Curtain of Sanity and Zubrick," in *National Lampoon* (April, 1991, and May, 1991). The book also contains some new material in the form of six newspaper-style strips in the back of the book; a two-page story called "Little Enid," starring a younger version of the character from *Ghost World*; and a four-page story about Clowes putting the book together, which also serves as a title page, a contents page, a copyright page, and a back-cover blurb, making the book entirely comics from cover to cover.

Plot

Twentieth Century Eightball is not a single narrative, and many of the strips are not even "stories" as such. Several are satires and think-pieces on a subject. "I Hate You Deeply" features Lloyd Llewellyn simply listing things he hates (the text acknowledges that he is acting as a mouthpiece for Clowes). Its companion piece, "I Love You Tenderly," starts off as a counterbalancing list of things Llewellyn loves, but drifts into a supplementary list of hates. "Art School Confidential" casts itself as an exposé of the pointlessness of art school, mocking the institution itself and the people who go there. "On Sports" explores sexual symbolism in sports, with explicit pornographic illustrations. "A

Daniel Clowes at the 2010 Alternative Press Expo in San Francisco, CA. (Guillaume Paumier)

811

Message to the People of the Future" is a brief survey of modern life addressed to people in the year 2293. There are also pieces on death ("My Suicide"), unconventional attractiveness ("Ugly Girls"), Clowes's hometown ("Chicago"), and religion ("Why I Hate Christians").

Several of the strips are observational. "The Stroll" and "Marooned on a Desert Island with the People from the Subway" are both stream-of-consciousness strips showing the point of view and thoughts of a character on an uneventful journey. "The Party" takes the same approach but changes the setting. Clowes goes on to subvert this observational style in "Just Another Day," in which he addresses the readers and ridicules them for identifying with the piece and then presents a series of increasingly absurd visions of the "real" Clowes. Only a few strips have a straightforward narrative: "Devil Doll?" concerns a teenage satanist who eventually finds redemption, and "The Happy Fisherman" is the surreal tale of a wandering fisherman who has a frozen carp stuck on his penis.

The shorter strips tend to be based around a one-joke character (or characters). These include "Sensual Santa," "Grip Glutz and Shamrock Squid," and the self-explanatory "Needled—k the Bug-F—-er.

Characters

- *Lloyd Llewellyn* is a sharp-suited film noir-style character who starred in his own book, which was written and drawn by Clowes before the *Eightball* series began. In his two *Eightball* strips, however, Llewellyn is used as a mouthpiece character for Clowes.
- *Zubrick* and *Pogeybait* are roommates. Zubrick is a misanthrope and borderline agoraphobic; Pogeybait is an eccentric with enormous hair and prominent underwear. They originated in a series of monthly adventures in *National Lampoon*, one of which is included in this collection.
- *Feldman*, a nerdy man who uses a mobility scooter, is noteworthy as he appears in two strips ("Feldman" and "Squirrel Girl and Candypants") and went on to be a character in the *Ghost World* (2001) film.

Artistic Style

Clowes's characteristic style has a cartoonlike quality uncluttered with simple, light lines. Although he has described himself as a "cartoonist," his narrative work tends to be subtler than his cartooning by presenting figures who are both plain striking in their slight physical imperfections. Nonetheless, the shorter strips in *Twentieth Century Eightball* have a wide variety of styles. Whereas Clowes's long narratives tend to use the most unobtrusive version of his style, the shorter strips often have an overt, baroque style befitting their broad and surreal humor.

While some strips use Clowes's "normal" style (the "observational" ones especially), much of *Twentieth Century Eightball* is cartoonlike and represents figures in a variety of different ways. "Playful Obsession," a parody of newspaper funnies and children's comics (the target being such strips' one-dimensional nature as well as the inherent obnoxiousness of Richie Rich), is a direct stylistic pastiche, including Ben-Day dots in the coloring; like any pastiche, the work's ability to reproduce the trappings of its target makes it funny. Others pieces, such as "Sensual Santa," seek to enhance the humor through visual grotesquerie.

Lloyd Llewellyn is sleekly depicted in a stripped-back pulp style, far neater and more angular than the typical Clowes figure. In "Why I Hate Christians," Clowes adopts a heavily stylized, 1960's-esque approach to drawing his central character using an oval-shaped head and almost cubist cartoon features. Both examples occur in strips that feature a Clowes avatar—perhaps allowing for a measure of detachment between artist and subject.

The stylistic experiments of these short strips fed back into Clowes's long-form work such as *Ice Haven* (2005) and *The Death Ray* (2011). The aesthetic shifts in these strips, as Clowes moves between central characters, allow him to present the world as those characters see it. Having started out as a disparate collection of material united only by its status as the product of a single writer-artist, *Eightball* eventually became a coherent entity while simultaneously retaining its original identity.

Themes

The strips in this collection are diverse, but the humor strips are largely written from a viewpoint of misanthropy, expressed for comic effect. The most obvious examples are the Lloyd Llewellyn strips "I Hate You Deeply" and "I Love You Tenderly," which mock their own misanthropy by bitterly complaining about "people with personality, magnetism, and charisma" in between more reasoned gripes and implicitly criticizing the author for hiding behind a cartoon character to make such criticisms.

The stream-of-consciousness strips are also disproportionately judgmental, reflecting people's tendency to regard themselves as reasonable and others as unreasonable. These are juxtaposed with parody strips such as "Playful Obsession" and "Needled—k the Bug-F—-er" that mock the way that humor strips tend to reduce their characters to a single characteristic, which is not that different from how people treat those they do not really know by judging them based on whatever they happen to be doing at the moment one encounters them.

The overall viewpoint of dissatisfaction with everything carries over into "Cool Your Jets," a strip in which two characters discuss the impossibility of finding the perfect woman, and "Give It Up!," which asserts that everyone's life is essentially futile. "Art School Confidential" targets everyone in an art school—the teachers and the students, the talented and the talentless, the professionals and the amateurs, the ugly and the beautiful, the men and the women. Clowes's satire is not tied to any specific agenda. It seeks to undermine almost everything, even himself and the act of undermining things. This is leavened only by sympathy for the underdog, expressed in "I Love You Tenderly" and in "Ugly Girls."

Impact

Since the underground comics movement of the 1960's, independent anthology comics generally featured work by a variety of creators. *Love and Rockets* was produced by a tight-knit creative team, but Peter Bagge's *Neat Stuff* (1985-1990) was the major forerunner of *Eightball* as an anthology in which diverse content was linked only by being the product of a single writer-artist. Progressing from the more focused *Lloyd Llewellyn*, Clowes used *Eightball* as a vehicle for almost anything that interested him.

The format has since become popular, with titles such as Adrian Tomine's *Optic Nerve* (1995-) and Chris Ware's *Acme Novelty Library* (2005). The former features low-key narratives of young people, similar to *Ghost World*, while the latter makes use of cartoon styles in a way that is similar to *Eightball* by playing up the contrast between style and subject matter. Alan Moore's *Tomorrow Stories* (1999-), written by Moore but illustrated by a variety of artists, features a similar mix of experimentation, parody, and humor and incorporates retro styling.

The influence of *Eightball* can even be seen in DC Comics' *Solo* series (2004-2006), which gave artists an issue each and allowed them to use any DC character. Many contributors elected to fill their issue with strips of varying genre, length, and style, demonstrating that this "authored" approach (which also incorporated pastiche) has reached the mainstream.

Films

Art School Confidential. Directed by Terry Zwigoff. United Artists/Mr. Mudd, 2006. The film is loosely based on the four-page strip from *Eightball*, issue 7, which had no story but was merely Clowes mocking his art school and fellow students. Scripted by Clowes, the film expands the view of art school seen in the original strip, including the student archetypes, the problems presented by art-school girls, the absurdity of what some students pass off as work, and students' desperate delusion of one day being successful. However the narrative spine bears more resemblance to another *Eightball* strip, "The Truth," in which an aspiring artist's conscious efforts to do quality work meet with failure before he stumbles on success accidentally. In the film, this kind of unwarranted success occurs twice—both when lead character Jerome (played by Max Minghella) is suspected of being a serial killer and when the undercover policeman trailing him is hailed as a naïve genius.

Eddie Robson

Further Reading
Clowes, Daniel. *Caricature* (2002).
Matt, Joe. *Peepshow* (1992-   ).
Ware, Chris. *Acme: Our Annual Report to Shareholders and Rainy Day Saturday Afternoon Fun Book, a Library of Novelty* (2005).

Bibliography
Hignite, M. Todd. *In the Studio: Visits with Contemporary Cartoonists*. New Haven, Conn.: Yale University Press, 2006.
Oakes, Kaya. *Slanted and Enchanted: The Evolution of Indie Culture*. New York: Henry Holt, 2009.
Sacks, Mike. *And Here's the Kicker: Conversations with 25 Top Humor Writers on Their Craft*. Cincinnati: Writer's Digest Books, 2009.

See also: *Ghost World*; *Ice Haven*; *David Boring*; *Like a Velvet Glove Cast in Iron*

U

Usagi Yojimbo

Author: Sakai, Stan
Artist: Stan Sakai (illustrator); Tom Luth (colorist)
Publisher: Fantagraphics Books; Mirage Comics; Dark Horse Comics
First Serial Publication: 1987-
First Book Publication: 1987-

Publication History

Usagi Yojimbo originated in small-press comics of the 1980's, first appearing in the anthropomorphic-animal anthology series *Albedo Anthropomorphics*. The series moved to Fantagraphics Books, which first included *Usagi Yojimbo* in its anthropomorphic-animal anthology *Critters* and later showcased the comic in its own series. The series rode the wave of success of black-and-white independent comics through the 1980's, until changes in the marketplace led creator Stan Sakai to take his samurai rabbit to Mirage Comics for a full-color run. When Mirage folded after sixteen issues, Sakai moved his series to Dark Horse Comics, which began carrying the title in 1996. The character of Miyamoto Usagi has also appeared as a guest star in a number of other titles. In 2011, Dark Horse released *Usagi Yojimbo: Yokai*, the only all-original *Usagi Yojimbo* graphic novel.

Although Sakai is a Japanese American artist creating comics in English for publication in the United States, he has noted in interviews that he is often considered a manga artist because *Usagi Yojimbo* is set in Japan and strongly influenced by Japanese culture and folklore.

Plot

Usagi Yojimbo is constructed as a slice-of-life picaresque. A samurai without portfolio, Usagi has no other agenda than to act according to his best judgment and to continue to improve himself as a person and a swordsman. Although there is an overarching plot of the series, in which Usagi opposes the schemes of the evil Lord Hikiji and other tyrannical or criminal fig-

---

> **Stan Sakai**
>
> Stan Sakai is synonymous with his long-running series *Usagi Yojimbo*, whose title character is a mercenary bunny rabbit: have sword, will hop. He introduced the character in 1984 and continues to publish it. Born in 1953 in Kyoto, Japan, Sakai has spent most of his life in the United States, first in Hawaii, where his family moved when he was two years old, and later in California, where he has long lived in Pasadena. Sakai got his start in comics as letterer for Sergio Aragonés's comic adventure, Groo the Wanderer.
>
> Though raised in the West, he acknowledges ties to his native country, having noted that Hawaii in particular has a strong Japanese culture. He has said that he is not much of a manga fan and has regularly distanced his own stories from manga. The cultural influences and associations of Sakai are quite filmic—his favorite movie is *Satomi Haddenden* (1959), a masterpiece of samurai cinema based on the epic novel *Nansō Satomi Hakkenden,* and he enjoys the work of other auteurs such as Akira Kurosawa and Hiroshi Inagaki.
>
> For *Usagi Yojimbo* and other works such as *47 Ronin*, Sakai has won five Eisner Awards, two Harvey Awards, the Inkwell "All-in-One" Award, and the Inkpot Award for Lifetime Achievement in the Field of Cartooning. Though well-recognized for his talents, Sakai is humble, saying he writes for himself and has "the best job in the world."

Stan Sakai, 2015. (Dhfujii, via Wikimedia Commons)

ures, the real goal of the story is to provide a window into the history and culture of seventeenth century Japan while telling bittersweet stories of heroism and humanity.

The two major elements that drive the world of *Usagi Yojimbo* are time and death. Unlike the characters in other anthropomorphic-animal comics, who tend to be immortal clowns or unchanging whimsical figures, the characters of *Usagi Yojimbo* live, age, and die. Wars and duels have casualties, characters have children who grow, and every character can learn and change with time and experience. Over the course of the series, Usagi evolves from a rather simple, stern figure whose behavior is guided by rigid Bushido principals into a well-rounded protagonist who offers commentary on many aspects of life. He progresses from early manhood to something approaching middle age.

Seventeenth century Japan, the other "star" of the series, was a pivotal era. Japan unified as a nation during that time and greatly restricted the use of gunpowder until the nineteenth century, ensuring the value of swordsmen like Usagi until contact with the West.

Volumes
- *Usagi Yojimbo: The Rōnin*, Volume 1 (1987). Collects short stories from *Albedo* and *Critters*.
- *Usagi Yojimbo: Samurai*, Volume 2 (1989). Collects issues 1-6 of the Fantagraphics series.
- *The Usagi Yojimbo Saga,* Volume 1 (2014). Collects volume 2 (1-16) and volume 3 (1-6).
- *The Usagi Yojimbo Saga,* Volume 2 (2015). Collects volume 3 (7-30) and *Usagi Yojimbo: Green Persimmon.*
- *The Usagi Yojimbo Saga,* Volume 3 (2015). Collects volume 3 (31-52).
- *The Usagi Yojimbo Saga,* Volume 4 (2015). Collects volume 3 (53-75).
- *The Usagi Yojimbo Saga,* Volume 5 (2015). Collects volume 3 (79-93) and *Usagi Yojimbo Color Special #1-3.*
- *The Usagi Yojimbo Saga,* Volume 6 (2016). Collects volume 3 (94-116).
- *The Usagi Yojimbo Saga,* Volume 7 (2016). Collects volume 3 (117-138) and "One Dark and Stormy Night."
- *The Usagi Yojimbo Saga: Legends* (2017) Collects *Space Usagi, Yokai,* and *Senso.*
- *The Usagi Yojimbo Saga,* Volume 8 (2019)

Characters
- *Miyamoto Usagi*, the protagonist, is an anthropomorphic male rabbit and a samurai with a powerful sense of honor and decency.
- *Ame Tomoe* is an anthropomorphic female samurai cat modeled on a historical figure. She is a recurring character in the series and often an ally of Usagi.
- *Murakami Gennosuke* is an anthropomorphic male rhinoceros *rōnin* with a severed nasal horn. Modeled on actor Toshiro Mifune, he is sometimes an ally of Usagi and sometimes an opponent.
- *Jotaro* is an anthropomorphic male child rabbit who is the unacknowledged son of Usagi by Mariko.

- *Zato-Ino* is an anthropomorphic blind male pig based on the main character of the Japanese *Zatoichi* film series. He is a masseur and swordsman.
- *Yagi* and *Gorogoro* are anthropomorphic goats who are based on the main characters of the manga series *Lone Wolf and Cub* (1970-1976), a disgraced samurai-turned-assassin and his infant son.
- *Mariko* is an anthropomorphic female rabbit from Usagi's home village and the lost love of his life. She maintains the masquerade that young Jotaro is her husband's son.
- *Jei*, a.k.a. *the Black Soul*, is an anthropomorphic male wolf armed with a black-bladed spear. He is an almost unkillable psychopath and religious fanatic who has battled Usagi on numerous occasions. Before his appearance in the comics and a fateful bargain, he was a priest named Jizonobu.
- *Lord Hebi* is an anthropomorphic male samurai snake and the vassal of Lord Hikiji.
- *Lord Hikiji* is the ruthless and ambitious primary villain of the series. He has never been depicted "onstage" in the later series, though he crosses over with other Sakai stories. In his one appearance, he is drawn as a human.
- *Lord Noriyuki* is an anthropomorphic male panda cub who is a young daimyo (feudal baron) Bottom of Form struggling to learn to do his noble duty.
- *Kitsune* is an anthropomorphic female fox and a thief whose path has crossed Usagi's on more than one occasion.
- *Sensei Katsuichi* is an anthropomorphic male samurai lion and swordplay trainer who has been a part of Usagi's adventures several times, generally as an ally. He was the rabbit's sword-training master.
- *Inspector Ishida* is an anthropomorphic male cat and a police detective who sometimes adventures alongside Usagi. He is based on Chinese Hawaiian police officer Chang Apana.
- *Sanshobo* is an anthropomorphic male bear who appears in a handful of Usagi stories. He is a monk/priest and a former samurai.
- *Sasuke the Demon Queller* is an anthropomorphic male fox who travels the land as an itinerant ghost- and monster-hunter. He sometimes shares adventures with Usagi.
- *Neko*, *Mogura*, and *Komori Ninja* are, respectively, anthropomorphic cat, mole, and bat ninja clans. They are generally both cannon-fodder opponents for Usagi and homages to the Japanese and American tradition of stagehand, garb-clad ninja assassins.
- *Tokage lizards* are small, ubiquitous lizard creatures doodled into many panels of the stories, offering lightly humorous nonverbal counterpoints to the goings-on. They are Sakai's most obvious tributes to cartoonist Sergio Aragonés.

Artistic Style

Although Sakai's work is classified as manga by some, there is little of the Disney-influenced manga style to his art. Sakai's early work in fanzines demonstrates his love of many comics figures of the 1960's and 1970's, including some of his peers. However, in *Usagi Yojimbo*, his art is primarily inspired by the work of collaborator Aragonés (best known for his work in *MAD* magazineand his series *Groo the Wanderer*, 1982-1984) and the visual styles of classical Japanese painters and filmmakers. Despite clean, spare lines and neatly symmetrical compositions, every panel is packed with detail and action, a Harvey Kurtzman-esque touch that has been a comedic trademark of *MAD* artists such as Aragonés. However, Sakai uses this bustling sea of detail less for laughs and more to emphasize the living, breathing world he creates.

Despite Sakai's considerable skill working with color, most of these stories are presented in black and white. The power of this visual choice is used to strong effect, though with far greater restraint than is seen in the often melodramatic Japanese-influenced artwork of Frank Miller. Much of Sakai's work resembles classic "funny animal" comic books and cartoons (down to the absence of blood amid the frequent violence), and he has continued to use narrative captions and thought balloons long after most mainstream superhero comics abandoned these "outmoded" storytelling devices. Be-

Usagi Yojimbo #1. (Dark Horse Comics/Stan Sakai)

cause it uses such straightforward methods, the art of *Usagi Yojimbo* perfectly complements the scripts, contributing to the series' unpretentious, highly successful method of storytelling.

Themes
To a certain extent, *Usagi Yojimbo* is an exploration by a third-generation American, examining the culture of his ancestors and showing it through his eyes. As Sakai's own Web site points out, *Usagi Yojimbo* is not an international success: It faces a tremendous uphill battle in Japan, where stories of samurai and of Miyamoto Musashi have burgeoned for centuries. Though *Usagi Yojimbo* is not published in Japan, the series has been published in 16 languages and is distributed in even more countries. Some of these translations include French, Italian, and Polish.

The samurai code of Bushido, and the ways in which it does or does not reflect the real lives of samurai (and others), is integral to the stories, as is the way everyday life works amid the seemingly rigid nature of feudal Japanese culture. Sakai seems to point out both the essential humanity behind all cultures and the fact that no set of ideas (samurai honor or other ideology) can completely explain all the modes of human expression. Sakai's characters are both Japanese and cartoon animals; above all else, however, they are people. Sakai achieves this empathic link for the reader, bringing his world to vivid life.

Usagi Yojimbo is a graphic narrative that examines what it is to live and be human, and, incidentally, it expresses wonder at the heroism of a long-ago place and time. Readers learn who Usagi is and what his place is in his world, which helps them understand more of their own life and world.

Impact
Standing at the intersection of traditional "funny animal" comics and the hypersexualized "furries," bridging the gap between 1980's black-and-white independent comics and modern mainstream comics with circulations almost as small, and joining East and West, *Usagi Yojimbo* is a graphic narrative that takes its comfortable place between worlds. Feted by both genre-only institutions such as the Cartoon Art Museum and broader cultural institutions such as the Japanese American National Museum (which hosted the 2011 exhibit "Year of the Rabbit: The Art of Stan Sakai's *Usagi Yojimbo*"), *Usagi Yojimbo* offers readers a mingling of "low" and "high" culture, with "funny books" that address everything from language to crafts, social mores, and personal responsibility.

The whimsical nature of *Usagi Yojimbo* puts it comfortably in the company of both *Groo the Wanderer* and *Teenage Mutant Ninja Turtles* (1984-1993), the latter of which has crossed over with *Usagi Yojimbo* on many occasions. Sakai's work is a smart, introspective take on Japanese culture, especially popular culture, with tributes to Godzilla, Gamera, and Akira Kurosawa. Although *Usagi Yojimbo* was preceded by both Mark Rogers' Samurai Cat stories (first published in 1984) and Larry Hama and Michael Golden's *Bucky O'Hare*, a series about an anthropomorphic rabbit warrior created in 1981, the comic owes no particular debt of influence to either of these. Perhaps the strongest influence *Usagi Yojimbo* has exerted on other creations is in its creator's quiet dedication to solid storytelling and painstaking research.

Further Reading

Laird, Peter, and Kevin Eastman. *Teenage Mutant Ninja Turtles* (1984-1993).

Sim, Dave. *Cerebus* (1977-2004).

Smith, Jeff. *Bone* (1991-2004).

Bibliography

Sakai, Stan. *The Art of Usagi Yojimbo: Twentieth Anniversary Edition*. Milwaukie, Oreg.: Dark Horse Books, 2004.

_____. *Usagi Yojimbo: The Special Edition*. Seattle: Fantagraphics Books, 2010.

Solomon, Charles. "Don't Get Between the Rabbit and His Sword." *Los Angeles Times*, November 25, 2005. http://articles.latimes.com/2005/dec/18/books/bk-solomon18.

See also: *Lone Wolf and Cub; Fist of the North Star; Blade of the Immortal*

V

Violent Cases

Author: Gaiman, Neil
Artist: Dave McKean (illustrator)
Publisher: Dark Horse Comics
First book publication: 1987

Publication History

Violent Cases, which began as a short story Neil Gaiman authored for a science fiction writer's workshop, was first published in black-and-white format in London in 1987 by Titan Books. Titan republished it in 1998. U.S. publisher Kitchen Sink Press also published it in 1998. Tundra published the first full-color edition (and the first American edition) in 1991, with a second edition following in 1992. Dark Horse Comics published an edition in 2003.

Plot

The nameless adult narrator reflects on the arm injury he suffered at the age of four while living in Portsmouth, England, and his ensuing meetings with an unnamed osteopath, a doctor who was once employed by famous Chicago gangster Al Capone. The boy and the doctor strike up a relationship. The narrator tries to remember events carefully so that he can present facts correctly, but he and his father cannot agree on (or remember) what the osteopath looked like.

The osteopath heightens the boy's curiosity about gangsters, and he is interested in knowing what Al Capone was like, what gangsters do for a living, and if they go to parties like children do. The osteopath tells the boy about Capone's violent actions but also about his generosity, such as spending $100,000 on flowers to honor the people he murdered, including a police chief.

The boy tells the osteopath (who apparently is not a licensed doctor but rather an apprentice who became skilled through practice and experience) that he is not looking forward to attending a birthday party at a hotel

Dave McKean. (By Niccolò Caranti, via Wikimedia Commons)

because he does not like the children, the bald magician, and the musical chairs party game. The osteopath informs the narrator's father that the boy's shoulder has healed successfully, so he does not have to return for more visits. However, as the boy is leaving, the osteopath makes the cryptic comment that he will see the boy again.

When the boy subsequently (and reluctantly) attends the birthday party, he moves away from the magician, fearing for his safety, and into the bar area of the hotel, where he encounters the osteopath. As the magician completes his act and the children play musical chairs, the osteopath tells the narrator more stories about Capone, until three men holding baseball bats and wearing hats take the doctor away, punishing him for abandoning Capone after the mobster was imprisoned for tax evasion. The osteopath never appears again. The title, *Violent Cases*, refers to the cases in which gangsters keep their machine guns; "violent" is a pun on "violin," for the violin cases that gangsters used to carry the guns.

Characters
- *Narrator* is an adult, but he recounts events from when he was four years old. The boy is curious about gangsters but fearful of other children. As an adult, he tries to recall the details of his encounters with Capone's osteopath. Memory and truth are important but elusive to him. As a child, he lived with his parents in his maternal grandparents' house. As an adult, the only relative with whom he deals is his father; their relationship seems distant. As an adult, he looks like Gaiman, inviting the possibility that the story is semiautobiographical.
- *Narrator's father* is a giant of a man, has a violent temper, and might have physically abused his son. The narrator cannot remember whether the injury was the result of an unfortunate accident or child abuse. The father pulled on his son's arm to drag him upstairs and put him to bed, while the boy wanted to walk downstairs. The nature of the injury suggests the father's angry disposition and cruelty toward his son. His continuous threats of forcing the boy out of his car to make him walk home exemplify his hot temper and symbolize the dysfunctional relationship between father and son.
- *The osteopath* confesses that he is not an educated doctor. He speaks with a central European accent and is most likely from Poland, although he lived for years in Chicago where he worked for Capone. He is defensive about leaving the employment of Capone after Capone is arrested and feels guilty and disloyal about it. He admires Capone, claiming, unconvincingly, that the gangster was benevolent because he contributed generously to the funerals of the men he murdered. The osteopath forgets periodically that he is speaking with a child, informing the four-year-old boy that he slept with his mentor's wife, describing men being clubbed to their bloody deaths by baseball bats, mentioning that Capone died of syphilis, and using foul language. When the osteopath hurts the child, readers should consider whether the pain comes from the normal process of a doctor's examination or whether the osteopath is cruelly and purposely causing the boy pain.
- *The magician* is bald and scary, at least from the perspective of the narrator as a four-year-old child. He makes loud noises in his magic act, which he performs at the birthday party. He seems unconcerned about frightening the boy. The magician speaks to the osteopath, which immediately makes the doctor cry. This happens before three men with baseball bats enter the hotel bar and suggests that the magician is somehow connected to Capone's henchmen. The magician wears stars, which are an important symbol in this graphic novel.

Artistic Style
Artist Dave McKean employs an expressionistic style to demonstrate tone and emotion. McKean uses mixed media, employing white chalk, charcoal, photographs, pen and ink, brush and ink, Ben-Day dots on the balloon for shading, and even masking tape. He seems to have even drawn on top of photographs. He draws lines on the face of the boy to show contrast; the boy poses in his new thick brown checked coat that the tailor has made. McKean creates drawings of Gaiman to hint that the boy could possibly be the author.

The movie posters that McKean draws link thematically to the impending doom of the osteopath. The poster advertising the film *The Man Who Knew Too Much* (1956) appears just as the osteopath is being captured by Capone's henchmen. Some of the characters are drawn realistically while others are in shadows, and the tailor seems more of a caricature than a real human being. The image of stars, drawn in various forms, permeates the graphic novel. McKean seems to have been influenced by the artistic style of illustrator Bill Sienkiewicz.

Themes

A significant theme in *Violent Cases* is memory and re-evaluation of the past. The narrator, now a grown man, wishes to recover his memory of the osteopath, whom he met on three occasions as a four-year-old child. The narrator and his father have markedly different memories of the doctor, including his physical appearance and his accent. The narrator wonders if the osteopath was gray haired or tubby; he cannot decide whether his memories are accurate or distorted.

A theme related to memory is fact versus fiction. The narrator wants to report the facts to the reader (he never does indicate who his audience is), yet he struggles to remember the past, thus becoming an unreliable, albeit captivating, speaker. Gaiman wrestles with the issue of reliable reporting, accuracy, and fact. For example, did the boy's father physically abuse him, or was his dislocated shoulder an unfortunate accident? Did his father dislocate his arm or merely sprain it? How does the incident on the staircase relate to the father's threat, once actually realized, that he would remove his son from the car and force him to walk? The narrator remarks, "I wouldn't want to gloss over the true facts. Without true facts, where are we?" However, the narrator cannot remember the facts and disagrees with his father about the osteopath. Gaiman leaves the reader to ponder what truth is and what is the figment of one's imagination, particularly when recovering a memory from previous decades and when recovering details from one's youth.

Another theme in the novel is violence. Capone and his henchmen are violent, yet they are also wealthy and generous. The henchmen kill people with baseball bats, leaving a trail of blood. Perhaps a connection exists between the murders of adults and the hurt suffered by children at parties when they lose at certain games. That is why Gaiman places the two scenes together in the same room and at the same time. The children are eliminated one by one, forced out of the game. The birthday girl cries after losing at musical chairs. The loss is a symbolically and emotionally violent act that makes the girl miserable during her party and explains why the narrator is afraid to participate.

Impact

The mid-1980's was an era when comics were beginning to be taken more seriously by adults. The genre was being written with more mature themes and topics, and writers and illustrators of this time brought with them pioneering methods to explore these issues. *Violent Cases,* with its complexity and sophistication, not only responded to this trend by addressing the issues of memory, truth, loyalty, and child abuse, but it served to influence many future comics professionals such as fantasy writer Gene Wolfe and colorist Daniel Vozzo. Furthermore, just as Gaiman was influenced significantly by comic book legend Alan Moore, Gaiman had a profound impact on fellow comics and fantasy writer Terry Pratchett.

Eric Sterling

Further Reading

Gaiman, Neil, and Dave McKean. *The Tragical Comedy or Comical Tragedy of Mr. Punch* (1994).

_____. *Signal to Noise* (1992).

Spiegelman, Art. *Maus: A Survivor's Tale.* (1986, 1991).

Bibliography

Gabilliet, Jean-Paul, and Bart Beaty and Nick Nguyen, trans. *Of Comics and Men: A Cultural History of American Comic Books*. Jackson: University Press of Mississippi, 2010.

Guillain, Charlotte. *Neil Gaiman: Rock Star Writer*. Chicago: Raintree, 2011.

Harvey, Robert C. *The Art of the Comic Book: An Aesthetic History*. Jackson: University Press of Mississippi, 1996.

McCabe, Joseph. *Hanging out with the Dream King: Conversations with Neil Gaiman and His Collaborators*. Seattle: Fantagraphics Books, 2004.

Petersen, Robert S. *Comics, Manga, and Graphic Novels: A History of Graphic Narratives*. Santa Barbara, Calif.: Praeger, 2011.

See also: *The Tragical Comedy or Comical Tragedy of Mr. Punch*; *Signal to Noise*; *Maus*

W

Walking Dead, The

Author: Kirkman, Robert
Artist: Charlie Adlard (illustrator); Tony Moore (illustrator); Ryan Ottley (penciller and cover artist); Cliff Rathburn (inker, colorist, and cover artist); Robert Kirkman (letterer); Rus Wooton (letterer); Tommy Lee Edwards (cover artist); Erik Larsen (cover artist)
Publisher: Image Comics
First serial publication: 2003-
First book publication: 2006-

Publication History

Robert Kirkman had self-published the series *Battle Pope* (2000) and created the superhero series *Invincible* (2003-   ) for Image Comics prior to pitching *The Walking Dead* to Image's publisher, Jim Valentino. Kirkman's aim was to create an open-ended postapocalyptic saga that used the zombie genre as a backdrop for a changing cast of characters. Valentino initially turned down Kirkman's pitch on the basis that serious zombie stories in comics did not sell. In order to persuade Valentino that the series would be successful, Kirkman lied and said that the zombie plague would eventually be revealed as an alien strategy to weaken the human race in preparation for a mass invasion of Earth. Valentino apparently did not notice that this was a plot lifted from the infamous cult film *Plan 9 from Outer Space* (1959). The series began with Kirkman scripting and Tony Moore providing the artwork; Charlie Adlard stepped in as illustrator after six issues.

Plot

The Walking Dead is a harrowing postapocalyptic adventure that follows a shifting band of survivors as they battle the undead and attempt to build a new life for themselves in a forever-altered world. In the opening sequence, Kentucky policeman Rick Grimes awakens in a hospital after being wounded on duty and finds himself the only living person in a city of the dead. On his way home, he encounters fellow survivors Morgan and Duane and learns of a camp outside the city where several other survivors have gathered. This group is led by Rick's former partner and best friend, Shane, and also includes his wife, Lori, and son, Carl. Shane is interested in Lori romantically and fears that Rick's return will displace him as group leader. Enraged, Shane attacks Rick, and Carl kills Shane.

Rick decides that the camp is unsafe, and the ragtag group takes to the road. Adding more members to their traveling convoy, they stop at a gated community that seems perfect but is overrun with zombies. They meet

---

Robert Kirkman

Robert Kirkman's *The Walking Dead* is one of the few genuine comics phenomena of the 2000's. Launched in 2003, the same year that he created the superhero saga *Invincible*, Kirkman's series helped ignite a wave of interest in zombies that culminated with the hit comic book series being transformed into a television series for AMC. Prior to his overnight success, Kirkman was little known in the comic book industry. He has subsequently gone on to produce a wide range of comics for Marvel, including *Captain America*, *Ultimate X-Men*, and *Irredeemable Ant-Man*. Kirkman's stories have been embraced for their unusual sense of plotting. In *The Walking Dead*, characters are introduced and dispensed with quickly, giving the series a highly unpredictable feeling. His work deals with dark themes concerning the battle for survival, and he has courted controversy for his inclusion of rape storylines in his comics.

Robert Kirkman speaking at the 2014 San Diego Comic Con International, for "The Walking Dead," at the San Diego Convention Center in San Diego, California. (By Gage Skidmore from Peoria, AZ, USA, via Wikimedia Commons)

still more survivors at a nearby farm; after spending some time there, tensions rise, and they leave to seek another new home. At the end of their rope, with supplies running out, they discover an abandoned prison with a few surviving inmates and believe that this is where they will stay and make a new life. The prison proves to be a wonderful temporary haven for the survivors.

While investigating a crashed helicopter, Rick and several others are taken to a survivors' community called Woodbury, led by a perverted lunatic known as the Governor. Under his rule, gladiatorial games are held with living and undead participants. He severs Rick's hand and rapes and tortures Rick's friend Michonne. Rick and the others escape with the help of a few Woodbury citizens and prepare for war. In the ensuing battle, many of the series' original survivors die, including Lori and her new baby, Judith. The prison is also rendered unsafe, forcing the few left alive to return to the road.

In the aftermath of the prison massacre, the remaining survivors disperse. Rick and Carl try to make it on their own. Carl has become a hardened young man and resents his father for allowing Lori and Judith to die; however, when Rick struggles with illness and needs Carl's help, Carl realizes that he still loves him. They eventually reunite with Michonne and several others.

Returning to the farm, the group encounters several survivors who are traveling to Washington, D.C., where one of them, a scientist, claims to have answers that will enable the government to stop the plague and save the world. The two groups join together and set off again, meeting a lone priest named Gabriel Stokes and a vicious group of cannibals.

Rick is suspicious of a newcomer named Aaron, who tells the group that he is a recruiter for a nearby walled community that offers food, safety, and the possibility of a stable future. Rick and company meet its leader, former congressman Douglas Monroe, and are welcomed into the slightly strange but idyllic neighborhood inside its walls. Rick is made constable of the community, and the others are assigned to various roles in the maintenance of their isolated world. After the community weathers internal crises and faces a marauding rival band of survivors and a zombie horde, Douglas realizes that the community needs a different leader: Rick.

Volumes
- *The Walking Dead:* Book One (2006). Collects issues 1-12. Rick Grimes awakens into a nightmarish reality, reunites with his family, and joins a group of survivors.
- *The Walking Dead:* Book Two (2007). Collects issues 13-24. Rick guides the survivors as they settle into postapocalyptic life at their new prison home. Relationships deepen, and a fragile stability is forged.
- *The Walking Dead:* Book Three (2007). Collects issues 25-36. Several of the survivors fall into the hands of the Governor, a twisted despot ruling a barbarous community that sets its sights on the prison.
- *The Walking Dead:* Book Four (2008). Collects issues 37-48. Rick and the group face devastating losses and the end of their hoped-for new

beginning as the Governor wages war on their prison haven.
- *The Walking Dead:* Book Five (2009). Collects issues 49-60. After leaving the prison, Rick recedes into himself and Carl is forced to become a harder, more mature person. They join old friends and a new group as they head to the East Coast.
- *The Walking Dead:* Book Six (2010). Collects issues 61-72. The survivors face a band of ferocious cannibals and are recruited to join a walled community outside Washington, D.C.
- *The Walking Dead:* Book Seven (2011). Collects issues 73-84. Rick and the group settle into life behind the walls but brace for the next potential attack.

Characters
- *Rick Grimes*, the protagonist, is a slender, sandy-haired former Kentucky policeman. A natural leader determined to protect his family and friends, he is dedicated to a moral and ethical code that he must violate at times in order to ensure survival. He struggles with the changes in himself and the horrible acts he sometimes commits for the good of the group.
- *Carl Grimes* is Rick's son. He has short black hair and wears Rick's old hat. He is forced to mature quickly in the world of the walking dead, developing a hard exterior, a surprising ability to kill when necessary, and a cynical outlook on life.
- *Andrea* is a young blond woman with freckles and a distinctive scar. She is a former law clerk and now an excellent sharpshooter. Originally traveling with Dale and her sister, Amy, she becomes close to Dale after her sister's death; the two become lovers. Following Dale's death, Andrea begins to wear his hat.
- *Michonne* is a former lawyer and fencing hobbyist who becomes a sword-wielding loner. She is raped and tortured by the Governor and mutilates him in revenge. She is Rick's deputy in the walled community and wants to leave the violence behind.
- *Glenn* is a young man who wears a baseball cap. A former pizza delivery boy with a talent for sneaking in and out of zombie-infested cities for supplies, he is an invaluable member of the survivors' group. He marries Maggie, the daughter of a farmer encountered on the way to the prison, and the two raise Carol's daughter, Sophia, after Carol's suicide.
- *Maggie* is a short-haired farmer's daughter who witnesses her entire family being killed by zombies. She struggles with depression and attempts suicide but eventually decides to make the most of life with her new husband, Glenn, and their adopted daughter, Sophia.
- *Morgan* is a middle-aged man who lost his wife and son. He is the first living person Rick encounters after awakening. When they meet again one year later, Rick persuades him to leave his undead son, Duane, whom he has been feeding. He joins the group in the walled community and begins a tentative relationship with Michonne.
- *Sergeant Abraham Ford* is a tall, muscular man with a large mustache. He struggles with his violent side and joins Rick's group as they enter the walled community, becoming part of the construction crew working to expand the protective walls.
- *Douglas Monroe* is a bald, elderly man with a white goatee. He is a former Ohio congressman and now the determined leader of the walled community. He is married to Regina but has taken advantage of the current situation by having affairs with a number of young women.
- *Shane* is Rick's best friend and partner. He takes care of Lori and Carl before Rick awakens and is the group's first leader. He wants a romantic relationship with Lori and fears Rick's return. He tries to kill Rick but is killed by Carl.
- *Lori Grimes* is Rick's wife. She has long black hair and a thin face. She gives birth to a daughter, Judith, who may or may not be Shane's child. Both are killed during the Governor's final assault on the prison.
- *Dale* is a slightly overweight older man with a scruffy gray beard and a distinctive fishing cap. His RV serves as the principal vehicle for Rick's group early in their travels. He travels initially

with sisters Amy and Andrea; following Amy's death, he and Andrea grow closer despite the significant difference in their ages. He loses one leg to a zombie attack and another to cannibals before dying.
- *Carol* is a young, deeply troubled blond woman with a daughter, Sophia. She was abused by her late husband. She eventually commits suicide by allowing a captured zombie to bite her.
- *The Governor* is a psychotic despot who controls the community of Woodbury. He rules with an iron fist, keeps severed reanimated heads for his own amusement, and has a perverted relationship with his undead daughter. His cruelty comes to an end when he dies during an assault on the prison.

Artistic Style

From the beginning of the series, the zombie apocalypse is portrayed in black and white with gray tones rather than in color, which creates a dark and oppressive atmosphere. The first six issues were illustrated by Moore, and his sharp-lined, often angular, elongated figures and almost cartoonish renditions of the characters give the series an underlying humorous tone that belies the story's gritty realism. Moore's art never shies away from the more horrifying aspects of the tale, and his style strikes a fitting balance between comical abstraction and terrifying reality.

Adlard, the illustrator beginning with issue 7, eschews Moore's light touch and sharp lines in favor of a fluid, slightly less defined approach. Adlard's work is darker, relying on heavy gray tones and softened figures to convey a world gone mad and life as a battle for survival. Adlard's depiction of the zombies also reaches a level of gruesome iconography that is instantly recognizable; he often depicts them as little more than emaciated shapes with hollow, white circles in place of eyes. While scenes typically take place in generic, ravaged suburban communities or nondescript rural areas, occasional sequences set in recognizable locations such as Washington, D.C., were created using photo references.

Themes

For all its horrific imagery and fanciful use of reanimated corpses, *The Walking Dead* is ultimately an examination of human nature at its most realistic, exploring the ways in which people react to their true potential and respond in the midst of extreme crisis. Although the zombies are a significant threat, the true monsters in *The Walking Dead* are human beings who resort to the most primal behavior in order to survive, at the cost of their morality, their ethics, and their very souls.

The conflict between rationality and animalism is also regularly addressed. Rick has an innate talent for leadership, but he struggles to balance thoughtful decision making with his tendency to react emotionally and violently. After the death of Rick's wife and baby, his sanity becomes a major focus of the comic. The series further inquires into the nature of humanity, asking if a person who disregards civilized behavior in favor of brutal self-interest is still human. Kirkman makes this aspect of the story clear when Rick tells his fellow survivors that it is they, and not the reanimated corpses, who are truly the "walking dead."

The absence of any explanation for the reanimation of the dead is a calculated choice by Kirkman that increases the sense of fear and hopelessness of the story. Characters debate the scientific and religious origins of the apocalypse, but they all must continue to exist in a world that offers no reasons and no respite.

Impact

The Walking Dead has had an enormous impact on both the horror genre specifically and the comic book industry in general. Demonstrating that it is possible to craft a long-running serialized comic book saga outside the stereotypical superhero genre, Kirkman and Image Comics shattered many preconceptions about the modern American comics industry and opened the door for numerous imitators. Kirkman became one of the most celebrated writers in the industry and a full partner in Image Comics with his imprint, Skybound. He also helped to revive the popularity of the comic book letters page, including in every issue an extensive section in which he engages with his readership.

The series' success led to the debut of a television adaptation that broke cable ratings records and drew more attention to the metaphorical power of the horror genre. Zombie stories have been a part of popular culture since the early 1930's, but the genre experienced a significant increase in mainstream popularity early in the twenty-first century, as indicated by the success of *The Walking Dead*, *Marvel Zombies* (2006-2010), and films such as *Zombieland* (2009). The crossover appeal of the series helped to energize the connection between comic books and other media, proving that the comics medium is a vital wellspring of storytelling that can appeal to a mass audience.

Television Series

The Walking Dead. Directed by Frank Darabont, et al. AMC Studios, 2010- . This series stars Andrew Lincoln as Rick Grimes. Its six-episode first season was hugely successful, and it was quickly renewed for a thirteen-episode second season. The show pushes commercial television boundaries with its gruesome violence but remains true to the spirit of the source material, focusing on the relationships and challenges faced by the survivors. Kirkman wrote the fourth episode and served as an executive producer, although the series diverges, sometimes drastically, from the comic book story lines.

Arnold T. Blumberg

Further Reading

Ennis, Garth. *Preacher* (1995-2000).

Kirkman, Robert. *Marvel Zombies* (2006-2010).

Vaughan, Brian K. *Y: The Last Man* (2002-2008).

Bibliography

Kim, Ann. "Graphic Grown Up." *Library Journal* 134, no. 13 (August, 2009): 20-22.

MacDonald, Heidi. "Image Comics Has New Kirkman Imprint." *Publishers Weekly* 257, no. 32 (August, 2010): 9.

Snellings, April. "My Apocalypse." *Rue Morgue* 104 (September, 2010): 20-21.

See also: *30 Days of Night; Elk's Run; Glacial Period; Zombies Versus Robots*

WALL, THE: GROWING UP BEHIND THE IRON CURTAIN

Author: Sís, Peter
Artist: Peter Sís (illustrator)
Publisher: Frances Foster Books
First book publication: 2007

Publication History

Picture-book artist Peter Sís was born and raised in Czechoslovakia during the Cold War and defected to the United States in 1982. He conceptualized *The Wall: Growing Up Behind the Iron Curtain* as a book that would relate to his American-born children his experiences of growing up under a totalitarian communist regime. Although Sís's previous picture books *The Three Golden Keys* and *Tibet Through the Red Box* were inspired by his childhood memories, *The Wall: Growing Up Behind the Iron Curtain* is by far his most autobiographical book.

The Wall: Growing Up Behind the Iron Curtain was published in 2007 by Frances Foster Books, an imprint of Farrar, Straus and Giroux. Marketed primarily as a nonfiction picture book for middle-school readers, it has been translated into several languages, including Czech, Danish, Russian, and Spanish.

Peter Sis, illustrator. (Courtesy of the John D. and Catherine T. MacArthur Foundation, via Wikimedia Commons)

Plot

Part memoir and part political history, *The Wall: Growing Up Behind the Iron Curtain* tells the story of Peter, a young boy growing up under Soviet-ruled Czechoslovakia. The book focuses on Peter's artistic development, following his transformation from a child who "drew what he was told" to a young adult who uses his art to survive and resist the oppressive atmosphere and policies of a communist society.

Peter was born with a passion for drawing. As a young boy, however, he unquestioningly follows the government's compulsory measures and accepts its propaganda. He becomes an enthusiastic member of the communist youth group Young Pioneers and willingly participates in government-sponsored activities. His artwork is strongly shaped by the communist doctrine, and he draws weapons of war and other symbols that express his allegiance to the communist government and the Soviet Union.

Later, Peter begins to question the oppressive nature of the government. His artwork becomes more personal, colorful, and dreamlike. He is, however, careful to keep his artwork a secret. During this period, he also gets a taste of "bits and pieces" of Western popular culture that manage to trickle through the Iron Curtain. Inspired by musicians such as the Beatles, he defies strict government policies by joining a rock-and-roll band.

In January, 1968, the new head of government, Alexander Dubček, enacts several reforms, including the lifting of censorship. His progressive policies result in the Prague Spring. Peter is thrilled by the freer influx of poetry, music, and entertainment from the West and the opportunities to travel abroad. On August 21, 1968, however, Soviet-led troops invade Czechoslovakia. Censorship, travel restrictions, and other prohibitive policies are reinstated, and Dubček and members of his government are sent off to the Soviet Union to be "re-educated." Despite the reinstitution of strict government policies, the Beach Boys are permitted to play a concert at Lucerna Hall in Prague. At the concert, while simultaneously listening to the Beach Boys' music and witnessing the police harass and beat up concertgoers, Peter comes to believe that true artistic freedom can be attained only in the United States.

As the government resumes surveillance and responds to dissidents with increasingly harsh measures, Peter fears that he could be punished for his artwork. He temporarily stops drawing and is conscripted into the army. He feels compelled to keep on drawing, as his artwork becomes his only source of hope. As he hears stories of his peers and prominent citizens being harassed, imprisoned, and tortured, he begins to have elaborate fantasies about escape. In the final sequence, Peter imagines his sketches and paintings coming together to form wings, buoying him and his bicycle over the Berlin Wall, away from the desolate, cruel landscape of communist Eastern Europe and toward the bright fields of the West and the distant outline of the United States. When the Berlin Wall falls in 1989, Peter feels that his and his fellow citizens' dreams of freedom are finally fulfilled.

Characters
- *Peter*, the protagonist, is a wide-eyed, smiling boy with a cowlick. He loves to draw and paint and is constantly holding a pencil, paintbrush, or sketching pad. As a young boy, he remains oblivious to the restrictive nature of the communist government. His expression of innocence and hopefulness later turns into an expression of horror, as he slowly comprehends the oppressive and brutal practices of the government. His artwork and journal entries also reflect the slow transformation of his political beliefs. Although the boy remains nameless in the text, Sís has clarified in interviews that the boy represents his young self.
- *The communist Czech government*, under the influence of Soviet leadership, is the antagonistic institution that enforces censorship and compels its citizens to comply with its strict policies. It subjects dissidents to severe forms of punishment. Members of the government and the secret police have piglike snouts and are constantly monitoring Czech citizens.
- *Alexander Dubček*, who became head of the Czech government in 1968, appears once in *The Wall* as a tiny bearded figure crossing a bridge and holding a winged "balloon" that symbolizes his commitment to reform and policy of openness. His balloon expands during the Prague Spring, as his liberal policies allow music, literature, and art to flourish. Soviet leadership strongly disapproves of his policies, and in 1969, he is removed from his position as head of government.

Artistic Style

Most illustrations in *The Wall: Growing Up Behind the Iron Curtain* are highly detailed pen-and-ink drawings. These black-and-white illustrations, with their stiff lines and intense use of hatching, signify the drabness, monotony, and conformity that characterized life under communist rule. Bright red communist symbols such as sickles, stars, and flags appear in many of these illustrations. Against black and white, the color red feels intrusive, menacing, and persistent, and communicates how Czech citizens have been forced to accept communism as a way of life.

In sharp contrast to these illustrations is the colorful world of the West. One double-page spread that depicts Peter's encounter with Western music, literature, and art during the Prague Spring is vividly colored and alludes to the Beatles' animated film *Yellow Submarine*. Despite the abundance of colors in this spread, Peter himself is drawn in black and white, indicating that he is still limited by government restrictions and that his worldview may still be shaped by communist doctrine. His paintings, however, begin to take on the bright colors that he associates with life in the West. His visions of the West, particularly the United States, are characterized by pastel colors and soft penciled lines, which contrast with the rigid, black-and-white quality of communist life.

Although Sís's illustrations include intricate drawings of buildings, cityscapes, and landscapes, he draws his characters in a cartoonlike fashion. Most notably, he caricatures the Czech government officials and secret police, emphasizing their base, brutish nature by drawing them with piglike snouts. Their animal appearance is reminiscent of comics creator Art Spiegelman's illustrations in *Maus* and refers to the slur "pig" often used against the police. The officials are often drawn hiding behind windows or in insets at the borders of the illustrations. This highlights their secretive but persistent intrusion into the private lives of Czech citizens.

The story uses a mixture of media and narrative voices, which results in a fragmentary narrative structure. Instead of organizing his memories into a simple linear narrative, Sís pastes together snippets, sketches, and snapshots of his early life. Running along the bottom of the pages is the primary narrative, which is written in curt sentences that provide few details. Illustrated panels of different sizes, each of which contains a different scene, provide details not mentioned in the textual narrative. Framing these illustrations are marginal notes, written in a more objective voice, that describe the policies and practices of the Czech government and outline events that took place in Europe during the Cold War. Occasionally, the entire narrative is interrupted by double-page spreads that feature excerpts from Sís's old journals. Bordering the journal excerpts are collages of photographs, communist ephemera, and Sís's early artwork. The fragmentary narrative structure speaks of Sís's struggle to come to terms with his childhood memories. The book's patchwork structure shows how Sís pieced together often painful memories to build a personal and national history. In mixing visual and textual modes, Sís shows that images, like language, can also be powerful, effective transmitters of memory and history.

Themes

The Wall: Growing Up Behind the Iron Curtain is a coming-of-age story that focuses on the artistic and political development of the protagonist. The power of art to uplift and liberate the individual is an important theme in the book. In linking Peter's artistic growth with his political awakening, *The Wall: Growing Up Behind the Iron Curtain* portrays art as a force that enlightens and empowers those who create and experience it. Art gives Peter respite from the oppressive conditions in his society and the means to resist such oppression. His constant compulsion to paint despite numerous prohibitions symbolizes the resilience of the individual's creative spirit. The story depicts popular culture as a similarly positive and subversive force that has the potential to uplift the masses and inspire them to perform acts of defiance.

The Wall: Growing Up Behind the Iron Curtain, however, asserts that art and creativity can truly flourish only in a free state. Sís's narrative shows that although Peter is still able to dream and create under communist rule, the pressure to conform and the atmosphere of fear prevents him from fully developing his creative potential. The book is a forceful critique of totalitarian rule, insisting that propaganda, censorship, and institutionalized conformity can only stifle the individual's moral, intellectual, and artistic growth. Communist policies, in emphasizing loyalty to state above all else, also undermine the institution of the family, for it encourages citizens to monitor and be suspicious of their own relatives. In contrast, capitalist society is depicted as celebrating individualism and encouraging its citizens to cultivate their knowledge and self-pride. *The Wall: Growing Up Behind the Iron Curtain* casts communist and capitalist societies as polar opposites and, in effect, suggests that capitalism is the ideal social system.

Impact

The Wall: Growing Up Behind the Iron Curtain is celebrated by children's literature critics for its experimentation with the picture-book form. Critics and reviewers have noted the book's use of graphic novel techniques, particularly the division of the page into panels and tiers. Its inventive layout, fragmentary narrative structure, and mixture of various techniques such as caricature, collage, and pen-and-ink illustration demonstrate the possibility of innovation with the picture-book form. The book's engagement with concepts such as violence and political oppression also challenges common notions of what material is appropriate for child readership. In *The Wall: Growing Up Behind the Iron Curtain*, as well as in his previous picture books, Sís pushes the boundaries of the picture-book genre. His books can be placed alongside the work of other innovative picture-book artists such as Anthony

Browne, David Macaulay, and David Wiesner. Because of its political content and its intertwining of memoir and history, *The Wall: Growing Up Behind the Iron Curtain* has also drawn comparisons with Marjane Satrapi's graphic memoir *Persepolis* (2003) and Art Spiegelman's Holocaust story, *Maus* (1986; 1991).

The Wall: Growing Up Behind the Iron Curtain has been widely lauded, especially in the United States, for its denouncement of censorship and celebration of artistic freedom. Many educators in the United States consider the book an effective tool in teaching young readers not only about Cold War history but also about concepts such as censorship and First Amendment rights. *The Wall: Growing Up Behind the Iron Curtain* has also been questioned for its dualistic representation of communist and capitalist societies. Sís acknowledges that the book has had a mixed reception in his former homeland. While playwright and former Czech Republic president Václav Havel proclaimed that *The Wall: Growing Up Behind the Iron Curtain* "is most of all about the will to live one's life in freedom and should be required reading for all those who take their freedom for granted," the book has also been criticized for its lack of nuance in representing life under Soviet rule. Sís maintains that the book is not only deliberate in highlighting the debilitating effects of totalitarian rule on the individual but also means to reveal his own naiveté as a child and adolescent, when he failed to recognize the oppressive nature of communist policies.

Lara Saguisag

Further Reading

Delisle, Guy. *Pyongyang: A Journey in North Korea* (2007).

Satrapi, Marjane. *Persepolis* (2003).

Spiegelman, Art. *Maus: A Survivor's Tale* (1986; 1991).

Bibliography

Maeots, Olga. "Behind the Wall Under the Red Star." *Bookbird: A Journal of International Children's Literature* 47, no. 3 (July, 2009): 46-53.

Marcus, Leonard S. "The Cold War Kid." Review of *The Wall: Growing Up Behind the Iron Curtain*, by Peter Sís. *The New York Times Book Review*, November 11, 2007. http://www.nytimes.com/2007/11/11/books/review/Marcus-t.html.

Scharioth, Barbara, and Nikola von Merveldt. "Peter Sís: A Quest for a Life in Truth." *Bookbird: A Journal of International Children's Literature* 47, no. 3 (July, 2009): 29-40.

Sís, Peter. "My Life with Censorship." *Bookbird: A Journal of International Children's Literature* 47, no. 3 (July, 2009): 42-45.

_____. "The Booklist Interview: Peter Sís." Interview by Jennifer Mattson. *Booklist* (January 1, 2008): 62.

See also: *Pyongyang*; *Waltz with Bashir*; *Persepolis*; *Maus*; *The Arrival*

Waltz with Bashir: A Lebanon War Story

Author: Folman, Ari
Artist: David Polonsky (illustrator); Ya'ara Buchman (illustrator); Michael Faust (illustrator); Asaf Hanuka (illustrator); Tomer Hanuka (illustrator)
Publisher: Metropolitan Books
First book publication: 2009

Publication History

Originally conceived and released as an Israeli animated documentary film in 2008 before being transformed into a graphic novel, *Waltz with Bashir* was published in English in 2009 by Henry Holt under the imprint Metropolitan Books. Metropolitan Books was established in 1995 to bring the public more controversial and unconventional titles in categories such as politics, current affairs, foreign fiction, and graphic novels. *Waltz with Bashir* also has been published in several other languages, including Hebrew, French, Spanish, German, and Danish.

Ari Folman, an Israeli writer, director, and producer for award-winning films and television series, is best known for his work in the documentary genre. Folman won Israeli Film Academy awards for the animation *Waltz with Bashir* and his feature film *Saint Clara*.

Artist David Polonsky has dabbled in many areas including portraits, sculpture, and illustrations (featured in every major newspaper and magazine in Israel). He has received numerous awards for his children's book illustrations and has also animated short films for television.

Plot

Waltz with Bashir is a nonfiction wartime testimony told through the eyes of filmmaker Ari Folman, who served as an Israel Defense Forces (IDF) soldier in 1982 during the Lebanese civil war (1975-1990). The graphic novel specifically centers on the September massacre of approximately three thousand Palestinian citizens in the Sabra and Shatila refugee camps. Historically, Israel was allied with the Lebanese Christian soldiers (known as the Phalangists) in order to occupy Lebanon up to and including Beirut with the aim of preventing Palestinian missile attacks against northern towns in Israel. Israeli minister of defense Ariel Sharon's secret motive was to strengthen the force against Israel's enemy Syria and maintain control by electing Bashir Gemayel, senior commander of the Phalangists, as the new Lebanese president. After Gemayel's appointment, he was assassinated by an unknown party assumed to be the Palestinians, the Syrians, or a collaboration of both forces. The Phalangists then conducted a three-day slaughter in Sabra and Shatila in retaliation for losing their beloved leader. Under the claim of purging the camps of Palestinian combat fighters—who were forced to evacuate weeks earlier—the militia members vengefully murdered remaining refugee occupants while the Israeli soldiers shot flares to provide light. The victims were largely ordinary citizens and included women, the elderly, and children. Although the Israeli soldiers did not officially carry out the Palestinian massacre, the government was held liable for not doing enough to stop the horror that occurred.

Ari Folman

Ari Folman is an Israeli filmmaker and television writer who made his name with the 1996 film *Saint Clara*, for which he won an Ophir Award. His 2008 animated documentary, *Waltz with Bashir*, debuted at the Cannes Film Festival. It tells the story of Folman's efforts to reconstruct his memories of his participation in the Shabra and Shatila massacre of thousands of Palestinian refugees in Lebanon in 1982. The film was adapted as a graphic novel by Folman and artist David Polonsky and released around the same time as the film. Folman's script is the effort of a middle-aged man to recall his thoughts, feelings, and experiences from twenty-five years earlier, and the work engages closely with themes of memory and loss. Since producing the graphic novel, Folman has returned to his career as a filmmaker.

Ari Folman at 43rd Karlovy Vary International Film Festival. (By Petr Novák, via Wikimedia Commons)

More than twenty years after the massacre, Folman must finally face his role in the slaughter. Folman's friend Boaz Rein-Buskila describes a recurring nightmare of being hunted by a pack of dogs that were killed in the massacre, prompting Folman's first vision. Picturing himself as a young man rising naked out of the water with two fellow Israeli soldiers, Folman realizes that although he remembers the basics of his military service, his time in Beirut is a black hole. Folman decides to reconstruct his repressed memories by interviewing other Israeli soldiers and witnesses to the massacre and by trying to comprehend (through the commentary of experts) how such selective amnesia could occur. During this process, his encounters demonstrate a similar trend since the other participants have hallucinations and nightmares related to the war but lack many details of their real contributions. For example, his friend Carmi Cna'an vividly recounts a dream where a beautiful woman swims to his military boat, carries him into the water, and takes his virginity. At that distance, Cna'an then watches as the boat explodes in flames and engulfs his military friends. However, despite being in Beirut and remembering instances of shooting like a maniac at unknown targets, he cannot remember his specific involvement in the massacre itself. As the interviews continue, Folman begins to dredge up real war memories such as transporting injured soldiers, his twenty-four-hour leave while trying to win back his former girlfriend, and his flight to Beirut after President Gemayel was assassinated. Ultimately, Folman cannot tell whether he helped fire the flares while the massacre was occurring or whether he merely watched them light up the sky, but the graphic novel ends by illustrating Folman's true location on the outskirts of the camps and providing photographic examples of the carnage he would have witnessed as aftermath.

Characters

- *Ari Folman*, the protagonist, is a middle-aged man who served in the Israel Defense Forces at the age of nineteen during the Lebanese civil war. Although on active duty while the massacre took place, he cannot recall his role in the slaughter. Years later, he attempts to fill in the missing scenes by interviewing witnesses to the Beirut invasion.
- *Boaz Rein-Buskila* is Folman's friend of thirty years. His recurring nightmare of being hunted by a pack of dogs—that ask for him by name to kill him—stems from his service in the Israel Defense Forces when he killed these animals so that the Palestinian soldiers would not be alerted and escape.
- *Ori Sivan* is Folman's childhood best friend, and Folman frequently confides in him and seeks his advice. He explains the workings of memory and how people create false memories or block out traumatic experiences.
- *Carmi Cna'an* is Folman's old friend. The two men grew apart after the war's end and his emigration twenty years earlier. Described as a genius with unlimited potential, he remembers

marching into Beirut but cannot recall the massacre.
- *Roni Dayag* is a biologist and former IDF soldier. Considered the classic antihero, he should have taken over when his tank commander was shot by a sniper. Unable to retaliate, he hides and eventually swims across the sea back to his regiment. He is plagued by survivor's guilt and feels like a deserter.
- *Shmuel Frenkel* is a champion fighter in Dennis Survival jujitsu and was Folman's cabin mate during the war. He performs a "waltz" in front of a huge poster of Lebanese president Bashir Gemayel: His motions appear dance-like, but he is actually shooting at Palestinian snipers and avoiding their gunfire.
- *Professor Zahava Solomon* is a world-renowned expert on war trauma. She explains dissociative events to Folman, wherein people who experience trauma perceive themselves outside the situation.
- *Ron Ben-Yishai* is considered Israel's foremost war correspondent. He telephones Minister of Defense Ariel Sharon to call for an end to the Palestinian slaughter, an ignored plea. He witnesses the aftermath by following the massacre survivors back into the camps.
- *Dror Harazi* is a former IDF soldier who was stationed on the front line outside the camps during the massacre and reported the massacre to his commander. He provides an account of the Beirut invasion.

Artistic Style

Waltz with Bashir is neatly arranged in rectangles and square panels. The only notable deviation from this pattern occurs during Ari's interview with the combat trauma expert, in which the overlapping, slanted arrangement mimics the nightmarish content of the pictures and how one's shield from true memory can dissolve into insanity. For both background and character depiction, Folman encouraged illustrator Polonsky, who completed 80 percent of the illustrations, to be as realistic as possible—including drawing the interviewees and other figures as they appear in real life—to foster emotional attachment in the audience. Since the subject matter is serious, however, Polonsky did not want his illustrations to appear too pretty and would frequently draw with his nondominant hand to avoid this result. In addition, in order to maintain audience focus on the realistic images, the dialogue is written in a simple font contained within unobtrusive, rectangular text boxes.

Although the illustrations all use a similar realistic style, there are three important variations. The most noticeable concerns the dream sequences, which are more vibrantly colored, contain unrealistic proportions, and seem more fantastical overall. Second, Folman's own memories appear less realistic since the figures are more exaggerated, strange, or cartoonlike in their appearance and facial expressions, heightening the unreliability of his own memory. Finally, as the story line becomes increasingly dark and violent when the massacre is addressed, the illustrations shift to dichromatic orange and black hues. This drastic change underscores the melancholy, horrific atmosphere until readers encounter photographs of the dead bodies. By purposefully concluding with photographer Robin Moyer's real-life images of the innocent Palestinian victims, Folman emphasizes the reality of the massacre and leaves readers to ponder the senseless destruction of war. Throughout the book, Polonsky uses the points of view of both Israelis and Palestinians—facing a Palestinian RPG missile, looking through binoculars as Phalangists shoot the refugees, and walking with Palestinian mourners through the camps—and this ending successfully shocks readers, forcefully reminding them of the brutal nature of life and humankind.

Themes

Folman continually addresses the unreliability of human memory, which forms the foundation of the plot since he begins interviewing other Israelis after having his first wartime flashback: rising naked out of the sea. Unable to determine this memory's accuracy or his true involvement during the massacre, Folman attempts to uncover his repressed memories and grasp how they become distorted or lost: Memory is dynamic (filling in false details or eliminating true ones) in order to shield one from trauma and harsh truths. The interview process reveals that Folman's selective amnesia is not unique. Many others involved in the war can recall only snippets of their participation. In times of horror, such disassociation from reality seems to be the only way to move forward and continue daily life.

Folman also highlights the senselessness of war. Rather than the glamour and glory presented in many American war films, *Waltz with Bashir* is told through the eyes of young, naïve common soldiers linked by the uncertainty of where they are going, who they are firing at, and why they are taking action. The men often fire frantically at an unseen enemy simply to have some perceived purpose. This theme is made especially apparent when Brigadier General Amos Yaron of the Israel Defense Forces puts a stop to the Palestinian massacre with only a few, brief sentences. Had the Israeli government heeded incoming reports earlier rather than waiting for eyewitness accounts, thousands of innocent victims could have been spared.

Impact

The graphic novel *Waltz with Bashir* achieved its status as a result of the success of Folman's animated documentary. Since the film received abundant critical praise, it seemed logical that the film (influenced stylistically by graphic novels) should be transformed into a graphic novel itself. Both formats have appealed to audiences based upon timely subject matter, unique perspective—trauma is based upon seeing the enemy's dead bodies rather than witnessing the killing of one's fellow soldiers—and the ambiguous political message where viewers individually interpret Israel's accountability in the camps.

Conversely, both the film and the graphic novel have been called propaganda for not illustrating enough Israeli responsibility for the massacre. Such critics see both works as an effort to depict the Israelis (rather than the Palestinians) as the victims, as they were shooting and crying during the event. Despite such accusations, the graphic novel leaves readers with images of the massacre's true victims. These images put both Folman's personal story and the animation into clear perspective, emphasizing that despite the use of an artistic style oftentimes reserved for fictional accounts, the slaughter of thousands of innocent people truly did occur.

Films

Waltz with Bashir. Directed by Ari Folman. Brigit Folman Film Gang, 2008. This animated documentary features all the characters voiced by the real interviewees, with the exceptions of Boaz Rein-Buskila and Carmi Cna'an, whose voices are dubbed by actors and whose real appearances were altered for anonymity. Since the graphic novel is a reverse adaptation of the film and both were created by Folman and Polonsky, the book differs only subtly. First, the dialogue had to be simplified to fit the pages, but the story line is the same in flow, mood, and ideas presented. Likewise, the film extends the carnage in the Sabra and Shatila refugee camps, using approximately fifty seconds of varied live footage shots for increased impact, whereas the book only has five photographs of the massacre. The film has received numerous international awards as well as six Israeli Film Academy awards (Best Film, Director, Screenplay, Editing, Art Direction, Sound).

Celeste Lempke

Further Reading

Sacco, Joe. *Footnotes in Gaza: A Graphic Novel* (2009).
_____. *Palestine* (2002).
Satrapi, Marjane. *Persepolis* (2003).

Bibliography

Mansfield, Natasha. "Loss and Mourning: Cinema's 'Language' of Trauma in *Waltz with Bashir*." *Wide Screen* 2, no. 1 (June, 2010).

Stewart, Garrett. "Screen Memory in *Waltz with Bashir*." *Film Quarterly* 63, no. 3 (Spring, 2010): 58-62.

Yosef, Raz. "War Fantasies: Memory, Trauma, and Ethics in Ari Folman's *Waltz with Bashir*." *Journal of Modern Jewish Studies* 9, no. 3 (November, 2010): 311-326.

See also: *Footnotes in Gaza*; *Palestine*; *Persepolis*

WE ARE ON OUR OWN

Author: Katin, Miriam
Artist: Miriam Katin (illustrator); Tom Devlin (cover artist)
Publisher: Drawn and Quarterly
First book publication: 2006

Publication History

We Are on Our Own, Miriam Katin's first full-length graphic novel, debuted toward the end of Katin's career as an illustrator and graphic artist. At the age of sixty-three and after a career as an animator for Disney and MTV, Katin introduced this compelling memoir about her and her mother during World War II. Katin is both author and illustrator of this single-volume work, relying heavily on her own memories and the experiences her parents recounted to her later in life. Originally published in 2006 by Drawn and Quarterly, the book has since been released in several additional languages through a variety of foreign publishers.

Plot

We Are on Our Own tells the story of Lisa (a representation of Katin and her childhood innocence) and her mother, Esther, who are forced to flee from their family home as the Nazis invade Hungary in 1944. They have lived comfortably as assimilated Jews, but to hide, they dress as peasants and flee to the countryside, where Esther tells a farmer and his wife that she and Lisa, who she professes is illegitimate, need a place to stay in exchange for work. The farmer takes them in; they are safe for a while, until Esther becomes the sexual "pet" of a Nazi soldier who has guessed her identity and who coerces her to sleep with him in exchange for keeping her secret. However, their cover is eventually blown, and Lisa and Esther flee to a winery, where Esther seeks work and a safe haven for herself and her daughter.

In 1945, the tide of the war turns, and the Soviets invade Hungary. The soldiers are rough and sexually abuse Esther; she discovers that she has been impregnated and heads with Lisa to the nearest town to seek an abortion. Tired, downtrodden, and terrified, she feels she is all alone, until she encounters David Blau, a family acquaintance and a kind soul, who takes her and Lisa in and helps them back on their feet. Though a romance threatens to blossom between Esther and David, Esther rejects David's advances and maintains that she will await her husband's return. As it turns out, Lisa's father, Károly, has been traveling across Hungary searching for his wife and daughter and trying desperately to follow their trail. Ultimately, David helps reunite Lisa's mother and father, even though it means that he cannot be with the woman with whom he has fallen in love. Peppered throughout the narrative are scenes from Lisa's adulthood, in which she is watching her own children play, either grappling with her faith and spirituality or just remembering the past.

Characters

- *Lisa* represents Katin's childhood self. Through her eyes, Katin introduces the terror and confusion of the wartime world and the resulting struggles with faith, as experienced by a child. Lisa's adult self is also depicted, though her adult character receives far less treatment.
- *Esther Levy*, Lisa's mother and a Jew who must flee her home as the Nazis approach, is a strong and savvy woman who does whatever is necessary to protect herself and her daughter during the war. Though faced with many troubling decisions and harsh treatment, she maintains her dignity and her hope that her family will one day be safely reunited.
- *Éva* is a Christian and a good friend of Esther who both helps Esther and Lisa flee and keeps Esther's affairs in order during and after the war. It is Éva who tells Esther's husband that the family has survived but is in hiding.
- *Anna* is the Levys' maid and another Christian friend who helps protect the family by lying for them about their sudden disappearance.
- *Károly Levy* is Esther's husband, who is absent for most of the story as he has been fighting in the war. He is introduced as a frail, war-weary

man, but one of dogged determination who will not give up his hopes of finding the family he has lost. Though his faith in God has wavered, he remains devoted to his wife and daughter.
- *David Blau* is a family acquaintance who first recognizes Lisa and Esther and helps them to safety. Though at first his assistance is largely altruistic, as Lisa and Esther settle into his family home he comes to care deeply for Esther. Nevertheless, his altruism prevails and, when Károly returns and is searching for his lost family, he is instrumental in bringing them together.
- *Mademoiselle Delachaux*, David Blau's family governess, helps to take over care of Lisa, first while her mother is in the hospital for her abortion and later as Lisa and Esther come to reside in the Blau family home. The governess teaches Lisa French and helps her return to the upper-middle-class lifestyle in which she would have been raised had the war not interrupted her childhood.

Artistic Style
Katin is the illustrator of her own memoir and renders images with such striking simplicity and insight that it seems possible they have come only from memory. Her pencil sketches have a cartoonlike quality to them, perhaps the product of Katin's career as an illustrator and cartoonist, but just as likely a depiction of the haziness of the finer details lost in childhood memory. The panels illustrating the wartime experiences of her childhood are rendered in black and white; the only color panels are those depicting her adulthood, which receives relatively sparse attention in comparison to her memories of her and her mother during the war.

The lettering of Katin's narrative is particularly intriguing. Though the text and thought bubbles are fairly standard throughout the story (spoken words appear in square text boxes and thoughts appear in wavy-lined bubbles), the text seems to waver, almost as if it were written with a shaking hand, which reflects the troubling nature of the subject matter.

> **Miriam Katin**
>
> Born in Hungary, Miriam Katin's family immigrated to Israel after the uprising of 1956 and then to the United States in 1963. She began publishing children's books in the 1990's and turned to producing comics in the 2000's. Though she has published short works in dozens of magazines and anthologies, she is best known for her 2006 graphic novel, *We Are on Our Own*. That book is a memoir of Katin's escape on foot, with her mother, from the Nazi invasion of Budapest. Told primarily from the point of view of a young girl living through incredible atrocities, *We Are on Our Own* mixes black-and-white sections drawn in uninked pencil with sequences set much later, drawn in extremely detailed pencil crayon. The sequences set during the war tend toward a greater degree of cartoonishness, while the color sequences are much more naturalistic. Throughout, Katin's use of pencils rather than inks tends to highlight the sketchily constructed nature of her images.

The panels are laid out primarily in squares that make comfortable use of the page space. They are not cluttered, but they leave little white space—only enough to distinguish the panels. The story is broken into "chapters" by single-image panels centered on a page of dark space that usually indicate specific changes in the course of Katin's life or in the tide of the war. When a specific event from her childhood relates in some way to a memory of her adulthood and her experience as a mother and wife, Katin interjects with a page of full-color illustrations. Though these sketches are no more detailed than the black-and-white images, the memories depicted therein seem sharper because of their brightness and vividness.

Themes
Set during the Nazi invasion of Hungary during World War II and the subsequent Soviet invasion toward the end of the war, *We Are on Our Own* addresses the profound effects of childhood traumas, particularly those

of the wartime experience, and the lasting effect they have on one's psyche. In crafting this memoir, Katin addresses many challenging subjects, including anti-Semitism, death, rape, abortion, and lost faith, as well as her mother's sometimes challenging choices. Through both her pencil sketches and her narration, Katin poignantly and sensitively provides insight without graphic imagery or violence.

Drawing on her own personal experiences as a child during World War II, as well as her understanding of her mother's experience as she tried to protect her young daughter, Katin crafts a compelling portrayal of the fears and questions of a child who is traumatized by what she is witnessing and is grasping for understanding. The reader sees the wartime world through the eyes of Lisa, a child and a projection of Katin as a toddler, who begins to piece the puzzle together through metaphor and understatement.

Katin also depicts the experiences of the adult that child grows to be, navigating the sometimes turbulent waters of marriage and parenthood and making choices for her own child. Through the interjected panels of her adult experiences, Katin reveals her struggles with spirituality and the loss of faith she experienced as a result of her childhood traumas. The contrast of the childhood experience and adult experience and her memories of each reveals a personal history that is saddening and inspiring and tells a largely universal story of the child's struggle to come to terms with traumas and the adult's struggle to maintain faith in spite of these experiences.

Impact

Published twenty years after the first installment of Art Spiegelman's *Maus* (1986), which tells of his father's experiences during World War II as a victim of the Nazis, Katin's *We Are on Our Own* cannot help but be compared to *Maus* and others in the body of literature chronicling the World War II experience of Jewish families and individuals. While the work itself has not yet had any profound influence on the graphic novels genre, Katin's debut draws together the artistic styles and thematic treatments of many of her predecessors, creating a finished product that is remarkable for the sensitivity with which it treats its subject matter as well as for the force of the narrative it conveys. More important, by publishing this story so late in her career, Katin sends the message that it is never too late to tell one's story and that sometimes such a story can better be told with images than with words. In that respect, Katin's work likely has a greater impact on the body of Holocaust and World War II literature than on the graphic novel genre or format. Nevertheless, hers remains an important voice in the graphic novel industry and will likely serve to inspire future writers as they craft their own memoirs and narratives.

Rachel E. Frier

Further Reading

Lemelman, Martin, and Martin Lemelman. *Mendel's Daughter* (2007).

Sfar, Joann. *Klezmer: Tales of the Wild East* (2006).

Spiegelman, Art. *Maus I: A Survivor's Tale: My Father Bleeds History* (1986, 1991).

Bibliography

David, Danya Sara. "Journeys of Faith and Survival: An Examination of Three Jewish Graphic Novels." M.A. thesis, University of British Columbia, 2008. https://circle.ubc.ca/bitstream/handle/2429/2453/ubc_2008_spring_david_danya_sara.pdf?sequence

Katin, Miriam. "In Plain Sight." *World Literature Today* 81, no. 6 (November/December, 2007): 14-18.

Vasvári, Louise O. "Women's Holocaust Memories/Memoirs: Trauma, Testimony, and the Gendered Imagination." In *Jewish Studies at Central European University*, edited by András Kovács and Michael I. Miller. Budapest: Central European University Press, 2008.

Vasvári, Louise O., and Steven Tötösy de Zepetnek. *Comparative Central European Holocaust Studies*. West Lafayette, Ind.: Purdue University Press, 2009.

See also: *Fun Home*; *Black Hole*; *Maus*; *A Jew in Communist Prague,* Volume I

What It Is

Author: Barry, Lynda
Artist: Lynda Barry (illustrator)
Publisher: Drawn and Quarterly
First book publication: 2008

Publication History

Lynda Barry's *What It Is* was first published in 2008 by Montreal-based comic book publisher Drawn and Quarterly. The large-format, full-color work was released in hardcover in the first and subsequent printings. A well-known writer and artist of comics for many years, Barry initially established herself as a cartoonist with her comic strip *Ernie Pook's Comeek*, which began in the *Chicago Reader* in 1979 and ran for nearly thirty years. She published book-length collections of comics and illustrated novels with such companies as Seattle-based Sasquatch Books and Simon and Schuster prior to working with Drawn and Quarterly, also serializing a number of her comics online. Her work, particularly *What It Is*, is especially noted for crossing genre boundaries.

Plot

What It Is blends memoir and writing exercises, performing as it instructs. As Barry delves deeply into her memory and reflects on the ways she uses images and words to tell stories, she poses questions that invite her readers to do the same. *What It Is* is as much an art book as it is a storybook and a workbook; artists, readers, and writers are all invited in, especially those who have struggled to overcome obstacles impeding their creativity. Barry's book is, in large part, about invention, and it discusses issues such as the genesis of ideas and the ways in which ideas can be accessed.

What It Is is roughly divided into two parts. The first part begins with a present-day Barry, under stress, frustrated, and bothered by everything in general and nothing in particular. She has a song stuck in her head, though she cannot remember where she heard it. While walking through a silhouetted forest, she contemplates the origins of thoughts and anxieties and wonders about the differences between the parts of her mind;

Lynda Barry presents on creativity to NASA employees. (By NASA Goddard Space Flight Center, via Wikimedia Commons)

she also ponders the fact that some ideas, experiences, and memories are immediately available, while others seem buried. Thus begins her journey into her memory, as she recalls childhood and adolescent experiences with drawing, singing, dancing, and writing. Interspersed between these memories and stories are questions about the nature of thought, writing, drawing, and storytelling.

Barry traces her history with art, moving from childhood through college. She recounts her moments of elation and self-doubt, from the thrill of having one of her drawings selected to hang on the wall of her elementary school classroom to her loss of confidence after erasing her work on a test so hard that she tore holes in the paper. She depicts her return to art in middle school and high school, and she recalls her college classes with Marilyn Frasca, a painting teacher whose way of connecting experiences, images, and memories to art greatly influences Barry.

In the second half of *What It Is*, Barry explains her creative process and poses questions to assist readers in their own explorations and creations. The creative process she outlines begins with lists, asking the reader to list, for example, the first ten cars he or she remembers from childhood. Building upon these lists, she next asks the reader to recall personal experiences, such as riding in one of the cars. She prompts the reader to think about movement within that memory and write down sensory experiences. All of the exercises are timed, creating the sense that *What It Is* is a writing workshop in book form.

Characters
- *Lynda Barry* is the author, narrator, and guide. Appearing at various ages, she is first seen as an adult, irritated and aggravated by something she cannot name. Throughout the majority of *What It Is*, however, she is portrayed as a past version of herself: a daydreaming child who believes that drawings and pictures have lives of their own; a young girl who takes hula lessons and gets lost in songs, stories, and television shows; an adolescent with a love of drawing who gives up after an experience with self-doubt and embarrassment leaves her with overwhelming shame and guilt; a junior high school student who begins to draw again, initially copying other artists' characters; and a college student studying art and trying to find and develop her own content, characters, and perspective.
- *The Gorgon* is an imaginary enemy from Barry's childhood, based on Medusa and developed from a horror movie Barry watched when she was eight years old. Barry suggests that the imaginary Gorgon helped her love her mother. The Gorgon appears to signify both internal and external obstacles.
- *Marilyn Frasca* is Barry's college art teacher, from whom she takes a painting class and learns about writing, particularly freewriting and journal keeping. Barry describes Frasca as mysterious, and although she remembers never getting any technical advice from her, she recalls a pivotal moment in which Frasca pointed out the teeth in Giotto's painting of the Madonna. The method that Barry outlines in *What It Is* is informed by what she learned with and through Frasca.

Artistic Style

What It Is plays with and pushes the boundaries of the graphic novel form. Some pages are collages; some are cut-and-paste. Identifiable comic panels do appear, but they are rare. Barry merges drawings with stamps and stickers with sketches. Her work is multidimensional, featuring revamped stationary, resituated excerpts from unidentifiable texts, ribbons and pieces of fabric, photographs and handwritten notes, paint, and glitter. The pages are bursting with color, and there are levels and depths of text to read.

Written pieces concerning Barry's past are printed on yellow legal paper, making them reminiscent of jotted and somewhat informal correspondence. Other words, sometimes relating directly to the rest of the page's content and sometimes trailing off in another direction as if representing a different thought, are written in cursive or typeset in various colors and inks. The text is surrounded with playful images of all sorts of creatures and objects, from mermaids and octopuses to birds and many-eyed monsters.

The bursting pages are not chaotic, though, and while the bits and pieces that make up the backgrounds and fill the margins may ask the reader to pause, they should not be considered distractions: *What It Is* encourages readers to let their minds wander, and the structure of the text, the use of images, the questions posed throughout, and the more straightforward directions and writing prompts are similarly encouraging.

Themes

What It Is concerns the accessing of one's creativity and imagination. The first section of the book chronicles moments from Barry's childhood and adolescence, tying these moments to themes of play, storytelling, and creativity. She recalls that she once imagined that the pictures taped to the walls of her early childhood home were able to move. She remembers trying to stay

> **Lynda Barry**
>
> Novelist and cartoonist Lynda Barry has categorized her work as "autobifictionalography" and combines dozens of narrative and artistic techniques to create both fiction and nonfiction stories, often in a dark but humorous manner. Barry's work—which is aimed at adults—often draws from her own life experiences and sometimes includes workbook sections for readers to create their own comics at home. Her artistic style is visually complex, combining brushwork with elaborate collage and other techniques.

still and focus, waiting to see what would change. She further recalls imagining that she saw a picture of a cat blink and notes that this image stuck in her memory. In describing such moments, Barry evokes the realm of imagination, the place in which memory and image meet creation. Play is essential to Barry's artistic process, and she additionally attempts to change the way she looks at the world, open herself to new experiences, and then remember, write, and draw those experiences.

Attention to vision and images informs the writing practice Barry details in the second half of the book, a workbook she calls "Writing the Unthinkable." The workbook provides space for readers to practice her method of invention and explore their own creative processes. Barry's method necessitates connecting with the unconscious creative impulse of childhood and working past the inner critic who tells the would-be artist that he or she is doing something poorly or incorrectly. Barry provides questions and prompts, word banks to draw from, and other sources of inspiration, but what she includes is not exhaustive. Readers can practice her method with any word or memory.

What It Is illuminates the way in which the imagination spirals, interrupting its own musings. The book asks questions of itself and its readers, combining collage with text to express the nature of the artistic process. The arrangements and aesthetics, then, support Barry's overarching ambition to follow the stream of thought and consciousness, allowing her mind to wander with questions and doodles and inviting readers to witness her creative process but also discover their own.

Impact

While *What It Is* is a difficult work to classify, its unconventional, genre-crossing blend of the graphic novel, "how-to" book, and memoir forms garnered it a great deal of critical acclaim. In 2009, the book won the Eisner Award for Best Reality-Based Work and the R. R. Donnelley Literary Award, awarded by the Wisconsin Library Association in recognition of the highest literary achievement by a Wisconsin author. Barry has taught classes and workshops across the United States based on the processes and questions she outlines in *What It Is*. These workshops, generally titled "Writing the Unthinkable," incorporate many of the sorts of creative exercises found in the book.

In 2010, Barry released *Picture This: The Near-Sighted Monkey Book*, also published by Drawn and Quarterly. This follow-up publication uses the same format as *What It Is* to examine the creative process of drawing, asking why an artist starts and sometimes stops a creative endeavor. Drawn and Quarterly went on to publish additional books by Barry, including *Blabber Blabber Blabber:* Volume 1 *of Everything* (2011), a collection of early works.

Marcy R. Isabella

Further Reading

Barry, Lynda. *One! Hundred! Demons!* (2002).
_____. *Picture This* (2010).
Kochalka, James. *The Cute Manifesto* (2005).

Bibliography

Elbow, Peter. *Writing Without Teachers*. 2d ed. New York: Oxford University Press, 1998.
McCloud, Scott. *Making Comics: Storytelling Secrets of Comics, Manga, and Graphic Novels*. New York: Harper, 2006.
_____. *Understanding Comics: The Invisible Art*. New York: HarperPerennial, 1993.

See also: *One! Hundred! Demons!; Fun Home; Embroideries*

When the Wind Blows

Author: Briggs, Raymond
Artist: Raymond Briggs (illustrator)
Publisher: Hamish Hamilton
First book publication: 1982

Publication History

When the Wind Blows, by British comics creator and children's author Raymond Briggs, was published as a hardcover simultaneously by Hamish Hamilton in Great Britain and by Shocken Books in the United States in 1982. It was then published by Penguin Books as a paperback in 1983. The book was reprinted each following year during the 1980's. *When the Wind Blows* has also enjoyed publication in several languages, including Chinese, Finnish, German, Japanese, Korean, Spanish, and Thai. The book's title was taken from the nursery rhyme and lullaby "Rock-a-Bye Baby."

Plot

On one level, the plot of *When the Wind Blows* seems deceptively simple. A retired couple, living somewhere in the English countryside, learn about an imminent nuclear attack. They follow government instructions about how to protect themselves and then the attack comes. The couple misunderstands the seriousness of their situation as they gradually succumb to radiation sickness. However, the strength of Briggs's work is in the subtlety of characterization of his two protagonists and the tension between the comedic elements and the bleak, almost unimaginable horror of the story.

The story opens with the retired Jim Bloggs returning to his wife Hilda at their house "Jimilda," full of news of impending war. They discuss the situation, revealing their naïveté when Jim thinks that the problems are being caused by "the ultimate determent" and when Hilda complains about a "preemptive strike" as if it is some kind of industrial action. Part of the black humor of the story comes from the fact that the various seemingly ridiculous precautions they then take—following these instructions blindly—were all taken from actual official leaflets. These include instructions to paint windows white, conflicting advice from government and county councils about whether to hang material on them, and instructions to get into a large paper bag before the bomb drops.

Jim goes to the local shops on his bike to try to buy a protractor to ensure that their shelter, made of house doors, is located at the correct angle to the wall. He and his wife reminisce about World War II and struggle to finalize their food and toilet arrangements, continuing to make simple mistakes. Jim believes that his hero from the war, Field Marshal Bernard "Monty" Montgomery, is still alive, and Hilda is writing a letter of complaint to the head of the KGB, who they think is named B. J. Key. Brief mention is made of other characters, such as the couple's son, Ron, who confuses them with his fatalistic view of the imminent attack, and Mr. Willis at the local shop, but they never make an appearance.

> **Raymond Briggs**
>
> A beloved children's book creator in the United Kingdom, where the film adaptation of his book *The Snowman* is shown on television every year at Christmas, Raymond Briggs has balanced work for young audiences and more serious reflections on political themes throughout his career. As a children's book creator, Briggs is best known for *Father Christmas*, *Fungus the Bogeyman*, and *The Snowman*, all of which are produced in the comics form. In 1980 he released the graphic novel *Gentleman Jim*, about the working-class couple Jim and Hilda Bloggs, who were based on his parents. The sequel to that work, *When the Wind Blows*, found the couple caught up in a nuclear war and was published to stunning acclaim. Briggs has also produced a graphic novel biography of his parents, *Ethel & Ernest*. Briggs's comics and graphic novels are distinctive for their detailed, cartoonish art, which is frequently produced with pencil crayon and cheerful colors that tend to ironize the downbeat nature of his stories.

After the bomb drops, Jim and Hilda are surprised to find that they have no power and water, and having left their shelter, they begin to feel increasingly unwell. They mistake the signs of radiation sickness for ailments that can be treated by a trip to the drugstore. On the final page, in twenty-four monochrome panels showing only the dark shelter where they are hiding, they attempt to pray, and Jim, rambling, attempts unsuccessfully to recite the Alfred, Lord Tennyson poem "The Charge of the Light Brigade" (1854) as they die.

Characters
- *Jim Bloggs*, addressed as "James" by his wife, is a portly, retired man. He is similar to, if not actually the same as, the title character of Briggs's earlier *Gentleman Jim* (1980). The reader learns that he was a child during World War II, a period he looks on with nostalgia as a simpler and more carefree time. He has a simplistic view of the world and trusting attitude toward authority. His life revolves around his wife, Hilda, and trips by bus to the public library or the shops.
- *Hilda Bloggs*, Jim's wife, has a view of the world that is, if anything, even more naïve than that of her husband. While Jim is keen to keep abreast of current events, Hilda believes that newspapers are "full of rubbish," except for the horoscopes. Some of Hilda and Jim's characteristics are taken from Briggs's parents, who feature directly in his later biographical graphic novel *Ethel and Ernest: A True Story* (1998).

Artistic Style

One of the striking things about *When the Wind Blows* is the fact that it is drawn largely in the familiar style Briggs had previously used for his highly successful children's books, including *Father Christmas* (1973) and *The Snowman* (1978). The two main characters are rotund, simply drawn and rendered, mainly in strong, bright watercolors enhanced by colored-pencil shading. This rather sedate and benign drawing style, combined with the dark nature of the story, creates a disjunction between form and content that makes the tragic events of the narrative seem even more shocking. In fact, it is possible to read the first few pages of the novel without realizing the bleak nature of the story that is about to unfold.

Most pages in the book contain seven rows of more than twenty densely packed panels. Briggs had originally tended to use a more traditional format with fewer than ten panels per page, but he was inspired to use this more intense layout after seeing small-scale reproductions of his earlier work. There are some exceptions to this dense page layout. When Jim and Hilda reminisce about World War II, larger balloon-shaped panels spread across the pages in colors that are literally rose-tinted. Early in the story, three dark-silhouetted double-page spreads depict a missile, military planes, and a nuclear submarine, respectively. These vast stark panels interrupt the narrative, bringing a massive dose of oppressive reality into the couple's comfortable, delusional world and helping to warn the reader of the dark events that are about to unfold. The nuclear explosion itself is rendered in a two-page spread that is almost pure white, with the smallest hint of red along the edges. Over the next two pages, the frames of the comic panels slowly reassert themselves, first as jagged white lines, and then fading in from red, the frames finally become rectangles again. The remainder of the story follows Briggs's usual drawing style and page layout, apart from two larger fantasy panels in which Jim imagines himself rescuing a beautiful girl and being confronted by a Russian soldier. As the couple's bodies gradually decay, the colors of the pages become increasingly muted and grayed until they are virtually just a dull monochrome.

Themes

The book essentially has two themes: the almost unimaginable horror of a nuclear attack and the misplaced trust of simple people in their incompetent, uncaring authorities.

Portrayals of nuclear war are comparatively rare in comics, although there were a spate of Cold War comics in the United States, including *Atom Age Combat* (1952) and *Atomic War* (1952-1953). Japanese reactions to the 1945 bombing of Hiroshima are addressed in Japanese manga such as Keiji Nakazama's *Barefoot Gen* (1973-1974) and Fumiyo Kouno's *Town of Evening Calm, Country of Cherry Blossoms* (2004). The earlier type of American comic tends to present nuclear war as winnable, while the later Japanese comics, perhaps unsurprisingly, concentrate on the sheer terror of the atomic bomb and its aftermath.

Briggs's portrayal of a nuclear attack with elements of black humor is unusual, if not unique, in the history of the medium. He portrays the political events that lead to the war as distant, and perhaps inevitable, and the attack is revealed gradually to the reader. Despite the increasing ghastliness of their situation, Briggs continuously introduces comedic elements as the couple makes a series of errors based on their fragile grasp of the situation in terms of both its origins and its implications.

Briggs's use of the simple, deluded lower-class couple to provide the humor in his story has been criticized as constituting an attack on the working classes, but he has stated that the ludicrously inadequate official guidelines were the target of his criticism, as well as the source of much of the humor. Having seen a documentary about precautions the population was meant to make in event of a nuclear war, Briggs obtained "Protect and Survive" and other leaflets produced by the authorities. When viewing Jim and Hilda's trust in these leaflets, it is certainly possible to see the couple as hopeless, naïve, and childlike in their simplistic approach to the situation. The question remains whether the humor in the story derives from Briggs simply making fun of the couple's stupidity. While their naïve mistakes are certainly part of the humor, the situation that they are in also engenders pathos, and Briggs clearly wants the reader to feel empathy for them.

Impact

It is clear that this work was aimed at adults, unlike Briggs's earlier books, which, although they tended to have a cynical edge, were aimed mainly at children. *Father Christmas* features a grumpy titular hero, *Fungus the Bogeyman* has a most disgusting central character, and even his popular *The Snowman* has a downbeat ending. Yet none of these stories approached the bleakness of *When the Wind Blows*.

Briggs's body of work has allowed him to occupy an unusual position in British publishing in that he is widely regarded as a children's author, even though all his most famous work is in a comic format. Even the most famous of British comic artists tend to be regarded as working in a lesser medium, where they are marginalized, but Briggs has escaped this entirely, and his work is often categorized with the more prestigious label of "picture books." This has meant that works such as *When the Wind Blows* tend to be reviewed in mainstream newspapers and are taken seriously by the British media. Briggs has received critical praise for both his children's books and his adult works such as *The Tin-Pot Foreign General and the Old Iron Woman* (1984), a satire on the Falklands War.

Copies of *When the Wind Blows* were sent by its British publishers to all members of the British parliament, where it received predictable praise or condemnation from those on either side of the political divide. The book was discussed in Parliament, and some of the more favorable comments it received from members of Parliament were included in later editions.

Films

When the Wind Blows. Directed by Jimmy T. Murakami. TVC London/Film Four International, 1986. This animated version was voiced by Sir John Mills and Dame Peggy Ashcroft, with music by Roger Waters and David Bowie. The book acted as a starting point for the artists' storyboards, with Briggs serving as consultant. There are two major differences from the book: the use of documentary footage to represent nostalgia for World War II and the depiction of the bomb drop itself in a lengthy and spectacular sequence of destruction that segues into black-and-white scenes of the couples' earlier happy life, before present reality intrudes again. The film was not as successful as the 1982 TVC animation of *The Snowman*, presumably because of its dark subject matter. Despite this, it was also adapted into a radio play and a West End theater production.

David Huxley

Further Reading

Briggs, Raymond. *Ethel and Ernest: A True Story* (1998).

_____. *The Snowman* (1978).

_____. *The Tin-Pot Foreign General and the Old Iron Woman* (1984).

Bibliography

Briggs, Raymond, and Nicolette Jones. *Blooming Books*. London: Jonathan Cape, 2003.

Cooke, Rachel. "Raymond Briggs: Big Kid, 'Old Git' and Still in the Rudest of Health." *The Observer* (August 9, 2008): 20-21.

Gravett, Paul "'Where Is the Use of a Book Without Pictures or Conversations?' Coming to Terms with the Graphic Novel in Europe." *Third Text* 21, no. 5 (September, 2007): 617-625.

Kilborn, Richard W. *Multimedia Melting Pot: Marketing "When the Wind Blows."* London: Comedia, 1986.

Wroe, Nicholas. "Profile: Raymond Briggs." *The Guardian*, December 17, 2004, p. 20.

See also: *Ethel and Ernest*; *The Snowman*

WHITEOUT

Author: Rucka, Greg
Artist: Steve Lieber (illustrator); Dave Gibbons (cover artist); Mike Mignola (cover artist); Frank Miller (cover artist); Matt Wagner (cover artist)
Publisher: Oni Press
First serial publication: 1998
First book publication: 1999

Publication History

Whiteout was originally serialized in four thirty-six-page issues published by Oni Press in 1998. The limited series was the first of several creations for Oni Press by writer Greg Rucka, who had previously established himself through his work on many titles for Marvel Comics and DC Comics as well as a series of novels featuring hard-nosed New York-based security consultant Atticus Kodiak. Artist Steve Lieber was known for his work on titles as *Hawkman* (1993-1996), *Conan the Usurper* (1997), and *Grendel Tales* (1997). The individual issues of *Whiteout* were slightly reformatted and published as a collected graphic novel in 1999. The following year, Rucka and Lieber collaborated to create a sequel, *Whiteout: Melt*.

Greg Rucka, comic-book writer and novelist, known for his period working in titles such as Queen and Country, Adventures of Superman, Wonder Woman *and the making of* Infinite Crisis. *(By Artemisboy, via Wikimedia Commons)*

Plot

After killing in self-defense a prisoner under her supervision, U.S. deputy marshal Carrie Stetko has been exiled to Antarctica and stationed at McMurdo, an American base. She is the sole law enforcement officer on the continent and one of just two women in a wasteland of ice and a sea of men. Despite the privation, the harsh environment agrees with her feisty, self-reliant personality.

The base is preparing to shut down for winter's eight months of darkness when a man's body is discovered on the ice. Carrie visits the scene, noticing core sample holes drilled nearby. Presumed to be a member of an international field-research team, the corpse is unidentifiable, its features obliterated. The body is brought back to McMurdo for autopsy. A footprint taken indicates the dead man is American Alexander Keller, a late addition to the research team.

Tracing the missing members of the team via radio link, Carrie flies with pilot Delfy to Victoria, the U.K. base, where researchers Siple and Mooney are staying. There, Carrie connects with Lily Sharpe, a British intelligence agent.

Following a lifeline, the women set off through whiteout conditions to the men's living quarters, where they discover Siple and Mooney, dead. Masked in winter gear, the killer stands over the bodies. He attacks the women with an ice hammer, knocking out Lily and chasing Carrie into the storm. The killer cuts the lifeline and leaves Carrie at the mercy of the elements. In zero visibility, Carrie stumbles upon a storage shed, crawls inside, and passes out. Lily regains consciousness, finds Carrie, and summons help.

Suffering from frostbite and exposure, Carrie is flown back to McMurdo, where the doctor amputates two fingers on her right hand. After recovering,

Carrie flies with Lily to the South Pole's Amundsen-Scott base, where missing researchers Wesselhoeft and Rubin have surfaced. Carrie encounters the supposedly deceased Keller and realizes that something went wrong in the identification process. She chases Keller, but he disappears outside. Meanwhile, Lily discovers the bodies of the freshly murdered Wesselhoeft and Rubin. Keller is eventually discovered and captured. With him is a cache of core samples; they are solid gold, worth thousands of dollars, and represent the motive for the murders.

Back at McMurdo, Carrie and Lily determine that the prisoner must have had an accomplice with flying skills. The only suspect is Haden, since Delfy's movements are accounted for. Haden attacks Lily, and she stabs him before collapsing. The doctor, also an accomplice in the gold-smuggling scheme, treats Haden and tries to persuade the wounded man to escape by snowmobile to a nearby base. Thinking the doctor wants the gold for himself, Haden attacks, but the doctor kills him with a wrench. Carrie interrogates Keller and confirms the doctor's role in the crimes. She confronts and arrests the doctor. He confesses that he has sewn another two hundred pounds of gold into the autopsied corpse, which is to be loaded onto a cargo plane removing the last of the departing base personnel. When the plane leaves, Carrie and Lily stay behind in Antarctica.

Characters
- *Carrie Stetko*, the protagonist, is a tough and determined U.S. deputy marshal. An attractive, freckled woman of about thirty, she is recently widowed. She has been relegated to Antarctica for killing a vicious rapist-murderer in her custody.
- *Brett MacEwan* is a U.S. marshal and Carrie's boss. A humorless, demanding middle-aged man, he is based in Hawaii.
- *"Furry"* is the doctor of McMurdo base, so nicknamed because of his untrimmed hair and beard. A stocky man in his fifties, he is one of Carrie's few friends in Antarctica, though he ultimately betrays her trust through his involvement in the crimes.
- *Lily Sharpe* is a British intelligence agent, though she never admits it. Tall, blond, attractive, and capable, she served in Macao before being posted to Antarctica.
- *Bates Rubin*, *Weiss*, *Siple*, *Mooney*, and *Isaac Wesselhoeft* are members of a field-research team working in Antarctica. They are murdered by Keller.
- *Alexander Keller* is a young American geologist-geophysicist and a co-conspirator in the gold-smuggling scheme. Clean-shaven with long blond hair, he is at first presumed dead but later discovered alive.
- *Lieutenant Byron Delfy* is a Naval Support Force Antarctica pilot. Young and friendly, he is a casual acquaintance of Carrie because of previous flights she has taken with him during her sojourn in Antarctica.
- *John Haden* is a pilot who flies out of Mawson base while serving Australian interests in Antarctica. A well-built, bearded man in his forties, he is a major conspirator in the murders.

Artistic Style
Appropriate to the stark setting, the artwork throughout *Whiteout* is entirely black and white, except for the cover of the collected series, drawn by Frank Miller, which displays the title in red beneath a high-contrast rendering of the heroine in an action pose. A splash page completed by a different artist introduces each of the collection's chapters. The first chapter's artwork, by Matt Wagner, is minimalist, placing a body with a head obscured by blood against a plain white background. The splash page for chapter 2, by Mike Mignola, is a chiaroscuro piece that shows a gun-wielding Carrie charging through a doorway. Chapter 3's introduction, the work of Dave Gibbons, is a highly realistic rendition of Lily rushing toward someone holding a gun in a gloved hand. Lieber, who illustrated and lettered the remainder of the volume, completed the chapter 4 splash page, which depicts Carrie supporting a battered Lily.

Lieber's style transitions smoothly from simple line art to highly refined close-ups and from silhouettes and rough blocks of light and shadow that indicate a faster pace to screened sketches that separate flashbacks from live action. Always readable, Lieber's drawings are realistic yet loose enough to retain a cartoonlike feel. Images are sufficiently detailed to set scenes and provide visual interest, but they are never so busy or overworked that they detract from narrative flow.

Layouts range from standard three- or four-tier pages for atmospheric expository or introspective scenes to wide horizontal panels for long views. Border-breaking verticals suspend time during fast-moving action scenes. Two-page spreads provide visual emphasis. Constantly shifting arrangements of panels of varying size and shape, presented from a variety of perspectives, not only help maintain interest but also underscore the book's tension: The reader does not know what to expect next.

Themes

Virtually every work of fiction concerns at least one of three conflicts: the protagonist versus one or more antagonists, the protagonist versus nature, or the protagonist versus himself or herself. *Whiteout* explores all three themes through terse plotting, appropriately stylized artwork, and narrative-advancing design.

First and foremost, *Whiteout* is a mystery. Protagonist Carrie Stetko, a law officer, is the only person in Antarctica with the authority to investigate crime. She must discover who has committed a series of murders and determine why and how the crimes were undertaken. In the course of pursuing her investigation to its conclusion, she is pitted against several wily, dangerous antagonists.

Second, Carrie operates in Earth's most hostile environment. Antarctica is an agoraphobic's nightmare: a monochromatic wilderness with few landmarks at best and a howling fury of white at worst. The climate outside is unforgiving; hypothermia, frostbite, disorientation, and death are everyday risks. The climate indoors is claustrophobic and equally unkind. An outsider because of her job and gender, Carrie works within a closed community primarily composed of men, many of whom subject her to subtle and blatant sexual harassment.

Finally, Carrie battles herself. A grieving widow with no solace from family or friends, a disgraced officer seeking redemption through work, and an isolated woman surrounded by potential enemies, she must summon up reserves of inner strength to overcome physical and emotional difficulties that would break lesser characters.

Impact

A worthy addition to modern comics, *Whiteout* upholds contemporary trends by depicting violence and incorporating rough language. The graphic novel is unusual in its introduction of a believable strong, intelligent, and conflicted woman who triumphs despite tremendous obstacles and retains her femininity while performing a typically male occupation in male-dominated surroundings. Carrie is a fully rounded character

---

Steve Lieber

Artist Steve Lieber broke into the American comics industry in the late 1990's, working with Marvel Comics on a *Conan* miniseries and with Dark Horse on a *Grendel* miniseries. His breakthrough work was on the acclaimed crime comic book series *Whiteout* (written by Greg Rucka) in 1999 and the sequel *Whiteout: Melt* in 2000. Subsequently adapted into a film, *Whiteout* is a murder mystery set in snowy Antarctica. In the mid-2000's, Lieber worked with writer Max Allan Collins on *On the Road to Perdition*, a sequel to Collins's acclaimed graphic novel, and continued to work with Rucka on projects for DC Comics. In 2006 he was hired by Marvel Comics to illustrate *Civil War: Frontline* (written by Paul Jenkins). Lieber is an accomplished artist working in a realist tradition. His images in *Whiteout* are carefully composed, and the strong black-and-white contrasts of interior scenes shift toward grays in the sequences set in snowy exteriors.

with a strong personality and distinctive, snappy speech patterns.

Whiteout is a realistic extension of the hard-boiled tradition. The two-fisted, sharp-tongued, angst-driven hero of yesteryear was updated and modernized for Rucka's earlier Atticus Kodiak novels. In *Whiteout*, the tough investigative crime fighter has been transformed into a woman. Rucka went on to further examine the feminine psyche in his British television-inspired and multiple Eisner Award-winning espionage series *Queen and Country* (2001-2007) and his noir-flavored *Stumptown* series (2009-).

The setting is likewise unusual. An intriguing venue for a mystery, the unrelenting sameness of Antarctica's terrain presents major visual challenges that illustrator Lieber skillfully solved. Rucka and Lieber were obviously compatible, and the two reunited for the sequel, *Whiteout: Melt*, and worked together on several other comics.

Films

Whiteout. Directed by Dominic Sena. Warner Brothers, 2009. This film adaptation stars Kate Beckinsale as Carrie Stetko and Tom Skerritt as the base doctor. The film differs from the graphic novel in two significant ways. First, Lily Sharpe is transformed into male investigator Robert Pryce (Gabriel Macht), eliminating the novel's competitive and sexual tension between the two female characters. Second, the plot is a hybrid, combining elements from *Whiteout* and *Whiteout: Melt*, two very different novels. This conflation of two stories resulted in a diluted, unfocused film that received neither commercial nor critical success.

Jack Ewing

Further Reading

Azzarello, Brian, and Eduardo Risso. *100 Bullets* (1999-2009).

Lapham, Dave. *Stray Bullets* (1995-2005).

Rucka, Greg, et al. *Queen and Country* (2001-2007).

Bibliography

Grant, Steven, and Stephen Mooney. *CSI: Crime Scene Investigation—Dying in the Gutters*. San Diego, Calif.: IDW, 2008.

Johnson, Nicholas. *Big Dead Place: Inside the Strange and Menacing World of Antarctica*. Los Angeles: Feral House, 2005.

See also: *Stray Bullets; Queen and Country; Richard Stark's Parker; Hard Boiled*

WHY I HATE SATURN

Author: Baker, Kyle
Artist: Kyle Baker (illustrator)
Publisher: DC Comics
First book publication: 1990

Publication History

Comics creator Kyle Baker began his career as an intern for Marvel Comics and spent several years inking various titles. An attempt at creating a newspaper strip led to the 1988 publication of *The Cowboy Wally Show* by Marlowe & Company, a Doubleday imprint. While the book sold few copies, it did lead to Baker receiving more work from Marvel, as well as DC Comics and First Comics.

Baker had initially set out to write a story that would appeal to a mainstream audience. He intended to sell the story as a script for a situation comedy, but eventually *Why I Hate Saturn* was published under Piranha Press, a DC Comics imprint. Piranha Press had begun one year earlier as an imprint through which DC Comics could publish stories outside the superhero genre, providing mainstream distribution for work that had an "underground" sensibility. The titles were mostly created by writers and artists not traditionally associated with superhero work or with comic books at all. However, the imprint lasted only a few years, ending in 1994, and Baker's situation comedy would be Piranha's most successful title.

Why I Hate Saturn was later re-released under Vertigo, another DC imprint, in 1998. Like Piranha Press, Vertigo specializes in alternative titles, although some titles do fit loosely into the superhero genre. Vertigo proved a more successful imprint (partially because it reused characters established in other books), and *Why I Hate Saturn* is still available through this imprint.

Plot

Anne Merkel, the story's protagonist, is a cynical, twenty-something New Yorker who writes for *Daddy-O*, a trendy magazine that she loathes. Although her column is popular, Anne recognizes the pointlessness of her work. Unfortunately, she lacks the drive to write something more meaningful, despite having a book contract to fulfill. She divides her time between getting drunk in bars with her friend, Rick, and getting drunk at home alone.

Anne's lifestyle is challenged by the arrival of her sister, Laura, who is bleeding from a gunshot wound. Needing a place where she can hide out for a while, Laura moves in with Anne. They grow increasingly annoyed with each other over the next several weeks until Laura leaves, never explaining the origin of her gunshot wound or why she had to hide.

Several days later, Anne is visited by Murphy Warner, a man interested in Laura's whereabouts. He gives Anne the diary of her former boyfriend, Frank. After reading it, she learns that Frank was in a relationship with Laura before he met Anne. Initially wary of Laura, who claimed to be the Queen of the Leather Astro-Girls of Saturn, Frank used a false name, Bob, on their first date and never told her his real name. Frank eventually left Laura, citing her delusion as one of his reasons. Three months later, he began dating Anne. Frank never realized that Anne was his former girlfriend's sister. Anne never realized that her sister's former boyfriend "Bob" was really Frank. After a year with Anne, Frank decided that he was still in love with Laura and left Anne to search for her.

Anne is contacted by Warner again. When she still refuses to help him find Laura, he uses his money and influence to have her fired from *Daddy-O*, after which the publishing house cancels her book contract and her apartment building is condemned. Anne then goes searching for Laura to warn her about Warner.

Anne eventually tracks her sister to San Francisco. Laura explains that she was in a relationship with Warner after Frank left her. Her gunshot wound was the result of Warner attacking her when she decided to end the relationship. While Laura and Anne try to figure how best to handle the situation, they discover that Frank has been murdered and Laura is considered the prime suspect. Realizing that the entire scenario has been orchestrated by Warner, the two of them decide to go into hiding.

Unfortunately, Anne and Laura are quickly tracked to a remote location in a desert, where they are surrounded by Warner and a hundred police officers. Laura demonstrates to Anne how one must sometimes use unconventional means to solve problems when she kills Warner and the police officers with a rocket launcher.

The story ends six months after Warner's death, with Laura hiding in Mexico and the newly self-confident Anne having written a best-selling novel.

Characters
- *Anne Merkel* is a young writer for *Daddy-O* magazine. Her work for the magazine is well-received and even leads to a publishing firm offering her a book contract, but her work habits are so poor that she rarely submits pieces in a timely fashion. She drinks to excess and is unwilling to make her life easier by performing mundane tasks such as acquiring a bank account or a state ID. She is usually sullen but also observant.
- *Rick* is Anne's best friend. He shares a similarly pessimistic worldview with Anne but uses his observations of the human condition to exploit people (specifically the various women he dates) rather than simply bemoan it.
- *Laura Merkel* is Anne's sister. Unlike Anne, she is an overly optimistic woman, a trait that causes her trouble throughout the story. She is environmentally aware but suffers from the delusion that she is Queen of the Leather Astro-Girls of Saturn.
- *Murphy Warner* is a former boyfriend of Laura. An extremely rich and powerful man, he wants Laura back as his girlfriend and possesses the means to ruin the life of anyone who does not cooperate with him. His obsession is so absolute that he is willing to resort to murder to achieve his goal.
- *Frank Roberts* is the former boyfriend of both Anne and Laura. By dating Laura under an assumed name, neither sister is aware that the other has had a relationship with him until long after he has left them both.

Artistic Style
Why I Hate Saturn is illustrated in black and white using a storyboard format, with both dialogue and internal monologue running either below or beside the corresponding panels. Faces are rendered with more detail than bodies or backgrounds. During dialogue scenes, the panels tend to close in on the speakers' faces. The combined effect of storyboard panel layout, detailed facial expressions, and close-up panels is that the artwork keeps the focus on dialogue rather than scenery. Anne's internal monologue scenes, on the other hand, either pull back the focus to whatever room Anne is occupying or "pull in" the focus to the point where the reader is actually seeing the thoughts in Anne's brain.

The character's clothing is also used to convey mood and disposition. Anne's bitter and cynical nature is reflected by the fact that she almost always wears black. Rick, being cynical yet determined to make the most of what he sees as a bad situation, alternates between black and white clothing, with quite a lot of gray. Laura, being far more optimistic, both in her views of people and of what she can do to improve the world around her, tends toward white or light-colored clothing. It is significant that in chapters 20 through 22, when Anne and Laura try disguising themselves, Anne switches to bright colors and Laura switches to black. Furthermore, they begin to switch philosophic viewpoints, with a brightly dressed Anne advocating passive resistance while a black-clad Laura dismisses the effectiveness of nonviolence, culminating in her murder of the police officers with a rocket launcher.

Themes
Why I Hate Saturn deals extensively with topics of identity: how people define those around them, how the media define people, and how people define themselves. Anne, Laura, and Rick all struggle with these issues, and each transcends the labels assigned by themselves and others.

All three characters begin the story somehow hampered by their assumptions about other people. Anne dismisses her co-workers, readers, and fellow New Yorkers as being shallow. When Laura arrives, Anne finds that she cannot dismiss her sister as being shallow as well, so instead dismisses her as insane. Laura is recovering from a terrible relationship when she first appears, her assumptions about the basic goodness of people having placed her in a life-threatening situation. Rick is cynically coasting from one exploitive relationship to another under the assumption that all women can be placed in one of three categories: beautiful/stupid, ugly/intelligent, or insane.

The media is shown defining people primarily by stereotypes or oversimplified labels. Anne receives a book deal from a publisher that defines her as a "female Charles Bukowski." Rick, an African American, is considered "not really black" because he is well-educated and speaks articulately. Laura is mistakenly labeled a murderer by media outlets controlled by her stalker, Murphy Warner.

All three characters transform when they choose to redefine themselves. Anne transforms into a bestselling author once she stops comparing herself with people she does not respect. Laura transforms from a drifter to a more dynamic character once she stops defining herself as a pacifist. Rick is able to have a romantic relationship with Anne once he ceases to be a self-centered exploiter.

Impact

While Kyle Baker had done both writing and illustration work for Marvel and DC Comics, he had not received much critical attention until the publication of *Why I Hate Saturn*. In 1991, the book received a Harvey Award for Best Graphic Album of Original Work. Following the book's publication, Baker began selling cartoons to a variety of magazines, doing animation work for several television shows, and receiving more writing offers.

Baker has continued writing and illustrating comics for Marvel, DC, and Image Comics. Among his work for these companies is an Eisner Award-winning series based on the Jack Cole-created character Plastic Man. He has received five Eisner Awards for Best Writer/Artist of Humor (1999, 2000, 2004, 2005, and 2006). He also founded his own company, Kyle Baker Publishing. Baker's books since *Why I Hate Saturn* have included *You Are Here* (1999), *I Die at Midnight* (2000), *King David* (2002), *Undercover Genie: The Irreverent Conjurings of an Illustrative Aladdin* (2003), and *Special Forces* (2007-).

Piranha Press imprint was noteworthy at the time it published *Why I Hate Saturn* for allowing many of its creators to retain the rights to their work—DC Comics traditionally published work-for-hire, as did its chief rival, Marvel Comics; however, the rights to *Why I Hate Saturn* still belong with DC Comics, not Baker. While the title has been considered for film adaptation on several occasions, Baker is not involved in any such project.

Michael Penkas

Further Reading

Baker, Kyle. *I Die at Midnight* (2000).
_____. *Plastic Man: Rubber Bandits* (2005).
_____. *You Are Here* (1998).

Bibliography

Kaplan, Arie. *Masters of the Comic Book Universe Revealed!* Chicago: Chicago Review Press, 2006.

McCloud, Scott. *Understanding Comics: The Invisible Art*. New York: HarperPerennial, 2009.

Nolen-Weathington, Eric, and Kyle Baker. *Kyle Baker*. Modern Masters 20. Raleigh, N.C.: TwoMorrows, 2009.

See also: *You Are Here*; *Wilson*

WILSON

Author: Clowes, Daniel
Artist: Daniel Clowes (illustrator)
Publisher: Drawn and Quarterly
First book publication: 2010

Publication History
Although Daniel Clowes has created several notable graphic novels from serialized comics, including *Ghost World* (1993-1997), *Wilson* is his first original full-length graphic novel. The stories that compose his other graphic novels initially appeared in serialized form in his series *Eightball* (1989-2004), and the stories were often slightly revised for publication in collected form. By contrast, *Wilson* arrived fully formed.

Clowes originally drew *Wilson* as a series of sketches while keeping vigil next to his father's hospital deathbed. The stick-figure drawings generated hundreds of comic strips that were mostly composed of boxes and word balloons, but they all centered on the same character. Upon Clowes's return to his drawing board, the bearded and bespectacled Wilson came to life. The character, originally envisioned as a younger version of Mr. Wilson from *Dennis the Menace*, and the novel, originally envisioned as a lost comic strip, soon both developed further into the story line of the finished work. Working without a publication contract, Clowes edited and refined *Wilson* to seventy-one full-page comic strips, leaving the reader to fill in the missing scenes implied in the narrative. Having years earlier promised Drawn and Quarterly a graphic novel, Clowes delivered *Wilson* to the publisher, which marked the author's first comics novel (Clowes strongly dislikes the term *graphic novel*) and his first publication with Drawn and Quarterly after being with Fantagraphics Books since the 1980's. Meeting Clowes's request for the thickest covers available, Drawn and Quarterly released *Wilson* as an oversized hardcover in the spring of 2010.

Plot
In the first panel of the novel, Wilson greets readers by declaring his love for humanity, a love not often, if ever, returned because of the way the misanthropic

Daniel Clowes at the 2006 San Diego Comic-Con Convention. (Sean Dejecacion, via Wikimedia Commons)

Wilson alienates nearly everyone around him with his blunt commentary. He is spurned by the people he encounters on the street and in coffee shops, and his closest relationship appears to be with Pepper, his dog. Wilson reflects on such matters as the death of his mother; how he ended up living in Oakland, California; and the fact that his former wife, Pippi, left him sixteen years ago. Seeking connections with his past, he sends a box of dog feces to the family of his former wife's sister and calls his father. Discovering that his father has cancer and is dying, Wilson leaves Pepper with Shelley, a dogsitter, and travels to Chicago to visit his father for the last time. Upon his father's death, Wilson reflects further on the direction of his own life. While visiting his old neighborhood in Chicago, he decides to find Pippi. After a search that includes encounters with his former sister-in-law, a cab driver, and a prostitute, Wilson goes to a diner to eat and finds Pippi working there as a waitress.

Certain that Pippi is a former drug addict and prostitute, Wilson woos her by joking that he has inherited a fortune from his father, a jest that Pippi seems to believe is true. She informs Wilson that she was pregnant when she left him and gave the baby up for adoption, and Wilson hires a private detective to find the now-teenage girl. Wilson and Pippi reunite with their daughter, Claire Cassidy, in a shopping mall in the suburbs, and the three take a long road trip together after Claire lies to her adopted parents about where she is going. After a visit to Pippi's sister's house, Pippi calls the police and turns Wilson in for kidnapping.

Wilson is convicted when both Pippi and Claire testify against him, and he spends six years in prison. Learning of Pippi's death from a drug overdose, Wilson returns to Oakland to retrieve Pepper and finds that she is also dead. With his last link to Pepper being Shelley, Wilson starts a seemingly loveless relationship with her, and the two move in together. Claire, who is now married and living in Alaska, contacts Wilson and informs him that he has a grandson, Jason. Though the relationship with Claire and her son appears to be superficial, Wilson seems elated to know that he has a legacy. Otherwise, he grinds his way through his days and continues to alienate those around him, including Shelley, with his caustic and blunt comments, while searching for a larger meaning in life, which he seemingly discovers on the last page.

Characters
- *Wilson*, the protagonist, is a balding, middle-aged white man with a mustache and a goatee who wears glasses and is talkative and blunt. Somehow subsisting without a job, he ages through the story as he tries to make sense of life, a quest that sends him looking into his past, which sets the plot into motion.
- *Pepper* is a small, white dog who is Wilson's closest companion. Wilson leaves her with Shelley, a dogsitter, when he travels to Chicago. Wilson is sent to prison for six years and is unable to retrieve Pepper before she dies of an illness a year before Wilson returns home.
- *Shelley* is a thin, almost gaunt, blond-haired, middle-aged white woman who works as a dogsitter. When Wilson returns from prison years after leaving his dog with her, she has taken on a new career, presumably as a real-estate agent, but is having trouble making ends meet. Consequently, she agrees to marry Wilson, but the relationship is passionless.
- *Pippi*, Wilson's former wife, is a chubby, middle-aged white woman who wears her long, blond hair in a ponytail. Thinking that Wilson has inherited money, she informs him that she was pregnant at the time she left and gave the daughter, Claire, up for adoption. She reunites with Wilson briefly to find Claire but ultimately turns him into the authorities for kidnapping. She later dies of a drug overdose.
- *Claire Cassidy*, Wilson and Pippi's daughter, is a brown-haired white woman who ages from adolescence to middle age. Given up by Pippi for adoption, she is raised by the Cassidys, a well-to-do suburban family. She testifies against Wilson in his trial, but he later forgives her when he discovers that he is a grandfather.

Artistic Style
With the cover featuring Wilson gazing curiously and directly at the reader, the character dominates the graphic novel that bears his name from the beginning. Though Clowes shifts illustration styles consistently in the novel (some chapters even appear to be homages to fellow cartoonists such as Ivan Brunetti and Chris Ware), Wilson remains recognizable whether he is drawn in a simpler cartoon form or in a more detailed mode. In fact, despite the stylistic range, readers familiar with Clowes's earlier work will find the illustration style in *Wilson* familiar.

Each page of the novel operates as a complete chapter and has a separate title at the top of the page. Within the six to eight panels of each page, Clowes utilizes the pacing of a classic Sunday newspaper comic strip. In the last panel of each chapter is a "payoff," whether a gag punch line typical of humor

> **Daniel Clowes**
>
> One of the most influential cartoonists of his generation, Daniel Clowes helped to define the alternative comics movement of the 1990's with his signature series *Eightball*. Although he began his career with the *Lloyd Llewellyn* series in 1986, it was with the creation of *Eightball* that Clowes became one of the most important voices in American comics. It was in the pages of that magazine that he serialized many of his best-known works, including *Like a Velvet Glove Cast in Iron*, *Ghost World*, *David Boring*, and *Ice Haven*. His more recent works have been published as a stand-alone graphic novel (*Wilson*) and serialized in the pages of *The New York Times* (*Mr. Wonderful*). In many ways, Clowes is the defining figure in the rise of the alternative comics movement and his work, with its themes of alienation and irony, helped to define a generational sensibility. Along with director Terry Zwigoff, Clowes was nominated for an Academy Award for the screenplay of the *Ghost World* film.

strips or, less often, a dramatic cliffhanger or poignant moment typical of dramatic strips. Aside from the chapter titles, no narration is utilized, and the story is told through dialogue between characters and monologue when Wilson speaks to himself aloud (no thought balloons appear). Occasionally, a sound effect appears in the art.

Clowes uses a range of colors on most pages, but a few chapters, such as "Fireside Chat," use only a single color over the black ink and white paper in a manner reminiscent of Clowes's work in *Ghost World*. Visually, motifs repeat as some earlier and later chapters parallel one another: Wilson walking through the streets of Oakland, staring at water, traveling (the shift from airplane to bus represents his reduced economic circumstances), and hassling a fellow customer at a coffee shop.

Themes

The bitter, ironic humor showcased in *Wilson* can alienate some readers and Wilson the character is often unlikeable. However, with the revelation of his fears and vulnerabilities, Wilson becomes a more sympathetic figure. Two major themes emerge. The first is the desire for human connection. Wilson consistently reaches out to the people around him, calling strangers "brother," "sister," "friend," and so forth, but, because of his unwillingness or inability to adhere to the unwritten rules of polite society, others avoid him. Ironically, many of the people avoiding Wilson hide behind technological devices such as telephones and computers, all of which are designed to communicate and certainly reduce the need for face-to-face contact.

The second major theme appears to be existential in Wilson's attempts to find meaning in life. This quest is seen most in scenes in which Wilson, in a symbolic act of cleansing and renewal, observes water and attempts to form a spiritual connection with it. The two themes merge as Wilson seems to find meaning through connections with others, connections often linked with water. For example, he compares his mother's absence after her death to never seeing the ocean again, and he seems happiest on the dock with his newfound family. It is significant that his relationship with Pippi disintegrates in front of an empty swimming pool. Once he has established a connection with something bigger than himself by having his family legacy continue through his grandson Jason, Wilson seems to live more in the present moment and has an epiphany late in life (and in the final chapter of *Wilson*) while staring at rain on a window. Whatever his epiphany, it is not shared with the reader, perhaps suggesting that each person must create her or his own meaning in life.

Impact

Wilson, well-received by critics and the public, landed on several year-end top-ten lists, including lists for general readers, which helped to verify graphic novels as commercially mainstream. Following *Wilson*'s success, Drawn and Quarterly summarily released another graphic novel by Clowes, *The Death-Ray*, in the fall of 2011. Clowes has also used Wilson the character in a short story, "Wilson in Day 16.412," which was originally published in *The New Yorker*. *Wilson* and Clowes were also nominated for several Eisner Awards in 2011.

Frederick A. Wright

Further Reading

Bagge, Peter. *Hate* (1990-1998).

Clowes, Daniel. *David Boring* (2002).

_____. *Like a Velvet Glove Cast in Iron* (2007).

Bibliography

Hajdu, David. *Heroes and Villains: Essays on Music, Movies, Comics, and Culture*. Cambridge, Mass.: Da Capo, 2009.

Hignite, M. Todd. *In the Studio: Visits with Contemporary Cartoonists*. New Haven, Conn.: Yale University Press, 2007.

Parille, Ken, and Isaac Cates, eds. *Daniel Clowes: Conversations*. Jackson: University Press of Mississippi, 2010.

See also: *Hate*; *David Boring*; *Ice Haven*; *Twentieth Century Eightball*; *Like a Velvet Glove Cast in Iron*

X

Xenozoic Tales

Author: Schultz, Mark
Artist: Mark Schultz (illustrator)
Publisher: Kitchen Sink Press; Marvel Comics; Flesk Publications
First serial publication: 1987-1996
First book publication: 1989

Publication History

Philadelphia-born Mark Schultz discovered comic books at age six, when he was drawn to the larger-than-life heroics typified by Tarzan and Superman. Over time, he supplemented his comics reading with the pulp works of Edgar Rice Burroughs and Robert E. Howard, while Al Williamson, Roy Krenkel, and Frank Frazetta proved to be artistic inspirations. As Schultz studied art, he also fell under the influence of classic American artists and illustrators such as Winslow Homer, Howard Pyle, N. C. Wyeth, Daniel Smith, Dean Cornwell, Herbert Morton Stoops, and Frank Hoban.

Although he dreamed of drawing comic book stories, Schultz attended Kutztown State College (now Kutztown University of Pennsylvania) before going to work as a commercial illustrator. As independent comic book publishing exploded in the 1980's, Schultz was finally inspired to make his dream a reality. He envisioned a postapocalyptic world set hundreds of years in the future, although technology would have stalled in modern times. The odd mix of cars and dinosaurs was on display in the twelve-page story "Xenozoic!," which he submitted to Denis Kitchen, founder of Kitchen Sink Press.

Xenozoic Tales proved successful enough to be adapted by CBS for Saturday morning television under the more familiar name of *Cadillacs and Dinosaurs*. Although it only lasted for one thirteen-episode season, it was successful enough to spawn a comic book based on the cartoon, published by Topps in 1994. Marvel Comics and Kitchen Sink Press also released reprints of the series under the *Cadillacs and Dinosaurs* title; Marvel's versions were color comic books, while Kitchen Sink Press put out three oversized black-and-white collections. In 2010, Flesh Publications packaged all the Schultz material in one volume.

Plot

By 1987, Earth was already experiencing a series of geologic upheavals that would alter the ecosystem. By the early twenty-first century, mankind was abandoning the surface for subterranean dwellings. By 2020, billions of humans had died and entire species had been rendered extinct almost overnight. Humans, too, were nearly extinct, making way for new life-forms to evolve. Those humans who remained found bunkers and hunkered down for survival.

The series picks up some 450 years later as humanity reemerges into a world unrecognizable by the reader. The Earth has become habitable for other life, including a wide range of formerly extinct creatures, from trilobites to mammoths. Somewhere along the way, Earth gained a second moon, which had its own effects on the planet's development.

The stories are set in this new Xenozoic (strange life) era and feature Jack "Cadillac" Tenrec. Jack is still in possession of technological skills, making him among the elite of the remaining human society. He is helping to rebuild the twentieth century from whatever parts have survived, notably Cadillacs, which he modifies to run on dinosaur guano in lieu of oil. Accompanying him on his adventures is the gorgeous scientist Hannah Dundee, who has secrets of her own. When not being chased by dinosaurs, Jack and Hannah must deal with corrupt humans as well as a new humanoid race

> **Mark Schultz**
>
> Mark Schultz is best known for his work in the 1980's as the writer/artist behind the *Xenozoic Tales* series of independent comics, featuring the adventures of a group of people living in a post-apocalyptic age in which dinosaurs and humans coexist. Schultz's visual style was influenced strongly by the artists affiliated with EC Comics in the 1950's and is notable for its highly realistic and detailed figure drawing. He relies on crosshatching and pen shading to create depth, and his work is highly illustrative, reminiscent of an earlier generation of magazine illustrators, such as Howard Pyle. His adventure comics also include a number of *Conan the Cimmerian* works, and, since 2004, he has been the writer of the *Prince Valiant* comic strip. He also wrote the unusual inter-company crossover, *Superman and Batman versus Aliens and Predator*.

that has genetic links to the reptiles and can telepathically chat with the dinosaurs.

Tenrec recognizes that, centuries before, humanity was somehow responsible for the cataclysm that altered the world. He considers it his personal responsibility to ensure that mankind has learned from its mistakes and can find a way to harmonize with the rebuilding world. While Tenrec looks after his "tribe," Hannah represents the city-state of Wassoon, although her role as an ambassador is viewed with skepticism by others. Each story stands on its own while slowly building a larger picture of the world and its current inhabitants.

Characters

- *Jack Tenrec* is a muscled, handsome brunet who is adept with mechanical objects. A master mechanic for his tribe, he adores rebuilding ancient automobiles, which he modifies to run on dinosaur waste, and has a large garage with a fleet of vehicles in various states of repair. He has a particular fondness for Cadillac convertibles. Tenrec is an excellent shot and has a unique understanding of the artifacts left behind by his ancestors. He is romantically and physically involved with Hannah Dundee but does not entirely trust her, given her enigmatic nature.
- *Hannah Dundee*, scientist and ambassador from the nearby city-state of Wassoon, fancies Jack Tenrec and accompanies him on his escapades. Shapely and raven-haired, she is adept with a gun and makes love with abandon. While living with Tenrec, she teaches his tribe farming techniques, but her real mission is to locate and raid the tribe's library for useful knowledge.
- *Lord Drumheller* is a haughty member of Tenrec's tribe who wants Hannah for himself. He repeatedly hunts Tenrec with the intent of killing him but fails with each effort.

Artistic Style

Though new to the comics scene at the time *Xenozoic Tales* was published, Schultz was aware of and greatly influenced by his predecessors in the tradition of adventure illustrations. At the same time, in the process of painstakingly and meticulously rendering his artistic vision, he was able to create something truly his own.

While Schultz's earliest work shows the influence of Eisner more than anyone else, Schultz fairly quickly developed a refinement and delicacy that more closely resembles the work of Williamson and Frazetta at their 1950's peaks. Drawing for black-and-white publication, Schultz adds a large amount of texture and detail, from clothing wrinkles to chipped wall plaster. He uses Zip-A-Tone judiciously to complement his line work, which can range from bold lines to feather-thin crosshatching.

Because his work is so meticulous and detailed, Schultz works slowly, which led to gaps between issues of *Xenozoic Tales*. Schultz has stated that he is ambivalent about his pacing, feeling that he is drawn to the meticulous work on display in *Xenozoic Tales* but that there are certain advantages to being less deliberate, including the ability to push a story forward. Nonetheless, he has been a steady writer and artist whose body of work has been recognized by his peers with numerous comics industry awards.

Themes

With *Xenozoic Tales*, Schultz wanted to create a comic book series that he would be inclined to read but that did not exist in the comics market at the time. While predominantly a swashbuckling series of adventures set in a fantastic future, *Xenozoic Tales* also highlights concerns about Earth's fragile ecosystem. Schultz makes the point repeatedly that humans nearly destroyed their symbiotic relationship with the Earth, and now that life is recovering, Jack Tenrec is determined to keep his fellow humans respectful of the planet. Schultz has stated that the environmentalist aspects of the story were late additions to his thematic shaping of the series, but that they are integral to the overall narrative purpose. The ecological angle, despite coming as late as it did, clearly has remained on Schultz's mind, as evidenced by the release of the 2010 illustrated novella.

Impact

Xenozoic Tales was one of many well-regarded comics to debut during an explosive period for independent comic books in the 1980's, thanks to the maturing direct-sales channel. However, its infrequent publishing schedule may have prevented it from gaining the attention it deserved. While such publishing gaps may have been unheard of for DC Comics or Marvel Comics at that time, they were not a problem for the smaller Kitchen Sink Press, which catered to the idiosyncrasies of its artists; Kitchen recognized Schultz's artistic power early on and allowed him to mature as a storyteller.

Although *Xenozoic Tales* debuted in early 1987, the fourteenth and final issue came out in fall 1996, nearly a decade later. As a result, although Schultz became an acclaimed and respected artist, his style was no longer in vogue. Instead, he is considered an "artist's artist," while readers' attentions were more commonly caught by the less realistic styles of the Image Comics creators who came to prominence during this period.

The series had minimal impact in the direct-sales channel, and even though it spawned an animated television series and a comic based on the cartoon, it did not inspire imitators. However, its sheer quality and overall dramatic excellence has seen it repeatedly repackaged and collected through the years.

Television Series

Cadillacs and Dinosaurs. De Souza Productions/Galaxy Films/Nelvana, 1993-1994. CBS aired one thirteen-episode season of the series, in part based on the enthusiasm of co-executive producers Steven E. de Souza and Sasha Harari. The show featured vocal work from David Keeley as Jack and Susan Roman as Hannah. Its ecological theme appealed to CBS, which emphasized this aspect more heavily than Schultz did in his stories. The series was not a hit, lasting but one season, due in part to preemptions on both coasts for Winter Olympics coverage in 1994. However, its visual appeal led to a variety of merchandise, including video games from Rocket Science Games and a Topps comic book.

Robert Greenberger

Further Reading

Gianni, Gary, Mark Schultz, and Harold R. Foster. *Hal Foster's Prince Valiant: Far from Camelot* (2008).

Schultz, Mark, Ariel Olivetti, and Todd Klein. *Superman and Batman Versus Aliens and Predator* (2007).

Williamson, Al, Mark Schultz, and Sergio Aragonés. *Al Williamson's Flash Gordon: A Lifelong Vision of the Heroic* (2009).

Bibliography

Allen, Mark. "Suspended Animation: *Xenozoic Tales*." *SciFiDimensions*, May 10, 2002. http://www.scifidimensions.com/May02/xenozoictales.htm.

Du Brow, Rick. "*Cadillacs* Cartoon Enters Brave New World." *Los Angeles Times*, February 12, 1994. http://articles.latimes.com/print/1994-02-12/entertainment/ca-22070_1_classic-cadillac.

Duin, Steve. "Mark Schultz." *The Oregonian*, February 26, 2008. http://blog.oregonlive.com/steveduin/2008/02/mark_schultz.html.

See also: *Age of Reptiles*; *A Contract with God, and Other Tenement Stories*; *Mouse Guard*

Y

YOSSEL
APRIL 19, 1943—A STORY OF THE WARSAW GHETTO UPRISING

Author: Kubert, Joe
Artist: Joe Kubert (illustrator)
Publisher: Ibooks
First book publication: 2003

Publication History

Yossel is Joe Kubert's fifth work created specifically for the graphic novel format and second dealing with the human cost of war, following *Fax from Sarajevo* (1996). However, because it deals with events involving Kubert's family, *Yossel* may be his most personal work. The graphic novel was first published in English in 2003. In 2005, Ehapa Press published a hardcover edition in German, Delcourt published an edition in French, and Public Square Books published a hardcover edition in Spanish. A new paperback edition was published by the DC Comics imprint Vertigo in May, 2011, as part of its *Joe Kubert Library* series.

Plot

Yossel was created as a stand-alone volume, a personal statement from Kubert on the Holocaust. Merging aspects of his professional life and family history with accounts of the Warsaw Uprising, *Yossel* tells of a young artist who lives in the Warsaw ghetto during the Nazi occupation of Poland. The novel begins with a rebel cell of Polish Jews huddled in a sewer, waiting to fight their Nazi oppressors. As they wait, young Yossel sketches and remembers.

A year after Kristallnacht, Yossel's life in Poland is uncertain but idyllic. Vaguely aware of the impending Nazi threat, he is preoccupied with the Sunday funnies and the few comic books he has seen. Drawing is his passion, to the chagrin of his Bar Mitzvah instructor, the rebbe.

One evening, a Nazi soldier comes to the door of Yossel's home in Yzeran and orders the family to leave immediately. Gathering what belongings they can, Yossel and his family join a ragtag parade of Jews bound for the Warsaw ghetto. As they trudge on, Yossel draws. After arriving at the ghetto and receiving orders from the Nazis, Yossel's father tells him that he is leaving to find the rest of their family. He returns at dawn, having failed in his efforts.

The family adapts to this new life. A Nazi takes notice of Yossel's drawings, and he becomes a favorite of the Nazi officers, which causes resentment in the ghetto community. Yossel's family is sent to the concentration camp at Auschwitz, but he remains behind to provide entertainment for the Nazis.

Allying with a band of rebels led by Mordecai,

Joe Kubert in The Israeli Cartoon Museum, Holon, Israel. (The Israeli Cartoon Museum/Alon Mitelman, via Wikimedia Commons)

Yossel uses his privileged position to convey information as ghetto conditions become dire. On his way to a rebel meeting, Yossel hears a gaunt man whispering in the shadows. The man has escaped from a concentration camp and told the rebels the truth about what has been happening in the camps. Revealing that he is the rebbe from Yzeran, the man tells Yossel of his family's death in the camps.

Mordecai calls for action. The rebels kill a Nazi guard and hide his body; emboldened by success, they assassinate six more. The Nazis retaliate, and the rebbe is found and hanged. In retribution, after his next session entertaining the Nazis, Yossel surreptitiously leaves two live hand grenades in the office complex, destroying it.

In the ensuing attacks, buildings are destroyed, and hundreds of Jews are killed. There are rumors that Nazi official Joseph Goebbels plans to level the ghetto. A regiment of Nazis arrives, fully armed and accompanied by tanks. Mordecai and his cadre decide that if they are to die, they will die like men.

After the rebel attack succeeds, the Nazis regroup and begin to burn the ghetto systematically, destroying it building by building. Clearing the way with a Molotov cocktail, Mordecai and his cadre retreat to the sewers, where the story began. The rebels' lives come to an inevitable end: Trapped in the sewers, they are killed with flamethrowers. A departing Nazi picks up Yossel's final drawing and considers it silently. He lets it fall into the sewer, where its lines blur into obscurity.

Characters

- *Yossel*, the protagonist, is a teenage Polish Jew who lives in the village of Yzeran until his family is relocated to the Warsaw ghetto. He is a talented artist fascinated with comics and fantasy illustrations. His art enables his survival in the ghetto and is a catalyst in his contribution to the underground.
- *Mordecai* is Yossel's protector after his parents are taken away. He is also the leader of the resistance cell that forms in the Warsaw ghetto. After hearing the rebbe's account of the atrocities occurring in the concentration camps, he tries in vain to convince the Jewish council, which controls the ghetto's population under the auspices of the Nazis, of the truth. When they refuse to listen, he decides to fight back.
- *The Rebbe* is the former rabbi of Yzeran. While in the concentration camp at Auschwitz, he survives through guile, hard work, and luck and sees the full extent of Nazi atrocity. After successfully escaping, he makes his way to the Warsaw ghetto, where he tells his tale to the rebels. He refuses to hide from the Nazis and is hanged.

Artistic Style

The art of *Yossel* was created using uninked pencils, rather than pencils and inks. This conscious choice by Kubert preserves the emotional integrity of the art. The value range is the result of mark making and erasure, techniques that create dark tones and highlights within the illustrations. The local color of the paper is preserved as an additional value. This further adds to the verisimilitude of the story, creating the sense that readers are privy to a personal sketchbook, an intimate experience.

Kubert's art is characterized by its high degree of visual energy, fine lines, and dynamically posed figures. His comics use the trompe l'oeil device of forced one-point perspective to great emotional effect. *Yossel* contains a particularly compelling example of this: In one scene, the rebbe is shown loading bodies into the ovens at the concentration camp. The full-page scene is shown from inside one of the ovens. The viewer sees prone feet on a slab, an open oven door, and rebbe and his co-workers standing beyond it.

Kubert eschews panel borders throughout the graphic novel, a technique used earlier by Will Eisner in his seminal work *A Contract with God* (1978). As a narrative device, the absence of borders usually results in a slower reading pace, but in the context of *Yossel*, it reinforces the sense of urgency and tension in the narrative. Borders do appear around text, which is digitally lettered in a font based on Kubert's own hand lettering. While this is occasionally jarring, as in the case of the typeset eviction notice depicted early in the novel, the disconnect it causes also has an emotional effect.

Within the narrative, readers also see Yossel's own art, which is rendered in a more tentative style than the rest of the book, lending an additional sense of authenticity to the work. Yossel's sketches take on nuances that reflect the narrative. Initially filled with heroes and monsters, his later sketches are influenced by his experiences in the ghetto. He creates fantasy art for his German oppressors, often depicting Nazis as superheroes, but this art is tinged with an urgency and resentment that they overlook.

Themes

Yossel follows in the tradition of Art Spiegelman's *Maus: A Survivor's Tale* (1986, 1991) and Eisner's *To the Heart of the Storm* (2000) in that it relates the intimate involvement of the creator's family with World War II. All three books deal with aspects of Judaism as it relates to World War II, and both *Yossel* and *Maus* are directly related to the Holocaust. The narrative of Kubert's novel is, in a sense, a cautionary tale. Yossel is clearly a stand-in for Kubert, who was an artistic teenager living in the United States at the time of the uprising in the Warsaw ghetto. This concept is reinforced by Kubert's introduction, in which he reveals that while he and his family emigrated from Poland when he was an infant, they were nearly unable to do so; he and his family could have shared the fate of Yossel and his parents.

Within the narrative, everyone who sees Yossel's art utters phrases such as "he draws like magic" and "I couldn't draw a straight line," echoing each other despite their differences. This reinforces the shared humanity of the Nazis and their Jewish captives, though the Nazis are unable to see it.

Readers are never told Yossel's surname, and almost no surnames appear in the narrative. This lack of family names, along with the image of Yossel's final drawings fading in the sewer, calls attention to the true goal of the Holocaust: the eradication of a people and their history. However, the narrative itself resists this attempt at eradication. Told in the first-person point of view and in past tense, the narrative makes readers privy to Yossel's thoughts and emotions despite his ultimate death, implying the survival and endurance of the spirit of the Polish Jews. The name Yossel, an intimate form of Yossef, is Hebrew for "he will enlarge" or "he will grow," which reinforces the conviction that the spirit of the Polish Jew lives on.

Impact

Critics received *Yossel* favorably, and the book is often used in classrooms to teach about the Holocaust. It is included in numerous lists of recommended books on the subject. The work is largely accessible to readers unaccustomed to the graphic novel form, though some report being put off by its more stark visual elements. Because of this, educators most often recommend its use in high school classes, as opposed to middle school classes.

The publication of this work was something of an event. As he has aged, Kubert has decreased his comics output, especially in comparison to his prodigious output as a younger man. He is one of a dozen or fewer major Golden Age comics artists who lived to see the medium mature. Of that number, most are in retirement or working in other fields, which gives an added significance to any new work by Kubert. His following work, *Jew Gangster* (2005), is also a veiled memoir of his youth. However, the newer work is based in observation, while *Yossel* remains a speculation.

Diana Green

Further Reading

Croci, Pascal. *Auschwitz* (2004).

Eisner, Will. *The Plot: The Secret Story of the Protocols of the Elders of Zion* (2005).

Speigelman, Art. *Maus: A Survivor's Tale* (1986, 1991).

Bibliography

Irving, Christopher. "Keeping Current with Joe Kubert." *Graphic NYC*, June 22, 2009. http://graphicnyc.blogspot.com/2009/03/keeping-current-with-joe-kubert.html.

Kaplan, Arie. *From Krakow to Krypton: Jews and Comic Books*. Philadelphia: Jewish Publication Society, 2008.

Schelly, Bill. *Man of Rock: A Biography of Joe Kubert*. Seattle: Fantagraphics Books, 2008.

Zuckerman, Samantha. "The Holocaust and the Graphic Novel: Using *Maus* and Its Narrative Forms to Bring Credence to the Medium." *Kedma*, no. 6 (Spring, 2008): 54-72. http://www.hillel.upenn.edu/kedma/06/zuckerman.pdf.

See also: *Maus; We Are on Our Own; Fax from Sarajevo*

YOU ARE HERE

Author: Baker, Kyle
Artist: Kyle Baker (illustrator)
Publisher: DC Comics
First book publication: 1999

> ### Kyle Baker
> Kyle Baker's widely diverse career as a writer-artist has ranged from hilarious all-ages observations about family life to adult satire and historical drama. An illustrator and animator, Baker often brings a cartoony, cinematic style to his work, such as graphic novels done in the style of movie storyboards and figures with exaggerated, distorted features and body language. His work ranges from silent, visually-based stories to dialogue-heavy tales featuring hilarious, punch line-heavy banter.

Publication History

You Are Here originated as a comic very different from the finished graphic novel. Creator Kyle Baker initially wrote a story about two friends, one of whom learns that material success does not necessarily lead to happiness. However, he felt the story had no real conflict, and he was unable to sell the idea to any publishers. Baker began to rework the plot by adding a more distinct villain and a more readily identifiable conflict. He also heightened tensions in the book by adding realistically deadly threats throughout the story.

Not wanting to see the nearly two dozen pages of art from his original story go unpublished, he began serializing them in *Instant Piano*, a 1994-1995 anthology comic to which he was already contributing. While those excerpts ran under the *You Are Here* title, Baker had already begun work on his revised story and was aware that he would never complete the original. He liked the name, however, and opted to keep it for his book, knowing *Instant Piano* readers would be looking for that title. The new story was noticeably different by page 3, so he felt confident that readers would not be disappointed by the change. Ultimately, *You Are Here* was published by DC Comics' Vertigo imprint in 1999.

Plot

In a serene cabin nestled in the woods, a body lies motionless in a bathtub overflowing with red liquid. Helen cheerfully enters the room to see how Noel is handling the tomato juice bath he is using to wash off the stench of a skunk. She then goes into the next room to repack Noel's suitcase. Her mother is somewhat abrasive about him, but Helen dismisses her barbs and talks with a deer that has wandered into the kitchen before coaxing Noel out of the bath to watch the sunset.

Noel visits his New York City apartment, only to find that his friend Oscar has been using it as a convenient location for one-night stands. After Oscar's lovers storm off, Oscar and Noel catch up at a nearby bar. Noel learns that his attempt to straighten out his life with Helen has been misinterpreted by his former colleagues, who believed he was in prison. Oscar takes Noel to meet his stripper girlfriend, Tracy, and the three go to a local diner. While watching television, Noel and Oscar learn that Vaughn Dreyfuss, a murderer whose wife Noel slept with, was recently released from prison and is actively looking for Noel.

Noel returns to his apartment, where Helen is waiting for him. She announces that she is pregnant; once Noel recovers from the shock, he proposes. Helen is thrilled. Planning to leave the city, they soon realize that their truck has been towed. After a trip to get Noel's license renewed, they again attempt to leave, only to run out of gas.

Noel and Helen walk to the nearest gas station and fill up a glass jar. Helen realizes the sun is about to set and races to find a good vantage point from which to watch. Still carrying the gasoline, Noel tries to keep up while perilously avoiding open flames. As they are about to watch the sunset, a mugger confronts them. Helen manages to convince him to wait and watch the sunset with them, but he robs them anyway.

Helen and Noel encounter Oscar and Tracy, and the latter suggests a carriage ride in Central Park. Helen drags Noel off as Oscar goes to make a phone call.

While on the phone, Oscar is accosted by Vaughn, who coerces Oscar to tell him where Noel is. Oscar points him to Central Park, and Vaughn thanks him before killing him.

While in the carriage with Helen, Noel spots Vaughn trailing them. Noel manages to frighten the horse into a gallop, but Vaughn follows closely. Helen and Noel lead a chase through Central Park, eventually hiding in and around the *Alice in Wonderland* sculpture.

They run into Tracy again and agree to drive her to her "simulated sex act" show. Helen is incredulous as Noel tells her of his former life as a jewel thief and explains the reason Vaughn is trying to kill him. Unable to cope with these revelations, Helen runs away. When the crowd of lust-filled men gathered to watch the show tries to rape Tracy, Noel intercedes, and he and Tracy manage to fight off the group.

As Noel returns to his apartment, a stranger hands him a series of faxes indicating that Vaughn is targeting Helen. Realizing where Helen is going, Noel races to reach the Staten Island Ferry, where Vaughn has already cornered her. Noel manages to sneak up on Vaughn, and the two fight, each inflicting the other with nearly fatal wounds. Noel finally triumphs, shooting the now-paralyzed Vaughn and throwing his body overboard.

Many months later, Noel visits his baby at the cabin. Both Helen and her mother are upset with him, though Helen's husband seems naïvely oblivious. As they banter back and forth, Tracy relaxes at Noel's apartment, reading a romance novel and casually sporting an engagement ring.

Characters
- *Noel Coleman* is a handsome and charismatic former jewel thief who is trying to start a new, more honest life as an artist. His years as a criminal in New York City have given him a decidedly grim and jaundiced view of humanity, and much of his attraction to Helen is based on that fact that she holds an opposite view of the world. Throughout the story, he tries desperately to protect Helen from the liars, cheats, crooks, and prostitutes that populate the city, even if he must lie to her to do so.
- *Helen Foster* is an eternal optimist with a broad smile and fiery red hair. She sees the bright side of everyone and everything, going so far as to compliment a mugger for allowing her to keep her wallet after stealing all her money at gunpoint. She remains almost naïvely cheerful throughout the story, despite seeing the seediest side of humanity.
- *Oscar* is Noel's old friend and partner. He is a self-infatuated womanizer with little respect for anyone. Stout, bald, and partially toothless, he is constantly on the lookout for a way to take advantage of any situation, though he frequently fails in that regard.
- *Vaughn Dreyfuss* is a murderer who was convicted a year before the story takes place. He is very clear about his intention to kill Noel, stating as much on national television. His Robert Mitchum-like good looks speak to his relentlessness and confidence, making him a grave threat to Noel and everyone he knows.

Artistic Style
Throughout the book, Baker uses techniques that both save him time and help serve the story. Though his figure work was created using traditional pen and ink, several of the background scenes were created using 3-D-rendering software. Baker cites his desire for speed and accuracy as the reason for his choice to use software in some scenes but not in others. Creating a digital model for the horse carriage, for example, was relatively simple, especially in comparison to drawing it by hand from many different perspectives. The ferry, however, would have been a more complex digital model and could be rendered traditionally just as easily.

Baker has also noted that part of the impetus behind *You Are Here* was his desire to spend hours sketching squirrels and trees in the park and sunrises and sunsets at the beach. Although most of the story takes place in New York City, Baker takes full advantage of natural settings, opening and closing the story in forested upstate New York and staging a twenty-page chase scene through the middle of Central Park. Apart from a few establishing shots, in fact, many of the city scenes feature no or minimal backgrounds, while all of the scenes that take place in nature are full of lush vegetation and wildlife.

Themes

Despite the external conflict represented by Vaughn, the biggest problem Noel faces in *You Are Here* is internal conflict. He loves Helen more for what she represents than who she is, and his desire to escape the life he led before he met her is his primary motivation. However, in attempting to cover up his past with lies and deceit, he inherently works against Helen's ideals of openness and honesty. The more he attempts to change his personality to match hers, the more his old traits emerge.

Helen is not without influence, however, as Noel realizes that his previous life as a jewel thief was decidedly immoral. While he does not become nearly as idealistic as Helen, she inadvertently proves to him that not everyone is as selfish and self-centered as Oscar and that many of the joys in life are simple ones.

Conversely, Noel and Helen's adventure affects Helen by showing her that even good men can be hurtful. Her implicit trust in the goodness of mankind is shattered when Noel kills the helpless Vaughn against her explicit wishes. Her saccharine goodness is brought down to a more realistic level in the last few pages, and she gains the ability to feel both positive and negative emotions. Baker's conclusion suggests both that neither end of the emotional spectrum is healthy and that everyone needs to find a middle ground in which he or she can experience pain and joy in equal measure.

Impact

Baker felt that his work immediately prior to *You Are Here*, particularly the work he did in Hollywood, was diluted by other contributors by the time it was released. While he did feel he learned a great deal from those experiences, he was not able to put all of it into practice until *You Are Here*. The book was Baker's first graphic novel to earn a profit, and he attributes much of its success to his decision not to target the broadest audience possible. The story does not follow a typical plot, instead relying on storytelling to captivate readers. Thus, the book became a turning point in Baker's career, prompting him to take more control of his stories and emphasize graphic novels over serialized comics. *You Are Here*'s success allowed Baker to turn down projects over which he had less control, such as an aborted "Noah's Ark" film, in favor of more graphic novels, such as *King David* (2002).

Sean Kleefeld

Further Reading

Baker, Kyle. *The Bakers: Do These Toys Belong Somewhere?* (2006).

_____. *Why I Hate Saturn* (1990).

McGruder, Aaron, Reginald Hudlin, and Kyle Baker. *Birth of a Nation: A Comic Novel* (2004).

Bibliography

Baker, Kyle. *How to Draw Stupid and Other Essentials of Cartooning*. New York: Watson-Guptill, 2008.

Baker, Kyle, and Eric Nolen-Weathington. *Kyle Baker*. Modern Masters Volume 20. Raleigh, N.C.: TwoMorrows, 2008.

Kaplan, Arie. *Masters of the Comic Book Universe Revealed!* Chicago: Chicago Review Press, 2006.

See also: *Why I Hate Saturn; A History of Violence; A Small Killing; Nat Turner*

You'll Never Know
Book One: A Good and Decent Man

Author: Tyler, C.
Artist: C. Tyler (illustrator)
Publisher: Fantagraphics Books
First serial publication: 2009-
First book publication: 2009

Publication History

Following her collections of short stories *The Job Thing* (1993) and *Late Bloomer* (2005), *You'll Never Know* is Carol Tyler's (known professionally as C. Tyler) first stand-alone project that focuses on a continuous storyline. The first installment of the trilogy, *You'll Never Know,* Book One*: A Good and Decent Man*, was published by Fantagraphics Books as a hardcover in 2009. In terms of book design, the choice of an oversized landscape format (12 × 10.5 inches) adds to the resemblance to a family photo album or scrapbook, and emphasizes the personal nature of the subject matter. Book One begins a trilogy that explores the life of the author's father (Chuck Tyler) during and after World War II. The first volume works as an introduction and establishes the main characters and their backgrounds without delving extensively into the core of the story. The second volume, *You'll Never Know,* Book Two*: Collateral Damage*, was published in 2010. The final installment, *You'll Never Know,* Book Three*: Soldier's Heart*, is set to be published in 2012.

Plot

The main narrative of *You'll Never Know* revolves around the biography of the author's father, Chuck Tyler, who worked as an army staff sergeant during World War II. Soon after entering the army, Chuck meets Hannah Yates, a striking beauty who works as a clerical secretary. Immediately, he falls head over heels for her and attempts to gain her attention by any means necessary. Luckily for him, his prankster ways work in his favor, winning Hannah's heart and hand before he is sent to Europe.

Simultaneously, *You'll Never Know,* Book One explores a second narrative in which the author recounts her daily life in Ohio, where she lives with her teenage daughter, Julia. In this story line, Tyler deals with the difficulties of single parenthood after her husband, cartoonist Justin Green, leaves her and her daughter for their former babysitter. Rather than resorting to finger pointing, the author concentrates on more significant issues at hand, such as the importance of father figures and the emotional toll caused by abandonment.

By becoming both the biographer of her father's life and an autobiographer, Tyler is able to weave two family narratives that span several decades. After numerous unsuccessful attempts at uncovering her father's secretive army past, Tyler receives an unexpected phone call from her father in which he suddenly recounts his wartime experiences. Overjoyed, she undertakes the role of historian and biographer, making a photo scrapbook of her father's past. Yet in spite of her father's sudden desire to share his personal history, Tyler still experiences difficulty in obtaining details about his dark times during the war. This is especially true in relation to an incident in Italy, a clear source of anguish and pain for Chuck. Narrative gaps, inaccuracy, and ambiguity in Chuck's recollections emphasize the emotional difficulty that arises when dealing with a traumatic past.

Although Tyler focuses on heavy themes such as war trauma and abandonment, the author cleverly incorporates a touch of humor to her work through funny commentary, self-ridicule, and a play with the comics form. Consequently, this lightens the tone of the first installment of her trilogy, contextualizing the story in terms of character backgrounds and setting up the narrative for a deepening of the complex relationship between father and daughter and past and present.

Characters

- *Charles William Tyler*, a.k.a. *Chuck*, is the main protagonist of the story. He is a World War II veteran and father of the author, Carol Tyler.

Chuck has a bald head, wears red suspenders, and smokes a pipe. He is a good problem solver and an excellent craftsman. He is quick-witted, resourceful, and pragmatic. As a young man in the army, he is portrayed as a trickster and troublemaker, constantly pulling stunts to gain attention. As a father, he is somewhat distant and short-tempered, making it difficult for Carol to gather information about his secretive past during World War II.

- *Carol Tyler* is a secondary protagonist. She is the author of *You'll Never Know* and the daughter of Chuck Tyler. In the book, she undertakes the role of biographer and autobiographer and narrates both her father's story and her own story. She is inquisitive, artistic, and devoted to her family.
- *Hannah Yates*, a secondary character, is Chuck's wife and Carol's mother. She usually wears glasses and a hat, and she goes by the nickname "Red" because of her hair color. Unlike Chuck, she is calm and patient and is portrayed as a quiet homemaker.
- *Julia Green*, a secondary character, is Carol's teenage daughter. She has long auburn hair and is between the ages of twelve and fifteen. In terms of plot, she serves mainly to advance the story line that revolves around Carol and her ex-husband's separation.
- *Justin Green*, a secondary character, is Carol's former husband and Julia's father. He is recognizable by his plaid shirts. He is present mainly within the narrative that recounts the difficulties that occurred after he left his family for another woman.

Artistic Style

You'll Never Know is produced with a custom-made palette of fifty-three inks and watercolors, giving the work a stunning vibrancy and richness. Tyler, who holds a graduate degree in painting from Syracuse University, demonstrates a mastery of watercolor techniques through her skilled understanding of line fluidity, lush colors, and dynamic composition. The book often emulates the scrapbook format with the use of mounted photo corners and picture frames. Similarly, the reproduction of memorabilia such as letters, maps, sketches, and photographs calls attention to the importance of memory in the work, a theme that is central to the initial impetus behind the work. Visually, the art showcases a great attention to detail through the incorporation of ornamentation in the book. For example, Tyler frequently draws detailed floral patterns, spirals, and textures to enliven her settings and backgrounds.

Because *You'll Never Know* is a graphic memoir, Tyler often plays with comics conventions, such as panel layouts and lettering. At times, she subtly leads readers to go against the usual reading direction and uses arrows to indicate a movement from the bottom of the page to the top. At other times, she drops the use of panels altogether and uses whole pages for single illustrations. In this way, Tyler clearly takes advantage of the dimensions of the book, amplifying the visual impact of her art through large and densely detailed illustrations. In terms of typography, Tyler uses three different lettering styles to reflect the various narratives in the book: cursive for her own narration, capital print letters for character dialogue, and regular print for her father's army scrapbook.

Themes

One of the main themes in *You'll Never Know, Book One: A Good and Decent Man* is seen in the legacy of trauma, where Chuck's difficult experience in the war has a considerable impact on the rest of his family. Tyler calls attention to the notion that not all scars are visible or explicit, since trauma frequently manifests itself in an implicit and unspoken manner. Questions about what triggers certain memories and what causes others to be repressed are constantly brought up in the text. By extension, musings on the nature of trauma deepen the meaning of the book's title, which comes to have a double meaning. On a surface level, *You'll Never Know* recalls Chuck and Hannah's early courtship by referencing a song by the same title that was popularized by Alice Faye in the 1940's. On a deeper level, the title emphasizes the incredible difficulty of truly knowing a person's private self, since Tyler's desire to uncover truth is met with her father's relentless desire to rid himself of his traumatic past by adopting a facade of stoic fortitude. Consequently, the work

> **Carol Tyler**
>
> Trained as a painter, Carol Tyler was attracted to the underground comics scene. She began producing comics in her thirties, publishing short pieces in *Weirdo*, *Wimmen's Comix*, and *Twisted Sisters*. Her first book, a collection of short stories about dead-end jobs titled *The Job Thing*, was published in 1993. *Late Bloomer*, a second collection of short stories, was published in 2005 and included her acclaimed short work "The Hannah Story," originally published in the anthology *Drawn and Quarterly*. In 2009 Tyler began publishing a three-volume book about her relationship with her father, a veteran of World War II. Tyler's drawings in these volumes are highly detailed and rendered with pen drawings and watercolors. She mixes traditional comics formats with illustrations that frame large text sections taken from letters and journals. Tyler is one of the most accomplished autobiographical cartoonists working in the form and, with her most recent work, has distinguished herself as a memoirist and journalist.

to media attention and positive reviews, the first installment of the trilogy was nominated for various awards, including two Eisners in 2010 for Best Writer/Artist of a Nonfiction Work and Best Painter/Multimedia Artist.

You'll Never Know is a Modern Age comic, produced in an era in which the graphic memoir has been a popular subgenre. It should be noted that Tyler was producing seminal works for several decades prior to *You'll Never Know*, contributing to major collections that are representative of the underground comics era, such as *Weirdo* (1981-1993), *Wimmen's Comix* (1972-1992), and *Twisted Sisters* (1994). In relation to other seminal comics, *You'll Never Know* is often likened to Art Spiegelman's *Maus: A Survivor's Tale* (1986, 1991) because of thematic similarities, including memory, family heritage, and World War II trauma. The story structures of the two works are also similar as both follow a parallel narrative that involves a complex relationship between a parent and a child. Although the two works possess many similarities, Tyler's *You'll Never Know*, Book One: *A Good and Decent Man* presents readers with a lighter tone and a more detailed and lively artistic style than *Maus* does.

Marie-Jade Menni

presents readers with an interesting tension between recollection and repression, a theme that is present throughout the trilogy.

Another important theme involves the complexity of memory. Throughout the story, memory is presented in a nonlinear and fragmented manner, as a process that is constantly under construction. The complex inner workings of memory are reflected in the narrative structure of the graphic memoir, which jumps between temporalities and character stories. Tyler frequently uses dialogue from one era to comment on another, where, for example, her father's dialogue about the past is juxtaposed with illustrations of the present, serving as a type of interpretation or critique of the action at hand.

Impact

The publication of Tyler's *You'll Never Know* trilogy has had a tremendous impact on the career of the author, becoming one of her most popular works. In addition

Further Reading

Spiegelman, Art. *Maus: A Survivor's Tale* (1986, 1991).

Tyler, Carol. *Late Bloomer* (2005).

———. *The Job Thing* (1993).

Bibliography

Rosenkranz, Patrick. "The ABCs of Autobio Comix." *The Comics Journal* (March 6, 2011). http://www.tcj.com/the-abcs-of-auto-bio-comix-2.

Tyler, Carol. "CR Sunday Interview: Carol Tyler." Interview by Tom Spurgeon. *The Comics Reporter*, July 5, 2009. http://www.comicsreporter.com/index.php/cr_sunday_interview_carol_tyler.

———. "The Fine Arts of Comics: Carol Tyler Interview." Interview by Mark Burbey. *The Comics Journal* 142 (June, 1991): 91-102.

———. "Interview: C. Tyler Pt. 1 (of 4)." Interview by Brian Heater. *The Daily Cross Hatch*, December 23,

2009. http://thedailycrosshatch.com/2009/12/23/interview-c-tyler-pt-1-of-4.

_____. "'You'll Never Know' Carol Tyler." Interview by Alex Dueben. *Comic Book Resources* (March 4, 2011). http://www.comicbookresources.com/?page=article&id=31136.

See also: *Maus*; *Alan's War*; *Last Day in Vietnam*; *Binky Brown Sampler*

Z

Zombies Vs. Robots

Author: Ryall, Chris
Artist: Ashley Wood (illustrator); Robbie Robbins (letterer)
Publisher: IDW Publishing
First book publication: 2008

Publication History

Chris Ryall and Ashley Wood, cocreators of the Eisner Award-nominated horror series *Doomed* (2005-2006), developed the miniseries *Zombies Vs. Robots* for IDW Publishing. According to Ryall, Wood had a simple idea: a series about zombies fighting robots. At the time, Ryall was the editor in chief and a regular writer at IDW, and Wood was a prominent artist for the company, working on such series as *Metal Gear Solid* (2004-2005) and *30 Days of Night (2002).*

Chris Ryall (left) with Ashley Wood. (Wikimedia Commons)

IDW released *Zombies Vs. Robots*, issues 1 and 2, in October and December, 2006. In 2007, the company published Ryall and Wood's three-part prequel titled "Which Came First?," featured in the miniseries *D'Airain Aventure* (2007).

In response to the reception of the *Zombies Vs. Robots* stories, IDW debuted *Zombies Vs. Robots Vs. Amazons*, issue 1, in September, 2007, a follow-up to the original series. Issues 2 and 3 were released in October, 2007, and February, 2008. "Which Came First?" and *Zombies Vs. Robots Vs. Amazons* have been released as hardcover collections and collected in trade paperbacks.

Plot

Revealed through dramatic art and darkly humorous text, the seemingly never-ending war between zombies ("braindead automatons") and robots ("brainless automatons") stems from an experiment at the Kirtland Underground Munitions Storage Complex in New Mexico, where three scientists (Herbert Throckmorton, Fritz Winterbottom, and Philippe Satterfield) have built various robots and developed a "trans-dimensional gateway." At the helm of the project is Satterfield, who embarks on a journey to the future. When Satterfield's plans go awry, Winterbottom, the second bravest of the three, dons a hulking "supersuit" akin to the one worn by Iron Man and passes through the gateway. Soon after, he encounters a group of zombies and retreats to the present. Meanwhile, Throckmorton activates his collection of robots, including one that seals the scientists' fate, and indirectly readies the robots for impending invasion of the zombie horde.

In the events that follow, the zombie outbreak consumes the human race, except for one baby girl, in the care of "guardbots," "warbots," and "docbots." As explained by an omniscient pressbot, the baby is labeled the last hope for humans. However, when the child's future takes a turn for the worse, one war-minded robot, "Bertie," tries to annihilate Earth's life-forms.

Surviving zombies make their way to the land of the Amazons. Soon after a group of young Amazons pry into the Queen's rituals, the undead infestation causes a royal shake-up and several significant deaths. The Amazons look to Bertie for protection, and the robot relies on help from Lady Vyssa, the Amazons' divine spectral intelligence. In the end, another race has been destroyed, but the robots' war does not seem to be over.

Volumes

- *Zombies Vs. Robots* (2007). Collects issues 1-2, or "Ghost in the Machine" and "Be All, End All." In this small collection, the human race has been destroyed by its advanced technology and the mysterious arrival of the undead commences.
- *Zombies Vs. Robots Vs. Amazons* (2008). Collects issues 1-3, or "Group Sects," "Bull Fight," and "Heir Force." This three-part installment centers on the unraveling of the Amazons, who, thanks to their gods, survived a nuclear holocaust aimed at destroying the zombies.
- *The Complete Zombies Vs. Robots* (2008). Collects "Which Came First?" from *D'Airain Adventure*, parts 1-3; *Zombies Vs. Robots*, issues 1-2; and *Zombies Vs. Robots Vs. Amazons*, issues 1-3. An expanded look at Ryall and Wood's mythology, collecting the complete *Zombies Vs. Robots* series and a three-part prequel featuring the origins of the zombie-robot war.
- *Zomnibus*, Volume 1 (2009). Collects *Zombies! Feast*, issues 1-5 (written by Shane McCarthy and illustrated by Chris Bolton); *Zombies! Eclipse of the Undead*, issues 1-4 (written by El Torres and illustrated by Yair Herrera); "Which Came First?" from *D'Airain Adventure*, parts 1-3; *Zombies Vs. Robots*, issues 1-2; and *Zombies Vs. Robots Vs. Amazons*, issues 1-3. This omnibus demonstrates the various approaches to zombie mythos and centers on the humans' futile efforts against the undead.

Characters

- *Philippe Satterfield*, an antagonist, is a stodgy scientist who, along with two other scientists, develops a time machine. His stubbornness and condescending attitude lead him to become the first to use the machine.
- *Fritz Winterbottom*, an antagonist, is a balding, relatively tall scientist who learns from Phillippe Satterfield's botched experiment, using a "supersuit" for his explorations. His voyage in time is said to be a cause of the zombie outbreak, in that he encounters the undead and tries to retreat to his former dimension.
- *Herbert Throckmorton*, a protagonist, is a bespectacled, timid scientist who works with Satterfield and Winterbottom. He befriends robots at Kirtland until the hulking Warbot-7G is activated. He designed the robot, which is "faster and more mentally acute" than most robots.
- *Pressbot-5*, a protagonist, is an omniscient robot who reports on the ongoing war between robots and zombies.
- *Zombies*, a collection of antagonists, are a variety of humans infected by an unknown virus, originating in another dimension. They shuffle slowly yet attack fiercely, infecting robots and anyone who is bitten or comes in contact with their blood.
- *Bertie*, a protagonist, is a cocksure warbot who is immune to the zombie virus. Always ready for battle, he is responsible for the destruction of most zombies and robots on Earth, and he is a saving grace for the Amazons when they are invaded by zombies.
- *Lady Vyssa*, a protagonist, is the Amazons' version of a robot, watching over the race's security since "the great bombs" fell on Earth. After befriending Bertie, she helps the robot resurrect other robots destroyed by the bombs.
- *Dhysa*, a protagonist, is the oldest daughter of the Amazon queen. She feels responsible for the zombie infestation, helping the surviving Amazons fight an uphill battle against their enemy.

Artistic Style

As the sole artist of *Zombies Vs. Robots* and *Zombies Vs. Robots Vs. Amazons*, Wood offers a mix of loosely defined expressionist sketches and paintings. He has a penchant for employing cool hues, favoring grays and blues, which align with the story's themes of despair and death as well as the artificial nature of the robots. Warm hues, accenting the darkness, pop up as a way to draw attention to bloodshed, zombie attacks, and other surprises.

In terms of pacing, Wood's sequential approach primarily consists of splash pages and large panels, creating room for battle sequences and exposition. Smaller panels are scattered throughout the story and, when created in a cluster, highlight smaller moments in time. Wood's approach to sound effects has a comical flair but also reflects the endless chaos on Earth.

Themes

The most prominent theme of *Zombies Vs. Robots* is the relationship between humans and technology. As the prequel shows, scientists devised artificially intelligent robots for war, time travel, medicine, and other tasks, such as sweeping and babysitting. The robots are aware of their abilities, establishing classes based on them and developing tensions among themselves as a result. Bertie, for example, loathes the weakness of older robot models. In the wake of the zombie outbreak, the robots outlive their makers, yet some seek to resurrect their creators. This type of irony plays up the humor of *Zombies Vs. Robots*.

War is a strong theme in the series. Though highly advanced, robots struggle against the unpredictable tactics of the undead's "brainlust."

Impact

The success of the *Zombies Vs. Robots* series helped fuel the trend of zombie stories common in the 2000's. Contemporary zombies stories include Image Comics' postapocalyptic series *The Walking Dead* (2003-   ); *Shaun of the Dead* (2004), a comical film about a zombie outbreak; and Marvel Comics' *Marvel Zombies* (2006-2010). *Pride and Prejudice and Zombies* came out in 2009, and several video games, including *Resident Evil 5* and *Dead Nation*, were released about the same time.

The success of *Zombies Vs. Robots* also fueled IDW's move further toward horror and science-fiction stories--particularly the *Zombies Vs. Robots* universe. In 2010, IDW released *Zombies Vs. Robots: Aventure*, a four-part anthology chronicling various human and robotic factions facing zombies before the nuclear holocaust; Ryall wrote the stories, and artists Menton Matthews III, Paul McCaffrey, and Gabriel Hernandez illustrated them. Wood contributed cover art. Wood also contributed covers to *Aventure*'s follow-up, *Zombies Vs. Robots: Undercity* (2011), a four-part story (penned by Ryall and illustrated by Mark Torres) centering on the U.S. president and his handpicked population.

Wood's other major work, *World War Robot* (2009), features industrialized military robots fighting alongside and against humans in a multi-front war on Earth, the Moon, and Mars. The story is told through Wood's oil paintings and accompanying text in the form of letters, field reports, and other accounts of the fictional war. Filmmaker Jerry Bruckheimer holds the rights to produce a film based on the series. Michael Bay, director of the *Transformers* (2007, 2009, 2011) movie series, has film rights to *Zombies Vs. Robots*.

Richard L. Shivener

Further Reading

Ryall, Chris, and Mark Torres. *Zombies Vs. Robots: Undercity* (2011).

Ryall, Chris, et al. *Zombies Vs. Robots: Aventure* (2010).

Wood, Ashley. *World War Robot* (2009).

Bibliography

Ryall, Chris. "In-Depth with IDW Publisher Chris Ryall." Interview by Alex Dueben. *Comic Book Resources*, January 17th, 2008. http://www.comicbookresources.com/?page=article&id=12330.

_____. "Chris Ryall's *Zombies Vs. Robots* Returns." *Comic Book Resources*, March 8, 2011. http://www.comicbookresources.com/?page=article&id=31209.

Manning, Shaun. "Ryall Vs. *Zombies Vs. Robots: Aventure.*" *Comic Book Resources*, December 9, 2009. http://www.comicbookresources.com/?page=article&id=23991.

Voger, Mark, et al. *The Dark Age: Grim, Great, and Gimmicky Post-Modern Comics.* Raleigh, N.C.: TwoMorrows, 2006.

See also: *Predator; Marvel Zombies; Walking Dead*

Zot!
The Complete Black and White Collection, 1987-1991

Author: McCloud, Scott; Ratafia, Ivy
Artist: Scott McCloud (illustrator); Bob Lappan (letterer)
Publisher: HarperCollins
First book publication: 2008

Publication History

The original *Zot!* comic books hit store shelves in 1984 under the logo of the now-defunct Eclipse Comics. The first ten installments were the only ones done in color, but creator Scott McCloud himself says, "Issue 11 was really a full reboot. We could have called it a 'New Number One,' but doing so was annoyingly fashionable in those days." The series ultimately ran for over thirty issues, with writer Ivy Ratafia providing some plot assistance to McCloud for later issues. Some additional comics were made by other creators with characters from *Zot!* in issues 10½ and 14½, and these are considered outside the main continuity.

Individual issues of *Zot!* have gone out of print, though some compilation books are available, the most recent being HarperCollins' 2008 *Zot! The Complete Black and White Collection, 1987-1991*. Compilation books of *Zot!* were released first by Eclipse Comics in 1990 and later by Kitchen Sink Press in 1997 and 1998; unfortunately, however, the one containing the final eight issues never made it to print.

An additional story of *Zot!* was later published on Scott McCloud's Web site. These sixteen digitally published installments use McCloud's concept of the "infinite canvas" and can still be read in their entirety at no charge on McCloud's site.

Plot

Zot! follows the trials and tribulations of the titular teen hero from a different world, which is described as the "the far-flung future of 1965," and Jenny, a teenager who lives in the "real" world. The interactions between the two characters and both worlds force them to fight supervillains and to face their own fears and doubts.

Scott McCloud at the Rhode Island School of Design, as part of his 50-state "Making Comics" tour. (By Grendelkhan, via Wikimedia Commons)

Friends from both worlds add their perspectives and often join in the adventures.

The compilation book has all but the first ten installments and divides the overarching story into two parts. The first part, titled "Heroes and Villains," focuses on Zot's world and how he deals with the traditional supervillains while Jenny watches and sometimes provides help. Jenny also deals with situations in her own world and meets new friends. The multitude of antagonists includes many memorable villains with unique motivations. Dr. Ignatius Rumbault Bellows, an inventor with steampunk creations, despises other forms of technology and launches attacks from his flying machines of doom. Zybox is a giant robot that can control other machines and encase other people within a *Matrix*-like simulation to keep them docile. The De-Evolutionaries, who hate technology and want humanity to "revert" to the trees, use a ray gun that turns people into monkeys. Dekko is an artist whose body had to be slowly replaced by machines. He has lost his sanity and now believes that the human condition needs to be eradicated. The Blotch is an overbearing evil CEO/mobster who uses loopholes and legal tricks to obtain more power. 9-Jack-9 is a powerful assassin for hire who can live and transport himself through anything electrical in an instant.

Part 2, titled "The Earth Stories," finds Zot unable to travel between worlds and stuck in Jenny's world. Individual installments focus more on Jenny and her friends and how their interactions with Zot help them face their own challenges. Relationships, homophobia, family troubles, bigotry, racism, class issues, and teen sex are discussed in a way that is not too preachy but still delivers an important message. Through it all, Zot is the fish out of water who can barely understand exactly what is going on, why the problems of humanity exist, and more important, why people cannot solve them. This naïveté has an effect on his friends, who are now forced to think about the world that they have accepted. This line of questioning is the first step toward helping them do something about the problems that one generally responds to with complaints or apathy.

Characters

- *Zot*, a.k.a. *Zachary T. Paleozogt*, is the protagonist and titular hero. He is a blond teenager who lives in a utopian world that mirrors the "real" one. He normally wears a shirt with a lightning bolt on it when not wearing his supersuit, which bears the same design. He is incredibly optimistic and confident, though somewhat confused as to how the world works. His main powers are flight and superstrength, and he has an array of high-tech contraptions to aid him against supervillains. His desire to make the world a better place and protect people is at the center of most plots.
- *Jenny*, a.k.a. *Jennifer Weaver*, is a brunet teenager that lives in the "real" world and hates it. She is Zot's friend and love interest and always tags along in his adventures. She is pessimistic about the world around her, which includes a mean older brother and mostly absent parents on the verge of a divorce, and would love to move to Zot's world eventually. The lightning bolt pendant she carries serves as a beacon for Zot and a means of communication between them. She is primarily a guide for the story as she helps Zot navigate in her world, and her questions in his world help the reader to understand this "alien" setting.
- *Terry*, a.k.a. *Theresa Veras*, is Jenny's best friend and confidant. She has dark, short hair and is mean to just about everyone but Jenny. She is cynical and does not seek solace or escape in going to Zot's world, no matter how much she hates her own. While Zot tries to give Jenny hope in the world, Terry often grounds Jenny's thoughts in apathy and even foreboding doom.
- *Woody*, a.k.a. *Woodrow Wilson Bernstein*, starts out as a short, gawky nerd but soon has a growth spurt that leaves him tall and handsome—and still somewhat geeky because he wears glasses. He is in love with Jenny and competes with Zot for her affection. Woody is a pensive realist with a bit of a self-esteem problem. He adds another dimension in Jenny's life and makes her think critically about her situation.
- *Max*, Zot's uncle and only family member, is an eccentric inventor who wears a lab coat and glasses. A father figure to Zot, he developed and invented many of the gadgets Zot uses, including his rocket boots, a robot butler named Peabody, his laser gun, and the machine that allows him to travel through worlds. He is analytical and values knowledge, to the point that he does not use labels such as "good" or "evil." His theoretical mind-set further complicates and influences how Jenny should see both worlds.

Artistic Style

McCloud did nearly all of the art and writing for *Zot!*, so the artistic style remains relatively uniform throughout the series. The first ten issues (which are not included in the 2008 compilation book and are quite hard to find) were originally rendered in color by Denis McFarling, while the remaining installments were done exclusively in black and white by McCloud. Bob Lappan did the lettering for the whole series.

Action panels are common, but splash pages of aspects and setting are present, creating a style that is often hailed as a combination of American comics and Japanese manga. The biggest variations of drawing styles are in the abstract and surreal visualizations of the villain Dekko.

Among the more interesting issues are those in the story arc "Getting to 99," a two-part installment that is reproduced in the compilation book as the rough "visual script" rather than the final version that readers originally saw in the comic. This installment was actually penciled by Chuck Austen, though conceived of and planned by McCloud. While it is in black and white, the scale of darkness and light directly represents Zot's and Jenny's worlds, respectively. Establishing panels contextualize the mood of the story, be it light or dark, and provide a wealth of information without a single piece of text.

Themes

At first, *Zot!* focuses on the traditional good-versus-evil battle that is quite common in works about superheroes. Later, as Zot and Jenny's relationship progresses, Zot's perspective on Jenny's world challenges how one looks at contemporary society. Family dynamics are also explored through Jenny's interactions with her parents and with the development of other characters. Zot's villains also serve as an allegory for current issues, including the evils of corrupting technologies, unchecked capitalism, and greed.

An overarching theme throughout *Zot!* is the importance of choosing optimism over cynicism when dealing with the problems of society. Zot is constantly hopeful and confident in his and Jenny's worlds that they can become better places. Jenny, on the other hand, is in a constant emotional struggle dealing with everyday life. Jenny's circle of friends and their problems add even more layers, and having Zot around leads them to challenge what they have accepted as "normal" and to change for the better.

Zot! is primarily a coming-of-age tale. The characters all face and overcome the challenges in their lives, and they all learn something about themselves in the process. Zot, Jenny, and the rest of their friends strive for maturity and finding a place within society. Part of that maturity involves not running away from one's problems no matter how hopeless the situation, which is why Zot encourages Jenny to stay in her world and give it a chance, despite all the bad things that end up happening. However, McCloud explains in author commentary that visiting Zot's utopian world is not symbolic of escapism or drug use, an interpretation critics have given when talking about this series.

Impact

Unfortunately, *Zot!* is mostly recognized as the comic series that Scott McCloud worked on before he wrote *Understanding Comics: The Invisible Art*, and few people have analyzed the compilation beyond the occasional book review. Reviewers Martha Cornog and Steve Raiteri of *Library Journal* praise McCloud's ability to "break down some barriers for superhero comics," while others say that he deconstructs the entire genre in an entertaining and thought-provoking way. As one of the few comics to use manga-style drawings and panels, McCloud was one of the first comics creators to blend American- and Japanese-style graphic storytelling and helped make it possible for future comics, films, and television programs to do the same.

Gabriel Romaguera

Further Reading

Eisner, Will, et al. *The Spirit* (1941-1952).
Tezuka, Osamu. *Astro Boy* (1952-1968).

Bibliography

Cornog, Martha, and Steve Raiteri. "Graphic Novels." *Library Journal*, September 15, 2008. http://www.libraryjournal.com/lj/ljinprint/currentissue/861882-403/graphic_novels_laugh_riot.html.csp.
Flagg, Gordon. "Zot! 1987-1991." Review of *Zot!*, by Scott McCloud. *Booklist* 105, no. 1 (September 1, 2008): 62.

McCloud, Scott. *Understanding Comics: The Invisible Art*. New York: HarperCollins, 2006.

See also: *A Contract with God, and Other Tenement Stories*

Appendixes

BIBLIOGRAPHY

Aamodt, Britt. *Superheroes, Strip Artists, and Talking Animals: Minnesota's Contemporary Cartoonists*. St. Paul: Minnesota Historical Society Press, 2011.

Abel, Jessica. "The Jessica Abel Interview." Interviewed by Greg Stump. *The Comics Journal* 270 (August, 2005): 68-106.

Abler, Thomas S. Review of *A Journey into Mohawk and Oneida Country, 1634-1635*. *Ethnohistory* 38, no. 3 (Summer, 1991): 340-343.

Abouet, Marguerite. "Drawing on the Universal in Africa: An Interview with Marguerite Abouet." Interview by Angela Ajayi. *Wild River Review*, February 9, 2011. http://www.wildriverreview.com/interview/drawing-universal-africa/marguerite-abouet/ajayi-angela.

Alaniz, Jose. "Speaking the 'Truth' of Sex: Moore and Gebbie's *Lost Girls*." *International Journal of Comic Art* 8, no. 2 (Fall, 2006): 307-318.

Allen, Mark. "Suspended Animation: *Xenozoic Tales*." *SciFiDimensions*, May 10, 2002. http://www.scifidimensions.com/May02/xenozoictales.htm.

Alsup, Janet. "One Female Reader Reading YAL: Understanding Norman Holland's Identity Themes Thirty Years Later." In *Young Adult Literature and Adolescent Identity Across Cultures and Classrooms: Contexts for the Literary Lives of Teens*. New York: Routledge, 2010.

Alter, Robert, and Frank Kermode. *The Literary Guide to the Bible*. Cambridge, Mass.: Belknap Press, 1999.

Alter, Robert. *The Art of Biblical Narrative*. New York: Basic Books, 1981.

_____. "Scripture Picture." Review of *The Book of Genesis*, by Robert Crumb. *New Republic* 240, no. 19 (October 21, 2009): 44-48.

Andelman, Bob. *Will Eisner: A Spirited Life*. Milwaukie, Ore.: M Press, 2005.

Anderson, Ho Che. "Interview with Ho Che Anderson." Interview by Dale Jacobs. *International Journal of Comic Art* 8, no. 2 (Fall, 2006): 363-86.

_____. "Rings True." *The Comics Journal* 182 (November, 1995): 103-105.

Andrae, Thomas. *Carl Barks and the Disney Comic Book: Unmasking the Myth of Modernity*. Jackson: University Press of Mississippi, 2006.

Apostolidès, Jean-Marie. *The Metamorphosis of Tintin, or, Tintin for Adults*. Translated by Jocelyn Hoy. Stanford, Calif.: Stanford University Press, 2010.

Arnold, Andrew D. "*Boring*'s Exciting Ride: A Comic-Book Saga Comes to a Resonant End." *Time* 155, no. 16 (April 24, 2000): 81. Available at http://www.time.com/time/magazine/article/0,9171,996711,00.html.

_____. "The Complex Simplicity of John Porcellino." *Time*, July 13, 2001. http://www.time.com/time/columnist/arnold/article/0,9565,167115,00.html.

_____. "From Ming to Kim." *Time*, September 23, 2005. http://www.time.com/time/columnist/arnold/article/0,9565,1108801,00.html.

_____. "No Bones About It." *Time*, September 17, 2004, 26-27. http://www.time.com/time/columnist/arnold/article/0,9565,698456,00.html.

_____. "The Original *Road to Perdition*." Review of *Road to Perdition*, by Max Allan Collins. *Time*, July 16, 2002. http://www.time.com/time/columnist/arnold/article/0,9565,321312,00.html.

_____. "Out of the Ballpark." Review of *The Golem's Mighty Swing* by James Sturm. *Time*, August 17, 2001. http://www.time.com/time/arts/article/0,8599,171550,00.html

_____. "Return of the Kings." *Time*, April 19, 2006. http://www.time.com/time/arts/article/0,8599,1184802,00.html.

_____. "What It Feels Like for a Girl." *Time*, October 11, 2002. http://www.time.com/time/arts/article/0,8599,364159,00.html.

Assouline, Pierre. *Hergé: The Man Who Created Tintin*. Translated by Charles Ruas. New York: Oxford University Press, 2009.

Attaboy. "Paul Pope: Ball in Play." *Hi-Fructose Magazine* 7 (2008): 54-61.

Attenberg, Jami. "Prime Cuts, Rare and Well Done." *Print* 61, no. 2 (March/April, 2007): 67.

Avermate, Roger. *Frans Masereel*. New York: Ritzzoli International, 1977.

Badman, Derik A. "The Golem's Mighty Swing." Review of *The Golem's Mighty Swing* by James Sturm. *MadInkBeard*, March 3, 2008. http://madinkbeard.com/archives/the-golems-mighty-swing.

Baker, Bill. Review of *Safe Area Goražde: The Special Edition*, by Joe Sacco. *ForeWord* October 17, 2010). http://www.forewordreviews.com/reviews/safe-area-gorazde.

Baker, Kyle, and Eric Nolen-Weathington. *Kyle Baker*. Modern Masters Volume 20. Raleigh, N.C.: TwoMorrows, 2008.

Baker, Kyle. *How to Draw Stupid and Other Essentials of Cartooning*. New York: Watson-Guptill, 2008.

Baldaev, Danzig. *Drawings from the Gulag*. London: FUEL, 2010.

Ball, David M., and Martha Kuhlman, eds. *The Comics of Chris Ware: Drawing Is a Way of Thinking*. Jackson: University Press of Mississippi, 2010.

Barker, Clive. Introduction to *30 Days of Night*. New York: IDW Publishing, 2003.

Barrier, J. Michael. *Carl Barks and the Art of the Comic Book*. New York: M. Lilien, 1981.

Barsanti, Chris. "PW Comics Week." *Publishers Weekly* 254, no. 23 (June 4, 2007): 36.

_____. "The Graphic Report." *Kirkus Reviews* 72, no. 19 (October 1, 2004).

Bartley, Aryn. "The Hateful Self: Substitution and the Ethics of Representing War." *Modern Fiction Studies* 54, no. 1 (2008): 50-71.

Baxter, Kathleen. "We're Just Wild About Harry: Master Magician Harry Houdini Still Fascinates and Mystifies Kids of All Ages." *School Library Journal*, April, 2010, p. 21.

Beaty, Bart. *David Cronenberg's "A History of Violence."* Toronto: University of Toronto Press, 2008.

_____. "Selective Mutual Reinforcement in the Comics of Chester Brown, Joe Matt, and Seth." In *Graphic Subjects: Critical Essays on Autobiography and Graphic Novels*, edited by Michael A. Chaney. Madison: University of Wisconsin Press, 2011.

_____. "The Strange Case of Lewis Trondheim." In *Unpopular Culture: Transforming the European Comic Book in the 1990's*. Toronto: University of Toronto Press, 2007.

_____. *Unpopular Culture: Transforming the European Comic Book in the 1990's*. Toronto: University of Toronto Press, 2007.

Beauchamp, Monte, ed. *The Life and Times of R. Crumb: Comments from Contemporaries*. New York: St. Martin's Griffin, 1998.

Bechdel, Alison. "An Interview with Alison Bechdel." Interview by Hillary L. Chute. *Modern Fiction Studies* 52, no. 4 (2006): 1004-1013.

_____. *The Indelible Alison Bechdel: Confessions, Comix, and Miscellaneous Dykes to Watch Out For*. Ithaca, N.Y.: Firebrand Books, 1998.

Beeler, Monique. "A Born Storyteller. The ABCs of Graphic Novelist and National Book Award Finalist Gene Yang '03." *Cal State East Bay Magazine*, Spring/Summer, 2009, 11-17.

Beirne, Rebecca. "*Dykes to Watch Out For* and the Lesbian Landscape." In *Lesbians in Television and Text After the Millennium*. New York: Palgrave Macmillan, 2008.

Benton, Mike. *Crime Comics: The Illustrated History*. Dallas, Tex.: Taylor, 1993.

Beronä, David A. "Breaking Taboos: Sexuality in the Work of Will Eisner and the Early Wordless Novels." *International Journal of Comic Art* 1, no. 1 (Spring/Summer, 1999): 90-103.

_____. *Wordless Books: The Original Graphic Novels*. New York: Abrams, 2008.

_____. "Wordless Comics: The Imaginative Appeal of *The System*." *Critical Approaches to Comics and Graphic Novels: Theories and Methods*, edited by Randy Duncan and Matthew J. Smith. New York: Routledge, 2011.

Berthold, Michael C. "Color Me Ishmael: Classics Illustrated Versions of *Moby-Dick*." *Word and Image* 9, no. 1 (January-March, 1993): 1-8.

Binelli, Mark. "Joe Sacco's Cartoon Violence." *Rolling Stone* 940 (January 22, 2004): 40-41.

Blincoe, Nicholas. "Cartoon Wars: The Israeli Occupation Gets Hard-Hitting Treatment from the Comic-Book Genius Joe Sacco in *Palestine*." *New Statesman*, January 6, 2003, p. 26.

Bloom, Harold. "Yahweh Meets R. Crumb." Review of *The Book of Genesis*, by Robert Crumb. *New York Review of Books* 56, no. 19 (December 3, 2009): 24-25.

Boatwright, Michael D. "Graphic Journeys: Graphic Novels' Representation of Immigrant Experiences." *Journal of Adolescent and Adult Literacy* 53, no. 6 (March, 2010): 468-476.

Boerner, Leigh Krietsch. "Ecology: A Story of Symbiosis." *Science* 324, no. 5932 (June, 2009): 1270.

Bogaert, Harmen Meyndertsz van den. *A Journey into Mohawk and Oneida Country, 1634-1635: The Journal of Harmen Meyndertsz van den Bogaert*. Translated and edited by Charles T. Gehring and William A. Starna. Syracuse, N.Y.: Syracuse University Press, 1988.

Booker, M. Keith. *May Contain Graphic Material: Comic Books, Graphic Novels, and Film*. New York: Praeger, 2007.

Boucher, Geoff. "Moebius on His Art, Fading Eyesight, and Legend: 'I Am Like a Unicorn.'" *Los Angeles Times Hero Complex*, April 2, 2011. http://herocomplex.latimes.com/2011/04/02/moebius-on-his-art-fading-eyesight-and-legend-i-am-like-a-unicorn.

Bowe, Marisa. "No Laughing Matter: Marisa Bowe on Joe Sacco." *Bookforum* (Summer, 2005): 26-57.

Bowers, Faubion. *Japanese Theatre*. New York: Hermitage House, 1952.

Boyd, Kevin. "2010 Outstanding Cartoonist: Michel Rabagliati." *The Joe Shuster Awards*, June 23, 2010. http://joeshusterawards.com/2010/06/23/2010-outstanding-cartoonist-michel-rabagliati.

Brayshaw, Chris. "The Struggle to Communicate." *The Comics Journal* 182 (November, 1995): 94-98.

Bredehoft, Thomas. "Comics Architecture, Multidimensionality, and Time: Chris Ware's *Jimmy Corrigan: The Smartest Kid on Earth*." *Modern Fiction Studies* 52, no. 4 (Winter, 2006): 869-890.

Brienza, Casey. "My Mommy Is in America and She Met Buffalo Bill." Review of *My Mommy Is in America and She Met Buffalo Bill*, by Jean Regnaud. *Graphic Novel Reporter*. http://www.graphicnovelreporter.com/content/my-mommy-america-and-she-met-buffalo-bill-review.

Briggs, Raymond, and Nicolette Jones. *Blooming Books*. London: Jonathan Cape, 2003.

Briggs, Raymond. "Big Kid, 'Old Git,' and Still in the Rudest of Health." Interview by Rachel Cooke. *The Observer* (August 9, 2008) http://www.guardian.co.uk/books/2008/aug/10/booksforchildrenandteenagers.

Brooker, Will. *Alice's Adventures: Lewis Carroll in Popular Culture*. New York: Continuum, 2004.

Brophy-Warren, Jamin. "Generation Vampire." *Wall Street Journal* 251, no. 97 (April 25, 2008): W2.

Brothers, David. "Jean 'Moebius' Giraud: Your Favorite Artist's Favorite Artist." *Comics Alliance*, April 22, 2011. http://comicsalliance.com/2011/04/22/jean-moebius-giraud-art.

Brown, Chester. "Chester Brown." Interview by Nicolas Verstappen. *du9: L'Autre Bande dessinée*, August, 2008. http://www.du9.org/Chester-Brown,1030.

———. "Getting Riel with Chester Brown." Interview by Guy Leshinski. *The Cultural Gutter*, January 5, 2006. http://www.theculturalgutter.com/comics/getting_riel_with_chester_brown.html.

Brown, Jeffrey. "When Jeffrey Was Brown: An Interview." Interview by Ian Brill. *Comic Book Galaxy*, 2010. http://www.comicbookgalaxy.com/jbrown.html.

Buhle, Paul. "History and Comics." *Reviews in American History* 35, no. 2 (June, 2007): 315-323.

———. "Walker in the Imagined City." *The Nation* 271, no. 11 (October 16, 2000): 29-32.

Burg, Steven L., and Paul S. Shoup. *The War in Bosnia-Herzegovina: Ethnic Conflict and International Intervention*. London: M. E. Sharpe, 2000.

Burns, Charles. "Charles Burns, Chip Kidd, Seth, and Chris Ware Panel." Interview by Jeet Heer. *Comics Journal*, March 31, 2010. http://classic.tcj.com/alternative/charles-burns-chip-kidd-seth-and-chris-ware-panel-part-one-of-three/.

———. "Charles Burns is *X'ed Out*." Interview by Alex Dueben. *Comic Book Resources*, October 18, 2010. http://www.comicbookresources.com/?page=article&id=28938.

Bush, Elizabeth. "*Robot Dreams*." Review of *Robot Dreams* by Sara Varon. *Bulletin of the Center for Children's Books* 61, no. 3 (November, 2007): 155.

Campbell, Eddie. "Campbell Interviews Lat: Part 1." *First Second*, January 11, 2007. http://firstsecondbooks.typepad.com/mainblog/2007/01/campbell_interv.html.

———. "Eddie Campbell." Interview by Dirk Deppey. *The Comics Journal* 273 (January, 2006): 66-114. Excerpt available at http://archives.tcj.com/273/i_campbell.html.

———. "What Is a Graphic Novel?" *World Literature Today* 81, no. 2 (March/April, 2007): 13.

Cannon, Kevin. "CR Sunday Interview: Kevin Cannon." Interview with Tom Spurgeon. *The Comics Reporter*, June 21, 2009. http://www.comicsreporter.com/index.php/cr_sunday_interview_kevin_cannon.

_____. "Kevin Cannon Talks *T-Minus* and *Far Arden*." Interview with Alex Dueben. *Comic Book Resources*, June 9, 2009. http://www.comicbookresources.com/?page=article&id=21527.

Carlin, John, Paul Karasik, and Brian Walker, eds. *Masters of American Comics*. New Haven, Conn.: Yale University Press, 2005.

Carroll, Lewis, John Tenniel, and Martin Gardner. *The Annotated Alice: "Alice's Adventures in Wonderland" and "Through the Looking-Glass."* New York: Norton, 2000.

Casey, Jim, and Stefan Hall. "The Exotic Other Scripted: Identity and Metamorphosis in David Mack's *Kabuki*." *ImageText: Interdisciplinary Comics Studies* 3, no. 1 (2006).

Castellucci, Cecil. "Creating Memorable Characters." In *2009 Children's Writer's and Illustrators Market*, edited by Alice Pope. Cincinnati: Writer's Digest Books, 2008.

Caturani, Khadijah. "*Palomar: The Heartbreak Soup Stories*: A Love and Rockets Book." Review of *Palomar: The Heartbreak Soup Stories*, by Gilbert Hernandez. *Library Journal* 129, no. 1 (January, 2004): 80.

Cavallaro, Dani. "The Brain in a Vat in Cyberpunk: The Persistence of the Flesh." *Studies in History and Philosophy of Biological and Biomedical Sciences* 35 (2004): 287-305.

Celayo, Armando, and David Shook. "Comic Adaptations of Literary Classics." *World Literature Today* 81, no. 2 (March/April, 2007): 33-36.

Celayo, Armando. "Monologues for the Coming Plague." Review of *Monologues for the Coming Plague*, by Anders Nilsen. *World Literature Today* 81, no. 2 (March, 2007): 70.

Chabon, Michael. Introduction to *Julius Knipl, Real Estate Photographer*. New York: Little, Brown, 1996.

Chalmers, John, and Sandra Marrs. "Lies, Letters, and the Strange Weather." Interview by Jennifer M. Contino. *Sequential Tart*. http://www.sequentialtart.com/archive/nov01/metaphrog.shtml.

_____. "The Metaphrog Interview." Interview by Gavin Lees. *The Comics Journal*, September 28, 2011. http://www.tcj.com/the-metaphrog-interview.

Chan, Suzette. "This Is the Story of Mariko Tamaki and Jillian Tamaki. So Read On." *Sequential Tart*. http://www.sequentialtart.com/archive/oct05/art_1005_3.shtml.

Chaney, Michael A. "Animal Subjects of the Graphic Novel." *College Literature* 38, no. 3 (Summer, 2011): 129-149.

_____. "Drawing on History in Recent African American Graphic Novels." *MELUS: The Journal of the Society for the Study of the Multi-Ethnic Literature of the United States* 32, no. 3 (2007): 175-200.

_____. "Terrors of the Mirror and the *Mise en Abyme* of Graphic Novel Autobiography." *College Literature* 38, no. 3 (Summer, 2011): 21-44.

Chenowith, Emily, and Jeff Zaleski. "*Blankets*." Review of *Blankets*, by Craig Thompson. *Publishers Weekly* 250, no. 33 (August 18, 2003): 60-61.

Chuen, Ooi Kok. "Lat: Then, Now, and Forever." *New Straits Times*, December 27, 2003, p. 5.

Chute, Hillary L. "Graphic Narrative as Witness: Marjane Satrapi and the Texture of Retracing." In *Graphic Women: Life Narrative and Contemporary Comics*. New York: Columbia University Press, 2010.

_____. *Graphic Women: Life Narrative and Contemporary Comics*. New York: Columbia University Press, 2010.

_____. "'The Shadow of a Past Time': History and Graphic Representation in *Maus*." *Twentieth Century Literature* 52, no. 2 (Summer, 2006): 199-230.

_____. "*Our Cancer Year, Janet and Me: An Illustrated Story of Love and Loss, Cancer Vixen: A True Story, Mom's Cancer, Blue Pills: A Positive Love Story, Epileptic,* and *Black Hole*." Review of *Cancer Vixen*, by Marisa Acocella Marchetto. *Literature and Medicine* 26, no. 2 (2008): 413-429.

_____. "The Texture of Retracing in Marjane Satrapi's *Persepolis*." *Women's Studies Quarterly* 36, no. 1/2 (Spring/Summer, 2008): 92-110.

Chute, Hillary, and Marie DeKoven. "Introduction: Graphic Narrative." *Modern Fiction Studies* 52, no. 4 (2006): 767-782.

Clarke, John Henrik, ed. *William Styron's Nat Turner: Ten Black Writers Respond*. Boston: Beacon Press, 1968.

Claudio, Esther. "*It's a Bird*—Steven T. Seagle and Teddy Kristiansen." *The Comics Grid*, March 7, 2011. http://www.comicsgrid.com/2011/03/steven-t-seagles-its-a-bird.

Clayton, Hamish, and Williams, Mark. "Smoke at Anchor: Dylan Horrocks' *Hicksville*." In *Floating Worlds: Essays on Contemporary New Zealand Fiction*, edited by Anna Jackson and Jane Stafford. Wellington, New Zealand: Victoria University Press, 2009.

Clough, Rob. "Art and Commerce: Skitzy." Review of *Skitzy*, by Don Freeman. *High-Low* (December 25, 2008). http://highlowcomics.blogspot.com/2008/12/art-and-commerce-skitzy.html

Clowes, Daniel, Ken Parille, and Isaac Cates. *Daniel Clowes: Conversations*. Jackson: University Press of Mississippi, 2010.

Clowes, Daniel, and Terry Zwigoff. *Ghost World: A Screenplay*. Seattle: Fantagraphics, 2001.

Clowes, Daniel. "And Here's the Kicker: Daniel Clowes Interview." Interview by Mike Sacks. *And Here's the Kicker*. http://www.andheresthekicker.com/ex_daniel_clowes.php.

———. "Conversation Four: Daniel Clowes." Interview by Mike Sacks. *McSweeney's*, 2009. http://www.mcsweeneys.net/links/sacks/clowes.html.

Coale, Mark. *Breaking the Panels: Over Seventy-Five Short Interviews from Around the Comics Industry*. Colora, Md.: O-Goshi Studios, 1998.

Cockburn, Patrick. "They Planted Hatred in Our Hearts." *The New York Times Book Review*, December 27, 2008, BR13.

Collins, Max Allan. "Just the Facts Ma'am: Max Collins Talks *Road to Perdition*." Interview by Arune Singh. *Comic Book Resources*, June 16, 2002. http://www.comicbookresources.com/?page=article&old=1&id=1240.

Constable, Liz. "Consuming Realities: The Engendering of Invisible Violences in Posy Simmonds's *Gemma Bovery*." *South Central Review* 19/20 (Winter, 2002): 63-84.

Coogan, Peter. "The Definition of the Superhero." In *A Comics Studies Reader*, edited by Jeet Heer and Kent Worcester. Jackson: University Press of Mississippi, 2009.

Cooke, Rachel. "Raymond Briggs: Big Kid, 'Old Git' and Still in the Rudest of Health." *The Observer* (August 9, 2008): 20-21.

Cooper, Dave. "The Dave Cooper Interview." Interview by Gary McEown. *The Comics Journal* 245 (August, 2002): 76-105.

———. "Dave Cooper." Interview by Nicolas Verstappen. *L'autre bande dessinée* (August, 2008). http://www.du9.org/Dave-Cooper,1028.

Cornell, Kevin. "The Curious Job of Kevin Cornell." *Bearskinrug*, August 13, 2008. http://www.bearskinrug.co.uk/_articles/2008/08/13/curious_job.

Cornog, Martha, and Steve Raiteri. "Graphic Novels." *Library Journal*, September 15, 2008. http://www.libraryjournal.com/lj/ljinprint/currentissue/861882-403/graphic_novels_laugh_riot.html.csp.

Couch, N. C. Christopher, and Stephen Weiner. *The Will Eisner Companion: The Pioneering Spirit of the Father of the Graphic Novel*. New York: DC Comics, 2004.

Coughlan, David. "Paul Auster's *City of Glass*: The Graphic Novel." *Modern Fiction Studies* 52, no. 4 (2006): 832-854.

Croonenborghs, Bart. "The Three Shadows of Cyril Pedrosa." *Broken Frontier*, May 28, 2008. http://www.brokenfrontier.com/lowdown/p/detail/the-three-shadows-of-cyril-pedrosa.

Crumb, Robert, and D. K. Holm, ed. *R. Crumb Conversations*. Jackson: University Press of Mississippi, 2004.

Crumb, Robert, and Peter Poplaski. *The R. Crumb Handbook*. London: MQ Publications, 2005.

Crumb, Robert. "R. Crumb, The Art of Comics No. 1." Interview by Ted Widmer. *Paris Review* 193 (Summer, 2010): 19-57.

Curtis, Michael. "Antisemitism." In *The Oxford Companion to the Politics of the World*, edited by Joel Krieger. New York: Oxford University Press, 1993.

Daly, Mark, and Rich Kreiner. "Seth, Brown, Matt." *The Comics Journal* 162 (1993): 51-56.

Dargis, Manohla. "A Savage and Sexy City of Pulp Fiction Regulars." *The New York Times*, April 1, 2005. http://movies.nytimes.com/2005/04/01/movies/01sin.html?_r=1&ex=1153281600&en=7e266ef33d532f3a&ei=5070&oref=slogin.

Dauber, Jeremy. "Comic Books, Tragic Stories: Will Eisner's American Jewish History." In *The Jewish Graphic Novel: Critical Approaches*, edited by Samantha Baskind and Ranen Omer-Sherman. Piscataway, N.J.: Rutgers University Press, 2010.

Dauncey, Hugh, ed. *French Popular Culture: An Introduction*. New York: Oxford University Press, 2003.

David, Danya Sara. "Journeys of Faith and Survival: An Examination of Three Jewish Graphic Novels." M.A. thesis, University of British Columbia, 2008. https://circle.ubc.ca/bitstream/handle/2429/2453/ubc_2008_spring_david_danya_sara.pdf?sequence.

Davies, Barry. *The Spycraft Manual: The Insider's Guide to Espionage Techniques*. London: Zenith Press 2005.

Davis, Mary Kemp. *Nat Turner Before the Bar of Judgment: Fictional Treatments of the Southampton Slave Insurrection*. Baton Rouge: Louisiana State University Press, 1999.

Davisson, Zack. "This Flame, This Carrot." *Comics Bulletin.* December 1, 2010. http://www.comicsbulletin.com/grind/129126934663262.htm.

De Jesús, Melinda. "Liminality and Mestiza Consciousness in Lynda Barry's *One Hundred Demons*." *MELUS* 29, no. 1 (Spring, 2004): 219-252.

_____. "Of Monsters and Mothers: Filipina American Identity and Maternal Legacies in Lynda Barry's *One Hundred Demons*." *Meridians: Feminism, Race, Transnationalism* 5, no. 1 (2004): 1-26.

Decker, Dwight R. "*Asterix*: 'These Frenchmen Are Crazy!'" *Comics Journal* 38 (February, 1978): 22-33.

Deitch, Kim. "An Interview with Kim Deitch." Interview by Jeffrey Ford. *Fantastic Metropolis* (October 9, 2002).

_____. "An Interview with Kim Deitch." Interview by Joshua Glenn. *Hilobrow* (August 3, 2010).

_____. "Underground Comix Come of Age: An Interview with Kim Deitch." Interview by Steven Heller. *AIGA: Journal of Graphic Design* 27 (March, 2007).

Delgado, Ricardo. Afterword to *Age of Reptiles: Tribal Warfare*. Milwaukie, Ore.: Dark Horse Comics, 1996.

Delisle, Guy. "A Talk with Guy Delisle: Looking for the Details." Interview by Ada Price. *Publishers Weekly*, October 20, 2009. http://www.publishersweekly.com/pw/by-topic/new-titles/adult-announcements/article/1868-a-talk-with-guy-delisle-looking-for-the-details-.html.

Di Liddo, Annalisa. *Alan Moore: Comics as Performance, Fiction as Scalpel*. Jackson: University Press of Mississippi, 2009.

Dodge, Chris. "The Revolution Will Not Be Photocopied." *Utne Reader* 107 (September/October, 2001): 23-25.

Doucet, Julie. "Julie Doucet." Interview by Andrea Juno. *Dangerous Drawings: Interviews with Comix and Graphix Artists*. New York: Juno Books, 1997.

_____. "Julie Doucet's Secretions: A Tête-à-Tête." Interview by the staff of *The Comics Journal*. *The Comics Journal* 141 (April, 1991): 98-99.

Drechsler, Debbie. "The Debbie Drechsler Interview." Interview by Gary Groth. *The Comics Journal* 249 (December, 2002): 82-107.

_____. "Debbie Drechsler." Interview by Nicholas Verstappen. *L'autre bande dessinée* (July, 2008). http://www.du9.org/Debbie-Drechsler,1018.

Driscoll, Catherine. "Girl Culture, Revenge, and Global Capitalism: Cybergirls, Riot Grrls, Spice Girls." *Australian Feminist Studies* 14, no. 29 (1999): 173-193.

Drooker, Eric. *Street Posters and Ballads: A Selection of Poems, Songs, and Graphics*. New York: Seven Stories Press, 1998.

Du Brow, Rick. "*Cadillacs* Cartoon Enters Brave New World." *Los Angeles Times*, February 12, 1994. http://articles.latimes.com/print/1994-02-12/entertainment/ca-22070_1_classic-cadillac.

DuBose, Mike S. "Holding Out for a Hero: Reaganism, Comic Book Vigilantes, and Captain America." *Journal of Popular Culture* 40, no. 6 (2007): 915-935.

Dubbs, Chris. *Space Dogs: Pioneers of Space Travel*. New York: Writer's Showcase, 2003.

Duffy, Damian, and John Jennings, eds. *Out of Sequence: Underrepresented Voices in American Comics*. Seattle: University of Washington Press, 2009.

Duin, Steve. "Mark Schultz." *The Oregonian*, February 26, 2008. http://blog.oregonlive.com/steveduin/2008/02/mark_schultz.html.

Durrant, Sabine. "Posy Simmonds: The Invisible Woman." *The Telegraph*, October 21, 2007. http://www.telegraph.co.uk/culture/books/3668684/Posy-Simmonds-the-invisible-woman.html.

Eisenstein, Paul. "Imperfect Masters: Rabbinic Authority in Joann Sfar's *The Rabbi's Cat*." In *The Jewish Graphic Novel: Critical Approaches*, edited by Samantha Baskind and Ranen Omer-Sherman. New Brunswick, N.J.: Rutgers University Press, 2008.

Eisner, Will, Frank Miller, and Charles Brownstein. *Eisner/Miller: A One-on-One Interview*. Milwaukie, Ore: Dark Horse Books, 2005.

Eisner, Will. "Comic and the New Literary: An Essay." *Inks: Cartoon and Comic Art Studies* 1, no. 2 (May, 1994): 2-5.

———. *Comics and Sequential Art: Principles and Practices from the Legendary Cartoonist*. New York: W. W. Norton, 2008.

———. *Graphic Storytelling and Visual Narrative*. New York: W. W. Norton, 2008.

———. *A Pictorial Arsenal of America's Combat Weapons*. New York: Sterling, 1960.

———. *Will Eisner's Shop Talk*. Milwaukie, Ore.: Dark Horse Comics, 2001.

Elbow, Peter. *Writing Without Teachers*. 2d ed. New York: Oxford University Press, 1998.

Englemann, Jonas. "'Picture This': Disease and Autobiographic Narration in the Graphic Novels of David B and Julie Doucet." In *Comics as a Nexus of Cultures: Essays on the Interplay of Media, Disciplines, and International Perspectives*, edited by Mark Berninger, Jochen Ecke, and Gideon Haberkorn. Jefferson, N.C.: McFarland, 2010.

Estren, Mark James. *A History of Underground Comics*. 3d ed. Berkeley, Calif.: Ronin, 1993.

Feiffer, Jules. *Backing into Forward: A Memoir*. New York: Doubleday, 2010.

———. "The Jules Feiffer Interview." Interview by Gary Groth. *The Comics Journal* 124 (1988).

Feine, Donald. R., and Robert Crumb. *Crumb Checklist of Work and Criticism, with a Biographical Supplement and a Full Set of Indexes*. Cambridge, Mass.: Boatner Norton Press, 1981.

Feltman, Matthew. "Phantom Towers: Crypto-Towers Haunting Dave McKean's *Cages* and *Mirrormask*." *ImageTexT: Interdisciplinary Comics Studies* 4, no. 1 (2008). http://www.english.ufl.edu/imagetext/archives/v4_1/feltman.

———. "The Art of Dave McKean." Interview by Dan Epstein. *Underground Online*. http://www.ugo.com/channels/freestyle/features/davemckean/default.asp.

Femia, Christine. "Percy Gloom." Review of *Percy Gloom*, by Cathy Malkasian. *Bust* 46 (August/September, 2007): 100.

Fialkov, Joshua, Noel Tuazon, and Scott A. Keating. *Elk's Run Bumper Edition*. Toronto: Speakeasy Comics, 2005.

Fialkov, Joshua. "Bug Talks *Tumor* with Joshua Hale Fialkov!" Interview by Mike L. Miller. *Ain't It Cool News*, November 9, 2009. http://www.aintitcool.com/node/43012.

Fischer, Craig, and Charles Hatfield. "Teeth, Sticks, and Bricks: Calligraphy, Graphic Focalization, and Narrative Braiding in Eddie Campbell's *Alec*." *SubStance* 40, no. 1 (2011): 70-93.

Fiske, Amy. "Blankets." Review of *Blankets*, by Craig Thompson. *Journal of Adolescent and Adult Literacy* 48, no. 2 (October, 2004): 178-179.

Flagg, Gordon. "Blankets." Review of *Blankets*, by Craig Thompson. *Booklist*, June 1, 2003, p. 1724.

———. "Paul Goes Fishing." Review of *Paul Goes Fishing*, by Michel Rabagliati. *Booklist*, March 15, 2008.

———. "Shenzhen: A Travelogue from China." Review of *Shenzhen: A Travelogue from China*, by Guy Delisle. *Booklist* 102, no. 22 (August 1, 2006): 60.

———. "Story Behind the Story: Hernandez's *Palomar*." *The Booklist* 100, no. 11 (February 1, 2004): 963.

———. "Zot! 1987-1991." Review of *Zot!*, by Scott McCloud. *Booklist* 105, no. 1 (September 1, 2008): 62.

Fletcher-Spear, Kristin. Review of *Life Sucks* by Jessica Abel and Gabe Soria. *Library Media Connection* 27, no. 2 (October, 2008): 76-77.

Forsdick, Charles, Laurence Grove, and Libbie McQuillan, eds. *The Francophone Bande Dessinée*. New York: Rodopi, 2005.

Frauenfelder, Mark. "Moebius." *Wired*, 2009. http://wired.com/wired/archive/2.01/moebius.html.

Freedman, Ariela. "Drawing on Modernism in Alison Bechdel's *Fun Home*." *Journal of Modern Literature* 32, no. 4 (Summer, 2009): 126-140.

Freeman, Don. *Come One, Come All!* New York: Rinehart, 1949.

———. "Oral History Interview with Don Freeman, 1965 June 4." Interview by Betty Hoag. *Smithsonian Archives of American Art*. http://www.aaa.si.edu/collections/interviews/oral-history-interview-don-freeman-12155.

French, Scot. *The Rebellious Slave: Nat Turner in American Memory.* Boston: Houghton Mifflin, 2004.

Frey, Nancy, and Douglas Fisher. *Teaching Visual Literacy: Using Comic Books, Graphic Novels, Anime, Cartoons, and More to Develop Comprehension and Thinking Skills.* Thousand Oaks, Calif.: Corwin Press, 2008.

Frye, Northrop, and Alvin A. Lee. *The Great Code: The Bible and Literature.* Toronto: University of Toronto Press, 2006.

Furey, Emmett. "CCI Xtra: Spotlight on Linda Medley." *Comic Book Resources,* July 25, 2006. http://www.comicbookresources.com/?page=article&id=7689.

Fussell, Paul. *The Great War and Modern Memory.* Reprint. New York: Sterling, 2009.

Gabilliet, Jean-Paul, Bart Beaty, and Nick Nguyen, trans. *Of Comics and Men: A Cultural History of American Comic Books.* Jackson: University Press of Mississippi, 2010.

Gaiman, Neil. "It's Good to Be Gaiman: A Revealing Interview with Newbery Winner Neil Gaiman." Interview by Roger Sutton. *School Library Journal,* March 1, 2009. http://www.schoollibraryjournal.com/article/CA6640441.html.

Gallo, Don, and Stephen Weiner. "Bold Books for Innovative Teaching: Show, Don't Tell—Graphic Novels in the Classroom." *English Journal* 94, no. 2 (November, 2004): 114-117.

Gardner, Jared. "Autobiography's Biography, 1972-2007." *Biography* 31, no. 1 (Winter, 2008): 1-26.

Geary, Rick. "The Power of Old-Fashioned Storytelling." In *The Education of a Comics Artist: Visual Narrative in Cartoons, Graphic Novels, and Beyond,* edited by Michael Dooley and Steven Heller. New York: Allworth Press, 2005.

Geis, Deborah R., ed. *Considering Maus: Approaches to Art Spiegelman's "Survivors Tale" of the Holocaust.* Tuscaloosa: University of Alabama Press, 2007.

George, Milo, ed. *R. Crumb.* Seattle, Wash.: Fantagraphics Books, 2004.

George, Milo, ed. *The Comics Journal Library, Volume Two: Frank Miller.* Fantagraphics Books, 2003.

Gilbert, Michael T., and Ken Quattro. "It Rhymes with Lust." *The Comics Journal* 277 (July, 2006): 78.

Gilland, Blue. "30 Days of Night/Tim Lebbon." Review of *30 Days of Night* by Steve Niles. *Dark Scribe Magazine,* October 22, 2007. Available at http://www.darkscribemagazine.com/reviews/30-days-of-night-tim-lebbon.html

Gipi. "Taken from Life: An Interview with Gipi." Interview by Nicole Rudick. *Words without Borders* (February, 2008). http://wordswithoutborders.org/article/taken-from-life-an-interview-with-gipi.

Goldsmith, Francisca. "*Percy Gloom.*" Review of *Percy Gloom,* by Cathy Malkasian. *Booklist* 103, no. 17 (May 1, 2007): 80.

_____. *The Readers' Advisory Guide to Graphic Novels.* Chicago: American Library Association, 2010.

Gonick, Larry. "Cartoon Larry Gonick—Curriculum Vitae." http://www.larrygonick.com/html/cv/cv.html.

_____. Interview by Matthew Surridge. *The Comics Journal* 224 (June, 2000): 34-68.

Goodman, George. "The Golem's Mighty Swing." Review of *The Golem's Mighty Swing* by James Sturm. *NINE: A Journal of Baseball History and Culture* 13, no. 1 (Fall, 2004): 149-151.

Gordon, Ian, Mark Jancovich, and Matthew P. McAllister. *Film and Comic Books.* Jackson: University Press of Mississippi, 2007.

Grammel, Scott. "Chester Brown: From the Sacred to the Scatological." *The Comics Journal* 135 (1990): 66-90.

Grant, Steven, and Stephen Mooney. *CSI: Crime Scene Investigation—Dying in the Gutters.* San Diego, Calif.: IDW, 2008.

Grant, Steven. "Permanent Damage: Issue 86." *Comic Book Resources,* May 7, 2003. http://www.comicbookresources.com/?page=article&id=14428.

Gravett, Paul. "Creator Profile: Nabiel Kanan." *Paul Gravett.* http://www.paulgravett.com/index.php/profiles/creator/nabiel_kanan.

_____. *Graphic Novels: Everything You Need to Know.* New York: Collins Designs, 2005

_____. "Posy Simmonds: A Literary Life." *The Comics Journal* 286 (November, 2007): 26-67.

_____. "'Where Is the Use of a Book Without Pictures or Conversations?' Coming to Terms with the Graphic Novel in Europe." *Third Text* 21, no. 5 (September, 2007): 617-625.

Green, Justin. "Comics and Catholics: Mark Burbey Interviews Justin Green." Interview by Mark Burbey. *The Comics Journal* 104 (January, 1986): 37-49.

Greenberg, Kenneth S., ed. *The Confessions of Nat Turner and Related Documents*. Boston: Bedford/St. Martins, 1996.

_____. *Nat Turner: A Slave Rebellion in History and Memory*. New York: Oxford University Press, 2003.

Grenville, Bruce, et al., eds. *Krazy! The Delirious World of Anime and Comics and Video Games and Art*. Berkeley: University of California Press, 2008.

Griffith, Paula E. "Graphic Novels in the Secondary Classroom and School Libraries." *Journal of Adolescent and Adult Literacy* 54 (November, 2010): 181-189.

Groensteen, Thierry. *The System of Comics*. Translated by Bart Beaty and Nick Nyugen. Jackson: University of Mississippi Press, 2007.

Groenwegen, David. "Royals Amok." *The Comics Journal* 218 (December, 1999): 31.

Gross, Milt, and Ari Y. Kelman. *Is Dis a System? A Milt Gross Comic Reader*. New York: New York University Press, 2009.

Gross, Milt, and Craig Yoe. *The Complete Milt Gross Comic Books and Life Story*. San Diego, Calif.: IDW, 2010.

Gross, Seymour L., and Eileen Bender. "History, Politics, and Literature: The Myth of Nat Turner." *American Quarterly* 23, no. 4 (October, 1971): 487-518.

Groth, Gary. Afterword to *Blackmark Thirtieth Anniversary Edition*. Milwaukie, Ore.: Fantagraphics Books, 2002.

_____. "Preface to Mid-Life Creative Imperatives (Part 1 of 3)." *The Comics Journal*, February 24, 2010. http://www.tcj.com/history/preface-to-independent-spirits-a-comics-perspective-part-1-of-3.

Grove, Lawrence. *Comics in French: The European Bande Dessinée in Context*. New York: Berghahn Books, 2010.

Guillain, Charlotte. *Neil Gaiman: Rock Star Writer*. Chicago: Raintree, 2011.

Gustines, George Gene. "Graphic Memories of Katrina's Ordeal." *The New York Times*, August 23, 2009, p. C1.

_____. "Hurricane Katrina: An Illustrated Story of Survival." Interview by Linda Wertheimer. National Public Radio, September 3, 2009. http://www.npr.org/templates/story/story.php?storyId=112506242.

_____. "A Quirky Superhero of the Comics Trade." *The New York Times*, November, 2006, 1-2.

Hajdu, David. *Heroes and Villains: Essays on Music, Movies, Comics, and Culture*. Cambridge, Mass.: Da Capo Press, 2009.

_____. "Joe Sacco and Daniel Clowes." In *Heroes and Villains: Essays on Music, Movies, Comics, and Culture*. Cambridge, Mass.: Da Capo Press, 2009.

Hamilton, Patrick. "Lost in Translation: Jessica Abel's *La Perdida*, the Bildungsroman, and 'That "Mexican" Feel.'" In *Multicultural Comics: From Zap to Blue Beetle*. Edited by Frederick Luis Aldama. Austin: University of Texas Press, 2010.

Hannon, Gerald. "Retro Man." *Toronto Life*, November 29, 2010, p. 1-5. http://www.torontolife.com/features/retro-man.

Harde, Roxanne. "'Give 'Em Another Circumcision': Jewish Masculinities in *The Golem's Mighty Swing*." In *The Jewish Graphic Novel: Critical Approaches*, edited by Samantha Baskind and Ranen Omer-Sherman. New Brunswick, N.J.: Rutgers University Press, 2008.

Harford, James J. *Korolev: How One Man Masterminded the Soviet Drive to Beat America to the Moon*. New York: Wiley, 1999.

Harris, Marla. "Borderlands: Places, Spaces, and Jewish Identity in Joann Sfar's *The Rabbi's Cat* and *Klezmer*." In *The Jewish Graphic Novel: Critical Approaches*, edited by Samantha Baskind and Ranen Omer-Sherman. New Brunswick, N.J.: Rutgers University Press, 2008.

_____. "Sex and the City: The Graphic Novel Series *Aya* as West African Comedy of Manners." *International Journal of Comic Art* 11, no. 2 (Fall, 2009): 119-135.

Harris, Miriam. "Cartoonists as Matchmakers: The Vibrant Relationship of Text and Image in the Work of Lynda Barry." In *Elective Affinities: Testing Word and Image Relationships*, edited by C. MacLeod and V. Plesch, eds. New York: Rodopi Press, 2009.

Harvey, Robert C. *The Art of the Comic Book: An Aesthetic History*. Jackson: University Press of Mississippi, 1996.

_____. "The Comic Book as Individual Expression: Harvey Kurtzman and the Revolution." In *The Art* of the Comic Book: An Aesthetic History*. Jackson: University Press of Mississippi, 1997.

_____. "Milt Gross: *Banana Oil* and the First Graphic Novel?" *The Comics Journal*, November 10, 2010. http://classic.tcj.com/top-stories/milt-gross-banana-oil-and-the-first-graphic-novel.

Hassell, Bravetta. "The Bold Outlines of a Plot." *The Washington Post*, July 16, 2006, p. D01.

Hatfield, Charles. *Alternative Comics: An Emerging Literature*. Jackson: University Press of Mississippi, 2005.

_____. "The Autobiographical Stories in *Yummy Fur*." *The Comics Journal* 210 (1999): 67.

_____. "Graphic Interventions: Form and Argument in Contemporary Comics." Ph.D. diss., University of Connecticut, 2000.

_____. "ImageSexT: A Roundtable on *Lost Girls*, A Review and a Response." *ImageTexT: Interdisciplinary Comics Studies* 3, no. 3 (2007).

_____. "The Presence of the Artist: Kim Deitch's *The Boulevard of Broken Dreams* Vis-à-Vis the Animated Cartoons." *ImageTexT: Interdisciplinary Comics Studies* 1, no. 1 (2004).

Hedges, Chris. "What War Looks Like." Review of *The Photographer: Into War-Torn Afghanistan with Doctors Without Borders*, by Didier Lefèvre and Emmanuel Guibert. *The New York Times*, May 24, 2009, BR5.

Heer, Jeet, and Kent Worcester. *A Comics Studies Reader*. Jackson: University Press of Mississippi, 2009.

Heer, Jeet. "The Incomplete Milt Gross." *The Comics Journal*, April 12, 2010. http://classic.tcj.com/history/the-incomplete-milt-gross.

Helford, Elyce Rae. "Postfeminism and the Female Action-Adventure Hero: Positioning Tank Girl." In *Future Females, The Next Generation: New Voices and Velocities in Feminist Science Fiction Criticism*, edited by Marleen S. Barr. Lanham, Md.: Rowman & Littlefield, 2000.

Herman, Daniel. *Gil Kane: Art and Interviews*. Neshannock, Pa.: Hermes Press, 2002.

Hernandez, Gilbert, Jaime Hernandez, and Mario Hernandez. "Pleased to Meet Them: The Hernandez Bros. Interview." Interview by Gary Groth, Robert Fiore, and Thom Powers. *The Comics Journal* 126 (January, 1989): 60-113.

Hernandez, Gilbert, and Jaime Hernandez. "The Hernandez Brothers." Interview by Neil Gaiman. *The Comics Journal* 178 (July, 1995): 91-123.

Hernandez, Gilbert. "*Palomar* and Beyond: An Interview with Gilbert Hernandez." Interview by Derek Parker Royal. *MELUS* 32, no. 3 (Fall, 2007): 221-246.

_____. "Gilbert Hernandez's *Palomar*." Interview by Heidi MacDonald. *Publishers Weekly* 250, no. 42 (October 20, 2003): S12.

_____. "Palomar and Beyond: An Interview with Gilbert Hernandez." Interview by Derek Parker Royal. *MELUS* 32, no. 3 (Fall, 2007): 221-246.

Hernandez, Jaime, and Gilbert Hernandez. *Ten Years of Love and Rockets*. Seattle: Fantagraphics Books, 1992.

Herodotus. *The Histories*. Translated by Aubrey de Sélincourt, revised by John M. Marincola. New York: Penguin Books, 1996.

Hignite, Todd. *The Art of Jaime Hernandez: The Secrets of Life and Death*. New York: Abrams ComicArts, 2010.

_____. "Daniel Clowes." *In the Studio: Visits with Contemporary Cartoonists*. New Haven, Conn.: Yale University Press, 2006.

_____. *In the Studio: Visits with Contemporary Cartoonists*. New Haven, Conn.: Yale University Press, 2007.

Hirsch, Marianne. "Editor's Column: Collateral Damage." *PLA* 119, no. 5 (October, 2004): 1209-1215.

Hitz, Frederick Porter. *The Great Game: The Myths and Reality of Espionage*. New York: Vintage Books, 2005.

Hoberman, J. "Gaslight: Ben Katchor's New Graphic Novel Is Set in a Shadowy New York of the 1830's." *The New York Times*, January 10, 1999. http://www.nytimes.com/books/99/01/10/reviews/990110.10hobermt.html.

_____. "Harvey Kurtzman's Hysterical Materialism." In *Masters of American Comics*, edited by John Carlin, Paul Karasik, and Brian Walker. Los Angeles: Hammer Museum and the Museum of Contemporary Art, 2005.

Hogan, John. "Cannon Fodder." *Graphic Novel Reporter*. http://graphicnovelreporter.com/content/cannon-fodder-interview.

Holm, D. K.. *Robert Crumb*. North Pomfret, Vt.: Pocket Essentials, 2005.

Horrocks, Dylan. "Sweeping Out the Lighthouse: An Interview with Dylan Horrocks." Interview by Tom Spurgeon. *The Comics Journal* 243 (May, 2002).

Horsley, Lee. *The Noir Thriller*. New York: Palgrave Macmillan, 2009.

Howard, Elise. "Neil Gaiman." *Horn Book Magazine* 85, no. 6 (November/December, 2009): 351-354.

Huxley, David. *Nasty Tales: Sex, Drugs, Rock 'n' Roll, and Violence in the British Underground*. Manchester, England: Critical Vision, 2001.

Imlah, Mick. "Tamara Drewe's Wessex." *The Times Literary Supplement*, November, 2007.

Irvine, Louise. *The Snowman Collector's Book*. Somerset, England: Richard Dennis, 2004.

Irving, Christopher. "Keeping Current with Joe Kubert." *Graphic NYC*, June 22, 2009. http://graphicnyc.blogspot.com/2009/03/keeping-current-with-joe-kubert.html.

_____. "Kim Deitch: A Novel Approach." *NYC Graphic*, January 5, 2010.

Jackson, Anna, and Jane Stafford. "Introduction: The Gaming Halls of the Imagination." In *Floating Worlds: Essays on Contemporary New Zealand Fiction*, edited by Anna Jackson and Jane Stafford. Wellington, New Zealand: Victoria University Press, 2009.

Jackson, Tom, and Emily S. Rueb. "From Dutch to Drawings." *The New York Times*, December 28, 2009. http://www.nytimes.com/interactive/2009/12/28/nyregion/200912-MOHAWK-ILLOS.html

Jansen, Sharon L. *Reading Women's Worlds from Christine de Pizan to Doris Lessing: A Guide to Six Centuries of Women Imagining Rooms of Their Own*. New York: Palgrave Macmillan, 2011.

Jason. "Interview with Jason." Interview by D. J. Douresseau. *Comic Book Bin*, June 15, 2004. http://www.comicbookbin.com/charlie32.html.

_____. "The Jason Interview." Interview by Matthias Wivel. *The Comics Journal* 294 (December, 2008): 28-77.

_____. "A Short Interview with Jason." Interview by Tom Spurgeon. *The Comics Reporter*, January 27, 2007. http://www.comicsreporter.com/index.php/resources/interviews/7393.

Jeffery, Keith. *The Secret History of MI6*. New York: Penguin, 2010.

Jeffrey, David Lyle, ed. *A Dictionary of Biblical Tradition in English Literature*. Grand Rapids, Mich.: W. B. Eerdmans, 2009.

Johnson, Charles. "Foreword: A Capsule History of Blacks in Comics." In *Still I Rise: A Graphic History of African Americans*, by Roland Laird, Taneshia Nash Laird, and Elihu Bey. New York: Sterling, 2009.

Johnson, Nicholas. *Big Dead Place: Inside the Strange and Menacing World of Antarctica*. Los Angeles: Feral House, 2005.

Johnson, R. Kikuo. "R. Kikuo Johnson Interview." Interview by Gary Groth. *The Comics Journal* 277 (July, 2006): 176.

Johnston, W. Robert. "Splash Panel Adventures!" *Smithsonian Studies in American Art* 3, no. 3 (Summer, 1989): 38-53.

Jones, Gerard, and Will Jacobs. *The Comic Book Heroes*. Rocklin, Calif.: Prima Books, 1997.

Jones, Malcolm. "New York's Comic-Book Hero." *Newsweek*, February 27, 2011. http://www.newsweek.com/2011/02/27/new-york-s-comic-book-hero.html.

Jones, Nicolette. *Raymond Briggs: Blooming Books*. London: Jonathan Cape, 2003.

Josipovici, Gabriel. Introduction to *Collected Stories*, by Franz Kafka. New York: A. A. Knopf, 1993.

Jourdain, Bill. "Comics' First Great African American Artist." *Golden Age of Comic Books*, June 17, 2009. http://goldenagecomics.org/wordpress/2009/06/17/comics-then-5-comics-first-great-african-american-artist.

Juneau, Thomas, and Mira Sucharov. "Narratives in Pencil: Using Graphic Novels to Teach Israeli-Palestinian Relations." *International Studies Perspectives* 11, no. 2 (May, 2010): 172-183.

Juno, Andrea. "Chester Brown." In *Dangerous Drawings: Interviews with Comix and Graphix Artists*. New York: Juno Books, 1997.

Kacyzne, Alter, and Marek Web. *Poyln: Jewish Life in the Old Country*. New York: Henry Holt, 2001.

Kafka, Franz. *The Great Wall of China, and Other Short Works*. Edited and translated by Malcolm Pasley. London: Penguin Books, 2002.

Kahn, Ariel. "Between Eros and Thanatos: Death and Desire in the Short Fiction of Koren Shadmi and Rutu Modan." *International Journal of Comic Art* 12, no. 1 (Spring, 2010): 157-182.

_____. "From Darkness into Light: Reframing Notions of Self and Other in Contemporary Israeli Graphic Narratives." In *The Jewish Graphic Novel: Critical Approaches*, edited by Samantha Baskind and Ranen Omer-Sherman. New Brunswick, N.J.: Rutgers University Press, 2008.

Kakutani, Michiko. "A Romantic Like Emma, Trapped in the Bourgeoisie." *The New York Times*, January 28, 2005. http://www.nytimes.com/2005/01/28/books/28book.html.

Kane, Gil. "Interview with Gil Kane, Part 1." *The Comics Journal* 186 (April, 1996): 88

Kanter, Albert. *Classics Illustrated*. New York: Gilberton, 1941-1971.

Kaplan, Arie. *From Krakow to Krypton: Jews and Comic Books*. Philadelphia: Jewish Publication Society, 2008.

_____. *Masters of the Comic Book Universe Revealed!* Chicago: Chicago Review Press, 2006.

Karasik, Paul. "Coffee with Paul Karasik." Interview by Bill Kartalopoulos. *Indy Magazine*, Spring, 2004. http://www.indyworld.com/indy/spring_2004/karasik_interview/index.html.

Katchor, Ben. "Ben Katchor." Interview by Alexander Theroux. *BOMB* 88 (Summer, 2004). http://bombsite.com/issues/88/articles/2668.

Katin, Miriam. "In Plain Sight." *World Literature Today* 81, no. 6 (November/December, 2007): 14-18.

Kessler, Peter. *The Complete Guide to Asterix*. London: Hodder Children's Books, 1995.

Khoury, George, ed. *The Extraordinary Works of Alan Moore*. Raleigh, N.C.: TwoMorrows, 2008.

Kilborn, Richard W. *Multimedia Melting Pot: Marketing "When the Wind Blows."* London: Comedia, 1986.

Kim, Ann. "Graphic Grown Up." *Library Journal* 134, no. 13 (August, 2009): 20-22.

Kim, Dong Hwa. "The Colors of Kim Dong Hwa: The 'Color' Trilogy." Interview by Michael C. Lorah. *Newsarama*, April 16, 2009. http://www.newsarama.com/comics/040916-Colors-First-SecondA.html.

Kitchen, Denis, and Paul Buhle. *The Art of Harvey Kurtzman: The Mad Genius of Comics*. New York: Abrams ComicArts, 2009.

Kitchen, Denis. "'Man, I'm Beat': Harvey Kurtzman's Frustrating Post-*Humbug* Freelance Career." *Comic Art* 7 (Winter, 2005): 3-16.

Koelling, Holly, and Betty Carter. *Best Books for Young Adults*. 3d ed. Chicago: American Library Association, 2007.

Korea Culture and Content Agency. *Manhwa: Another Discovery in Asian Comics*. Seoul: Communication Books, 2007.

_____. *Manhwa 100: A New Era for Korean Comics*. Seoul: C&C Revolution, 2008.

Koslowski, Rich. "Rich Koslowski Counts Down to *Three Fingers*: *3 Geeks* Creator Tackles an Animation Icon." Interview by Beau Yarbrough. *Comic Book Resources*, May 6, 2002. http://www.comicbookresources.com/?page=article&id=1114.

Kreiner, Rich. "Lust for Life, Man! Twenty-Five Years of Eddie Campbell." *The Comics Journal* 220 (February, 2000): 45-56.

Krich, John. "Cartoonists—Malaysia: Lats of Laughs." *Far Eastern Economic Review*, April 15, 2004, p. 40.

Kuper, Peter. "This Is Not a Comic Book: Jarret Lovell Interviews Graphic Artist Peter Kuper." Interview by Jarret Lovell. *Crime Media Culture* 2 (April, 2006): 75-83.

_____. *Speechless*. Marietta, Ga.: Top Shelf Productions, 2001.

Kyler, Carolyn. "Mapping a Life: Reading and Looking at Contemporary Graphic Memoir." *The CEA Critic* 72, no. 3 (Spring/Summer, 2010): 2-20.

Lamm, Spencer, et al. *The Matrix Comics*. Brooklyn, N.Y.: Burlyman, 2003.

Lees, Gavin. "Graphic Youth: *Louis: Night Salad* by Metaphrog." Review of *Louis: Night Salad*, by John Chalmers and Sandra Marrs. *The Comics Journal*, February 21, 2011. http://classic.tcj.com/alternative/louis-night-salad-by-Metaphrog.

Lehmann-Haupt, Christopher. "Mum, Dad, and Not Always So Merry Old England." *The New York Times*, September 23, 1999.

Lemberg, Jennifer. "Closing the Gap in Alison Bechdel's *Fun Home*." *Women's Studies Quarterly* 36, nos. 1/2 (2008): 129-140.

Lent, John A. "Cartooning in Malaysia and Singapore: The Same, but Different." *International Journal of Comic Art* 5, no. 1 (Spring, 2003): 256-289.

_____. "Out of Africa: The Saga of Exiled Cartoonists in Europe." *Scan: Journal of Media Arts Culture* 5, no. 2 (September, 2008).

_____. "The Varied Drawing Lots of Lat, Malaysian Cartoonist." *The Comics Journal* 211 (April, 1999): 35-39.

Leong, Tim. Interview with Brian K. Vaughan. *Comic Foundry*, July 6, 2006. Available at http://comicfoundry.com/?p=1522.

Lesk, Andrew. "Redrawing Nationalism: Chester Brown's *Louis Riel: A Comic-Strip Biography*." *Journal of Graphic Novels and Comics* 1, no. 1 (June, 2010): 63-81.

Levin, Bob. "Good Ol' Chester Brown: A Psycho-Literary Exploration of *Yummy Fur*." *The Comics Journal* 162 (1993): 45-49.

_____. *Outlaws, Rebels, Freethinkers, and Pirates: Essays on Cartoons and Cartoonists*. Seattle: Fantagraphics Books, 2005.

_____. "Rice, Beans, and Justin Greens." *The Comics Journal* 203 (April, 1998): 101-107.

Levy, Ariel. "*Cancer Vixen: A True Story*." Review of *Cancer Vixen: A True Story*, Marisa Acocella Marchetto. *The New York Times Book Review*, October 22, 2006, 30.

Ligotti, Thomas, Stuart Moore, and Joe Harris. *The Nightmare Factory*. New York: Harper Paperbacks, 2007.

Lindenmuth, Brian. "The Fall (and Rise) of the Crime Comic." *Mulholland Books*, December 14, 2010. http://www.mulhollandbooks.com/2010/12/14/a-history-of-and-appreciation-for-crime-comics.

Ling, Chuan-Yao, and David Shook. "*Shenzhen: A Travelogue from China*." *World Literature Today* 81, no. 2 (March/April, 2007): 65.

Lister, Sam. "Playgrounds, Gardens, Communities, Worlds: Dylan Horrocks's *Hicksville*." *Journal of New Zealand Literature* 25 (2007): 138-163.

Little, Jason. "An Interview with Jason Little." Interview by Mark Bryant. *Popimage*, Fall, 1999. http://www.beecomix.com/comics/infoframes.htm.

Locke, Vince. "Interview by Will Colling for The Nexus," August 5, 2005. http://insidepulse.com/2005/08/05/39887.

_____. *Visions: Drawings and Paintings*. Plymouth, Mich.: Caliber Press, 1992.

"Lost Girl." Review of *Lost Girl*, by Nabiel Kanan. *Publishers Weekly*, January 1, 2003. http://www.publishersweekly.com/978-1-56163-229-9.

Lukich, Mike. "Ice Haven," *PopMatters*, February 6, 2006. http://www.popmatters.com/comics/ice-haven.shtml.

Lutes, Jason. "Back to the City: Jason Lutes on Berlin 2." Interview by Michael C. Lorah. *Newsarama*, October 1, 2008. http://www.newsarama.com/comics/100801-Berlin2.html

_____. "Walrus Comix Presents: An Exclusive Interview with Artist Extraordinaire, Missoula, Montana's Comix Laureate Jason Lutes." *Walrus Comix*. http://www.walruscomix.com/interviewlutes.html.

Lutes, Jean M. "Lynching Coverage and the American Reporter-Novelist." *American Literary History* 19, no. 2 (Summer, 2007): 456-481.

Lyga, Allyson A. W., and Barry Lyga. *Graphic Novels in Your Media Center: A Definitive Guide*. Westport, Conn.: Libraries Unlimited, 2004.

MacDonald, Heidi. "Image Comics Has New Kirkman Imprint." *Publishers Weekly* 257, no. 32 (August, 2010): 9.

_____. "Image Takes a 'Chance'." *Publishers Weekly* 249, no. 37 (2002): 34.

Maeots, Olga. "Behind the Wall Under the Red Star." *Bookbird: A Journal of International Children's Literature* 47, no. 3 (July, 2009): 46-53.

Malek, Amy. "Memoir as Iranian Exile Cultural Production: A Case Study of Marjane Satrapi's *Persepolis* Series." *Iranian Studies* 39, no. 3 (2006): 353-380.

Mangum, Teresa, and K. Corey Creekmur. "A Graphic Novel Depicting War as an Interspecies Event: *Pride of Baghdad*." *Society and Animals* 15, no. 4 (2007): 405-408.

Manning, Shaun. "Justin Green on *Binky Brown*." *Comic Book Resources*, January 22, 2010. http://www.comicbookresources.com/?page=article&id=24518.

_____. "Ricardo Delgado on *Age of Reptiles: The Journey*." Comic Book Resources, September 18, 2009. http://www.comicbookresources.com/?page=article&id=22978.

_____. "Ryall vs. *Zombies Vs. Robots: Adventure*." *Comic Book Resources*, December 9, 2009. http://www.comicbookresources.com/?page=article&id=23991.

Mansfield, Natasha. "Loss and Mourning: Cinema's 'Language' of Trauma in *Waltz with Bashir*." *Wide Screen* 2, no. 1 (June, 2010).

Marchetto, Marisa Acocella. *Cancer Vixen*. *Glamour*, August, 2006. http://www.glamour.com/health-fitness/2006/08/cancer-vixen-cartoon.

Marcus, Leonard S. "The Cold War Kid." Review of *The Wall: Growing Up Behind the Iron Curtain*, by Peter Sís. *The New York Times Book Review*, November 11, 2007. http://www.nytimes.com/2007/11/11/books/review/Marcus-t.html.

Marshall, Monica. *Joe Sacco*. New York: Rosen, 2005.

Martindale, Kathleen. "Back to the Future with *Dykes to Watch Out For* and *Hothead Paisan*." In *Un/popular Culture: Lesbian Writing After the Sex Wars*. Albany: State University of New York, 1997.

Matt, Joe. "Interview with Joe Matt." Interview by Christopher Brayshaw. *Comics Journal* 183 (January, 1996): 47-75.

Maughan, Shannon. "*Pedro and Me*." Review of *Pedro and Me*, by Judd Winick. *Publishers Weekly* 247, no. 38 (September 1, 2000): 37.

Mazzucchelli, David. Interview by Frank Young. *Comics Journal* 152 (August, 1992): 114-119.

_____. "Three Questions for David Mazzucchelli." Interview by Bill Kartalopoulos. *Indy Magazine*, Spring, 2004. http://www.indyworld.com/indy/spring_2004/mazzucchelli_interview/index.html.

McCabe, Joseph. *Hanging out with the Dream King: Conversations with Neil Gaiman and His Collaborators*. Seattle: Fantagraphics Books, 2004.

McCarthy, Tom. *Tintin and the Secret of Literature*. London: Granta Books, 2006.

McCloud, Scott. "Introduction." In *Larry Marder's Beanworld Book 1: Wahoolazuma!* Milwaukie, Ore.: Dark Horse Books, 2009.

McCloud, Scott. *Making Comics: Storytelling Secrets of Comics, Manga, and Graphic Novels*. New York: Harper, 2006.

_____. *Understanding Comics: The Invisible Art*. New York: HarperPerennial, 2010.

McElhatton, Greg. "My Mommy Is in America and She Met Buffalo Bill." Review of *My Mommy Is in America and She Met Buffalo Bill*, by Jean Regnaud. *Read About Comics*, February 18, 2009. http://www.readaboutcomics.com/2009/02/18/my-mommy-is-in america.

McGovern, Celeste. "You've Come a Long Way, Baby." *Alberta Report/Newsmagazine* 22, no. 33 (July, 1995): 24.

McInnes, Gavin. "Gavin McInnes Explains Dave Cooper." *Juxtapoz* 113 (June, 2010): 132-142.

McIntee, David. *Beautiful Monsters: The Unofficial and Unauthorized Guide to the Alien and Predator Films*. Surrey, England: Telos, 2005.

McKean, Dave, and Neil Gaiman. *Dustcovers: The Collected Sandman Covers, 1989-1997*. New York: Vertigo, 1998.

McKean, Dave. "Dave McKean on *Arkham Asylum* and *Cages*." Interview. *Comics Career* 2, no. 1 (1990). http://www.comicscareer.com/?page_id=55.

McKeever, Ted. "Finishing *Transit* and More—Talking to Ted McKeever." Interview by Vaneta Rogers. *Newsarama*, September 18, 2008. http://www.newsarama.com/comics/090818-TedMcKeever.html.

McKinney, Mark, ed. *History and Politics in French Language Comics and Graphic Novels*. Jackson: University Press of Mississippi, 2008.

_____. *History and Politics in French-Language Comics and Graphic Novels*. Jackson: University Press of Mississippi, 2008.

Medley, Linda. "Linda Medley Interview." Interview by Eric Evans. *The Comics Journal* 218 (December, 1999): 93-105.

Medley, Mark. "Bryan Lee O'Malley's Finest Hour." *National Post*, July 20, 2010. http://arts.nationalpost.com/2010/07/20/bryan-lee-omalleys-finest-hour.

Mescallado, Ray. "Easy Comparisons." *The Comics Journal* 182 (November, 1995): 99-102.

Messner-Loebs, William. "Bill Messner-Loebs: A Career Retrospective (Part I)." Interview by Darren Schroeder. *Comics Bulletin*. http://www.comicsbulletin.com/storytelling/95852385995680.htm.

Mikkonen, Kai. "Presenting Minds in Graphic Narratives." *Partial Answers: Journal of Literature and the History of Ideas* 6, no. 2 (June, 2008): 301-321.

Miller, Ann. *Reading Bande Dessinée: Critical Approaches to French-Language Comic Strip*. Chicago: Intellect Books, 2007.

Miller, Ann, and Murray Pratt. "Transgressive Bodies in the Work of Julie Doucet, Fabrice Neaud, and Jean-Christophe Menu: Towards a Theory of the AutobioBD." *Belphegor: Popular Literature and Media Culture* 4, no. 1 (November, 2004).

Miller, Frank, and Hal Schuster. *Frank Miller*. San Bernardino, Calif.: Borgo Press, 1986.

Millidge, Gary Spencer, and Smoky Man, eds. *Alan Moore: Portrait of an Extraordinary Gentleman*. Marietta, Ga.: Top Shelf Productions, 2003.

Milliken, Joe. "Just Like Magic: The Center for Cartoon Studies Publishes Its First Graphic Novel." *Vermont Guardian*, April 27, 2007. http://www.vermontguardian.com/culture/042007/Cartoon-Studies.shtml.

Modan, Rutu. "An Interview with Rutu Modan." Interview by Joe Sacco. *The Comics Journal,* no. 288 (February, 2008): 29-38.

Moffett, Matthew L. "Buddy Does Seattle." *School Library Journal* 51, no. 9 (September, 2005): 242.

Moltenbray, Karen. "Witches' Brew: Mainframe Entertainment Mixes Up a Wide Range of Graphic Styles to Create a Unique Look for *Scary Godmother*." *Computer Graphics World* 26, no. 10 (October, 2003).

Montero, Patrick. "Comic Book Artist Jeffrey Brown: More Than Meets the Eye." *New York Daily News*, November 1, 2007. http://articles.nydailynews.com/2007-11-01/entertainment/17905837_1_comics-fantagraphics-graphic-novel.

Moody, Rick. "*Epileptic*: Disorder in the House." *The Best American Comics Criticism*. Edited by Ben Schwartz. Seattle, Wash.: Fantagraphics Books, 2010.

Moore, Alan. "Alan Moore Interview." Interview by Brad Stone. Comic Book Resources, October 22, 2001. http://www.comicbookresources.com/?page=article&id=511.

_____. *From Hell: The Compleat Scripts*. Falston, Md.: Bordlerlands Press, 2000.

Moore, Anne Elizabeth, ed. *The Best American Comics 2007*. Boston: Houghton Mifflin, 2007.

Moore, Stuart. "Graphic Violence: A Talented New Generation of Writers Brings Crime to the Comics." *Mystery Scene* 77 (2002): 32-35.

Moore, Terry. "The Terry Moore Interview." Interview by Dirk Deppey. *The Comics Journal* 276 (May, 2006): 60.

Morgenstern, Karl. "On the Nature of the Bildungsroman." Translated by Tobias Boes. *PMLA: Publications of the Modern Language Association of America* 124, no. 2 (March, 2009): 647-659.

Morris, Janice. "Suspended Animation." Review of *Exit Wounds*, by Rutu Modan. *Canadian Literature* 197 (Summer, 2008): 166-167.

Mozaffari, Nahid. Review of *Journey from the Land of No*, *Lipstick Jihad*, and *Embroideries*. *Women's Studies Quarterly* 34, nos. 1/2 (Spring/Summer, 2006): 516-527.

Mullins, Katie. "Questioning Comics: Women and Autocritique in Seth's *It's a Good Life, If You Don't Weaken*." *Canadian Literature* 203 (Winter, 2009): 11-29.

Mulman, Lisa Naomi. "A Tale of Two Mice: Graphic Representations of the Jew in Holocaust Narrative." In *The Jewish Graphic Novel: Critical Approaches*, edited by Samantha Baskind and Ranen Omer-Sherman. Piscataway, N.J.: Rutgers University Press, 2010.

Murray, Mike. "Which Was More Important Sir, Ordinary People Getting Electricity or the Rise of Hitler? Using *Ethel and Ernest* with Year Nine." *Teaching History* 107 (June, 2002): 20-25.

Nashawaty, Chris. "Comix Trip." *Entertainment Weekly* 239 (September, 1994): 47.

National Commission on Terrorist Attacks upon the United States. *The 9/11 Commission Report: Final Report of the National Commission on Terrorist Attacks upon the United States*. New York: W. W. Norton, 2004.

Neace, Melissa. "*Pedro and Me: Friendship, Loss, and What I Learned*." Review of *Pedro and Me*, by Judd Winick. *Library Media Connection* 23, no. 7 (April/May, 2005): 54.

Nelson, Arvid. "Arvid Nelson talks *Rex Mundi*." Interview by David Press. *Comic Book Resources*, July 18, 2008. http://www.comicbookresources.com/?page=article&id=17297.

_____. "Nelson Talks *Rex Mundi* and Religion." Interview by Edward Carey. *Comic Book Resources*, September 17, 2008. http://www.comicbookresources.com/?page=article&id=18089.

Neufeld, Josh. "Post-Katrina Depicted in Comic Strips." Interview by Farai Chideya. National Public Radio, August 24, 2007. http://www.npr.org/templates/story/story.php?storyId=13928549.

Newman, Lee. "Trading Up: The Complete Essex County." *Broken Frontier*, January 13, 2010. http://www.brokenfrontier.com/lowdown/p/detail/trading-up-the-complete-essex-county.

Nilsen, Anders. "An Interview with Anders Nilsen." Interview by Matthew Baker. *Nashville Review* (April 1, 2011). http://www.vanderbilt.edu/english/nashvillereview/archives/1902.

Nolen-Weathington, Eric, and Kyle Baker. *Kyle Baker*. Modern Masters 20. Raleigh, N.C.: TwoMorrows, 2009.

Nolen-Weathington, Eric. *Charles Vess*. Modern Masters 11. New York: TwoMorrows, 2007.

_____. *Jeff Smith*. Modern Masters 25. New York: TwoMorrows, 2011.

Nye, Russell B. "*Asterix* Revisited." *Comics Journal* 72 (May, 1982): 59-65.

"O'Connor, George: *Journey into Mohawk Country*." *Kirkus Reviews* 74, no. 17 (September 1, 2006): 910.

O'English, Lorena, J. Gregory Matthews, and Elizabeth Blakesley Lindsay. "Graphic Novels in Academic Libraries: From *Maus* to Manga and Beyond." *The Journal of Academic Librarianship* 32, no. 2 (March, 2006): 173-182.

O'Malley, Bryan Lee. "Bryan Lee O'Malley." Interview by Jason Heller. *The Onion AV Club*, November 9, 2007. http://www.avclub.com/articles/bryan-lee-omalley,14171.

_____. *Scott Pilgrim and the Infinite Sadness*. Portland, Ore.: Oni, 2009.

Oakes, Kaya. *Slanted and Enchanted: The Evolution of Indie Culture*. New York: Henry Holt, 2009.

Oates, Stephen B. *The Fires of Jubilee: Nat Turner's Fierce Rebellion*. New York: Harper, 1975.

Oh, Sandra. "Sight Unseen: Adrian Tomine's *Optic Nerve* and the Politics of Recognition." *MELUS* 32, no. 3 (2007): 129-151.

Oklahoma History Center. "James Vance: Writer/Editor, Tulsa." *The Uncanny Adventures of Okie Cartoonists*. http://www.okiecartoonists.org/jvance.html.

Olsen, Stephen P. *The Library of Graphic Novelists: Neil Gaiman*. New York: Rosen, 2005.

Op de Beeck, Nathalie. "Found Objects: (Jem Cohen, Ben Katchor, Walter Benjamin)." *Modern Fiction Studies* 52, no. 4 (Winter, 2006): 807-831.

Orbán, Katalin. "Trauma and Visuality: Art Spiegelman's *Maus* and *In the Shadow of No Towers*." *Representations* 97 (Winter, 2007): 57-89.

Paparone, Lesley. "Art and Identity in Mark Kalesniko's Mail Order Bride." *MELUS* 32, no. 3 (Fall, 2007): 201-220.

Parille, Ken, and Isaac Cates, eds. *Daniel Clowes: Conversations*. Jackson: University Press of Mississippi, 2010.

Parille, Ken. "A Cartoon World." *Boston Review*, January/February, 2006.

_____. "What's This One About? A Re-Reader's Guide to Daniel Clowes's *David Boring*." In *Best American Comics Criticism*, edited by Ken Schwartz. Seattle, Wash.: Fantagraphics Books, 2010.

Pearl, Monica B. "Graphic Language: Redrawing the Family (Romance) in Alison Bechdel's *Fun Home*." *Prose Studies* 30, no. 3 (2008): 286-304.

Pedrosa, Cyril. "There's No Such Thing as a Graphic Novel." *First Second Books: Doodles and Dailies*, April 14, 2008. http://firstsecondbooks.typepad.com/mainblog/cyril_pedrosa_guest_blogger.

Pekar, Harvey. "*Maus* and Other Topics." *The Comics Journal* 113 (December, 1986): 54-57.

_____. Introduction to *The Best American Comics 2006*. Boston: Houghton Mifflin Harcourt, 2006.

"Percy Gloom." Review of *Percy Gloom*, by Cathy Malkasian. *Publishers Weekly* 254, no. 23 (June 4, 2007): 36.

"Percy Gloom." Review of *Percy Gloom*, by Cathy Malkasian. *Kirkus Reviews* 75, no. 12 (June 15, 2007): 8.

Petersen, Robert S. *Comics, Manga, and Graphic Novels: A History of Graphic Narratives*. Santa Barbara, Calif.: Praeger, 2011.

Phegley, Keil. "Emmanuel's Travels: Guibert Talks *Alan's War*." Comic Book Resources, May 8, 2009. http://comicbookresources.com?page=article&id=21146.

Phipps, Keith. "*Lost Girl*." Review of *Lost Girl*, by Nabiel Kanan. *A.V. Club*, March 29, 2002. http://www.avclub.com/articles/nabiel-kanan-lost-girl,6301.

Pilcher, Tim. *Erotic Comics 2: A Graphic History from the Liberated '70's to the Internet*. New York: Abrams, 2008.

Poodle, Amy. "Jim Woodring's FraAOOOO-OOOOOIIIIink: Detourning the Dream Factory." *Mindless Ones*, May 9, 2008. http://mindlessones.com/2008/05/09/fraaooooooooooiiiiink-detourning-the-dream-factory/#more-224.

Pope, Paul. *100%*. New York: DC Comics, 2005.

———. "Paul Pope Interview, Part 1." Interview by Ray Mescallado. *The Comics Journal* 191 (November, 1996): 98-118.

———. *Pulphope: The Art of Paul Pope*. Richmond, Va.: AdHouse Books, 2007.

Poplaski, Peter, ed. *The R. Crumb Coffee Table Art Book*. Boston: Little, Brown, 1997.

Porcellino, John. "A Comic Strip Interview with Comic Artist John Porcellino." Interview by Noah Van Sciver. *The Comics Journal* 299 (August, 2009): 14-16.

———. "Interview: John Porcellino." Interview by Jason Heller. *A.V. Club*, July, 2011. http://www.avclub.com/articles/john-porcellino,14096.

Postema, Barbara. "Mind the Gap: Absence as Signifying Function in Comics." Ph.D. dis., Michigan State University, 2010.

Publishers Weekly. Review of *The Curious Case of Benjamin Button: A Graphic Novel*, by Nunzio DeFilippis and Christina Weir. 255, no. 39 (2008): 65.

Publishers Weekly. "Shenzhen: A Travelogue from China." *Publishers Weekly* 253, no. 37 (September 18, 2006): 42.

Pulda, Molly. "The Grandmother Paradox: Mary McCarthy, Michael Ondaatje, and Marjane Satrapi." *A/B: Auto/Biography Studies* 22, no. 2 (Winter, 2007): 230-249.

Rabin, Nathan. "My Year of Flops Case File 24 *Mystery Men*." *A.V. Club*, April 17, 2007. http://www.avclub.com/articles/my-year-of-flops-case-file-24-mystery-men,15144.

Raeburn, Daniel K. *Chris Ware*. New Haven, Conn.: Yale University Press, 2004.

Raney, Vanessa. "Review of Charles Burns' *Black Hole*." *ImageTexT: Interdisciplinary Comics Studies* 2, no. 1 (2005).

Reed, Calvin. "More Comics from Disney—Duh." *Publishers Weekly* 252, no. 9 (February 28, 2005).

Repetti, Massimo. "African Wave: Specificity and Cosmopolitanism in African Comics." *African Arts* 40, no. 2 (June, 2007): 16-35.

Review of *Life Sucks* by Jessica Abel and Gabe Soria. *Publishers Weekly* 255, no. 8 (February 25, 2008): 59.

Rhode, Michael G., ed. *Harvey Pekar: Conversations*. Jackson: University Press of Mississippi, 2008.

Richards, Dave. "Joy of the Pride: Vaughan Talks *Pride of Baghdad*." *Comic Book Resources*, September 11, 2006. Available at http://www.comicbookresources.com/?page=article&id=8051

Rieff, David. "Bosnia Beyond Words." *The New York Times Book Review*, December 24, 2000. http://www.nytimes.com/2000/12/24/books/bosnia-beyond-words.html?scp=1&sq=Bosnia+Beyond+Words&st=cse&pagewanted=all.

Roback, Diane. "About Our Cover Artist." *Publishers Weekly* 254, no. 28 (2007): 1.

Robbins, Trina. *From Girls to Grrrlz: A History of Women's Comics from Teens to Zines*. San Francisco: Chronicle Books, 1999.

———. *The Great Women Cartoonists*. New York: Watson-Guptill, 2001.

Robinson, Alex. "Alex Robinson." Interview by Gavin J. Grant. *Indie Bound*. http://www.indiebound.org/author-interviews/robinsonalex.

———. "Alex Robinson Chat Transcript." Interview by Brian Cronin, Brandon Harvey, and Adam P. Knave. *Comic Book Resources*, September 8, 2008. http://goodcomics.comicbookresources.com/2008/09/08/alex-robinson-chat-transcript.

———. "The Alex Robinson Interview." Interview by Tom Crippen. *The Comics Journal* 293 (November, 2008): 64-99.

———. "Alex's Robinson's *Tricked*." Interview by Hilary Goldstein. *IGN*, March 17, 2005. http://comics.ign.com/articles/596/596989p1.html.

———. "New Tricks: An Interview with Alex Robinson." Interview by John Hogan. *Graphic Novel Reporter*. http://graphicnovelreporter.com/content/new-tricks-interview-alex-robinson-interview.

Robinson, James. Introduction to *Leave It to Chance: Monster Madness and Other Stories*. Orange, Calif.: Image Comics, 2003.

———. Introduction to *Leave It to Chance: Shaman's Rain*. Orange, Calif.: Image Comics, 2002.

Robinson, Tasha. "Bill Sienkiewicz: *Stray Toasters*." Review of *Stray Toasters*, by Bill Sienkiewicz. *A.V. Club*, October 14, 2003. http://www.avclub.com/articles/bill-sienkiewicz-stray-toasters,5404.

Romney, Jonathan. "Tanked Up on Attitude." *New Statesman and Society* 8, no. 358 (June, 1995): 35.

Rosa, Don. "Don Rosa Part 1." Interview by Dana Gabbard. *The Comics Journal* 183 (January, 1996): 82.

_____. *The Life and Times of Scrooge McDuck Companion*. Timonium, Md.: Gemstone, 2006.

Rosenblatt, Adam, and Andrea A. Lunsford. "Critique, Caricature, and Compulsion in Joe Sacco's Comics Journalism." In *The Rise of the American Comics Artist: Creators and Contexts*, edited by Paul Williams and James Lyons. Jackson: University Press of Mississippi, 2010.

Rosenkranz, Patrick. "The ABCs of Autobio Comix." *The Comics Journal* (March 6, 2011). http://www.tcj.com/the-abcs-of-auto-bio-comix-2.

_____. *Rebel Visions: The Underground Comix Revolution, 1963-1975*. Seattle, Wash.: Fantagraphics Books, 2002.

Roth, Laurence. "Drawing Contracts: Will Eisner's Legacy." *The Jewish Quarterly Review* 97, no. 3 (Summer, 2007): 463-484.

Royal, Derek Parker. "Sequential Sketches of Ethnic Identity: Will Eisner's *A Contract with God* as Graphic Cycle." *College Literature* 38, no. 3 (Summer, 2011): 150-167.

_____. "There Goes the Neighborhood: Cycling Ethnoracial Tension in Will Eisner's *Dropsie Avenue*." *Shofar* 29, no. 2 (Winter, 2011): 120-145.

Royal, Derek Parker. "To Be Continued ... : Serialization and Its Discontent in the Recent Comics of Gilbert Hernandez." *International Journal of Comic Art* 11, no. 1 (Spring, 2009): 262-280.

Rubenstein, Anne. "Matters of Conscience: A Howard Cruse Interview." *The Comics Journal* 182 (November, 1995): 106-118.

Rubin, Brian P. "*Richard Stark's Parker: The Hunter*." Review of *Richard Stark's Parker: The Hunter*, by Darwyn Cooke. *Graphic Novel Reporter*. http://www.graphicnovelreporter.com/content/richard-starks-parker-hunter-review.

Rugg, Jim. "Cecil Interviews *Plain Janes* Co-Creator Jim Rugg." Interview by Cecil Castellucci. *Newsarama*, May 18, 2007. http://blog.newsarama.com/2007/05/18/cecil-interviews-plain-janes-co-creator-jim-rugg.

_____. "Jim Rugg Aims to Catch Your Eye with *Plain Janes*." Interview by Arune Singh. *Comic Book Resources*, December 28, 2006. http://www.comicbookresources.com/?page=article&id=8952.

Runton, Andy. "Into the Woods: Andy Runton Talks 'Owly.'" Interview by Shaun Manning. *Comic Book Resources* (December 11, 2007). http://www.comicbookresources.com/?page=article&id=12132.

_____. "Declaration of Independents: Andy Runton." Interview by Karen Maeda. *Sequential Tart* (September, 2004). http://www.sequentialtart.com/archive/sept04/doi_0904.shtml.

_____. "What a Hoot: Runton Talks Owly." Interview by Justin Jordan. *Comic Book Resources* (February 23, 2007). http://www.comicbookresources.com/?page=article&id=9435.

Russell, Benjamin. Review of *The Curious Case of Benjamin Button: A Graphic Novel*, by Nunzio DeFilippis and Christina Weir. *School Library Journal* 55, no. 1 (2009): 135.

Ryall, Chris. "Chris Ryall's *Zombies Vs. Robots* Returns." *Comic Book Resources*, March 8, 2011. http://www.comicbookresources.com/?page=article&id=31209.

_____. "In-Depth with IDW Publisher Chris Ryall." Interview by Alex Dueben. *Comic Book Resources*, January 17th, 2008. http://www.comicbookresources.com/?page=article&id=12330.

Ryken, Leland, James C. Wilhoit, and Trempor Longman III, eds. *Dictionary of Biblical Imagery*. Downers Grove, Ill.: InterVarsity Press, 1998.

Ryken, Leland, and Trempor Longman III, eds. *A Complete Literary Guide to the Bible*. Grand Rapids, Mich.: Zondervan, 2010.

Ryken, Leland. *The Literature of the Bible*. Grand Rapids, Mich.: Zondervan, 1981.

Sís, Peter. "My Life with Censorship." *Bookbird: A Journal of International Children's Literature* 47, no. 3 (July, 2009): 42-45.

_____. "The Booklist Interview: Peter Sís." Interview by Jennifer Mattson. *Booklist* (January 1, 2008): 62.

Sabin, Roger. *Adult Comics: An Introduction*. London: Routledge, 2011.

_____. *Comics, Comix, and Graphic Novels: A History of Comic Art*. London: Phaidon Press, 2001.

Saccio, Tatjana, and Dennis Seese. "Tag Team Review No. 9: Ted McKeever's *Transit*." Review of *Transit*, by Ted McKeever. *Library Journal*, December 17, 2008. http://www.libraryjournal.com/article/CA6623680.html.

Sacco, Joe. *Safe Area Goražde: The War in Eastern Bosnia 1992-1995*. Seattle, Wash.: Fantagraphics Books, 2000.

Sacks, Mike. *And Here's the Kicker: Conversations with 25 Top Humor Writers on Their Craft*. Cincinnati: Writer's Digest Books, 2009.

Salaman, Jeff. "The Kane Mutiny: Paul Grist Rewrites the Detective Story with *Kane*." *Spin*, July, 1997, 46.

Salisbury, Martin. "Brian Biggs." In *Play Pen: New Children's Book Illustration*. London: Laurence King, 2007.

Sanders, Joe Sutliff. "*Essex County*." Review of *Essex County*. *Teacher Librarian* 36, no. 3 (2009): 25.

———. "A Western Legend." *Teacher Librarian* 37, no. 1 (2009): 29.

Sante, Luc. "The Gentrification of Crime." *The New York Times Review of Books*, March 28, 1985.

Satrapi, Marjane. "Interview with Marjane Satrapi." Interview by Robert Root. *Fourth Genre: Explorations in Nonfiction* 9, no. 2 (Fall, 2007): 147-157.

———. "*Persepolis*: A State of Mind." *Literal, Latin American Voices* 13 (Summer, 2008): 44-47.

Scharioth, Barbara, and Nikola von Merveldt. "Peter Sís: A Quest for a Life in Truth." *Bookbird: A Journal of International Children's Literature* 47, no. 3 (July, 2009): 29-40.

Schelly, Bill. *Man of Rock: A Biography of Joe Kubert*. Seattle, Wash.: Fantagraphics Books, 2008.

Schmitz-Emans, Monika. "Kafka in European and U.S. Comics Inter-medial and Inter-cultural Transfer Processes." *Revue de littérature comparée*, no. 312 (2004): 485-505.

Schneider, Greice. "Comics and Everyday Life: From *Ennui* to Contemplation." *European Comic Art* 3, no. 1 (2010): 37-63.

Schumacher, Michael. *Will Eisner: A Dreamer's Life in Comics*. New York: Bloomsbury, 2010.

Schumer, Arlen. *The Silver Age of Comic Book Art*. Portland, Ore.: Collectors Press, 2003.

Schuytema, Paul C. "Looking for a Hero: Modern Comic Book Characters Toil in an Imperfect World." *Omni* 16, no. 12 (1994): 27.

Schwartz, Ben, ed. *The Best American Comics Criticism*. Seattle: Fantagraphics, 2010.

Schwartz, E. A. "A Journey into Mohawk and Oneida Country, 1634-1635: The Journal of Harmen Meyndertsz van den Bogaert." *The American Indian Quarterly* 18, no. 1 (Winter, 1994): 119. http://find.galegroup.com.libproxy.uml.edu/itx/start.do?prodId=AONE.

Schwarz, Gretchen, and Christina Crenshaw. "Old Media, New Media: The Graphic Novel as Bildungsroman." *Journal of Media Literacy Education* 3, no. 1 (2011).

Schweitzer, Darrell, ed. *The Neil Gaiman Reader*. Rockville, Md.: Wildside Press, 2007.

Scott, Gini Graham. *Homicide by the Rich and Famous: A Century of Prominent Killers*. Westport, Conn.: Praeger, 2005.

Screech, Matthew. "Constructing the Franco-Belgian Hero: Hergé's *Aventures de Tintin*." In *Masters of the Ninth Art: Bandes Dessinées and Franco-Belgian Identity*. Liverpool, England: Liverpool University Press, 2005.

———. *Masters of the Ninth Art: Bandes Dessinées and Franco-Belgian Identity*. Liverpool, England: Liverpool University Press, 2005.

Seagle, Steven T. "Sex and Death: The Steven T. Seagle Interview." Interview by Shaun Manning. *Comics Bulletin*. http://www.comicsbulletin.com/features/113807922497512.htm.

Seneca, Matt. "Your Monday Panel 15: *Le garage hérmetique de Jerry Cornelius* episode 26 (1988), page 1, panel 1. Drawn by Moebius." *Death to the Universe*, June 7, 2010. http://deathtotheuniverse.blogspot.com/2010/06/your-monday-panel-15.html.

Serchay, David S. *The Librarian's Guide to Graphic Novels for Adults*. New York: Neal-Schuman, 2010.

Seven, John. "Motel Art Improvement Service Goes from Web to Print." *Publisher's Weekly*, December 14, 2010. http://www.publishersweekly.com/pw/by-topic/book-news/comics/article/45504-motel-art-improvement-service-goes-from-web-to-print.html.

Shaer, Matthew. "Graphic Novels, All Grown Up." *Christian Science Monitor*, June 27, 2008. http://www.csmonitor.com/The-Culture/Arts/2008/0627/p13s01-algn.html.

Shandler, Jeffrey. *Adventures in Yiddishland: Postvernacular Language and Culture*. Berkeley: University of California Press, 2008.

Shanower, Eric. "Twenty-First Century Troy." In *Classics and Comics*, edited by George Kovacs and C. W. Marshall. New York: Oxford University Press, 2011.

Shasha, David. "Rediscovering the Arab Jewish Past." *The American Muslim*, October 26, 2005. http://www.theamericanmuslim.org.

Sheehy, Donald G. Afterword to *The Curious Case of Benjamin Button: A Graphic Novel*, by Nunzio DeFilippis and Christina Weir. Philadelphia: Quirk Books, 2008.

Sherman, Bill. "Graphic Novel Review: *The Plain Janes* by Cecil Castellucci and Jim Rugg." Review of *The Plain Janes*, by Cecil Castellucci and Jim Rugg. *Graphic Novel Review*, May 23, 2007. http://blogcritics.org/books/article/graphic-novel-review-the-plain-janes.

Sheyahshe, Michael A. *Native Americans in Comic Books: A Critical Study*. Jefferson, N.C.: McFarland, 2008.

Shook, David. "*Shortcomings*." *World Literature Today* 82, no. 3 (2008): 65-66.

"*Shutterbug Follies*." Review of *Shutterbug Follies*, by Jason Little. *Librarianaut*, March 24, 2009. http://librarianaut.com/2009/03/24/book-review-shutterbug-follies.

Siddiqi, Asif A. *Sputnik and the Soviet Space Challenge*. Gainesville: University Press of Florida, 2003.

Siegel, Alexis. Afterword to *Notes for a War Story*. New York: First Second, 2007.

Sieruta, Peter D. "Pedro and Me." Review of *Pedro and Me*, by Judd Winick. *Horn Book Magazine* 76, no. 6 (November/December, 2000): 775-776.

Siggins, Maggie. *Louis Riel: A Life of Revolution*. Toronto: HarperCollins, 1994.

Sim, Dave. Introduction to *Flaming Carrot Comics Presents Flaming Carrot, Man of Mystery*! Milwaukie, Ore.: Dark Horse Comics, 2008.

Simmonds, Posy. "Posy Simmonds." Interview by Daneet Steffens. *Mslexia* 37 (April/May/June, 2008). https://secure.svr9-speedyservers.com/~mslexia/magazine/interviews/interview_37.php.

Singh, Arune. "Collins' 'Road' to the Future." Review of *Road to Perdition*, by Max Allan Collins. *Comic Book Resources*, August 7, 2002. http://www.comicbookresources.com/?page=article&id=1373.

Skilling, Pierre. "The Good Government According to Tintin: Long Live Old Europe?" In *Comics as Philosophy*, edited by Jeff McLaughlin. Jackson: University Press of Mississippi, 2005.

Skinn, Dez. *Comix: The Underground Revolution*. New York: Thunder's Mouth Press, 2004.

Small, David. "David Small Talks with The White Rabbit's Grandniece." Interview by Danica Davidson. *The Comics Journal*, October 6, 2010. http://classic.tcj.com/interviews/david-small-talks-with-the-white-rabbits-grandniec/.

_____. "The Powells.com Interview with David Small." Interview by Dave Weich. *Powell's Books*, August 13, 2009. http://www.powells.com/blog/?p=7543.

_____. "Why I Write. . . ." *Publishers Weekly* 256, no. 35 (August 31, 2009): 23-25.

Smart, James. "*Richard Stark's Parker: The Outfit*, Adapted and Illustrated by Darwyn Cooke." Review of *Richard Stark's Parker: The Outfit*, by Darwyn Cooke. *The Guardian*, November 26, 2010.

Smith, Jeff. *The Art of Bone*. Milwaukie, Ore.: Dark Horse Comics, 2007.

_____. *Bone Handbook*. New York: Graphix, 2010.

_____. "Interview with Jeff Smith." Interview by Jeff Mason. *Indy Magazine*, January 21, 1994.

_____. "Introduction." In *Larry Marder's Beanworld Book 3: Remember Here When You Are There!* Milwaukie, Ore.: Dark Horse Books, 2009.

Smith, Paul. Introduction to *Leave It to Chance: Trick or Treat and Other Stories*. Orange, Calif.: Image Comics, 2002.

Snellings, April. "My Apocalypse." *Rue Morgue* 104 (September, 2010): 20-21.

Snodgrass, Mary Ellen. *Encyclopedia of Gothic Literature*. New York: Facts On File, 2005.

Soh, Chunghee Sarah. "Prostitutes Versus Sex Slaves: The Politics of Representing the 'Comfort Women.'" In *Legacies of the Comfort Women of World War II*, edited by Margaret Stetz and Bonnie Oh. Armonk, N.Y.: M.E. Sharpe, 2001.

Song, Hyoung Song. "'How Good It Is to Be a Monkey': Comics, Racial Formation, and American Born Chinese." *Mosaic: A Journal for the Interdisciplinary Study of Literature* 43, no. 1 (March, 2010): 73-92.

Sorensen, Lita. *Bryan Talbot*. New York: Rosen, 2005.

Spiegelman, Art. "Gloomy Toons." Review of *Flood! A Novel in Pictures* by Eric Drooker. *The New York Times Book Review*, December 27, 1992.

_____. "A Problem of Taxonomy." *The New York Times Book Review*, December 29, 1991. http://www.nytimes.com/1991/12/29/books/l-a-problem-of-taxonomy-37092.html.

Sperb, Jason. "Removing the Experience: Simulacrum as an Autobiographical Act in *American Splendor*." *Biography* 29, no. 1 (Winter, 2006): 123-139.

Spurgeon, Tom. "Kane #20." *The Comics Journal* 206 (April, 1988): 36-37.

Squier, Susan M. "So Long as They Grow Out of It: Comics, The Discourse of Developmental Normalcy and Disability." *Journal of Medical Humanities* 29, no. 2 (June, 2008): 71-88.

Stafford, Tim. *Teaching Visual Literacy in the Primary Classroom: Comic Books, Film, Television, and Picture Narratives*. New York: Routledge, 2010.

Steinberg, Sybil S. Review of *Dear Julia,*, by Brian Biggs." *Publishers Weekly*, March 6, 2000: 84.

Stewart, Garrett. "Screen Memory in *Waltz with Bashir*." *Film Quarterly* 63, no. 3 (Spring, 2010): 58-62.

Stiles, Steve. "His Name Is Kane: A Master of the Comics Field." *stevestiles.com*. http://stevestiles.com/kane2.htm.

Stout, Tim. "*It Rhymes with Lust* Story Structure." *Tim Stout*. http://timstout.wordpress.com/story-structure/it-rhymes-with-lust-story-structure.

Styron, William. *The Confessions of Nat Turner*. New York: Random House, 1968.

Sulprizio, Chiara. "*Eros* Conquers All: Sex and Love in Eric Shanower's *Age of Bronze*." In *Classics and Comics*, edited by George Kovacs and C. W. Marshall. New York: Oxford University Press, 2011.

Szadkowski, Joseph. "For Illustrator, Brush Is Mightier Than Word." *Washington Times*, September 29, 2007.

_____. "Master of Sequential Art Influences Generations." *Washington Times*, September 22, 2007.

Tabachnick, Stephen E. "A Comic-Book World." *World Literature Today* 81, no. 2 (March/April, 2007): 24.

_____. "The Graphic Novel and the Age of Transition: A Survey and Analysis." *English Literature in Transition, 1880-1920* 53, no. 1 (2010): 3-28.

_____. *Teaching the Graphic Novel*. New York: Modern Language Association of America, 2009.

Talbot, Bryan. *The Adventures of Luther Arkwright*. Milwaukie, Ore.: Dark Horse Books, 2007.

_____. *The Art of Bryan Talbot*. New York: NBM, 2007.

_____. "Engraving the Void and Sketching Parallel Worlds: An Interview with Bryan Talbot." Interview by Roger Whitson. *ImageTexT Interdisciplinary Comics Studies* 3, no. 2 (2007). http://www.english.ufl.edu/imagetext/archives/v3_2/talbot.

Tamaki, Jillian. "The Jillian Tamaki Interview." Interview by Chris Randle. *The Comics Journal*, July 5, 2011. http://www.tcj.com/the-jillian-tamaki-interview.

Tamaki, Mariko. "Graphic Scenes: In Conversation with Mariko Tamaki." Interview by Zoe Whittal. *Herizons* 22, no. 2 (2008): 37.

Tan, Shaun. "A Conversation with Illustrator Shaun Tan." Interview by Chuan-Yao Ling. *World Literature Today* 82, no. 5 (September/October, 2008): 44-47.

_____. "Silent Voices: Illustration and Visual Narrative." The 2009 Colin Simpson Memorial Lecture, March 28, 2009. http://www.asauthors.org/scripts/cgiip.exe/WService=ASP0016/ccms.r?PageId=10216.

_____. *Sketches from a Nameless Land: The Art of "The Arrival."* Melbourne: Lothian, 2010.

Taylor, Craig. "Girls' World." *The Guardian*, November 3, 2001, pp. 60-67.

Taylor, Jessica. "Skim, a Beautiful Graphic Novel." *Xtra!*, March 13, 2008. http://www.xtra.ca/public/Toronto/Skim_a_beautiful_graphic_novel-4468.aspx.

"TCJ 300 Conversations: David Mazzucchelli and Dash Shaw." *Comics Journal*, December, 16, 2009. http://classic.tcj.com/tcj-300/tcj-300-conversations-david-mazzucchelli-dash-shaw/

Tensuan, Theresa. "Comic Visions and Revisions in the Work of Lynda Barry and Marjane Satrapi." *Modern Fiction Studies* 52, no. 4 (Winter, 2006): 947-964.

"The Way I See It: Raymond Briggs—Artists Tackle Ten Existential Questions." *New Statesman* 136 (December 17, 2007): 72.

Thompson, Craig. "Interview with Craig Thompson, Parts 1 and 2." Interview by Brian Heater. *The Daily Cross Hatch*, May 28, 2007.

Thompson, Jill. "Interview: Jill Thompson Talks *Scary Godmother*, *Beasts of Burden*, and More." *MTV Geek*, March 7, 2011. http://geek-news.mtv.com/2011/03/07/interview-jill-thompson-talks-scary-godmother-beasts-of-burden-and-more.

_____. "Jill Thompson Interview." *Westfield Comics*, June, 2001. http://westfieldcomics.com/wow/low/low_int_050.html.

Tomine, Adrian. "Adrian Tomine." Interview by Nicole Rudick. *The Believer*, October, 2007, 42-51. http://www.believermag.com/issues/200710/?read=interview_tomine.

Tong, Ng Suat. "A Short Walk Through the Unifactor: Jim Woodring, Frank, and *Weathercraft*." *The Hooded Utilitarian*, July 6, 2010. http://www.tcj.com/hoodedutilitarian/2010/07/a-short-walk-through-the-unifactor-jim-woodring-frank-and-weathercraft.

_____. "Flopsy, Mopsy, Cotton-tail, and Helen." *The Comics Journal*, no. 1777 (May, 1995): 50-52.

Tramountanas, George A. "Strangers No More, as Moore Brings *Strangers in Paradise* to an End." *Comic Book Resources*, March 17, 2006. http://www.comicbookresources.com/?page=article&id=6652.

True, Everett. Introduction to *Buddy Does Seattle*, by Peter Bagge. Seattle: Fantagraphics Books, 2005.

Turner, Julia. "The Trouble with Drawing Dick Cheney: Ernie Colón and Sid Jacobson, the Comic Book Vets Behind *The 9/11 Report: A Graphic Adaptation*." *Slate* 10 (September 11, 2006). http://www.slate.com/id/2149231.

Tyler, Carol. "CR Sunday Interview: Carol Tyler." Interview by Tom Spurgeon. *The Comics Reporter*, July 5, 2009. http://www.comicsreporter.com/index.php/cr_sunday_interview_carol_tyler.

_____. "The Fine Arts of Comics: Carol Tyler Interview." Interview by Mark Burbey. *The Comics Journal* 142 (June, 1991): 91-102.

_____. "Interview: C. Tyler Pt. 1 (of 4)." Interview by Brian Heater. *The Daily Cross Hatch*, December 23, 2009. http://thedailycrosshatch.com/2009/12/23/interview-c-tyler-pt-1-of-4.

_____. "'You'll Never Know' Carol Tyler." Interview by Alex Dueben. *Comic Book Resources* (March 4, 2011). http://www.comicbookresources.com/?page=article&id=31136.

Vance, James. "A Short Interview with James Vance." Interview by Tom Spurgeon. *The Comics Reporter*, August 13, 2006. http://www.comicsreporter.com/index.php/resources/interviews/5875.

Varnum, Robin, and Christina T. Gibbons. *The Language of Comics: Word and Image*. Jackson: University Press of Mississippi, 2007.

Vasvári, Louise O. "Women's Holocaust Memories/Memoirs: Trauma, Testimony, and the Gendered Imagination." In *Jewish Studies at Central European University*, edited by András Kovács and Michael I. Miller. Budapest: Central European University Press, 2008.

Vasvári, Louise O., and Steven Tötösy de Zepetnek. *Comparative Central European Holocaust Studies*. West Lafayette, Ind.: Purdue University Press, 2009.

Venezia, Antonio. "New New (Graphic) Journalism." *Radical Philosophy* 161 (May/June, 2010): 58-60.

Verheiden, Mark, and Mark Nelson. "Writer and Artist: Mark Verheiden and Mark Nelson." Interview by David Anthony Kraft. *Aliens: Comics Interview Special Edition*, 1988, 3-27.

Versaci, Rocco. "Creating a 'Special Reality': Comic Books Versus Memoir." In *This Book Contains Graphic Language: Comics as Literature*. New York: Continuum, 2007.

_____. "The 'New Journalism' Revisited: Comics Versus Reportage." In *This Book Contains Graphic Language: Comics as Literature*. New York: Continuum, 2007.

Vessels, Joel E. *Drawing France: French Comics and the Republic*. Jackson: University Press of Mississippi, 2010.

Vishniac, Roman. *A Vanished World*. New York: Farrar, Straus, and Giroux, 1999.

Voger, Mark, et al. *The Dark Age: Grim, Great, and Gimmicky Post-Modern Comics*. Raleigh, N.C.: TwoMorrows, 2006.

Vollmar, Rob. "The Importance of Being Bacchus." *The Comics Journal* 273 (January, 2006): 62-65.

Von Busak, Richard. "Memoirs of a Catholic Boyhood: Birth of the Comic Book Autobiography." *Metroactive*, 1995. http://www.metroactive.com/papers/metro/10.12.95/comics-9541.html.

Wagner, Hank, Christopher Golden, and Stephen R. Bissette. *Prince of Stories: The Many Worlds of Neil Gaiman*. New York: St. Martin's Griffin, 2009.

Wagner, John. "Interview by La Placa Rifa and W. R. Logan for The Class of '79." http://www.2000ad.nu/classof79/jw_interview.htm.

Walker, Tristram. "Graphic Wounds: The Comics Journalism of Joe Sacco." *Journeys* 11, no. 1 (Summer, 2010): 69-88.

Waller, Reed, and Kate Worley. "An Interview with Reed Waller and Kate Worley." Interview by Rich Kreiner. *Comics Journal* 143 (July, 1991): 93-100.

Wandtke, Terrence R. "Frank Miller Strikes Again and Batman Becomes a Postmodern Anti-Hero: The Tragi(Comic) Reformulation of the Dark Knight." In *The Amazing Transforming Superhero! Essays on the Revision of Characters in Comic Books, Film, and Television*. Jefferson, N.C.: McFarland, 2007.

Wandtke, Terrence R. *The Amazing Transforming Superhero! Essays on the Revision of Characters in Comic Books, Film, and Television*. Jefferson, N.C.: McFarland, 2007.

Ware, Chris, ed. "King Cat." In *McSweeney's Quarterly 13*. San Francisco: McSweeney's Quarterly, 2004.

Warner, Chris. *Aliens/Predator: Panel to Panel*. Milwaukie, Ore.: Dark Horse Comics, 2006.

Warren, Rosalind. "Alison Bechdel." In *Dyke Strippers: Lesbian Cartoonists A to Z*. Pittsburgh: Cleis Press, 1995.

Watson, Julia. "Autographic Disclosures and Genealogies of Desire in Alison Bechdel's *Fun Home*." *Biography* 30, no. 1 (2008): 27-57.

Watson, Sasha. "The Graphic Reality of a Stricken Land." *Los Angeles Times*, May 31, 2009.

_____. "Sons Against Fathers in *Elk's Run*." *Publisher's Weekly*, March 13, 2007. http://www.publishersweekly.com/pw/by-topic/new-titles/adult-announcements/article/14188-sons-against-fathers-in-elk-s-run-.html.

Weiland, Jonah. "Catching Up on *Elk's Run* with Johsua Fialkov." *Comic Book Resources*, September 20, 2005. http://www.comicbookresources.com/?page=article&id=5689.

_____. "The Horror of It All: Fialkov Talks *Western Tales of Terror* and *Elk's Run*." *Comic Book Resources*, December 21, 2004. http://www.comicbookresources.com/?page=article&old=1&id=4579.

Weiner, Stephen. "Dreams Deferred in a Harsh Landscape: Essex County, Volume 2: Ghost Stories." *Boston Globe*, March 8, 2008.

_____. *Faster Than a Speeding Bullet: The Rise of the Graphic Novel*. New York: Nantier Beall Minoustchine, 2003.

Weschler, Lawrence. "A Wanderer in the Perfect City." *The New Yorker* 69, no. 25 (August 9, 1993): 58-66.

Wheeler, Andrew. Review: "*Journey, Volume 1* by William Messner-Loebs." Review of *Journey: The Adventures of Wolverine MacAlistaire, Volume 1* by William Messner-Loebs. *Comicmix.com*, September 22, 2008. http://www.comicmix.com/news/2008/09/22/review-journey-vol-1-by-william-messner-loebs.

_____. "Review: *Three Shadows* by Cyril Pedrosa." Review of *Three Shadows*, by Cyril Pedrosa. *Comic Mix*, April 2, 2008. http://www.comicmix.com/news/2008/04/02/review-three-shadows-by-cyril-pedrosa.

Whitlock, Gillian. "From Tehran to Tehrangeles: The Generic Fix of Iranian Exilic Memoirs." *Ariel: A Review of International English Literature* 39, no. 1/2 (2008): 7-27.

Whyte, Murray. "King's Life in Pictures of Every Kind." *The New York Times*, August 10, 2003. http://www.nytimes.com/2003/08/10/arts/art-architecture-king-s-life-in-pictures-of-every-kind.html.

Wiacek, Win. "Omaha the Cat Dancer Complete Set." Review of *Omaha the Cat Dancer*, by Reed Waller and Kate Worley. *ComicsReview*, April 30, 2011. http://www.comicsreview.co.uk/nowreadthis/2011/04/30/omaha-the-cat-dancer-complete-set-part-i-2.

Wiater, Stanley, and Stephen Bissette. *Comic Book Rebels: Conversations with the Creators of the New Comics*. New York: Donald I. Fine, 1993.

Wild, Abigail. "Punks of Publishing." *The Herald Scotland*, September 18, 2004.

Willard, Thomas. "Occultism." *The Handbook of the Gothic*. 2d ed. Edited by Marie Mulvey Roberts. New York: New York University Press, 2009.

Willett, Perry. "The Cutting Edge of German Expressionism: The Woodcut Novel of Frans Masereel and Its Influences." In *A Companion to the Literature of*

German Expressionism, edited by Neil H. Donahue. Rochester, N.Y.: Camden House, 2005.

Winick, Judd. "Judd Remembers." *Advocate*, no. 820 (September 12, 2000).

Witek, Joseph. *Comic Books as History: The Narrative Art of Jack Jackson, Art Spiegelman, and Harvey Pekar*. Jackson: University Press of Mississippi, 1989.

_____. "From Genre to Medium: Comics and Contemporary American Culture." In *Rejuvenating the Humanities*, edited by Ray B. Browne and Marshall W. Fishwick. Bowling Green, Ohio: Bowling Green State University Popular Press, 1992.

Withrow, Steven, and Alexander Danner. *Character Design for Graphic Novels*. Burlington, Mass.: Focal Press, 2007.

Witzke, Sean. "Emma Peel Sessions 50: Because It's Everything, Though Everything Was Never the Deal." *Supervillain*, February 20, 2011, http://supervillain.wordpress.com/2011/02/20/emma-peel-sessions-50-because-its-everything-though-everything-was-never-the-deal.

Wivel, Matthias. "David B. Interview." *The Comics Journal* 275 (March, 2006). http://archives.tcj.com/275/i_davidb.html.

Wolchik, Susan L. "Czechoslovakia." In *The Oxford Companion to the Politics of the World*, edited by Joel Krieger. New York: Oxford University Press, 1993.

Wolk, Douglas. "Alan Moore's 'Literary' Porn." *Publishers Weekly* 253, no. 18 (May 1, 2006): 22-23.

_____. "Chester Brown: The Outsider." In *Reading Comics: How Graphic Novels Work and What They Mean*. New York: Da Capo Press, 2007.

_____. "Drawing Fire." *Print* 62, no. 1 (February, 2008): 76-83.

_____. *Reading Comics: How Graphic Novels Work and What They Mean*. Cambridge, Mass.: Da Capo Press, 2008.

_____. "Shades of Meaning." Review of *Asterios Polyp* by David Mazzucchelli. *The New York Times Book Review*, July 26, 2009, p. 11.

_____. "This Sweet Sickness: David B.'s *Epileptic* Lays Bare the Author's Tortured Muse—and Transfigures the Graphic Novel." *The New York Magazine*, May 2005. http://nymag.com/nymetro/arts/books/reviews/10851.

Woo, Benjamin. "Reconsidering Comics Journalism: Information and Experience in Joe Sacco's *Palestine*." In *The Rise and Reason of Comics and Graphic Literature: Critical Essays on the Form*, edited by Joyce Goggin and Dan Hassler-Forest. Jefferson, N.C.: McFarland, 2010.

Wroe, Nicholas. "Profile: Raymond Briggs." *The Guardian*, December 17, 2004, p. 20.

Yang, Andrew. "Globality in Comics." *197* (Summer, 2008): 193-194, 201.

Yang, Gene Luen. "Printz Award Winner Speech." *Young Adult Library Services* 6, no. 1 (Fall, 2007): 11-13.

_____. Review of *The Arrival*, by Shaun Tan. *The New York Times*, November 11, 2007. http://www.nytimes.com/2007/11/11/books/review/Yang-t.html.

Yarbrough, Beau. "San Diego, Day 2: *Leave It to Chance* Returns in 2002." *Comic Book Resources*, July 20, 2001. http://www.comicbookresources.com/?page=article&id=87

Yosef, Raz. "War Fantasies: Memory, Trauma, and Ethics in Ari Folman's *Waltz with Bashir*." *Journal of Modern Jewish Studies* 9, no. 3 (November, 2010): 311-326.

Zaleski, Jeff. "Comics! Books! Films!: The Many Faces of Neil Gaiman: The Arts and Ambitions of Neil Gaiman" *Publishers Weekly* 250, no. 30 (July, 2003): 46.

_____. "Mail Order Bride." *Publishers Weekly* 242, no. 22 (May 28, 2001): 51.

Zeigler, James. "Too Cruel: The Diseased Teens and Mean Bodies of Charles Burns's *Black Hole*." *Scan: Journal of Media Arts Culture* 5, no. 2 (September, 2008).

Zuckerman, Samantha. "The Holocaust and the Graphic Novel: Using *Maus* and Its Narrative Forms to Bring Credence to the Medium." *Kedma*, no. 6 (Spring, 2008): 54-72. http://www.hillel.upenn.edu/kedma/06/zuckerman.pdf.

GUIDE TO ONLINE RESOURCES

Center for Cartoon Studies
http://www.cartoonstudies.org/

A two-year institution based in White River Junction, Vermont, offering a Masters in Fine Arts degree program dedicated to elevating the cartooning profession. Provides a thoughtful meditation on the artistic value and role of comics in our society.

The Comic Book Database
http://www.comicbookdb.com/index.php

An online, user-created database, ComicBookDB compiles all things comics-related. Helpful in answering specific questions regarding issue numbers, contributors, character backgrounds, and series history. A useful resource for reference or cataloging.

Comic Book Legal Defense Fund
http://cbldf.org/

A nonprofit organization, founded in 1986, dedicated to fighting censorship and preserving freedom of expression in the drawing, writing, selling, and reading of comics.

Comic Book Resources
http://www.comicbookresources.com/

An online magazine devoted to comics and their adaptations in television, film, and video games, CBR provides comics-related news coverage and articles from comics writers, artists, and critics. Backed by Comic-Con International.

The Comics Journal
http://www.tcj.com/

A print and online magazine about comics featuring interviews, editorials, in-depth reporting, regular columns, industry news, and hard-line reviews. A blog highlights new content on the website.

The Comics Reporter
http://www.comicsreporter.com/

A useful collection of comics industry news, complete with commentary. Created and maintained by Tom Spurgeon, former editor of *The Comics Journal*. Publishes regular interviews with comics creators and reviews of recent publications.

Comics Worth Reading
http://comicsworthreading.com/

A collection of independent reviews of comics, graphic novels, and manga written from a predominantly female perspective. Established in 1999 by longtime comics fan and critic Johanna Draper Carlson, CWR provides up-to-date news coverage on the comics industry.

Diamond Bookshelf
http://www.diamondbookshelf.com/public/

A database hosted by the world's largest comic book distributor, Diamond Bookshelf is an informative resource for librarians and teachers. The site includes bestsellers, information on new and upcoming titles, and core lists by age group, as well as sample lesson plans and articles on using graphic novels in education and literacy.

Good Comics for Kids (SLJ blog)
http://blog.schoollibraryjournal.com/goodcomicsforkids

A blog maintained by *School Library Journal*, Good Comics for Kids reviews and recommends children's and all-ages comics, graphic novels, and manga.

Graphic Novel Reporter
http://www.graphicnovelreporter.com/

An offshoot of BookReporter.com, Graphic Novel Reporter is an online resource aimed at librarians. In addition to providing resources to help librarians collect and promote graphic novels in their libraries, GNR publishes feature articles and reviews useful to those with a cursory knowledge of graphic novels, comics, and manga.

Graphic Novels in Libraries listserv (GNLIB-L)
http://www.angelfire.com/comics/gnlib/

An email discussion group for librarians to ask questions and advise other librarians on graphic novels in their libraries—topics include popular titles, recommending graphic novels, shelving, resources, reading level, etc.

Graphic Novels: Resources for Teachers & Librarians
http://library.buffalo.edu/libraries/asl/guides/graphic-novels/index.php

An excellent starting point for librarians and teachers who want to become more comfortable with understanding, selecting, and recommending graphic novels for young adult patrons or students. Provides useful information on graphic novels publishers, formats, and genres.

Houston Public Library Graphic Books Next Reads Newsletters
http://www.nextreads.com/Display2.aspx?SID=797a1db1-f3d7-44c8-bb75-5176f6987699&N=388932

An online publication created by the staff at Houston Public Library, the bi-monthly newsletters *Graphic Books* and *Teen Graphic Books* highlight a thematic array of graphic novel titles, old and new.

Lambiek Comiclopedia
http://www.lambiek.net/

A collection of entries on over 11,000 comic artists from around the world, Comiclopedia has been maintained by the Lambiek comics shop in Amsterdam since 1994. Complete with representative illustrations, Comiclopedia is an excellent resource on comics contributors and their works.

Newsarama
http://www.newsarama.com/comics/

An online source for comics industry news, comic reviews, previews, press releases, articles, and commentary, Newsarama has covered comics for fans daily since 1998.

No Flying, No Tights
http://www.noflyingnotights.com/index2.html
No Flying, No Tights: Sidekicks
http://www.noflyingnotights.com/sidekicks/
No Flying, No Tights: The Lair
http://www.noflyingnotights.com/lair/

An online collection created by YA librarian Robin Brenner in 2002, the site features reviews of graphic novels and manga for teens. In addition to a blog, two more age-specific sister sites have been launched that review graphic novels and manga for kids (Sidekicks) and adults (The Lair).

Sequential Tart
http://www.sequentialtart.com/

A monthly webzine on comics and the comics industry, *Sequential Tart* is written with special attention paid to women as creators, characters, and fans—but is of interest to any comics enthusiast.

YALSA Great Graphic Novels for Teens
www.ala.org/yalsa/ggnt

This ann otated list has been compiled annually since 2007 by a Young Adult Library Services Association special committee. Great Graphic Novels for Teens provides graphic novels (published in the previous 16 months) recommendations for teen readers.

Timeline

c. 15000-12000 B.C.E.	Polychromatic prehistoric art, represented in the form of cave paintings of bison and deer, is created in a cave complex in Altamira, Spain. Other cave paintings date as far back as 25000 B.C.E.
c. 1070	The Bayeux Tapestry, an embroidered cloth which communicates the 1066 Norman conquest of England through hundreds of images and words, is created.
1401	In what is considered a pivotal event of the Renaissance, artists such as Lorenzo Ghiberti, Filippo Brunelleschi, and Donatello participate in a competition to decorate the bronze doors of the Baptistery of San Giovanni in Florence, Italy, by telling the biblical story of the sacrifice of Isaac.
18th-19th century	English poet and artist William Blake reinvigorates the medieval illuminated book, leading to much imitation later in the twentieth century. Cited as an influence by many graphic novelists, Blake would later make an appearance in the seminal *Watchmen* (1986), among other graphic novels.
1837	Swiss schoolmaster Rudolphe Töpffer creates what is considered by many historians to be the first known comic book, *The Adventures of Obadiah Oldbuck*.
1895	American comic strip writer Richard F. Outcault, considered by many to be the foremost inventor of the comic strip, creates *The Yellow Kid*.
1919	Flemish artist Frans Masereel creates the "image novel" *Mon Livre d'Heures* (*Passionate Journey*), one of more than twenty wordless and woodcut novels he would create throughout his career.
1929	Working in wood engravings, American artist Lynd Ward creates *God's Man*, one of six wood-engraved novels he would produce between 1929 and 1937 that depict the troubled American landscape.
1930	American illustrator and artist Milt Gross publishes *He Done Her Wrong The Great American Novel and Not a Word in It--No Music Too*; a visual novel with no text, it is often regarded as the second American graphic novel.
c.1938	Beginning of the Golden Age of Comic Books, which marks the mainstream arrival of the comic book.
1938	The comic book series *Action Comics*, which introduces the "superhero" character of Superman, debuts.
1939	The character of "The Bat-Man" is introduced in *Detective Comics* #27. The company producing the comic will eventually adopt the name DC Comics.

1939	The comic book series *Marvel Comics* is released. Timely will later be renamed Marvel.
1941	Captain America makes his first appearance in *Captain America Comics* #1, battling the Axis alliance of ongoing World War II. That same year, Wonder Woman, the first female superhero, is also introduced.
1950	St. John Publications releases the "picture novel" *It Rhymes with Lust*, written by Arnold Drake and Leslie Waller (as Drake Waller), as part of a short-lived experiment in creating a mature comic book series for adults using a small paperback format.
1952	Humor magazine *MAD*, originally a comic book, makes its debut. Edited by Harvey Kurtzman, the magazine would have a strong influence on the underground comics movement.
1954	Dr. Fredric Wertham, an outspoken opponent of comics, publishes *Seduction of the Innocent*, which links depictions of crime and horror in comics to juvenile delinquency.
1954	The Comics Code, a self-imposed censorship system on comics in the United States, is created.
1956	Beginning of the Silver Age of Comic Books, a period during which many of the conventions of the modern comic medium are established and many Golden Age characters such as the Flash and Green Lantern are revamped.
1962	Frank Stack's *The Adventures of Jesus*, a satirical view of the religious beliefs and society of Middle America, is published. It is regarded as the first underground comic ever published.
1964	The term "graphic novel" is coined by writer Richard Kyle in a newsletter circulated to all members of the Amateur Press Association.
1968	In what is considered another significant step for the graphic novel medium, artist Gil Kane and writer Archie Goodwin collaborate on *His Name Is . . . Savage*, which Kane self-published.
1968	Robert Crumb, the leading figure of the underground comics movement, self-publishes his first solo comic, *Zap Comix*. Its publication is often regarded as the beginning of the underground "comix" movement.
c.1970	Beginning of the Bronze Age of Comic Books, a period marked by an increasing drive for realism and social relevance in comics
1970	Underground comics publishing pioneer Kitchen Sink Press is founded.

1972	Underground comics strip *Fritz the Cat*, by Robert Crumb, is adapted into an animated comedy film, becoming the first animated film to receive an X rating. Though Crumb took issue with many aspects of the film, it would become the most successful independent animated film of all time.
1976	Author and illustrator Richard Corben's *Bloodstar*, generally considered the first self-proclaimed "graphic novel," is published by Morning Star Press. It is adapted from a short story entitled "The Valley of the Worm" by pulp writer Robert E. Howard.
1976	Harvey Pekar's *American Splendor*, a landmark title in both the graphic novel medium and the Underground Comix movement, begins publication.
1977	Early alternative comics publisher WaRP Graphics (later Warp Graphics) is incorporated, and begins publication of the long-running *Elfquest* series.
1978	Will Eisner's *A Contract with God*, considered by many to be the first "graphic novel," is published. That same year, Marvel Comics releases *The Silver Surfer*, considered by many to be the first work in graphic novel format.
1981	The Hernandez brothers, Gilbert and Jamie, self-publish the first issue of *Love and Rockets*. Fantagraphics begins publishing the comic book series one year later.
c. 1985	Beginning of the Modern Age of Comics, a period which ushers in more mature themes and revisionist approaches and introduces longer-form works and better-known artists.
1986	Art Spiegelman's *Maus*, considered one of the most significant graphic novels ever produced, is published.
1986	Dark Horse Comics, the largest independent comic book publisher, is founded.
1987	DC Comics collects the twelve issues of author Alan Moore's *Watchmen* as a trade paperback. Along with *Maus* and *Batman The Dark Knight Returns* (1986), it becomes part of a trio of graphic novels of the 1980's that brings the concept mainstream attention outside of the comics field.
1988	Named in honor of cartoonist Will Eisner, the Will Eisner Comic Industry Awards are created, which recognize creative and outstanding achievement in American comic books.
1992	*Maus* becomes the first graphic novel to win the Pulitzer Prize.
1992	Comic book publisher Image Comics is founded by several renowned illustrators who broke from Marvel in a dispute over character copyrights.

2001	The film *Ghost World* is released to critical acclaim, becoming one of the first mainstream adaptations of an indie comic and earning alternative comic author Daniel Clowes an Academy Award nomination for Best Adapted Screenplay.
2006	Gene Yang's *American Born Chinese* becomes the first graphic novel nominated for a National Book Award.
2009	Fordham University hosts the first Graphic Novels in Education Conference.
2001	The graphic novel series *Persepolis*, Marjane Satrapi's autobiographical account of growing up in Iran, wins the Angoulême International Comics Festival Coup de Coeur Award. The graphic novel series would later win several other awards, including the first Fernando Buesa Blanco Peace Prize in 2003 for its stance against totalitarianism.
2005	Scholastic Inc., the world's largest publisher of children's books, announces the creation of a new graphic novel imprint, Graphix.
2005	*Watchmen* is the only graphic novel listed on *Time* magazine's "The 100 Best English Language Novels from 1923 to the Present."
2006	Gene Yang's *American Born Chinese* becomes the first graphic novel nominated for a National Book Award. It would later win the Michael L. Printz award for excellence in Young Adult literature.
2006	Alison Bechdel's *Fun Home* is a finalist for the National Book Critics Circle Award.
2009	Fordham University hosts the first Graphic Novels in Education Conference.
2009	*The New York Times* introduces three different best-seller lists for graphic novels: hardcover, softcover, and manga.
2015	*El Deafo*, by Cece Bell becomes the first graphic novel to win a Newbery Medal
2015	*This One Summer*, by Mariko Tamaki and Jillian Tamaki, becomes the first graphic novel named as Caldecott Medal Honor book
2017	*March*, by John Lewis, Andrew Aydin and Nate Powell becomes the first graphic novel to win a National Book Award

Major Awards

Bill Finger Award for Achievement in Comic Book Writing

Awarded annually at Comic-Con International since 2005, the Bill Finger Award committee selects a living and a deceased writer to recognize for their body of work.

2005	Jerry Siegel Arnold Drake	2012	Frank Doyle Steve Skeates
2006	Alvin Schwartz Harvey Kurtzman	2013	Steve Gerber Don Rosa
2007	Gardner Fox George Gladier	2014	Robert Kanigher Bill Mantlo Jack Mendelsohn
2008	Archie Goodwin Larry Lieber	2015	Don McGregor John Stanley
2009	John Broome Frank Jacobs	2016	Richard E. Hughes Elliot S! Maggin
2010	Gary Friedrich Otto Binder	2017	Jack Kirby William Messner-Loebs
2011	Del Connell Bob Haney	2018	Joye Hummel Murchison Kelly Dorothy Roubicek Woolfolk

Eisner Awards

Named in honor of cartoonist Will Eisner, the Eisner Awards were first granted in 1988. Category nominees are selected by a committee, and then final winners are chosen by representatives from all fields of the comics industry.

1988

Best Writer/Artist or Writer/Artist Team	*Watchmen*	Alan Moore and Dave Gibbons
Best Writer	*Watchmen*	Alan Moore
Best Single Issue (or One-Shot)	*Gumby Summer Fun Special #1*	Bob Burden and Art Adams
Best New Series	*Concrete*	Paul Chadwick
Best Limited Series or Story Arc	*Watchmen*	Alan Moore and Dave Gibbons
Best Graphic Album	*Watchmen*	Alan Moore and Dave Gibbons
Best Continuing Series	*Concrete*	Paul Chadwick

Best Black & White Series	*Concrete*	Paul Chadwick
Best Artist	*Nexus*	Steve Rude
Best Art Team	*Space Ghost Special*	Steve Rude, Willie Blyberg, and Ken Steacy

1989

Best Writer/Artist or Writer/Artist Team	*Concrete*	Paul Chadwick
Best Writer	*Batman: The Killing Joke*	Alan Moore
Best Single Issue (or One-Shot)	*Kings in Disguise #1*	James Vance and Dan Burr
Best New Series	*Kings in Disguise*	James Vance and Dan Burr
Best Limited Series or Story Arc	*Silver Surfer*	Stan Lee and Jean "Moebius" Giraud
Best Graphic Album	*Batman: The Killing Joke*	Alan Moore and Brian Bolland
Best Continuing Series	*Concrete*	Paul Chadwick
Best Black & White Series	*Concrete*	Paul Chadwick
Best Artist	*Batman: The Killing Joke*	Brian Bolland
Best Art Team	*Excalibur*	Alan Davis and Paul Neary

1990 – No Awards Given

1991

Best Writer/Artist or Writer/Artist Team	*Hard Boiled*	Frank Miller and Geof Darrow
Best Writer	*Sandman*	Neil Gaiman
Best Single Issue (or One-Shot)	*Concrete Celebrates Earth Day*	Paul Chadwick, Charles Vess, and Jean "Moebius" Giraud
Best Limited Series or Story Arc	*Give Me Liberty*	Frank Miller and Dave Gibbons
Best Inker		Al Williamson
Best Graphic Album—Reprint	*Sandman: The Doll's House*	Neil Gaiman and various artists

Best Graphic Album—New	*Elektra Lives Again*	Frank Miller and Lynn Varley
Best Continuing Series	*Sandman*	Neil Gaiman and various artists
Best Black & White Series	*Xenozoic Tales*	Mark Schultz
Best Artist	*Nexus*	Steve Rude

1992

Best Writer/Artist or Writer/Artist Team	*The Incredible Hulk*	Peter David and Dale Keown
Best Writer	*Sandman Books of Magic, Miracleman*	Neil Gaiman
Best Single Issue (or One-Shot)	*Sandman #22-#28: "Season of Mists"*	Neil Gaiman and various artists
Best Limited Series or Story Arc	*Concrete: Fragile Creature*	Paul Chadwick
Best Inker	*Batman Versus Predator*	Adam Kubert
Best Humor Publication	*Groo the Wanderer*	Mark Evanier and Sergio Aragonés
Best Graphic Album—Reprint	*Maus II*	Art Spiegelman
Best Graphic Album—New	*To the Heart of the Storm*	Will Eisner
Best Cover Artist	*Animal Man*	Brian Bolland
Best Continuing Series	*Sandman*	Neil Gaiman and various artists
Best Comics-Related Periodical	*Comics Buyer's Guide*	edited by Don and Maggie Thompson
Best Comics-Related Book	*From "Aargh!" to "Zap!": Harvey Kurtzman's Visual History of the Comics*	Harvey Kurtzman, edited by Howard Zimmerman
Best Comic Strip Collection	*Calvin and Hobbes: The Revenge of the Baby-Sat*	Bill Watterson
Best Coloring	*Legends of the Dark Knight, 2112, and Akira*	Steve Oliff

Best Artist	*Batman: Judgment on Gotham*	Simon Bisley
Best Anthology	*Dark Horse Presents*	edited by Randy Stradley

1993

Best Writer/Artist Team	*Nexus: The Origin*	Mike Baron and Steve Rude
Best Writer/Artist	"Sin City" *Dark Horse Presents*	Frank Miller
Best Writer	*Miracleman; Sandman*	Neil Gaiman
Best Single Issue (or One-Shot)	*Nexus: The Origin*	Mike Baron and Steve Rude
Best Short Story	"Two Cities," in *Xenozoic Tales #12*	Mark Schultz
Best Serialized Story	"From Hell" in *Taboo*	Alan Moore and Eddie Campbell
Best Publication Design	*Sandman: Season of Mists*	designed by Dave McKean
Best Penciller/Inker, Color	*Fairy Tales of Oscar Wilde; Robin 3000; Legends of the Dark Knight: "Hothouse"*	P. Craig Russell
Best Penciller/Inker, Black & White	"Sin City" *Dark Horse Presents*	Frank Miller
Best Penciller	*Nexus: The Origin*	Steve Rude
Best Painter/Multimedia Artist	*Aliens: Tribes*	Dave Dorman
Best Limited Series or Story Arc	*Grendel: War Child*	Matt Wagner and Patrick McEown
Best Lettering	*The Sandman Demon*	Todd Klein
Best Inker	*Batman: Sword of Azrael*	Kevin Nowlan
Best Humor Publication	*Bone*	Jeff Smith
Best Graphic Album—Reprint	*Sin City*	Frank Miller

Best Graphic Album—New	*Signal to Noise*	Neil Gaiman and Dave McKean
Best Cover Artist	*Animal Man; Wonder Woman*	Brian Bolland
Best Continuing Series	*Sandman*	Neil Gaiman and various artists
Best Comics-Related Publication	*Comics Buyer's Guide*	edited by Don and Maggie Thompson
Best Comic Strip Collection	*Calvin and Hobbes: Attack of the Deranged Mutant Killer Monster Snow Goons*	Bill Watterson
Best Coloring	*Legends of the Dark Knight #28-#30; Martian Manhunter: American Secrets; James Bond 007: Serpent's Tooth; Spawn*	Steve Oliff/Olyoptics
Best Archival Collection/Project	*Carl Barks Library album series*	
Best Anthology	*Taboo*	edited by Steve Bissette

1994

Best Writer/Artist	*Bone*	Jeff Smith
Best Writer	*Sandman; Death: The High Cost of Living*	Neil Gaiman
Best Single Issue (or One-Shot)	*Batman Adventures: Mad Love*	Paul Dini and Bruce Timm
Best Short Story	"The Amazing Colossal Homer," in *Simpsons Comics #1*	Steve Vance, Cindy Vance, and Bill Morrison
Best Serialized Story	*Bone #8-10: "The Great Cow Race"*	Jeff Smith
Best Publication Design	*Marvels*	designed by Comicraft
Best Penciller/Inker or Penciller/Inker Team	*Sandman #50*	P. Craig Russell
Best Painter/Multimedia Artist	*Marvels*	Alex Ross

Best Limited Series or Story Arc	*Marvels*	Kurt Busiek and Alex Ross
Best Lettering	*The Shadow; Dark Joker: The Wild; The Sandman Demon, Jonah Hex: Two-Gun Mojo, Hellblazer*	Todd Klein
Best Humor Publication	*Bone*	Jeff Smith
Best Graphic Album—Reprint	*Cerebus: Flight (Mothers and Daughters, Book 1)*	Dave Sim and Gerhard
Best Graphic Album—New	*A Small Killing*	Alan Moore and Oscar Zarate
Best Cover Artist	*Animal Man; Wonder Woman; Legends of the Dark Knight #50*	Brian Bolland
Best Continuing Series	*Bone*	Jeff Smith
Best Comics-Related Publication	*Understanding Comics*	Scott McCloud
Best Coloring	*Spawn*	Steve Oliff and Reuben Rude (Olyoptics)
Best Archival Collection/Project	*Complete Little Nemo in Slumberland,* Volume 6	Winsor McCay
Best Anthology	*Dark Horse Presents*	edited by Randy Stradley

1995

Best Writer/Artist-Humor	*Bone*	Jeff Smith
Best Writer/Artist	*Hellboy: Seeds of Destruction*	Mike Mignola
Best Writer	*From Hell*	Alan Moore
Best Single Issue (or One-Shot)	*Batman Adventures Holiday Special*	Paul Dini, Bruce Timm, Ronnie Del Carmen, and others
Best Short Story	"The Babe Wore Red" in *Sin City: The Babe Wore Red and Other Stories*	Frank Miller

Best Serialized Story	"The Life and Times of Scrooge McDuck" in Uncle Scrooge #285-296	Don Rosa
Best Publication Design	The Acme Novelty Library	designed by Chris Ware
Best Penciller/Inker or Penciller/Inker Team	Martha Washington Goes to War	Dave Gibbons
Best Painter/Multimedia Artist	Mystery Play	Jon J. Muth
Best New Series	Too Much Coffee Man	Shannon Wheeler
Best Limited Series or Story Arc	Sin City: A Dame to Kill For	Frank Miller
Best Lettering	Batman vs. Predator II; The Demon, Sandman; Uncle Scrooge	Todd Klein
Best Humor Publication	Bone	Jeff Smith
Best Graphic Album—Reprint	Hellboy: Seeds of Destruction	Mike Mignola
Best Graphic Album—New	Fairy Tales of Oscar Wilde, Volume 2	P. Craig Russell
Best Cover Artist	Hellblazer	Glenn Fabry
Best Continuing Series	Bone	Jeff Smith
Best Comics-Related Publication	Hero Illustrated	
Best Coloring	Martha Washington Goes to War	Angus McKie
Best Archival Collection/Project	The Christmas Spirit	Will Eisner
Best Anthology	Big Book of Urban Legends	edited by Andy Helfer

1996

Best Writer/Artist—Humor	Groo	Sergio Aragonés
Best Writer/Artist—Drama	Stray Bullets	David Lapham

Best Writer	*From Hell*	Alan Moore
Best Single Issue (or One-Shot)	*Kurt Busiek's Astro City #4: "Safeguards"*	Kurt Busiek and Brent Anderson
Best Short Story	*"The Eltingville Comic-Book, Science-Fiction, Fantasy, Horror, and Role-Playing Club in Bring Me the Head of Boba Fett"* in *Instant Piano #3*	Evan Dorkin
Best Serialized Story	*Strangers in Paradise #1-8*	Terry Moore
Best Publication for a Younger Audience	*Batman & Robin Adventures*	Paul Dini, Ty Templeton, and Rick Burchett
Best Publication Design	*The Acme Novelty Library*	designed by Chris Ware
Best Penciller/Inker or Penciller/Inker Team	*The Big Guy and Rusty the Boy Robot*	Geof Darrow
Best Painter/Multimedia Artist	*Batman: Manbat*	John Bolton
Best New Series	*Kurt Busiek's Astro City*	Kurt Busiek and Brent Anderson
Best Limited Series or Story Arc	*Sin City: The Big Fat Kill*	Frank Miller
Best Lettering	*Groo; Usagi Yojimbo*	Stan Sakai
Best Humor Publication	*Milk & Cheese #666*	Evan Dorkin
Best Graphic Album—Reprint	*The Tale of One Bad Rat*	Bryan Talbot
Best Graphic Album—New	*Stuck Rubber Baby*	Howard Cruse
Best Cover Artist	*Kurt Busiek's Astro City*	Alex Ross
Best Continuing Series	*Acme Novelty Library*	Chris Ware
Best Comics-Related Periodical/Journalism	*The Comics Journal*	
Best Comics-Related Book	*Alex Toth*	edited by Manuel Auad
Best Coloring	*The Acme Novelty Library*	Chris Ware
Best Archival Collection/Project	*The Complete Crumb Comics, Volume 11*	R. Crumb
Best Anthology	*The Big Book of Conspiracies*	edited by Bronwyn Taggart

1997

Best Writer/Artist—Humor	*Walt Disney's Comics & Stories; Uncle Scrooge*	Don Rosa
Best Writer/Artist—Drama	*Hellboy: Wake the Devil*	Mike Mignola
Best Writer	*From Hell; Supreme*	Alan Moore
Best Single Issue (or One-Shot)	*Kurt Busiek's Astro City,* Volume 2, #1: "Welcome to Astro City"	Kurt Busiek, Brent Anderson, and Will Blyberg
Best Short Story	"Heroes," in *Batman: Black & White* #4	Archie Goodwin and Gary Gianni
Best Serialized Story	*Starman* #20-23: "Sand and Stars"	James Robinson, Tony Harris, Guy Davis, and Wade von Grawbadger
Best Publication for a Younger Audience	*Leave It to Chance*	James Robinson and Paul Smith
Best Publication Design	*Acme Novelty Library* #7	designed by Chris Ware
Best Penciller/Inker or Penciller/Inker Team	*Book of Ballads and Sagas; Sandman* #75	Charles Vess
Best Penciller	*Nexus: Executioner's Song*	Steve Rude
Best Painter/Multimedia Artist	*Kingdom Come*	Alex Ross
Best New Series	*Leave It to Chance*	James Robinson and Paul Smith
Best Limited Series or Story Arc	*Kingdom Come*	Mark Waid and Alex Ross
Best Lettering	*The Sandman; Death: The Time of Your Life; House of Secrets; The Dreaming; Batman; The Spectre; Kingdom Come*	Todd Klein
Best Inker	*Spider-Man, Untold Tales of Spider-Man* #17-18	Al Williamson
Best Humor Publication	*Sergio Aragonés Destroys DC and Sergio Aragonés Massacres Marvel*	Mark Evanier and Sergio Aragonés

Best Graphic Album—Reprint	*Stray Bullets: Innocence of Nihilism*	David Lapham
Best Graphic Album—New	*Fax from Sarajevo*	Joe Kubert
Best Cover Artist	*Kingdom Come; Kurt Busiek's Astro City*	Alex Ross
Best Continuing Series	*Kurt Busiek's Astro City*	Kurt Busiek, Brent Anderson, and Will Blyberg
Best Comics-Related Periodical/Journalism	*The Comics Journal*	
Best Comics-Related Book	*Graphic Storytelling*	Will Eisner
Best Coloring	*Preacher; Death: The Time of Your Life; Dr. Strangefate; Challengers of the Unknown*	Matt Hollingsworth
Best Archival Collection/Project	*Tarzan: The Land That Time Forgot and The Pool of Time*	Russ Manning
Best Anthology	*Batman: Black and White*	edited by Mark Chiarello and Scott Peterson

1998

Best Writer/Artist—Humor	*Bone*	Jeff Smith
Best Writer/Artist	*Hellboy: Almost Colossus; Hellboy Christmas Special; Hellboy Jr. Halloween Special*	Mike Mignola
Best Writer	*Hitman; Preacher; Unknown Soldier; Blood Mary: Lady Liberty*	Garth Ennis
Best U.S. Edition of International Material	*Gon Swimmin'*	Masahi Tanaka
Best Single Issue (or One-Shot)	*Kurt Busiek's Astro City* Volume 2 #10: "Show 'Em All"	Kurt Busiek, Brent Anderson, and Will Blyberg
Best Short Story	"The Eltingville Comic Book, Science-Fiction, Fantasy, Horror and Role-Playing Club In: The Marathon Men" in *Dork! #4*	Evan Dorkin

Best Serialized Story	*Kurt Busiek's Astro City*, Volume 2, #4-9: "Confession"	Kurt Busiek, Brent Anderson, and Will Blyberg
Best Publication for a Younger Audience	*Batman & Robin Adventures*	Ty Templeton, Brandon Kruse, Rick Burchett, and others
Best Publication Design	*Kingdom Come deluxe slip-cover edition*	art director Bob Chapman/DC design director Georg Brewer
Best Penciller/Inker or Penciller/Inker Team	*Elric: Stormbringer; Dr. Strange: What Is It That Disturbs You, Stephen?*	P. Craig Russell
Best Painter/Multimedia Artist	*Uncle Sam*	Alex Ross
Best New Series	*Castle Waiting*	Linda Medley
Best Limited Series or Story Arc	*Batman: The Long Halloween*	Jeph Loeb and Tim Sale
Best Lettering	*Batman, Batman: Poison Ivy; The Dreaming, House of Secrets, The Invisibles, Uncle Sam; Uncle Scrooge Adventures; Castle Waiting*	Todd Klein
Best Humor Publication	*Gon Swimmin'*	Masahi Tanaka
Best Graphic Album—Reprint	*Sin City: That Yellow Bastard*	Frank Miller
Best Graphic Album—New	*Batman & Superman Adventures: World's Finest*	Paul Dini, Joe Staton, and Terry Beatty
Best Cover Artist	*Kurt Busiek's Astro City; Uncle Sam*	Alex Ross
Best Continuing Series	*Kurt Busiek's Astro City*	Kurt Busiek, Brent Anderson, and Will Blyberg
Best Comics-Related Periodical/Journalism	*The Comics Journal*	
Best Comics-Related Book	*The R. Crumb Coffee Table Art Book*	edited by Pete Poplaski
Best Coloring	*The Acme Novelty Library*	Chris Ware
Best Archival Collection/Project	*Jack Kirby's New Gods*	Jack Kirby
Best Anthology	*Hellboy Christmas Special*	edited by Scott Allie

1999

Best Writer/Artist—Humor	*You Are Here*	Kyle Baker
Best Writer/Artist	*300*	Frank Miller
Best Writer	*Kurt Busiek's Astro City; Avengers*	Kurt Busiek
Best U.S. Edition of International Material	*Star Wars: A New Hope—Manga*	Hisao Tamaki
Best Single Issue (or One-Shot)	*Hitman #34: "Of Thee I Sing"*	Garth Ennis, John McCrea, and Garry Leach
Best Short Story	*"Devil's Advocate" in Grendel: Black, White, and Red #1*	Matt Wagner and Tim Sale
Best Serialized Story	*Usagi Yojimbo #13-22: "Grasscutter"*	Stan Sakai
Best Publication for a Younger Audience	*Batman: The Gotham Adventures*	Ty Templeton, Rick Burchett, and Terry Beatty
Best Publication Design	*Batman Animated*	designed by Chip Kidd
Best Penciller/Inker or Penciller/Inker Team	*Superman for All Seasons; Grendel Black, White, and Red #1*	Tim Sale
Best Painter/Multimedia Artist	*Superman: Peace on Earth*	Alex Ross
Best New Series	*Inhumans*	Paul Jenkins and Jae Lee
Best Limited Series or Story Arc	*300*	Frank Miller and Lynn Varley
Best Lettering	*Castle Waiting; House of Secrets; The Invisibles; The Dreaming, etc.*	Todd Klein
Best Humor Publication	*Groo*	Sergio Aragonés and Mark Evanier
Best Graphic Album—Reprint	*Batman: The Long Halloween*	Jeph Loeb and Tim Sale
Best Graphic Album—New	*Superman: Peace on Earth*	Paul Dini and Alex Ross
Best Cover Artist	*The Invisibles*	Brian Bolland
Best Continuing Series	*Preacher*	Garth Ennis and Steve Dillon

Best Comics-Related Periodical/Journalism	*The Comics Journal*	
Best Comics-Related Book	*Batman: Animated*	Paul Dini and Chip Kidd
Best Coloring	*300*	Lynn Varley
Best Archival Collection/Project	*Plastic Man Archives*, Volume 1	Jack Cole
Best Anthology	*Grendel: Black, White, and Red*	Matt Wagner, edited by Diana Schutz

2000

Best Writer/Artist—Humor	*I Die at Midnight;* "*Letitia Lerner, Superbaby's Babysitter*" in *Elseworlds 80-Page Giant*	Kyle Baker
Best Writer/Artist	*Eightball*	Dan Clowes
Best Writer	*League of Extraordinary Gentlemen, Promethea, Tom Strong, Tomorrow Stories, Top Ten*	Alan Moore
Best U.S. Edition of International Material	*Blade of the Immortal*	Hiroaki Samura
Best Single Issue (or One-Shot)	*Tom Strong #1: "How Tom Strong Got Started"*	Alan Moore, Chris Sprouse, and Al Gordon
Best Short Story	"*Letitia Lerner, Superman's Baby Sitter*" in *Elseworlds 80-Page Giant*	Kyle Baker
Best Serialized Story	*Tom Strong #4-7*	(Saveen/Ingrid Weiss time travel arc) by Alan Moore, Chris Sprouse, Al Gordon, and guest artists
Best Publication for a Younger Audience	*Simpsons Comics*	various
Best Publication Design	*300*	designed by Mark Cox
Best Penciller/Inker or Penciller/Inker Team	"*Jack B. Quick*" in *Tomorrow Stories*	Kevin Nowlan
Best Painter/Multimedia Artist	*Batman: War on Crime*	Alex Ross

Best New Series	*Top Ten*	Alan Moore, Gene Ha, and Zander Cannon
Best Limited Series or Story Arc	*Whiteout: Melt*	Greg Rucka and Steve Lieber
Best Lettering	*Promethea, Tom Strong, Tomorrow Stories, Top Ten; The Dreaming, Gifts of the Night, The Invisibles, Sandman Presents: Lucifer*	Todd Klein
Best Humor Publication	*Bart Simpson's Treehouse of Horror*	Jill Thompson, Oscar González Loyo, Steve Steere Jr., Scott Shaw!, Sergio Aragonés, and Doug TenNapel
Best Graphic Album—Reprint	*From Hell*	Alan Moore and Eddie Campbell
Best Graphic Album—New	*Acme Novelty Library #13*	Chris Ware
Best Cover Artist	*Batman: No Man's Land; Batman: Harley Quinn; Batman: War on Crime; Kurt Busiek's Astro City; ABC Alternate #1 covers*	Alex Ross
Best Continuing Series	*Acme Novelty Library*	Chris Ware
Best Comics-Related Periodical/Journalism	*Comic Book Artist*	
Best Comics-Related Book	*The Sandman: The Dream Hunters*	Neil Gaiman and Yoshitaka Amano
Best Coloring	*The Authority; Planetary*	Laura Dupuy
Best Archival Collection/Project	*Peanuts: A Golden Celebration*	
Best Anthology	*Tomorrow Stories*	Alan Moore, Rick Veitch, Kevin Nowlan, Melinda Gebbie, and Jim Baikie

2001

Best Writer/Artist—Humor	*Maakies, Sock Monkey*	Tony Millionaire
Best Writer/Artist	*Age of Bronze*	Eric Shanower

Best Writer	*The League of Extraordinary Gentlemen, Promethea, Tom Strong, Top Ten, Tomorrow Stories*	Alan Moore
Best U.S. Edition of International Material	*Lone Wolf and Cub*	Kazuo Koike and Goseki Kojima
Best Single Issue (or One-Shot)	*Promethea #10: "Sex, Stars, and Serpents"*	Alan Moore, J. H. Williams III, and Mick Gray
Best Short Story	*"The Gorilla Suit" in Streetwise*	Sergio Aragonés
Best Serialized Story	*100 Bullets #15-18: "Hang Up on the Hang Low"*	Brian Azzarello and Eduardo Risso
Best Publication for a Younger Audience	*Scary Godmother: The Boo Flu*	Jill Thompson
Best Publication Design	*Jimmy Corrigan*	designed by Chris Ware
Best Penciller/Inker or Penciller/Inker Team	*Ring of the Nibelung*	P. Craig Russell
Best Painter/Multimedia Artist	*Scary Godmother*	Jill Thompson
Best New Series	*Powers*	Brian Michael Bendis and Michael Avon Oeming
Best Limited Series or Story Arc	*The Ring of the Nibelung*	P. Craig Russell, with Patrick Mason
Best Lettering	*Promethea, Tom Strong, Tomorrow Stories, Top 10; The Invisibles Dreaming; Castle Waiting*	Todd Klein
Best Humor Publication	*Sock Monkey,* Volume 3	Tony Millionaire
Best Graphic Album—Reprint	*Jimmy Corrigan*	Chris Ware
Best Graphic Album—New	*Safe Area Goražde*	Joe Sacco
Best Cover Artist	*Batman: Gotham Knights; The Flash; The Invisible*	Brian Bolland
Best Continuing Series	*Top 10*	Alan Moore, Gene Ha, and Zander Cannon
Best Comics-Related Book	*Wonder Woman: The Complete History*	Les Daniels

Best Coloring	*Acme Novelty Library #14*	Chris Ware
Best Archival Collection/Project	*The Spirit Archives,* Volumes 1 and 2	Will Eisner
Best Anthology	*Drawn & Quarterly,* Volume 3	edited by Chris Oliveros

2002

Best Writer/Artist—Humor	*Dork*	Evan Dorkin
Best Writer/Artist	*Eightball*	Dan Clowes
Best Writer	*Powers; Alias; Daredevil; Ultimate Spider-Man*	Brian Michael Bendis
Best U.S. Edition of International Material	*Akira*	Katsuhiro Otomo
Best Single Issue (or One-Shot)	*Eightball #22*	Dan Clowes
Best Short Story	"The Eltingville Club in 'The Intervention'" in *Dork #9*	Evan Dorkin
Best Serialized Story	*Amazing Spider-Man #30-35:* "Coming Home"	J. Michael Straczynski, John Romita Jr., and Scott Hanna
Best Publication for a Younger Audience	*Herobear and the Kid*	Mike Kunkel
Best Publication Design	*Acme Novelty Library #15*	designed by Chris Ware
Best Penciller/Inker or Penciller/Inker Team	*100 Bullets*	Eduardo Risso
Best Painter/Multimedia Artist	*Rose*	Charles Vess
Best New Series	*Queen & Country*	Greg Rucka and Steve Rolston
Best Limited Series or Story Arc	*Hellboy: Conqueror Worm*	Mike Mignola
Best Lettering	*Promethea; Tom Strong's Terrific Tales; Tomorrow Stories; Top 10; Greyshirt; The Sandman Presents: Everything You Always Wanted to Know About Dreams But Were Afraid to Ask; Detective Comics; The Dark Knight Strikes Again; Castle W*	Todd Klein

Best Humor Publication	*Radioactive Man*	Batton Lash, Abel Laxamana, Dan De Carlo, Mike DeCarlo, and Bob Smith
Best Graphic Album—Reprint	*Batman: Dark Victory*	Jeph Loeb and Tim Sale
Best Graphic Album—New	*The Name of the Game*	Will Eisner
Best Cover Artist	*Detective Comics; 100 Bullets*	Dave Johnson
Best Continuing Series	*100 Bullets*	Brian Azzarello and Eduardo Risso
Best Comics-Related Periodical/Journalism	*Comic Book Artist*	edited by Jon Cooke
Best Comics-Related Book	*Peanuts: The Art of Charles M. Schulz*	edited by Chip Kidd
Best Coloring	*Ruse; Ministry of Space*	Laura DePuy
Best Archival Collection/Project	*Akira*	Katsuhiro Otomo
Best Anthology	*Bizarro Comics*	edited by Joey Cavalieri

2003

Best Writer/Artist—Humor	*House at Maakies Corner*	Tony Millionaire
Best Writer/Artist	*Age of Bronze*	Eric Shanower
Best Writer	*Powers; Alias; Daredevil; Ultimate Spider-Man*	Brian Michael Bendis
Best U.S. Edition of International Material	*Dr. Jekyll & Mr. Hyde*	Robert Louis Stevenson, adapted by Jerry Kramsky and Lorenzo Mattotti
Best Single Issue (or One-Shot)	*The Stuff of Dreams*	Kim Deitch
Best Short Story	"The Magician and the Snake" in *Dark Horse Maverick: Happy Endings*	Katie Mignola and Mike Mignola
Best Serialized Story	*Fables #1-5: "Legends in Exile"*	Bill Willingham, Lan Medina, and Steve Leialoha
Best Publication for a Younger Audience	*Herobear and the Kid*	Mike Kunkel

Best Publication Design	*Batman: Nine Lives*	designed by Amie Brockway-Metcalf
Best Penciller/Inker or Penciller/Inker Team	*League of Extraordinary Gentlemen*	Kevin O'Neill
Best Painter/Multimedia Artist	*Wolverine: Netsuke*	George Pratt
Best New Series	*Fables*	Bill Willingham, Lan Medina, Mark Buckingham, and Steve Leialoha
Best Limited Series or Story Arc	*League of Extraordinary Gentlemen*, Volume 2	Alan Moore and Kevin O'Neill
Best Lettering	*Dark Knight Strikes Again; Detective Comics; Wonder Woman: The Hiketeia; Fables; Human Target: Final Cut; Promethea; Tom Strong; Castle Waiting*	Todd Klein
Best Humor Publication	*The Amazing Screw-On Head*	Mike Mignola
Best Graphic Album—Reprint	*Batman: Black and White*, Volume 2	edited by Mark Chiarello and Nick J. Napolitano
Best Graphic Album—New	*One! Hundred! Demons!*	Lynda Barry
Best Cover Artist	*Wonder Woman*	Adam Hughes
Best Continuing Series	*Daredevil*	Brian Michael Bendis and Alex Maleev
Best Comics-Related Publication (Periodical or Book)	*B. Krigstein*, Volume 1	Greg Sadowski
Best Coloring	*Hellboy: Third Wish; The Amazing Screw-on Head; Star Wars: Empire; Human Target: Final Cut; Doom Patrol; Tom Strong; Captain America*	Dave Stewart
Best Archival Collection/Project	*Krazy & Ignatz*	George Herriman
Best Anthology	*SPX 2002*	

2004

Best Writer/Artist—Humor	*Plastic Man; The New Baker*	Kyle Baker
Best Writer/Artist	*Blankets*	Craig Thompson
Best Writer	*The League of Extraordinary Gentlemen; Promethea; Smax, Tom Strong; Tom Strong's Terrific Tales*	Alan Moore
Best U.S. Edition of International Material	*Buddha,* Volumes 1 and 2	Osamu Tezuka
Best Single Issue (or One-Shot)	*Conan: The Legend #0*	Kurt Busiek and Cary Nord
Best Single Issue (or One-Shot)	*The Goon #1*	Eric Powell
Best Short Story	"Death" in *The Sandman: Endless Nights*	Neil Gaiman and P. Craig Russell
Best Serialized Story	*Gotham Central #6-10:* "Half a Life"	Greg Rucka and Michael Lark
Best Publication for a Younger Audience	*Walt Disney's Uncle Scrooge*	various
Best Publication Design	*Mythology: The DC Comics Art of Alex Ross*	designed by Chip Kidd
Best Penciller/Inker or Penciller/Inker Team	*Planetary; Planetary/Batman: Night on Earth; Hellboy Weird Tales*	John Cassaday
Best Painter/Multimedia Artist	"Stray" in *The Dark Horse Book of Hauntings*	Jill Thompson
Best New Series	*Plastic Man*	Kyle Baker
Best Limited Series or Story Arc	*Unstable Molecules*	James Sturm and Guy Davis
Best Lettering	*Detective Comics; Fables; The Sandman: Endless Nights; Tom Strong; Promethea; 1602*	Todd Klein
Best Humor Publication	*Formerly Known as the Justice League*	Keith Giffen, J. M. DeMatteis, Kevin Maguire, and Joe Rubinstein
Best Graphic Album—Reprint	*Batman Adventures: Dangerous Dames and Demons*	Paul Dini, Bruce Timm, and others

Best Graphic Album—New	*Blankets*	Craig Thompson
Best Cover Artist	*Batgirl; Fables*	James Jean
Best Continuing Series	*100 Bullets*	Brian Azzarello and Eduardo Risso
Best Comics-Related Periodical/Journalism	*Comic Book Artist*	edited by Jon B. Cooke
Best Comics-Related Book	*The Art of Hellboy*	Mike Mignola
Best Coloring	*Batman; Wonder Woman; 100 Bullets*	Patricia Mulvihill
Best Archival Collection/Project	*Krazy and Ignatz, 1929-1930*	George Herriman, edited by Bill Blackbeard
Best Anthology	*The Sandman: Endless Nights*	Neil Gaiman and others, edited by Karen Berger and Shelly Bond

2005

Best Writer/Artist—Humor	*Plastic Man*	Kyle Baker
Best Writer/Artist	*Concrete: The Human Dilemma*	Paul Chadwick
Best Writer	*Y: The Last Man; Ex Machina; Runaways*	Brian K. Vaughan
Best U.S. Edition of Foreign Material	*Buddha*, Volumes 3-4	Osamu Tezuka
Best Single Issue (or One-Shot)	*Eightball #23: "The Death Ray,"*	Dan Clowes
Best Short Story	*"Unfamiliar"* in *The Dark Horse Book of Witchcraft*	Evan Dorkin and Jill Thompson
Best Serialized Story	*Fables #19-27: "March of the Wooden Soldiers"*	Bill Willingham, Mark Buckingham, and Steve Leialoha
Best Publication Design	*The Complete Peanuts*	designed by Seth
Best Penciller/Inker	*Astonishing X-Men; Planetary; I Am Legion: The Dancing Faun*	John Cassaday
Best Penciller/Inker	*WE3*	Frank Quitely

Best Painter/Multimedia Artist (interior art)	*It's a Bird...*	Teddy Kristiansen
Best New Series	*Ex Machina*	Brian K. Vaughan, Tony Harris, and Tom Fesiter
Best Limited Series	*DC: The New Frontier*	Darwyn Cooke
Best Lettering	*Promethea; Tom Strong; Tom Strong's Terrific Tales; Wonder Woman; Books of Magick: Life During Wartime; Fables; WE3; Creatures of the Night*	Todd Klein
Best Humor Publication	*The Goon*	Eric Powell
Best Graphic Album—Reprint	*Bone One Volume Edition*	Jeff Smith
Best Graphic Album—New	*The Originals*	Dave Gibbons
Best Digital Comic	*Mom's Cancer*	Brian Fies
Best Cover Artist	*Fables; Green Arrow; Batgirl*	James Jean
Best Continuing Series	*The Goon*	Eric Powell
Best Comics-Related Periodical	*Comic Book Artist*	edited by Jon B. Cooke
Best Comics-Related Book	*Men of Tomorrow: Geeks, Gangsters, and the Birth of the Comic Book*	Gerard Jones
Best Coloring	*Daredevil; Ultimate X-Men; Ultimate Six; Captain America; Conan; BPRD; DC: The New Frontier*	Dave Stewart
Best Archival Collection/Project	*The Complete Peanuts*	edited by Gary Groth
Best Anthology	*Michael Chabon Presents The Amazing Adventures of the Escapist*	edited by Diana Schutz and David Land

2006

Best Writer/Artist—Humor	*Plastic Man; The Bakers*	Kyle Baker
Best Writer/Artist	*Shaolin Cowboy*	Geof Darrow
Best Writer	*Promethea; Top Ten: The Forty-Niners*	Alan Moore

Best U.S. Edition of Foreign Material	*The Rabbi's Cat*	Joann Sfar
Best Single Issue (or One-Shot)	*Solo #5*	Darwyn Cooke
Best Short Story	"Teenage Sidekick" in *Solo #3*	Paul Pope
Best Serialized Story	*Fables #36-38, 40-41* "Return to the Homelands"	Bill Willingham, Mark Buckingham, and Steve Leialoha
Best Reality-Based Work	*It Was the War of the Trenches*	Kyle Baker
Best Publication for a Younger Audience	*Owly: Flying Lessons*	Andy Runton
Best Publication Design (tie)	*Acme Novelty Library Annual Report to Shareholders*	Chris Ware
Best Publication Design (tie)	*Little Nemo in Slumberland: So Many Splendid Sundays*	Philippe Ghielmetti
Best Penciller/Inker	*Astonishing X-Men; Planetary*	John Cassaday
Best Painter/Multimedia Artist (interior art)	*Hip Flask: Mystery City*	Ladronn
Best New Series	*All Star Superman*	Grant Morrison and Frank Quitely
Best Limited Series	*Seven Soldiers*	Grant Morrison and various artists
Best Lettering	*Wonder Woman; Justice; Seven Soldiers #0; Desolation Jones; Promethea; Top Ten: The Forty-Niners; Tomorrow Stories Special; Fables; 1602: New World*	Todd Klein
Best Graphic Album—Reprint	*Black Hole*	Charles Burns
Best Graphic Album—New	*Top Ten: The Forty Niners*	Alan Moore and Gene Ha
Best Digital Comic	*PVP*	Scott Kurtz
Best Cover Artist	*Fables; Runaways*	James Jean
Best Continuing Series	*Astonishing X-Men*	Joss Whedon and John Cassaday
Best Comics-Related Periodical	*Comic Book Artist*	edited by Jon B. Cooke
Best Comics-Related Book	*Eisner/Miller*	edited by Charles Brownstein and Diana Schutz

Independents & Underground Classics   MAJOR AWARDS

Best Coloring	*Acme Novelty Library #16*	Chris Ware
Best Archival Collection/Project—Strips	*The Complete Calvin & Hobbes*	Bill Watterson
Best Archival Collection/Project—Comic Books	*Absolute Watchmen*	Alan Moore and Dave Gibbons
Best Anthology	*Solo*	edited by Mark Chiarello

2007

Best Writer/Artist—Humor	*Billy Hazelnuts; Sock Monkey: The Inches Incident*	Tony Millionaire
Best Writer/Artist	*Batman: Year 100*	Paul Pope
Best Writer	*Captain America; Daredevil; Criminal*	Ed Brubaker
Best U.S. Edition of International Material—Japan	*Old Boy*	Garon Tsuchiya and Nobuaki Minegishi
Best U.S. Edition of International Material	*The Left Bank Gang*	Jason
Best Single Issue (or One-Shot)	*Batman/The Spirit #1: "Crime Convention"*	Jeph Loeb and Darwyn Cooke
Best Short Story	*"A Frog's Eye View"* in *Fables: 1001 Nights of Snowfall*	Bill Willingham and James Jean
Best Reality-Based Work	*Fun Home*	Alison Bechdel
Best Publication for a Younger Audience	*Gumby*	Bob Burden and Rick Geary
Best Publication Design	*Absolute DC: The New Frontier*	Darwyn Cooke
Best Penciller/Inker or Penciller/Inker Team	*Fables*	Mark Buckingham/Steve Leialoha
Best Painter/Multimedia Artist (interior art)	*"A Dog and His Boy"* in The Dark Horse Book of Monsters; *"Love Triangle"* in Sexy Chix; *"Fair Division,"* in Fables: 1001 Nights of Snowfall	Jill Thompson
Best New Series	*Criminal*	Ed Brubaker and Sean Phillips
Best Limited Series or Story Arc	*Batman: Year 100*	Paul Pope

Best Lettering	*Fables; Jack of Fables; Fables: 1001 Nights of Snowfall; Pride of Baghdad; Testament; Fantastic Four: 1602; Eternals; Lost Girls*	Todd Klein
Best Humor Publication	*Flaming Carrot Comics*	Bob Burden
Best Graphic Album—Reprint	*Absolute DC: the New Frontier*	Darwyn Cooke
Best Graphic Album—New	*American Born Chinese*	Gene Luen Yang
Best Digital Comic	*Sam and Max*	Steve Purcell
Best Cover Artist	*Fables, Jack of Fables; Fables: 1001 Nights of Snowfall*	James Jean
Best Continuing Series	*All Star Superman*	Grant Morrison and Frank Quitel
Best Comics-Related Periodical/Journalism	*Alter Ego*	edited by Roy Thomas
Best Comics-Related Book	*The Art of Brian Bolland*	Joe Pruett
Best Coloring	*BPRD; Conan; The Escapists; Hellboy; Action Comics; Batman/The Spirit; Superman*	Dave Stewart
Best Archival Collection/Project—Strips	The Complete Peanuts, 1959-1960, 1961-1962	Charles Schulz
Best Archival Collection/Project—Comic Books	*Absolute Sandman*, Volume 1	Neil Gaiman and various
Best Anthology	*Fables: 1001 Nights of Snowfall*	Bill Willingham and various

2008

Best Writer/Artist—Humor	*The Goon*	Eric Powell
Best Writer/Artist	*Acme Novelty Library #18*	Chris Ware
Best Writer	*Captain America; Criminal; Daredevil; Immortal Iron Fist*	Ed Brubaker
Best U.S. Edition of International Material—Japan	*Tekkonkinkreet: Black & White*	Taiyo Matsumoto

Best U.S. Edition of International Material	*I Killed Adolf Hitler*	Jason
Best Single Issue (or One-Shot)	*Justice League of America #11: "Walls"*	Brad Meltzer and Gene Ha
Best Short Story	*"Mr. Wonderful"* in *New York Times Sunday Magazine*	Daniel Clowes
Best Reality-Based Work	*Satchel Paige: Striking Out Jim Crow*	James Sturm and Rich Tommaso
Best Publication for Teens	*Laika*	Nick Abadzis
Best Publication for Kids	*Mouse Guard: Fall 1152* and *Mouse Guard: Winter 1152*	David Petersen
Best Publication Design	*Process Recess 2*	James Jean and Chris Pitzer
Best Penciller/Inker or Penciller/Inker Team	*Y: The Last Man*	Pia Guerra/Jose Marzan, Jr.
Best Painter/Multimedia Artist (interior art)	*The Goon: Chinatown*	Eric Powell
Best New Series	*Buffy the Vampire Slayer, Season 8*	Joss Whedon, Brian K. Vaughan, Georges Jeanty, and Andy Owens
Best Limited Series or Story Arc	*The Umbrella Academy*	Gerard Way and Gabriel Bá
Best Lettering	*Justice, Simon Dark; Fables, Jack of Fables; Crossing Midnight; League of Extraordinary Gentlemen: The Black Dossier; Nexus*	Todd Klein
Best Humor Publication	*Perry Bible Fellowship: The Trial of Colonel Sweeto and Other Stories*	Nicholas Gurewitch
Best Graphic Album—Reprint	*Mouse Guard: Fall 1152*	David Petersen
Best Graphic Album—New	*Exit Wounds*	Rutu Modan
Best Digital Comic	*Sugarshock!*	Joss Whedon and Fabio Moon
Best Cover Artist	*Fables; The Umbrella Academy; Process Recess 2; Superior Showcase 2*	James Jean

Best Continuing Series	*Y: The Last Man*	Brian K. Vaughan, Pia Guerra, and Jose Marzan, Jr.
Best Comics-Related Periodical/Journalism	*Newsarama*	produced by Matt Brady and Michael Doran
Best Comics-Related Book	*Reading Comics: How Graphic Novels Work and What They Mean*	Douglas Wolk
Best Coloring	*BPRD; Buffy the Vampire Slayer; Cut; Hellboy; Lobster Johnson; The Umbrella Academy; The Spirit*	Dave Stewart
Best Archival Collection/Project—Strips	*Complete Terry and the Pirates,* Volume 1	Milton Caniff
Best Archival Collection/Project—Comic Books	*I Shall Destroy All the Civilized Planets!*	Fletcher Hanks
Best Anthology	*5*	Gabriel Bá, Becky Cloonan, Fabio Moon, Vasilis Lolos, and Rafael Grampa

2009

Best Writer/Artist	*Acme Novelty Library #19*	Chris Ware
Best Writer	*Fables, House of Mystery*	Bill Willingham
Best U.S. Edition of International Material—Japan	*Dororo*	Osamu Tezuka
Best U.S. Edition of International Material	*The Last Musketeer*	Jason
Best Short Story	"Murder He Wrote" in *The Simpsons' Treehouse of Horror #14*	Ian Boothby, Nina Matsumoto, and Andrew Pepoy
Best Reality-Based Work	*What It Is*	Lynda Barry
Best Publication for Teens	*Coraline*	Neil Gaiman, adapted by P. Craig Russell
Best Publication for Kids	*Tiny Titans*	Art Baltazar and Franco
Best Publication Design	*Hellboy Library Editions*	Cary Grazzini and Mike Mignola

Best Penciller/Inker or Penciller/Inker Team	*BPRD*	Guy Davis
Best Painter/Multimedia Artist (interior art)	*Magic Trixie; Magic Trixie Sleeps Over*	Jill Thompson
Best New Series	*Invincible Iron Man*	Matt Fraction and Salvador Larocca
Best Limited Series or Story Arc	*Hellboy: The Crooked Man*	Mike Mignola and Richard Corben
Best Lettering	*Acme Novelty Library #19*	Chris Ware
Best Humor Publication	*Herbie Archives*	"Shane O'Shea" (Richard E. Hughes) and Ogden Whitney
Best Graphic Album—Reprint	*Hellboy Library Edition*, Volumes 1 and 2	Mike Mignola
Best Graphic Album—New	*Swallow Me Whole*	Nate Powell
Best Digital Comic	*Finder*	Carla Speed McNeil
Best Cover Artist	*Fables; The Umbrella Academy*	James Jean
Best Continuing Series	*All Star Superman*	Grant Morrison and Frank Quitely
Best Comics-Related Periodical/Journalism	*Comic Book Resources*	produced by Jonah Weiland
Best Comics-Related Book	*Kirby: King of Comics*	Mark Evanier
Best Coloring	*Abe Sapien: The Drowning; BPRD; The Goon; Hellboy; Solomon Kane; The Umbrella Academy; Body Bags; Captain America: White*	Dave Stewart
Best Archival Collection/Project—Strips	*Little Nemo in Slumberland: Many More Splendid Sundays*	Winsor McCay
Best Archival Collection/Project—Comic Books	*Creepy Archives*	
Best Anthology	*Comic Book Tattoo: Narrative Art Inspired by the Lyrics and Music of Tori Amos*	edited by Rantz Hoseley

2010

Best Writer/Artist–Nonfiction	*Footnotes in Gaza*	Joe Sacco
Best Writer/Artist	*Asterios Polyp*	David Mazzucchelli
Best Writer	*Captain America; Daredevil; Marvels Project; Criminal; Incognito*	Ed Brubaker
Best U.S. Edition of International Material—Asia	*A Drifting Life*	Yoshihiro Tatsumi
Best U.S. Edition of International Material	*The Photographer*	Emmanuel Guibert, Didier Lefevre, and Frédéric Lemerier
Best Single Issue (or One-Shot)	*Captain America #601: "Red, White, and Blue-Blood"*	Ed Brubaker and Gene Colan
Best Short Story	"Urgent Request" in *The Eternal Smile*	Gene Luen Yang and Derek Kirk Kim
Best Reality-Based Work	*A Drifting Life*	Yoshihiro Tatsumi
Best Publication for Teens	*Beasts of Burden*	Evan Dorkin and Jill Thompson
Best Publication for Kids	*The Wonderful Wizard of Oz hc*	L. Frank Baum, Eric Shanower, and Skottie Young
Best Publication Design	*Absolute Justice*	Curtis King and Josh Beatman
Best Penciller/Inker or Penciller/Inker Team	*Detective Comics*	J. H. Williams III
Best Painter/Multimedia Artist (interior art)	*Beasts of Burden; Magic Trixie and the Dragon*	Jill Thompson
Best New Series	*Chew*	John Layman and Rob Guillor
Best Limited Series or Story Arc	*The Wonderful Wizard of Oz*	Eric Shanower and Skottie Young
Best Lettering	*Asterios Polyp*	David Mazzuccheilli
Best Humor Publication	*Scott Pilgrim* Volume 5: *Scott Pilgrim vs. the Universe*	Bryan Lee O'Malley
Best Graphic Album—Reprint	*Absolute Justice*	Alex Ross, Jim Krueger, and Doug Braithewaite
Best Graphic Album—New	*Asterios Polyp*	David Mazzucchelli
Best Digital Comic	*Sin Titulo*	Cameron Stewart

Best Cover Artist	*Detective Comics*	J. H. Williams III
Best Continuing Series	*The Walking Dead*	Robert Kirkman and Charles Adlard
Best Comics-Related Periodical/Journalism	*The Comics Reporter*	produced by Tom Spurgeon
Best Comics-Related Book	*The Art of Harvey Kurtzman: The Mad Genius of Comics*	Denis Kitchen and Paul Buhle
Best Coloring	Abe Sapien; BPRD; The Goon; Hellboy; Solomon Kane; Umbrella Academy; Zero Killer; Detective Comics; Luna Park	Dave Stewart
Best Archival Collection/Project—Strips	*Bloom County: The Complete Library*, Volume 1	Berkeley Breathed, edited by Scott Dunbier
Best Archival Collection/Project—Comic Books	*The Rocketeer: The Complete Adventures* deluxe ed.	Dave Stevens, edited by Scott Dunbier
Best Anthology	*Popgun* Volume 3	edited by Mark Andrew Smith, D. J. Kirkbride, and Joe Keatinge
Best Adaptation from Another Work	*Richard Stark's Parker: The Hunter*	Darwyn Cooke

2011

Best Writer/Artist	*Richard Stark's Parker: The Outfit*	Darwyn Cooke
Best Writer	*Lock & Key*	Joe Hill
Best U.S. Edition of International Material—Asia	*Naoki Urasawa's 20th Century Boys*	Naoki Urasawa
Best U.S. Edition of International Material	*It Was the War of the Trenches*	Jacques Tardi
Best Single Issue (or One-Shot)	*Hellboy: Double Feature of Evil*	Mike Mignola and Richard Corben
Best Short Story	"Post Mortem" in *I Am an Avenger* #2	Greg Rucka and Michael Lark
Best Reality-Based Work	*It Was the War of the Trenches*	Jacques Tardi
Best Publication for Teens	*Smile*	Raina Telgemeier

Best Publication for Kids	*Tiny Titans*	Art Baltazar and Franco
Best Publication Design	*Dave Stevens' The Rocketeer Artist's Edition*	designed by Randall Dahlk
Best Penciller/Inker or Penciller/Inker Team	*The Marvelous Land of Oz*	Skottie Young
Best Painter/Multimedia Artist (interior art)	*Blacksad*	Juanjo Guarnido
Best New Series	*American Vampire*	Scott Snyder, Stephen King, and Rafael Albuquerque
Best Limited Series	*Daytripper*	Fábio Moon and Gabriel Bá
Best Lettering	*Fables; The Unwritten; Joe the Barbarian; iZombie; Tom Strong and the Robots of Doom; SHIELD; Driver for the Dead*	Todd Klein
Best Humor Publication	*I Thought You Would Be Funnier*	Shannon Wheeler
Best Graphic Album—Reprint	*Wednesday Comics*	edited by Mark Chiarello
Best Graphic Album—New	*Return of the Dapper Men*	Jim McCann and Janet Lee
Best Graphic Album—New	*Wilson*	Daniel Clowes
Best Digital Comic	*Abominable Charles Christopher*	Karl Kerschl
Best Cover Artist	*Hellboy; Baltimore: The Plague Ships*	Mike Mignola
Best Continuing Series	*Chew*	John Layman and Rob Guillory
Best Comics-Related Periodical/Journalism	*Comic Book Resources*	produced by Jonah Weiland
Best Comics-Related Book	*75 Years of DC Comics: The Art of Modern Mythmaking*	Paul Levitz
Best Coloring	*Hellboy; BPRD; Baltimore; Let Me In; Detective Comics; Neil Young's Greendale; Daytripper; Joe the Barbarian*	Dave Stewart
Best Archival Collection/Project—Strips	*Archie: The Complete Daily Newspaper Strips, 1946–1948*	Bob Montana, edited by Greg Goldstein

Independents & Underground Classics   MAJOR AWARDS

Best Archival Collection/Project—Comic Books	*Dave Stevens' The Rocketeer Artist's Edition*	edited by Scott Dunbier
Best Anthology	*Mouse Guard: Legends of the Guard*	edited by Paul Morrissey and David Petersen
Best Adaptation from Another Work	*The Marvelous Land of Oz*	L. Frank Baum, adapted by Eric Shanower and Skottie Young

2012

Best Writer/Artist	*Habibi*	Craig Thompson
Best Writer	*Irredeemable, Incorruptible; Daredevil*	Mark Waid
Best U.S. Edition of International Material—Asia	*Onward Towards Our Noble Deaths*	Shigeru Mizuki
Best U.S. Edition of International Material	*The Manara Library, vol. 1: Indian Summer and Other Stories*	Milo Manara with Hugo Pratt
Best Single Issue	*Daredevil #7*	Mark Waid, Paolo Rivera, and Joe Rivera
Best Short Story	"The Seventh" in *Richard Stark's Parker: The Martini Edition*	Darwyn Cooke
Best Reality-Based Work	*Green River Killer: A True Detective Story*	Jeff Jensen and Jonathan Case
Best Publication for Young Adults	*Anya's Ghost*	Vera Brosgol
Best Publication for Kids	*Snarked*	Roger Langridge
Best Publication for Early Readers	*Dragon Puncher Island*	James Kochalka
Best Publication Design	*Jim Henson's Tale of Sand*	Eric Skillman
Best Penciller/Inker or Penciller/Inker Team	*Jim Henson's Tale of Sand*	Ramón K. Pérez
Best Limited Series	*Criminal: The Last of the Innocent*	Ed Brubaker and Sean Phillips
Best Lettering	*Usagi Yojimbo*	Stank Sakai
Best Humor Publication	*Milk & Cheese: Dairy Products Gone Bad*	Evan Dorkin
Best Graphic Album—Reprint	*Richard Stark's Parker: The Martini Edition*	Darwyn Cooke
Best Graphic Album—New	*Jim Henson's Tale of Sand*	original screenplay by Jim Henson and Jerry Juhl, adapted by Ramón K. Pérez

941

Best Digital Comic	Battlepug	Mike Norton
Best Cover Artist	*Black Panther; Lone Ranger, Lone Ranger/Zorro; Dark Shadows; Warlord of Mars; Archie Meets Kiss*	Francesco Francavilla
Best Continuing Series	*Daredevil*	Mark Waid, Paolo Rivera, and Joe Rivera
Best Comics-Related Periodical/ Journalism	The Comics Reporter	Tom Spurgeon
Best Comics-Related Book	*MetaMaus*	Art Spiegelman
Best Coloring	*iZombie; Madman All-New Giant-Size Super-Ginchy Special*	Laura Allred
Best Archival Collection/Project—Strips	*Walt Disney's Mickey Mouse* vols. 1-2	Floyd Gottfredson, edited by David Gerstein and Gary Groth
Best Archival Collection/Project—Comic Books	*Walt Simonson's The Mighty Thor Artist's Edition*	Walt Simonson
Best Anthology	*Dark Horse Presents*	Mike Richardson
Best Educational/Academic Work	*Cartooning: Philosophy & Practice*	Ivan Brunetti
Best Educational/Academic Work	*Hand of Fire: The Comics Art of Jack Kirby*	Charles Hatfield

2013

Best Writer/Artist	*Building Stories*	Chris Ware
Best Writer	*Saga*	Brian K. Vaughan
Best U.S. Edition of International Material—Asia	*Naoki Urasawa's 20th Century Boys*	Naoki Urasawa
Best U.S. Edition of International Material	*Blacksad: Silent Hell*	Juan Diaz Canales and Juanjo Guarnido
Best Single Issue	*The Mire*	Becky Cloonan
Best Short Story	"Moon 1969: The True Story of the 1969 Moon Launch" in Tales Designed to Thrizzle #8	Michael Kupperman
Best Reality-Based Work	*Annie Sullivan and the Trials of Helen Keller*	Joseph Lambert
Best Reality-Based Work	*The Carter Family: Don't Forget This Song*	Frank M. Young and David Lasky

Best Publication for Teens	*A Wrinkle in Time*	Madeleine L'Engle, adapted by Hope Larson
Best Publication for Kids	*Adventure Time*	Ryan North, Shelli Paroline, and Braden Lamb
Best Publication for Early Readers	*Babymouse for President*	Jennifer L. Holm and Matthew Holm
Best Publication Design	*Building Stories,*	Chris Ware
Best Penciler/Inker	*Hawkeye*	David Aja
Best Penciler/Inker	*Daredevil*; *Rocketeer: Cargo of Doom*	Chris Samnee
Best Painter/Multimedia Artist	*Blacksad*	Juanjo Guarnido
Best New Series	*Saga*	Brian K. Vaughan and Fiona Staples
Best Lettering	*Building Stories*	Chris Ware
Best Humor Publication	*Darth Vader and Son*	Jeffrey Brown
Best Graphic Album—Reprint	*King City*	Brandon Graham
Best Graphic Album—New	*Building Stories*	Chris Ware
Best Educational/Academic Work	*Lynda Barry: Girlhood Through the Looking Glass*	Susan E. Kirtley
Best Digital Comic	*Bandette*	Paul Tobin and Colleen Coover
Best Cover Artist	*Hawkeye*	David Aja
Best Continuing Series	*Saga*	Brian K. Vaughan and Fiona Staples
Best Comics-Related Periodical/Journalism	The Comics Reporter	edited by Tom Spurgeon,
Best Comics-Related Book	*Marvel Comics*: *The Untold Story*	Sean Howe
Best Coloring	*Batwoman*; *Fatale*; *BPRD, Conan the Barbarian*; *Hellboy in Hell*; *Lobster Johnson*; *The Massive*	Dave Stewart
Best Archival Collection/Project—Strips	*Pogo, vol. 2: Bona Fide Balderdash*	Walt Kelly, edited by Carolyn Kelly and Kim Thompson
Best Archival Collection/Project—Comic Books	*David Mazzucchelli's Daredevil Born Again: Artist's Edition*	edited by Scott Dunbier
Best Anthology	*Dark Horse Presents*	edited by Mike Richardson

Best Adaptation from Another Medium	*Richard Stark's Parker: The Score*	adapted by Darwyn Cooke
Russ Manning Promising Newcomer Award	Russel Roehling	
Bob Clampett Humanitarian Award	Chris Sparks and Team Cul deSac	
Will Eisner Spirit of Comics Retailer Award	Challengers Comics + Conversation, Chicago, IL	
Hall of Fame		
Lee Falk, Al Jaffee, Mort Meskin, Trina Robbins, Spain Rodriguez, Joe Sinnott		

2014

Best Writer/Artist	*Love and Rockets New Stories #6*	Jaime Hernandez
Best Writer	*Saga*	Brian K. Vaughan
Best U.S. Edition of International Material—Asia	*The Mysterious Underground Men*	Osamu Tezuka
Best U.S. Edition of International Material	*Goddam This War! by Jacques Tardi and Jean-Pierre Verney*	
Best Single Issue	*Hawkeye #11: "Pizza Is My Business"*	Matt Fraction and David Aja
Best Short Story	"Untitled," in *Love and Rockets New Stories #6*	Gilbert Hernandez
Best Scholarly/Academic Work	*Black Comics: Politics of Race and Representation*	edited by Sheena C. Howard and Ronald L. Jackson II
Best Reality-Based Work	*The Fifth Beatle: The Brian Epstein Story*	Vivek J. Tiwary, Andrew C. Robinson, and Kyle Baker
Best Publication for Teens	*Battling Boy*	Paul Pope
Best Publication for Kids	*The Adventures of Superhero Girl*	Faith Erin Hicks
Best Publication for Early Readers	*Itty Bitty Hellboy*	Art Baltazar and Franco
Best Publication Design	*Genius, Illustrated: The Life and Art of Alex Toth*	designed by Dean Mullaney
Best Penciller/Inker or Penciller/Inker Team	*The Wake*	Sean Murphy
Best Painter/Multimedia Artist	*Saga*	Fiona Staples
Best New Series	*Sex Criminals*	Matt Fraction and Chip Zdarsky

Best Limited Series	*The Wake*	Scott Snyder and Sean Murphy
Best Lettering	*Richard Stark's Parker: Slayground*	Darwyn Cooke
Best Humor Publication	*Vader's Little Princess*	Jeffrey Brown
Best Graphic Album—Reprint	*RASL*	Jeff Smith
Best Graphic Album—New	*The Property*	Rutu Modan
Best Digital/Webcomic	*The Oatmeal*	Matthew Inman
Best Cover Artist	*Hawkeye*	David Aja
Best Continuing Series	*Saga*	Brian K. Vaughan and Fiona Staples
Best Comics-Related Periodical/Journalism	*Comic Book Resources*	produced by Jonah Weiland
Best Comics-Related Book	*Genius, Illustrated: The Life and Art of Alex Toth*	Dean Mullaney and Bruce Canwell
Best Coloring	*The Manhattan Projects, Nowhere Men, Pretty Deadly, Zero; The Massive; Tom Strong; X-Files Season 10; Captain Marvel, Journey into Mystery; Numbercruncher; Quantum and Woody*	Jordie Bellaire
Best Archival Collection/Project—Strips	*Tarzan: The Complete Russ Manning Newspaper Strips, vol. 1*	edited by Dean Mullaney
Best Archival Collection/Project—Comic Books	*Will Eisner's The Spirit Artist's Edition*	edited by Scott Dunbier
Best Anthology	*Dark Horse Presents*	edited by Mike Richardson
Best Adaptation from Another Medium	*Richard Stark's Parker: Slayground*	Donald Westlake, adapted by Darwyn Cooke
Russ Manning Promising Newcomer Award	Aaron Conley	
Bob Clampett Humanitarian Award	Joe Field	
Bill Finger Award for Excellence in Comics Writing	Robert Kanigher, Bill Mantlo, Jack Mendelsohn	
Will Eisner Spirit of Comics Retailer Award	Legend Comics & Coffee, and All Star Comics	
Hall of Fame		
Orrin C. Evans, Irwin Hasen, Hayao Miyazaki, Sheldon Moldoff, Alan Moore, Dennis O'Neil, Bernie Wrightson		

2015

Best Writer/Artist	*Sisters*	Raina Telgemeier
Best Writer	*Avatar: The Last Airbender* (Dark Horse); *The Shadow Hero* (First Second)	Gene Luen Yang
Best U.S. Edition of International Material—Asia	*Showa 1939–1944* and *Showa 1944–1953: A History of Japan*	Shigeru Mizuki (Drawn & Quarterly)
Best U.S. Edition of International Material	*Blacksad: Amarillo*	Juan Díaz Canales & Juanjo Guarnido (Dark Horse)
Best Single Issue (or One-Shot)	*Beasts of Burden: Hunters and Gatherers*	Evan Dorkin & Jill Thompson (Dark Horse)
Best Short Story	"When the Darkness Presses"	Emily Carroll
Best Scholarly/Academic Work	*Graphic Details: Jewish Women's Confessional Comics in Essays and Interviews*	edited by Sarah Lightman (McFarland)
Best Reality-Based Work	*Hip Hop Family Tree,* vol. 2	Ed Piskor (Fantagraphics)
Best Publication for Teens (ages 13-17)	*Lumberjanes*	Shannon Watters, Grace Ellis, Noelle Stevenson, & Brooke A. Allen (BOOM! Box)
Best Publication for Kids (ages 8-12)	*El Deafo*	Cece Bell (Amulet/Abrams)
Best Publication for Early Readers (up to age 7)	*The Zoo Box*	Ariel Cohn & Aron Nels Steinke (First Second)
Best Publication Design	*Little Nemo: Dream Another Dream*	designed by Jim Rugg (Locust Moon)
Best Penciller/Inker	*Saga*	Fiona Staples
Best Painter/Multimedia Artist (interior art)	*The Sandman: Overture*	J. H. Williams III
Best New Series	*Lumberjanes*	Shannon Watters, Grace Ellis, Noelle Stevenson, & Brooke A. Allen (BOOM! Box)
Best Limited Series	*Little Nemo: Return to Slumberland*	Eric Shanower & Gabriel Rodriguez (IDW)

Best Lettering	*Usagi Yojimbo: Senso, Usagi Yojimbo Color Special: The Artist*	Stan Sakai
Best Humor Publication	*The Complete Cul de Sac*	Richard Thompson (Andrews McMeel)
Best Graphic Album—Reprint	Through the Woods	Emily Carroll (McElderry Books)
Best Graphic Album—New	*This One Summer*	Mariko Tamaki & Jillian Tamaki (First Second)
Best Digital/Web Comic	*The Private Eye*	Brian Vaughan & Marcos Martin
Best Continuing Series	*Saga*	Brian K. Vaughan & Fiona Staples (Image)
Best Comics-Related Periodical/Journalism	Comics Alliance	edited by Andy Khouri, Caleb Goellner, Andrew Wheeler, & Joe Hughes
Best Comics-Related Book	*Genius Animated: The Cartoon Art of Alex Toth*, vol. 3	Dean Mullaney & Bruce Canwell (IDW/LOAC)
Best Coloring	*Hellboy in Hell; BPRD; Abe Sapien; Baltimore; Lobster Johnson; Witchfinder; Shaolin Cowboy; Aliens: Fire and Ston*	Dave Stewart
Best Archival Collection/Project—Strips (at least 20 Years Old)	*Winsor McCay's Complete Little Nemo*	edited by Alexander Braun (TASCHEN)
Best Archival Collection/Project—Comic Books (at least 20 Years Old)	*Steranko Nick Fury Agent of S.H.I.E.L.D. Artist's Edition*	edited by Scott Dunbier (IDW)
Best Anthology	*Little Nemo: Dream Another Dream*	edited by Josh O'Neill, Andrew Carl, & Chris Stevens (Locust Moon)
Best Adaptation from Another Medium	*Richard Stark's Parker: Slayground*	Donald Westlake, adapted by Darwyn Cooke
Bob Clampett Humanitarian Award	Bill & Kayre Morrison	
Russ Manning Promising Newcomer Award	Jorge Corona	
Russ Manning Promising Newcomer Award	Greg Smallwood	

Bill Finger Award for Excellence in Comics Writing	Don McGregor, John Stanley	
Will Eisner Spirit of Comics Retailer Award	Packrat Comics, Hilliard, Ohio	owned by Jamie Colegrove and Teresa Colegrove
Hall of Fame		
Judges' Choices	Marge (Marjorie Henderson Buell), Bill Woggon	
Elected	John Byrne, Chris Claremont, Denis Kitchen, Frank Miller	

2016

Best Writer/Artist	*Invisible Ink: My Mother's Secret Love Affair with a Famous Cartoonist*	Bill Griffith
Best Writer	*Southern Bastards*; *Men of Wrath*; *Doctor Strange*; *Star Wars*; *Thor*	Jason Aaron
Best U.S. Edition of International Material—Asia	*Showa, 1953–1989: A History of Japan*	Shigeru Mizuki (Drawn & Quarterly)
Best U.S. Edition of International Material	*The Realist*	Asaf Hanuka (BOOM! Studios/Archaia)
Best Single Issue/One-Shot	*Silver Surfer* #11: "Never After"	Dan Slott and Michael Allred (Marvel)
Best Short Story	"Killing and Dying" in *Optic Nerve* #14	Adrian Tomine
Best Reality-Based Work	*March: Book Two*	John Lewis, Andrew Aydin, and Nate Powell (Top Shelf/IDW)
Best Publication for Teens (ages 13-17)	*SuperMutant Magic Academy*	Jillian Tamaki (Drawn & Quarterly)
Best Publication for Kids (ages 9-12)	*Over the Garden Wall*	Pat McHale, Amalia Levari, and Jim Campbell (BOOM! Studios/KaBOOM!)
Best Publication for Early Readers (up to age 8)	*Little Robot*	Ben Hatke (First Second)
Best Publication Design	*Sandman Gallery Edition*	designed by Josh Beatman/Brainchild Studios
Best Penciller/Inker or Penciller/Inker Team	*Paper Girls*	Cliff Chiang

Best Painter/Multimedia Artist	*Descender*	Dustin Nguyen
Best New Series	*Paper Girls*	Brian K. Vaughan and Cliff Chiang (Image)
Best Limited Series	*The Fade Out*	Ed Brubaker and Sean Phillips (Image)
Best Lettering	*Trashed*	Derf Backderf
Best Humor Publication	*Step Aside, Pops: A Hark! A Vagrant Collection*	Kate Beaton (Drawn & Quarterly)
Best Graphic Album—Reprint	*Nimona*	Noelle Stevenson (Harper Teen)
Best Graphic Album—New	*Ruins*	Peter Kuper (SelfMadeHero)
Best Digital/Webcomic	*Bandette*	Paul Tobin and Colleen Coover (Monkeybrain/comiXology)
Best Cover Artist	*Hawkeye, Karnak, Scarlet Witch*	David Aja
Best Continuing Series	*Southern Bastards*	Jason Aaron and Jason Latour (Image)
Best Comics-Related Periodical/Journalism	*Hogan's Alley*	edited by Tom Heintjes
Best Comics-Related Book	*Harvey Kurtzman: The Man Who Created Mad and Revolutionized Humor in America*	Bill Schelly (Fantagraphics)
Best Coloring	*The Autumnlands, Injection, Plutona, Pretty Deadly, The Surface, They're Not Like Us, Zero* (Image); *The X-Files* (IDW); *The Massive* (Dark Horse); *Magneto, Vision*	Jordie Bellaire
Best Archival Collection/Project—Strips	*The Eternaut*	Héctor Germán Oesterheld and Francisco Solano Lòpez, edited by Gary Groth and Kristy Valenti (Fantagraphics)
Best Archival Collection/Project—Comic Books	*Walt Kelly's Fairy Tales*	edited by Craig Yoe (IDW)
Best Anthology	*Drawn & Quarterly, Twenty-Five Years of Contemporary, Cartooning, Comics, and Graphic Novels*	edited by Tom Devlin (Drawn & Quarterly)

Best Adaptation from Another Medium	*Two Brothers*	Fábio Moon and Gabriel Bá (Dark Horse)
Best Academic/Scholarly Work	*The Blacker the Ink: Constructions of Black Identity in Comics and Sequential Art*	edited by Frances Gateward and John Jennings
Hall of Fame		
Judges' Choices	Carl Burgos, Tove Jansson	
Voters' Choices	Lynda Barry, Rube Goldberg, Matt Groening, Jacques Tardi	

2017

Best Writer/Artist	*The Art of Charlie Chan Hock Chye*	Sonny Liew (Pantheon)
Best Writer	*Paper Girls, Saga* (Image)	Brian K. Vaughan
Best Webcomic	*Bird Boy*	Anne Szabla
Best U.S. Edition of International Material—Asia	*The Art of Charlie Chan Hock Chye*	Sonny Liew (Pantheon)
Best U.S. Edition of International Material	*Moebius Library: The World of Edena*	Jean "Moebius" Giraud et al. (Dark Horse)
Best Single Issue/One-Shot	*Beasts of Burden: What the Cat Dragged In*	Evan Dorkin, Sarah Dyer, and Jill Thompson (Dark Horse)
Best Short Story	"Good Boy," in *Batman Annual #1*	Tom King and David Finch
Best Reality-Based Work	*March (Book Three)*	John Lewis, Andrew Aydin, and Nate Powell (Top Shelf)
Best Publication for Teens (ages 13-17)	*The Unbeatable Squirrel Girl*	Ryan North and Erica Henderson (Marvel)
Best Publication for Kids (ages 9-12)	*Ghosts*	Raina Telgemeier (Scholastic)
Best Publication for Early Readers (up to age 8)	*Narwhal: Unicorn of the Sea*	Ben Clanton (Tundra)
Best Publication Design	*The Art of Charlie Chan Hock Chye*	designed by Sonny Liew (Pantheon)

Best Penciller/Inker or Penciller/Inker Team	*Saga*	Fiona Staples
Best Painter/Multimedia Artist (interior art)	*Wonder Woman: The True Amazon* (DC); *Beasts of Burden: What the Cat Dragged In*	Jill Thompson
Best New Series	*Black Hammer*	Jeff Lemire and Dean Ormston (Dark Horse)
Best Limited Series	*The Vision*	Tom King and Gabriel Walta (Marvel)
Best Lettering	*Clean Room, Dark Night, Lucifer* (Vertigo/DC); *Black Hammer*	Todd Klein
Best Humor Publication	*Jughead*	Chip Zdarsky, Ryan North, Erica Henderson, and Derek Charm
Best Graphic Album—Reprint	*Demon*	Jason Shiga (First Second)
Best Graphic Album—New	*Wonder Woman: The True Amazon*	Jill Thompson (DC Comics)
Best Digital Comic	*Bandette*	Paul Tobin and Colleen Coover
Best Cover Artist (for multiple covers)	*Saga*	Fiona Staples
Best Continuing Series	*Saga*	Brian K. Vaughan and Fiona Staples (Image)
Best Comics-Related Periodical/Journalism	The A.V. Club comics coverage, including Comics Panel, Back Issues, and Big Issues	Oliver Sava et al.
Best Comics-Related Book	*Krazy: George Herriman, A Life in Black and White*	Michael Tisserand
Best Coloring	*Cry Havoc, Paper Girls, The Wicked + The Divine* (Image); *Black Widow, The Mighty Thor, Star-Lord*	Matt Wilson
Best Archival Collection/Project—Strips (at least 20 years old)	*Chester Gould's Dick Tracy, Colorful Cases of the 1930s*	edited by Peter Maresca (Sunday Press)
Best Archival Collection/Project—Comic Books (at least 20 Years Old)	*The Complete Wimmen's Comix*	edited by Trina Robbins, Gary Groth, and J. Michael Catron (Fantagraphics)

Best Anthology	*Love Is Love*	edited by Sarah Gaydos and Jamie S. Rich (IDW/DC)
Best Academic/Scholarly Work	*Superwomen: Gender, Power, and Representation*	Carolyn Cocca
Hall of Fame		
Judges' Choices	Milt Gross, H. G. Peter, Antonio Prohias, Dori Seda	
Voters' Choices	Gilbert Hernandez, Jaime Hernandez, George Pérez, Walt Simonson, Jim Starlin	

2018

Best Writer/Artist	*My Favorite Thing Is Monsters*	Emil Ferris
Best Writer	*Batman, Batman Annual #2, Batman/Elmer Fudd Special #1, Mister Miracle*	Tom King
Best Writer	*Monstress*	Marjorie Liu
Best U.S. Edition of International Material—Asia	*My Brother's Husband, vol. 1*, by Gengoroh Tagame,	translated by Anne Ishii
Best U.S. Edition of International Material	*Run for It: Stories of Slaves Who Fought for the Freedom*	Marcelo D'Salete, translated by Andrea Rosenberg (Fantagraphics)
Best Single Issue/One-Shot	*Hellboy: Krampusnacht*	Mike Mignola and Adam Hughes (Dark Horse)
Best Short Story	"A Life in Comics: The Graphic Adventures of Karen Green," in *Columbia Magazine* (Summer 2017)	Nick Sousanis
Best Reality-Based Work	*Spinning*	Tillie Walden (First Second)
Best Publication for Teens (ages 13-17)	*Monstress*	Marjorie Liu and Sana Takeda (Image)
Best Publication for Kids (ages 9–12)	*The Tea Dragon Society*	Katie O'Neill (Oni)
Best Publication for Early Readers (up to age 8)	*Good Night, Planet*	Liniers (Toon Books)

Best Publication Design	*Akira 35th Anniversary Edition*	designed by Phil Balsman, Akira Saito (Veia), NORMA Editorial, and MASH•ROOM (Kodansha)
Best Penciller/Inker or Penciller/Inker Team	*Mister Miracle*	Mitch Gerads
Best Painter/Multimedia Artist (interior art)	*Monstress*	Sana Takeda
Best New Series	*Black Bolt*	Saladin Ahmed and Christian Ward (Marvel)
Best Limited Series	*Black Panther: World of Wakanda*	Roxane Gay, Ta-Nehisi Coates, and Alitha E. Martinez (Marvel)
Best Lettering	*Usagi Yojimbo, Groo: Slay of the Gods*	Stan Sakai
Best Humor Publication	*Baking with Kafka*	Tom Gauld (Drawn & Quarterly)
Best Graphic Album—Reprint	*Boundless*	Jillian Tamaki (Drawn & Quarterly)
Best Graphic Album—New	*My Favorite Thing Is Monsters*	Emil Ferris (Fantagraphics)
Best Cover Artist	*Monstress*	Sana Takeda
Best Continuing Series	*Monstress*	Marjorie Liu and Sana Takeda (Image)
Best Comics-Related Periodical/Journalism:	*The Comics Journal*	edited by Dan Nadel, Timothy Hodler, and Tucker Stone
Best Comics-Related Book	*How to Read Nancy: The Elements of Comics in Three Easy Panels*	Paul Karasik and Mark Newgarden (Fantagraphics)
Best Coloring	*My Favorite Thing Is Monsters*	Emil Ferris
Best Archival Collection/Project—Strips	*Celebrating Snoopy*	Charles M. Schulz, edited by Alexis E. Fajardo and Dorothy O'Brien (Andrews McMeel)
Best Archival Collection/Project—Comic Books	*Akira 35th Anniversary Edition*	Katsuhiro Otomo, edited by Haruko Hashimoto, Ajani Oloye, and Lauren Scanlan (Kodansha)

Best Anthology	*Elements: Fire, A Comic Anthology by Creators of Color*	edited by Taneka Stotts
Best Adaptation from Another Medium	*Kindred*	Octavia Butler, adapted by Damian Duffy and John Jennings (Abrams ComicArts)
Best Academic/Scholarly Work	*Latinx Superheroes in Mainstream Comics*	Frederick Luis Aldama (University of Arizona Press)
Best Writer/Artist	*My Favorite Thing Is Monsters*	Emil Ferris
Best Writer	*Batman, Batman Annual #2, Batman/ Elmer Fudd Special #1, Mister Miracle*	Tom King
Hall of Fame		
Judges' Choices	Carol Kalish, Jackie Ormes	
Voters' Choices	Charles Addams, Karen Berger, Dave Gibbons, Rumiko Takahashi	

Glyph Comics Awards

Presented annually at the East Coast Black Age of Comics Convention, the Glyph Comics Awards were established in 2006 to honor the best works published in the comic industry which are either created by or are about people of color.

2006

Story of the Year	*Nat Turner*	Kyle Baker, writer and artist
Best Writer	*Lucifer's Garden of Verses: Darlin' Niki*	Lance Tooks
Best Artist	*Nat Turner*	Kyle Baker
Best Male Character	Huey Freeman; *The Boondocks*	Aaron McGruder
Best Female Character	Darlin' Niki, *Lucifer's Garden of Verses: Darlin' Niki*	Lance Tooks
Rising Star Award	*The Roach*	Robert Roach
Best Reprint Publication	*Birth of a Nation*	
Best Cover	*Nat Turner #1*	Kyle Baker, illustrator

Best Comic Strip or Webcomic	*The K Chronicles*	Keith Knight, writer and artist
Fan Award for Best Comic	*Black Panther: Who Is the Black Panther?*	Reginald Hudlin, John Romita, Jr., Klaus Janson, Axel Alonso

2007

Story of the Year	*Stagger Lee*	Derek McCulloch, writer, Shepherd Hendrix, artist
Best Writer	*Stagger Lee*	Derek McCulloch
Best Artist	*The Bakers*	Kyle Baker
Best Male Character	Stagger Lee, *Stagger Lee*	Derek McCulloch, writer, Shepherd Hendrix, artist; inspired by the life of Lee Shelton
Best Female Character	Thomasina Lindo, *Welcome to Tranquility*	co-created by Gail Simone, writer, Neil Googe, artist
Rising Star Award	*Spike, Templar, Arizona*	
Best Reprint Publication	*Deogratias: A Tale of Rwanda*	
Best Cover	*Stagger Lee*	Shepherd Hendrix, artist
Best Comic Strip or Webcomic	*The K Chronicles*	Keith Knight, writer and artist
Fan Award for Best Comic	*Storm*	Eric Jerome Dickey, David Yardin & Lan Medina and Jay Leisten & Sean Parsons

2008

Story of the Year	*Sentences: The Life of MF Grimm*	Percy Carey, writer, Ronald Wimberly, artist
Best Writer	*Satchel Paige: Striking Out Jim Crow*	James Sturm
Best Artist	*Nat Turner: Revolution*	Kyle Baker
Best Male Character	Emmet Wilson, *Satchel Paige: Striking Out Jim Crow*	co-created by James Sturm, writer, and Rich Tommaso, artist
Best Female Character	Amanda Waller, *Checkmate*	Greg Rucka, writer, Joe Bennett & Jack Jadson, artists
Rising Star Award	*Aya*	Marguerite Abouet

Best Reprint Publication	*Aya*	
Best Cover	*Sentences: The Life of MF Grimm*	Ronald Wimberly, illustrator
Best Comic Strip or Webcomic	*The K Chronicles*	Keith Knight, story and art
Fan Award for Best Comic	*Fantastic Four: The New Fantastic Four*	Dwayne McDuffie, writer, Paul Pelletier & Rick Magyar, artists

2009

Story of the Year	*Bayou*	Jeremy Love, writer and artist
Best Writer	*Bayou*	Jeremy Love
Best Artist	*Bayou*	Jeremy Love
Best Male Character	Black Lightning, *Final Crisis: Submit*	Grant Morrison, writer, Matthew Clark, Norm Rapmund, Rob Hunter, and Don Ho, artists
Best Female Character	Lee Wagstaff, *Bayou*	Jeremy Love, writer and artist
Rising Star Award	*The Hole: Consumer Culture*	Damian Duffy & John Jennings
Best Reprint Publication	*Me and the Devil Blues V1*	
Best Cover	*Unknown Soldier #1*	Igor Kordey, illustrator
Best Comic Strip or Webcomic	*Bayou,*	Jeremy Love, writer and artist
Fan Award for Best Comic	*Vixen: Return of the Lion*	G. Willow Wilson, writer, Cafu, artist

2010

Story of the Year	*Unknown Soldier #13-14*	Joshua Dysart, writer, Pat Masioni, artist
Best Writer	*Archie & Friends*	Alex Simmons
Best Artist	*World of Hurt*	Jay Potts
Best Male Character	Isaiah Pastor, *World of Hurt*	created by Jay Potts, writer and artist
Best Female Character	Aya, *Aya: The Secrets Come Out*	created by Marguerite Abouet, writer, Clement Oubrerie, artist
Rising Star Award	*World of Hurt*	Jay Potts

Best Reprint Publication	*Aya: The Secrets Come Out*	
Best Cover	*Luke Cage Noir #1*	Tim Bradstreet, illustrator
Best Comic Strip or Webcomic	*The K Chronicles*	Keith Knight, writer and artist
Fan Award for Best Comic	*Luke Cage Noir*	Mike Benson & Adam Glass, writers, Shawn Martinbrough, artist

2011

Story of the Year	*Fist Stick Knife Gun*	Geoffrey Canada, writer, Jamar Nicholas, artist
Best Writer	*Unknown Soldier*	Joshua Dysart
Best Artist	*BB Wolf and the 3 LPs*	Richard Koslowski
Best Male Character	*Geoff, Fist Stick Knife Gun*	Geoffrey Canada, writer, Jamar Nicholas, artist
Best Female Character	*Selena, 28 Days Later*	Michael Alan Nelson, writer; Declan Shalvey & Marek Oleksicki, artists
Rising Star Award	*Fist Stick Knife Gun*	Jamar Nicholas
Best Reprint Publication	*Superman vs. Muhammad Ali Deluxe HC*	
Best Cover	*Unknown Soldier #15*	Dave Johnson, illustrator
Best Comic Strip or Webcomic	*The K Chronicles*	Keith Knight, writer and artist
Fan Award for Best Comic	*Captain America/Black Panther: Flags of Our Fathers*	Reginald Hudlin, writer, Denys Cowan, artist

2012

Story of the Year	*Princeless*	Jeremy Whitley, writer, M. Goodwin, artist
Best Writer	*Princeless*	Jeremy Whitley
Best Artist	*Ultimate Comics: Spider-Man*	Sara Pichelli

Best Male Character	Miles Morales, *Ultimate Comics: Spider-Man*	Brian Michael Bendis, writer, Sara Pichelli, artist; inspired by the character created by Stan Lee & Steve Ditko
Best Female Character	Adrienne, *Princeless*	created by Jeremy Whitley, writer, and M. Goodwin, artist
Rising Star Award	*Watermelon*	Whit Taylor
Best Cover	*Chew* #27	Rob Guillory
Best Comic Strip or Webcomic	*Fungus Grotto*	Ms. Shatia Hamilton, story and art

2013

Story of the Year	*Monsters 101*	Muhammad Rasheed, writer and artist
Best Writer	*Shadowlaw*	Brandon Easton
Best Artist	*Ultimate Comics: Spider-Man* #6	Chris Samnee
Best Male Character	Mort, *Monsters 101*	Muhammad Rasheed, writer and artist
Best Female Character	Dyana, *Night Stalker*	Orlando Harding, writer; David Miller, artist
Rising Star Award	*H.O.P.E.*	Raymond Ayala
Best Cover	*Indigo: Hit List 1.0*	Charlie Goubile and Mshindo Kuumba I, artists
Best Comic Strip or Webcomic	*Mama's Boyz*	Jerry Craft, writer and artist
Fan Award for Best Comic	*Ascended: The Omega Nexus*	Roger Reece and Jerry Reece, writers

2014

Story of the Year	*Watson and Holmes* #6	Brandon Easton, writer; N. Steven Harris, artist
Best Writer	*Watson and Holmes* #6	Brandon Easton
Best Artist	*Watson and Holmes* #6	N. Steven Harris

Best Male Character	Jack Maguire, *Nowhere Man: You Don't Know Jack*	Jerome Walford, writer and artist
Best Female Character	Ajala, *Ajala: A Series of Adventures*	Robert Garrett, writer; N. Steven Harris, artist
Rising Star Award	*OneNation #1*	Alverne Ball, writer; Jason Reeves and Luis Guerrero, artists
Best Reprint Publication	*Martin Luther King and the Montgomery Story*	Fellowship of Reconciliation/Top Shelf Productions
Best Cover	*Route 3 #2: A Date… A Destiny*	Robert Jeffrey, writer; Sean Hill, artist
Best Comic Strip or Webcomic	*The Adigun Ogunsanwo*	Carles C. J. Juzang, writer and artist
Fan Award for Best Comic	*Watson and Holmes #6*	Brandon Easton, writer; N. Steven Harris, artist

2015

Story of the Year	*Shaft*	David F. Walker, writer; Bilquis Evely, artist
Best Writer	*Day Black*	Keef Cross
Best Artist	*Artifacts*	Nelson Blake 2
Best Male Character	Bass Reeves, *Bass Reeves: Tales of the Talented Tenth*	Joel Christian Gill, writer and artist
Best Female Character	Ajala Storm; *Ajala: A Series of Adventures*	
Rising Star Award	*OneNation: Old Druids*	Alverne Ball and Jason Reeves, writers; Lee Moyer and Ari Syahrazad, artists
Best Reprint Publication	*TechWatch*	Chameleon Creations
Best Cover	*Offset #1- The Man Who Travels with a Piece of Sugarcane*	Tristan Roach

Best Comic Strip or Webcomic	*Kamikaze*	Alan and Carrie Tupper, writers and artists; Havana Nguyen, artist
Fan Award for Best Comic	*OneNation: Safehouse*	Jason Reeves, writer; Samax Amen and Deon de Lange, artists

2016

Story of the Year	*Brotherman:-Dictator of Discipline: Revelation*	Guy A. Sims, writer; Dawud Anyabwile, artist
Best Writer	*(H)afrocentric*	Juliana "Jewels" Smith
Best Artist	*Brotherman: Dictator of Discipline: Revelation*	Dawud Anyabwile
Best Male Character	Arron Day (Blackjack), *Blackjack: There Came a Dark Hunter*	Alex Simmons, writer; Tim Fielder, artist
Best Female Character	Moon Girl, *Moon Girl & Devil Dinosaur*	Brandon Monclare and Amy Reeder, writers; Natacha Bustos and Amy Reeder, artists
Rising Star Award	*Bounce!*	Chuck Collins, writer and artist
Best Reprint Publication	*Concrete Park vol. 2: R-E-S-P-E-C-T*	Dark Horse Comics
Best Cover	*Blue Hand Mojo: Dust to Dust*	John Jennings, writer and artist
Best Comic Strip or Webcomic	*Bounce!*	Chuck Collins, writer and artist
Fan Award for Best Comic	*Bounce!* Chuck Collins, writer and artist	

2017

Story of the Year	*March*, Book Three	John Lewis and Andrew Aydin, writers; Nate Powell, artist
Best Writer	*March*, Book Three	John Lewis and Andrew Aydin, writers
Best Artist	*Black Panther*	Brian Stelfreeze

Best Male Character	Matt Trakker, *M.A.S.K.- Mobile Armored Strike Kommand*	Brandon Easton, writer; Tommy Vargas and Tommy Lee Edwards, artists
Best Female Character	Lily Brown, *Malice in Ovenland* vol. 1	Micheline Hess, writer and artist
Rising Star Award	*Tuskegee Heirs: Flames of Destiny*	Marcus Williams and Greg Burnham, writers; Marcus Williams, artist
Best Reprint Publication	*E.X.O.- The Legend of Wale Williams. Part One*	YouNeek Studios
Best Cover	*Black* #1	Kwanza Osajyefo, writer; Khary Randolph, artist
Best Comic Strip or Webcomic	*Tuskegee Heirs: Flames of Destiny*	Marcus Williams and Greg Burnham, writers; Marcus Williams, artist
Fan Award for Best Comic	*M.A.S.K.- Mobile Armored Strike Kommand*	Brandon Easton, writer; Tommy Vargas and Tommy Lee Edwards, artists

2018

Story of the Year	*Matty's Rocket: Book One*	Tim Fielder, writer and artist
Best Writer	*Leon: Protector of the Playground*	Jamar Nicholas
Best Artist	*Princess Love ♥ Pon*	Shauna J. Grant
Best Male Character	Is'nana the Were-Spider, *Is'nana the Were-Spider*	Greg Anderson-Elysee, writer; Daryl Toh, artist
Best Female Character	Matty Watty, *Matty's Rocket: Book One*	Tim Fielder
Rising Star Award	*Is'nana the Were-Spider*	Greg Anderson-Elysee, writer; Daryl Toh, artist
Best Reprint Publication	*Moon Girl and Devil Dinosaur V3: Smartest There Is*	Marvel
Best Cover	*Matty's Rocket*	Tim Felder, writer and artist
Best Comic Strip or Webcomic	*(H)afrocentric*, vols. 1-4	Juliana "Jewels" Smith

| Fan Award for Best Comic | *Is'nana the Were-Spider* | Greg Anderson-Elysee, writer; Daryl Toh, artist |

Harvey Awards

Named for artist and writer Harvey Kurtzman, the Harvey Awards were established in 1988 to honor the best works published in the comics industry. Comic book professionals vote for the final winners in each category.

1988

Best American Edition of Foreign Material	*Moebius*	Jean "Moebius" Giraud
Best Artist	*Watchmen*	Dave Gibbons
Best Cartoonist	*Concrete*	Paul Chadwick
Best Colorist	*Watchmen*	John Higgins
Best Continuing or Limited Series	*Watchmen*	Alan Moore and Dave Gibbons
Best Domestic Reprint Project	*The Spirit*	Will Eisner
Best Graphic Album	*Watchmen*	Alan Moore and Dave Gibbons
Best Inker	*Daredevil*	Al Williamson
Best Letterer	*American Flagg!*	Ken Bruzenak
Best New Series	*Concrete*	Paul Chadwick
Best Single Issue or Story	*Watchmen #9*	Alan Moore and Dave Gibbons
Best Writer	*Watchmen*	Alan Moore
Special Award for Excellence in Presentation	*Watchmen*	Alan Moore and Dave Gibbons

1989

Best American Edition of Foreign Material	*Incal*	Alejandro Jodorowsky and Jean "Moebius" Giraud
Best Artist	*Batman: The Killing Joke*	Brian Bolland
Best Cartoonist	*Concrete*	Paul Chadwick
Best Colorist	*Batman: The Killing Joke*	John Higgins
Best Continuing or Limited Series	*Love & Rockets*	Gilbert and Jaime Hernandez

Best Domestic Reprint Project	*The Complete Crumb Comics*	Robert Crumb
Best Graphic Album	*Batman: The Killing Joke*	Alan Moore and Brian Bolland
Best Inker	*Daredevil*	Al Williamson
Best Letterer	*Mr. Monster*	Ken Bruzenak
Best New Series	*Kings in Disguise*	Vance and Burr
Best Single Issue or Story	*Batman: The Killing Joke*	Alan Moore, Brian Bolland, and John Higgins
Best Writer	*Love & Rockets*	Gilbert Hernandez
Special Award for Excellence in Presentation	*Hardboiled Detective Stories*	Charles Burns
Special Award for Humor in Comics		Bill Watterson

1990

Best American Edition of Foreign Material	*Akira*	Katsuhiro Otomo
Best Anthology	*A1*	
Best Artist	*Xenozoic Tales*	Mark Schultz
Best Biographical, Historical or Journalistic Presentation	*The Comics Journal*	
Best Cartoonist		Chester Brown
Best Colorist	*Akira*	Steve Oliff
Best Continuing or Limited Series	*Love & Rockets*	Gilbert and Jaime Hernandez
Best Domestic Reprint Project	*The Complete Little Nemo in Slumberland*	Winsor McCay
Best Graphic Album	*Ed the Happy Clown*	Chester Brown
Best Inker	*Daredevil*	Al Williamson
Best Letterer	*Black Kiss*	Ken Bruzenak
Best New Series	*Eightball*	
Best New Talent		Jim Lee
Best Single Issue or Story	*Eightball #1*	Dan Clowes

Best Syndicated Strip or Panel	*Calvin and Hobbes*	Bill Watterson
Best Writer	*Love & Rockets*	Gilbert Hernandez
Special Award for Excellence in Presentation	*Arkham Asylum*	Grant Morrison and Dave McKean
Special Award for Humor in Comics		Sergio Aragones

1991

Best American Edition of Foreign Material	*Lt. Blueberry*	Jean "Moebius" Giraud
Best Anthology	*RAW*	edited by Francoise Mouly and Art Spiegelman
Best Artist	*World's Finest*	Steve Rude
Best Biographical, Historical or Journalistic Presentation	*The Comics Journal*	edited Gary Groth and Helena Harvilicz
Best Cartoonist	*Hate*	Peter Bagge
Best Colorist	*Akira*	Steve Oliff
Best Continuing or Limited Series	*Eightball*	Dan Clowes
Best Domestic Reprint Project	*The Complete Crumb Comics*	Robert Crumb
Best Graphic Album of Previously Published Work	*Warts and All*	Drew Friedman
Best Inker	*Fafhrd and the Grey Mouser*	Al Williamson
Best Letterer	*Eightball*	Daniel Clowes
Best New Series	*Hate*	Peter Bagge
Best New Talent		Julie Doucet
Best Original Graphic Album	*Why I Hate Saturn*	Kyle Baker
Best Single Issue or Story	*Eightball #3*	Dan Clowes
Best Syndicated Strip or Panel	*Calvin and Hobbes*	Bill Watterson
Best Writer	*Sandman*	Neil Gaiman
Special Award for Excellence in Presentation	*Complete Little Nemo in Slumberland*	Winsor McKay
Special Award for Humor in Comics		Sergio Aragones

1992

Best American Edition of Foreign Material	*Akira*	Katsuhiro Otomo
Best Anthology	*Dark Horse Presents*	edited by Randy Stradley
Best Artist	*Xenozoic Tales*	Mark Schultz
Best Biographical, Historical or Journalistic Presentation	*The Comics Journal*	edited by Gary Groth and Helena Harvilicz; art directed by Dale Yarger
Best Cartoonist	*Cerebus*	Dave Sim
Best Colorist	*Akira*	Steve Oliff
Best Continuing or Limited Series	*Eightball*	Dan Clowes
Best Domestic Reprint Project	*The Complete Crumb Comics*	Robert Crumb
Best Graphic Album of Previously Published Work	*Maus II*	Art Spiegelmen
Best Inker	*Love & Rockets*	Jaime Hernandez
Best Letterer	*Sandman*	Todd Klein
Best New Series	*Cages*	Dave McKean
Best New Talent		Joe Quesada
Best Original Graphic Album	*To the Heart of the Storm*	Will Eisner
Best Single Issue or Story	*Xenozoic Tales #11*	Mark Schultz and Steve Stile
Best Syndicated Strip or Panel	*Calvin and Hobbes*	Bill Watterson
Best Writer	*Sandman*	Neil Gaiman
Special Award for Excellence in Presentation	*Complete Little Nemo in Slumberland*	Winsor McKay
Special Award for Humor in Comics		Sergio Aragones

1993

Best American Edition of Foreign Material	*Akira*	Katsuhiro Otomo
Best Anthology	*Dark Horse Presents*	edited by Randy Stradley

Best Artist	*Xenozoic Tales*	Mark Schultz
Best Biographical, Historical or Journalistic Presentation	*The Comics Journal*	edited by Gary Groth and Frank Young; art directed by Dale Yarger
Best Cartoonist	*Invisible People*	Will Eisner
Best Colorist	*Tantalizing Stories Presents Frank in the River*	Jim Woodring
Best Continuing or Limited Series	*Sandman*	Neil Gaiman and various artists
Best Domestic Reprint Project	*The Complete Crumb Comics*	Robert Crumb
Best Graphic Album of Previously Published Work	*Hey Look!*	Harvey Kurtzman
Best Inker	*Spider-Man 2099*	Al Williamson
Best Letterer	*Sandman*	Todd Klein
Best New Series	*Madman*	Michael Dalton Allred
Best Original Graphic Album	*Fairy Tales of Oscar Wilde* Volume 1	P. Craig Russell and Oscar Wilde
Best Single Issue or Story	*Tantalizing Stories Presents Frank in the River*	Jim Woodring and Mark Martin
Best Syndicated Strip or Panel	*Calvin and Hobbes*	Bill Watterson
Best Writer	*Invisible People*	Will Eisner
Special Award for Excellence in Presentation	*Batman: Night Cries*	Archie Goodwin and Scott Hampton
Special Award for Humor in Comics		Sergio Aragones

1994

Best American Edition of Foreign Material	*Billie Holiday*	Jose Munoz and Carlos Sampayo
Best Anthology	*Blab!*	edited by Monte Beauchamp
Best Artist	*Marvels*	Alex Ross
Best Biographical, Historical or Journalistic Presentation	*Understanding Comics*	Scott McCloud; edited by Mark Martin
Best Cartoonist	*Bone*	Jeff Smith

Best Colorist	*Spawn*	Steve Oliff
Best Continuing or Limited Series	*Marvels*	Kurt Busiek and Alex Ross
Best Domestic Reprint Project	*Complete Little Nemo in Slumberland* Volume 6	Winsor McCay
Best Graphic Album of Previously Published Work	*Complete Bone Adventures*	Jeff Smith
Best Inker	*Spider-Man 2099*	Al Williamson
Best Letterer	*Spawn*	Tom Orzechowski
Best New Series	*Captain Sternn*	Bernie Wrightson and Shephard Hendrix
Best Original Graphic Album	*Understanding Comics*	Scott McCloud
Best Single Issue or Story	*Batman: Mad Love*	Paul Dini and Bruce W. Timm
Best Syndicated Strip or Panel	*Calvin and Hobbes*	Bill Watterson
Best Writer	*Understanding Comics*	Scott McCloud
Special Award for Excellence in Presentation	*Marvels*	Kurt Busiek and Alex Ross
Special Award for Humor in Comics		Jeff Smith

1995

Best American Edition of Foreign Material	*Druuna: Carnivora*	Paolo Eleuteri Serpieri
Best Anthology	*Dark Horse Presents*	edited by Bob Schreck and Randy Stradley
Best Artist	*Hellboy*	Mike Mignola
Best Biographical, Historical or Journalistic Presentation	*The Comics Journal*	edited by Gary Groth and Frank Young
Best Cartoonist	*Bone*	Jeff Smith
Best Colorist	*Spawn*	Steve Oliff/Olyoptics
Best Continuing or Limited Series	*From Hell*	Alan Moore and Eddie Campbell
Best Domestic Reprint Project	*The Complete Crumb Comics*	Robert Crumb

Best Graphic Album of Previously Published Work	*Marvels*	Kurt Busiek and Alex Ross
Best Inker	*Spider-Man 2099*	Al Williamson
Best Letterer	*Sandman*	Todd Klein
Best New Series	*Acme Novelty Library*	Chris Ware
Best Original Graphic Album	*Our Cancer Year*	Harvey Pekar, Joyce Brabner, and Frank Stack
Best Single Issue or Story	*Marvels #4*	Kurt Busiek and Alex Ross
Best Syndicated Strip or Panel	*Calvin and Hobbes*	Bill Watterson
Best Writer	*From Hell*	Alan Moore
Special Award for Excellence in Presentation	*Acme Novelty Library*	Chris Ware
Special Award for Humor in Comics		Sergio Aragones

1996

Best American Edition of Foreign Material	*Akira*	Katsuhiro Otomo
Best Anthology	*Drawn & Quarterly*	edited by Marina Lesenko
Best Artist	*Hellboy*	Mike Mignola
Best Biographical, Historical or Journalistic Presentation	*Crumb*	directed by Terry Zwigoff
Best Cartoonist	*Bone*	Jeff Smith
Best Colorist	*Acme Novelty Library*	Chris Ware
Best Continuing or Limited Series	*Sin City*	Frank Miller
Best Cover Artist	*Kurt Busiek's Astro City #1*	Alex Ross
Best Domestic Reprint Project	*The Complete Crumb Comics*	Robert Crumb
Best Graphic Album of Previously Published Work	*Hellboy: The Wolves of St. August*	Mike Mignola
Best Inker	*Superman vs. Aliens*	Kevin Nowlan
Best Letterer	*Acme Novelty Library*	Chris Ware

Best New Series	*Astro City*	Kurt Busiek and Brent Anderson
Best New Talent		Adrian Tomine
Best Original Graphic Album	*Stuck Rubber Baby*	Howard Cruse
Best Single Issue or Story	*Astro City #1*	Kurt Busiek and Brent Anderson
Best Syndicated Strip or Panel	*Calvin and Hobbes*	Bill Watterson
Best Writer	*From Hell*	Alan Moore
Special Award for Excellence in Presentation	*Acme Novelty Library*	Chris Ware
Special Award for Humor in Comics		Evan Dorkin

1997

Best American Edition of Foreign Material	*Gon*	Masashi Tanaka
Best Anthology	*Dark Horse Presents*	edited by Bob Schreck
Best Artist	*Kingdom Come*	Alex Ross
Best Biographical, Historical or Journalistic Presentation	*The Comics Journal*	edited by Gary Groth and Tom Spurgeon
Best Cartoonist	*Bone*	Jeff Smith
Best Colorist	*Acme Novelty Library*	Chris Ware
Best Continuing or Limited Series	*Eightball*	Dan Clowes
Best Cover Artist	*Kingdom Come #1*	Alex Ross
Best Domestic Reprint Project	*Batman: The Dark Knight Returns — 10th Anniversary Hardcover Edition*	Frank Miller
Best Graphic Album of Previously Published Work	*Astro City: Life in the Big City*	Kurt Busiek and Brent Anderson
Best Inker	*Xenozoic Tales*	Mark Schultz
Best Letterer	*Eightball*	Dan Clowes
Best New Series	*Leave It to Chance*	James Robinson and Paul Smith
Best New Talent		Jessica Abel
Best Original Graphic Album	*Fax from Sarajevo*	Joe Kubert

Best Single Issue or Story	*Acme Novelty Library #7*	Chris Ware
Best Syndicated Strip or Panel	*Dilbert*	Scott Adams
Best Writer	*Eightball*	Dan Clowes
Special Award for Excellence in Presentation	*Acme Novelty Library*	Chris Ware
Special Award for Humor in Comics		Sergio Aragones

1998

Best American Edition of Foreign Material	*Drawn & Quarterly*	various creators
Best Anthology	*Dark Horse Presents*	edited by Bob Schreck and Jamie S. Rich
Best Artist	Body of work in 1997 including *Elric: Stormbringer* and *Dr. Strange: What Is It That Disturbs You Stephen?*	P. Craig Russell
Best Biographical, Historical or Journalistic Presentation	*The Comics Journal*	edited by Gary Groth
Best Cartoonist	Body of work in 1997 including *Sergio Aragones' Louder Than Words*	Sergio Aragones
Best Colorist	Body of work in 1997 including *Acme Novelty Library*	Chris Ware
Best Continuing or Limited Series	*Kurt Busiek's Astro City*	Kurt Busiek and Brent Anderson
Best Cover Artist	*Kurt Busiek's Astro City; Batman: Legends of the Dark Knight #100; Squadron Supreme*	Alex Ross
Best Domestic Reprint Project	*Jack Kirby's New Gods*	Jack Kirby
Best Graphic Album of Previously Published Work	*Batman Black & White Collected*	various
Best Inker	Body of work in 1997 including *Black Hole*	Charles Burns

Best Letterer	Body of work in 1997 including *Ka-Zar, Castle Waiting,* and *Uncle Sam*	Todd Klein
Best New Series	*Penny Century*	Jaime Hernandez
Best New Talent		Steven Weissman
Best Original Graphic Album	*Sin City: Family Values*	Frank Miller
Best Single Issue or Story	*Eightball #18*	Dan Clowes
Best Syndicated Strip or Panel	*Mutts*	Patrick McDonnell
Best Writer	Body of work in 1997 including *Kurt Busiek's Astro City, Avengers,* and *Thunderbolts*	Kurt Busiek
Special Award for Excellence in Presentation	*Acme Novelty Library*	Chris Ware
Special Award for Humor in Comics		Sergio Aragones

1999

Best American Edition of Foreign Material	*A Jew in Communist Prague*	Vittorio Giardino
Best Anthology	*Oni Double Feature*	edited by Bob Schreck
Best Artist	*Penny Century*	Jaime Hernandez
Best Biographical, Historical or Journalistic Presentation	*The Comics Journal*	edited by Gary Groth and Tom Spurgeon
Best Cartoonist	*Bone*	Jeff Smith
Best Colorist	*300*	Lynn Varley
Best Continuing or Limited Series	*300*	Frank Miller and Lynn Varley
Best Cover Artist	*Kurt Busiek's Astro City, Superman Forever, Superman: Peace on Earth*	Alex Ross
Best Domestic Reprint Project	*DC Archives: Plastic Man*	Jack Cole
Best Graphic Album of Previously Published Work	*Cages*	Dave McKean
Best Inker	*Black Hole*	Charles Burns

Best Letterer	Body of work in 1998 including *House of Secrets* and *Captain America*	Todd Klein
Best New Series	*The Spirit: The New Adventures*	edited by Catherine Garnier
Best New Talent		Kevin Smith
Best Original Graphic Album	*You Are Here*	Kyle Baker
Best Single Issue or Story	*Penny Century #3*	Jaime Hernandez
Best Syndicated Strip or Panel	*For Better or For Worse*	Lynn Johnston
Best Writer	Body of work in 1998 including *From Hell* and *Supreme*	Alan Moore
Special Award for Excellence in Presentation	*Acme Novelty Library*	Chris Ware
Special Award for Humor in Comics		Sergio Aragones

2000

Best American Edition of Foreign Material	*Star Wars: The Manga*	Toshiki Kudo and Shin-Ichi Hiromoto
Best Anthology	*Tomorrow Stories*	edited by Scott Dunbier
Best Artist	*Hellboy: Box Full of Evil*	Mike Mignola
Best Biographical, Historical or Journalistic Presentation	*The Comics Journal*	
Best Cartoonist	*Bone*	Jeff Smith
Best Colorist	*Acme Novelty Library*	Chris Ware
Best Continuing or Limited Series	*Acme Novelty Library*	Chris Ware
Best Cover Artist	*Acme Novelty Library*	Chris Ware
Best Domestic Reprint Project	*DC Archive Series*	edited by Dale Crain
Best Graphic Album of Previously Published Work	*From Hell*	Alan Moore and Eddie Campbell
Best Inker	*Penny Century*	Jaime Hernandez
Best Letterer	*Acme Novelty Library*	Chris Ware

Best New Series	*Weasel*	Dave Cooper
Best New Talent		Craig Thompson
Best Original Graphic Album	*Batman: War on Crime*	Paul Dini and Alex Ross
Best Single Issue or Story	*Acme Novelty Library #13*	Chris Ware
Best Syndicated Strip or Panel	*Peanuts*	Charles Schulz
Best Writer	*League of Extraordinary Gentlemen*	Alan Moore
Special Award for Excellence in Presentation	*Acme Novelty Library #13*	Chris Ware
Special Award for Humor in Comics		Sergio Aragones

2001

Best American Edition of Foreign Material	*Lone Wolf & Cub*	Kazuo Koike and Goseki Kojima
Best Anthology	*Drawn & Quarterly* Volume 3 #1	edited by Chris Oliveros
Best Artist	*Penny Century*	Jaime Hernandez
Best Biographical, Historical or Journalistic Presentation	*The Comics Journal*	
Best Cartoonist	*MAD Magazine*	Al Jaffee
Best Colorist	*The Authority*	Laura DePuy
Best Continuing or Limited Series	*Acme Novelty Library*	Chris Ware
Best Cover Artist	*Wonder Woman*	Adam Hughes
Best Domestic Reprint Project	*The Spirit Archives*	Will Eisner
Best Graphic Album of Previously Published Work	*Jimmy Corrigan*	Chris Ware
Best Inker	*Black Hole*	Charles Burns
Best Letterer	*Castle Waiting*	Todd Klein
Best New Series	*Luba's Comics and Stories*	Gilbert Hernandez
Best New Talent		Michel Rabagliati
Best Original Graphic Album	*Last Day in Vietnam*	Will Eisner

Best Single Issue or Story	*Superman & Batman: World's Funniest*	Evan Dorkin and various artists
Best Syndicated Strip or Panel	*Mutts*	Patrick McDonnell
Best Writer	*Promethea*	Alan Moore
Special Award for Excellence in Presentation	*Jimmy Corrigan*	Chris Ware
Special Award for Humor in Comics		Sergio Aragones

2002

Best American Edition of Foreign Material	*Lone Wolf & Cub*	Kazuo Koike and Goseki Kojima
Best Anthology	*Bizarro*	
Best Artist	*100 Bullets*	Eduardo Risso
Best Biographical, Historical or Journalistic Presentation	*Jack Cole and Plastic Man*	
Best Cartoonist		Dan Clowes
Best Colorist	*Acme Novelty Library*	Chris Ware
Best Continuing or Limited Series	*100 Bullets*	
Best Cover Artist	*Wonder Woman*	Adam Hughes
Best Domestic Reprint Project	*The Spirit Archives*	Will Eisner
Best Graphic Album of Previously Published Work	*Lone Wolf & Cub*	Kazuo Koike and Goseki Kojima
Best Inker	*Black Hole*	Charles Burns
Best Letterer	*Acme Novelty Library*	Chris Ware
Best New Series	*La Perdida*	
Best New Talent		Jason
Best Original Graphic Album	*Golem's Mighty Swing*	James Sturm
Best Single Issue or Story	*Eightball #22*	Dan Clowes
Best Syndicated Strip or Panel	*Mutts*	Patrick McDonnell
Best Writer	*100 Bullets*	Brian Azzarello

Special Award for Excellence in Presentation	*Spirit Archives*	
Special Award for Humor in Comics		Evan Dorkin

2003

Best American Edition of Foreign Material	*Lone Wolf & Cub*	Kazuo Koike and Goseki Kojima
Best Anthology	*Comics Journal Summer Special 2002*	
Best Artist	*100 Bullets*	Eduardo Risso
Best Biographical, Historical or Journalistic Presentation	*B. Krigstein* Volume 1	
Best Cartoonist	*Bone*	Jeff Smith
Best Colorist	*Hellboy*	Dave Stewart
Best Continuing or Limited Series	*League of Extraordinary Gentlemen*	Alan Moore and Kevin O'Neill
Best Cover Artist	*Wonder Woman*	Adam Hughes
Best Domestic Reprint Project	*Krazy and Ignatz*	George Herrimann
Best Graphic Album of Previously Published Work	*20th Century Eightball*	Daniel Clowes
Best Inker	*Love & Rockets*	Jaime Hernandez
Best Letterer	*Promethea*	Todd Klein
Best New Series	*Rubber Necker*	Nick Bertozzi
Best New Talent		Nick Bertozzi
Best Original Graphic Album	*Cartoon History of the Universe* Volume 3	Larry Gonick
Best Single Issue or Story	*League of Extraordinary Gentlemen* Volume II #1	Alan Moore and Kevin O'Neill
Best Syndicated Strip or Panel	*Mutts*	Patrick McDonnell
Best Writer	*Promethea*	Alan Moore
Special Award for Excellence in Presentation	*Krazy and Ignatz*	

| Special Award for Humor in Comics | | Evan Dorkin |

2004

Best American Edition of Foreign Material	*Persepolis*	Marjane Satrapi
Best Anthology	*Drawn & Quarterly #5*	edited by Chris Oliveros
Best Artist	*Blankets*	Craig Thompson
Best Biographical, Historical or Journalistic Presentation	*Comic Art Magazine*	
Best Cartoonist	*Blankets*	Craig Thompson
Best Colorist	*Acme Novelty Datebook*	Chris Ware
Best Continuing or Limited Series	*League of Extraordinary Gentlemen* Volume II	Alan Moore and Kevin O'Neill
Best Cover Artist	*Black Hole*	Charles Burns
Best Domestic Reprint Project	*Krazy and Ignatz*	George Herrimann
Best Graphic Album of Previously Published Work	*Louis Riel*	Chester Brown
Best Inker	*Black Hole*	Charles Burns
Best Letterer	*Cerebus*	Dave Sim
Best New Series	*Plastic Man*	Kyle Baker
Best New Talent		Derek Kirk Kim
Best Original Graphic Album	*Blankets*	Craig Thompson
Best Single Issue or Story	*Gotham Central #6-10*	Greg Rucka and Michael Lark
Best Single Issue or Story	*Love & Rockets #9*	Gilbert and Jaime Hernandez
Best Syndicated Strip or Panel	*Maakies*	Tony Millionaire
Best Writer	*Louis Riel*	Chester Brown
Special Award for Excellence in Presentation	*Acme Novelty Datebook*	Chris Ware
Special Award for Humor in Comics		Tony Millionaire

2005

Best American Edition of Foreign Material	*Buddha*	Osamu Tezuka
Best Anthology	*Michael Chabon Presents: The Amazing Adventures of the Escapist*	edited by Diana Schutz
Best Anthology	*McSweeney's Quarterly Concern #13*	edited by Chris Ware
Best Artist	*DC: The New Frontier*	Darwyn Cooke
Best Biographical, Historical or Journalistic Presentation	*Comic Book Artist*	edited by Jon B. Cooke
Best Cartoonist	*Bone*	Jeff Smith
Best Colorist	*DC: The New Frontier*	Dave Stewart
Best Continuing or Limited Series	*The New Frontier*	Darwyn Cooke
Best Cover Artist	*Fables*	James Jean
Best Domestic Reprint Project	*The Complete Peanuts 1950-52*	Charles Schulz
Best Graphic Album of Previously Published Work	*Bone: Volume One Collection*	Jeff Smith
Best Inker	*Black Hole*	Charles Burns
Best Letterer	*Wonder Woman*	Todd Klein
Best New Series	*Michael Chabon Presents: The Amazing Adventures of the Escapist*	
Best New Talent		Andy Runton
Best Original Graphic Album	*Blacksad 2*	Juajono Guardno and Juan Diaz Canales
Best Single Issue or Story	*Eightball #23*	Dan Clowes
Best Syndicated Strip or Panel	*Mutts*	Patrick McDonald
Best Writer	*Eightball*	Daniel Clowes
Special Award for Excellence in Presentation	*The Complete Peanuts 1950-52*	Charles Schulz

Special Award for Humor in Comics		Kyle Baker

2006

Best American Edition of Foreign Material	*Buddha*	Osamu Tezuka
Best Anthology	*Solo*	
Best Artist	*Promethea*	J. H. Williams III
Best Biographical, Historical or Journalistic Presentation	*The Comics Journal*	
Best Cartoonist	*Acme Novelty Library #16*	Chris Ware
Best Colorist	*Astonishing X-Men*	Laura Martin
Best Continuing or Limited Series	*Runaways*	Brian K. Vaughan
Best Cover Artist	*Fables*	James Jean
Best Domestic Reprint Project	*Little Nemo in Slumberland: So Many Splendid Sundays*	
Best Graphic Album of Previously Published Work	*Black Hole*	Charles Burns
Best Inker	*Black Hole*	Charles Burns
Best Letterer	*Acme Novelty Library #16*	Chris Ware
Best New Series	*Young Avengers*	
Best New Talent		R. Kikuo Johnson
Best New Talent		Roberto Aguirre-Sacasa
Best Online Comics Work	*American Elf*	James Kochalka
Best Original Graphic Album	*Tricked*	Alex Robinson
Best Single Issue or Story	*Love & Rockets* Volume 2 #15	Gilbert and Jaime Hernandez
Best Syndicated Strip or Panel	*Maakies*	Tony Millionaire
Best Writer	*Captain America*	Ed Brubaker
Special Award for Excellence in Presentation	*Little Nemo in Slumberland: So Many Splendid Sundays*	Winsor McKay
Special Award for Humor in Comics		Kyle Baker

2007

Best American Edition of Foreign Material	*Abandon the Old in Tokyo*	Yoshihiro Tatsumi
Best American Edition of Foreign Material	*Moomin*	Tove Jansson
Best Anthology	*Flight,* Volume 3	
Best Artist	*All-Star Superman*	Frank Quitely
Best Biographical, Historical or Journalistic Presentation	*Art Out of Time*	
Best Cartoonist	*Love & Rockets*	Jaime Hernandez
Best Colorist	*American Born Chinese*	Lark Pien
Best Continuing or Limited Series	*Daredevil*	Ed Brubaker and Michael Lark
Best Cover Artist	*Fables*	James Jean
Best Domestic Reprint Project	*Complete Peanuts*	Charles Schulz
Best Graphic Album of Previously Published Work	*Absolute New Frontier*	Darwyn Cooke
Best Inker	*Eternals*	Danny Miki
Best Letterer	*Usagi Yojimbo*	Stan Sakai
Best New Series	*The Spirit*	
Best New Talent		Brian Fies
Best Online Comics Work	*Perry Bible Fellowship*	Nicholas Gurewitch
Best Original Graphic Album	*Pride of Baghdad*	Brian K. Vaughn and Nino Henrichon
Best Single Issue or Story	*Civil War #1*	
Best Syndicated Strip or Panel	*The K Chronicles*	Keith Knight
Best Writer	*Daredevil*	Ed Brubaker
Special Award for Excellence in Presentation	*Lost Girls*	
Special Award for Humor in Comics		Bryan Lee O'Malley

2008

Best American Edition of Foreign Material	*Eduardo Risso's Tales of Terror*	Eduardo Risso
Best Anthology	*Popgun* Volume 1	edited by Joe Keatinge and Mark Andrew Smith
Best Artist	*All-Star Superman*	Frank Quitely
Best Biographical, Historical or Journalistic Presentation	*Reading Comics: How Graphic Albums Work and What They Mean*	Douglas Wolk
Best Cartoonist	*The Spirit*	Darwyn Cooke
Best Colorist	*Thor*	Laura Martin
Best Continuing or Limited Series	*All Star Superman*	
Best Cover Artist	*Hellboy*	Mike Mignola
Best Domestic Reprint Project	*Complete Peanuts*	Charles Schulz
Best Graphic Album of Previously Published Work	*Captain America Omnibus* Volume 1	Ed Brubaker, Steve Epting, and Mike Perkins
Best Inker	*Witchblade*	Kevin Nowlan
Best Letterer	*Daredevil*	Chris Eliopoulos
Best New Series	*Umbrella Academy*	
Best New Talent		Vasilis Lolos
Best Online Comics Work	*Perry Bible Fellowship*	Nicholas Gurewitch
Best Original Graphic Album	*Scott Pilgrim Gets It Together*	Bryan Lee O'Malley
Best Single Issue or Story	*All Star Superman #8*	
Best Syndicated Strip or Panel	*Doonesbury*	Garry Trudeau
Best Writer	*Y: The Last Man*	Brian K. Vaughan
Special Award for Excellence in Presentation	*EC Archives*	Various
Special Award for Humor in Comics		Nicholas Gurewitch

2009

Best American Edition of Foreign Material	*Gus and His Gang*	Chris Blain
Best Anthology	*Comic Book Tattoo*	edited by Rantz Hoseley and Tori Amos
Best Artist	*Umbrella Academy*	Gabriel Ba
Best Biographical, Historical or Journalistic Presentation	*Kirby: King of Comics*	Mark Evanier,
Best Cartoonist	*Tall Tales*	Al Jaffee
Best Colorist	*Umbrella Academy*	Dave Stewart
Best Continuing or Limited Series	*All Star Superman*	
Best Cover Artist	*Fables*	James Jean
Best Domestic Reprint Project	*Complete Peanuts*	Charles Schulz
Best Graphic Album of Previously Published Work	*Nat Turner*	Kyle Baker
Best Inker	*Thor*	Mark Morales
Best Letterer	*Marvel 1985*	John Workman
Best New Series	*Echo*	
Best New Talent		Bryan J.L. Glass
Best Online Comics Work	*High Moon*	Scott O. Brown, Steve Ellis, and David Gallaher
Best Original Graphic Album	*Too Cool To Be Forgotten*	Alex Robinson
Best Single Issue or Story	*Y: The Last Man #60*	Brian Vaughan and Pia Guerra
Best Syndicated Strip or Panel	*Mutts*	Patrick McDonnell
Best Writer	*All-Star Superman*	Grant Morrison
Special Award for Excellence in Presentation	*Kirby: King of Comics*	Mark Evanier
Special Award for Humor in Comics		Al Jaffee

2010

Best American Edition of Foreign Material	*The Art of Osamu Tezuka: The God of Manga*	Helen McCarthy
Best Anthology	*Wednesday Comics*	
Best Artist	*The Book of Genesis*	Robert Crumb
Best Biographical, Historical or Journalistic Presentation	*Art of Harvey Kurtzman*	Denis Kitchen and Paul Buhle
Best Cartoonist	*Richard Stark's Parker: The Hunter*	Darwyn Cooke
Best Colorist	*The Rocketeer: The Complete Adventures*	Laura Martin
Best Continuing or Limited Series	*The Walking Dead*	
Best Cover Artist	*Hellboy: The Bride from Hell*	Mike Mignola
Best Domestic Reprint Project	*The Rocketeer: The Complete Adventures*	Dave Stevens
Best Graphic Album of Previously Published Work	*Mice Templar,* Volume 1	Bryan J.L. Glass and Michael Avon Oeming
Best Inker	*Amazing Spider-Man*	Klaus Janson
Best Letterer	*Asterios Polyp*	David Mazzucchelli
Best New Series	*Chew*	
Best New Talent		Rob Guillory
Best Online Comics Work	*PVP*	Scott Kurtz
Best Original Graphic Album	*Asterios Polyp*	David Mazucchelli
Best Original Graphic Publication for Younger Readers	*The Muppet Show Comic Book*	
Best Single Issue or Story	*Asterios Polyp*	David Mazucchelli
Best Syndicated Strip or Panel	*Mutts*	Patrick McDonnell
Best Writer	*The Walking Dead*	Robert Kirkman
Special Award for Excellence in Presentation	*The Rocketeer: The Complete Adventures*	Dave Stevens
Special Award for Humor in Comics		Bryan Lee O'Malley

2011

Best American Edition of Foreign Material	*Blacksad*	Juan Diaz Canales and Juanjo Guarnido
Best Anthology	*Popgun #4*	edited by D.J. Kirkbride, Anthony Wu, and Adam P. Knave
Best Artist	*Richard Stark's Parker: The Outfit*	Darwyn Cooke
Best Biographical, Historical or Journalistic Presentation	*The Art of Jaime Hernandez: The Secrets of Life and Death*	edited by Todd Hignite
Best Cartoonist	*Richard Stark's Parker: The Outfit*	Darwyn Cooke
Best Colorist	*Cuba: My Revolution*	Jose Villarrubia
Best Continuing or Limited Series	*Love and Rockets,* Volume 3	Jaime and Gilbert Hernandez
Best Cover Artist	*Hellboy*	Mike Mignola
Best Domestic Reprint Project	*Dave Stevens' The Rocketeer Artist's Edition*	designed by Randall Dahlk and edited by Scott Dunbier
Best Graphic Album of Previously Published Work	*Beasts of Burden: Animal Rites*	Evan Dorkin and Jill Thompson
Best Inker	*Thor*	Mark Morales
Best Letterer	*Thor*	John Workman
Best New Series	*American Vampire*	Scott Snyder, Stephen King, and Rafael Albuquerque
Best New Talent	*Thor: The Mighty Avenger*	Chris Samnee
Best Online Comics Work	*Hark! A Vagrant*	Kate Beaton
Best Original Graphic Album	*Scott Pilgrim,* Volume 6: *Scott Pilgrim's Finest Hour*	Bryan Lee O'Malley
Best Original Graphic Publication for Younger Readers	*Tiny Titans*	Art Baltazar and Franco Aureliani
Best Single Issue or Story	*Daytripper*	Fabio Moon and Gabiel Ba
Best Syndicated Strip or Panel	*Doonesbury*	Garry Trudeau
Best Writer	*Thor: The Mighty Avenger*	Roger Landridge

Special Award for Excellence in Presentation	*Dave Stevens' The Rocketeer Artist's Edition*	designed by Randall Dahlk and edited by Scott Dunbier
Special Award for Humor in Comics	*The Muppet Show*	Roger Langridge

2012

Best American Edition of Foreign Material	*The Manara Library vol. 1: Indian Summer and Other Stories*	Milo Manara
Best Anthology	*Dark Horse Presents*	edited by Mike Richardson
Best Artist or Penciller	*Batwoman*	J.H. Williams
Best Biographical, Historical, or Journalistic Presentation	*Genius Isolated: The Life and Art of Alex Toth*	Dean Mullaney and Bruce Canwell
Best Cartoonist	*Hark! A Vagrant*	Kate Beaton
Best Colorist	*Hellboy: The Fury*	Dave Stewart
Best Continuing or Limited Series	*Daredevil*	Mark Waid and Paolo Rivera
Best Cover Artist	*Batwoman*	J.H. Williams
Best Domestic Reprint Project	*Walt Simonson's The Mighty Thor, Artist's Edition*	IDW Publishing
Best Graphic Album of Original Work	*Jim Henson's Tale of Sand*	Ramón Pérez and Jim Henson
Best Graphic Album of Previously Published Work	*The Death-Ray*	Daniel Clowes
Best Inker	*Daredevil*	Joe Rivera
Best Letterer	*Fear Itself*	Chris Eliopoulos
Best New Series	*Daredevil*	Mark Waid and Paolo Rivera
Best New Talent	*Ultimate Spider-Man*	Sara Pichelli

Best Online Comics Work	*Battlepug*	Mike Norton
Best Original Graphic Publication for Younger Readers	*Anya's Ghost*	Vera Brosgol
Best Single Issue or Story	*Jim Henson's Tale of Sand*	Ramón Pérez
Best Syndicated Strip or Panel	*Cul de Sac*	Richard Thompson
Best Writer	*Daredevil*	Mark Waid
Special Award for Excellence in Presentation	*Walt Simonson's The Mighty Thor, Artist's Edition*	IDW Publishing
Special Award for Humor in Comics	*Hark! A Vagrant*	Kate Beaton

2013

Best American Edition of Foreign Material	*Blacksad: A Silent Hell*	Juan Diaz Canales and Juanjo Guarnido
Best Anthology	*Dark Horse Presents*	edited by Mike Richardson
Best Artist or Penciller	*Saga*	Fiona Staples
Best Biographical, Historical, or Journalistic Presentation	*Robot 6*	Comic Book Resources
Best Cartoonist	*Love and Rockets: New Stories*	Jaime Hernandez
Best Colorist	*Saga*	Fiona Staples
Best Continuing or Limited Series	*Saga*	Brian K. Vaughan and Fiona Staples
Best Cover Artist	*Hawkeye*	David Aja
Best Domestic Reprint Project	*David Mazzucchelli's Daredevil Born Again: Artist's Edition*	edited by Scott Dunbier

Best Graphic Album of Original Work	*Richard Stark's Parker: The Score*	Darwyn Cooke
Best Graphic Album of Previously Published Work	*Alien: The Illustrated Story*	Archie Goodwin and Walter Simonson
Best Inker	*Captain America*	Klaus Janson
Best Letterer	*Fables*	Todd Klein
Best New Series	*Saga*	Brian K. Vaughan and Fiona Staples
Best Online Comics Work	*Battlepug*	Mike Norton
Best Original Graphic Publication for Younger Readers	*Adventure Time*	Ryan North
Best Single Issue or Story	*Saga #1*	Brian K. Vaughan and Fiona Staples
Best Syndicated Strip or Panel	*Dick Tracy*	Mike Curtis and Joe Staton
Best Writer	*Saga*	Brian K. Vaughan
Most Promising New Talen	*Avengers Arena*	Dennis Hopeless
Special Award for Excellence in Presentation	*Building Stories*	Chris Ware
Special Award for Humor in Comics	*Adventure Time*	Ryan North

2014

Best American Edition of Foreign Material	*Attack on Titan*	Hajime Isayama
Best Anthology	*Dark Horse Presents*	edited by Mike Richardson
Best Artist or Penciller	*Saga*	Fiona Staples
Best Biographical, Historical, or Journalistic Presentation	*The Fifth Beatle: The Brian Epstein Story*	Vivek Tiwary, Andrew Cornell Robinson, Kyle Baker

Best Cartoonist	*Battling Boy*	Paul Pope
Best Colorist	*Hellboy: The Midnight Circus*	Dave Stewart
Best Continuing or Limited Series	*Saga*	Brian K. Vaughan and Fiona Staples
Best Cover Artist	*Saga*	Fiona Staples
Best Domestic Reprint Project	*The Best of Comix Book: When Marvel Comics Went Underground*	edited by Denis Kitchen and John Lind
Best Graphic Album of Original Work	*The Fifth Beatle: The Brian Epstein Story*	Vivek Tiwary, Andrew Cornell Robinson, Kyle Baker
Best Graphic Album of Previously Published Work	*Mouse Guard Volume Three: The Black Axe*	David Petersen
Best Inker	*All New X-Men*	Wade Von Grawbadger
Best Letterer	*Rachel Rising*	Terry Moore
Best New Series	*Sex Criminals*	Matt Fraction and Chip Zdarsky
Best Online Comics Work	*Battlepug*	Mike Norton
Best Original Graphic Publication for Younger Readers	*Adventure Time*	Ryan North
Best Single Issue or Story	*Pizza Is My Business, Hawkeye #11*	Matt Fraction and David Aja
Best Syndicated Strip or Panel	*Dick Tracy*	Mike Curtis and Joe Staton
Best Writer	*Saga*	Brian K. Vaughan
Most Promising New Talen	*Sex Criminals*	Chip Zdarsky
Special Award for Excellence in Presentation	*The Best of Comix Book: When Marvel Comics Went Underground*	John Lind

Special Award for Humor in Comics	*Adventure Time*	Ryan North

2015

Best American Edition of Foreign Material	*Blacksad: Amarillo*	Juan Diaz Canales and Juanjo Guarnido
Best Anthology	*Dark Horse Presents*	edited by Mike Richardson
Best Artist or Penciller	*Saga*	Fiona Staples
Best Biographical, Historical, or Journalistic Presentation	*Teenage Mutant Ninja Turtles: The Ultimate Visual History*	Andrew Farago
Best Cartoonist	*Rachel Rising*	Terry Moore
Best Colorist	*Hellboy in Hell*	Dave Stewart
Best Continuing or Limited Series	*Saga*	Brian K. Vaughan and Fiona Staples
Best Cover Artist	*Saga*	Fiona Staples
Best Domestic Reprint Project	*Nick Fury, Agent of S.H.I.E.L.D. Artist's Edition*	edited by Jim Steranko
Best Graphic Album of Original Work	*Jim Henson's The Musical Monsters of Turkey Hollow*	Roger Langridge and Jim Henson
Best Graphic Album of Previously Published Work	*Mouse Guard: Baldwin the Brave and other tales*	Peter Petersen
Best Inker	*Batman*	Danny Miki
Best Letterer	*Afterlife with Archie*	Jack Morelli
Best New Series	*Southern Bastards*	Image Comics
Best Online Comics Work	*The Private Eye*	Brian K. Vaughan, Marcos Martin, Muntsa Vicente, Panel Syndicate
Best Original Graphic Publication for Younger Readers	*Lumberjanes*	Shannon Watters, Grace Ellis, and Noelle Stevenson

Best Single Issue or Story	"Breaking Out" in Dark Horse Presents #35	Dark Horse Comics
Best Syndicated Strip or Panel	*Dick Tracy*	Mike Curtis and Joe Staton
Best Writer	*Daredevil*	Mark Waid
Most Promising New Talent	"Kill Me" from Dark Horse Presents	Chad Lambert
Special Award for Excellence in Presentation	*Little Nemo: Dream Another Dream*	Andrew Carl, Josh O'Neill, Chris Stevens
Special Award for Humor in Comics	*Sex Criminals*	Chip Zdarsky

2016

Best American Edition of Foreign Material	*Two Brothers*	Dark Horse Comics
Best American Edition of Foreign Material	*Corto Maltese: Beyond the Windy Isles*	IDW Publishing
Best Anthology	*Peanuts: A Tribute to Charles M. Schulz*	BOOM! Studios
Best Artist or Penciller	*Saga*	Fiona Staples
Best Biographical, Historical, or Journalistic Presentation	*March: Book Two*	Top Shelf Productions
Best Cartoonist	*Usagi Yojimbo*	Stan Sakai
Best Colorist	*Silver Surfer*	Laura Allred
Best Continuing or Limited Series	*Saga*	Brian K. Vaughan and Fiona Staples
Best Cover Artist	*Saga*	Fiona Staples
Best Domestic Reprint Project	*Crimson vol. 1*	BOOM! Studios
Best Graphic Album of Original Work	*March: Book Two*	Top Shelf Productions

Best Graphic Album of Previously Published Work	*The Less Than Epic Adventures of TJ and Amal*	Iron Circus Comics
Best Inker	*Dark Knight III: The Master Race*	Klaus Janson
Best Letterer	*Ragnarok*	John Workman
Best New Series	*Paper Girls*	Image Comics
Best Online Comics Work	*Battlepug*	Mike Norton
Best Original Graphic Publication for Younger Readers	*Lumberjanes*	Shannon Watters, Grace Ellis, and Noelle Stevenson
Best Single Issue or Story	*Peanuts: A Tribute to Charles M. Schulz*	BOOM! Studios
Best Syndicated Strip or Panel	*Bloom County*	Berkeley Breathed
Best Writer	*Saga*	Brian K. Vaughan
Most Promising New Talent	*The Vision*	Tom King
Special Award for Excellence in Presentation	*Peanuts: A Tribute to Charles M. Schulz*	Scott Newman
Special Award for Humor in Comics	*Sex Criminals*	Chip Zdarsky

Ignatz Awards

Named in honor of the mouse from George Herriman's comic strip *Krazy Kat*, the Ignatz Awards were established in 1997 to recognize excellence in comics publishing by small press creators. Winners are chosen by attendees of the annual Small Press Expo convention.

1997

Outstanding Artist	*Palookaville*	Seth	Drawn & Quarterly
Outstanding Graphic Novel or Collection	*It's A Good Life If You Don't Weaken*	Seth	Drawn & Quarterly
Outstanding Story	*From Hell*	Alan Moore and Eddie Campbell	Kitchen Sink Press
Promising New Talent	*Nowhere*	Debbie Dreschler	Drawn & Quarterly

Outstanding Series	*Acme Novelty Library*	Chris Ware	Fantagraphics
Outstanding Comic	*Eightball #17*	Dan Clowes	Fantagraphics
Outstanding Mini-Comic	*The Perfect Planet*	James Kochalka	

1998

Outstanding Artist	*Cerebus*	Dave Sim	Aardvark-Vanaheim
Outstanding Graphic Novel or Collection	*Ghost World*	Dan Clowes	Fantagraphics
Outstanding Story	"Ghost World" serialized in *Eightball*	Dan Clowes	Fantagraphics
Promising New Talent	*Finder*	Carla Speed McNeil	Lightspeed Press
Outstanding Series	*Acme Novelty Library*	Chris Ware	Fantagraphics
Outstanding Comic	*Acme Novelty Library #9*	Chris Ware	Fantagraphics
Outstanding Mini-Comic	*Amy Unbounded*	Rachel Hartman	

1999

Outstanding Artist	*Liberty Meadows #1*	Frank Cho	Insight Studios Group
Outstanding Graphic Novel or Collection	*Cages*	Dave McKean	Kitchen Sink Press
Outstanding Story	"David Boring" *Eightball #20*	Dan Clowes	Fantagraphics
Promising New Talent	*Fireball #7*	Brian Ralph	Fort Thunder
Outstanding Series	*The Extended Dream of Mr. D*	Max	Drawn & Quarterly
Outstanding Comic	*Liberty Meadows #1*	Frank Cho	Insight Studio Group
Outstanding Mini-Comic	*Fireball #7*	Brian Ralph	

2000

Outstanding Artist	*Weasel*	Dave Cooper	Fantagraphics

Outstanding Graphic Novel or Collection	*From Hell*	Alan Moore and Eddie Campbell	Eddie Campbell Comics
Outstanding Story	*"Jimmy Corrigan, Smartest Kid on Earth" Acme Novelty Library*	Chris Ware	Fantagraphics
Promising New Talent	*Boswash*	Nick Bertozzi	Luxurious Comics
Outstanding Series	*Weasel*	Dave Cooper	Fantagraphics
Outstanding Comic	*The Acme Novelty Library No. 13*	Chris Ware	Fantagraphics
Outstanding Mini-Comic	*LowJinx #2: Understanding the Horrible Truth About Re-inventing Mini Comics (The Bastard Format)*	various, edited by Kurt Wolfgang	
Outstanding Debut Award	*Dork #8*	Evan Dorkin	Slave Labor Graphics

2001

Awards Cancelled

2002

Outstanding Artist	*Artichoke Tales #1, Non #5*	Megan Kelso	Highwater Books and Red Ink Press
Outstanding Graphic Novel or Collection	*The Golem's Mighty Swing*	James Sturm	Drawn & Quarterly
Outstanding Story	*Trenches*	Scott Mills	Top Shelf
Promising New Talent	*Catch as Catch Can*	Greg Cook	Highwater Books
Outstanding Series	*Sketchbook Diaries*	James Kochalka	Top Shelf
Outstanding Comic	*Eightball #22*	Dan Clowes	Fantagraphics
Outstanding Mini-Comic	*Artichoke Tales #1*	Megan Kelso	
Outstanding Online Comic	*Bee*	Jason Little	www.beecomix.com
Outstanding Debut Award	*Pulpatoon Pilgrimage*	Joel Priddy	AdHouse Books

2003

Outstanding Artist	*Shutterbug Follies*	Jason Little	Doubleday
Outstanding Graphic Novel or Collection	*Three Fingers*	Rich Koslowski	Top Shelf
Outstanding Story	*Flee*	Jason Shiga	Sparkplug Comic Books
Promising New Talent	*Same Difference and Other Stories*	Derek Kirk Kim	self-published
Outstanding Series	*Black Hole*	Charles Burns	Fantagraphics
Outstanding Comic	*Rubber Necker #2*	Nick Bertozzi	Alternative Comics
Outstanding Mini-Comic	*I Am Going to Be Small*	Jeffrey Brown	
Outstanding Online Comic	*American Elf*	James Kochalka	http://www.americanelf.com
Outstanding Debut Award	*Studygroup12 #3*	edited by Zack Soto	

2004

Outstanding Artist	*Blankets*	Craig Thompson,	Top Shelf
Outstanding Graphic Novel or Collection	*Blankets*	Craig Thompson	Top Shelf
Outstanding Story	"Glenn Ganges" *Drawn and Quarterly Showcase* Book 1	Kevin Huizenga	Drawn & Quarterly
Promising New Talent	*Kramers Ergot #4*	Lauren Weinstein	Avodah Books
Outstanding Series	*Finder*	Carla Speed McNeil	Lightspeed Press
Outstanding Comic	*Eightball #23*	Dan Clowes	Fantagraphics
Outstanding Mini-Comic	*Lucky #3*	Gabrielle Bell	

Outstanding Online Comic	*American Elf*	James Kochalka	http://www.americanelf.com
Outstanding Debut Award	*Teen Boat #6: VOTE BOAT*	Dave Roman and John Green	Cryptic Press

2005

Outstanding Artist	*Epileptic, Babel*	David B.	Drawn & Quarterly
Outstanding Anthology or Collection	*Diary of a Mosquito Abatement Man*	John Porcellino	La Mano
Outstanding Graphic Novel	*Persepolis 2: The Story of a Return*	Marjane Satrapi	Pantheon
Outstanding Story	*Dogs and Water*	Anders Nilsen	Drawn & Quarterly
Promising New Talent	*Owly*	Andy Runton	Top Shelf
Outstanding Series	*Finder*	Carla Speed McNeil	Lightspeed Press
Outstanding Comic	*Or Else #1*	Kevin Huizenga	Drawn & Quarterly
Outstanding Mini-Comic	*Phase 7*	Alec Longstreth	
Outstanding Online Comic	*Perry Bible Fellowship*	Nicholas Gurewitch	http://www.pbfcomics.com/
Outstanding Debut Award	*Will You Still Love Me If I Wet The Bed?*	Liz Prince	Top Shelf
Outstanding Artist	*Billy Hazelnuts*	Tony Millionaire	Fantagraphics

2006

Outstanding Anthology or Collection	*Black Hole*	Charles Burns	Pantheon
Outstanding Graphic Novel	*Tricked*	Alex Robinson	Top Shelf
Outstanding Story	*Ganges #1*	Kevin Huizenga	Fantagraphics
Promising New Talent	*Salamander Dream, Gray Horses*	Hope Larson	

Outstanding Series	*Owly*	Andy Runton	Top Shelf
Outstanding Comic	*Schizo #4*	Ivan Brunetti	Fantagraphics
Outstanding Mini-Comic	*Monsters*	Ken Dahl	
Outstanding Online Comic	*Perry Bible Fellowship*	Nicholas Gurewitch	http://www.pbfcomics.com/
Outstanding Debut Award	*Class of '99*	Josh Eiserike	self-published

2007

Outstanding Artist	*Love & Rockets*	Jaime Hernandez	Fantagraphics
Outstanding Anthology or Collection	*Curses*	Kevin Huizenga	Drawn & Quarterly
Outstanding Graphic Novel	*Don't Go Where I Can't Follow*	Anders Nilsen	Drawn & Quarterly
Outstanding Story	*"Felix" Drawn & Quarterly Showcase Vol. 4*	Gabrielle Bell	Drawn & Quarterly
Promising New Talent	*The Blot*	Tom Neely	I Will Destroy You
Outstanding Series	*The Mourning Star*	Kazimir Strzepek	Bodega Distribution
Outstanding Comic	*Optic Nerve #11*	Adrian Tomine	Drawn & Quarterly
Outstanding Mini-Comic	*P.S. Comics #3*	Minty Lewis	
Outstanding Online Comic	*Achewood*	Chris Onstad	http://www.achewood.com/
Outstanding Debut Award	*Papercutter #6*	edited by Alec Longstreth	Tugboat Press

2008

Outstanding Artist	*Do Not Disturb My Waking Dream*	Laura Park	self-published
Outstanding Anthology or Collection	*Papercutter #7*	edited by Greg Means	Tugboat Press

Outstanding Graphic Novel	*Skim*	Mariko Tamaki and Jillian Tamaki	Groundwood Books
Outstanding Story	*The Thing About Madeleine*	Lilli Carre	self-published
Promising New Talent	*How to Understand Israel in 60 Days or Less*	Sarah Glidden	self-published
Outstanding Series	*Snake Oil*	Chuck Forsman	self-published
Outstanding Comic	*Snake Oil #1*	Chuck Forsman	self-published
Outstanding Mini-Comic	*Bluefuzz*	Jesse Reklaw	
Outstanding Online Comic	*Achewood*	Chris Onstad	http://www.achewood.com/
Outstanding Debut Award	*Swallow Me Whole*	Nate Powell	Top Shelf

2009

Outstanding Artist	*Swallow Me Whole*	Nate Powell	Top Shelf
Outstanding Anthology or Collection	*Kramer's Ergot #7*	ed. Sammy Harkham	Buenaventura Press
Outstanding Graphic Novel	*Acme Novelty Library #19*	Chris Ware	Drawn & Quarterly
Outstanding Story	*"Willy," Papercutter #10*	Damien Jay	Tugboat Press
Promising New Talent	*Woman King*	Colleen Frakes	self-published
Outstanding Series	*Uptight*	Jordan Crane	Fantagraphics
Outstanding Comic	*Uptight #3*	Jordan Crane	Fantagraphics
Outstanding Mini-Comic	*Stay Away from Other People*	Lisa Hanawalt	
Outstanding Online Comic	*Year of the Rat*	Cayetano Garza	http://magicinkwell.com/?p=68

2010

Outstanding Artist	*Alec: The Years Have Pants*	Eddie Campbell	Top Shelf
Outstanding Anthology or Collection	*Masterpiece Comics*	R. Sikoryak	Drawn & Quarterly
Outstanding Graphic Novel	*Market Day*	James Sturm	Drawn & Quarterly
Outstanding Story	*Monsters*	Ken Dahl	Secret Acres
Promising New Talent	"The Orphan Baiter," *Papercutter #13*	Matt Wiegle	Tugboat Press
Outstanding Series	*Ganges,*	Kevin Huizenga	Fantagraphics
Outstanding Comic	*I Want You*	Lisa Hanawalt	Buenaventura Press
Outstanding Mini-Comic	*Rambo 3.5*	Jim Rugg	
Outstanding Online Comic	*Troop 142*	Mike Dawson	http://troop142.mike-dawsoncomics.com/index.html/

2011

Outstanding Artist	*I Will Bite You*	Joseph Lambert	Secret Acres
Outstanding Graphic Novel or Collection	*Gaylord Phoenix*	Edie Fake	Secret Acres
Outstanding Story	"Browntown" from *Love and Rockets: New Stories #3*	Jaime Hernandez	Fantagraphics
Promising New Talent	*House of Twelve Monthly #3*	Darryl Ayo Brathwaite	Comixology
Outstanding Series	*Everything Dies*	Box Brown	Microcosm Publishing
Outstanding Comic	*Lose #3*	Brendan Leach	Koyama Press
Outstanding Mini-Comic	*Ben Died of a Train*	Box Brown	Self-published
Outstanding Anthology or Collection	*I Will Bite You*	Joseph Lambert	Secret Acres

| Outstanding Online Comic | *Hark! A Vagrant* | Kate Beaton | www.harkavagrant.com |

2012

Outstanding Artist	*Love and Rockets: New Stories*	Jaime Hernandez	Fantagraphics Books
Outstanding Graphic Novel or Collection	*Big Questions*	Anders Nilsen	Drawn & Quarterly
Outstanding Story	"Return to Me" from *Love and Rockets: New Stories #4*	Jaime Hernandez	Fantagraphics Books
Promising New Talent	*Hot Dog Beach*	Lale Westvind	Self-published
Outstanding Series	*Love and Rockets: New Stories*	The Hernandez Brothers	Fantagraphics Books
Outstanding Comic	*Pterodactyl Hunters*	Brendan Leach	Top Shelf Productions
Outstanding Mini-Comic	*The Monkey in the Basement and Other Delusions*	Corinne Mucha	Retrofit
Outstanding Anthology or Collection	*Hark! A Vagrant*	Kate Beaton	Drawn & Quarterly
Outstanding Online Comic	*SuperMutant Magic Academy*	Jillian Tamaki	Now available through Drawn & Quarterly

2013

Outstanding Artist	Michael DeForge	*Lose #4*	Koyama Press
Outstanding Graphic Novel or Collection	Ulli Lust	*Today is the Last Day of the Rest of Your Life*	Fantagraphics Books
Outstanding Story	John Martz	*Gold Star*	Retrofit Comics
Promising New Talent	Sam Alden	*Hawaii 1997 & Haunter*	Self-published
Outstanding Series	Michael DeForge	*Lose*	Koyama Press

Outstanding Comic	Ethan Rilly	*Pope Hats #3*	AdHouse Books
Outstanding Mini-Comic	Charles Forsman	*The End of the Fucking World #16*	Fantagraphics Books
Outstanding Anthology or Collection	Michael DeForge	*Very Casual*	Koyama Press
Outstanding Online Comic	*SuperMutant Magic Academy*	Jillian Tamaki	Now available through Drawn & Quarterly

2014

Outstanding Artist	Sam Bosma	*Fantasy Basketball*	Nobrow
Outstanding Graphic Novel or Collection	Jillian and Mariko Tamaki	*This One Summer*	First Second Books
Outstanding Story	Meredith Gran	"Brownout Biscuit" from *Octopus Pie: Dead Forever*	www.octopuspie.com
Promising New Talent	Cathy G. Johnson	*Jeremiah; Boy Genius; Until It Runs Clear*	Self-published
Outstanding Series	Jason Shiga	*Demon*	First self-published on-line, print: First Second Books
Outstanding Comic	Sam Alden	*Wicked Chicken Queen*	Retrofit/Big Planet
Outstanding Mini-Comic	Sophie Goldstein	*House of Women*	Fantagraphics Books
Outstanding Anthology or Collection	edited by Robert Kirby	*QU33R*	Northwest Press
Outstanding Online Comic	Evan Dahm	*Vattu*	rice-boy.com/vattu

2015

Outstanding Artist	Emily Carroll	*Through the Woods*	Simon & Schuster

Outstanding Graphic Novel or Collection	Sophie Goldstein	*The Oven*	AdHouse Books
Outstanding Story	Jillian Tamaki	"Sex Coven" in *Frontier* #7	Youth in Decline
Promising New Talent	Sophia Foster-Dimino	*Sphincter, Sex Fantasy*	
Outstanding Series	Sophia Foster-Dimino	*Sex Fantasy*	Koyama Press
Outstanding Comic	Sophie Goldstein	*The Oven*	AdHouse Books
Outstanding Mini-Comic	Sophia Foster-Dimino	*Sex Fantasy #4*	Koyama Press
Outstanding Anthology or Collection	Eleanor Davis	*How To Be Happy*	Fantagraphics Books
Outstanding Online Comic	Lilli Carré	*The Bloody Footprint*	New York Times

2016

Outstanding Artist	Tillie Walden	*The End of Summer*	Avery Hill
Outstanding Graphic Novel or Collection	Lisa Hanawalt	*Hot Dog Taste Test*	Drawn & Quarterly
Outstanding Story	Noah Van Sciver	*My Hot Date*	Kilgore Books & Comics
Promising New Talent	Tillie Walden	*I Love This Part*	Avery Hill
Outstanding Series	Keiler Roberts	*Powdered Milk*	Self-published
Outstanding Comic	Sam Bosma	*Fantasy Sports #1*	Nobrow
Outstanding Mini-Comic	Carolyn Nowak	*Radishes*	Self-published
Outstanding Anthology or Collection	Kate Beaton	*Step Aside Pops*	Drawn & Quarterly
Outstanding Online Comic	Meredith Gran	*Octopus Pie*	www.octopuspie.com

Russ Manning Promising Newcomer Award

Awarded annually at Comic-Con International since 1982, The Manning Award is given to a new comics artist who displays exceptional talent.

1982	Dave Stevens
1983	Jan Duursema
1984	Steve Rude
1985	Scott McCloud
1986	Art Adams
1987	Eric Shanower
1988	Kevin Maguire
1989	Richard Piers Raynor
1990	Dan Brereton
1991	Daerick Gross
1992	Mike Okamoto
1993	Jeff Smith
1994	Gene Ha
1995	Edvin Biukovic
1996	Alexander Maleev
1997	Walk Holcomb
1998	Matt Vander Pool
1999	Jay Anceleto
2000	Alan Bunce
2001	Goran Sudzuka
2002	Tan Eng Huat
2003	Jerome Opena
2004	Eric Wight
2005	Chris Bailey
2006	R. Kikuo Johnson
2007	David Peterson
2008	Cathy Malkasian
2009	Eleanor Davis
2010	Marian Churchland
2011	Nate Simpson
2012	Tyler Crook
2013	Russel Roehling
2014	Aaron Conley
2015	Jorge Corona
	Greg Smallwood
2016	Dan Mora
2017	Anne Szabla

WORKS BY ARTIST

Abadzis, Nick
Laika (illustrator), 460

Abel, Jessica
La Perdida (illustrator), 465

Adlard, Charlie
Walking Dead, The (illustrator), 858

Alexander, Jason Shawn
Queen and Country (illustrator), 664

Anderson, Ho Che
King: A Comics Biography (illustrator), 452

Aragones, Sergio
Aliens (illustrator), 42

Ashburn, Bryn
Curious Case of Benjamin Button, The (letterer), 189

B., David (pseudonym of Pierre-François Beauchard)
Epileptic (illustrator), 235, 238

Bagge, Peter
Aliens (illustrator), 42
Hate (illustrator), 336

Baker, Kyle
Nat Turner (illustrator), 566
Why I Hate Saturn (illustrator), 888
You Are Here (illustrator), 903

Baker, Matt
It Rhymes with Lust (illustrator), 386

Baresh, Paul
Mail Order Bride (letterer), 530

Barry, Lynda
One! Hundred! Demons! (illustrator), 588
What It Is (illustrator), 875

Beauchard, Pierre-François. *See* **B., David**

Bechdel, Alison
Dykes to Watch Out For (illustrator), 216
Fun Home: A Family Tragicomic (illustrator), 285

Beletsky, Misha
Jew of New York, The: A Historical Romance (cover artist), 410

Bell, Gabrielle
Lucky (illustrator), 525

Berberian, Charles
Get a Life (illustrator), 295

Bertozzi, Nick
Houdini: The Handcuff King (illustrator), 365

Bicksler, Dennis
Cancer Vixen (colorist), 144

Biggs, Brian
Dear Julia (illustrator), 201

Bissette, Stephen
Aliens (illustrator), 44
Swamp Thing (illustrator), 44

Blanc-Dumont, Michel
Blueberry (illustrator), 107

Blanchard, Jim
Hate (inker), 336

Bleeker, James
Journey: The Adventure of Wolverine MacAlistaire (letterer), 419

Bravo, Émile
My Mommy Is in America and She Met Buffalo Bill (illustrator), 562

Breton, Florence
Blueberry (colorist), 107

Briggs, Raymond
Ethel and Ernest (illustrator), 240
Snowman, The (illustrator), 750
When the Wind Blows (illustrator), 879

Brown, Chester
Ed the Happy Clown (illustrator), 221
I Never Liked You (illustrator), 378
Louis Riel: A Comic-Strip Biography (illustrator), 512
Playboy, The (illustrator), 644

Brown, Jeffrey
Clumsy (illustrator), 167

Brownrigg, Chris
Love and Rockets (colorist), 517

Bruno, Mario
Aya of Yopougon (colorist), 70

Bruno, Philippe
Aya of Yopougon (colorist), 70

Buchman, Ya'ara
Waltz with Bashir: A Lebanon War Story (illustrator), 867

Budgett, Greg
American Splendor: From Off the Streets of Cleveland (illustrator), 51

Burchett, Rick
Queen and Country (illustrator), 664

Burden, Bob
Flaming Carrot Comics (illustrator), 261

Burns, Charles
Black Hole (illustrator), 94

Burns, Ian
It Was the War of the Trenches (letterer), 397

Burr, Dan
Kings in Disguise (illustrator), 456

Byrne, John
Aliens (illustrator), 42

Campbell, Eddie
Alec: The Years Have Pants (illustrator), 33
Bacchus (illustrator), 75
From Hell: Being a Melodrama in Sixteen Parts (illustrator), 279

Campbell, Jim
Age of Reptiles (colorist), 21

Cannon, Kevin
Far Arden (illustrator), 248

Chalenor, Chris
Tank Girl (colorist), 806

Churilla, Brian
Rex Mundi (penciller), 677

Clowes, Daniel
David Boring (illustrator), 193
Ghost World (illustrator), 299
Ice Haven (illustrator), 369
Like a Velvet Glove Cast in Iron (illustrator), 486
Twentieth Century Eightball (illustrator), 849
Wilson (illustrator), 891

Colan, Gene
Predator (illustrator), 652

Colón, Ernie
9/11 Report, The: A Graphic Adaptation (illustrator), 575

Cooke, Darwyn
Richard Stark's Parker (illustrator), 683

Cooper, Dave
Suckle: The Status of Basil (illustrator), 780

Corben, Richard
Aliens (illustrator), 42

Cornell, Kevin
Curious Case of Benjamin Button, The (illustrator), 189

Corteggiani, François
Blueberry (illustrator), 107

Cox, Jeromy
Leave It to Chance (colorist), 474
Rex Mundi (colorist), 677

Crumb, Robert
American Splendor: From Off the Streets of Cleveland (illustrator), 51
Book of Genesis, The (illustrator), 120
Complete Fritz the Cat, The (illustrator), 179
Kafka (illustrator), 438

Cruse, Howard
Stuck Rubber Baby (illustrator), 776

Daigle-Leach, Susan
Life and Times of Scrooge McDuck, The (colorist), 479

Dalle-Rive, Fanny
Epileptic (letterer), 235

Darrow, Geoff
Hard Boiled (illustrator), 322

David B. *See* **B., David**

Davis, Guy
Rex Mundi (penciller, inker, cover artist), 677

Dean, Dan
Mail Order Bride (letterer), 530

Deitch, Kim
Boulevard of Broken Dreams, The (illustrator), 125

Del Carmen, Ronnie
Aliens (illustrator), 42

Delgado, Ricardo
Age of Reptiles (illustrator), 21

Delisle, Guy
Burma Chronicles (illustrator), 134
Pyongyang: A Journey in North Korea (illustrator), 660
Shenzhen (illustrator), 713

Deluze, Eve
Epileptic (letterer), 235
Persepolis (letterer), 631

DeVille, Ellie
Tale of One Bad Rat, The (letterer), 794

Devine, Carol
Ethel and Ernest (cover artist), 240

Devlin, Tom
Aya of Yopougon (letterer), 70
We Are on Our Own (cover artist), 871

Di Bartolo, Jim
Rex Mundi (illustrator), 677

Dionnet, Jannick
Blueberry (colorist), 107

Dorkin, Evan
Predator (illustrator), 652

Doucet, Julie
Long Time Relationship (illustrator), 491

Dranski, John
Queen and Country (letterer), 664

Drechsler, Debbie
Summer of Love, The (illustrator), 785

Drooker, Eric
Flood! A Novel in Pictures (illustrator), 267

Dumm, Gary G.
American Splendor: From Off the Streets of Cleveland (illustrator), 51

Dupuy, Philippe
    Get a Life (illustrator), 295
    Haunted (illustrator), 342

Eaton, Jeremy
    Harum Scarum (letterer), 326

Edwards, Tommy Lee
    Walking Dead, The (cover artist), 858

Eisner, Will
    Contract with God, A (illustrator), 184
    Dropsie Avenue (illustrator), 212
    Last Day in Vietnam: A Memory (illustrator), 470
    Minor Miracles: Long Ago and Once Upon a Time Back When... (illustrator), 548

Faust, Michael
    Waltz with Bashir: A Lebanon War Story (illustrator), 867

Feiffer, Jules
    Tantrum (illustrator), 810

Felix, Phil
    Blueberry (letterer), 107

Fernandez, Leandro
    Queen and Country (illustrator), 664

Ferreyra, Juan
    Rex Mundi (illustrator), 677

Findakly, Brigitte
    Harum Scarum (colorist), 326
    Rabbi's Cat, The (colorist), 671

Fletcher, Jared K.
    Plain Janes, The (letterer), 641
    Sloth (letterer), 743

Follet, René
    Blueberry (illustrator), 107

Fraysic
    Blueberry (colorist), 107

Freeman, Don
    Skitzy: The Story of Floyd W. Skitzafroid (illustrator), 739

Freeman, George
    Leave It to Chance (inker), 474

Gale, Janet
    Blueberry (colorist), 107

Gallant, Gregory.

See **Seth Geary, Rick**
    Treasury of Victorian Murder, A (illustrator), 839

Gebbie, Melinda
    Lost Girls (illustrator), 501

Giardino, Vittorio
    Jew in Communist Prague, A: Loss of Innocence (illustrator), 406

Gibbons, Dave
    Whiteout (cover artist), 883

Gillain, Joseph. *See* **Jijé Gipi (pseudonym of Gianni Pacinotti)**
    Notes for a War Story (illustrator), 579

Giraud, Claudine
    Blueberry (colorist), 107

Giraud, Jean.

 See **MoebiusGonick, Larry**
    Cartoon History of the Universe, The (illustrator), 149

Green, Justin
    Binky Brown Sampler (illustrator), 89

Grenier, Amie
    Leave It to Chance (letterer), 474

Grist, Paul
    Kane (illustrator), 448

Grønevet, Kristian
Jar of Fools (cover artist), 402

Gross, Milt
He Done Her Wrong (illustrator), 347

Guibert, Emmanuel
Alan's War: The Memories of G.I. Alan Cope (illustrator), 29
Photographer, The: Into War-Torn Afghanistan with Doctors Without Borders (illustrator), 636

Guinan, Paul
Aliens (illustrator), 42

Hamilton, Tim
Aliens (penciller), 42

Hanley, Jason
Elk's Run (letterer), 225

Hanuka, Asaf
Waltz with Bashir: A Lebanon War Story (illustrator), 867

Hanuka, Tomer
Waltz with Bashir: A Lebanon War Story (illustrator), 867

Hawthorne, Mike
Queen and Country (illustrator), 664

Heisler, Michael
Blueberry (letterer), 107

Henrichon, Niko
Pride of Baghdad: Inspired by a True Story (illustrator), 656

Henry, Flint
Aliens (penciller), 42
Hergé Adventures of Tintin, The (illustrator), 10

Hernandez, Gilbert
Love and Rockets (illustrator), 517
Palomar: The Heartbreak Soup Stories (illustrator), 606
Sloth (illustrator), 743

Hernandez, Jaime
Love and Rockets (illustrator), 517

Hernandez, Mario
Love and Rockets (illustrator), 517

Hewlett, Jamie
Tank Girl (illustrator), 806

Hillyer, Ed
Bacchus (illustrator), 75

Hollingsworth, Matthew
Queen and Country (cover artist), 664

Horrocks, Dylan
Bacchus (illustrator), 75
Hicksville (illustrator), 356

Hurtt, Brian
Queen and Country (illustrator), 664

J., Eric (pseudonym of Eric Johnson)
Rex Mundi (illustrator), 677

Jackson, Jack
Hey, Wait... (illustrator), 352
Jason (pseudonym of John Arne Sæterøy), 355
Lost Cause: John Wesley Hardin (illustrator), 493

Jijé (pseudonym of Joseph Gillain)
Blueberry (letterer), 107

Johnson, Eric. *See* **J., Eric**

Johnson, Jeff
Hate (colorist), 336
Love and Rockets (colorist), 517

Johnson, Paul
Aliens (illustrator), 42

Johnson, R. Kikuo
Night Fisher (illustrator), 572

Jones, Kelley
Aliens (illustrator), 42

Kalesniko, Mark
Mail Order Bride (illustrator), 530

Kanan, Nabiel
Lost Girl (illustrator), 497

Kane, Gil
Blackmark (illustrator), 99

Katchor, Ben
Jew of New York, The: A Historical Romance (illustrator), 410
Julius Knipl, Real Estate Photographer (illustrator), 429

Katin, Miriam
We Are on Our Own (illustrator), 871

Keating, Scott A.
Elk's Run (colorist), 225

Kidd, Chip
Jew of New York, The: A Historical Romance (cover artist), 410
Sin City (cover artist), 730

Kim Dong Hwa
Color Trilogy, The (illustrator), 171

Kindzierski, Jessica
Strangers in Paradise (cover artist), 757

Klein, Todd
Castle Waiting (letterer), 153
It's a Bird... (letterer), 390
Life and Times of Scrooge McDuck, The (letterer), 479
Lost Girls (letterer), 501
Pride of Baghdad: Inspired by a True Story (letterer), 656

Konot, Sean
Queen and Country (letterer), 664

Koslowski, Rich
Three Fingers (illustrator), 818

Kristiansen, Teddie
Bacchus (illustrator), 75

Kristiansen, Teddy H.
It's a Bird... (illustrator), 390

Kubert, Joe
Fax from Sarajevo (illustrator), 252
Yossel: April 19, 1943 – A Story of the Warsaw Ghetto Uprising (illustrator), 900

Kublick, Wes
Bacchus (illustrator), 75

Kuper, Peter
Give It Up!: And Other Short Stories (illustrator), 305
System, The (illustrator), 790

Kuramoto, John
David Boring (illustrator), 193

Kurtzman, Harvey
Harvey Kurtzman's Jungle Book (illustrator), 331

Kusa, Brittany
It Was the War of the Trenches (letterer), 397

Lapham, David
Stray Bullets (illustrator), 763

Lapham, Maria
Stray Bullets (cover artist), 763

Lappan, Bob
Road to Perdition (letterer), 687

Lappan, Robert
History of Violence, A (colorist), 361

Larsen, Erik
Kampung Boy (illustrator), 443
Lat, 446
Walking Dead, The (cover artist), 858

Leach, Gary
  Life and Times of Scrooge McDuck, The (colorist), 479

Lees, Gavin
  It Was the War of the Trenches (letterer), 397

Lefèvre, Didier
  Photographer, The: Into War-Torn Afghanistan with Doctors Without Borders (cover artist), 636

Legris, Claude
  Hard Boiled (colorist), 322

Lemercier, Frédéric
  Photographer, The: Into War-Torn Afghanistan with Doctors Without Borders (colorist), 636

Lemire, Jeff
  Complete Essex County, The (illustrator), 175

Lieber, Steve
  Whiteout (illustrator), 883

Little, Jason
  Shutterbug Follies (illustrator), 722

Locke, Vince
  History of Violence, A (illustrator), 361

Lopez, Kenny
  Blueberry (letterer), 107

Lutes, Jason
  Berlin: City of Stones (illustrator), 85
  Jar of Fools (illustrator), 402

Mack, David
  Kabuki (illustrator), 433

Mahnke, Doug
  Aliens (penciller and inker), 42

Major, Guy
  Queen and Country (colorist), 664

Malkasian, Cathy
  Percy Gloom (illustrator), 623

Marchetto, Marisa Acocella
  Cancer Vixen (illustrator), 144

Marder, Larry
  Tales of the Beanworld: A Most Peculiar Comic Book Experience (illustrator), 798

Marrs, Sandra
  Louis (illustrator), 506

Martin, Joe
  Kabuki (letterer), 433

Masereel, Frans
  Passionate Journey (illustrator), 611

Mathieu, Marc-Antoine
  Dead Memory (illustrator), 197

Matt, Joe
  Poor Bastard, The (illustrator), 647

Mays, Rick
  Kabuki (illustrator), 433

Mazzucchelli, David
  Asterios Polyp (illustrator), 60
  City of Glass (illustrator), 163

McKean, Dave
  Cages (illustrator), 139
  Signal to Noise (illustrator), 726
  Tragical Comedy or Comical Tragedy of Mr. Punch, The (illustrator), 831
  Violent Cases (illustrator), 854

McKeever, Ted
  Metropol: The Complete Series + Metropol A.D. (illustrator), 543
  Transit (illustrator), 835

McNeil, Carla Speed
  Queen and Country (illustrator), 664

Medley, Linda
Castle Waiting (illustrator), 153

Menu, Jean-Christophe
Epileptic (cover artist), 235

Merrien, Céline
Alan's War: The Memories of G.I. Alan Cope (letterer), 29
Persepolis (letterer), 631

Messner-Loebs, William
Journey: The Adventure of Wolverine MacAlistaire (illustrator), 419

Mignola, Mike
Aliens (penciller), 42
Whiteout (cover artist), 883

Miller, Frank
Sin City (illustrator), 730
300 (illustrator), 822
Whiteout (cover artist), 883

Millet, Jason
Rex Mundi (colorist), 677

Mitten, Christopher
Queen and Country (illustrator), 664

Modan, Rutu
Exit Wounds (illustrator), 244

Moebius (pseudonym of Jean Giraud)
Airtight Garage of Jerry Cornelius (illustrator), 26
Aliens (illustrator), 42
Blueberry (illustrator), 107

Moore, Marcus
Bacchus (illustrator), 75

Moore, Terry
Strangers in Paradise (illustrator), 757

Moore, Tony
Walking Dead, The (illustrator), 858

Morse, Scott
Queen and Country (cover artist), 664

Mullins, Peter
Bacchus (illustrator), 75

Nelson, Mark A.
Aliens (illustrator), 42

Neufeld, Josh
A.D.: New Orleans After the Deluge (illustrator), 1

Nilsen, Anders
Monologues for the Coming Plague (illustrator), 552

Norrie, Christine
Queen and Country (inker), 664

Norton, Mike
Queen and Country (illustrator), 664

Novak, James
Stray Toasters (letterer), 768

Novak, Jim
Blueberry (letterer), 107

Novgorodoff, Danica
Photographer, The: Into War-Torn Afghanistan with Doctors Without Borders (cover artist), 636

Oakley, Bill
Blueberry (letterer), 107

O'Connor, George
Journey into Mohawk Country (illustrator), 424

O'Malley, Brian Lee
Queen and Country (inker), 664
Scott Pilgrim (illustrator), 707

Ortho
Glacial Period (letterer), 309

Osrin, Ray
It Rhymes with Lust (inker and letterer), 386

Osten, James A.
Journey: The Adventure of Wolverine MacAlistaire (letterer), 419

Ottley, Ryan
Walking Dead, The (penciller and cover artist), 858

Oubrerie, Clément
Aya of Yopougon (illustrator), 70

Pacinotti, Gianni. *See* **Gipi**

Patton, Rhea
Love and Rockets (colorist), 517

Pedrosa, Cyril
Three Shadows (illustrator), 826

Petersen, David
Mouse Guard (illustrator), 556

Phillips, Steven John
Incognegro: A Graphic Mystery (cover artist), 374

Pien, Lark
American Born Chinese (colorist), 47

Pleece, Warren
Incognegro: A Graphic Mystery (illustrator), 374
Life Sucks (illustrator), 483

Polonsky, David
Waltz with Bashir: A Lebanon War Story (illustrator), 867

Pope, Paul
Ballad of Doctor Richardson, The (illustrator), 81

Porcellino, John
Diary of a Mosquito Abatement Man (illustrator), 209
Perfect Example (illustrator), 627

Post, April
Bacchus (illustrator), 75

Prado, Miguelanxo
Streak of Chalk (illustrator), 772

Rabagliati, Michel
Paul (illustrator), 615

Rathburn, Cliff
Walking Dead, The (inker, colorist, and cover artist), 858

Rayner, Richard Piers
Road to Perdition (illustrator), 687

Rehm, Dirk
Dead Memory (letterer), 197
Pyongyang: A Journey in North Korea (letterer), 660
Shenzhen (letterer), 713

Reynolds, Eric
Hate (inker), 336

Robbins, Robbie
30 Days of Night (letterer), 814

Robins, Clem
Incognegro: A Graphic Mystery (letterer), 374

Robinson, Alex
Box Office Poison (illustrator), 130
Tricked (illustrator), 844

Rodriguez, Spain
American Splendor: From Off the Streets of Cleveland (illustrator), 51

Rolston, Steve
Queen and Country (illustrator), 664

Rosa, Don
Life and Times of Scrooge McDuck, The (illustrator), 479

Rouge, Michel
Blueberry (illustrator), 107

Rugg, Jim
Plain Janes, The (illustrator), 641

Runton, Andy
Owly (illustrator), 596

Sacco, Joe
American Splendor: From Off the Streets of Cleveland (illustrator), 51
Fixer, The: A Story from Sarajevo (illustrator), 256
Footnotes in Gaza: A Graphic Novel (illustrator), 271
Palestine (illustrator), 602
Safe Area Goražde (illustrator), 699

Sakai, Stan
Queen and Country (illustrator), 664

Saladino, Gaspar
Blueberry (letterer), 107

Sale, Tim
Queen and Country (cover artist), 664

Samnee, Chris
Queen and Country (illustrator), 664

Sæterøy, John Arne. See **Jason**

Satrapi, Marjane
Chicken with Plums (illustrator), 158
Embroideries (illustrator), 230
Persepolis (illustrator), 631

Schultz, Mark
Xenozoic Tales: Cadillacs and Dinosaurs (illustrator), 896

Scotese, Petra
Blueberry (colorist), 107

Seth (pseudonym of Gregory Gallant)
It's a Good Life, If You Don't Weaken: A Picture Novella (illustrator), 393

Sfar, Joann
Rabbi's Cat, The (illustrator), 671

Shamray, Gerry
American Splendor: From Off the Streets of Cleveland (illustrator), 51

Shanower, Eric
Age of Bronze: The Story of the Trojan War (illustrator), 16

Sherwood, Doug
Queen and Country (letterer), 664

Sienkiewicz, Bill
Stray Toasters (illustrator), 768

Simmonds, Posy
Gemma Bovery (illustrator), 290
Tamara Drewe (illustrator), 802

Sinclair, James
Age of Reptiles (colorist), 21

Sis, Peter
Wall, The: Growing Up Behind the Iron Curtain (illustrator), 863

Small, David
Stitches: A Memoir (illustrator), 753

Smith, Jeff
Bone (illustrator), 115

Smith, Jordan
Alice in Sunderland: An Entertainment (cover artist), 38

Smith, Paul
Leave It to Chance (illustrator), 474

Smulkowski, Scarlett
Blueberry (colorist), 107

Snyder, John K., III
Queen and Country (illustrator), 664

Spiegelman, Art
In the Shadow of No Towers (illustrator), 382
Maus: A Survivor's Tale (illustrator), 538

Spoons, Bwana
Tricked (cover artist), 844

Stack, Frank
American Splendor: From Off the Streets of Cleveland (illustrator), 51
Our Cancer Year (illustrator), 592

Stamatiadis, Steve
Bacchus (illustrator), 75

Starr, Roxanne
Flaming Carrot Comics (letterer), 261

Stassen, Jean-Philippe
Deogratias: A Tale of Rwanda (illustrator), 205

Stewart, Dave
Queen and Country (colorist), 664
Rex Mundi (colorist, cover artist), 677

Sturm, James
Golem's Mighty Swing, The (illustrator), 313
Market Day (illustrator), 534

Sycamore, Hilary
Journey into Mohawk Country (colorist), 424
Laika (colorist), 460
Life Sucks (colorist), 483

Talbot, Bryan
Adventures of Luther Arkwright, The (illustrator), 6
Alice in Sunderland: An Entertainment (illustrator), 38
Tale of One Bad Rat, The (illustrator), 794

Talon, Durwin
Queen and Country (cover artist), 664

Tamaki, Jillian
Skim (illustrator), 735

Tan, Shaun
Arrival, The (illustrator), 56

Tardi, Jacques
It Was the War of the Trenches (illustrator), 397

Templesmith, Ben
30 Days of Night (illustrator), 814

Thompson, Craig
Blankets: An Illustrated Novel (illustrator), 103
Good-Bye, Chunky Rice (illustrator), 318

Thompson, Jill
Scary Godmother: The Boo Flu (illustrator), 704

Tomine, Adrian
Shortcomings (illustrator), 717

Tran-Le, Evelyne
Blueberry (colorist), 107

Trondheim, Lewis
Harum Scarum (illustrator), 326

Tuazon, Noel
Elk's Run (illustrator), 225

Tyler, Carol
You'll Never Know Book One: A Good and Decent Man (illustrator), 906

Uderzo, Albert
Asterix (illustrator), 65

Vance, William (pseudonym of William van Cutsem)
Blueberry (illustrator), 107

van Cutsem, William. See **Vance, William**

Varley, Lynn
Sin City (colorist, cover artist), 730
300 (colorist), 822

Varon, Sara
Robot Dreams (illustrator), 691

Vess, Charles
Rose: Prequel to Bone (illustrator), 695

Vrana, Michel
Jar of Fools (cover artist), 402

Wagner, Matt
Whiteout (cover artist), 883

Ware, Chris
Jimmy Corrigan: The Smartest Kid on Earth (illustrator), 414

Warner, Chris
Predator (illustrator), 652

Warnock, Brett
Tricked (cover artist), 844

Weissman, Steven
Love and Rockets (colorist), 517

Wheatley, Doug
Aliens (illustrator), 42

Wiesenfeld, Josh
Strangers in Paradise (inker), 757

Williams, J. H., III
Rex Mundi (cover artist), 677

Winick, Judd
Pedro and Me: Friendship, Loss, and What I Learned (illustrator), 620

Woodring, Jim
Frank Book, The (illustrator), 275

Woodring, Mary
Hate (colorist), 336

Wooton, Rus
Walking Dead, The (letterer), 858

Workman, John
Hard Boiled (letterer), 322

Wrightson, Bernie
Aliens (illustrator), 42

Yang, Gene Luen
American Born Chinese (illustrator), 47

Yeates, Samuel
Lost Cause: John Wesley Hardin (cover artist), 493

Zabel, Joe
American Splendor: From Off the Streets of Cleveland (illustrator), 51

Zamajtuk, Jason
Cancer Vixen (colorist), 144

Zarate, Oscar
Small Killing, A (illustrator), 746

Zingarelli, Mark
American Splendor: From Off the Streets of Cleveland (illustrator), 51

WORKS BY AUTHOR

Abadzis, Nick
Laika, 460

Abel, Jessica
La Perdida, 465
Life Sucks, 483

Abouet, Marguerite
Aya of Yopougon, 70

Anderson, Ho Che
King: A Comics Biography, 452

Auster, Paul
City of Glass, 163

B., David (pseudonym of Pierre-François Beauchard)
Epileptic, 235, 238

Bagge, Peter
Aliens, 42
Hate, 336

Baker, Kyle
Nat Turner, 566
Why I Hate Saturn, 888
You Are Here, 903

Barry, Dan
Predator, 652

Barry, Lynda
One! Hundred! Demons!, 588
What It Is, 875

Beauchard, Pierre-François. *See* **B., David**

Bechdel, Alison
Dykes to Watch Out For, 216
Fun Home: A Family Tragicomic, 285

Bell, Gabrielle
Lucky, 525

Berberian, Charles
Get a Life, 295

Bertozzi, Nick
Houdini: The Handcuff King, 365

Biggs, Brian
Dear Julia, 201

Bissette, Stephen
Aliens, 42

Bogaert, Harmen Meyndertsz van den
Journey into Mohawk Country, 424

Brabner, Joyce
Our Cancer Year, 592

Briggs, Raymond
Ethel and Ernest, 240
Snowman, The, 750
When the Wind Blows, 879

Brown, Chester
Ed the Happy Clown, 221
I Never Liked You, 378
Louis Riel: A Comic-Strip Biography, 512
Playboy, The, 644

Brown, Jeffrey
Clumsy, 167

Burden, Bob
Flaming Carrot Comics, 261

Burns, Charles
Black Hole, 94

Byrne, John
Aliens, 42

Campbell, Eddie
Alec: The Years Have Pants, 33
Bacchus, 75
From Hell: Being a Melodrama in Sixteen Parts, 279

Campbell, Mark
Bacchus, 75

Cannon, Kevin
Far Arden, 248

Castellucci, Cecil
Plain Janes, The, 641

Chalmers, John
Louis, 506

Charlier, Jean-Michel
Blueberry, 107

Clowes, Daniel
David Boring, 193
Ghost World, 299
Ice Haven, 369
Like a Velvet Glove Cast in Iron, 486
Twentieth Century Eightball, 849
Wilson, 891

Collins, Max Allan
Road to Perdition, 687

Cooper, Dave,
Suckle: The Status of Basil, 780

Corteggiani, François
Blueberry, 107

Crécy, Nicolas de
Glacial Period, 309

Crumb, Robert
Book of Genesis, The, 120
Complete Fritz the Cat, The, 179

Cruse, Howard
Stuck Rubber Baby, 776

Darrow, Geoff

David B. *See* **B., David**

DeFilippis, Nunzio,
Curious Case of Benjamin Button, The, 189

Deitch, Kim
Boulevard of Broken Dreams, The, 125

Deitch, Simon
Boulevard of Broken Dreams, The, 125

Delgado, Ricardo
Age of Reptiles, 21

Delisle, Guy
Burma Chronicles, 134
Pyongyang: A Journey in North Korea, 660
Shenzhen, 713

Dixon, Chuck
Predator, 652

Dorkin, Evan
Predator, 652

Doucet, Julie
Long Time Relationship, 491

Drake, Arnold,
It Rhymes with Lust, 386

Drechsler, Debbie
Summer of Love, The, 785

Drooker, Eric
Flood! A Novel in Pictures, 267

Dupuy, Philippe
Get a Life, 295
Haunted, 342

Eisner, Will
Contract with God, A, 184
Dropsie Avenue, 212
Last Day in Vietnam: A Memory, 470
Minor Miracles: Long Ago and Once Upon a Time Back When..., 548

Feiffer, Jules
Tantrum, 810

Fialkov, Joshua Hale
Elk's Run, 225

Fitzgerald, F. Scott
Curious Case of Benjamin Button, The, 189

Folman, Ari
Waltz with Bashir: A Lebanon War Story, 867

Freeman, Don
Skitzy: The Story of Floyd W. Skitzafroid, 739

Gaiman, Neil
Signal to Noise, 726
Tragical Comedy or Comical Tragedy of Mr. Punch, The, 831
Violent Cases, 854

Gallant, Gregory. *See* **Seth**

Geary, Rick,
Treasury of Victorian Murder, A, 839

Giardino, Vittorio
Jew in Communist Prague, A: Loss of Innocence, 406

Gipi (pseudonym of Gianni Pacinotti)
Notes for a War Story, 579

Giraud, Jean. *See* **Moebius**

Gonick, Larry
Cartoon History of the Universe, The, 149

Goodwin, Archie
Blackmark, 99

Goscinny, René
Asterix, 65

Green, Justin
Binky Brown Sampler, 89

Grist, Paul
Kane, 448

Gross, Milt
He Done Her Wrong, 347

Guibert, Emmanuel
Alan's War: The Memories of G.I. Alan Cope, 29

Guinan, Paul
Aliens, 42

Hergé
Adventures of Tintin, The, 10

Hernandez, Gilbert
Love and Rockets, 517
Palomar: The Heartbreak Soup Stories, 606
Sloth, 743

Hernandez, Jaime
Love and Rockets, 517

Hernandez, Mario
Love and Rockets, 517

Horrocks, Dylan
Bacchus, 75
Hicksville, 356

Jackson, Jack
Lost Cause: John Wesley Hardin, 493

Jacobson, Sid
9/11 Report, The: A Graphic Adaptation, 575

Jason (pseudonym of John Arne Sæterøy)
Hey, Wait…, 352

Johnson, Mat
Incognegro: A Graphic Mystery, 374

Johnson, R. Kikuo
Night Fisher, 572

Johnston, Antony
Queen and Country, 664

Kafka, Franz
Give It Up!: And Other Short Stories, 305

Kalesniko, Mark
Mail Order Bride, 530

Kanan, Nabiel
Lost Girl, 497

Kane, Gil
Blackmark, 99

Karasik, Paul
City of Glass, 163

Katchor, Ben
Jew of New York, The: A Historical Romance, 410
Julius Knipl, Real Estate Photographer, 429

Katin, Miriam
We Are on Our Own, 871

Kim Dong Hwa
Color Trilogy, The, 171

Kirkman, Robert
Walking Dead, The, 858

Kubert, Joe
Fax from Sarajevo, 252
Yossel: April 19, 1943 – A Story of the Warsaw Ghetto Uprising, 900

Kublick, Wes
Bacchus, 75

Kuper, Peter
Give It Up!: And Other Short Stories, 305
System, The, 790

Kurtzman, Harvey
Harvey Kurtzman's Jungle Book, 331

Lapham, David
Stray Bullets, 763
Lat, 446
Kampung Boy, 443

Lefèvre, Didier
Photographer, The: Into War-Torn Afghanistan with Doctors Without Borders, 636

Lemire, Jeff
Complete Essex County, The, 175

Little, Jason
Shutterbug Follies, 722

Locke, Vince
History of Violence, A, 361

Lutes, Jason
Berlin: City of Stones, 85
Houdini: The Handcuff King, 365
Jar of Fools, 402

Mack, David
Kabuki, 433

Mairowitz, David Zane
Kafka, 438

Malkasian, Cathy
Percy Gloom, 623

Marchetto, Marisa Acocella
Cancer Vixen, 144

Marder, Larry
Tales of the Beanworld: A Most Peculiar Comic Book Experience, 798

Martin, Alan
Tank Girl, 806

Masereel, Frans
Passionate Journey, 611

Mathieu, Marc-Antoine
Dead Memory, 197

Matt, Joe
Poor Bastard, The, 647

Mazzucchelli, David
Asterios Polyp, 60
City of Glass, 163

McKean, Dave
Cages, 139

McKeever, Ted
Metropol: The Complete Series + Metropol A.D., 543
Transit, 835

Medley, Linda
Castle Waiting, 153

Messner-Loebs, William
Journey: The Adventure of Wolverine MacAlistaire, 419

Miller, Frank
Hard Boiled, 322
Sin City, 730
300, 822

Modan, Rutu
Exit Wounds, 244

Moebius (pseudonym of Jean Giraud)
Airtight Garage of Jerry Cornelius, 26
Aliens, 42
Blueberry, 107

Moore, Alan
From Hell: Being a Melodrama in Sixteen Parts, 279
Lost Girls, 501
Small Killing, A, 746

Moore, Marcus
Bacchus, 75

Moore, Terry
Strangers in Paradise, 757

Nelson, Arvid
Rex Mundi, 677

Neufeld, Josh
A.D.: New Orleans After the Deluge, 1

Niles, Steve
30 Days of Night, 814

Nilsen, Anders
Monologues for the Coming Plague, 552

O'Malley, Brian Lee
Scott Pilgrim, 707

Pacinotti, Gianni. *See* **Gipi**

Pedrosa, Cyril
Three Shadows, 826

Pekar, Harvey
American Splendor: From Off the Streets of Cleveland, 51
Our Cancer Year, 592

Petersen, David
Mouse Guard, 556

Pope, Paul
Ballad of Doctor Richardson, The, 81

Porcellino, John
Diary of a Mosquito Abatement Man, 209
Perfect Example, 627

Prado, Miguelanxo
Streak of Chalk, 772

Rabagliati, Michel
Paul, 615

Regnaud, Jean
My Mommy Is in America and She Met Buffalo Bill, 562

Robinson, Alex
Box Office Poison, 130
Tricked, 844

Robinson, James
Leave It to Chance, 474

Rosa, Don
Life and Times of Scrooge McDuck, The, 479

Rucka, Greg
Queen and Country, 664
Whiteout, 883

Runton, Andy
Owly, 596

Sacco, Joe
Fixer, The: A Story from Sarajevo, 256
Footnotes in Gaza: A Graphic Novel, 271
Palestine, 602
Safe Area Goražde, 699

Sæterøy, John Arne. *See* **Jason**

Satrapi, Marjane
Chicken with Plums, 158
Embroideries, 230
Persepolis, 631

Schultz, Mark
Xenozoic Tales: Cadillacs and Dinosaurs, 896

Seagle, Steven T.
It's a Bird..., 390

Seth (pseudonym of Gregory Gallant)
It's a Good Life, If You Don't Weaken: A Picture Novella, 393

Sfar, Joann
Rabbi's Cat, The, 671

Shanower, Eric
Age of Bronze: The Story of the Trojan War, 16

Sienkiewicz, Bill
Stray Toasters, 768

Simmonds, Posy
Gemma Bovery, 290
Tamara Drewe, 802

Sis, Peter
Wall, The: Growing Up Behind the Iron Curtain, 863

Small, David
Stitches: A Memoir, 753

Smith, Jeff
Bone, 115
Rose: Prequel to Bone, 695

Soria, Gabe
Life Sucks, 483

Spiegelman, Art
In the Shadow of No Towers, 382
Maus: A Survivor's Tale, 538

Stark, Richard (pseudonym of Donald E. Westlake)
Richard Stark's Parker, 683

Stassen, Jean-Philippe
Deogratias: A Tale of Rwanda, 205

Sturm, James
Golem's Mighty Swing, The, 313
Market Day, 534

Talbot, Bryan
Adventures of Luther Arkwright, The, 6
Alice in Sunderland: An Entertainment, 38
Tale of One Bad Rat, The, 794

Tamaki, Mariko, 737
Skim, 735

Tan, Shaun
Arrival, The, 56

Tardi, Jacques
It Was the War of the Trenches, 397

Thompson, Craig
Blankets: An Illustrated Novel, 103
Good-Bye, Chunky Rice, 318

Thompson, Jill
Scary Godmother: The Boo Flu, 704

Tomine, Adrian
Shortcomings, 717

Trondheim, Lewis
Harum Scarum, 326

Tyler, Carol
You'll Never Know Book One: A Good and Decent Man, 906

Uderzo, Albert
Asterix, 65

Vance, James
Kings in Disguise, 456
Omaha the Cat Dancer, 583

Varon, Sara
Robot Dreams, 691

Vaughan, Brian K.
Pride of Baghdad: Inspired by a True Story, 656

Verheiden, Mark
Aliens, 42
Predator, 652

Wagner, John
History of Violence, A, 361

Waller, Drake (pseudonym of Arnold Drake and Leslie Waller)
It Rhymes with Lust, 386

Waller, Reed
Omaha the Cat Dancer, 583

Ware, Chris
Jimmy Corrigan: The Smartest Kid on Earth, 414

Weir, Christina
Curious Case of Benjamin Button, The, 189

Westlake, Donald E. *See* **Stark, Richard**

White, Daren
Bacchus, 75

Wilson, Colin
Blueberry, 107

Winick, Judd
Pedro and Me: Friendship, Loss, and What I Learned, 620

Woodring, Jim
Frank Book, The, 275

Worley, Kate
Omaha the Cat Dancer, 583

Yang, Gene Luen
American Born Chinese, 47

WORKS BY PUBLISHER

Abstract Studio
Strangers in Paradise, 757

Alfred A. Knopf
Cancer Vixen, 144
Tantrum, 810

Am Oved (Hebrew publisher)
Exit Wounds, 244

Antarctic Press
Box Office Poison, 130
Strangers in Paradise, 757

Archaia Studios Press
Mouse Guard, 556

Avon Books
City of Glass, 163

Ballantine Books
Harvey Kurtzman's Jungle Book, 331

Bantam Books
Blackmark, 99

Baronet Books
Contract with God, A, 184

Beanworld Press
Tales of the Beanworld: A Most Peculiar Comic Book Experience, 798

Bélier Press
Complete Fritz the Cat, The, 179

Berita
Kampung Boy, 443

Black Eye Productions
Dear Julia, 201

Boom! Studios
Life and Times of Scrooge McDuck, The, 479

Caliber Press
Kabuki, 433

Cartoon Books
Bone, 115
Castle Waiting, 153
Rose: Prequel to Bone, 695

Casterman (French publisher)
Adventures of Tintin, The, 10
It Was the War of the Trenches, 397

Coconino Press (Italian publisher)
Exit Wounds, 244
Notes for a War Story, 579

Conundrum Press (English publisher)
Paul, 615

Cornélius (French publisher)
Haunted, 342

Daewon Culture Industry (Korean publisher)
Color Trilogy, The, 171

Dancing Elephant Press
Kane, 448

Dark Horse Comics
Adventures of Luther Arkwright, The, 6
Age of Reptiles, 21
Alice in Sunderland: An Entertainment, 38
Aliens, 42
American Splendor: From Off the Streets of Cleveland, 51
Bacchus, 75
Cages, 139
Dead Memory, 197
Fax from Sarajevo, 252
Flood! A Novel in Pictures, 267
Hard Boiled, 322
It Rhymes with Lust, 386
Last Day in Vietnam: A Memory, 470
Rex Mundi, 677

Signal to Noise, 726
Sin City, 730
Tale of One Bad Rat, The, 794
Tales of the Beanworld: A Most Peculiar Comic Book Experience, 798
Tank Girl, 806
300, 822
Violent Cases, 854

DC Comics
American Splendor: From Off the Streets of Cleveland, 51
History of Violence, A, 361
Incognegro: A Graphic Mystery, 374
It's a Bird..., 390
Minor Miracles: Long Ago and Once Upon a Time Back When..., 548
Plain Janes, The, 641
Pride of Baghdad: Inspired by a True Story, 656
Road to Perdition, 687
Stuck Rubber Baby, 776
System, The, 790
Tragical Comedy or Comical Tragedy of Mr. Punch, The, 831
Why I Hate Saturn, 888
You Are Here, 903

Delcourt (French publisher)
Burma Chronicles, 134
Dead Memory, 197
Three Shadows, 826

Doubleday
Cartoon History of the Universe, The, 149
He Done Her Wrong, 347
Shutterbug Follies, 722

Dover
Passionate Journey, 611

Drawn and Quarterly
Aya of Yopougon, 70
Berlin: City of Stones, 85
Burma Chronicles, 134
Ed the Happy Clown, 221
Exit Wounds, 244
Fixer, The: *A Story from Sarajevo*, 256
Get a Life, 295
Golem's Mighty Swing, The, 313
Haunted, 342
Hicksville, 356
I Never Liked You, 378
It's a Good Life, If You Don't Weaken: A Picture Novella, 393
Jar of Fools, 402
Long Time Relationship, 491
Louis Riel: A Comic-Strip Biography, 512
Lucky, 525
Market Day, 534
Paul, 615
Perfect Example, 627
Playboy, The, 644
Poor Bastard, The, 647
Pyongyang: A Journey in North Korea, 660
Shenzhen, 713
Shortcomings, 717
Skitzy: The Story of Floyd W. Skitzafroid, 739
Summer of Love, The, 785
We Are on Our Own, 871
What It Is, 875

Dupuis (French publisher)
Deogratias: A Tale of Rwanda, 205
Photographer, The: *Into War-Torn Afghanistan with Doctors Without Borders*, 636

Eclipse Comics
Tales of the Beanworld: A Most Peculiar Comic Book Experience, 798

Eddie Campbell Comics
Bacchus, 75

Editions Albert-René
Asterix, 65

Editions Dargaud (French publisher)
Asterix, 65
Blueberry, 107
Harum Scarum, 326
Rabbi's Cat, The, 671

El Capitán
Stray Bullets, 763

Independents & Underground Classics   WORKS BY PUBLISHER

Fanfare/Ponent Mon
My Mommy Is in America and She Met Buffalo Bill, 562

Fantagraphics Books
Blackmark, 99
Boulevard of Broken Dreams, The, 125
Castle Waiting, 153
Frank Book, The, 275–278
Ghost World, 299
Harum Scarum, 326
Hate, 336
He Done Her Wrong, 347
Hey, Wait…, 352
It Was the War of the Trenches, 397
Kafka, 438
King: A Comics Biography, 452
Like a Velvet Glove Cast in Iron, 486
Love and Rockets, 517
Mail Order Bride, 530
Monologues for the Coming Plague, 552
Night Fisher, 572
Palestine, 601
Palomar: The Heartbreak Soup Stories, 606
Percy Gloom, 623
Safe Area Goražde, 699
Suckle: The Status of Basil, 780
Twentieth Century Eightball, 849
You'll Never Know Book One: A Good and Decent Man, 906

Firebrand Books
Dykes to Watch Out For, 216

First Second Books
Alan's War: The Memories of G.I. Alan Cope, 29
American Born Chinese, 47
Color Trilogy, The, 171
Deogratias: A Tale of Rwanda, 205
Journey into Mohawk Country, 424
Laika, 460
Life Sucks, 483
Notes for a War Story, 579
Photographer, The: Into War-Torn Afghanistan with Doctors Without Borders, 636
Robot Dreams, 691
Three Shadows, 826

Flesk Publications
Xenozoic Tales: Cadillacs and Dinosaurs, 896

Four Walls Eight Windows
Flood! A Novel in Pictures, 267
Our Cancer Year, 592

Frances Foster Books
Wall, The: Growing Up Behind the Iron Curtain, 863

Gallimard (French publisher)
Aya of Yopougon, 70
My Mommy Is in America and She Met Buffalo Bill, 562

Gemstone Publishing
Life and Times of Scrooge McDuck, The, 479

Gollancz
Tragical Comedy or Comical Tragedy of Mr. Punch, The, 831

Groundwood Books
Skim, 735

Hachette
Asterix, 65

Hamish Hamilton
When the Wind Blows, 879

HarperCollins
Cartoon History of the Universe, The, 149

Harrier Comics
Bacchus, 75

Harry N. Abrams
Nat Turner, 566

Harvey Pekar
American Splendor: From Off the Streets of Cleveland, 51

1023

Henry Holt
Pedro and Me: Friendship, Loss, and What I Learned, 620

Highwater Books
Perfect Example, 627

Hill and Wang
9/11 Report, The: A Graphic Adaptation, 575

Horse Press
Ballad of Doctor Richardson, The, 81

Houghton Mifflin
Dykes to Watch Out For, 216
Fun Home: A Family Tragicomic, 285

Hyperion Paperbacks for Children
Houdini: The Handcuff King, 365

Ibooks
Yossel: April 19, 1943 – A Story of the Warsaw Ghetto Uprising, 900

Icon Books
Kafka, 438

IDW Publishing
Journey: The Adventure of Wolverine MacAlistaire, 419
Richard Stark's Parker, 683
30 Days of Night, 814

Image Comics
Age of Bronze: The Story of the Trojan War, 16
Bone, 115
Kabuki, 433
Kane, 448
Leave It to Chance, 474
Metropol: The Complete Series + Metropol A.D., 543
Rex Mundi, 677
Strangers in Paradise, 757
Transit, 835
Walking Dead, The, 858

Jippi Forlag (Norwegian publisher)
Hey, Wait…, 352

Jonathan Cape
Ethel and Ernest, 240
Tamara Drewe, 802

Kitchen Sink Press
Black Hole, 94
Cages, 139
Cartoon History of the Universe, The, 149
Contract with God, A, 184
Dropsie Avenue, 212
Harvey Kurtzman's Jungle Book, 331
Kings in Disguise, 456
Lost Cause: John Wesley Hardin, 493
Lost Girls, 501
Xenozoic Tales: Cadillacs and Dinosaurs, 896

La Mano
Diary of a Mosquito Abatement Man, 209

L'Association (French publisher)
Alan's War: The Memories of G.I. Alan Cope, 29
Chicken with Plums, 158
Embroideries, 230
Epileptic, 235
Persepolis, 631
Pyongyang: A Journey in North Korea, 660
Shenzhen, 713

Last Gasp
Binky Brown Sampler, 89

Les Editions de la Pasteque (French publisher)
Paul, 615

Les Humanoïdes Associés (French publisher)
Airtight Garage of Jerry Cornelius, 26
Get a Life, 295

Little, Brown
Adventures of Tintin, The, 10
Julius Knipl, Real Estate Photographer, 429

Lothian Books
Arrival, The, 56

Independents & Underground Classics — WORKS BY PUBLISHER

Marvel Comics
- *Airtight Garage of Jerry Cornelius*, 26
- *Stray Toasters*, 768
- *Xenozoic Tales: Cadillacs and Dinosaurs*, 896

Marvel ICON Comics
- *Kabuki*, 433

Metaphrog
- *Louis*, 506

Metropolitan Books
- *Footnotes in Gaza: A Graphic Novel*, 271
- *Waltz with Bashir: A Lebanon War Story*, 867

Musée du Louvre (French publisher)
- *Glacial Period*, 309

NBM
- *Cages*, 139
- *Give It Up!: And Other Short Stories*, 305
- *Glacial Period*, 309
- *Jew in Communist Prague*, A: Loss of Innocence, 406
- *Lost Girl*, 497
- *Omaha the Cat Dancer*, 583
- *Streak of Chalk*, 772
- *Treasury of Victorian Murder*, A, 839

Norma Editorial (Spanish publisher)
- *Streak of Chalk*, 772

Olio
- *Castle Waiting*, 153

Oni Press
- *Queen and Country*, 664
- *Scott Pilgrim*, 707
- *Whiteout*, 883

Pantheon Books
- *A.D.: New Orleans After the Deluge*, 1
- *Asterios Polyp*, 60
- *Black Hole*, 94
- *Boulevard of Broken Dreams*, The, 125
- *Chicken with Plums*, 158
- *David Boring*, 193
- *Embroideries*, 230
- *Epileptic*, 235
- *Gemma Bovery*, 290
- *Ice Haven*, 369
- *Jew of New York*, The: A Historical Romance, 410
- *Jimmy Corrigan: The Smartest Kid on Earth*, 414
- *La Perdida*, 465
- *Maus: A Survivor's Tale*, 538
- *Persepolis*, 631
- *Rabbi's Cat*, The, 671
- *In the Shadow of No Towers*, 382

Paquet Editions (French publisher)
- *Mail Order Bride*, 530

Penguin
- *Tank Girl*, 806

Ponet Mon (Spanish publisher)
- *Mail Order Bride*, 530

Poptoon (Korean publisher)
- *Mail Order Bride*, 530

Random House
- *Snowman*, The, 750

Rip Off Press
- *Cartoon History of the Universe*, The, 149

Rizzoli Lizard (Italian publisher)
- *Jew in Communist Prague*, A: Loss of Innocence, 406

Sasquatch Books
- *One! Hundred! Demons!*, 588

Sirius Entertainment
- *Scary Godmother: The Boo Flu*, 704

Top Shelf
- *Alec: The Years Have Pants*, 33
- *Blankets: An Illustrated Novel*, 103
- *Box Office Poison*, 130
- *Clumsy*, 167
- *Complete Essex County*, The, 175
- *Dear Julia*, 201
- *Far Arden*, 248

Good-Bye, Chunky Rice, 318
From Hell: Being a Melodrama in Sixteen Parts, 279
Lost Girls, 501
Owly, 596
Three Fingers, 818
Tricked, 844

Tundra
Cages, 139

Vertigo
Sloth, 743

VG Graphics
Signal to Noise, 726
Small Killing, A, 746

Villard
Elk's Run, 225

Vortex Comics
Ed the Happy Clown, 221
Transit, 835

W. W. Norton
Book of Genesis, The, 120
Kings in Disguise, 456
Stitches: A Memoir, 753

INDEX

Note: Page numbers in **bold** indicate main discussion. Character page numbers reflect their description only. Additional information about the character can be found in the plot section of the referenced article. Names without qualifiers are characters. * indicates real person with sidebar.

A

*Abadzis, Nick, 437
Abbas (Hamid): *A.D.: New Orleans After the Deluge,* 2
Abberline, Frederick: *From Hell: Being a Melodrama in Sixteen Parts,* 272
Abbess Clarice: *Castle Waiting,* 150
Abby. *See* Nolan, Abigail
Abdel Nasser, Jemal (Gamal): *Footnotes in Gaza: A Graphic Novel,* 260
Abdi: *Chicken with Plums,* 155
Abel: *Book of Genesis, The,* 188
*Abel, Jessica, 441
Abernathy, Ralph: *King: A Comics Biography,* 432
Abigail: *Mouse Guard,* 529
*Abouet, Marguerite, 73
Abraham (Abram): *Book of Genesis, The,* 117
Abram. *See* Abraham
Abraracourcix. *See* Vitalstatistix
absence of color: *Lost Girl,* 475
Abu Ammar. *See* Arafat, Yasir
abuse, child. *See* child abuse or exploitation
abuse, domestic. *See* domestic abuse, as core theme
acceptance, as core theme: *Castle Waiting,* 152
Achilles: *Age of Bronze: The Story of the Trojan War,* 17
Ackermann: *It Was the War of the Trenches,* 385
Acorn, Jemmy: *Journey: The Adventure of Wolverine MacAlistaire,* 403
Adam: *Book of Genesis, The,* 118
Adjoua: *Aya of Yopougon,* 72
Adjutant, Rackham: *Castle Waiting,* 158
A.D.: New Orleans After the Deluge, **1–4**
adolescence, as core theme: *Black Hole,* 93; *Blankets: An Illustrated Novel,* 101;
adventure genre: *Adventures of Tintin, The,* 9–14; *Age of Reptiles,* 23; *Asterix,* 68; *Bacchus,* 78; *Ed the Happy Clown,* 215; *Far Arden,* 240; *Harum Scarum,* 319
Adventures of Luther Arkwright, The, **5–8**
Adventures of Tintin, The, **9–14**
advertisements, artistic: *Jimmy Corrigan: The Smartest Kid on Earth,* 399

Afghanistan: *Photographer, The: Into War-Torn Afghanistan with Doctors Without Borders,* 602
African woman: *Rabbi's Cat, The,* 633
afternoon tea: *Embroideries,* 222
Agamemnon: *Age of Bronze: The Story of the Trojan War,* 17
Age of Bronze: The Story of the Trojan War, **16–20**
Age of Reptiles, **15–19**
aging. *see* maturation and aging
Ahmed, Awad Mohammed: *Footnotes in Gaza: A Graphic Novel,* 260
AIDS: *Black Hole,* 95
Airtight Garage of Jerry Cornelius, **24–27**
Akemi: *Kabuki,* 417
Alan's War: The Memories of G.I. Alan Cope, **28–31**
Albert: *Aya of Yopougon,* 74
Alberta. *See* Jezanna
Albert Victor, Prince (Prince Eddy): *From Hell: Being a Melodrama in Sixteen Parts,* 272
Alcazar, General: *Adventures of Tintin, The,* 11
Alec: The Years Have Pants, **32–36**
Aleron: *Rex Mundi,* 639
Alexis: *Queen and Country,* 628
Ali: *Pride of Baghdad: Inspired by a True Story,* 620
Alibabic, Munir: *Fixer, The: A Story from Sarajevo,* 247
Alice: *Lucky,* 499
Alice from *Alice's Adventures in Wonderland. See* Fairchild, Lady Alice
Alice in Sunderland: An Entertainment, **37–40**
alienation, as core theme: *American Born Chinese,* 48; *Ballad of Doctor Richardson, The,* 84; *Give It Up!: And Other Short Stories,* 298; *Hate,* 330. *See also* prejudice and discrimination
Alien King: *Aliens,* 43
Aliens, **41–45**
Alison, Aunt: *Louis,* 483
allegory, nature of: *Cages,* 139; *Three Shadows,* 794; *Tragical Comedy or Comical Tragedy of Mr. Punch, The,* 798
Alms, Harold: *Julius Knipl, Real Estate Photographer,* 412

1027

al-Rashid, Shaykh Ibrahim: *Rex Mundi*, 639

al-Shehhi, Marwan: *9/11 Report, The: A Graphic Adaptation*, 544

alternative genre: *Airtight Garage of Jerry Cornelius*, 24-27; *Arrival, The*, 59-62; *Asterios Polyp*, 63-66; *Black Hole*, 93-96; *Cages*, 137-140; *Complete Essex County, The*, 170-173; *Complete Fritz the Cat, The*, 174-178; *Dead Memory*, 190-193; *Dropsie Avenue*, 179-182; *Dykes to Watch Out For*, 209-213; *Ed the Happy Clown*, 214-217; *Ghost World*, 290-295; *Give It Up!: And Other Short Stories*, 296-299; *Harvey Kurtzman's Jungle Book*, 323-326; *Hate*, 327-331; *Hey, Wait...*, 340-342; *Hicksville*, 343-346; *Ice Haven*, 359-362; *Jar of Fools*, 388-390; *Jew in Communist Prague, A: Loss of Innocence*, 391-394; *Jimmy Corrigan: The Smartest Kid on Earth*, 398-401; *Julius Knipl, Real Estate Photographer*, 411-413; *Like a Velvet Glove Cast in Iron*, 463-466; *Long Time Relationship*, 467-469; *Lost Girl*, 474-476; *Lost Girls*, 477-481; *Love and Rockets*, 491-497; *Mail Order Bride*, 502-505; *Metropol: The Complete Series + Metropol A.D.*, 514-517; *Monologues for the Coming Plague*, 522-525; *Night Fisher*, 540-542; *Omaha the Cat Dancer*, 551-555; *One! Hundred! Demons!*, 556-559; *Palomar: The Heartbreak Soup Stories*, 573-576; *Passionate Journey*, 577-580; *Percy Gloom*, 591-594; *Plain Janes, The*, 605-607; *Signal to Noise*, 683-686; *Skim*, 692-695; *Skitzy: The Story of Floyd W. Skitzafroid*, 696-699 *Sloth*, 700-703; *Small Killing, A*, 704-707; *Strangers in Paradise*, 722-726; *Streak of Chalk*, 736-739; *Suckle: The Status of Basil*, 745-748; *Summer of Love, The*, 753-755; *System, The*, 756-759; *Tale of One Bad Rat, The*, 760-763; *Tantrum*, 776-779; *Three Fingers*, 784-787; *Tragical Comedy or Comical Tragedy of Mr. Punch, The*, 796-799; *Tricked*, 807-810; *Twentieth Century Eightball*, 811-814; *When the Wind Blows*, 842-845; *Why I Hate Saturn*, 850-852; *Wilson*, 853-856

altruism, as core theme: *Burma Chronicles*, 136

Alysha: *Elk's Run*, 218

Amalia: *Kafka*, 421

Amazing Ernesto. *See* Weiss, Ernie

Amber: *Far Arden*, 239

Amelia: *Stray Bullets*, 729

American Born Chinese, **46-49**

American Dream, as core theme: *Dropsie Avenue*, 214; *Hate*, 207

American Indians. *See* Native Americans

American Splendor: From Off the Streets of Cleveland, **50-54**

Ames, Mr.: *Ice Haven*, 360

Ammar: *Palestine*, 570

Amos, Uncle: *Minor Miracles: Long Ago and Once Upon a Time Back When...*, 519

amputation: *Haunted*, 334

Ana: *Streak of Chalk*, 736

André, Grandfather: *Epileptic*, 228

Andrea: *Walking Dead, The*, 825

Andy: *Poor Bastard, The*, 611

Angel: *Cages*, 139; *Owly*, 140

Angel (Michael O'Sullivan, Sr.): *Road to Perdition*, 646

Angel Face (Marmaduke O'Shaughnessy): *Blueberry*, 109

Angelic Woman: *Suckle: The Status of Basil*, 745

Angel of Death. *See* Azrael

Angus: *Lucky*, 500

animal characters: *Deogratias: A Tale of Rwanda*, 198-201; *Glacial Period*, 300-303; *Harum Scarum*, 319-333; *Haunted*, 332-335; *Laika*, 437-440; *Maus: A Survivor's Tale*, 509-513; *Mouse Guard*, 526-530; *Owly*, 564-568; *Rabbi's Cat, The*, 632-636; *Three Fingers*, 784-786

animalism, as core theme: *Walking Dead, The*, 826

animation, evolution of: *Boulevard of Broken Dreams, The*, 123

Anna: *Berlin: City of Stones*, 87; *We Are on Our Own*, 836

Anne: *Lost Girl*, 478

Anne, Princess (and later Queen): *Adventures of Luther Arkwright, The*, 6

Annie: *Paul*, 582

Anoosh, Uncle: *Persepolis*, 598

Antelope: *Pride of Baghdad: Inspired by a True Story*, 620

anthropomorphism: *Complete Fritz the Cat, The*, 176

antiheroic: *Fixer, The: A Story from Sarajevo*, 257-258; *Flaming Carrot Comics*, 248

Anti-Semitism, as core theme: *Golem's Mighty Swing, The*, 305; *Jew in Communist Prague, A: Loss of Innocence*, 391; *We Are on Our Own*, 838. *See also* Judaism apocalypse, as core theme: *Blackmark*, 99; *Metropol: The Complete Series + Metropol A.D.*, 516; *Rex Mundi*, 640; *Signal to Noise*, 785; *Walking Dead, The*, 826; zombie, *Walking Dead, The*, 826

Apollinaria: *Deogratias: A Tale of Rwanda*, 198

appearance, surface, as core theme: *Cancer Vixen*, 562; *Curious Case of Benjamin Button, The*, 185; *Dead Memory*, 192; *Why I Hate Saturn*, 851

appearance *vs.* reality, as core theme: *Queen and Country*, 630

Applejack, Celia: *Stray Bullets*, 729

Applejack, Virginia (Amy Racecar): *Stray Bullets*, 727

Arafat, Yasir (Abu Ammar): *Footnotes in Gaza: A Graphic Novel*, 260

Archangel of Death. *See* O'Sullivan, Michael, Sr.

Archer, Ms.: *Skim*, 692

architecture: *It's a Good Life, If You Don't Weaken: A Picture Novella*, 380

Arisztidescu, Radu: *Life Sucks*, 460

Arkwright, Luther: *Adventures of Luther Arkwright, The*, 6

Armwhistle, Carhorn: *Three Fingers*, 785

Arrival, The, **59–62**

Arshadian, Amineh: *Embroideries*, 223

art, as core theme: *Gemma Bovery*, 283; *Glacial Period*, 302; *Ice Haven*, 361; *Signal to Noise*, 685; *Strangers in Paradise*, 725; *Tale of One Bad Rat, The*, 762

Arthur, Grandfather: *Tragical Comedy or Comical Tragedy of Mr. Punch, The*, 797

artistic journey: *Alec: The Years Have Pants*, 34

artistic style. *See artistic style* section in specific articles; specific artistic style elements such as panels

Aryeh, Uncle: *Exit Wounds*, 235

Ashraf (the Lion): *Footnotes in Gaza: A Graphic Novel*, 260

Assurancetourix. *See* Cacofonix

Asterios Polyp, **63–66**

Asterix, **67–71**

Asterix (Astérix): *Asterix*, 67

Atta, Mohammed: *9/11 Report, The: A Graphic Adaptation*, 544

attitude changes, as core theme: *Cancer Vixen*, 143

Augustine: *Deogratias: A Tale of Rwanda*, 199

Aunt Alison: *Louis*, 483

Aunt Ruthie: *Exit Wounds*, 235

Aunt Sarah: *It's a Bird...*, 377

Auster, Paul (character): *City of Glass*, 159

authenticity, as core theme: *Poor Bastard, The*, 613; *Skim*, 692; *Tricked*, 809

autobiographical genre: *Alan's War: The Memories of G.I. Alan Cope*, 28; *Alec: The Years Have Pants*, 32; *American Splendor: From Off the Streets of Cleveland*, 50; *Binky Brown Sampler*, 89; *Blankets: An Illustrated Novel*, 101; *Box Office Poison*, 125; *Burma Chronicles*, 133; *Cancer Vixen*, 141; *Clumsy*, 162; *Contract with God, A*, 179; *Diary of a Mosquito Abatement Man*, 202; *Dropsie Avenue*, 205; *Epileptic*, 226; *Fixer, The: A Story from Sarajevo*, 242; *Flood! A Novel in Pictures*, 255; *Fun Home: A Family Tragicomic*, 276; *Get a Life*, 286; *Good-Bye, Chunky Rice*, 311; *Haunted*, 332; *I Never Liked You*, 367; *It's a Bird...*, 377; *It's a Good Life, If You Don't Weaken: A Picture Novella*, 380; *Kampung Boy*, 442; *Last Day in Vietnam: A Memory*, 445; *Long Time Relationship*, 467; *Lucky*, 489; *Minor Miracles: Long Ago and Once Upon a Time Back When...*, 518; *My Mommy Is in America and She Met Buffalo Bill*, 531; *One! Hundred! Demons!*, 556; *Our Cancer Year*, 560; *Palestine*, 569; *Paul*, 581; *Pedro and Me: Friendship, Loss, and What I Learned*, 588; *Perfect Example*, 595; *Persepolis*, 598; *Playboy, The*, 608; *Poor Bastard, The*, 611; *Pyongyang: A Journey in North Korea*, 622; *Safe Area Goražde*, 659; *Shenzhen*, 671; *Stitches: A Memoir*, 718; *Twentieth Century Eightball*, 811; *Wall, The: Growing Up Behind the Iron Curtain*, 828; *Waltz with Bashir: A Lebanon War Story*, 832; *We Are on Our Own*, 836; *What It Is*, 839; *You'll Never Know Book One: A Good and Decent Man*, 867

Aya: *Aya of Yopougon*, 72

Aya of Yopougon, **72–76**

Aye, Maung: *Burma Chronicles*, 134

Azarael, Isaac: *Jew of New York, The: A Historical Romance*, 396

Azrael (Angel of Death): *Chicken with Plums*, 155

Azzi: *Embroideries*, 244

B

*B., David (pseudonym of Pierre-François Beauchard), 238, *Epileptic*, 226

Bacchus: *Bacchus*, 80

Bacchus, **77-81**
background style: *A.D.: New Orleans After the Deluge,* 2-3; *Aya of Yopougon,* 72; *Chicken with Plums,* 154; *City of Glass,* 158; *Dear Julia,* 194; *Dropsie Avenue,* 205; *Ed the Happy Clown,* 214; *Far Arden,* 238; *Give It Up!: And Other Short Stories,* 296; *He Done Her Wrong,* 336; *From Hell: Being a Melodrama in Sixteen Parts,* 271; *Kabuki,* 414; *Life and Times of Scrooge McDuck, The,* 454; *Monologues for the Coming Plague,* 522; *Our Cancer Year,* 560; *Pedro and Me: Friendship, Loss, and What I Learned,* 588; *Playboy, The,* 608; *Poor Bastard, The,* 611; *Rose: Prequel to Bone,* 652; *Tale of One Bad Rat, The,* 760; *Tank Girl,* 772; *30 Days of Night,* 780
*Bagge, Peter, 330
Bajramovic, Ismet (Celo): *Fixer, The: A Story from Sarajevo,* 247
Bakalites, The: *Airtight Garage of Jerry Cornelius,* 25
*Baker, Kyle, 535
Baker, Mary Beth (Tambi): *Strangers in Paradise,* 724
Ballad of Doctor Richardson, The, **82-85**
balloons. *See* speech bubbles (balloons)
Balsaad: *Rose: Prequel to Bone,* 654
Balzamo: *Blackmark,* 98
Barbara: *Hard Boiled,* 316
Barnes, Dave: *Black Hole,* 94
Baron. *See* Old Man
Barry, grandmother of Lynda: *One! Hundred! Demons!,* 556
*Barry, Lynda, 556
Barry, Lynda (character): *One! Hundred! Demons!,* 556; *What It Is,* 839
Barry, mother of Lynda: *One! Hundred! Demons!,* 556
Bartleby: *Bone,* 113
baseball: *Golem's Mighty Swing, The,* 304-307
Basil: *Suckle: The Status of Basil,* 745
Batts, Leonard: *Hicksville,* 344
Bauer, Captain Rolf: *Lost Girls,* 479
Baumhoffer: *Blueberry,* 109
Beachard, Florence: *Epileptic,* 227
Beachard, Jean-Christophe: *Epileptic,* 227
Beachard, Marie-Claire: *Epileptic,* 227
Beagle Boys: *Life and Times of Scrooge McDuck, The,* 455
Beam, Ray: *Tricked,* 808
Beanish: *Tales of the Beanworld: A Most Peculiar Comic Book Experience,* 765

Beatty, Daniel (New Man): *Houdini: The Handcuff King,* 356
Beauchard, Pierre-François. *See* B., David
beauty, feminine, as core theme: *Color Trilogy, The,* 173
Beaver, Goodman: *Harvey Kurtzman's Jungle Book,* 324
Bechdel, Alison (character): *Fun Home: A Family Tragicomic,* 276
Bechdel, Bruce: *Fun Home: A Family Tragicomic,* 276
Bechdel, Helen: *Fun Home: A Family Tragicomic,* 278
Bee: *Shutterbug Follies,* 680
Begovic, Dr. Alija: *Safe Area Goražde,* 660
Bell, Duncan: *Leave It to Chance,* 449
*Bell, Gabrielle, 498
Bell, Gabrielle (character): *Lucky,* 498
Bell, Henry (Hershl Bloom): *Golem's Mighty Swing, The,* 304
Bell, Ormond: *Julius Knipl, Real Estate Photographer,* 412
Ben: *Blankets: An Illustrated Novel,* 102; *Tale of One Bad Rat, The,* 760
Bender, Kate: *Treasury of Victorian Murder, A,* 805
Bendix, Will: *Leave It to Chance,* 449
Benedetto, Richie: *History of Violence, A,* 340
Ben Gurion, David: *Footnotes in Gaza: A Graphic Novel,* 260
Benina: *Deogratias: A Tale of Rwanda,* 199
Benny: *Contract with God, A,* 180
Ben-Yishai, Ron: *Waltz with Bashir: A Lebanon War Story,* 834
Berlin: City of Stones, **86-88**
Bernard: *Percy Gloom,* 591
Berto: *Streak of Chalk,* 736
*Bertozzi, Nick, 355
Bessehl, Emile: *Far Arden,* 239
Beth: *Lost Girl,* 475
betrayal: *Box Office Poison,* 126
Big Daddy: *Stray Toasters,* 733
Big Fish: *Tales of the Beanworld: A Most Peculiar Comic Book Experience,* 765
*Biggs, Brian, 194
Big Nose: *Age of Reptiles,* 21
bigotry. *See* prejudice and discrimination
Billie (Newt): *Aliens,* 41
Billings: *Like a Velvet Glove Cast in Iron,* 463

Binet: *It Was the War of the Trenches,* 384
Binky Brown Sampler, **89–92**
bin Laden, Osama: *9/11 Report, The: A Graphic Adaptation,* 543
Bintou: *Aya of Yopougon,* 72
biographical genre: *Chicken with Plums,* 154; *Embroideries,* 154; *Epileptic,* 226; *Ethel and Ernest,* 231; *Fun Home: A Family Tragicomic,* 276; *Houdini: The Handcuff King,* 355; *Jew of New York, The: A Historical Romance,* 395; *Kafka,* 419; *King: A Comics Biography,* 431; *Laika,* 437; *La Perdida,* 441; *Lost Cause: John Wesley Hardin,* 470; *Louis Riel: A Comic-Strip Biography,* 487; *Maus: A Survivor's Tale,* 509; *You'll Never Know Book One: A Good and Decent Man,* 867
Bird Lady: *Monologues for the Coming Plague,* 522
*Bissette, Stephen, 44
Bjørn: *Hey, Wait...,* 340
B. K.: *Journey: The Adventure of Wolverine MacAlistaire,* 402
Black Boxes: *Dead Memory,* 191
Black Hole, **93–96**
Blackmark: *Blackmark,* 98
Blackmark, **97–100**
Blake: *Blueberry,* 109
Blanche: *Hard Boiled,* 316
Blankets: An Illustrated Novel, **101–104**
Blank-Faced Man: *Monologues for the Coming Plague,* 523
Blau, David: *We Are on Our Own,* 837
Bloch, Frederick (Freddie): *Kings in Disguise,* 435
Bloggs, Hilda: *When the Wind Blows,* 843
Bloggs, Jim: *When the Wind Blows,* 843
Bloom, Hershl. *See* Bell, Henry
Blue Back: *Age of Reptiles,* 21
Blueberry, **105–111**
Blue Eyes. *See* Delia
Blyss, Dr.: *Stitches: A Memoir,* 720
Boats, Mr.: *American Splendor: From Off the Streets of Cleveland,* 52
Boaz: *Airtight Garage of Jerry Cornelius,* 25
Bob. *See* Grey, Danny
body image: *Love and Rockets,* 496
body language: *Bone,* 118; *Footnotes in Gaza: A Graphic Novel,* 259; *Glacial Period,* 300; *Jar of Fools: A Picture Story,* 388; *Plain Janes, The,* 606.; *Robot Dreams,* 649; *Skim,* 692; *Sloth,* 700; *Stitches: A Memoir,* 718

Boggs, Detective Roger: *Stray Bullets,* 730
Bone, **112–116**
Bone, Fone: *Bone,* 115
Bone, Phonciple "Phoney": *Bone,* 114
Bone, Smiley: *Bone,* 115
Bongsoon: *Color Trilogy, The,* 166
Bonner, Senator Calvin: *Omaha the Cat Dancer,* 552
Booga: *Tank Girl,* 772
Book of Genesis, The, **117–120**
Boom'r Band: *Tales of the Beanworld: A Most Peculiar Comic Book Experience,* 764
Booth, John Wilkes: *Treasury of Victorian Murder, A,* 805
Borden, Lizzie: *Treasury of Victorian Murder, A,* 805
Boring, David: *David Boring,* 188
Boris: *It's a Good Life, If You Don't Weaken: A Picture Novella,* 381
Borzhak, Morris: *Julius Knipl, Real Estate Photographer,* 412
Bosco: *Deogratias: A Tale of Rwanda,* 199
Bosnian War (1992-1995): *Fax from Sarajevo,* 243–
Bosun, The: *Three Shadows,* 793
Bouedaue, Veronica (Rachel Hampton; Beverly Pace): *Strangers in Paradise,* 725
Boulevard of Broken Dreams, The, **121–124**
de Bourville, Vattier: *Glacial Period,* 301
Bouvreuil: *It Was the War of the Trenches,* 385
Bovery, Charles: *Gemma Bovery,* 282
Bovery, Gemma: *Gemma Bovery,* 292
Box Office Poison, **125–127**
boy: *Small Killing, A,* 704; *Tragical Comedy or Comical Tragedy of Mr. Punch, The,* 797
Brabner, Joyce (character): *American Splendor: From Off the Streets of Cleveland,* 52; *Our Cancer Year,* 560
Bradley, Babs: *Hate,* 329
Bradley, Betty: *Hate,* 329
Bradley, Brad: *Hate,* 329
Bradley, Butch: *Hate,* 329
Bradley, Harold William, Jr. (Buddy): *Hate,* 328
brand parodies: *Dykes to Watch Out For,* 212
Braun, Elga: *Berlin: City of Stones,* 87
Braun, Gudrun: *Berlin: City of Stones,* 87
Braun, Heinz: *Berlin: City of Stones,* 87
Braun, Otto: *Berlin: City of Stones,* 87
de Bressigny, Hervé: *Gemma Bovery,* 282
Briggs, Ernest: *Ethel and Ernest,* 231
Briggs, Ethel: *Ethel and Ernest,* 232
Briggs, Julie: *Ethel and Ernest,* 232

*Briggs, Raymond, 231
Brit: *Suckle: The Status of Basil,* 746
Brobson, Doctor: *A.D.: New Orleans After the Deluge,* 2
Broken Nose (1). *See* Blueberry
Broken Nose (2): *Age of Reptiles,* 21
Bronson: *Richard Stark's Parker,* 643
Brother Philip: *Deogratias: A Tale of Rwanda,* 199
Brown, Binky: *Binky Brown Sampler,* 90
Brown, Chester (character): *I Never Liked You,* 368; *Playboy, The,* 368
Brown, Gordon: *Playboy, The,* 609
*Brown, Jeffrey, 162
Brown, Leonard "Stinky": *Hate,* 328
Brown, mother of Chester: *I Never Liked You,* 368
Brown, Ruby: *Dropsie Avenue,* 207
brushwork: *Airtight Garage of Jerry Cornelius,* 26; *Elk's Run,* 219; *It Rhymes with Lust,* 596; *La Perdida,* 596;
bubbles. *See* speech bubbles (balloons)
Buddy. *See* Bradley, Harold William, Jr.
Bug-a-Boo: *Scary Godmother: The Boo Flu,* 664
Bukk: *Pride of Baghdad: Inspired by a True Story,* 620
Bullocks-Femur, Gwynnethina Casey: *Strangers in Paradise,* 724
Bunny, Bartholomew Baxter "Buggy" III: *Three Fingers,* 785
Burger, Dick: *Hicksville,* 344
Burma Chronicles, **133–136**
Burmese dictatorship: *Burma Chronicles,* 135
*Burns, Charles, 93
Bush, George W.: *9/11 Report, The: A Graphic Adaptation,* 544; *In the Shadow of No Towers,* 371
Button, Benjamin: *Curious Case of Benjamin Button, The,* 184
Button, Roger: *Curious Case of Benjamin Button, The,* 184
Button, Roscoe: *Curious Case of Benjamin Button, The,* 184
Butzo: *Fax from Sarajevo,* 243
Byrne, Sister Margaret: *Complete Essex County, The,* 171

C

"C": *Queen and Country,* 628
Caco. *See* Topalovic, Musan
Cacofonix (Assurancetourix): *Asterix,* 69
Cadillacs and Dinosaurs. See Xenozoic Tales
Cages, **137–140**
Cain: *Book of Genesis, The,* 118
Caitlin: *Lost Girl,* 475
Calculus, Cuthbert (Tryphon Tournesol): *Adventures of Tintin, The,* 10
Calderon, Heraclio: *Love and Rockets,* 495
Callahan, Nancy: *Sin City,* 688
Calloway, Lily. *See* Chihuahua Pearl
Cameron, Kimberly Keiko (Skim): *Skim,* 693
Campbell, Annie: *Alec: The Years Have Pants,* 33
*Campbell, Eddie, 34
Campbell, Eddie (Alec MacGarry, character): *Alec: The Years Have Pants,* 32
Camp Koala: *Tank Girl,* 774
Canard, Anna: *Skim,* 693
Cancer Vixen, **141–144**
Candy (Uriel): *Metropol: The Complete Series + Metropol A.D.,* 515
*Cannon, Kevin, 238
capitalism, as core theme: *Jew of New York, The: A Historical Romance,* 396; *Wall, The: Growing Up Behind the Iron Curtain,* 830
Caprice: *Tricked,* 809
captions: *Cartoon History of the Universe, The,* 146
captivity, as core theme: *Jew in Communist Prague, A: Loss of Innocence,* 393
caricature: *Box Office Poison,* 126
Carl: *Incognegro: A Graphic Mystery,* 364
Carmichael: *Ice Haven,* 361
Carnelian, Lewis. *See* Cornelius, Jerry
Carol: *Tantrum,* 777; *Walking Dead, The,* 826
Carrie: *I Never Liked You,* 369
Carter, Frederick: *Richard Stark's Parker,* 643
cartographic feel: *Hicksville,* 345
Cartoon History of the Universe, The, **145–148**
Cash, Izzy: *Contract with God, A,* 180; *Dropsie Avenue,* 180
Cassidy, Claire: *Wilson,* 854
Castafiore, Bianca: *Adventures of Tintin, The,* 11
*Castellucci, Cecil, 605
Castle Waiting, **149–152**
Cat: *Flood! A Novel in Pictures,* 256
Cat Goddess Bast: *Glacial Period,* 301
Cavendish, Alistair: *Far Arden,* 240
Celo. *See* Bajramovic, Ismet; Delalic, Ramiz
censorship, as core theme: *Burma Chronicles,* 135

Century, Penny. *See* García, Beatríz
Chace, Tara: *Queen and Country,* 627
Chalky, Harvard: *Stray Toasters,* 733
Chang, later Cheng, Angela: *Queen and Country,* 629
change. *See* transformation and change, as core theme
Chantal: *Get a Life,* 287
chaos tamed, as core theme: *Adventures of Tintin, The,* 12
Chapman, Annie: *From Hell: Being a Melodrama in Sixteen Parts,* 273
chapter differences: *Ice Haven,* 361
character emotion. *See* emotions and emotional expression
characters. *See plot within specific articles; specific characters; specific titles*
charcoal drawing style: *Shenzhen,* 673
Charlene: *Complete Fritz the Cat, The,* 175
Charles: *Ice Haven,* 360
*Charlier, Jean-Michel, 110
Chascarrillo, Margarita Luisa "Maggie": *Love and Rockets,* 494
Chau, Knives: *Scott Pilgrim,* 668
Chelo: *Love and Rockets,* 492; *Palomar: The Heartbreak Soup Stories,* 493
Cheney, Dick: *9/11 Report, The: A Graphic Adaptation,* 545
Chess, Sir: *Castle Waiting,* 151
Chet: *It's a Good Life, If You Don't Weaken: A Picture Novella,* 381
Chet (Chester Brown, character): *Poor Bastard, The,* 612
Cheun: *Shenzhen,* 672
chiaroscuro style: *City of Glass,* 160
Chicken with Plums, **154–157**
Chief Beeferman: *Harvey Kurtzman's Jungle Book,* 325
Chief Inspector: *Harum Scarum,* 320
Chihuahua Pearl (Lily Calloway): *Blueberry,* 107
child abuse and exploitation: *Small Killing, A,* 821
child abuse or exploitation: *One! Hundred! Demons!,* 556
Chimp, Chester: *Three Fingers,* 785
Chinese-box fish: *Frank Book, The,* 266
Chinese pictographs: *American Born Chinese,* 48
Chini: *Blueberry,* 109
Chin-Kee: *American Born Chinese,* 47
Cho, Master: *Color Trilogy, The,* 167

Chong-Chen, Chang: *Adventures of Tintin, The,* 11
Choovanski, Katina Marie (Katchoo): *Strangers in Paradise,* 724
Christian religion. *See* religion and faith
Christie: *Hard Boiled,* 316
Chuck, Captain: *Good-Bye, Chunky Rice,* 312
Chula: *Age of Reptiles,* 21
Chung-Myung: *Color Trilogy, The,* 167
Chunky Rice: *Good-Bye, Chunky Rice,* 312
Churchill, Winston, First Lord of the Admiralty: *Rex Mundi,* 639
Cindy: *Plain Janes, The,* 606
City of Glass, **158–161**
cityscape: *Julius Knipl, Real Estate Photographer,* 412
Clarice: *Dykes to Watch Out For,* 210
Clarice, Abbess: *Castle Waiting,* 151
Clarke, Beatrice: *Three Fingers,* 785
clear-line drawing style: *A.D.: New Orleans After the Deluge,* 3;
Clement: *Get a Life,* 287
Clinton, Bill: *9/11 Report, The: A Graphic Adaptation,* 544
Clive: *Louis,* 484
close-ups: *Boulevard of Broken Dreams, The,* 126;
clothing and accessories: *Shortcomings,* 684
*Clowes, Daniel, 811
Clumsy, **162–165**
Clytemnestra, Queen of the Nile (Mabel): *Castle Waiting,* 150
Cobb, Andy: *Tamara Drewe,* 769
Cochise: *Blueberry,* 106
Coleman, Noel: *You Are Here,* 865
Coleslaw, Enid: *Ghost World,* 292
Coleslaw, father of Enid: *Ghost World,* 292
collage: *Alice in Sunderland: An Entertainment,* 38
collecting, as core theme: *It's a Good Life, If You Don't Weaken: A Picture Novella,* 381
*Collins, Max Allan, 646
Collins, Mr.: *Houdini: The Handcuff King,* 356
color, accent: *Fun Home: A Family Tragicomic,* 293
color, contrasting: *Journey into Mohawk Country,* 408
color, cover: *Mail Order Bride,* 503
color, palettes for day and night: *Deogratias: A Tale of Rwanda,* 199
color, pastel: *Small Killing, A,* 705
color, primary: *Asterios Polyp,* 62;

color, specific combinations: *Age of Reptiles*, 26;
color, text: *Market Day*, 507
Color Trilogy, The, **166–169**
comedy. *See* humor
comic strip format: *Blankets: An Illustrated Novel*, 102
coming-of-age, as core theme: *Deogratias: A Tale of Rwanda*, 200;
commentary on French society: *Asterix*, 69
commercialism, as core theme: *Boulevard of Broken Dreams, The*, 123
communal living, as core theme: *Castle Waiting*, 152
communication, as core theme: *I Never Liked You*, 368; *Streak of Chalk*, 738
community: *Ice Haven*, 361
Complete Essex County, The, **170–173**
Complete Fritz the Cat, The, **174–178**
computer-generated art. *See* digital and computer-generated art
conflict, as core theme: *Last Day in Vietnam: A Memory*, 447
connection. *See* relationships
Connie: *I Never Liked You*, 368
Conrad: *Mouse Guard*, 527
consumerism, as core theme: *Hard Boiled*, 317
Contract with God, A, **179–182**
contrasts, artistic: *Bone*, 114; *I Never Liked You*, 368; *Sloth*, 701; *Strangers in Paradise*, 725; *Tank Girl*, 774
control, as core theme: *Bone*, 115
*Cooke, Darwyn, 642
*Cooper, Dave, 745
cooperation, as core theme: *Tales of the Beanworld: A Most Peculiar Comic Book Experience*, 766
Cope, Alan: *Alan's War: The Memories of G.I. Alan Cope*, 29
Cornelius, Jerry (Lewis Carnelian): *Airtight Garage of Jerry Cornelius*, 24
Corrigan, Amy: *Jimmy Corrigan: The Smartest Kid on Earth*, 399
Corrigan, J.: *Jimmy Corrigan: The Smartest Kid on Earth*, 399
Corrigan, James Reed: *Jimmy Corrigan: The Smartest Kid on Earth*, 399
Corrigan, James William: *Jimmy Corrigan: The Smartest Kid on Earth*, 340
Corrigan, Jimmy: *Jimmy Corrigan: The Smartest Kid on Earth*, 340

Corrigan, William: *Jimmy Corrigan: The Smartest Kid on Earth*, 341
corruption, as core theme: *Aliens*, 45; *Three Shadows*, 794
corrupt policeman: *System, The*, 757
counterculture values, as core theme: *Binky Brown Sampler*, 91; *Complete Fritz the Cat, The*, 175
Cousin Irving: *Minor Miracles: Long Ago and Once Upon a Time Back When...*, 519
cover art, notable: *Age of Bronze: The Story of the Trojan War*, 22; *Mail Order Bride*, 504; *Night Fisher*, 513; *Our Cancer Year*, 562
Craft, Elmer: *Journey: The Adventure of Wolverine MacAlistaire*, 403
Craig: *Blankets: An Illustrated Novel*, 101
Craig's parents: *Blankets: An Illustrated Novel*, 102
"Crazy" Bones: *Dropsie Avenue*, 180
Crazy Connor. *See* Looney, Connor
creation, acts of: *Airtight Garage of Jerry Cornelius*, 25; *Cages*
*Crécy, Nicolas de, 300
crime: *Treasury of Victorian Murder, A*, 804
crime fiction genre: *David Boring*, 189
Crocker, Paul: *Queen and Country*, 627
Cromwell, Nathaniel: *Adventures of Luther Arkwright, The*, 7
cross-hatching. *See* hatching
*Crumb, Robert, 50
Crumb, Robert (character): *American Splendor: From Off the Streets of Cleveland*, 52
*Cruse, Howard, 740
Cubic Man: *Monologues for the Coming Plague*, 523
Cully, Dinah Lucina: *Castle Waiting*, 151
cultural issues, as core theme: *American Born Chinese*, 48;
Curious Case of Benjamin Button, The, **183–186**
Current, Eddy: *Metropol: The Complete Series + Metropol A.D.*, 515
cursive text: *Embroideries*, 224
cut-and-paste: *Signal to Noise*, 840; *What It Is*, 840
cuteness as metaphor: *Good-Bye, Chunky Rice*, 312
cyberpunk aesthetic: *Hard Boiled*, 317
cycles, as core theme: *Alice in Sunderland: An Entertainment*, 39; *Robot Dreams*, 650
Cynthia: *Dykes to Watch Out For*, 211
Czechoslovakia: *Wall, The: Growing Up Behind the Iron Curtain*, 828

D

Dad. *See* Small, Edward "Ed"
Dahlia: *Stray Toasters,* 733
daily life, as core theme: *American Splendor: From Off the Streets of Cleveland,* 53;
daily newspaper comic strips: *Gemma Bovery,* 283; *He Done Her Wrong,* 338
Dale: *Walking Dead, The,* 826
Dalxtré, Larc: *Airtight Garage of Jerry Cornelius,* 26
Damon: *Plain Janes, The,* 606
Dandel: *Good-Bye, Chunky Rice,* 311
Danielle: *American Splendor: From Off the Streets of Cleveland,* 52
Danny: *American Born Chinese,* 47
Danton: *Hicksville,* 344
dark. *See* color, dark tones
Darke, Oscar: *Kane,* 429
Dark Eye: *Age of Reptiles,* 21
Darnell (Mansell): *A.D.: New Orleans After the Deluge,* 2
*Darrow, Geoff, 315
Dave: *Blankets: An Illustrated Novel,* 102
David: *Far Arden,* 239;
David B. *See* B., David
David Boring, **187–189**
Davies, Greg: *Box Office Poison,* 126
Davies, Maggie Hole: *Small Killing, A,* 705
Davies, Sherman: *Box Office Poison,* 125
Dayag, Roni: *Waltz with Bashir: A Lebanon War Story,* 834
Dayan, Moshe: *Footnotes in Gaza: A Graphic Novel,* 260
Dead Memory, **190–193**
Dear Julia, **194–197**
Death (character): *Flaming Carrot Comics,* 251
death, as core theme: *Ethel and Ernest,* 232;
deception, as core theme: *Tricked,* 809
*DeFilippis, Nunzio, 184
*Deitch, Kim, 121
Delachaux, Mademoiselle: *We Are on Our Own,* 837
Delalic, Ramiz (Celo): *Fixer, The: A Story from Sarajevo,* 247
Delfy, Lieutenant Byron: *Whiteout,* 847
*Delgado, Ricardo, 20
Delia (Blue Eyes): *Sin City,.* 688
*Delisle, Guy, 133

Delisle, Guy (character): *Burma Chronicles,* 134; *Pyongyang: A Journey in North Korea,* 136
Delisle, Louis: *Burma Chronicles,* 134
Delisle, Nadège: *Burma Chronicles,* 134
Delores: *Our Cancer Year,* 561
Demon: *Suckle: The Status of Basil,* 746
Denise: *A.D.: New Orleans After the Deluge,* 2
Deogratias: *Deogratias: A Tale of Rwanda,* 198
Deogratias: A Tale of Rwanda, **198–201**
depression, as core theme: *Perfect Example,* 596
Deputy White (Francis Jefferson-White): *Incognegro: A Graphic Mystery,* 364
DeRoc, Andre: *Omaha the Cat Dancer,* 554
Derringer, Ivy: *Aliens,* 43
desire, as core theme: *Black Hole,* 95
Desrosiers, Jean-Louis: *Paul,* 582
destiny, as core theme: *Give It Up!: And Other Short Stories,* 298
detailed depictions in art: *Adventures of Tintin, The,* 278;
Dexter, Captain John: *Kane,* 429
dialect: *American Splendor: From Off the Streets of Cleveland,* 52
dialogue: *Asterix,* 70; *Blueberry,* 106
Diamant, Dora: *Kafka,* 421
Diary of a Mosquito Abatement Man, **202–204**
digital and computer-generated art: *Summer of Love, The,* 754
Dilios: *300,* 789
Dillon, Dr. Joe: *Stitches: A Memoir,* 719
Dillon, Mrs. Irene: *Stitches: A Memoir,* 719
Dimas: *Streak of Chalk,* 737
Director: *Signal to Noise,* 684
discrimination. *See* prejudice and discrimination
disguise: *Incognegro: A Graphic Mystery,* 365
dissatisfaction: *Twentieth Century Eightball,* 813
distance, as style element: *Deogratias: A Tale of Rwanda,* 199
distortions in style: *Cages,* 138
Divjak, Jovan: *Fixer, The: A Story from Sarajevo,* 244
Doctor, The. *See* Brobson, Doctor
Doe, John (Miroslaw Raminski): *Plain Janes, The,* 606.,
dog: *System, The,* 757
dog: *Haunted,* 757
Dogmatix (Idéfix): *Asterix,* 69
Dollin, Matt: *Harvey Kurtzman's Jungle Book,* 324

domestic abuse, as core theme: *Castle Waiting,* 151
domestic abuse as core theme: *Castle Waiting,* 151
Dominguez, Ray: *Love and Rockets,* 492
Dominique: *Paul,* 528
Dongchul: *Color Trilogy, The,* 167
Donovan, Michael Steven. *See* Blueberry
Doodley, Chet: *Ed the Happy Clown,* 215
Doppelmeyer, Rebecca: *Ghost World,* 294
Doris: *Cages,* 138
Dorothy from *The Wonderful Wizard of Oz. See* Gale, Miss Dorothy
double-page spreads: *Asterios Polyp,* 337;
double splash pages: *Black Hole,* 95
*Doucet, Julie, 468
Down, Captain Lucius: *Rose: Prequel to Bone,* 653
Downs, Lucius: *Bone,* 113
*Drake, Arnold, 374
Dreamishness: *Tales of the Beanworld: A Most Peculiar Comic Book Experience,* 765
dreams and dream-like: *Get a Life,* 288
*Drechsler, Debbie, 753
Drewe, Tamara: *Tamara Drewe,* 768
Dreyfuss, Vaughn: *You Are Here,* 865
*Drooker, Eric, 257
Dropsie Avenue, **205–208**
drug dealer: *System, The,* 758
Drumheller, Lord: *Xenozoic Tales: Cadillacs and Dinosaurs,* 857
drunken subway operator: *System, The,* 758
duality, as core theme: *Asterios Polyp,* 65;l
Dubcek, Alexander: *Wall, The: Growing Up Behind the Iron Curtain,* 829
Dube, Francie and Peter: *Paul,* 583
Dubrovsky, Yelena: *Laika,* 438
duck: *Haunted,* 449
Duck, Dapper: *Three Fingers,* 785
Duck, Donald: *Life and Times of Scrooge McDuck, The,* 456
Ducon: *It Was the War of the Trenches,* 385
Duksam: *Color Trilogy, The,* 167
Dumont, Gabriel: *Louis Riel: A Comic-Strip Biography,* 489
Dundee, Hannah: *Xenozoic Tales: Cadillacs and Dinosaurs,* 857
Dunham, Keith: *Summer of Love, The,* 754
Dupont and Dupond. *See* Thompson and Thompson
Dupuy, mother of Phillippe: *Haunted,* 332

*Dupuy, Philippe, 332
Dupuy, Phillippe (character): *Haunted,* 332
duty, sense of: *Age of Bronze: The Story of the Trojan War,* 16
Dykes to Watch Out For, **209–213**
dynamism in art. *See* energetic artistic style

E

Ecarano, Alex: *Pedro and Me: Friendship, Loss, and What I Learned,* 589
Eddie: *Contract with God, A,* 180
Eddington, Damon: *Aliens,* 43
Eddowes, Catherine: *From Hell: Being a Melodrama in Sixteen Parts,* 273
Eddy, Prince. *See* Albert Victor, Prince
Edin: *Safe Area Goražde,* 660
Edith, Granny: *My Mommy Is in America and She Met Buffalo Bill,* 532
Ed the Happy Clown: *Ed the Happy Clown,* 215
Ed the Happy Clown: The Definitive Ed Book, **214–217**
Eggskull (Jedediah): *Blueberry,* 109
egoism, as core theme: *Houdini: The Handcuff King,* 356
Ehwa: *Color Trilogy, The,* 167
Ehwa's mother: *Color Trilogy, The,* 167
"eight pager": *Lost Girls,* 479
*Eisner, Will, 518
Elandos (Lopez): *Omaha the Cat Dancer,* 553
Elassouli, Abed: *Footnotes in Gaza: A Graphic Novel,* 260
El Gordo: *La Perdida,* 442
El-Horani, Dr. Abdullah: *Footnotes in Gaza: A Graphic Novel,* 260
Eliza: *Black Hole,* 94
Elk's Run, **218–221**
Elliot, Chaplain Captain Plimey: *Alan's War: The Memories of G.I. Alan Cope,* 29
Ellis, John: *Ghost World,* 292
El-Najeeli, Mohammed Atwa: *Footnotes in Gaza: A Graphic Novel,* 260
Embroideries, **222–225**
Emira: *Safe Area Goražde,* 660
Emmis, Shloyma: *Minor Miracles: Long Ago and Once Upon a Time Back When...,* 519
emptiness: *Louis Riel: A Comic-Strip Biography,* 488
English Canadian: *Shenzhen,* 673
Enoch. *See* Notochord, Jasper

entertainment industry: *Complete Fritz the Cat, The,* 176
environment. *See* nature and the environment
Ephialtes: *300,* 788
Epileptic, **226–230**
Esau: *Book of Genesis, The,* 118
escape, as core theme: *Flood! A Novel in Pictures,* 269; *Sloth,* 257
escarole: *Haunted,* 333
Eskimo hunter: *Flood! A Novel in Pictures,* 256
Esteban: *Glacial Period,* 301
Esther: *Sin City,* 688
Ethel and Ernest, **231–233**
ethics. *See* morality and ethics
ethnic identity: *La Perdida,* 443
ethnoracial conflict, as core theme: *Dropsie Avenue,* 207
European comic style: *Jar of Fools,* 389;
Eva: *We Are on Our Own,* 836
evangelist and his son: *System, The,* 758
Eve: *Book of Genesis, The,* 118
evolution, as core theme: *Tales of the Beanworld: A Most Peculiar Comic Book Experience,* 766
Exit Wounds, **234–237**
expectations, as core theme: challenging, in *Scary Godmother: The Boo Flu,* 664
exploration, as core theme: *Far Arden,* 240
expressionist style: *Violent Cases,* 821
Eyeball Kid: *Bacchus,* 78

F

facial expressions: *Age of Reptiles,* 22;
Facincani, Rob: *Black Hole,* 94
Fairchild, Lady Alice (Alice from *Alice's Adventures in Wonderland*): *Lost Girls,* 478
Fairfax, Harry: *Adventures of Luther Arkwright, The,* 6
fairy tales, as core theme: *Castle Waiting,* 151
faith. *See* religion and faith
Fajer: *Pride of Baghdad: Inspired by a True Story,* 620
Falconer, Chance: *Leave It to Chance,* 450
Falconer, Lucas: *Leave It to Chance,* 450
fame, as core theme: *Three Fingers,* 786
family relationships. *See* relationships, family
Fanta: *Aya of Yopougon,* 73
fantasy genre: *Airtight Garage of Jerry Cornelius,* 26–26

fantasy vs. reality, as core theme: *American Splendor: From Off the Streets of Cleveland,* 53;
Far Arden, **238–241**
Farley, Steve (Stevie): *Summer of Love, The,* 754
Farzaneh: *Chicken with Plums,* 155
fascism, as core theme: *Adventures of Tintin, The,* 12
Father: *Snowman, The,* 716
Faucheux: *It Was the War of the Trenches,* 385
Faux Pa: *Frank Book, The,* 264
Fax from Sarajevo, **242–245**
fear, as core theme: *Black Hole,* 95
Featherskill, Edie: *Cages,* 138
Fedayee, The: *Footnotes in Gaza: A Graphic Novel,* 260
feelings. *See* emotions and emotional expression
*Feiffer, Jules, 776
Feinbroyt, Yosl: *Jew of New York, The: A Historical Romance,* 396
Feldman: *Twentieth Century Eightball,* 812
Féli. *See* Félicité
Félicité (Féli): *Aya of Yopougon,* 74
Felix: *Get a Life,* 297; *Notes for a War Story,* 549
Felix, Kate: *Kane,* 429
Fell, Dr. Hieronymous: *Castle Waiting,* 151
female characters and issues: *Black Hole,* 96;
female superhero genre: *Love and Rockets,* 494
feminine beauty, as core theme: *Color Trilogy, The,* 169
femme fatale: *It Rhymes with Lust,* 375
Femur, Frederick "Freddie" Stanley: *Strangers in Paradise,* 724
Fernande, Grandmother: *Epileptic,* 228
*Fialkov, Joshua Hale, 218
fictional world overinvolvement: *Flaming Carrot Comics,* 253
fiction genre. *See specific graphic novels; specific types of fiction*
Fields, Police Officer: *Houdini: The Handcuff King,* 357
film-noir style. *See* noir style
filmstrip: *Shutterbug Follies,* 680
Finkel, Dr.: *Jew in Communist Prague, A: Loss of Innocence,* 392
Finkel, Edith: *Jew in Communist Prague, A: Loss of Innocence,* 392
Finkel, Jonas: *Jew in Communist Prague, A: Loss of Innocence,* 492
Finkler, Mr.: *Market Day,* 507

1037

Finkler's son-in-law: *Market Day*, 507
Firedog: *Glacial Period*, 301
Fixer, The (Neven): *Fixer, The: A Story from Sarajevo*, 247
Fixer, The: A Story from Sarajevo, **246-249**
Flaming Carrot: *Flaming Carrot Comics*, 250-254
Flaming Carrot Comics, **250-254**
flashbacks: *Adventures of Luther Arkwright, The*, 7; *City of Glass*, 160; *Deogratias: A Tale of Rwanda*, 198 467
Flavor, Irving: *Box Office Poison*, 126
flight, as core theme: *Dear Julia*, 196
Flood! A Novel in Pictures, **255-258**
Flosso, Al: *Jar of Fools*, 389
Flowers, Ramona: *Scott Pilgrim*, 668
Flutter: *Owly*, 565
Foley, Jimmy: *Hate*, 329
Follett, JoAnne: *Omaha the Cat Dancer*, 554
*Folman, Ari, 832
Fontaine, Fred: *Boulevard of Broken Dreams, The*, 122
Footnotes in Gaza: A Graphic Novel, **259-262**
foreground style: *Rose: Prequel to Bone*, 654
Formulaic Companion: *Louis*, 482
Fortuna: *Far Arden*, 239
Foster, father of Loren: *Night Fisher*, 240
Foster, Helen: *You Are Here*, 865
Foster, Loren: *Night Fisher*, 540
Fouquet, Fabrice: *Pyongyang: A Journey in North Korea*, 623.
Fournot, Dr. Juliette: *Photographer, The: Into War-Torn Afghanistan with Doctors Without Borders*, 603
framing: *Dropsie Avenue*, 207
Franco, Gabriel: *Exit Wounds*, 235
Franco, Koby: *Exit Wounds*, 235
Frank: *Frank Book, The*, 264
Frank, R.: *Mail Order Bride*, 503
Frank Book, The, **263-266**
Frankie: *Poor Bastard, The*, 613
Frasca, Marilyn: *What It Is*, 840
Fred: *Perfect Example*, 596
Freddie. *See* Bloch, Frederick
free association: *Harum Scarum*, 346
freedom, as core theme: *Blueberry*, 108
*Freeman, Don, 696
Freer, Lillian: *Boulevard of Broken Dreams, The*, 122
free will, as core theme: *Color Trilogy, The*, 516
French language: *Aya of Yopougon*, 75

Frenchman. *See* Sergeant
Frenkel, Shmuel: *Waltz with Bashir: A Lebanon War Story*, 834
friendship, as core theme: *Fax from Sarajevo*, 253; Fritz: *Complete Fritz the Cat, The*, 175
Fritz (Rosalba Martinez): *Love and Rockets*, 492
Frobes, Barry: *Small Killing, A*, 705
Frogmouth. *See* Solis, Vivian
From Hell: Being a Melodrama in Sixteen Parts, **271-275**
frontier life, as core theme: *Journey: The Adventure of Wolverine MacAlistaire*, 404
full-page panels: *Cancer Vixen*, 168;
function of art, as core theme: *Glacial Period*, 302
Fun Home: A Family Tragicomic, **276-280**
Furious, Mr.: *Flaming Carrot Comics*, 252
Furry: *Whiteout*, 847

G

Gabriel. *See* Humphrey
Gabriel, Grandfather: *Epileptic*, 228
Gaedel, Stephen: *Box Office Poison*, 126
Gail: *Sin City*, 689
*Gaiman, Neil, 726
Gale, Miss Dorothy (Dorothy from *The Wonderful Wizard of Oz*): *Lost Girls*, 478
*Gallant, Gregory (Seth), 380
gallerist: *Cages*, 138
Garbanzo, Professor (Proffy): *Tales of the Beanworld: A Most Peculiar Comic Book Experience*, 765
García, Beatríz (Penny Century): *Love and Rockets*, 494
Garfield, James A.: *Treasury of Victorian Murder, A*, 805
Gaspard: *It Was the War of the Trenches*, 385
gay characters. *See* homosexuality
Gazenko, Oleg: *Laika*, 438
*Geary, Rick, 803
Geat: *Like a Velvet Glove Cast in Iron*, 464
*Gebbie, Melinda, 479
Gemma Bovery, **281-285**
gender identity, as core theme: *Aya of Yopougon*, 75
gender roles, as core theme: *Castle Waiting*, 152
General, The: *Kabuki*, 414
generational issues: *Embroideries*, 224
genocide: *Deogratias: A Tale of Rwanda*, 198;

geometrical shapes: *Dead Memory*, 192; *Exit Wounds*, 234
Georg: *Kafka*, 420
George: *Last Day in Vietnam: A Memory*, 446
Gerbs: *Playboy, The*, 609
Gerritsen, Marten: *Journey into Mohawk Country*, 408
gestures, of adolescents: *Summer of Love, The*, 770
Getafix (Panoramix): *Asterix*, 69
Get a Life, **286–289**
Ghassan: *Palestine*, 570
Ghost World, **290–295**
Gianelli, Father: *Dropsie Avenue*, 207
Giardelli, Nick: *Stray Bullets*, 729
*Giardino, Vittorio, 391
Ginger: *Dykes to Watch Out For*, 210
*Gipi (pseudonym of Gianni Pacinotti), 547
*Giraud, Jean (Mobius), 24
Girl/Young Woman: *Passionate Journey*, 578
Giuliano: *Notes for a War Story*, 548
Give It Up!: And Other Short Stories, **296–299**
Glacial Period, **300–303**
Glass, Emma: *Strangers in Paradise*, 725
Glass, Esperanza Leticia (Hopey): *Love and Rockets*, 494
Glenn: *Walking Dead, The*, 825
Gloom, Percy: *Percy Gloom*, 592
God: *Book of Genesis, The*, 118
Godfrey: *Like a Velvet Glove Cast in Iron*, 464
Gold, Abie: *Contract with God, A*, 181
Goldberg, David: *Ice Haven*, 360
Goldie: *Contract with God, A*, 180
Goldstein, Rabbi: *Dropsie Avenue*, 207
Golem's Mighty Swing, The, **304–307**
*Gonick, Larry, 145
good and evil, as core theme: *Adventures of Tintin, The*, 12
Good-Bye, Chunky Rice, **311–314**
Good Girl Art: *It Rhymes with Lust*, 375
Goofy Sermon Jerk: *Tales of the Beanworld: A Most Peculiar Comic Book Experience*, 766
Goofy Surveillance Jerks: *Tales of the Beanworld: A Most Peculiar Comic Book Experience*, 766
Goofy Survey Jerks: *Tales of the Beanworld: A Most Peculiar Comic Book Experience*, 765
Gorgon, The: *What It Is*, 840
*Goscinny, René, 67
gossip: *Embroideries*, 223

Goulbat, Hershel: *Jew of New York, The: A Historical Romance*, 396
government issues: *9/11 Report, The: A Graphic Adaptation*, 546
Graad: *Airtight Garage of Jerry Cornelius*, 26
Grace: *Hicksville*, 344
Grandfather André: *Epileptic*, 228
Grandfather Arthur: *Tragical Comedy or Comical Tragedy of Mr. Punch, The*, 797
Grandfather Gabriel: *Epileptic*, 228
Grandmother: *Embroideries*, 223
Grandmother Fernande: *Epileptic*, 228
Grandparents: *Stitches: A Memoir*, 719
Gran'ma Ben. *See* Harvestar, Rose
Gran'Ma'Pa: *Tales of the Beanworld: A Most Peculiar Comic Book Experience*, 765
Grant, Ulysses S.: *Blueberry*, 106
graphic journalism: *Footnotes in Gaza: A Graphic Novel*, 261
Graves, Gideon Gordon: *Scott Pilgrim*, 668
Gray, Thomas Ruffin: *Nat Turner*, 537
Grayson, Sergeant: *Blueberry*, 109
Great Red Dragon: *Rose: Prequel to Bone*, 654
greed, as core theme: *Flood! A Novel in Pictures*, 257;
Greek mythology: *Asterios Polyp*, 65
Green, Julia: *You'll Never Know Book One: A Good and Decent Man*, 868
*Green, Justin, 89
Green, Justin (character): *You'll Never Know Book One: A Good and Decent Man*, 868
Greg: *American Born Chinese*, 48
Grégoire: *Aya of Yopougon*, 74
Gregor: *Glacial Period*, 301
Grete: *Kafka*, 420
Grey, Danny (Bob): *Alec: The Years Have Pants*, 33
grief, as core theme: *My Mommy Is in America and She Met Buffalo Bill*, 533
Grimaldi: *Harum Scarum*, 320
Grimes, Carl: *Walking Dead, The*, 825
Grimes, Lori: *Walking Dead, The*, 825
Grimes, Rick: *Walking Dead, The*, 825
Grisn, Reverend: *Transit*, 800
*Grist, Paul, 428
gritty style: *Fax from Sarajevo*, 244;
Grofeld: *Richard Stark's Parker*, 643
*Gross, Milt, 336
group of forest friends: *Haunted*, 333

Grubert, Major: *Airtight Garage of Jerry Cornelius*, 25
*Guibert, Emmanuel, 28
Guibert, Emmanuel (character): *Alan's War: The Memories of G.I. Alan Cope*, 29
guilt, as core theme: *Hey, Wait...*, 342
Guiteau, Charles Julius: *Treasury of Victorian Murder, A*, 805
Gull, Sir William Withey: *From Hell: Being a Melodrama in Sixteen Parts*, 272
Gustavson, Mr.: *Houdini: The Handcuff King*, 357
Gwendolyn: *Mouse Guard*, 528

H

Haddock, Captain: *Adventures of Tintin, The*, 10
Haden, John: *Whiteout*, 847
Hafley: *Far Arden*, 239
Hagar: *Book of Genesis, The*, 119
Halloween: *Scary Godmother: The Boo Flu*, 663
hallucinatory images: *Frank Book, The*, 264
Hamfist: *Haunted*, 333
Hamid (Abbas): *A.D.: New Orleans After the Deluge*, 2
Hamilton, George Cecil III: *Hate*, 329
Hampton, Rachel. *See* Bouedaue, Veronica
Hanka: *Jew in Communist Prague, A: Loss of Innocence*, 392
Hannah: *Scary Godmother: The Boo Flu*, 663
Happy Hooligan: *In the Shadow of No Towers*, 371
Harazi, Dror: *Waltz with Bashir: A Lebanon War Story*, 834
Hard Boiled, **315–318**
Hardiman, Beth: *Tamara Drewe*, 769
Hardiman, Nicholas: *Tamara Drewe*, 769
Hardin, John Wesley: *Lost Cause: John Wesley Hardin*, 471
Harmensz: *Glacial Period*, 302
Harris, Amelia: *American Born Chinese*, 48
Harrow, Bette: *Richard Stark's Parker*, 644
Hartigan, John: *Sin City*, 688
Harum Scarum, **319–322**
Harvestar, Briar (Hooded One): *Bone*, 113
Harvestar, Rose (Gran'ma Ben): *Bone*, 114; *Rose: Prequel to Bone*, 652
Harvey Kurtzman's Jungle Book, **323–326**
hashing: *Lost Girl*, 475
hatching: *Adventures of Luther Arkwright, The*, 7
Hate, **327–331**
Haunted, **332–335**

Hayashi, Miko: *Shortcomings*, 676
headlines: *Dykes to Watch Out For*, 362
healing, as core theme: *Complete Essex County, The*, 173
He Done Her Wrong, **336–339**
heiress, the: *He Done Her Wrong*, 337
Hektor: *Age of Bronze: The Story of the Trojan War*, 16
Helen: *Age of Bronze: The Story of the Trojan War*, 16
Heller, Dr.: *Flaming Carrot Comics*, 251
Helmut: *It Was the War of the Trenches*, 385
Hemphill, Police Officer: *Houdini: The Handcuff King*, 357
Henry: *Nat Turner*, 536
Heraclio: *Palomar: The Heartbreak Soup Stories*, 575
*Hergé, 9
Herman, Numi: *Exit Wounds*, 235
Hermes: *Bacchus*, 80
*Hernandez, Gilbert, 496
*Hernandez, Jaime, 496
hero, as core theme: *Metropol: The Complete Series + Metropol A.D.*, 515
hero, the: *He Done Her Wrong*, 337
heroine, the: *He Done Her Wrong*, 337
Herschel: *American Splendor: From Off the Streets of Cleveland*, 52
Hersh, Frimme: *Contract with God, A*, 180
Hervé: *Aya of Yopougon*, 74
Hey, Wait..., **340–342**
Heyoka: *Tales of the Beanworld: A Most Peculiar Comic Book Experience*, 766
Hickok, Wild Bill: *Blueberry*, 109
Hicks (Wilks): *Aliens*, 43
Hicks, Mrs.: *Hicksville*, 344
Hicksville, **343–346**
Hine, Shelley: *Omaha the Cat Dancer*, 554
historical criticism, as core theme: *Cartoon History of the Universe, The*, 151
historical fiction genre: *Berlin: City of Stones*, 87;
historical references: *Adventures of Luther Arkwright, The*, 5
history genre: *A.D.: New Orleans After the Deluge*, 1
history of comics and cartoons: *It's a Good Life, If You Don't Weaken: A Picture Novella*, 381
History of Violence, A, **347–350**
Hitch, Captain: *Leave It to Chance*, 450
Hobbs: *Leave It to Chance*, 451

Hokama, Shane: *Night Fisher,* 540
Hole, Maggie: *Small Killing, A,* 705
Hole, Timothy: *Small Killing, A,* 705
holidays: *Scary Godmother: The Boo Flu,* 532;
Holmes, H. H. *See* Mudgett, Herman W.
homage: *Box Office Poison,* 126;
    homecoming, as core theme: *Good-Bye, Chunky Rice,* 313
homeless old man: *System, The,* 757
Homer: *Blueberry,* 109
homosexuality: *Aya of Yopougon,* 75
honesty, as core theme: *Clumsy,* 164
Honey Lou: *Harvey Kurtzman's Jungle Book,* 324
Hooded One. *See* Harvestar, Briar
Hoover, J. Edgar: *King: A Comics Biography,* 432
hope, as core theme: *Blankets: An Illustrated Novel,* 103
Hopey. *See* Glass, Esperanza Leticia
Hornet, Mrs.: *Skim,* 693
*Horrocks, Dylan, 345
horror genre: *Aliens,* 44
Hospital Nurse: *Stitches: A Memoir,* 719
hotel porter: *Shenzhen,* 672
Houdini, Bess: *Houdini: The Handcuff King,* 356
Houdini, Harry: *Houdini: The Handcuff King,* 356
Houdini: The Handcuff King, **335–338**
Housang: *Chicken with Plums,* 156
Huet: *It Was the War of the Trenches,* 385
Huey: *Shutterbug Follies,* 680
Huey, Dewey, and Louie: *Life and Times of Scrooge McDuck, The,* 456
Huff, Firmin: *Dead Memory,* 191
Huld, Arnold: *Elk's Run,* 219
Hulk: *Glacial Period,* 301
human connection. *See* relationships
human existence, as core theme: *Bacchus,* 81
humanity, aspects of, as core theme: *Aliens,* 45;
humor, as core theme: *Asterix,* 70; *Blueberry,* 110;
Humphrey (Gabriel): *Metropol: The Complete Series + Metropol A.D.,* 515
hunger artist: *Give It Up!: And Other Short Stories,* 297
Huron. *See* Taro
Hussey, Mike: *Stray Bullets,* 730
hypocrisy, as core theme: *Omaha the Cat Dancer,* 554

I

Ian: *Stray Bullets,* 729
Ice Haven, **359–362**
Idéfix. *See* Dogmatix
identity, as core theme: *Arrival, The,* 61; *Fun Home: A Family Tragicomic,* 279; *Ghost World,* 393-294; *Hard Boiled,* 317; *Kabuki,* 418; *La Perdida,* 443; *Lost Girl,* 475–476; *Maus: A Survivor's Tale,* 512; *Skim,* 694; *Stuck Rubber Baby,* 743
Ignace: *Aya of Yopougon,* 73
Ilium, Willy: *Asterios Polyp,* 64
illness, as core theme: *It's a Bird...,* 379; *Stitches: A Memoir,* 730;
illuminated manuscript: *Mouse Guard,* 529
imagery: *Palomar: The Heartbreak Soup Stories,* 575
imagination, as core theme: *Arrival, The,* 61; *Boulevard of Broken Dreams, The,* 123; *Snowman, The,* 715; *What It Is,* 840
impressionism: *Contract with God, A,* 181; *Good-Bye, Chunky Rice,* 313
Incognegro (Zane Pinchback): *Incognegro: A Graphic Mystery,* 364
Incognegro: A Graphic Mystery, **363–366**
independence, as core theme: *Notes for a War Story,* 549; *Tales of the Beanworld: A Most Peculiar Comic Book Experience,* 766
Indian cab driver: *System, The,* 758
I Never Liked You, **367–369**
Infinite City, The: *Dead Memory,* 190
ink and water technique: *Alan's War: The Memories of G.I. Alan Cope,* 30
inking style: *Blackmark,* 98-99; *Dropsie Avenue,* 207; *Hate,* 327; *Ice Haven,* 361; *Kings in Disguise,* 439; *Lost Cause: John Wesley Hardin,* 471; *Passionate Journey,* 578; *Perfect Example,* 607;
Inno. *See* Innocent
innocence, as core theme: *Ice Haven,* 361; *Notes for a War Story,* 459; *Safe Area Goražde,* 661;
Innocent (Inno): *Aya of Yopougon,* 72-75
Inspector Ruffhaus: *Harum Scarum,* 320
interracial couple: *System, The,* 757
In the Shadow of No Towers, **370–373**
intolerance. *See* prejudice and discrimination
introductions: 267

Iphigenia: *Age of Bronze: The Story of the Trojan War,* 16-17
Iran: *Persepolis,* 598–599
Irane: *Chicken with Plums,* 154–155
Iraq: *Pride of Baghdad: Inspired by a True Story,* 619–621
Ireneaux, Emile-Jean: *Rex Mundi,* 639
Iron Henry: *Castle Waiting,* 150
irony: *Dead Memory,* 192; *Harum Scarum,* 319--322
Irving, Cousin: *Minor Miracles: Long Ago and Once Upon a Time Back When...,* 518
Isaac: *Book of Genesis, The,* 117
Ishmael: *Book of Genesis, The,* 117
Islam: *Persepolis,* 600; *Rabbi's Car, The,* 635; *Rex Mundi,* 640
isolation. *See* loneliness and isolation
Israel. *See* Jacob
Israeli-Palestinian conflict: *Exit Wounds,* 236; *Footnotes in Gaza: A Graphic Novel,* 261
It Rhymes with Lust, **374–376**
It's a Bird..., **377–379**
It's a Good Life, If You Don't Weaken: A Picture Novella, **380–383**
It Was the War of the Trenches, **384–387**
Izetbegovic, Alija: *Fixer, The: A Story from Sarajevo,* 247

J

J., John: *Perfect Example,* 596
Jack: *Lost Girl,* 475
Jack (Iron Jack Rafferty; Jackie Boy): *Sin City,* 688
Jackie Boy: *Sin City,* 689
*Jackson, Jack, 470–471
Jack the Bellboy: *American Splendor: From Off the Streets of Cleveland,* 51
Jack the Ripper: *From Hell: Being a Melodrama in Sixteen Parts,* 271
Jacob (Israel): *Book of Genesis, The,* 119
*Jacobson, Sid, 543–545
Jacques: *Get a Life,* 287
Jakin, Houm: *Airtight Garage of Jerry Cornelius,* 25
James: *Plain Janes, The,* 602
James, Jesse: *Kings in Disguise,* 435
Jane: *Plain Janes, The,* 606
Jane (Main Jane): *Plain Janes, The,* 606
Jar of Fools, **388–390**

Jarrah, Ziad: *9/11 Report, The: A Graphic Adaptation,* 545
Jasmine: *Dykes to Watch Out For,* 211
*Jason (pseudonym of John Arne Sæterøy), 218, 220
Jasper: *Lucky,* 499, 501
Jay: *Hate,* 329
Jayne: *Plain Janes, The,* 606
Jean: *My Mommy Is in America and She Met Buffalo Bill,* 532
Jean, Daddy of: *My Mommy Is in America and She Met Buffalo Bill,* 532
Jean, Monsieur: *Get a Life,* 287
Jedediah. *See* Eggskull
Jeff: *Clumsy,* 168
Jeffers, Marcus: 374
Jefferson-White, Francis (Deputy White): *Incognegro: A Graphic Mystery,* 364
Jennifer (Rival Cartoon Girl): *Cancer Vixen,* 142
Jenson, Susan "Susie." *See* Omaha
Jeremy: *It's a Bird...,* 378
Jeri: *Aliens,* 43
Jerome: *Life Sucks,* 460
Jesenská, Milena: *Kafka,* 421
Jessica: *Suckle: The Status of Basil,* 742
Jet Girl: *Tank Girl,* 773–774
Jew in Communist Prague, A: Loss of Innocence, **391–394**
Jewish identity, as core theme: *Contract with God, A,* 181
  See also Judaism
Jew of New York, The: A Historical Romance, **395–397**.
Jezanna (Alberta): *Dykes to Watch Out For,* 211
Jill: *Poor Bastard, The,* 613
Jiminez, Pipo: *Love and Rockets,* 495
Jimmy Corrigan: The Smartest Kid on Earth, **718–721**
Joachim: *Three Shadows,* 793
jobs and work, as core theme: *Skitzy: The Story of Floyd W. Skitzafroid,* 698
Joel: *Hate,* 329
Joey: *Stray Bullets,* 729
John: *Playboy, The,* 609
Johnson, Lyndon B.: *King: A Comics Biography,* 432
*Johnson, Mat, 363
*Johnson, R. Kikuo, 540
Johnson, Susan "Susie." *See* Omaha
Joker: *Kings in Disguise,* 435

Jon: *Hey, Wait...*, 340
Jones, Matt: *Elk's Run*, 219
Josef K: *Kafka*, 421
Joseph: *Book of Genesis, The*, 119; *Glacial Period*, 301
Josh: *Ghost World*, 292
Joshua: *Metropol: The Complete Series + Metropol A.D.*, 515
Josie: *Ed the Happy Clown: The Definitive Ed Book*, 215
Joubert, Raymond: *Gemma Bovery*, 282
journalism: *Photographer, The: Into War-Torn Afghanistan with Doctors Without Borders*, 604; *Safe Area Goražde*, 661–662;
journey, as core theme: *Far Arden*, 240; *Good-Bye, Chunky Rice*, 312; *Journey into Mohawk Country*, 407; *Journey: Life and Times of Scrooge McDuck, The*, 454; *Pyongyang: A Journey in North Korea*, 623–624; *Three Shadows*, 793
Journey into Mohawk Country, **407–410**
Journey: The Adventure of Wolverine MacAlistaire, **402–406**
Joyce: *Tantrum*, 777
Judaism: *Golem's Mighty Swing, The*, 313–317; *Jew in Communist Prague, A: Loss of Innocence*, 406–409; *Yossel: April 19, 1943 – A Story of the Warsaw Ghetto Uprising*, 862. See also Anti-Semitism, as core theme; Jewish identity
Judith, Miss: *30 Days of Night*, 872
Juka. See Prazina, Jusuf
Jules César. See Julius Caesar
Julia: *Dear Julia*, 195; *Signal to Noise*, 684
Julie: *Blankets: An Illustrated Novel*, 102
Julien: *Lucky*, 500
Juliette (Ma'am): *Glacial Period*, 301
Julius: *Deogratias: A Tale of Rwanda*, 199
Julius Caesar (Jules César): *Asterix*, 69
Julius Knipl, Real Estate Photographer, **411–413**
justice. See law and justice
juxtapositions: *Give It Up!: And Other Short Stories*, 297

K

K: *Kafka*, 421
K., Josef: *Kafka*, 421
Kabeiroi, The: *Bacchus*, 78
Kabuki, **414–418**
Kabuki (Ukiko Kai): *Kabuki*, 435
Kafka, **438–442**

Kafka, Franz (as inspiration): *Give It Up!: And Other Short Stories*, 296
Kafka, Franz (character): *Kafka*, 420
Kafka, Hermann: *Kafka*, 420
*Kalesniko, Mark, 502
Kalloway, Jack (Kalo): *It's a Good Life, If You Don't Weaken: A Picture Novella*, 381
Kalloway, Mrs.: *It's a Good Life, If You Don't Weaken: A Picture Novella*, 381
Kalo. See Kalloway, Jack
Kampung Boy, **424–427**
*Kanan, Nabiel, 474
Kane: *Kane*, 428
Kane, **428–430**
Karen: *Cages*, 138
Karkes, Professor Ferdinand: *David Boring*, 188
Kassandra: *Age of Bronze: The Story of the Trojan War*, 17
Katchoo. See Choovanski, Katina Marie
*Katchor, Ben, 395
Kate: *Queen and Country*, 629
*Katin, Miriam, 836
Katt, Chuck. See Tabey, Charles, Jr.
Katze, Freidrich Von: *Three Fingers*, 785
Katzenjammer Kids: *In the Shadow of No Towers*, 371
Kaufman, Tom: *Hate*, 329
Kawula, Kevin: *One! Hundred! Demons!*, 557
Keiffer, Hans: *Journey: The Adventure of Wolverine MacAlistaire*, 403
Keiffer, Ilse: *Journey: The Adventure of Wolverine MacAlistaire*, 403
Keiko (Scarab): *Kabuki*, 416–417
Keller, Alexander: *Whiteout*, 847
Kelly: *Blueberry*, 109
Kelly, Marie Jeanette. See Kelly, Mary Jane
Kelly, Mary Jane (Marie Jeanette Kelly): *From Hell: Being a Melodrama in Sixteen Parts*, 272
Ken: *It's a Good Life, If You Don't Weaken: A Picture Novella*, 381
Kennedy, John F.: *King: A Comics Biography*, 432
Kenzie: *Mouse Guard*, 528
Kerney, Ned: *Three Fingers*, 785
Ketzelbourd, Moishe: *Jew of New York, The: A Historical Romance*, 396
Kevin: *Sin City*, 689
Kevin (Kwame): *A.D.: New Orleans After the Deluge*, 2

Khaled: *Footnotes in Gaza: A Graphic Novel*, 544
Khalid Sheikh Mohammed: *9/11 Report, The: A Graphic Adaptation*, 576–577
Khambehl, Stanislav: *Harum Scarum*, 320–321
Khan, Bassir: *Photographer, The: Into War-Torn Afghanistan with Doctors Without Borders*, 603
Khan, mother of Nasser Ali: *Chicken with Plums*, 155
Khan, Nasser Ali: *Chicken with Plums*, 154
Khatchatourian, Oleg: *Shutterbug Follies*, 680
Kierkegaard, Hildy: *Box Office Poison*, 12
Kim: *Poor Bastard, The*, 612
Kim, Alice: *Shortcomings*, 676
*Kim Dong Hwa, 166
King, Coretta Scott: *King: A Comics Biography*, 432
King, Martin Luther, Jr.: *King: A Comics Biography*, 432
King: A Comics Biography, **431–433**
King Kush: *Ballad of Doctor Richardson, The*, 84
King Lion: *Three Fingers*, 785
King of Spain. *See* Sammy
Kings in Disguise, **434–436**
Kinney, David: *Queen and Country*, 629
*Kirkman, Robert, 823
Kishon, Nathan: *Jew of New York, The: A Historical Romance*, 395
Knipl, Julius: *Julius Knipl, Real Estate Photographer*, 412
Kohler, John Jr.: *Elk's Run*, 219
Kohler, John Sr.: *Elk's Run*, 219
Kohler, Sara: *Elk's Run*, 219
Kópen, Emile: *Hicksville*, 344
Korea: *Color Trilogy, The*, 166; *Pyongyang: A Journey in North Korea*, 622
Korolev, Sergei: *Laika*, 438
*Koslowski, Rich, 784
Kowolsky, Hiram: *Adventures of Luther Arkwright, The*, 6
Kozlonowski, Beth: *Stray Bullets*, 729
Kraml, Wanda: *David Boring*, 188
Kris: *Playboy, The*, 609
Kristi: *Perfect Example*, 596
*Kubert, Joe, 242, 860
Kubert, Joe (character): *Fax from Sarajevo*, 243
Kubert, Muriel: *Fax from Sarajevo*, 243
Kudryavka. *See* Laika
Kukol, Mr.: *Houdini: The Handcuff King*, 356

Kunzo, Vervel (Man in an India Rubber Suit): *Jew of New York, The: A Historical Romance*, 396
Kupe: *Hicksville*, 344
*Kuper, Peter, 756
*Kurtzman, Harvey, 323
Kwame (Kevin): *A.D.: New Orleans After the Deluge*, 2
Kyu, Mr.: *Pyongyang: A Journey in North Korea*, 623
Kyung Seo: *Mail Order Bride*, 503

L

La Croex, Jeromus: *Journey into Mohawk Country*, 425
Lady, the. *See* Suu Kyi, Aung San
Lafont: *It Was the War of the Trenches*, 385
Laika, **437–440**
Laika (Kudryavka): *Laika*, 438
Landra: *Mouse Guard*, 529
landscapes: *It's a Good Life, If You Don't Weaken: A Picture Novella*, 381; *Tale of One Bad Rat, The*, 726; *Wall, The: Growing Up Behind the Iron Curtain*, 829
L'Angelier, Pierre Emile: *Treasury of Victorian Murder, A*, 805
language, as core theme: *City of Glass*, 158; *Dead Memory*, 190; *Flood! A Novel in Pictures*, 256; *I Never Liked You*, 369; *Summer of Love, The*, 755; *Treasury of Victorian Murder, A*, 805
Lao-Tsu, Wong: *American Born Chinese*, 48
Laparik, Mrs.: *Jew in Communist Prague, A: Loss of Innocence*, 392
La Perdida, **441–444**
*Lapham, David, 727
Lasker, Skim: *Richard Stark's Parker*, 644
Last Day in Vietnam: A Memory, **445–447**
Latin America: *La Perdida*, 441–444; *Love and Rockets*, 491–496; *Palomar: The Heartbreak Soup Stories*, 573–576
Laura: *Blankets: An Illustrated Novel*, 102; *Like a Velvet Glove Cast in Iron*, 464; *Poor Bastard, The*, 613
law and justice, as core themes: *Ed the Happy Clown: The Definitive Ed Book*, 216; *Kafka*, 422
layout style: *Adventures of Tintin, The*, 12; *Asterios Polyp*, 65; *Asterix*, 70; *Blackmark*, 99; *Box Office Poison*, 126–127; *Dear Julia*, 196; *Elk's Run*, 220; *Get a Life*, 288; *Harum Scarum*, 321; *Haunted*, 334;

Independents & Underground Classics   INDEX

He Done Her Wrong, 338–339; *Hicksville*, 345; *Houdini: The Handcuff King*, 357; *It Was the War of the Trenches*, 386; *Jimmy Corrigan: The Smartest Kid on Earth*, 400–401; *Leave It to Chance*, 451–452; *Life and Times of Scrooge McDuck, The*, 457; *Lost Cause: John Wesley Hardin*, 472; *Mouse Guard*, 529–530; *Persepolis*, 600–601; *Playboy, The*, 609–610; *Rex Mundi*, 640; *Robot Dreams*, 651–652; *Tank Girl*, 774; *When the Wind Blows*, 843–844; *Whiteout*, 848; *You'll Never Know Book One: A Good and Decent Man*, 868–867
leadership, as core theme: *Tales of the Beanworld: A Most Peculiar Comic Book Experience*, 766
Leah: *Book of Genesis, The*, 119
Leave It to Chance, **448–453**
Leavenworth, Lisa: *Hate*, 329
Lebanon: *Waltz with Bashir: A Lebanon War Story*, 832
LeBeuf, Jimmy: *Complete Essex County, The*, 171–172
LeBeuf, Lawrence: *Complete Essex County, The*, 172
LeBeuf, Lou: *Complete Essex County, The*, 172
LeBeuf, Mary: *Complete Essex County, The*, 172
LeBeuf, Vince: *Complete Essex County, The*, 172
Leeds, Kevin: *Stray Bullets*, 729
Lees, Robert: *From Hell: Being a Melodrama in Sixteen Parts*, 273
Legyscapo, Leopold: *Dear Julia*, 195
*Lemire, Jeff, 170
Lender, Claire: *Jar of Fools*, 389
Lender, Nathan: *Jar of Fools*, 389
Lenz, Sasha: *Shortcomings*, 719
Leo: *A.D.: New Orleans After the Deluge*, 2; *Dear Julia*, 195; *Percy Gloom*, 592–593; *Tantrum*, 777
Leo (Leopold Legyscapo): *Dear Julia*, 195
Leonidas: *300*, 788
Leopard: *Age of Reptiles*, 20
lesbian characters. See homosexuality
Lestrade, Beatrice Dorothy: *Box Office Poison*, 126
lettering: *Adventures of Tintin, The*, 12; *Diary of a Mosquito Abatement Man*, 204; *Elk's Run*, 220; *Kurtzman's Jungle Book*, 325; *Ice Haven*, 361; *It's a Good Life, If You Don't Weaken: A Picture Novella*, 382; *Julius Knipl, Real Estate Photographer*, 412; *Kafka*, 419; *La Perdida*, 439; *Night Fisher*, 541; *One! Hundred! Demons!*, 558; *Plain Janes, The*, 607; *In the Shadow of No Towers*, 382; *Signal to Noise*, 685; *30 Days of Night*, 782; *Tragical Comedy or Comical Tragedy of Mr. Punch, The*, 498; *We Are on Our Own*, 837; *You'll Never Know Book One: A Good and Decent Man*, 868
Letterman, David: *American Splendor: From Off the Streets of Cleveland*, 52
Letushim, Enoch: *Jew of New York, The: A Historical Romance*, 396
Lev, Buttercup: *Golem's Mighty Swing, The*, 305
Levine, Bob: *Small Killing, A*, 705
Levy, Esther: *We Are on Our Own*, 836
Levy, Karoly: *We Are on Our Own*, 836–837
liberation. See freedom
Lieam: *Mouse Guard*, 528
*Lieber, Steve, 846
life and art, as core themes: *Gemma Bovery*, 283–284
Life and Times of Scrooge McDuck, The, **454–458**
life as transitory, as core theme: *Three Shadows*, 794–795
life experience, as core theme: *Burma Chronicles*, 135–136; *Mouse Guard*, 529–530; *Notes for a War Story*, 549
Life Sucks, **459–462**
Lightfoot: *Leave It to Chance*, 450
Like a Velvet Glove Cast in Iron, **463–466**
Lila: *Percy Gloom*, 592
Lil Bro: *System, The*, 757
Lincoln, Abraham: *Treasury of Victorian Murder, A*, 805
line style: *A.D.: New Orleans After the Deluge*, 3; *Airtight Garage of Jerry Cornelius*, 26; *Notes for a War Story* 548;. See also clear-line drawing style
Ling, Pam: *Pedro and Me: Friendship, Loss, and What I Learned*, 589
linguistic shift: *La Perdida*, 443
Lin the illustrator, Mr.: *Shenzhen*, 672
Lion, the. See Ashraf
lions: *Pride of Baghdad: Inspired by a True Story*, 619
Lisa: *It's a Bird...*, 378; *We Are on Our Own*, 836
Lise: *Three Shadows*, 793
Lita: *Perfect Example*, 596; *Sloth*, 701
literature: *Gemma Bovery*, 283; *Streak of Chalk*, 737
*Little, Jason, 679
Little Blue: *Owly*, 566
Little Killer (Stefano): *Notes for a War Story*, 548
Livonia: *Good-Bye, Chunky Rice*, 311
Llewellyn, Lloyd: *Twentieth Century Eightball*, 812

1045

*Locke, Vince, 347
Lodewijk, Martin: *Fax from Sarajevo,* 243
Lois: *Dykes to Watch Out For,* 210
loneliness and isolation, as core theme: *Ballad of Doctor Richardson, The,* 84; *Blankets: An Illustrated Novel,* 103; *Boulevard of Broken Dreams, The,* 123; *Give It Up!: And Other Short Stories,* 298; *Haunted,* 334–335; *Ice Haven,* 361–362; *Louis Riel: A Comic-Strip Biography,* 489
Long, Jody: *Tamara Drewe,* 769
long-haired gamer: *System, The,* 758
Long Jaw: *Age of Reptiles,* 20
Long Liz. *See* Stride, Elizabeth
Long Time Relationship, **467–469**
Looney, Connor (Crazy Connor): *Road to Perdition,* 647
Looney, John: *Road to Perdition,* 647
Lopez. *See* Elandos
Lord, Ava: *Sin City,* 689
Lord of the Locusts: *Rose: Prequel to Bone,* 652
Los Angeles: *Hard Boiled,* 315–317
loss, as core theme: *A.D.: New Orleans After the Deluge,* 3; *Asterios Polyp,* 65; *Chicken with Plums,* 156; *Ghost World,* 293–294; *Good-Bye, Chunky Rice,* 313; *Haunted,* 334–335; *Ice Haven,* 361–362; *Like a Velvet Glove Cast in Iron,* 465; *My Mommy Is in America and She Met Buffalo Bill,* 533; *Percy Gloom,* 593; *Robot Dreams,* 650–651; *Snowman, The,* 716
Lost Cause: John Wesley Hardin, **470–473**
Lost Girl, **474–476**
Lost Girls, **477–481**
Lot: *Book of Genesis, The,* 177
Loudermilk, Clay: *Like a Velvet Glove Cast in Iron,* 464
Louis: *Louis,* 484; *Three Shadows,* 793
Louis, **482–486**
Louis Riel: A Comic-Strip Biography, **487–490**
Louis XXII, King of France: *Rex Mundi,* 639
Louvre museum, Paris: *Glacial Period,* 300–301
love, as core theme: *Color Trilogy, The,* 169; *Dykes to Watch Out For,* 212; *Ethel and Ernest,* 233; *Fax from Sarajevo,* 244; *Gemma Bovery,* 283–284; *He Done Her Wrong,* 338–339; *Jar of Fools,* 390; *Journey into Mohawk Country,* 408–409; *Omaha the Cat Dancer,* 554; *Passionate Journey,* 579–580; *Pedro and Me: Friendship, Loss, and What I Learned,* 590; *Percy Gloom,* 593; *Scott Pilgrim,* 669; *30 Days of Night,* 782–783; *Three Shadows,* 794–795; *Tricked,* 809. *See also* relationships
Love and Rockets, **491–497**
Lovett, Detective Jimmy: *Kane,* 429
loyalty, as core theme: *Pyongyang: A Journey in North Korea,* 623–624; *Wall, The: Growing Up Behind the Iron Curtain,* 830
Luba: *Love and Rockets,* 491; *Palomar: The Heartbreak Soup Stories,* 573
Lucas: *Streak of Chalk,* 737
Lucha Libre wrestler, female: *Haunted,* 333
Lucha Libre wrestler, male: *Haunted,* 333
Lucha Libre wrestlers: *Haunted,* 333
Lucie: *Paul,* 583
Lucky: *Frank Book, The,* 264
Lucky, **498–501**
*Lutes, Jason, 86
Lyla: *Shutterbug Follies,* 680
Lyllith: *Blackmark,* 99
Lynda: *Small Killing, A,* 705
Lyons, John: *Perfect Example,* 596
Lysenko, Gropius: *Aliens,* 43–44

M

Ma'am. *See* Juliette
Mabel. *See* Clytemnestra, Queen of the Nile
MacAlistaire, Joshua: *Journey: The Adventure of Wolverine MacAlistaire,* 403
Macdonald, John A.: *Louis Riel: A Comic-Strip Biography,* 488
MacEwan, Brett: *Whiteout,* 847
MacGarry, Alec (Eddie Campbell): *Alec: The Years Have Pants,* 34
MacGuffin, Detective: *System, The,* 757
*Mack, David, 414
madness, as core theme: *Sin City,* 690
Maggie: *Walking Dead, The,* 825
magic, as core theme: *Jar of Fools,* 390
Magical Realism: *Sloth,* 701
magician: *Violent Cases,* 820
Mahmed: *Photographer, The: Into War-Torn Afghanistan with Doctors Without Borders,* 603
Maier, Lili: *Summer of Love, The,* 754
Maier, Pearl: *Summer of Love, The,* 754
Mail Order Bride, **502–505**
Main Jane (Jane): *Plain Janes, The,* 606

*Mairowitz, David Zane, 419
Maiselles, Rabbi Albert: *Rex Mundi*, 639
Maison, Georgette: *Alec: The Years Have Pants*, 34
Major, Stiffly: *Asterios Polyp*, 64
major, the: *Last Day in Vietnam: A Memory*, 446
Major, Ursula: *Asterios Polyp*, 64
male creature, a: *Haunted*, 333
Malka: *Rabbi's Cat, The*, 634
*Malkasian, Cathy, 591
Malvina: *Airtight Garage of Jerry Cornelius*, 25
Mama. *See* Small, Betty
Mamadou: *Aya of Yopougon*, 74
Mammal, Arthur: *Julius Knipl, Real Estate Photographer*, 412
man, a: *Flood! A Novel in Pictures*, 256; *Passionate Journey*, 578
Mandeville, Baronet Aristide de: *Rex Mundi*, 639
Manfred: *Three Shadows*, 793
manga styling: *Hate*, 329; *Kabuki*, 417–418; *Scott Pilgrim*, 668–667; *Transit*, 801
Manhog: *Frank Book, The*, 264
Man in an India Rubber Suit. *See* Kunzo, Vervel
Man in White: *Rex Mundi*, 639
Mansell (Darnell): *A.D.: New Orleans After the Deluge*, 2
Manute: *Sin City*, 689–690
manwah style: *Color Trilogy, The*, 168
Man Who Couldn't Stop, The: *Ed the Happy Clown: The Definitive Ed Book*, 215
Manzi, Little Lou: *History of Violence, A*, 348
maps: *Cartoon History of the Universe, The*, 146; *Jimmy Corrigan: The Smartest Kid on Earth*, 400; *9/11 Report, The: A Graphic Adaptation*, 545
Maracas, Fetor: *Julius Knipl, Real Estate Photographer*, 412
Marah, Abel: *Jew of New York, The: A Historical Romance*, 395–396
*Marchetto, Marisa Acocella, 141
Marchetto, Marisa Acocella (character): *Cancer Vixen*, 142
Marchetto, Silvano: *Cancer Vixen*, 142
*Marder, Larry, 764
Margaret: *Percy Gloom*, 592
Marie: *Lucky*, 499; *Paul*, 583
Marin, Father Gérard, S. J.: *Rex Mundi*, 638
Marjane: *Chicken with Plums*, 155
Marjane (Marji): *Embroideries*, 223

Marji. *See* Marjane (Marji)
Market Day, **506–508**
Markus: *Persepolis*, 600
Marlowe, Roderick: *30 Days of Night*, 782
Marnie: *Blackmark*, 98–99
Marquises of Aragon, Navarre, and Catalonia: *Rex Mundi*, 639
marriage, as core theme: *Ethel and Ernest*, 232; *Houdini: The Handcuff King*, 357; *Mail Order Bride*, 504; *Our Cancer Year*, 562
*Marrs, Sandra, 482
Martel, Charles, Mayor of the Court: *Rex Mundi*, 639
Martin, Crawfish: *Journey: The Adventure of Wolverine MacAlistaire*, 404
Martinez, Petra: *Love and Rockets*, 495
Martinez, Rosalba (Fritz): *Love and Rockets*, 495
Marv: *Sin City*, 689
Marvin: *Minor Miracles: Long Ago and Once Upon a Time Back When...*, 519
Mary: *Poor Bastard, The*, 612–613
Mary (Wolf Marie): *Journey: The Adventure of Wolverine MacAlistaire*, 404
masculinity: *Notes for a War Story*, 549
*Masereel, Frans, 577
mask and disguise: *Kabuki*, 418
Masson, Audrey: *It Rhymes with Lust*, 375
Masson, Rust: *It Rhymes with Lust*, 375
Master Cho: *Color Trilogy, The*, 168
Mat: *Kampung Boy*, 425
Mathers, Michaela: *Incognegro: A Graphic Mystery*, 364
*Mathieu, Marc-Antoine, 190
Mat's father: *Kampung Boy*, 425
Mat's grandmother: *Kampung Boy*, 425
Mat's mother: *Kampung Boy*, 444
*Matt, Joe, 611
Matt, Joe (character): *Poor Bastard, The*, 612
Matthew, Novate Inquisitor: *Rex Mundi*, 639
Matthews, Katie: *Skim*, 693
maturation and aging, as core theme: *Color Trilogy, The*, 169; *Curious Case of Benjamin Button, The*, 185; *Ethel and Ernest*, 232; *Rose: Prequel to Bone*, 654–655; *Suckle: The Status of Basil*, 747; *Tale of One Bad Rat, The*, 762; *Tantrum*, 778. *See also* adolescence; coming-of-age
Maus: A Survivor's Tale, **509–513**
Maya: *Age of Reptiles*, 22

Mazure: *It Was the War of the Trenches,* 385
*Mazzucchelli, David, 63
McCarthy, Dwight: *Sin City,* 689
McClure, Jimmy: *Blueberry,* 108
McConey: *Harum Scarum,* 320
McDuck, Hortense: *Life and Times of Scrooge McDuck, The,* 456
McDuck, Scrooge: *Life and Times of Scrooge McDuck, The,* 456
McGraw, Bobby: *Stray Bullets,* 729
McGraw, Janet: *Stray Bullets,* 729
McGregor, Sam and Ruth: *Tale of One Bad Rat, The,* 761
McKay, Handy: *Richard Stark's Parker,* 644
*McKean, Dave, 137, 683
McKenna, Edie: *History of Violence, A,* 348
meaning of life, as core theme: *Hate,* 330; *Ice Haven,* 361-362
media, role of: *Incognegro: A Graphic Mystery,* 363-366; *Why I Hate Saturn,* 851
medicine, as core theme: *Epileptic,* 299; *Journey into Mohawk Country,* 408-409
*Medley, Linda, 149, 151
Mednick, Si: *Harvey Kurtzman's Jungle Book,* 324-325
melancholy: *Lost Cause: John Wesley Hardin,* 472
Melba: *Minor Miracles: Long Ago and Once Upon a Time Back When...,* 519
Melorra: *Ghost World,* 293
Memo: *La Perdida,* 442
memoir genre: *Cancer Vixen,* 144. See also autobiographical genre
memory, as core theme: *Small Killing, A,* 706; *Tragical Comedy or Comical Tragedy of Mr. Punch, The,* 798; *Violent Cases,* 822; *You'll Never Know Book One: A Good and Decent Man,* 869
Mendelman: *Market Day,* 507
Menelaus: *Age of Bronze: The Story of the Trojan War,* 17
mental illness, as core theme: *Louis Riel: A Comic-Strip Biography,* 489
Meor brothers: *Kampung Boy,* 425
Merkel, Anne: *Why I Hate Saturn,* 851
Merkel, Laura: *Why I Hate Saturn,* 851
Merle: *Life Sucks,* 460
mermaid: *Tragical Comedy or Comical Tragedy of Mr. Punch, The,* 797

Mersh: *Minor Miracles: Long Ago and Once Upon a Time Back When...,* 519
*Messner-Loebs, William, 402, 405
Metropol: The Complete Series + Metropol A.D., **514-517**
Mexican drug culture: *La Perdida,* 443
Michelle: *A.D.: New Orleans After the Deluge,* 2
Michonne: *Walking Dead, The,* 825
midlife crisis, as core theme: *Tantrum,* 778
Midnight: *Mouse Guard,* 528-529
migration, as core theme: *Age of Reptiles,* 22-23; *Arrival, The,* 61
Miho: *Sin City,* 690
Miller, Dave: *Life Sucks,* 460
*Miller, Frank, 315, 687, 788, 846
Miller, Lisa: *Scott Pilgrim,* 668
Milly: *Pedro and Me: Friendship, Loss, and What I Learned,* 589
Milou. See Snowy
Mina: *Chicken with Plums,* 155
Minder One: *Queen and Country,* 629
Minder Three: *Queen and Country,* 629
minimalism: *Diary of a Mosquito Abatement Man,* 204; *Hicksville,* 344; *Monologues for the Coming Plague,* 524
Minor Miracles: Long Ago and Once Upon a Time Back When..., **518-521**
miracles, as core theme: *Minor Miracles: Long Ago and Once Upon a Time Back When...,* 520
Miranda: *Lucky,* 499
Mirza: *Chicken with Plums,* 155
Mishkin, Al: *Boulevard of Broken Dreams, The,* 122
Mishkin, Nathan: *Boulevard of Broken Dreams, The,* 122
Mishkin, Ted: *Boulevard of Broken Dreams, The,* 122
missing woman: *System, The,* 758
mixed media. See multimedia
Mizell, Elizabeth: *Hate,* 329
Mo: *Dykes to Watch Out For,* 210
Mo (Moishe Strauss): *Golem's Mighty Swing, The,* 305
*Modan, Rutu, 234, 236
*Moebius (pseudonym of Jean Giraud), 24, 25
Mohad, Samuel: *Airtight Garage of Jerry Cornelius,* 25
mole, a: *Kafka,* 421
Moncrief, Hildegarde: *Curious Case of Benjamin Button, The,* 184

Mondo, Herk: *Aliens,* 43
money, as core theme: *System, The,* 758–759
Monkey King of Flower Fruit Mountain: *American Born Chinese,* 47
Monologues for the Coming Plague, **522–525**
Monroe, Douglas: *Walking Dead, The,* 825
Monster: *Stray Bullets,* 729
Mooney: *Whiteout,* 847
*Moore, Alan, 271, 477, 704
Moore, Alan (character): *Alec: The Years Have Pants,* 34
Moore, Penny: *Alec: The Years Have Pants,* 34
*Moore, Terry, 722, 725
Moorish influence: *Rabbi's Cat, The,* 634
morality and ethics, as core theme: *Richard Stark's Parker,* 644–645
Mordecai: *Yossel: April 19, 1943 – A Story of the Warsaw Ghetto Uprising,* 861
Morgan: *Walking Dead, The,* 825
Morgan, Beth: *Complete Essex County, The,* 172
Moricant, Grand Inquisitor Gervase: *Rex Mundi,* 639
Morris, Bob: *Cancer Vixen,* 142
mortality, as core theme: *Three Shadows,* 794–795. *See also* death
Mortician: *Shutterbug Follies,* 680
Morton, Uncle: *Tragical Comedy or Comical Tragedy of Mr. Punch, The,* 797
Mother: *Snowman, The,* 716
mother tyrannosaur: *Age of Reptiles,* 22
motion and movement, in art: *Skitzy: The Story of Floyd W. Skitzafroid,* 698
Mouly, Françoise: *Maus: A Survivor's Tale,* 510; *In the Shadow of No Towers,* 371
Mousa, Mohammed Yousef Shaker: *Footnotes in Gaza: A Graphic Novel,* 260
Mouse Guard, **526–530**
movie posters: *Violent Cases,* 821–822
Mozaffar: *Chicken with Plums,* 155
Mudgett, Herman W. (H. H. Holmes): *Treasury of Victorian Murder, A,* 805
Mueller, Marthe: *Berlin: City of Stones,* 87
Muench, Gerhart: *Alan's War: The Memories of G.I. Alan Cope,* 29
Muench, Vera: *Alan's War: The Memories of G.I. Alan Cope,* 29
Müller, Doctor J. W.: *Adventures of Tintin, The,* 11

Mullins, Pete (contributing artist): *From Hell: Being a Melodrama in Sixteen Parts,* 271
multiculturalism, as core theme: *American Born Chinese,* 48
multimedia: *Cages,* 139; *King: A Comics Biography,* 433; *Stray Toasters,* 734
multiple artists: *Aliens,* 41; *Queen and Country,* 626
Muni, Joey: *History of Violence, A,* 348
Murad, Comrade Commissioner: *Jew in Communist Prague, A: Loss of Innocence,* 392
Murphy, Cory: *Pedro and Me: Friendship, Loss, and What I Learned,* 589
Murphy, Yahtzi: *Hate,* 329
Murphys: *Stitches: A Memoir,* 719
Murray, Leon: *Stray Bullets,* 729
music, references to popular: *Love and Rockets,* 496
Muskegon, Tina: *Like a Velvet Glove Cast in Iron,* 464
My Mommy Is in America and She Met Buffalo Bill, **531–534**
mystery, as core theme: *Chicken with Plums,* 156; *Exit Wounds,* 236; *From Hell: Being a Melodrama in Sixteen Parts,* 274; *Predator,* 617; *Shutterbug Follies,* 681; *Streak of Chalk,* 738–739
mystery genre: *David Boring,* 188; *Exit Wounds,* 236; *Incognegro: A Graphic Mystery,* 364, 365–366; *Rex Mundi,* 638; *Shutterbug Follies,* 679; *Tragical Comedy or Comical Tragedy of Mr. Punch, The,* 796–797; *Whiteout,* 848
myth and legend, as core theme: *Asterios Polyp,* 65; *Bacchus,* 78, 81; *Binky Brown Sampler,* 91; *Flood! A Novel in Pictures,* 257; *From Hell: Being a Melodrama in Sixteen Parts,* 274; *Rose: Prequel to Bone,* 655

N

Nahid: *Chicken with Plums,* 155
Nahum, Jules: *Rabbi's Cat, The,* 632
Najmudin: *Photographer, The: Into War-Torn Afghanistan with Doctors Without Borders,* 603
Nakai, Enoch: *Predator,* 616
Nakamura, Suzy: *American Born Chinese,* 47
nameless former prisoner, the: *Jew in Communist Prague, A: Loss of Innocence,* 392
naming, as core theme: *City of Glass,* 160
Naomi: *Palestine,* 570
narration: *Age of Reptiles,* 22; *Airtight Garage of Jerry Cornelius,* 26

narrative boxes: *Black Hole,* 95
Narrator's father: *Violent Cases,* 821
Natalie: *Tantrum,* 777
nationalism, as core theme: *La Perdida,* 443
Nat Turner, **535-539**
nature and the environment, as core theme: *Diary of a Mosquito Abatement Man,* 204; *Night Fisher,* 541;
Naybors, Harry: *Ice Haven,* 361
*Nelson, Arvid, 640
Netley, John: *From Hell: Being a Melodrama in Sixteen Parts,* 273
*Neufeld, Josh, 3
Neunier, Michele: *My Mommy Is in America and She Met Buffalo Bill,* 533
Neven. *See* Fixer, The
New Man. *See* Beatty, Daniel
Newt (Billie): *Aliens,* 42
Newton, Winsor: *Boulevard of Broken Dreams, The,* 122
New York City: *Flood! A Novel in Pictures,* 257
Jew of New York, The: A Historical Romance, 396
. *See also* World Trade Center Twin Towers
New Zealand: *Hicksville,* 344
Nicholls, Polly: *From Hell: Being a Melodrama in Sixteen Parts,* 273
Nick: *Tricked,* 808
Nigel: *Transit,* 801
Night Fisher, **540-542**
*Niles, Steve, 780
*Nilsen, Anders, 524
Nina: *Stray Bullets,* 728
9/11 Report, The: A Graphic Adaptation, **543-546**
Nitti, Frank: *Road to Perdition,* 647
Nixon. *See* Seltz, Carl
Nixon, E. D.: *King: A Comics Biography,* 432
Noah: *Book of Genesis, The,* 118
Noah, Major Mordecai: *Jew of New York, The: A Historical Romance,* 396
Noah-like character: *Flood! A Novel in Pictures,* 256
Noel: *Ballad of Doctor Richardson, The,* 83
noir style: *Ghost World,* 364;
noise of daily life, as core theme: *Signal to Noise,* 685
Nolan, Abigail (Abby): *Stray Toasters,* 733
Noone, Sammy: *Stuck Rubber Baby,* 742
Noor: *Pride of Baghdad: Inspired by a True Story,* 620
Norabelle: *One! Hundred! Demons!,* 557
Norah: *Tantrum,* 777

Norbert: *Aliens,* 43
North Korea: *Pyongyang: A Journey in North Korea,* 623
nostalgia, as core theme: *Kampung Boy,* 426
Notes for a War Story, **547-550**
Notochord, Jasper (Enoch): *Metropol: The Complete Series + Metropol A.D.,* 515
nuclear war: *When the Wind Blows,* 843
nudity: *Mail Order Bride,* 583; *Paul,* 583
numbered pages: *Embroideries,* 224

O

Obélix. *See* Obelix
Obelix (Obélix): *Asterix,* 68
objectivity, as core theme: *Footnotes in Gaza: A Graphic Novel,* 261
O'Brien, Sean: *Dropsie Avenue,* 206
obsession, as core theme: *Dear Julia,* 196; *It's a Good Life, If You Don't Weaken: A Picture Novella,* 381; *Jew of New York, The: A Historical Romance,* 396
Octobriana: *Adventures of Luther Arkwright, The,* 7
O'Dea, Esther: *Jar of Fools,* 389
Odysseus: *Age of Bronze: The Story of the Trojan War,* 16
Ofelia: *Love and Rockets,* 495
Officer Hogan: *Houdini: The Handcuff King,* 356
O'Gilt, Goldie: *Life and Times of Scrooge McDuck, The,* 456
old lady, an: *Haunted,* 333
Old Man, The (Baron): *Three Shadows,* 793
Old Zeph: *Blackmark,* 98
Olemaun, Deputy Stella: *30 Days of Night,* 781
Olemaun, Sheriff Eben: *30 Days of Night,* 782
Olga: *Kafka,* 421
Olivares, Carla: *La Perdida,* 442
Olivares, Rod: *La Perdida,* 442
Omaha (Jenson or Johnson, Susan "Susie"): *Omaha the Cat Dancer,* 553
Omaha the Cat Dancer, **551-555**
*O'Malley, Brian Lee, 669
One Claw: *Age of Reptiles,* 21
One! Hundred! Demons!, **556-559**
One Thousand, Mr.: *Like a Velvet Glove Cast in Iron,* 464
oppression, as core theme: *Burma Chronicles,* 135; *Jew in Communist Prague, A: Loss of Innocence,* 393;

Omaha the Cat Dancer, 554; *Palestine,* 571; *Pyongyang: A Journey in North Korea,* 623
ordinary life. *See* daily life
Oriole, Francis: *Jew of New York, The: A Historical Romance,* 396
Orley: *Stuck Rubber Baby,* 742
Orly: *Exit Wounds,* 235
Orson: *Scary Godmother: The Boo Flu,* 663; *Stray Bullets,* 728
Ortiz, Eulalio (Speedy): *Love and Rockets,* 494
Oscar: *La Perdida,* 442; *You Are Here,* 865
Oscura: *Age of Reptiles,* 22
O'Shaughnessy, Marmaduke. *See* Angel Face
osteopath: *Violent Cases,* 821
ostracism. *See* alienation, as core theme
O'Sullivan, Michael, Jr.: *Road to Perdition,* 647
O'Sullivan, Michael, Sr. (Archangel of Death; the Angel): *Road to Perdition,* 647
Other Guy: *Monologues for the Coming Plague,* 523
Ottla: *Kafka,* 421
Our Cancer Year, **560–563**
overlapping characters: *System, The,* 757
overlapping panels: *In the Shadow of No Towers,* 372
Owly: *Owly,* 566
Owly, **564–568**

P

P., John: *Perfect Example,* 596
Paar, Dot: *David Boring,* 188
Pace, Beverly. *See* Bouedaue, Veronica
pacing: *Bone,* 185
Pacinotti, Gianni. *See* Gipi
page as chapter: *Wilson,* 853
page layout. *See* layout
Paige, Victor: *Golem's Mighty Swing, The,* 305
Palermo, Polo: *Dropsie Avenue,* 206
Palestine. *See* Israeli-Palestinian conflict
Palestine, **569–572**
Palmer, Guffie: *Blueberry,* 109
Palomar: The Heartbreak Soup Stories, **573–576**
panels, size of. *See* size of panels
panel transitions: *Deogratias: A Tale of Rwanda,* 199
panoramic views: *A.D.: New Orleans After the Deluge,* 2
Panoramix. *See* Getafix
Papa John: *Stitches: A Memoir,* 719
Papavasilou, Daisy: *Shutterbug Follies,* 680

Papineau, Ken: *Complete Essex County, The,* 171
Papineau, Lester: *Complete Essex County, The,* 171
parallel lines: *Boulevard of Broken Dreams, The,* 123
parallel universe: *Julius Knipl, Real Estate Photographer,* 413
Paris: *Age of Bronze: The Story of the Trojan War,* 18
Parker: *Richard Stark's Parker,* 644
Parker, Darcy: *Strangers in Paradise,* 723
Parker, Lynn: *Richard Stark's Parker,* 644
Parks, Rosa: *King: A Comics Biography,* 432
parody: *Complete Fritz the Cat, The,* 177
Parvine: *Chicken with Plums,* 156; *Embroideries,* 223
passing: *Incognegro: A Graphic Mystery,* 364
Passionate Journey, **577–580**
past as influence: *Box Office Poison,* 126
Patella, Miss: *Jew of New York, The: A Historical Romance,* 396
Patience, Prudence, and Plenty: *Castle Waiting,* 150
patriotism, as core theme: *It Was the War of the Trenches,* 386
Patzi: *Alan's War: The Memories of G.I. Alan Cope,* 30
Paul: *Glacial Period,* 301
Paul, **581–584**
Paula: *Palestine,* 570
Paul's Family Members: *Paul,* 583
Pearson, Keith: *Black Hole,* 94
Pedro and Me: Friendship, Loss, and What I Learned, **588–590**
*Pedrosa, Cyril, 792
*Pekar, Harvey, 584
Pekar, Harvey (character): *American Splendor: From Off the Streets of Cleveland,* 50
Pekar, Lennie: *Our Cancer Year,* 561
pen and ink: *Hey, Wait...,* 342
pencilwork. *See* line style
Pepper: *Wilson,* 854
Pepper, Anna Dellyne: *Stuck Rubber Baby,* 741
Pepper, Les: *Stuck Rubber Baby,* 742
Pepper, Reverand Harland: *Stuck Rubber Baby,* 742
Percy Gloom, **591–594**
Perfect Example, **595–597**
Performer, The: *Alice in Sunderland: An Entertainment,* 38
Persepolis, **598–601**
perseverance, as core theme: *Scary Godmother: The Boo Flu,* 664

1051

perspective, artistic: *Exit Wounds,* 235;
perzine. *See* autobiographical genre
Peter: *Wall, The: Growing Up Behind the Iron Curtain,* 829
Peters, Helen Francine: *Strangers in Paradise,* 729
Peters, Julie: *Skim,* 693
*Petersen, David, 528
Pettibone, Mr.: *Scary Godmother: The Boo Flu,* 663
Pharos, Dr.: *Julius Knipl, Real Estate Photographer,* 412
Phelps, Autumn: *Shortcomings,* 677
Phil: *Blankets: An Illustrated Novel,* 102
Philip, Brother: *Deogratias: A Tale of Rwanda,* 199
Philips, General Homer: *Predator,* 617
Phoebe: *Tricked,* 808
Photographer, The: Into War-Torn Afghanistan with Doctors Without Borders, **602–604**
photographs: *Adventures of Tintin, The,* 12
Photoshop: *Summer of Love, The,* 754
picture book: *Arrival, The,* 40
Picture Man, The: *Color Trilogy, The,* 169
Pierrot, Grandpa: *My Mommy Is in America and She Met Buffalo Bill,* 533
Pig. *See* de Bourville, Vattier
Pike, Suzette: *Three Shadows,* 793
Pilgrim, Scott: *Scott Pilgrim,* 668
Pilgrim, Stacey: *Scott Pilgrim,* 668
Pilgrim, The: *Alice in Sunderland: An Entertainment,* 38
Pinchback, Alonzo (Pinchy): *Incognegro: A Graphic Mystery,* 364
Pinchback, Zane (Incognegro): *Incognegro: A Graphic Mystery,* 364
Pinchy. *See* Pinchback, Alonzo
Pine, Kim: *Scott Pilgrim,* 668
Pinkerton, Allan: *Blueberry,* 109
Pipo: *Palomar: The Heartbreak Soup Stories,* 574
Pippi: *Wilson,* 854
Plain Janes, The, **605–607**
Plantard de St. Clair, David-Louis: *Rex Mundi,* 639
Plantard de St. Clair, Lady Isabelle: *Rex Mundi,* 639
Plaster, Rodney: *Shutterbug Follies,* 680
Playboy, The, **608–610**
playful style: *What It Is,* 840. *See also* humor
plesiosaur: *Age of Reptiles,* 22
plot. *See* plot section in specific articles
Pogeybait: *Twentieth Century Eightball,* 812

point of view shifts: *King: A Comics Biography,* 489
police: *Flood! A Novel in Pictures,* 256
policeman, corrupt: *System, The,* 757
police officer: *Give It Up!: And Other Short Stories,* 297
Police Officer Fields: *Houdini: The Handcuff King,* 357
Police Officer Hemphill: *Houdini: The Handcuff King,* 357
Police Officer Sanchez: *Plain Janes, The,* 606
politics, as core theme: *Adventures of Tintin, The,* 12
Polk, Melanie: *Stuck Rubber Baby,* 742
Polk, Toland: *Stuck Rubber Baby,* 742
Polly Jane: *Plain Janes, The,* 606
Polyp, Asterios: *Asterios Polyp,* 64
Polyp, Ignazio: *Asterios Polyp,* 64
Poor Bastard, The, **611–614**
*Pope, Paul, 82
*Porcellino, John, 202
Porcellino, John (character): *Diary of a Mosquito Abatement Man,* 203
pornography: *Lost Girls,* 479
Portly Pig: *Three Fingers,* 785
Possey: *Owly,* 566
Postman, the: *Louis,* 484
Potter, Helen: *Tale of One Bad Rat, The,* 761
Potter, Mr. Harold: *Lost Girls,* 761
Potter, Mrs. Wendy (Wendy from *Peter Pan*): *Lost Girls,* 478
Potters, The: *Tale of One Bad Rat, The,* 761
Poulbot, Madame: *Get a Life,* 287
poverty: *Epileptic,* 229
power, as core theme: *Adventures of Luther Arkwright, The,* 7
*Prado, Miguelanxo, 738
Prazina, Jusuf (Juka): *Fixer, The: A Story from Sarajevo,* 247
Precious: *Like a Velvet Glove Cast in Iron,* 464
Precocious, Mr.: *Tank Girl,* 774
Predator: *Predator,* 617
Priam: *Age of Bronze: The Story of the Trojan War,* 17
Prichard, Dr. Edward William: *Treasury of Victorian Murder, A,* 804
Pride of Baghdad: Inspired by a True Story, **619–621**
Prince Eddy. *See* Albert Victor, Prince
Princess Anne. *See* Anne, Princess (and later Queen)
Professor. *See* Swatchell
Proffy. *See* Garbanzo, Professor

Proto: *Age of Reptiles*, 21
Prunier: *It Was the War of the Trenches*, 386
Psychologist: *Stitches: A Memoir*, 719
P.T.O. (the strange girl): *Lost Girl*, 475
publication history. *See* publication history section in specific articles
pulp magazine artistic style: *Blackmark*, 99
Punch, Mr.: *Tragical Comedy or Comical Tragedy of Mr. Punch, The*, 797
Punch and Judy: *Tragical Comedy or Comical Tragedy of Mr. Punch, The*, 797
Punter, The: *Alice in Sunderland: An Entertainment*, 38
puppet show: *Tragical Comedy or Comical Tragedy of Mr. Punch, The*, 798
Pupshaw: *Frank Book, The*, 264
Pyongyang: A Journey in North Korea, **622–625**

Q

Queen and Country, **626–631**
Quenneville, Anne: *Complete Essex County, The*, 172
Quetzal: *Age of Reptiles*, 21
Quidnunc, Clean: *Louis*, 484
Quidnunc, Jerk: *Louis*, 484
quilt squares: *Blankets: An Illustrated Novel*, 103
Qin, David (Yousaka Takahashi): *Strangers in Paradise*, 724
Quince: *Leave It to Chance*, 451
Quinn, Daniel: *City of Glass*, 159

R

*Rabagliati, Michel, 581
Rabbi's Cat, The, **632–636**
rabbi's rabbi: *Rabbi's Cat, The*, 634
Raccoon: *Robot Dreams*, 650
Raccoon, Mrs.: *Owly*, 566
race and racism: *Incognegro: A Graphic Mystery*, 364–366; *King: A Comics Biography*, 431. *See also* prejudice and discrimination
Racecar, Amy. *See* Applejack, Virginia
Rachel: *Book of Genesis, The*, 119; *Market Day*, 507
Radloff, Toby: *American Splendor: From Off the Streets of Cleveland*, 52
Rafael. *See* Raffi
Rafferty, Iron Jack. *See* Jack
Raffi (Rafael): *Dykes to Watch Out For*, 211
rain: *Sin City*, 690
Raina: *Blankets: An Illustrated Novel*, 102

Raina's parents: *Blankets: An Illustrated Novel*, 102
Raines, Ginger: *Stuck Rubber Baby*, 742
Raminski, Miroslaw. *See* Doe, John
Rand: *Mouse Guard*, 529
Randolph, A. Philip: *King: A Comics Biography*, 432
Rankins, Mark and Wizzy: *Gemma Bovery*, 282
Raphael: *It's a Bird...*, 378
Rapid Rodriguez: *Three Fingers*, 785
Rashid: *Pride of Baghdad: Inspired by a True Story*, 620
Rastapopoulos, Roberto: *Adventures of Tintin, The*, 11
Rat: *Tale of One Bad Rat, The*, 761
rat creatures: *Bone*, 114
rationality, as core theme: *Walking Dead, The*, 826
Raul: *Streak of Chalk*, 737
Rayburn, Simon: *Queen and Country*, 629
Raymond: *Ethel and Ernest*, 232
Reagan, Ronald: *Ed the Happy Clown: The Definitive Ed Book*, 215
realistic style: *History of Violence, A*, 349; *Kings in Disguise*, 435; *Like a Velvet Glove Cast in Iron*, 465; *Night Fisher*, 541; *9/11 Report, The: A Graphic Adaptation*, 545; *Waltz with Bashir: A Lebanon War Story*, 834. *See also* photorealistic style; surrealistic style
reality. *See* fantasy *vs.* reality
Real Pa: *Frank Book, The*, 264
Reba: *Minor Miracles: Long Ago and Once Upon a Time Back When...*, 519
Rebbe, The: *Yossel: April 19, 1943 – A Story of the Warsaw Ghetto Uprising*, 861
Rebekah: *Book of Genesis, The*, 119
rebellion, as core theme: *Pyongyang: A Journey in North Korea*, 624
Rebibo, Raymond: *Rabbi's Cat, The*, 634
rebirth, as core theme: *A.D.: New Orleans After the Deluge*, 3
Redbreast, Regis P.: *Three Fingers*, 785
Reddear, John: *Skim*, 693
Red Dragon: *Bone*, 114
redemption and atonement, as core themes: *Give It Up!: And Other Short Stories*, 298
Red Neck (Red Wooley): *Blueberry*, 109
Reed: *Signal to Noise*, 684
reflection, as core theme: *Alan's War: The Memories of G.I. Alan Cope*, 30

Regis: *Photographer, The: Into War-Torn Afghanistan with Doctors Without Borders*, 603
Rein-Buskila, Boaz: *Waltz with Bashir: A Lebanon War Story*, 833
relationships, as core themes. *See specific types of relationships below*
relationships, family: *Chicken with Plums*, 156; *Fax from Sarajevo*, 244; *Fun Home: A Family Tragicomic*, 279; *Jimmy Corrigan: The Smartest Kid on Earth*, 400; *Lost Girl*, 475–476; *Nat Turner*, 537; *Omaha the Cat Dancer*, 554; *Persepolis*, 600–601; *Rabbi's Cat, The*, 635; *Stitches: A Memoir*, 720; *Stray Toasters*, 734
relationships, forming: *It's a Good Life, If You Don't Weaken: A Picture Novella*, 381
relationships, friend. *See* friendship, as core theme
relationships, human and God: *Book of Genesis, The*, 119–120
relationships, human and machinery: *Dead Memory*, 192
relationships, male and female: *Suckle: The Status of Basil*, 747. *See also* marriage; romance
relationships, parent and child: *Home after Dark*, 354
relationships, self to society: *Berlin: City of Stones*, 88
relationships, sexual: *Contract with God, And Other Tenement Stories, A*, 181; *Dykes to Watch Out For*, 212
relationships, trust in: *Box Office Poison*, 126
relationships between characters: *Blankets: An Illustrated Novel*, 103; *Box Office Poison*, 126; *Get a Life*, 288; *Long Time Relationship*, 469; *Lucky*, 500; *Poor Bastard, The*, 613; *Strangers in Paradise*, 725–726; *Tamara Drewe*, 770; *Tricked*, 809
relationships between parents: *Ethel and Ernest*, 232; *Houdini: The Handcuff King*, 357
release, as core theme: *Ballad of Doctor Richardson, The*, 84–85
religion and faith, as core theme: *Aliens*, 45; *American Born Chinese*, 48; *Binky Brown Sampler*, 91; *Blankets: An Illustrated Novel*, 103; *Ed the Happy Clown: The Definitive Ed Book*, 216; *Journey into Mohawk Country*, 408–409; *Rabbi's Cat, The*, 635; *Rex Mundi*, 640. *See also* Islam; Judaism; spirituality
religious genre: *Contract with God, A*, 181; *Golem's Mighty Swing, The*, 306; *Market Day*, 508; *Rabbi's Cat, The*, 635

renewal, as core theme: *Alice in Sunderland: An Entertainment*, 39
repeated panels: *Castle Waiting*, 151; *Hey, Wait...*, 341–342
Resnick, Mal: *Richard Stark's Parker*, 644
responsibility, as core theme: *Small Killing, A*, 706; *Tantrum*, 778
restaurant cook: *Shenzhen*, 673
Reubens, Isabel Ortiz "Izzy": *Love and Rockets*, 494
revenge and retribution, as core theme: *Road to Perdition*, 648
reversal of fortune, as core theme: *David Boring*, 189
Rex Mundi, **637–641**
Reynard: *Blackmark*, 98–99
Reza: *Chicken with Plums*, 155; *Persepolis*, 600
Rhodes, Chris: *Black Hole*, 94
Rhodes, Dr.: *Our Cancer Year*, 561
Rhyton: *Glacial Period*, 301
Ricardo: *La Perdida*, 442
Richard: *Pyongyang: A Journey in North Korea*, 623; *Tricked*, 808
Richardson, Dr. Jefferson: *Ballad of Doctor Richardson, The*, 83
Richard Stark's Parker, **642–645**
Rick: *Why I Hate Saturn*, 851
Rick Holstrum (Rick the Dick): *Black Hole*, 94–95
Rick the Dick. *See* Rick Holstrum
Riel, Louis: *Louis Riel: A Comic-Strip Biography*, 488
Riki: *Safe Area Goražde*, 660
Ringding, Johnny: *Harvey Kurtzman's Jungle Book*, 324
Rival Cartoon Girl. *See* Jennifer
Rivera, Angel: *Love and Rockets*, 494
Rivera, Lily: *Tricked*, 808
Rizzo, Marie: *Minor Miracles: Long Ago and Once Upon a Time Back When...*, 519
Road to Perdition, **646–648**
Roark, Patrick Henry: *Sin City*, 689
Roark, Senator: *Sin City*, 690
Robert: *Photographer, The: Into War-Torn Afghanistan with Doctors Without Borders*, 603
Roberts, Frank: *Why I Hate Saturn*, 851
*Robinson, Alex, 125
*Robinson, James, 448
Robot: *Robot Dreams*, 650
Robot Dreams, **649–651**
Rocky: *Owly*, 566

Rogers, Mary: *Treasury of Victorian Murder, A*, 805
Roibin: *Mouse Guard*, 529
Roland: *Paul*, 583
role of artist in society: *Market Day*, 508
ROM: *Dead Memory*, 191
romance, as core theme: *Ballad of Doctor Richardson, The*, 84; *Cages*, 139; *Color Trilogy, The*, 169; *Exit Wounds*, 236
romance genre: *Ballad of Doctor Richardson, The*, 84; *Box Office Poison*, 125; *Color Trilogy, The*, 169; *Gemma Bovery*, 282; *Skim*, 694
Romeo: *Sloth*, 701
Ron: *Queen and Country*, 629
Ron (Ronacles): *Stray Bullets*, 730
Ronacles. *See* Ron
*Rosa, Don, 454
Rose: *Stray Bullets*, 729
Rose: Prequel to Bone, **652–655**
Rossmann, Karl: *Kafka*, 421
Rougeur, Monsieur: *Lost Girls*, 479
Rubicon, Victor: *Julius Knipl, Real Estate Photographer*, 412
Rubin, Bates: *Whiteout*, 847
*Rucka, Greg, 626, 630, 846
rumor: *Burma Chronicles*, 135–136
Rumsfeld, Donald: *9/11 Report, The: A Graphic Adaptation*, 545
*Runton, Andy, 564
Rush, Ellen: *Cages*, 138
Rush, Jonathan: *Cages*, 138
Russian Jew: *Rabbi's Cat, The*, 634
Russo, Valerie "Val": *Hate*, 329
Rustemagic, Edina: *Fax from Sarajevo*, 243
Rustemagic, Ervin: *Fax from Sarajevo*, 243
Rustemagik, Egon: *Stray Toasters*, 733
Rustin, Bayard: *King: A Comics Biography*, 432
Ruth: *Good-Bye, Chunky Rice*, 312
Ruthie: *It's a Good Life, If You Don't Weaken: A Picture Novella*, 381; *Tantrum*, 777
Ruthie, Aunt: *Exit Wounds*, 235
Rwanda: *Deogratias: A Tale of Rwanda*, 198–200
Ryan, Nicholas: *Treasury of Victorian Murder, A*, 804
Ryuichi Kai: *Kabuki*, 416

S

Sabarsky, Leo: *Cages*, 138
*Sacco, Joe, 246

Sacco, Joe (character): *Fixer, The: A Story from Sarajevo*, 247; *Footnotes in Gaza: A Graphic Novel*, 260; *Palestine*, 570; *Safe Area Goražde*, 660
Sadie: *Mouse Guard*, 528
Safa: *Pride of Baghdad: Inspired by a True Story*, 620
Safe Area Goražde, **659–662**
St. Clair, Jim: *Richard Stark's Parker*, 644
St. George: *Leave It to Chance*, 451
Sally: *Lost Girl*, 475
Sam: *Cancer Vixen*, 142; *Harvey Kurtzman's Jungle Book*, 324
Sameh: *Palestine*, 570
Samia: *Dykes to Watch Out For*, 211
Sammy (King of Spain): *Kings in Disguise*, 435
Samsa, Gregor: *Kafka*, 420–421
Sam the Meatman: *Transit*, 801
Sanchez, Officer: *Plain Janes, The*, 606
Santo: *Age of Reptiles*, 21
Sara: *Streak of Chalk*, 737
Sarah: *Blankets: An Illustrated Novel*, 102
Sarah (Sarai): *Book of Genesis, The*, 118
Sarah, Aunt: *It's a Bird...*, 378
Sarai. *See* Sarah
Sarakiel: *Metropol: The Complete Series + Metropol A.D.*, 515
sarcasm: *Scott Pilgrim*, 669
Sasser, Sean: *Pedro and Me: Friendship, Loss, and What I Learned*, 589
*Sæterøy, John Arne (Jason), 340
satire: *Asterix*, 70; *Curious Case of Benjamin Button, The*, 185; *Gemma Bovery*, 284; *Harvey Kurtzman's Jungle Book*, 325–326; *Twentieth Century Eightball*, 813
Satrapi (character): *Embroideries*, 223
Satrapi, Ebi (character): *Persepolis*, 600
Satrapi, grandmother of Marjane (character): *Persepolis*, 600
*Satrapi, Marjane, 154, 156, 222, 598
Satrapi, Marjane (character): *Chicken with Plums*, 155; *Persepolis*, 599–600
Satrapi, Taji (character): *Persepolis*, 600
Saunders, Lieutenant: *Leave It to Chance*, 451
Saunière, Julien: *Rex Mundi*, 638
Saxon: *Mouse Guard*, 528
Scarab. *See* Keiko
Scary Godmother: *Scary Godmother: The Boo Flu*, 663
Scary Godmother: The Boo Flu, **663–665**

Schaefer, Detective: *Predator*, 617
Schmidt, Otto: *Berlin: City of Stones*, 87
Schultz, Doc: *Louis Riel: A Comic-Strip Biography*, 488
*Schultz, Mark, 857, 858
Schwartz, David: *Berlin: City of Stones*, 87
science fiction genre: *Adventures of Luther Arkwright, The*, 5–7; *Airtight Garage of Jerry Cornelius*, 26; *Aliens*, 44; *Ballad of Doctor Richardson, The*, 85; *Blackmark*, 97–99; *Dead Memory*, 190–191; *Tank Girl*, 772–773
Scott, Thomas: *Louis Riel: A Comic-Strip Biography*, 488
Scott Pilgrim, **666–670**
scrapbook format: *Curious Case of Benjamin Button, The*, 185; *Tank Girl*, 774; *You'll Never Know Book One: A Good and Decent Man*, 867, 868
Scribble-Face: *Monologues for the Coming Plague*, 523
Scruggs, Mr.: *Contract with God, A*, 180
*Seagle, Steven T., 377
Sébastien: *Aya of Yopougon*, 74
second-person narration: *Fixer, The: A Story from Sarajevo*, 247–248
Séguier, Pierre: *Glacial Period*, 301
self-awareness, as core theme: *Lost Girls*, 480
self-centeredness, as core theme: *Glacial Period*, 302-303
self-deception, as core theme: *Tricked*, 809
self-discovery, as core theme: *Bone*, 115
self-image, as core theme: *Scott Pilgrim*, 669
self-interest, as core theme: *Jew of New York, The: A Historical Romance*, 397
self-sacrifice: *Maus: A Survivor's Tale*, 512
Selimbegovic, Vildania: *Fixer, The: A Story from Sarajevo*, 247
Selladore: *Julius Knipl, Real Estate Photographer*, 412
Seltz, Becky: *Hard Boiled*, 316
Seltz, Carl (Nixon): *Hard Boiled*, 316
sentimentality: *Good-Bye, Chunky Rice*, 312
September 11, 2001 terrorist attacks: *In the Shadow of No Towers*, 370–371; *9/11 Report, The: A Graphic Adaptation*, 543–546
Sergeant (Frenchman): *Deogratias: A Tale of Rwanda*, 206–207
Serpent, The: *Book of Genesis, The*, 118
Serra, Miguel: *Sloth*, 701

Seth (character): *It's a Good Life, If You Don't Weaken: A Picture Novella*, 381; *Poor Bastard, The*, 612
*Seth (pseudonym of Gregory Gallant), 380
Seth's mother: *It's a Good Life, If You Don't Weaken: A Picture Novella*, 381
setting. *See plot section of specific graphic novels*
Seven Bowing Bystanders: *Houdini: The Handcuff King*, 356
Severing, Kurt: *Berlin: City of Stones*, 87
sexuality, as core theme: *Aya of Yopougon*, 75; *Binky Brown Sampler*, 91; *Black Hole*, 96; *Contract with God, A*, 181; *Embroideries*, 224–225; *Fun Home: A Family Tragicomic*, 279; *Lost Girls*, 480; *Love and Rockets*, 496; *Omaha the Cat Dancer*, 554; *Shortcomings*, 677–678; *Stuck Rubber Baby*, 743; *Suckle: The Status of Basil*, 747
*Sfar, Joann, 632
Sfar, Rabbi Abraham: *Rabbi's Cat, The*, 633–634
Sfar, Sheikh Muhammed: *Rabbi's Cat, The*, 634
Sfar, Zlabya: *Rabbi's Cat, The*, 634
shading: *Contract with God, A*, 181; *Dropsie Avenue*, 207; *Harvey Kurtzman's Jungle Book*, 325; *Ice Haven*, 361; *Life Sucks*, 460; *Maus: A Survivor's Tale*, 510–511; *Pyongyang: A Journey in North Korea*, 623
shadow styles: *Hicksville*, 344; *It's a Good Life, If You Don't Weaken: A Picture Novella*, 381; *Jew of New York, The: A Historical Romance*, 396; *Minor Miracles: Long Ago and Once Upon a Time Back When...*, 519–520; *Three Shadows*, 794
Shaftsbury, Elton: *Contract with God, A*, 180
Shah, Aider: *Photographer, The: Into War-Torn Afghanistan with Doctors Without Borders*, 603
Shah-Leshy, Inanna: *Signal to Noise*, 684
Shandra: *Blackmark*, 99
Shane: *Walking Dead, The*, 825
Shanks, Armitage "Army": *Far Arden*, 239
*Shanower, Eric, 15, 16
Sharett, Moshe (Moshe Shertok): *Footnotes in Gaza: A Graphic Novel*, 260
Sharon, Ariel: *Footnotes in Gaza: A Graphic Novel*, 260
Sharpe, Lily: *Whiteout*, 847
Shaw, Rob: *Omaha the Cat Dancer*, 554
Shelley: *Wilson*, 854
Shenzhen, **671–674**
Shepard, Rowena: *Dropsie Avenue*, 206

sheriff: *Incognegro: A Graphic Mystery,* 364
Shertok, Moshe. *See* Sharett, Moshe
Shirl, Monk: *It Rhymes with Lust,* 375
Shlock, Lucifer: *Harvey Kurtzman's Jungle Book,* 324
Shortcomings, **675–678**
Shoveler: *Flaming Carrot Comics,* 252
Shrdlu, Etaoin: *Harvey Kurtzman's Jungle Book,* 325
Shtarkah, Jacob: *Contract with God, A,* 180
Shutterbug Follies, **679–682**
Siamese: *Kabuki,* 417
Sickert, Walter: *From Hell: Being a Melodrama in Sixteen Parts,* 273
*Sienkiewicz, Bill, 732
Signal to Noise, **683–686**
silhouettes: *Life and Times of Scrooge McDuck, The,* 456–457
Silver, Bradley: *Strangers in Paradise,* 725
Silver, Griffin: *Strangers in Paradise,* 725
*Simmonds, Posy, 281, 283, 768
Simone, Granny: *My Mommy Is in America and She Met Buffalo Bill,* 533
simplicity of style: *My Mommy Is in America and She Met Buffalo Bill,* 533; *Perfect Example,* 596; *Persepolis,* 600; *Robot Dreams,* 650; *300,* 790
Simpson: *Bacchus,* 80
Sin, Mr.: *Pyongyang: A Journey in North Korea,* 623
Sina: *Age of Reptiles,* 21
Sin City, **687–691**
singer in the subway: *System, The,* 758
single page spread. *See* full-page panels
single page stories: *Alec: The Years Have Pants,* 34–35
Siple: *Whiteout,* 847
*Sis, Peter, 828
Sissoko, Bonaventure: *Aya of Yopougon,* 74
Sissoko, Moussa: *Aya of Yopougon,* 74
Sister Margaret Byrne: *Complete Essex County, The,* 172
Sivan, Ori: *Waltz with Bashir: A Lebanon War Story,* 833
size of characters: *Complete Essex County, The,* 172–173; *Rabbi's Cat, The,* 634
size of graphic novel: *Ballad of Doctor Richardson, The,* 84; *Hicksville,* 344; *Mouse Guard,* 529; *Notes for a War Story,* 548; *Photographer, The: Into War-Torn Afghanistan with Doctors Without Borders,* 603–604; *In the Shadow of No Towers,* 372–373;

Suckle: The Status of Basil, 746–747; *Tragical Comedy or Comical Tragedy of Mr. Punch, The,* 798
size of panels: *Age of Reptiles,* 22; *City of Glass,* 159; *Friends with Boys,* 269; *Get a Life,* 288; *Ghost World,* 293; *Skim,* 693–694; *Snowman, The,* 716; *Stitches: A Memoir,* 720
Skeetes, Bob: *Ghost World,* 292
sketchiness: *Alec: The Years Have Pants,* 34–35; *Elk's Run,* 219
Skim, **692–695**
Skim (Kimberly Keiko Cameron): *Skim,* 693
Skitzafroid, Mr.: *Skitzy: The Story of Floyd W. Skitzafroid,* 697–698
Skitzafroid, Mrs.: *Skitzy: The Story of Floyd W. Skitzafroid,* 698
Skitzy: The Story of Floyd W. Skitzafroid, **696–699**
Sky: *I Never Liked You,* 368
slapstick: *He Done Her Wrong,* 337, 338
Slave: *Three Shadows,* 793–794
slavery: *Nat Turner,* 537–538
Sloth, **700–703**
Small, Betty (Mama): *Stitches: A Memoir,* 719
*Small, David, 351, 718
Small, David (character): *Stitches: A Memoir,* 719
Small, Edward "Ed" (Dad): *Stitches: A Memoir,* 719
Small, Ted: *Stitches: A Memoir,* 719
Small Killing, A, **704–707**
Smith, Adam: *Elk's Run,* 219
Smith, Danny: *Dropsie Avenue,* 206
*Smith, Jeff, 112, 115, 652
Smith, Madeleine: *Treasury of Victorian Murder, A,* 805
Smith, Mr.: *Houdini: The Handcuff King,* 356
(S)mother: *Cancer Vixen,* 142
Snake Eye: *Age of Reptiles,* 21
snow: *Blankets: An Illustrated Novel,* 102, 103; *Sin City,* 690
Snowman: *Snowman, The,* 716
Snowman, The, **715–717**
Snowy (Milou): *Adventures of Tintin, The,* 11
social bonds, as core theme: *Alec: The Years Have Pants,* 35
social class: *One! Hundred! Demons!,* 558
social criticism, as core theme: *Metropol: The Complete Series + Metropol A.D.,* 516
social environment changes, as core theme: *Cancer Vixen,* 143

social roles, as core themes: *Kafka,* 421
sociocultural considerations. *See* cultural issues, as core theme
Solander, Jain: *Castle Waiting,* 150
soldiers: *Flood! A Novel in Pictures,* 256. *See also* war
Solidus, Professor: *Jew of New York, The: A Historical Romance,* 396
Soliman, Professor: *Rabbi's Cat, The,* 634
Solis, Vivian (Frogmouth): *Love and Rockets,* 494
Soloman, Boyd: *Dear Julia,* 195
Solomon: *Good-Bye, Chunky Rice,* 312
Solomon, Professor Zahava: *Waltz with Bashir: A Lebanon War Story,* 834
Sonnenschein, Hana: *Asterios Polyp,* 64
Soor, Lisa: *Skim,* 693
sound effects (onomatopoetic): *Far Arden,* 240; *Nat Turner,* 537; *Wilson,* 855
the South: *Incognegro: A Graphic Mystery,* 363–365
space travel: *Laika,* 439
Spanish Scott: *Stray Bullets,* 729
Sparrow: *Dykes to Watch Out For,* 210
Sparrowdark: *Journey: The Adventure of Wolverine MacAlistaire,* 404
Spears, General Thomas A. W.: *Aliens,* 43
Specialist: *Three Fingers,* 785
spectacle: *Golem's Mighty Swing, The,* 305, 306
speech, as core theme: *I Never Liked You,* 368–369. *See also* language
speech bubbles (balloons): *American Splendor: From Off the Streets of Cleveland,* 48; *Box Office Poison,* 126; *Chicken with Plums,* 156; *Epileptic,* 228; *Harvey Kurtzman's Jungle Book,* 325; *Scary Godmother: The Boo Flu,* 663–664; *Shutterbug Follies,* 681; *Signal to Noise,* 685
speed lines: *Book of Genesis, The,* 119; *Skitzy: The Story of Floyd W. Skitzafroid,* 698
Speedy. *See* Ortiz, Eulalio
Spiegelman, Anja: *Maus: A Survivor's Tale,* 510
*Spiegelman, Art, 370, 509, 511
Spiegelman, Art (character): *Maus: A Survivor's Tale,* 510; *In the Shadow of No Towers,* 371
Spiegelman, Mala: *Maus: A Survivor's Tale,* 510
Spiegelman, Nadja: *In the Shadow of No Towers,* 371
Spiegelman, Vladek: *Maus: A Survivor's Tale,* 510
spirit, as core theme: *Scary Godmother: The Boo Flu,* 664
spirituality. *See* religion and faith

spirituality, as core theme: *Alan's War: The Memories of G.I. Alan Cope,* 30; *Rabbi's Cat, The,* 635. *See also* religion and faith
splash pages: *Black Hole,* 95; *Minor Miracles: Long Ago and Once Upon a Time Back When...,* 519–520; *Scary Godmother: The Boo Flu,* 663–664
Sponge Boy: *Flaming Carrot Comics,* 252
Spook, Mr.: *Tales of the Beanworld: A Most Peculiar Comic Book Experience,* 765
spray paint: *System, The,* 758
Spud: *Transit,* 800
Square Robot: *Robot Dreams,* 650
Squeaky Toy Rat: *Tank Girl,* 774
Stanislas, Father Prior: *Deogratias: A Tale of Rwanda,* 199
Stanton, Duke: *Blueberry,* 109
*Stassen, Jean-Philippe, 198
status of comics as medium: *Hicksville,* 346
STDs (sexually transmitted disease): *Black Hole,* 95
Stefano. *See* Little Killer
Stegman, Arthur: *Richard Stark's Parker,* 644
Stelios: *300,* 789
stencils: *System, The,* 758
Stephen: *It's a Good Life, If You Don't Weaken: A Picture Novella,* 381
stereotypes: *Owly,* 567; *Skitzy: The Story of Floyd W. Skitzafroid,* 698. *See also* prejudice and discrimination
Stern, Clint: *Richard Stark's Parker,* 644
Stetko, Carrie: *Whiteout,* 847
Steve: *It's a Bird...,* 378; *Tricked,* 808
Steve's dad: *It's a Bird...,* 378
Steve's mom: *It's a Bird...,* 378
Stevie: *Tank Girl,* 774
Stevie (Steve Farley): *Summer of Love, The,* 754
Stillman, Peter Jr.: *City of Glass,* 159
Stillman, Peter Sr.: *City of Glass,* 159
Stillman, Virginia: *City of Glass,* 159
Stills, Steven: *Scott Pilgrim,* 668
Stitches: A Memoir, 718–721
stockbroker: *System, The,* 757
storyboards: *American Splendor: From Off the Streets of Cleveland,* 52; *Persepolis,* 600; *Why I Hate Saturn,* 851
story line shifts: *King: A Comics Biography,* 433
storytelling, as core theme: *Alice in Sunderland: An Entertainment,* 39; *Castle Waiting,* 151; *Gemma Bovery,* 283

strange girl. *See* P.T.O.
Strangers in Paradise, **722–726**
Strauss, Moishe (Mo): *Golem's Mighty Swing, The,* 305
Strauss, Noah (Zion Lion): *Golem's Mighty Swing, The,* 305
Stray Bullets, **727–731**
Stray Toasters, **732–735**
Streak of Chalk, **736–739**
stream of consciousness: *Monologues for the Coming Plague,* 523–524; *Twentieth Century Eightball,* 813
Stride, Elizabeth (Long Liz): *From Hell: Being a Melodrama in Sixteen Parts,* 273
strippers: *System, The,* 757
Stuart: *Dykes to Watch Out For,* 211
Stuck Rubber Baby, **740–744**
*Sturm, James, 304, 506
Sub Girl: *Tank Girl,* 774
Suckle: The Status of Basil, **745–748**
Sue-Yun: *Life Sucks,* 460
suffering, as core theme: *Asterios Polyp,* 65
Summer of Love, The, **753–755**
Sun, Wei-Chen: *American Born Chinese,* 47
Sunoo: *Color Trilogy, The,* 168
superheroes: *Jimmy Corrigan: The Smartest Kid on Earth,* 400; *Leave It to Chance,* 452
superhero genre: *Hicksville,* 345; *Tank Girl,* 772–773
Superman: *It's a Bird...,* 378
supernatural genre: *Sloth,* 702
surrealistic style: *Flaming Carrot Comics,* 252; *Like a Velvet Glove Cast in Iron,* 465; *Love and Rockets,* 495–496
survival, as core theme: *A.D.: New Orleans After the Deluge,* 3; *Age of Reptiles,* 22; *David Boring,* 189; *Harum Scarum,* 321; *Minor Miracles: Long Ago and Once Upon a Time Back When...,* 520; *Plain Janes, The,* 607; *Predator,* 617; *Walking Dead, The,* 826
Susette: *Skitzy: The Story of Floyd W. Skitzafroid,* 698
Susie: *It's a Good Life, If You Don't Weaken: A Picture Novella,* 381
Suu Kyi, Aung San (the Lady): *Burma Chronicles,* 135
Svenson, Sven: *Dropsie Avenue,* 207
Swallow, Miss: *Tantrum,* 777
Swatchell (Professor): *Tragical Comedy or Comical Tragedy of Mr. Punch, The,* 797
sword and sorcery, as core theme: *Blackmark,* 99

Sydney: *Dykes to Watch Out For,* 211
Sylvia: *Small Killing, A,* 705
symbolic imagery: *Color Trilogy, The,* 168; *Epileptic,* 228; *Mail Order Bride,* 503; *Stitches: A Memoir,* 720
System, The, **756–759**

T

Tabey, Charles, Jr. (Chuck Katt): *Omaha the Cat Dancer,* 553
Tabey, Charles, Sr.: *Omaha the Cat Dancer,* 553–554
Tabey, Maria Elandos: *Omaha the Cat Dancer,* 554
Taji: *Chicken with Plums,* 155; *Embroideries,* 223
Tale of One Bad Rat, The, **760–763**
Tales of the Beanworld: A Most Peculiar Comic Book Experience, **764–767**
talisman: *Black Hole,* 95
*Tamaki, Jillian, 692, 693
*Tamaki, Mariko, 692, 693
Tamar: *Book of Genesis, The,* 119
Tamara Drewe, **768–771**
Tamássy, Madame Flóra: *Rex Mundi,* 639
Tambri. *See* Baker, Mary Beth
Tammy: *Percy Gloom,* 592
Tammy, father of: *Percy Gloom,* 593
Tammy, mother of: *Percy Gloom,* 593
Tammy, parents of: *Percy Gloom,* 593
*Tan, Shaun, 59
Tanaka, Ben: *Shortcomings,* 676
Tank Girl, **772–775**
Tank Girl (Rebecca Buck): *Tank Girl,* 773
Tantrum, **776–779**
*Tardi, Jacques, 384
Tarmooti, Doctor: *Julius Knipl, Real Estate Photographer,* 412
Taro (Huron): *Ballad of Doctor Richardson, The,* 84
Tato: *Streak of Chalk,* 737–738
Taylor: *30 Days of Night,* 782
Taylor, Creed: *Lost Cause: John Wesley Hardin,* 471
Teach'm, Mr.: *Tales of the Beanworld: A Most Peculiar Comic Book Experience,* 765
technology, as core theme: *Dead Memory,* 192
teenagers. *See* adolescence, as core theme
Telchines, The: *Bacchus,* 80
Teniers, Baron Robert: *Rex Mundi,* 639
Tenrec, Jack: *Xenozoic Tales: Cadillacs and Dinosaurs,* 858

1059

terror, as core theme: *Black Hole,* 93, 95
terrorism: *9/11 Report, The: A Graphic Adaptation,* 544, 545; *In the Shadow of No Towers,* 372
testing boundaries, as core theme: *Lost Girl,* 475
Texas history: *Lost Cause: John Wesley Hardin,* 470, 472
texture: *Blackmark,* 99; *Xenozoic Tales: Cadillacs and Dinosaurs,* 858
Thea: *Dykes to Watch Out For,* 211
themes. *See specific core themes such as* loss
Theo: *Get a Life,* 287
Theresa: *Clumsy,* 163
Theseus, Joe: *Bacchus,* 80
30 Days of Night, **780–783**
*Thompson, Jill, 663
Thompson, Victor: *Aliens,* 43
Thompson and Thompson (Dupont and Dupond): *Adventures of Tintin, The,* 11
Thorn: *Bone,* 114
thought bubbles (balloons): *American Splendor: From Off the Streets of Cleveland,* 52; *Houdini: The Handcuff King,* 357; *Kane,* 430; *Palestine,* 570; *Plain Janes, The,* 606; *Summer of Love, The,* 755; *We Are On Our Own,* 837. *See also* captions
3-D: *You Are Here,* 865
three-dimensional appearance: *Rose: Prequel to Bone,* 654
Three Fingers, **784–787**
300, **788–791**
Three Shadows: *Three Shadows,* 794
Three Shadows, **792–795**
Three Tooth: *Age of Reptiles,* 21
Throop, Alecto: *Aliens,* 44
time, interwoven: *Jimmy Corrigan: The Smartest Kid on Earth,* 399–340
time line: *9/11 Report, The: A Graphic Adaptation,* 543, 545
Tintin: *Adventures of Tintin, The,* 11
Tiny: *Owly,* 566
Todd: *Stray Toasters,* 733
tolerance, as core theme: *System, The,* 759
Tolliver and Dayne: *Castle Waiting,* 151
Tom: *Lucky,* 499
Tomassen, Willem: *Journey into Mohawk Country,* 408
*Tomine, Adrian, 675
Tom the foreigner: *Shenzhen,* 673
Toni: *Dykes to Watch Out For,* 211

Topalovic, Musan (Caco): *Fixer, The: A Story from Sarajevo,* 247
Torrino, John: *History of Violence, A,* 348
Tournesol, Tryphon. *See* Calculus, Cuthbert
Tournon, Genevieve: *Rex Mundi,* 639
traditionalism, as core theme: *Aya of Yopougon,* 75
Tragical Comedy or Comical Tragedy of Mr. Punch, The, **796–799**
transformation and change, as core theme: *Incognegro: A Graphic Mystery,* 365; *Kafka,* 422; *Small Killing, A,* 706
Transit, **800–802**
transition, as core theme: *Kings in Disguise,* 436; *Palomar: The Heartbreak Soup Stories,* 575–576
transitions in style: *Whiteout,* 847–848
translators: *Shenzhen,* 672
traumatic event, as core theme: *Deogratias: A Tale of Rwanda,* 200; *Kafka,* 422; *Maus: A Survivor's Tale,* 512; *You'll Never Know Book One: A Good and Decent Man,* 868–869
Traun: *Transit,* 801
travel. *See* journey
Travers, Joseph: *Nat Turner,* 537
Treasury of Victorian Murder, A, **803–806**
Trent, Ellinore: *Journey: The Adventure of Wolverine MacAlistaire,* 404
Tricked, **807–810**
Trinity: *Metropol: The Complete Series + Metropol A.D.,* 515
Trish: *Poor Bastard, The,* 612
*Trondheim, Lewis, 319
trust in relationships: *Box Office Poison,* 126
Tsi-Nah-Pah. *See* Blueberry
Tsukiko: *Kabuki,* 416
Tumlinson, Joe: *Lost Cause: John Wesley Hardin,* 471
Turner, father of Nat: *Nat Turner,* 536
Turner, mother of Nat: *Nat Turner,* 536
Turner, Nat: *Nat Turner,* 536
Turner, wife of Nat: *Nat Turner,* 536
Turtle: *Pride of Baghdad: Inspired by a True Story,* 620
Twentieth Century Eightball, **811–814**
24-Hour Comics Day: *Far Arden,* 240
Two Nose: *Age of Reptiles,* 21–22
two unnamed women: *Embroideries,* 224
*Tyler, Carol, 867, 869
Tyler, Carol (character): *You'll Never Know Book One: A Good and Decent Man,* 868

Tyler, Charles William "Chuck": *You'll Never Know Book One: A Good and Decent Man*, 867–868
tyrannosaur mother: *Age of Reptiles*, 22
Tze-Yo-Tzuh: *American Born Chinese*, 47

U

Ukiko Kai. *See* Kabuki
Uncle Amos: *Minor Miracles: Long Ago and Once Upon a Time Back When...*, 519
Uncle Anoosh: *Persepolis*, 600
Uncle Aryeh: *Exit Wounds*, 235
Uncle Morton: *Tragical Comedy or Comical Tragedy of Mr. Punch, The*, 797
Unifactor (place): *Frank Book, The*, 263–265
unnamed boy: *Minor Miracles: Long Ago and Once Upon a Time Back When...*, 519
unnamed friend: *Playboy, The*, 609
unnamed guide: *Cartoon History of the Universe, The*, 146
unnamed man: *Flood! A Novel in Pictures*, 256
unnamed protagonist: *Arrival, The*, 60
unnamed soldier-narrator: *It Was the War of the Trenches*, 385
unnamed woman: *Flood! A Novel in Pictures*, 256
unnamed women, two: *Embroideries*, 224
urbanization and modernism, as core theme: *Aya of Yopougon*, 75; *Palomar: The Heartbreak Soup Stories*, 575
Uriel. *See* Candy

V

vampires: *Life Sucks*, 461; *30 Days of Night*, 781–782
*Vance, James, 434, 435
*van Cutsem, William (William Vance), 105
Van Damme, Madame: *Like a Velvet Glove Cast in Iron*, 464
van den Bogaert, Harmen Meyndertsz: *Journey into Mohawk Country*, 407–408
van der Platz, Violet: *Ice Haven*, 361
Van Dropsie family: *Dropsie Avenue*, 206
*Varon, Sara, 649
Vastenov: *Rabbi's Cat, The*, 634
*Vaughan, Brian K., 619
Vela, Margo: *Leave It to Chance*, 449
Velasquez, Ed: *Box Office Poison*, 126
Velasquez, Rosa: *Life Sucks*, 460
Venetia: *Deogratias: A Tale of Rwanda*, 199

Verifax, Mike: *Harvey Kurtzman's Jungle Book*, 324
Veronique: *Get a Life*, 287
*Vess, Charles, 652
Vester, Sly Jr.: *Three Fingers*, 785
Vickery, Mr.: *Houdini: The Handcuff King*, 356
Victoria, Queen of England: *From Hell: Being a Melodrama in Sixteen Parts*, 273
Victorio: *Blueberry*, 109
Vida: *Ice Haven*, 361
village boy: *It Was the War of the Trenches*, 385
village *vs.* modern life, as core theme: *Kampung Boy*, 426
villain, the: *He Done Her Wrong*, 337
Villaseñor, Tonantzín: *Love and Rockets*, 495; *Palomar: The Heartbreak Soup Stories*, 575
Vincente: *30 Days of Night*, 782
Vincente, Mister: *Harum Scarum*, 321
Vint, Gustave: *Julius Knipl, Real Estate Photographer*, 412
violence, artistic: *Glacial Period*, 302
violence, as core theme: *Predator*, 617; *Road to Perdition*, 647; *Violent Cases*, 822
violence, as response to occupation: *Palestine*, 571
violence, domestic, as core theme: *Castle Waiting*, 152
violence, fictional connected to real-life: *Black Hole*, 93, 96
violence, gradual increase in: *History of Violence, A*, 349
violence, historical: *Treasury of Victorian Murder, A*, 805
violence, realistic: *From Hell: Being a Melodrama in Sixteen Parts*, 274
violence, sexual: *Like a Velvet Glove Cast in Iron*, 465
Violence, Thelonius: *Harvey Kurtzman's Jungle Book*, 324
violence, victims and perpetrators: *Deogratias: A Tale of Rwanda*, 199-200
Violent Cases, **820–822**
Violet, Dr. Montana: *Stray Toasters*, 733
Vitalstatistix (Abraracourcix): *Asterix*, 69
vulnerability and frailty, as core theme: *Clumsy*, 163–164

W

Wack, Jack: *Metropol: The Complete Series + Metropol A.D.*, 515

waiter, the: *Last Day in Vietnam: A Memory*, 446
Walking Dead, The, **823-827**
Wall, The: Growing Up Behind the Iron Curtain, **828-831**
Wallace: *Sin City*, 689
*Waller, Drake (pseudonym of Arnold Drake and Leslie Waller), 374
*Waller, Leslie, 374
Walter, Bertrand: *Harum Scarum*, 320
Walter, Dr.: *Harum Scarum*, 320
Waltz with Bashir: A Lebanon War Story, **832-835**
Wang, Jin: *American Born Chinese*, 47
war, as core theme: *Alan's War: The Memories of G.I. Alan Cope*, 30; *Blackmark*, 99; *Fax from Sarajevo*, 244; *Fixer, The: A Story from Sarajevo*, 248; *It Was the War of the Trenches*, 386; *Last Day in Vietnam: A Memory*, 447; *Notes for a War Story*, 549; *Photographer, The: Into War-Torn Afghanistan with Doctors Without Borders*, 639; *Predator*, 602; *Pride of Baghdad: Inspired by a True Story*, 620-621; *Rex Mundi*, 640; *Safe Area Goražde*, 659-660; *300*, 788; *Waltz with Bashir: A Lebanon War Story*, 834-835; *When the Wind Blows*, 843-844
*Ware, Chris, 398
war genre: *Alan's War: The Memories of G.I. Alan Cope*, 28-30
Warner, Murphy: *Why I Hate Saturn*, 851
Warren, Peaceful: *Castle Waiting*, 151
Warren, Sir Charles: *From Hell: Being a Melodrama in Sixteen Parts*, 273
watercolor: *Curious Case of Benjamin Button, The*, 185; *Elk's Run*, 219; *Julius Knipl, Real Estate Photographer*, 412; *Notes for a War Story*, 548; *Signal to Noise*, 684-685; *Small Killing, A*, 705; *When the Wind Blows*, 843; *You'll Never Know Book One: A Good and Decent Man*, 868
We Are on Our Own, **836-838**
Weber, Hal: *It Rhymes with Lust*, 375
Weiss: *Whiteout*, 847
Weiss, Ernie: *Jar of Fools*, 389
Weldon, Donald: *Queen and Country*, 629
Wells, Wallace: *Scott Pilgrim*, 668
Wendy: *Sin City*, 689
Wendy from *Peter Pan*. *See* Potter, Mrs. Wendy
Wes: *Life Sucks*, 460
Wesselhoeft, Isaac: *Whiteout*, 847
western genre: *Blueberry*, 105-110

Westerns, as influence: *Fixer, The: A Story from Sarajevo*, 248
What It Is, **839-841**
Wheeler, Monty: *Mail Order Bride*, 503
Wheeler, Mr.: *Mail Order Bride*, 503
Wheeler, Riley: *Stuck Rubber Baby*, 742
When the Wind Blows, **842-845**
Whim: *Frank Book, The*, 264
whispering: *La Perdida*, 443
White, Walter, 363
white-on-black format: *Playboy, The*, 609
Whiteout, **846-849**
white space. *See* open space
Whitman, Whitey: *David Boring*, 188
Why I Hate Saturn, **850-852**
Wilde, Dr.: *Like a Velvet Glove Cast in Iron*, 464
Wilder, Random: *Ice Haven*, 361
Wilks (Hicks): *Aliens*, 43
Will: *Nat Turner*, 537
Willeford, Mr.: *Hard Boiled*, 316
Wilson: *Wilson*, 854
Wilson, **853-856**
Winick, Bobbi: *Pedro and Me: Friendship, Loss, and What I Learned*, 589
*Winick, Judd, 588
Winick, Judd (character): *Pedro and Me: Friendship, Loss, and What I Learned*, 589
Winick, Michael: *Pedro and Me: Friendship, Loss, and What I Learned*, 589
Winston: *Complete Fritz the Cat, The*, 175
Wolf Marie (Mary): *Journey: The Adventure of Wolverine MacAlistaire*, 404
Wolverine (Joshua MacAlistaire): *Journey: The Adventure of Wolverine MacAlistaire*, 403
Wolzendorf, Franz: *Berlin: City of Stones*, 87
woman, a: *Flood! A Novel in Pictures*, 255
women as social conscience: *Aya of Yopougon*, 75. *See also* female characters and issues
wonder of life, as core theme: *Alec: The Years Have Pants*, 35
Wong, Eve: *Mail Order Bride*, 503
woodcut style: *Castle Waiting*, 151; *Chicken with Plums*, 156; *Contract with God, A*, 181; *Flood! A Novel in Pictures*, 256; *Long Time Relationship*, 468; *Mouse Guard*, 529; *Passionate Journey*, 577-579; *Three Shadows*, 794; *Treasury of Victorian Murder, A*, 805

*Woodring, Jim, 263
Wooley, Red. *See* Red Neck
word balloons. *See* speech bubbles (balloons)
word images: *System, The,* 758
wordless comics: *Hey, Wait...,* 341; *Skitzy: The Story of Floyd W. Skitzafroid,* 698
wordless panels: *Houdini: The Handcuff King,* 357; *Life and Times of Scrooge McDuck, The,* 457
words and objects as interchangeable: *City of Glass,* 160
words to indicate actions: *Tank Girl,* 774
World Trade Center Twin Towers: *Asterios Polyp,* 65; *9/11 Report, The: A Graphic Adaptation,* 544; *In the Shadow of No Towers,* 371
World War I: *It Was the War of the Trenches,* 384–386
World War II: *We Are on Our Own,* 837–838; *Yossel: April 19, 1943 – A Story of the Warsaw Ghetto Uprising,* 862
*Worley, Kate, 551
Wormy: *Owly,* 566
wounded GI, the: *Last Day in Vietnam: A Memory,* 446
Wurstmacher, Hans: *Three Fingers,* 785
Wylde, Rose: *Adventures of Luther Arkwright, The,* 6

X

Xenozoic Tales: Cadillacs and Dinosaurs, **857–859**
Xerxes: *300,* 789

Y

*Yang, Gene Luen, 46
Yates, Hannah: *You'll Never Know Book One: A Good and Decent Man,* 868
Yazdovsky, Vladimir: *Laika,* 438–439
Yellow Bastard: *Sin City,* 690
Yetchem the Archer: *Airtight Garage of Jerry Cornelius,* 25
Yiddish New York, as core theme: *Julius Knipl, Real Estate Photographer,* 413
York, Colonel Ed: *Treasury of Victorian Murder, A,* 805

Yossel: *Yossel: April 19, 1943 – A Story of the Warsaw Ghetto Uprising,* 861
Yossel: April 19, 1943 – A Story of the Warsaw Ghetto Uprising, **860–863**
You Are Here, **864–866**
You'll Never Know Book One: A Good and Decent Man, **867–870**
Young Boy (James): *Snowman, The,* 715-716
young gay man: *System, The,* 758
Yousaka Takahashi. *See* Quin, David
Yousef, Ramzi: *9/11 Report, The: A Graphic Adaptation,* 544
YouTube: *Alan's War: The Memories of G.I. Alan Cope,* 30
Yvette: *My Mommy Is in America and She Met Buffalo Bill,* 532

Z

Zabel, Sam: *Hicksville,* 344
Zamora, Mr.: *Pedro and Me: Friendship, Loss, and What I Learned,* 589
Zamora, Pedro: *Pedro and Me: Friendship, Loss, and What I Learned,* 589
*Zarate, Oscar, 704
Zékinan: *Aya of Yopougon,* 74
Zill: *Pride of Baghdad: Inspired by a True Story,* 620
Zion Lion. *See* Strauss, Noah
Zip-A-Tone patterns: *Blackmark,* 99; *Lost Cause: John Wesley Hardin,* 471; *Xenozoic Tales: Cadillacs and Dinosaurs,* 858
zoetrope: *Jimmy Corrigan: The Smartest Kid on Earth,* 400
zombies: *Walking Dead, The,* 823, 825, 826
zoom, as style: *City of Glass,* 160; *Pyongyang: A Journey in North Korea,* 623
Zorro: *Harvey Kurtzman's Jungle Book,* 324
Zubrick: *Twentieth Century Eightball,* 812